Encyclopedia of American Parties, Campaigns, and Elections

Republican presidential nomination in 1808, DeWitt Clinton allowed himself to be adopted by the Federalists as their presidential candidate. It was an odd coupling. Although he was defeated, Clinton fared better, excluding John Adams, than any other Federalist presidential candidate between 1796 and 1816: 7 states with 89 Electoral College votes were carried by the Federalist ticket of Clinton and Jared Ingersol of Pennsylvania, the vice-presidential nominee, to 11 states and 128 Electoral College ballots for the Republicans. This flirtation with the Federalists, however, was to give Clinton difficulty in New York politics for the rest of his life. His apostasy, and his use of the spoils system to advance his own policies rather than his party's interests, were never forgiven by Tammany Hall, and only occasionally as political expediency required by the party's Van Buren faction. Nonetheless, Clinton was able to secure the Republican nomination and fashion gubernatorial victories, albeit often narrow ones, in 1817 and 1820, again in 1824 and 1826, having declined to seek reelection in 1822. Death came to DeWitt Clinton at the Governor's House in Albany on February 11, 1828. *See*: ELECTIONS: 1812.

Reference: Dorothie Bobbé, *DeWitt Clinton* (New York: Minton, Balch, 1933).

CLINTON, WILLIAM JEFFERSON (BILL) (1946–) is the forty-second president of the United States. Bill Clinton was born in Hope, Arkansas, to Virginia and William Jefferson Blythe. William Blythe, a traveling salesman, died in an auto accident before Bill Clinton was born. Clinton's mother Virginia then married Roger Clinton, a car dealer, when Bill was four years old. Clinton was raised as a Baptist. As a young man, he considered becoming a musician, a teacher, or a preacher. He decided on becoming a politician. His career choice was reinforced in 1963, when he met President John F. Kennedy as a member of a Boys' State delegation to Washington, D.C. In 1968, Clinton graduated from Georgetown University; he then studied at Oxford as a Rhodes scholar for two years. He returned to the United States and earned a law degree from Yale Law School in 1973. While at Yale, he married another law student, Hillary Rodham. After law school Clinton joined the faculty of the University of Arkansas School of Law.

Clinton started his active political career by running for Arkansas' Third Congressional District seat in 1974, and lost to the incumbent Republican. In 1976, Clinton ran the presidential campaign of Jimmy Carter in Arkansas, and he was elected state attorney general. In 1978, Clinton sought and won the Arkansas Democratic gubernatorial nomination, and went on to win the general election. He was 32 years old, the youngest governor in Arkansas history. In his first term, Clinton raised state taxes and fees, and, as a result of those tax increases, he was defeated by Republican Frank White in 1980. Clinton started his comeback by apologizing for trying to do too much too soon in his first term. In 1982, Clinton was once again elected governor of Arkansas, and this time he set out to reform education. The term of the governor of Arkansas was increased

Encyclopedia of American Parties, Campaigns, and Elections

William C. Binning,
Larry E. Esterly, and
Paul A. Sracic

GREENWOOD PRESS
Westport, Connecticut • London

Library of Congress Cataloging-in-Publication Data

Binning, William C.
    Encyclopedia of American parties, campaigns, and elections /
    William C. Binning, Larry E. Esterly, and Paul A. Sracic.
       p.   cm.
    Includes bibliographical references (p.) and index.
    ISBN 0–313–30312–6 (alk. paper)
    1. United States—Politics and government—Dictionaries.
    2. Politicians—United States—Biography—Dictionaries.
    I. Esterly, Larry E. (Larry Eugene), 1938– . II. Sracic, Paul A.
    III. Title.
    JK9.B56   1999
    324'.0973'03—dc21   98–46810

British Library Cataloguing in Publication Data is available.

Library of Congress Catalog Card Number: 98–46810
ISBN: 0–313–30312–6

First published in 1999

Greenwood Press, 88 Post Road West, Westport, CT 06881
An imprint of Greenwood Publishing Group, Inc.
www.greenwood.com

Printed in the United States of America

The paper used in this book complies with the
Permanent Paper Standard issued by the National
Information Standards Organization (Z39.48–1984).

10 9 8 7 6 5 4 3 2

To our families:
Maureen and Patrick Binning, and Katie Cuttitta
Donna Esterly
Susan, Katya, and Anna Sracic

Contents

Introduction

The purpose of the *Encyclopedia of American Parties, Campaigns, and Elections* is to provide journalists, teachers, students, and citizens with a comprehensive guide to the language of contemporary American politics. This is no easy task, for the language of politics, like any other specialized language, is filled with complex terms whose meanings, though grounded in history, continue to evolve. So, for example, the citizen who wants to understand a term like "gerrymandering" ought to know something about the eighteenth century politician Elbridge Gerry, and even more about current debates over voting districts and voting rights. Yet this is not the sort of information that is currently available in most political encyclopedias. Instead, existing encyclopedias tend to focus on particular elements within politics—for instance, political parties. Moreover, they are often written for political scholars and are therefore inaccessible to the average reader.

This encyclopedia is different in that it is intended for both the professional and the amateur. Much of this book consists of easy-to-understand explanations of both common and complex political terms. We also provide brief biographies of major political figures, descriptions of significant political parties and movements, and explanations of important cases about elections and campaign finance law decided by the Supreme Court of the United States. Finally, under the term "elections" the reader will find a detailed account of the presidential elections and campaigns held since the Constitution was ratified in 1788.

For ease of use, all of the entries are arranged alphabetically. To aid those who are seeking a more comprehensive understanding of American politics, we have cross-referenced related entries. In addition, after most of the entries, we have provided a list of books and/or articles that might be helpful to those wishing to learn more about a selected topic. A detailed index is located at the end of this encyclopedia.

When writing an encyclopedia of this type, the most difficult challenge is to decide what to leave in and what to leave out. In making these decisions, our overall rule of thumb was to err on the side of contemporary terms and issues. Our hope is that, in the process, we have developed a reference work that will be relevant and useful to both the student of government and the average citizen. If we have managed to succeed in this we will have accomplished a great deal.

Although the authors alone accept responsibility for any errors which remain in this text, our appreciation must be expressed to the several individuals who have assisted us at various points in the writing process. Linda Babinec and Tanisha Miller gave generous amounts of their time to proofreading and photocopying early drafts of this encyclopedia. Our particular thanks is extended to Donna Esterly, who in the first stages of preparing this work gave valuable editorial assistance.

A

ABSENTEE BALLOT. State law permits voters to cast ballots by mail when they are physically unable to go to the polls. Usually age, illness, or absence from the county on election day is sufficient to qualify for an absentee ballot. In most states self-declaration is all that is required. Years ago, the absentee ballot request had to be notarized and written medical justification was required. Laws have become more liberal in recent years. For example, in the state of Washington the elderly and the disabled are placed on a permanent absentee voter list and are sent ballots in the mail without having to make a formal request. The absentee voter needs to meet state registration requirements. The number of absentee ballots cast in elections has been increasing.

Absentee votes can determine the outcome of an election. Political parties spend time and money cultivating absentee voters by sending previous absentee voters applications for future elections along with a party slate card. Recently, the state of Oregon initiated vote-by-mail elections. *See*: REGISTRATION, VOTER; VOTE-BY-MAIL.

Reference: Richard Smolka and Ronald Michaelson, "Election Legislation," in *The Book of the States*, Vol. 30 (Lexington, Ky.: Council of State Governments, 1994).

ADAMS, JOHN (1735–1826) was born in what is now Quincy, Massachusetts, on October 30, 1735, graduated from Harvard in 1755, and "read" the law, subsequently taking up its practice in 1758. Early on adopting the patriot cause, he was elected in 1774 to the first continental congress, where two years later he was assigned to the committee given responsibility for drafting the Declaration of Independence. At the further assignment of the continental congress Adams was to devote more than a decade (1777–1788) to various European diplomatic missions, only occasionally interrupting his stay there to return home, as in 1779 when he served as a member of the Massachusetts constitutional convention, becoming in effect the author of that state's first constitution. Adams was not to return permanently to the United States until June of 1788. Less than a year later, as a result of the first meeting of the Electoral College under the newly adopted Constitution, he was elected to the vice-presidency. During his two terms Adams was to suffer many of the frustrations that were to burden his successors in that office. Not invited by President Washington to be an active participant in executive department decision making, Adams was left to perform the one duty constitutionally assigned to vice-presidents, presiding, without benefit of vote other than to break ties, over the proceedings of the U.S. Senate. Even though Adams did on a record-setting 31 occasions cast such tie-breaking votes, he came to regard the vice-presidential role as no more than that of a "cipher." With Washington declining consideration of a third term Adams became, among Federalists (Alexander Hamilton's opposition notwithstanding), the anticipated choice to succeed the departing president. The presidential election of 1796, however, was to be the first characterized by competing party tickets: Adams and Thomas Pinckney of South Carolina as vice-presidential candidate for the Federalists; Thomas Jefferson and Aaron Burr of New York as the Republican nominees. Because of the prevailing language in the Constitution with regard to the functioning of the Electoral College, the balloting resulted in the peculiarity of Adams, with 71 votes, being elected president and his Republican rival Jefferson, with 68 votes, the second highest number, winning the vice-presidency (after further problems in the election of 1800, the constitutional provisions for the Electoral College were to be altered by the adoption of the Twelfth Amendment in 1804). The dilemmas of the Adams administration were largely ones of national defense and foreign policy. Attempting to enforce a position of neutrality between and among warring European powers, Adams drew the fire of Hamilton and many other Federalists who preferred stronger ties with Great Britain and, from the other side, of Thomas Jefferson and the Republicans, who were equally ardent in their calls for support of revolutionary France. The enactment in 1798 of the much-criticized Alien and Sedition Acts was seen by many, particularly Republican leaders, as an attempt by the Adams administration and the Federalist Congress to silence and remove political opposition. Buffeted on all fronts, John Adams nonetheless chose to seek reelection in 1800. Once again the Electoral College misfired, with Jefferson and Burr, the respective Republican presidential and vice-presidential candidates, each receiving an equal number of votes, 73, to Adams's total of 65. Thus was the presidential election thrown into the U.S. House of Representatives where, ironically, lame-duck Federalists were yet in the majority. It was not until the thirty-sixth ballot that the House was to elect Thomas Jefferson as president of the United States. While the House was thus preoccupied, Adams and the Federalist Senate were active in the attempt to safeguard party control of the national judiciary. Among Adams's court nominations confirmed by the Senate was that of Secretary of State John Marshall to become Chief Justice of the U.S. Supreme Court. No decision of John Adams's presidency was to have a greater impact on American political and constitutional development. Not waiting for the formal ceremonies inaugurating Jefferson, and Burr as vice-president, Adams withdrew to his farm in Massachusetts where he was to live out a quarter century of retirement. His death came while his son, John Quincy, occupied the White House, on July 4, 1826, the fiftieth anniversary of American independence, and on the same day as the death in Virginia of his patriot colleague and sometime rival Thomas Jefferson. *See*: ELECTIONS: 1796, 1800.

References: Ralph Adams Brown, *The Presidency of John Adams* (Lawrence: University Press of Kansas, 1975); John E. Ferling, *John Adams: A Life* (Knoxville: University of Tennessee Press, 1992); Page Smith, *John Adams*, 2 vols. (Garden City, N.Y.: Doubleday, 1962).

ADAMS, JOHN QUINCY (1767–1848). Son of a president, father of a distinguished diplomat, grandfather of historians. For more than a century members of the Adams family made and recorded the history of the United States. Born in what is now Quincy, Massachusetts, on July 11, 1767, a son of John and Abigail Adams, the young John Quincy was given an early exposure to the fields of diplomacy and foreign relations. Educated in Europe while his father was on diplomatic missions there, the precocious Adams, age fourteen, became secretary to Francis Dana, first U.S. minister to Russia, and subsequently to his father, minister to Great Britain, 1781–1785. Returning to the United States in the latter year, he was to graduate from Harvard in 1787, study the law, be admitted to the Massachusetts bar in 1790, and in that year establish his practice in Boston. Diplomacy, however, was to prevail over the law. In 1794 he returned to Europe, President Washington having appointed the 27-year-old lawyer as minister to the Netherlands. When his father succeeded to the presidency in 1797, John Quincy was reassigned to Prussia, where he remained until the Jeffersonian Republicans came to power in 1801. Returning to the United States, John Quincy was to launch his own political career in the party of his father. Elected to the Massachusetts Senate as a Federalist in 1802, that body, in turn, elected Adams the following year to the U.S. Senate. With characteristic Adams independence he was to prove an unreliable Federalist, supporting Republican tariff measures and the Embargo Act of 1807. Losing the confidence of the Massachusetts legislature, Adams resigned from his Senate seat in 1808. No longer anathema to the Republicans, two successive presidents, Madison and Monroe, were to draw on his diplomatic skills: minister to Russia, 1809–1814; chief of the American Peace Commission at Ghent in 1814, responsible for the negotiated conclusion to the War of 1812; minister to Great Britain, 1815–1817; and secretary of state, 1817–1825—assignments constituting an unparalleled record in the conduct of the new nation's diplomacy. As secretary of state two accomplishments gave particular distinction to that record: the Adams-Onis Treaty of 1819, in which Spain ceded the Floridas to the United States, and promulgation of the Monroe Doctrine in 1823, in which the United States declared Latin America closed to further foreign colonization or military intrusion. Beginning with the election of 1808, a pattern of inheritance had developed in presidential politics whereby the secretary of state was presumed to be the leading contender to succeed to the executive office. With the demise of the Federalists and the absence of any newly organized opposition party, a number of regional and factional presidential candidates emerged in 1824. Some party leaders from the West advanced the name of Henry Clay of Kentucky, others that of the hero of the battle of New Orleans, Andrew Jackson of Tennessee; the Republican congressional caucus nominated William H. Crawford of Georgia; New England interests came forward with the candidacy of Secretary of State John Quincy Adams. Such a diverse field produced no candidate with an Electoral College majority; thus, as constitutionally required, the presidential election was transferred to the U.S. House of Representatives, each state delegation to cast one vote among the three candidates advanced on the basis of their having secured the greatest number of Electoral College ballots: Jackson, 99 ballots from eleven states; Adams, 84 ballots from seven states; Crawford, 41 ballots from three states. Clay, with but 37 ballots from three states, was eliminated from House consideration. He was, however, as a highly influential member of that body, to play a key role in the presidential determination. Preferring someone other than Jackson, his rival from the West, Clay became active in his support of Adams, who on the first balloting in the House, on February 8, 1825, secured election: thirteen state delegations voting for the secretary of state, seven supporting Jackson, and four delegations giving votes to Crawford. Inaugurated, with John C. Calhoun of South Carolina as vice-president, on March 4, 1825, Adams almost immediately was to make an appointment ordaining the failure of his presidency. Selecting Henry Clay as secretary of state, he infuriated the Jacksonians. With their candidate having secured the largest popular vote, having carried more states than any of the other contenders of 1824, they now claimed an election stolen from them in the House of Representatives on the basis of a ''corrupt bargain'': Clay had delivered the White House to Adams in trade for the secretary of stateship, thereby placing himself high on the ladder of future presidential succession. Almost immediately Jackson's supporters organized for the election of 1828, fashioning from remnants of the old Jeffersonian Republican Party (joined by frontier democrats) a new, popularly based Democratic Party. Adams by personality and program was ill equipped to meet such a challenge. His advocacy of an extensive program of nationally funded internal improvements, of initiatives in the fields of education, science, and exploration, gained little congressional support; in House and Senate, Adams became a president without a party. In 1828, in order to compete with the Democratic national ticket of Jackson and Vice-President John C. Calhoun, an administration party, the National Republicans, nominated Adams for a second presidential term, joining him with the vice-presidential nominee, Secretary of the Treasury Richard Rush of Pennsylvania. The election result, marking a significant step in the further democratization of American politics, was a decisive Democratic Party victory: nearly 650,000 popular votes were cast for the Jackson-Calhoun ticket, fifteen states with 178 Electoral College votes were carried; Adams, with 500,000 popular votes, carried but nine states with 83 Electoral College ballots. Thus, as with his father, John Quincy Adams was to be a one-term president, caught, again as with his father, in one of the critical realigning elections of American political history. His retirement, however, was to be a distinguished one. Elected in 1830 to the U.S. House of Representatives, voters in the twelfth congressional district of Massachusetts were on an additional eight consecutive occasions to return him to that body. He was in the House, as in his successful argument before the U.S. Supreme Court in the *Amistad* case in 1841, an ardent voice in opposition to slavery. Related to the latter issue, Adams opposed annexation of Texas as a slave state and the subsequent war with Mexico (1846–1848). Stricken while at his desk on the House floor on February 21, 1848, Adams was carried to the private chambers of the Speaker where he died on February 23, 1848. *See*: ELECTIONS: 1824, 1828.

References: Samuel Flagg Bemis, *John Quincy Adams and the Foundations of American Foreign Policy, John Quincy Adams and the Union* (New York: Knopf, 1949, 1956); Mary W. M. Hargreaves, *The Presidency of John Quincy Adams* (Lawrence: University Press of Kansas, 1985); Paul C. Nagel, *John Quincy Adams: A Public Life, A Private Life* (New York: Knopf, 1997).

ALIENATION is a concept that has evolved in Western political thought. It dates back to ancient times. One of the more recent philosophical views was expressed by Karl Marx, who used the term as descriptive of man's current condition, determined from the Industrial Revolution, where mechanization and the routine of work separated man from creative activity. The Marxist use of the word has fallen out of fashion.

In contemporary politics the word now refers to an individual who does not participate in politics because the individual believes he/she cannot affect the political system. A person who is alienated believes that one's actions have no influence on government, so one does not vote. Alienation is often used as an explanation for the lack of participation and low voter turnout.

Reference: George Lichtheim, ''Alienation,'' in *International Encyclopedia of the Social Sciences*, Vol. 1, David Sills, ed. (New York: Crowell and Macmillan, 1968).

AMERICAN INDEPENDENT PARTY was a third-party movement created by Alabama Governor George Wallace for the presidential election of 1968. The party was on the ballot in 50 states. Wallace was critical of the civil rights laws that had been passed under the Johnson administration, including the Civil Rights Act and the Voting Rights Act. The Wallace political movement was a reaction to these federal laws in the South. Wallace and his party were proponents of the Tenth Amendment of the U.S. Constitution which guarantees that: "the powers not delegated to the United States by the constitution, nor prohibited by it to the states are reserved to the states respectively, or to the people." The party also criticized the federal judicial system. In the 1968 presidential election, Wallace won five states, garnering 46 electoral college votes, and received 13% of the total votes cast for president. There was a distinct possibility that the Wallace campaign would deny the major parties an Electoral College majority. In 1968, the Republican nominee, Richard Nixon, won a majority of the Electoral College votes. In 1972, Wallace sought the presidential nomination of the Democratic Party but was paralyzed by an assassination attempt. *See*: WALLACE, GEORGE CORLEY.

Reference: A. James Reichley, *The Life of the Parties: A History of American Political Parties* (New York: The Free Press, 1992).

ANTHONY, SUSAN B. (1820–1906) was a founder and the leading figure in the women's suffrage movement in the nineteenth century. Susan B. Anthony was born into a Quaker family in Adams, Massachusetts. Her father was active in the temperance movement and the family were staunch abolitionists. Some of Susan's brothers were active with John Brown in Kansas.

Susan B. Anthony was influenced by Elizabeth Cady Stanton to take up the cause of women's rights. Stanton would be a lifelong friend and ally of Anthony's. At first, they tried to join women's suffrage with the abolition movement. This effort failed, and the suffragettes came to oppose the Fourteenth and Fifteenth Amendments because of the use of the word "male," which had never been used in the Constitution. Anthony and Stanton created the National Women's Suffrage Association in 1869. There was a rival American Woman Suffrage Association.

In 1872 Susan B. Anthony and sixteen other women registered to vote, and voted in the 1872 general election in Rochester, New York. They were arrested and charged with violating federal law. Associate Justice of the Supreme Court Ward Hunt heard the case. Susan was fined $100 and costs. She refused to pay; she hoped to bring her case to a higher court. The case was dropped.

Susan B. Anthony dedicated her life to the women's suffrage movement. She made her living lecturing on the topic. She was recognized as a very able organizer. In 1890 the two suffrage organizations united as the National American Suffrage Organizations. Anthony became the president in 1892. She believed that the solution to women's rights was a constitutional amendment and she lobbied in Washington from 1879 to 1891. The first Senate floor vote on women's suffrage took place in 1887.

Susan B. Anthony was active until her final years. She died in 1906 in Rochester, New York. She left her estate to the suffrage movement and never saw her life's goal fulfilled. *See*: GENDER GAP; NINETEENTH AMENDMENT; WOMEN'S SUFFRAGE.

References: Katherine Anthony, *Susan B. Anthony: Her Personal History and Her Era* (Garden City, N.Y.: Doubleday, 1954); Beverly Beeton, *Women Vote in the West: The Women Suffrage Movement, 1869–1896* (New York: Garland Publishing, 1896).

ANTI-MASONIC PARTY was a political party organized in upstate New York in 1827. The Anti-Masonic Party was the country's first third party. It was quite active in Pennsylvania and parts of New England. The party was mobilized by anti-Jacksonians against the Masons who were viewed with suspicion by those who held to a literal interpretation of the Bible. The party had particular strength in Vermont where it campaigned for temperance, Sunday blue laws, and free public education. In 1835, the Anti-Masons won the governorship of Pennsylvania. The major strategist for the Anti-Masons in New York was Thurlow Reed, a newspaper editor in Rochester, New York. He was able to gain the support of business interests for his party. While working for the Anti-Masons, Reed developed ties to William Henry Seward and Thaddeus Stevens of Pennsylvania.

This Anti-Masonic Party was the first party to hold a national convention; the other parties soon followed their lead. In 1831, at their National Convention in Baltimore, the Anti-Masons nominated William Wirt for president. Thurlow Weed soon recognized that the Anti-Masons were not going to be a strong enough force to challenge the Democratic-Republican Party, and he left the Anti-Masons to join the Whig Party. *See*: NATIONAL PARTY CONVENTION; WHIG PARTY.

References: Ralph M. Goldman, *The National Party Chairmen and Committees: Factionalism at the Top* (Armonk, N.Y.: M. E. Sharpe, 1990); Charles McCarthy, *The Antimasonic Party: A Study of Political Antimasonry in the United States, 1827–1840*, vol. 1, *Annual Report of the American Historical Association for the Year 1902* (Washington, D.C.: Government Printing Office, 1903); A. James Reichley, *The Life of the Parties: A History of American Political Parties* (New York: The Free Press, 1992).

APPROVAL RATING is the response to a closed-in poll question asking the respondents to rate the performance of the incumbent. It is most frequently used to rate the president. The question might have a range from strongly approve to strongly disapprove. Pollsters have asked this question for decades, so a current incumbent's approval rating can be compared to previous incumbents at various points in their term. A low approval rating of an incumbent suggests that the incumbent will be vulnerable in a subsequent election. President Bill Clinton enjoyed a high approval rating throughout most of 1996, which was an indication he would be reelected. *See*: POLL.

Reference: Michael W. Traugott and Paul J. Lavrakas, *The Voter's Guide to Election Polls* (Chatham, N.J.: Chatham House, 1996).

APPROVAL VOTING is a proposed election system in which voters can vote for as many candidates on the ballot for a particular office as they want, but a voter can only cast one vote per candidate. The candidate with the highest vote total wins. This permits the voter to vote for the candidates he/she approves of and avoids the wasted-vote problem. This electoral system has received a great deal of attention by students of elections, but has never been adopted.

Reference: Peter C. Fishburn, ''Social Choice and Pluralitylike Electoral Systems,'' in *Electoral Laws and Their Political Consequences*, Bernard Grofman and Arend Lijphart, eds. (New York: Agathon Press, 1986).

ARMEY, RICHARD K. (DICK) (1940–   ) currently serves as majority leader of the House Republicans, and member of Congress from the Twenty-Sixth District in Texas. Dick Armey was born in Cando, North Dakota. He earned an AB degree from Jamestown College in 1963, and a Ph.D. in Economics from the University of Oklahoma in 1969. He served as chairman of the Economics Department at North Texas State University from 1977 until 1983.

Armey says he tired of petty academic politics, and while watching C-SPAN, decided he could do a better job than the officials he was watching, and ran for Congress in 1984. He was a political novice, and took the Republican nomination by default, since no one thought incumbent Tom Vandergriff could be unseated. Surprisingly, Armey won by a vote of 51% to 49%. Armey's election reflects the changing politics of the South. A part of the district Armey currently represents was in New Dealer Sam Rayburn's district.

One of Armey's first successes was the creation of the Base Closure Commissions. These commissions determine which military bases should be closed, and Congress must then vote on the entire package. Armey opposed President Bush's budget summit. In 1992 Armey challenged Republican Conference chairman Jerry Lewis, who had supported Bush's budget package. Armey won the number three leadership position in the House by a vote of 88 to 84. In that leadership struggle Armey enjoyed the support of the House freshmen. When Newt Gingrich developed the idea of a Contract with America, Armey responded enthusiastically. Armey wrote parts of the Contract, and he campaigned tirelessly for the 1994 GOP congressional candidates, who ran on the Contract. When the Republicans captured the majority, Armey was elected Majority Leader without opposition. He has become the nuts and bolts operator of the new majority.

Armey is an opponent of farm subsidies, and he favors a flat tax. He has been elected by large margins, garnering 74% of the vote in 1996. *See*: CONTRACT WITH AMERICA; GINGRICH, NEWT(ON).

Reference: Michael Barone and Grant Ujifusa, *The Almanac of American Politics 1998* (Washington, D.C.: National Journal, 1997).

ARTHUR, CHESTER A. (1830–1886). Never having held an elective public office before being chosen as vice-president of the United States, Arthur was to succeed to the executive office at the death of President Garfield on September

19, 1881. Born in Fairfield, Vermont into the family of a Baptist clergyman on October 5, 1830, Arthur was graduated Phi Beta Kappa from Union College in 1848. Settling in New York City as a law clerk, he was admitted to the bar in 1854. Strong in his anti-slavery views he early joined the newly formed Republican Party, attending its first national convention in 1856. In New York, Arthur came to be a key figure in the organizational politics of the state party, becoming virtually second-in-command in the political machine of Roscoe Conkling. Even though a machine politician to the core, Arthur acquired a reputation for personal honesty, and when in office was committed to thorough record-keeping and a scrupulous accounting of the use of public funds. Serving during the Civil War years as Quartermaster General of New York, in 1871 he was appointed by President Grant to one of the most personally lucrative and patronage-rich positions in the national government, collector of the port of New York where two-thirds of the nation's tariff revenue was generated. Even though his administration of the customhouse was, by then current standards, competent, in a demonstration of his opposition to both the spoils system and the Conkling machine, President Hayes suspended Arthur from the collectorship in 1878. Two years later, when the Republican convention of 1880 became deadlocked between Conkling's "stalwart" faction attempting a third nomination for former president Grant and "half breed" forces supporting Senator James G. Blaine of Maine, delegates turned on the thirty-sixth ballot to "dark horse" candidate James A. Garfield of Ohio. To appease disgruntled "stalwarts," Chester A. Arthur was given the vice-presidential nomination. Winning an election exceptionally close in the popular vote, Garfield and Arthur were inaugurated on March 4, 1881. Garfield, however, was to serve but six months in the presidency. The victim of an assassination attempt on July 2, he died on September 19, 1881. Arthur assumed the presidential office under a cloud of public distrust. Garfield's attacker, a disappointed office seeker, had cried out as he fired at the president, "I am a stalwart, and Arthur will be president." Seeking to dispel any suspicion that either he or the Conkling machine had any part in the assassination, which clearly they had not, Arthur severed ties with his New York associates. Even though unconvinced that the spoils system could not work with both honesty and efficiency, Arthur nonetheless accepted the Pendleton Civil Service Reform Act, signing it into law on January 16, 1883. To further demonstrate his commitment to the combat of political corruption, Arthur lent the full support of his administration to federal prosecution of those allegedly involved in the star route mail frauds, many of whom were established "stalwarts." The jury acquittal of the major defendants on June 14, 1883 was a devastating political blow for Arthur. Throughout his presidency, and largely shielded from public attention, Arthur suffered increasingly bad health. As such, he chose in 1884 not to be an active candidate for his party's presidential nomination, even as he had considerable support particularly among Republican business leaders in New York and other major cities. Upon leaving the presidency, Arthur returned to his business interests and law practice in New York

City. Now diagnosed as suffering from Bright's disease, a condition which had been suspected during his White House illnesses, Arthur died on November 18, 1886, some 20 months after the end of his presidency. *See*: ELECTIONS: 1880; GARFIELD, JAMES A.

References: Justus D. Doenecke, *The Presidencies of James A. Garfield and Chester A. Arthur* (Lawrence: University Press of Kansas, 1981); Thomas C. Reeves, *Gentleman Boss, the Life of Chester Alan Arthur* (New York: Knopf, 1975).

ASSESSMENT. In older, urban machine-style parties, public employees who received patronage appointments paid a regular assessment to the party. The amount paid was calculated as a percentage of their salary. Some political party organizations actually instituted a payroll deduction. This was the case for the Cincinnati Republican Party Organization for many years. This practice of assessing public employees has fallen into disuse with the decline of urban political parties and the rise of Civil Service. *See*: MACHINE POLITICS; *RUTAN* v. *THE REPUBLICAN PARTY OF ILLINOIS* (1990).

Reference: Anne Freedman, *Patronage: An American Tradition* (Chicago: Nelson-Hall, 1994).

AT-LARGE ELECTION SYSTEM is an election system where all of the members of a governing body are selected by all of the voters of a jurisdiction. The Electoral College is an at-large system. The entire state votes for all of the electors, except for Maine and Nebraska, which use congressional districts for distributing Electoral College votes.

At-large election systems are frequently used in American cities where the voters cast votes for more than one member of the city council. The candidates are ranked by total votes received, and then are awarded seats until all of the seats have been distributed. Typically, voters are permitted to cast only one vote for each candidate, and the voters have as many votes as there are seats available. This type of election system was promoted by the Progressive Reform movement to break the stranglehold of the political bosses on American cities. The reformers believed that city council members elected at-large would take a city-wide approach to issues, rather than the narrow view of a specific part of the city. The at-large system has been criticized for favoring candidates of the majority population and making it difficult for minority candidates to win seats.

The at-large election system has been used for the election of members of state legislatures in some states. In 1967, Congress prohibited at-large elections for members of the House of Representatives, except in states where only one member is elected. *See*: CUMULATIVE VOTING; PROPORTIONAL REPRESENTATION; SINGLE-MEMBER DISTRICT; WARD.

Reference: Joseph F. Zimmerman, "Enhancing Representational Equity in Cities," in *United States Electoral Systems: Their Impact on Women and Minorities*, Wilma Rule and Joseph F. Zimmerman, eds. (Westport, Conn.: Greenwood Press, 1992).

ATWATER, LEE (1951–1991) served as chairman of the Republican National Committee (RNC) from 1989 to 1991. Atwater was born in Atlanta, Georgia and was raised in Columbia, South Carolina. He received an AB degree from Newberry College in 1973. While at Newberry he served as an intern in the office of Strom Thurmond, which increased his appetite for politics, and he became active in College Republicans.

After college, Atwater started a political consulting business. He was a very skillful Republican campaign consultant and became noted for his use of negative campaign tactics. He gained national attention by managing Ronald Reagan's 1980 primary campaign in South Carolina. He later managed George Bush's presidential campaign in 1988. Atwater was criticized for using coded racial themes in the Willie Horton ads against Michael Dukakis. With the support of President Bush, Atwater became RNC Chair after the 1988 campaign. He was the first professional political consultant to head up a national party. *See*: ELECTIONS: 1988; NEGATIVE ADVERTISING; REPUBLICAN NATIONAL COMMITTEE (RNC).

AUSTRALIAN BALLOT was introduced in the United States in the late nineteenth century. It is a secret general election ballot. It is also used for primaries. This ballot is printed, distributed, paid for, and counted by the government. Prior to the introduction of the Australian ballot, the parties supplied the ballots to the voters, and voting was not secret. With the introduction of the Australian ballot, the states began to acquire authority to regulate political parties. This ballot was first used in Australia in 1858. All of the states in the United States have used the Australian ballot since 1888.

References: Leon D. Epstein, *Parties in the American Mold* (Madison: University of Wisconsin Press, 1986); Jerrold G. Rusk, "The Effect of the Australian Ballot Reform on Split Ticket Voting: 1876–1908," *American Political Science Review*, Vol. 64 (1970).

B

BABY BOOMERS is the name used to describe the generation born after the end of World War II. Millions were born in the United States between 1946 and 1964. It is estimated that there are 75 million baby boomers. The population group has had a tremendous impact on American culture, the economy, and the political system. A large number of schools were built to accommodate them in the 1950s, and they flooded colleges and universities in the 1960s. They protested the Vietnam War and created a free-spirited youth culture in the 1960s. It is expected that they will have a tremendous impact on the entitlement programs such as Social Security and Medicare when they begin to retire.

Many experts predict that future politics will be driven by a generational struggle as younger voters, who will have to pay the cost of the entitlements demanded by the retired baby boomers, resist the added tax burden. President Bill Clinton was the first ''boomer'' to serve as president of the United States.

Reference: Paul C. Light, *Baby Boomers* (New York: W. W. Norton, 1988).

BAKER **v.** *CARR,* 369 U.S. 186 (1962) is a threshold case in which it was announced that courts were competent to review legislative apportionments. Sixteen years earlier, in the case of *Colegrove* v. *Green* (1946), the Supreme Court had refused to entertain a challenge to an Illinois apportionment statute, arguing that to do so would violate the ''political questions'' doctrine.

This case involved a challenge to the apportionment of the Tennessee General Assembly. The legislature in that state had not been reapportioned since 1901, even though the population had both grown and shifted in the prior 60 years. In a stunning reversal of *Colegrove*, the Court directed the Federal District Court in Tennessee to hear the challenge and, if appropriate, fashion a remedy.

Although the decision in *Baker* is a narrow one resolving only the question of justiciability, the removal of the "political questions" barrier to judicial examination of state apportionments made possible the establishment of the principle of "one person, one vote" in *Gray* v. *Sanders* (1963), *Reynolds* v. *Sims* (1964), and *Wesberry* v. *Sanders* (1964). All of the subsequent reapportionment cases are therefore really the progeny of *Baker. See: COLEGROVE* v. *GREEN* (1946); *GRAY* v. *SANDERS* (1963); POLITICAL QUESTIONS DOCTRINE; REAPPORTIONMENT; *REYNOLDS* v. *SIMS* (1964); *WESBERRY* v. *SANDERS* (1964).

Reference: Gene Graham, *One Man, One Vote: Baker v. Carr and the American Levellers* (Boston: Little, Brown, 1972).

BALANCED TICKET is a slate of candidates offered by a political party that reflects ethnic, gender, racial, and geographic diversity. In the era of urban machines the party slate represented ethnic diversity. It was expected that every ethnic group represented on the slate would vote for the entire ticket.

In national party presidential tickets attention has been given to sectional or geographic regions of the country when selecting a vice-presidential candidate. Today, attention is often given to gender and racial representation. The capacity of state and local parties to slate candidates has diminished with the introduction of the primary and the weakened state of political parties. *See*: VICE-PRESIDENTIAL SELECTION.

BALLOT, LONG is a ballot with a long list of federal, state, and local candidates to be selected by the voters. This type of ballot was promoted in the era of Jacksonian democracy. Today, reformers believe that voters with so many choices will not make well-informed choices and that many voters will simply follow the party cue. Reformers in the Progressive Era attempted to reduce the number of public offices elected on the long ballot. They promoted the idea of having more professional administrators appointed to public office and having fewer officials elected to state and local government positions. *See*: BALLOT, SHORT.

BALLOT, OFFICE BLOCK is a type of general election ballot that groups candidates by the office they are seeking, rather than by party. This is the most common ballot type used by states today. This is also known as the Massachusetts ballot. This ballot form encourages ticket splitting. *See*: BALLOT, PARTY COLUMN; SPLIT-TICKET VOTING.

Reference: Jack L. Walker, "Ballot Forms and Voter Fatigue: An Analysis of the Office Block and Party Column Ballots," *Midwest Journal of Political Science*, Vol. 10 (1966).

BALLOT, PARTY COLUMN is a general election ballot form that groups candidates by party. All candidates are listed in a column under a party label.

A voter can pull one lever, or make one mark, and cast a vote for all of the candidates offered by a particular party. This type of ballot form is also called the Indiana ballot, where it is still used. This type of ballot encourages straight-ticket voting. In 1988, in the state of Indiana, the Democrats were concerned that their popular candidate for governor, Evan Bayh, would lose because Indiana Senator Dan Qualye was the Republican Party's vice-presidential nominee and that would lead Indiana voters to cast a single vote for the entire Republican ticket. That did not happen. Bayh was elected. *See*: BALLOT, OFFICE BLOCK.

Reference: Jack L. Walker, "Ballot Forms and Voter Fatigue: An Analysis of the Office Block and Party Column Ballots," *Midwest Journal of Political Science*, Vol. 10 (1966).

BALLOT, SHORT is a ballot that contains candidates for only a few offices to be filled by the voters in a particular election. The expectation of the Progressive Reformers, who promoted the short ballot, was that voters would make more informed choices if they could restrict their attention to the qualifications and the positions of the candidates for a few offices. The reformers argued that more public offices should be filled by appointment of professional administrators with the result that better qualified personnel would serve in state and local government. This ballot, like the other Progressive reforms, was directed at weakening party machines that controlled the nominations of the offices in elections where long ballots were used. In recent decades, state governments have reduced the number of statewide elected officials. *See*: BALLOT, LONG.

BALLOT ACCESS. State law defines the requirements for a party or an independent candidate to gain a position on the ballot. States often have restrictive ballot access laws for independent candidates. The candidates are required to collect a given number of signatures to qualify for the ballot. For new political parties there are usually two requirements: first, the new party must circulate a petition and collect the signatures of a certain percentage of the registered voters to qualify; and second, to retain ballot access status the party must receive a certain percentage of the vote in the general election. If the new party does not achieve the defined percentage, the party will have to circulate petitions to regain ballot access. The ballot access laws are seen by some as barriers to third parties put up by the two major parties. However, defenders of the strict ballot access laws point out that more lenient ballot access laws would lead to a cluttered ballot.

Proponents of easing ballot access for third parties and independent candidates argue that the leaders of the two parties intentionally create ballot access barriers to restrict competition from both third parties and primary challengers. In 1996 it was estimated that a third party would have to collect 1,600,000 signatures to gain access to the presidential ballot in every state. To have the opportunity to file a slate of candidates for every federal and state office a third party would have to gather 3,500,000 signatures. An independent candidate for president would have to gather 186,000 signatures. The requirement is further complicated by established windows for circulating petitions.

In many states, ballot access laws make it difficult not only for third parties and independents, but also for candidates seeking major party nominations. In 1996 only three of eight Republican presidential candidates attempted to overcome the barriers required to enter the New York Republican presidential primary. Of those three candidates Patrick Buchanan was unable to qualify for one-third of New York's districts, and Steve Forbes was only able to get on the ballot through a court challenge to the rules. Only the New York State Republican Party favored presidential candidate Bob Dole was able to qualify. *See*: THIRD PARTIES.

References: E. Joshua Rosenkranz, *Voter Choice '96: A 50-State Report Card on the Presidential Elections* (New York: Brennen Center for Justice at New York University School of Law, 1996); *Ballot Access News*, Richard Winger, ed., P.O. Box 470296, San Francisco, CA 94147.

BANDWAGON EFFECT is the tendency of voters to support the expected winner. The effect of polls published before election day might lead voters to a "herd effect" where the undecided voters go with the predicted winner. Proposals such as uniform poll closing in states, and an effort by Congress to restrict the announcement of exit polls before West Coast polls are closed were designed to mitigate the bandwagon effect. In 1996 the national TV networks projected an Electoral College reelection victory for President Clinton before the polls closed on the West Coast. The projection was made with states where polls had closed. There was no claim that the projection affected the outcome of the election in the West, since Clinton had held a substantial lead in the polls in California before the election. Also, the undecided voters did not break for Clinton. Both Dole and Perot made substantial gains with the undecided voters in the closing days of the 1996 election. A counterinfluence to the bandwagon effect is the underdog effect.

The bandwagon effect may be more evident in presidential nominations where party activists and contributors move to support the winners of the early primaries.

BARBOUR, HALEY was elected chairman of the Republican National Committee on January 29, 1993 on the third ballot. Barbour succeeded the ineffective Rich Bond, who had been selected by President Bush to chair the party after the death of the skillful Lee Atwater.

Barbour was a native of Yazoo, Mississippi where he was born in 1947. He started in politics as executive director of the Mississippi Republican Party. Barbour earned his law degree from the University of Mississippi. In 1982 he was the Republican nominee for the Senate against John C. Stennis. He lost that election. Prior to his election to the party chairmanship, he was a Washington lobbyist.

Haley Barbour had significant success in rebuilding the Republican Party. Under his leadership the Republicans made tremendous gains. Since 1992, as Barbour himself said: "We've gone from 176 seats in the House to 227, from 43 in the Senate to 55, from 18 governors to 32, and we have increased the number of Republicans by 500 net in the state legislatures."

Barbour is viewed as one of the most successful national GOP chairmen since Ray Bliss. His one major shortcoming was not winning the White House in 1996. Barbour was not only a skillful organizer and strategist, but an effective spokesman for the GOP on national media talk shows. *See*: REPUBLICAN NATIONAL COMMITTEE.

Reference: Alan Greenblatt, "Barbour: A Tough Act to Follow," *Congressional Quarterly Weekly Report*, Vol. 55 (January 25, 1997).

BARNBURNERS are political activists who take extreme measures in an attempt to achieve their goals. Barnburners do not calculate the consequences of their strategies and tactics. Their actions may cost more than the benefits derived. Some view the harsh language of Patrick Buchanan at the 1992 Republican convention as barnburning. This term is derived from the example of a farmer who was so radical that he burned down his barn to get rid of the rats.

In U.S. party history, the Barnburners were a faction of the Democratic Party that in 1846 supported the Wilmot Proviso which prohibited slavery in the territory acquired from Mexico. The faction of the Democratic Party in New York State that supported the Wilmot Proviso were called Barnburners. They were so-named because they did not seem to care that their position would split the party and bring about a general election defeat. At the 1848 Democratic convention the New York delegation was evenly divided between the Barnburners and the Hunkers (so-named because it was said that they hunkered for spoils), the latter group not wanting to lose voter support in the South over the slavery issue. *See*: ELECTIONS: 1848.

Reference: A. James Reichley, *The Life of the Parties: A History of American Political Parties* (New York: The Free Press, 1992).

BARNSTORM. Barnstorming by a political candidate in a campaign is making many campaign stops in a short period of time. Candidates frequently barnstorm the country or the state in the closing days of a campaign. It is derived from the idea of going from barn to barn. In nineteenth-century campaigns the barn was a site for itinerant entertainers, and politics was a form of entertainment in that era.

In 1996, Republican presidential nominee Bob Dole barnstormed in the final days of the campaign. He flew around the country holding late-night and early morning campaign rallies, hoping to ignite his campaign. He also demonstrated that despite his age, he had the stamina and energy for the presidency. Many analysts think this final push by Dole energized the Republican base vote and contributed to retaining the Republican majorities in both the House and Senate, despite Dole's defeat.

Reference: William Safire, *Safire's New Political Dictionary* (New York: Random House, 1993).

***BEER* v. *U.S.*,** 425 U.S. 130 (1976) is a case that established a relative (non-absolute) standard for evaluating claims of discriminatory redistricting under section 5 of the Voting Rights Act. In *Beer*, the Supreme Court declared that the federal district court was to apply a principle of "non-retrogression" when deciding whether or not to grant preclearance to areas covered by section 5 of the Voting Rights Act. In practice, this meant that covered areas would not have to provide for proportionate representation of minority populations in their redistricting plans. The only requirement was that redistricting plans could not provide less representation for minority groups.

The case itself involved voting districts for the New Orleans city council. Although 45% of the city's population was African American, the redistricting plan submitting to the federal court for preclearance under the Voting Rights Act was likely to result in only one minority representative on the seven-seat city council. Although the lower court initially refused to approve the plan, the U.S. Supreme Court overturned that decision, noting that there were no African Americans currently sitting on the New Orleans city council. Therefore, even though African Americans did not enjoy proportionate representation, their situation had not retrogressed. *See*: PRECLEARANCE; REAPPORTIONMENT; VOTING RIGHTS ACT.

BELLWETHER is a region of the country where the voting behavior reflects the nation's sentiment as a whole. A bellwether is a predictor of the sentiment of the country and consequently predicts and reflects the national election outcome. In 1996 the *New York Times* ran a series of articles on the political views of the citizens of Stark County (Canton, Ohio), which from past voting patterns is a bellwether county in a battleground state for American presidential elections. In 1996, Clinton carried Stark County for the second time. Another bellwether county is Peoria, Illinois, which Clinton also carried in 1996. He was the first Democrat to carry that county since Lyndon Baynes Johnson in 1964. Clinton carried Macomb County in Michigan, a county of socially conservative blue-collar Reagan Democrats.

Reference: Rhodes Cook, "Clinton's Easy Second-Term Win Riddles GOP Electoral Map," *Congressional Quarterly Weekly Report*, Vol. 54 (November 9, 1996).

BENCHMARK POLL is a major poll done on behalf of a candidate early in the campaign. The poll is done months before the campaign starts to determine the name identification of the candidates, and what percentage of the electorate is committed to particular candidates. The poll is often designed to determine partisan alignment, ideology, and demographic characteristics of the electorate. The benchmark poll also tests possible campaign themes. The themes that have the greatest appeal in the poll will be developed for use in the campaign. *See*: TRACKING POLLS.

Reference: Nelson W. Polsby and Aaron Wildavsky, *Presidential Elections: Strategies and Structures in American Politics*, 9th ed. (Chatham, N.J.: Chatham House, 1996).

BLACK CAUCUS refers to a group of African-American members of the House of Representatives who meet regularly to discuss issues and develop a common agenda. The Black Caucus was formed in 1969 with nine members. The group was funded as a legislative service organization until the Republican majority of the 104th Congress determined that in order to save money, legislative service organizations would no longer be funded. The Black Caucus continued to exist without public funds to support it.

There are 39 black members of the House of Representatives in the 105th Congress. All of the African-American House members are Democrats, except Oklahoma Republican Representative J. C. Watts, who is not a member of the Black Caucus.

The leader of the Black Caucus in the 105th Congress is fiery Representative Maxine Waters from Los Angeles, California. Her immediate predecessor was Kweisi Mfume of Maryland, who now heads the NAACP. *See*: MAJORITY-MINORITY DISTRICT; *MILLER* v. *JOHNSON* (1995); *SHAW* v. *RENO* (1993).

BLACK VOTING. The attainment of the right to vote by African Americans was a long and difficult struggle. The ratification of the post–Civil War U.S. constitutional amendments was the beginning of black enfranchisement. These amendments included the Fourteenth Amendment guaranteeing all Americans equal protection of the law, and the Fifteenth Amendment, which banned denying the right to vote on the basis of "race, color or previous condition of servitude." At the end of reconstruction, Southern white politicians devised various ways to restrict black voting. These restrictions included: literacy tests, poll taxes, and implementation of the all-white Democratic primary.

The Supreme Court found the white primary unconstitutional in *Smith* v. *Allright* (1944). The Civil Rights movement in the 1960s led to enactment of the Civil Rights Act and the Voting Rights Act. There are no longer any legal barriers to black voting.

After the Civil War, black Americans were overwhelmingly Republican. Blacks began to vote Democratic in the 1930s, and became part of the New Deal coalition. However, many blacks remained Republican. For example, in 1956, 39% of blacks voted for Dwight D. Eisenhower. Blacks deserted the

Republican Party in 1964 because the Republican nominee, Barry Goldwater, opposed the Civil Rights Act.

In 1996, 84% of black voters voted for Clinton, 12% voted for Dole, and 4% for Ross Perot. Black voters have become one of the strongest and most reliable voting groups for the Democratic Party. *See*: VOTING RIGHTS ACT.

References: Lucius J. Barker and Mack H. Jones, *African Americans and the American Political System*, 3rd ed. (Englewood Cliffs, N.J.: Prentice-Hall, 1994); Rufus P. Browning, Dale Rogers Marshall, and David Tabb, *Racial Politics in American Cities*, 2nd ed. (New York: Longman, 1997).

BLAINE, JAMES G. (1830–1893), to his political admirers "the plumed knight," to his detractors "the continental liar from the State of Maine," the future presidential candidate was born on a farm near West Brownsville, Pennsylvania on January 31, 1830. Entering Washington College at age thirteen, he was graduated in 1847. Teaching first in Kentucky, then in Philadelphia, Blaine was to relocate in Augusta, Maine, where in 1854 he became editor of the *Kennebec Journal*. Originally planning to become a lawyer, Blaine settled into a newspaperman's career, exchanging the latter within but a few years for that of the politician. Active in organizing the Republican Party in Maine, becoming its state chairman, the young editor, age 29, was elected to the Maine legislature in 1859, becoming House Speaker in 1861. Leaving the state legislature in 1863, having been elected to the U.S. House of Representatives, Blaine was to become Speaker in 1869, serving in that role until the coming of the Democratic majority of 1875. Widely regarded as the most likely Republican candidate for the presidency in 1876, Blaine was to be denied the nomination. Charged in the spring of 1876 (on the basis of the partial disclosure of the so-called "Mulligan Letters") with having secured improper financial benefit through the sale of bonds for the Little Rock and Fort Smith Railroad, and even though making a spirited defense of his actions on the House floor, Blaine became tarnished goods at the Republican convention in Cincinnati in June of 1876, and the delegates gave a fourth ballot nomination to Ohio governor Rutherford B. Hayes. While unacceptable in Cincinnati, such was not the case in Augusta, Maine where the state's governor appointed Blaine to fill an unexpired term in the U.S. Senate. Blaine's career in House and Senate was marked by his party leadership, not by his legislative product. While not a radical Republican, Blaine did oppose President Hayes's decision in April of 1877 to remove the last of federal troops from southern states, thus ending the period of military reconstruction. Blaine believed that to leave the newly freed black man unprotected in his civil and voting rights was to ensure violation of those rights by the post-reconstruction state governments of the South. Blaine, by conviction and by a calculation of his party's advantage, was, through the remainder of his career, to maintain an advocacy of full citizenship rights for black Americans. Again a candidate for the Republican presidential nomination in 1880, Blaine was again denied; the convention became deadlocked between the senator's "half breed" supporters and "stalwarts" attempting to nominate former president Ulysses S. Grant; delegates turned on the thirty-sixth ballot to dark horse compromise nominee James A. Garfield of Ohio. Successful in the election, President Garfield invited Blaine to join the cabinet as secretary of state. Blaine's tenure was, however, to be brief. Within three months of "stalwart" Vice-President Chester A. Arthur succeeding to the presidency because of Garfield's assassination, Blaine resigned his cabinet post, on December 12, 1881. Out of politics, Blaine turned to the writing of his memoirs, the first volume of which was published in 1884. That same year unflagging supporters brought his name once again to a Republican national convention, and, reinforcing the old adage, on this the third attempt Blaine forces prevailed. Blaine himself was a somewhat reluctant candidate, sensing that 1884 was unlikely to be a Republican year. Yet the presidential contest was exceptionally close, one of the closest in the nation's history. Democratic Party candidate Governor Grover Cleveland of New York, and his running mate Thomas A. Hendricks of Indiana, eked out a popular vote plurality of but 26,000 votes from among ten million cast, carrying 20 states and 219 Electoral College ballots to 18 states and 182 votes in the Electoral College for Blaine and Republican vice-presidential candidate Senator John A. Logan of Illinois. The campaign and election of 1884 revolved more around the issue of candidate character than substantive policy issues. The "Mulligan Letters" disclosed in 1876 were resurrected to haunt the Blaine candidacy; additional materials revealed included a letter in which Blaine, asking an associate to provide him with a letter of exoneration, ended his request with the postscript, "Best regards to the Mrs." followed by "Burn this letter." The "Mulligan Letters," nearly a decade old, continued to have weight and, by Blaine's further evasions, reinforced the public image of a man of questionable integrity. Democrats, hoping to benefit from the contrast of a candidate known for his independence and honesty relative to a duplicitous, perhaps corrupt, partisan, received their own jolt when in July newspapers revealed that Cleveland was the father of an illegitimate child for whom he acknowledged responsibility. Cleveland, however, turned the revelation to his advantage; doubting the true paternity of the child he nonetheless confirmed his acceptance of responsibility, instructing his campaign aids and advisors to simply "tell the truth." In such a close election from among many factors there is usually one cited, more often than all the others, as being responsible for gaining the victory or causing the defeat. Analysts have tended to point to one such incident, late in the campaign, which possibly sealed Blaine's fate. In New York City, Blaine met, on the morning of October 29, with a group of the city's Protestant clergymen. There the Rev. Samuel Burchard, acting as spokesman for the group, referred alliteratively to the Democrats as the party of "Rum, Romanism, and Rebellion." Perhaps not actually hearing the remark, Blaine made no comment. Within the day, however, the slander was on the streets, and despite Blaine's subsequent disavowal, it was irretrievable as to the damage inflicted on his candidacy among Catholic voters. Blaine was to lose New York State and its Electoral College ballots by but 1,200 votes; had the state been carried, Blaine, on the basis of the Electoral College count, would have won the presidency. Analysts have suggested that the Rev. Burchard's comment deflected from Blaine sufficient numbers of Irish Catholic votes in New York City alone to have produced the defeat. Returning to his home in Augusta, Blaine continued to work on the second volume of his memoirs, subsequently published in 1886. When Blaine embarked on an extended European tour in 1887–1888, many felt that it was a prelude to yet another bid for a Republican presidential nomination. Such, however, was not the case. Letting it be known that he was not to be considered as a candidate, Blaine endorsed and later campaigned for Benjamin Harrison of Indiana, successful both at the convention and in the fall election. Again invited to join the cabinet as secretary of state, Blaine's tenure was to prove longer than in 1881. At the State Department, Blaine's major interest, and accomplishment, was in Latin American affairs where he argued for trade reciprocity and general goodwill between the United States and its hemispheric neighbors to the south. Out of such efforts emerged the Inter-American Conferences of 1889 and 1890, forerunners of the Pan American Union. The increasingly strained relationship between President Harrison and his secretary of state (based on personality, not policy differences) led to Blaine's resignation on June 4, 1892. In failing health, Blaine died in Washington, D.C., on January 27, 1893, eight months after leaving the cabinet. *See*: ELECTIONS: 1884.

References: James G. Blaine, *Twenty Years of Congress: From Lincoln to Garfield*, 2 vols. (Norwich, Conn.: Henry Bill, 1884–1886); David S. Muzzey, *James G. Blaine, A Political Idol of Other Days* (New York: Dodd, Mead, 1935).

BLOODY SHIRT. The "Bloody Shirt" was waved by the Republicans in the election campaigns of the post–Civil War period. They did it to remind voters that it was the Democrats who had not fully supported the war effort, and consequently they were responsible for the death and destruction that resulted from the Civil War. This emotional campaign tactic was effective, and the Republicans dominated American national elections from 1864 until 1874.

Reference: John Calvin Batchelor, *"Ain't You Glad You Joined the Republicans?" A Short History of the GOP* (New York: Henry Holt, 1996).

BLUE DOG COALITION is a group of moderate Democratic members of the House of Representatives who meet regularly to advance a moderate agenda in Congress. Over 60% of this informal caucus group comes from the South. Blue Dog is an antonym of "Yellow Dog Democrat" which is used to describe an unswerving party loyalist. *See*: DEMOCRAT; YELLOW DOG.

Reference: http://www.house.gov/collinpeterson/bluedog/purpose.htm.

BOSS is a political leader, usually a party leader, who leads a disciplined and hierarchically organized political organization. A boss, typically, is able to control party nominations and consequently, has patronage in the form of public jobs and contracts to award to his supporters to maintain his organization. There were a number of urban bosses in early twentieth-century American history. A few of the more notable political bosses in American urban history include: William M. "Boss" Tweed of New York's Tammany Hall; Ed Kelly of Chicago in the 1940s; Frank Hague of Newark, New Jersey in the 1940s; and Edward Crump of Memphis, who served from the 1930s to the 1950s. Chicago Mayor Richard J. Daley was one of the last effective urban bosses. Daley's organization controlled party nominations and elections. It is estimated that he controlled 35,000 patronage jobs. This type of party leader is disappearing in America as a result of the direct primary, the short ballot, civil service law, and candidate-centered politics. *See*: MACHINE POLITICS; TAMMANY HALL.

References: Ralph G. Martin, *The Bosses* (New York: Putnam, 1964); Martin Shefter, "The Emergence of the Political Machine: An Alternative View," in *Theoretical Perspectives on Urban Politics*, Willis D. Hawley et al. (Englewood Cliffs, N.J.: Prentice-Hall, 1976).

BOUNCE, CONVENTION is a significant gain in the polls for the presidential nominee that result from the national party's conventions. The last five presidential challengers have had an average gain of ten points as a result of their party's national conventions. In 1992, William Clinton enjoyed the largest bounce for a challenger—15%. Incumbents also enjoy a bounce; however, the average is not as large as the challenger's average bounce. Since 1960 all presidential nominees have gained support from their national party conventions except Hubert Humphrey in 1968, who declined 7% in the polls because of the disruptions at the 1968 Democratic National Convention. Bob Dole received a bounce in the polls of 9% from the 1996 Republican National Convention in San Diego. The gain in the polls from the convention bounce does not usually persist. *See*: NATIONAL PARTY CONVENTION.

BRYAN, WILLIAM JENNINGS (1860–1925), three times the presidential nominee of the Democratic Party, three times defeated, the "Great Commoner," was a commanding figure in that raucous period of American politics stretching from the days of Cleveland and McKinley to those of Wilson and Harding. Born on the threshold of the Civil War on March 19, 1860 in Salem, Illinois, Bryan was not to leave that state for Nebraska until 1887. By then he had completed his study at Chicago's Union College of Law, had "read" the law in the Jacksonville offices of Lyman Trumbull, friend to Lincoln and himself a U.S. Senator, and had been in 1883 duly admitted to the bar. Lincoln, Nebraska seemed to Bryan not only to offer greater promise than Illinois for his practice of law, but more importantly, for his passion of politics. The latter promise was all but immediately fulfilled. In 1890 in the throes of agrarian depression the heretofore rock-ribbed Republican first congressional district sent the youthful Bryan, age

30, to the U.S. House of Representatives, narrowly reelecting him in 1892.
Having already established his reputation as a spellbinding speaker, Bryan found
in Washington a national stage on which to showcase his oratorical skills in
arguing the cause of the common man, farmer, and laborer. Instead of running
for reelection to the House in 1894, Bryan sought election by the Nebraska
legislature to the U.S. Senate. In this he was unsuccessful. But it was at this
time that Bryan found his issue: not merely the economic value, but the political
and moral virtue, of silver over gold. In what strikes Americans a century later
as an exotic and all but unfathomable debate, the competing claims of the two
metals were the energizing force for a decade of often bitter class warfare in
the political arena. Bryan was a champion of silver, much as established interests, with no small amount of promotion from industrialist and politico Mark
Hanna, discovered in William McKinley the savior of gold. Silverites, not
"gold-bugs," controlled the Chicago convention of the Democrats in 1896, and
William Jennings Bryan, relying on the power of both his voice and his message,
came to control the silverites: "You shall not press down upon the brow of
labor this crown of thorns; you shall not crucify mankind upon a cross of gold."
In no small part on the strength of these words, convention delegates on their
fifth ballot made Bryan, age 36, the Democratic presidential nominee, the youngest man ever to be nominated by a major political party. Within weeks Bryan
was also to become the nominee of both the Populist and National Silver parties.
Throughout the campaign, the Populist nomination created considerable difficulty for Bryan. The Populists, at their Baltimore convention, had given the
party's vice-presidential nomination to Georgia firebrand and agrarian radical
Tom Watson. Chicago Democrats, on the other hand, a few weeks earlier had
balanced their national ticket in traditional fashion, joining the youthful midwesterner at the head of the ticket with an eastern, relatively conservative Democrat, the older Arthur Sewall, established shipbuilder of Bath, Maine. To
prevent further defection of "Gold Democrats" in the east and industrial midwest, without alienating Populists of the South and agrarian midwest or voters
of the silver producing states, was no small challenge, even to a man of Bryan's
remarkable political and oratorical skills. This difficulty was enhanced by the
type of campaign Bryan chose to wage; the only choice that could have been
made by someone relying for success upon use of his greatest asset, his voice.
He criss-crossed the country by rail, a record-setting estimated 18,000 miles,
delivering hundreds of speeches to enthralled crowds of, as he saw it, the common man. His basic theme rarely varied, only the stridency of its presentation:
as president he would attack those great concentrations of wealth in the United
States that stifled economic opportunity for farmer and laborer; he would attack
that same concentration as it stifled for the common man a democratic politics;
and, always and foremost, advocacy of silver as the means by which these larger
objectives were to be accomplished. Election day saw William McKinley, the
Republican presidential nominee, who conducted a "front porch" campaign,
with Mark Hanna transporting thousands by rail to the McKinley home in Can-

ton, Ohio, emerge the solid victor. McKinley and his running mate Garret A. Hobart of New Jersey secured a popular vote plurality of nearly 600,000 votes, carrying 23 states with 271 Electoral College votes to 22 states and 176 ballots in the Electoral College for Bryan. Even though he lost, some analysts would regard the 1896 election as a prelude of things to come for the Democrats. While he did not dramatically move farmers, small businessmen, industrial and railway workers into Democratic Party ranks in 1896, he did pave the way for such a voter realignment to be initiated in 1912 with Woodrow Wilson's New Freedom, and eventually solidified with Franklin D. Roosevelt's New Deal of the 1930s. Further, on the strength of the 1896 returns Bryan was to secure recognition as his party's foremost national spokesman, virtually insuring his renomination in 1900. As Democrats assembled in Kansas City in 1900, no compelling reason emerged to part company with Bryan and he was unanimously renominated for the presidency on the convention's first ballot. The issue of silver, however, was another matter. Economic recovery had largely silenced the battle of the metals. Only Bryan's direct intervention kept the silver plank in the Democratic platform, and then only by the narrowest of margins. As he entered upon his campaign, Bryan, too, sensed the demise of silver as the great issue that could drive his message as it had four years earlier. Bryan, the pragmatist, while continuing with his crusade against concentrated wealth and his advocacy of the interests of the common man, simply dropped silver from his repertoire. To some degree substituted for the latter was his argument against American imperialism as he saw it emerging following the end of the Spanish-American War in August of 1898. Anti-imperialism, however, never gained the widespread emotional response that had been given to silver four years earlier. The result was an election defeat slightly more decisive than in 1896. Bryan, with his running mate, the former vice-president of the United States during the second Cleveland administration, Adlai E. Stevenson of Illinois, failed once again to bring about voter realignment; the Republican national ticket of McKinley and vice-presidential nominee Governor Theodore Roosevelt of New York, improving on its showing of four years earlier, ran up a popular vote plurality of more than 800,000, winning 28 states and 292 ballots in the Electoral College to 17 states and 155 Electoral College votes for the Democrats. Reacting to two successive Bryan defeats, moderate and conservative forces reclaimed control of the national Democratic Party, the 1904 nomination going not to Bryan but to Judge Alton B. Parker of New York. With the national economy performing in solid fashion, and given the personal popularity of Theodore Roosevelt, who was now in the White House following the McKinley assassination in 1901, Bryan calculated that 1904 was unlikely to be promising of Democratic Party success. How right he was. The party's 1904 ticket of Parker and his 80-year-old running mate Henry G. Davis, "the grand old man" of West Virginia politics, went down to resounding defeat. It was now the turn of Bryan and the progressive wing to reclaim party organizational control. This accomplished, Bryan once again secured a first ballot presidential nomination at the Denver convention of 1908.

The campaign waged by Bryan and his running mate John W. Kern of Indiana was in terms of its message the most controlled and moderate of Bryan's three attempts at the presidency. Using the theme "Shall the People Rule?" Bryan urged the direct election of U.S. Senators and numerous other electoral reforms. Silver as an issue was abandoned and his economic message generally softened; the Democratic Party, he reassured voters, was no enemy but rather the friend of industry, portraying the party as "the steadfast protector of that wealth which represents a service to society." The result of this moderation was Bryan's worst presidential election defeat; the Republican candidate, Secretary of War William Howard Taft of Ohio, and vice-presidential nominee Congressman James S. Sherman of New York, captured a popular vote plurality in excess of one million votes, carrying 29 states with 321 Electoral College ballots to 17 states and 162 votes in the Electoral College for Bryan-Kern. Bryan, sensing that he would never again lead his party's national ticket, now returned to what had become for him routine, traveling the lecture circuit where he would long remain in demand, writing editorials for the weekly newspaper *The Commoner* which he had founded in 1901, and arguing the populist cause within the Democratic Party. At age 48, the mantle of party elder statesman seemed about to shroud the "Great Commoner." There was to be, however, a last hurrah. Breaking a stalemate at the Baltimore convention of 1912, Bryan, in abandoning the candidacy of Champ Clark of Missouri, paved the way for the forty-sixth ballot nomination of Woodrow Wilson, the former academician and now governor of New Jersey, who was to go forward to election day victory over a deeply divided Republican Party. Despite Wilson's misgivings, and attempts to divert him to an ambassadorship, Bryan was appointed secretary of state, even though he, himself, preferred an assignment to the Treasury Department. Bryan, with Wilson's support, set about a noble task: to have the nations of the world renounce war, and one by one, enter into treaties for the "advancement of peace." Bryan's task, of course, was to be thwarted by the war clouds gathering in Europe. After August of 1914, as Wilson, proclaiming American neutrality (something to which Bryan wholly subscribed), gradually moved toward European intervention, the gulf between the president and his secretary of state widened, and Bryan resigned his post on June 8, 1915. While remaining personally and politically loyal to the president, Bryan with his usual vigor took up the cause of nonintervention and pacifism. On the lecture circuit and from the editorial page he added to this cause those of women's suffrage, prohibition, and religious fundamentalism, including a frontal attack on the Darwinian theory of evolution. It was this latter cause that proved to be his last, and to some of his longtime friends and supporters the most disconcerting. In the summer of 1925, Bryan became a participant in what came to be known as the "Scopes Trial," a case involving a high school science teacher, John T. Scopes, charged with teaching the theory of evolution in his biology classes in violation of provisions in Tennessee law. Scopes's defense was taken up by the nation's leading trial lawyer Clarence Darrow. While Bryan and his colleagues for the prosecution were to

enjoy victory in the court's decision, the confrontation between Bryan and Darrow, anticipated by so many, was severely disappointing to Bryan's fundamentalist followers. While still in Tennessee, arranging to have published his closing
argument which for procedural reasons he had been unable to deliver in the
courtroom, Bryan was fatally stricken on July 26, 1925. The body of the "Great
Commoner" was returned to Washington, D.C., for burial in Arlington National
Cemetery. *See*: ELECTIONS: 1896, 1900, 1908.

References: Paolo E. Coletta, *William Jennings Bryan*, 3 vols. (Lincoln: University of
Nebraska Press, 1964–1969); Louis W. Koenig, *Bryan: A Political Biography* (New
York: Putnam's, 1971).

BUCHANAN, JAMES (1791–1868) was born near Mercersburg, Pennsylvania
on April 23, 1791, and attended Dickinson College from which he graduated in
1809. Studying the law in Lancaster, Pennsylvania, where he would establish
his practice, Buchanan was admitted to the bar in 1812. Beginning his political
career as one of the last of the Federalists, Buchanan was elected to the U.S.
House of Representatives in 1820 and was to serve there until 1831, his political
allegiance shifting to the Jacksonian Democrats. His long political career was
to be marked by an emphasis on diplomatic service and foreign policy issues,
beginning in 1831 with his appointment by President Jackson as minister to
Russia. Returning from St. Petersburg in 1833 he was elected by the Pennsylvania legislature to a seat in the U.S. Senate where he later chaired the Senate
Foreign Relations Committee. Leaving the Senate in 1845, Buchanan joined the
cabinet, appointed secretary of state by President James K. Polk. In that role
Buchanan had to deal with two major territorial controversies: the confrontation
(peacefully concluded) with Great Britain as to control of the Oregon Territory
with establishment of the northern border at the forty-ninth parallel; the confrontation with Mexico (settled by war) as to possession of territories in the
southwest and resolved by the Treaty of Guadalupe Hidalgo in 1848, which
restored peace and forced Mexico to cede to the United States (in exchange for
fifteen million dollars) California and the vast New Mexico Territory. Attempting to resurrect the pattern of presidential succession whereby secretaries of state
stood first in line for selection to the executive office, Buchanan was a major,
but unsuccessful, candidate for the Democratic presidential nomination in 1848,
losing to Lewis Cass of Michigan. With Cass's subsequent defeat and the Whig
Party returned to power, Buchanan resumed his practice of law in Lancaster.
Again a candidate for his party's nomination in 1852, Buchanan was again
denied. With the Democratic victory, however, Buchanan found himself returned
to diplomatic service, accepting President Pierce's appointment as minister to
Great Britain. Perhaps the most notable feature of his four-year tour of duty was
the attempt made in 1854 by the U.S. ministers to Great Britain, Spain, and
France, meeting at Ostend in Belgium at the instruction of Secretary of State
William L. Marcy, to arrange for U.S. purchase of Cuba from Spain; failing

that, to proclaim the right of American military intervention there in the event of internal unrest (particularly a slave revolt which would have the potential of spreading to the American South). The "Ostend Manifesto" was subsequently repudiated by the Pierce administration, the secretary of state claiming that his ministers had gone beyond their instructions. The manifesto was, however, to do significant damage to Buchanan's future political career in that it characterized him among abolitionists, and even among more moderate anti-slavery advocates, as another one of the "northern men of southern principles," willing to go to significant lengths to protect the South's "peculiar institution." Buchanan, while personally opposed to slavery, took the position popular with so many within his party: slavery was constitutionally protected in those states where it existed and could be changed only at the initiative of those state governments. As to its extension into the territories (and within new states as they should come to be carved out of those territories), that was to be determined, case by case, on the basis of an exercise in "popular sovereignty" by those living within the territories. In effect, Buchanan subscribed to the Compromise of 1850, including vigorous federal enforcement of the fugitive slave law. When the Pierce administration, accepting the Kansas-Nebraska Act of 1854, destroyed the last vestiges of the Compromise of 1820 and opened the way to the possibility of slavery's extension into Kansas Territory, Pierce's renomination, now adamantly opposed by anti-slavery Democrats, became politically impossible. Buchanan was advanced as an acceptable alternative, not damaged by "Bleeding Kansas" in that he was removed from both the issue and the event by performance of his ambassadorial duties in London. Nominated on the convention's seventeenth ballot, "Old Buck" was joined on the Democratic national ticket with John C. Breckinridge of Kentucky as the party's vice-presidential candidate. With the disintegration of the Whig Party following the elections of 1852, Buchanan and the Democrats faced for the first time a newly organized competitor, a Republican Party born of the slavery issue and composed of Northern Whigs, defecting anti-slavery Democrats, and many of those who in the recent past had been associated with the Liberty Party or, subsequently, the Free-Soil movement. The new party had nominated "the Pathfinder of the West," soldier and explorer John C. Frémont of California. Finessing the slavery issue for one last time, the Democrats won a solid victory over Frémont and his running mate, former U.S. Senator from New Jersey William L. Dayton; Buchanan posting a popular vote plurality just shy of 500,000 votes, and carrying 19 states with 174 Electoral College ballots. In losing, the Republicans registered a respectable first showing, gathering more than 1,300,000 popular votes, gaining 114 Electoral College ballots from 11 states. The "Know-Nothing," American Party presidential candidacy of former president Millard Fillmore, with his vice-presidential running mate Andrew Jackson Donelson of Tennessee, drew nearly 900,000 popular votes and carried the state of Maryland with its 8 Electoral College ballots. Buchanan began his presidency with the expectation that in the case *Scott* v. *Sandford* (1857), commonly to become known as the Dred Scott case, the U.S. Supreme Court could do what presidents, congresses, and parties had heretofore been unable to do: impose a definitive solution to the slavery problem, one which, in respect of the high court's role as "giver of the law," the American people would obediently accept. The Court's decision, in March of 1857 but days after Buchanan's inauguration, declaring, among other holdings, that Congress had no constitutional authority to legislatively restrict slavery in the territories of the United States, far more than resolving the issue once and for all as Buchanan had hoped, merely added fuel to the raging fire. Buchanan himself further contributed to the conflagration when in 1858 he sought, unsuccessfully, congressional approval for Kansas's admission to the Union as a slave state, based on his acceptance of the submitted Lecompton Constitution, a document seen by anti-slavery forces as having been jerry-rigged and without legitimacy. Just as Kansas had destroyed the political career and presidency of Franklin Pierce, so, in effect, it now consumed James Buchanan. With the Republican presidential victory of November 1860, awaiting Lincoln's inauguration in March, and as state after Southern state seceded from the Union, Buchanan, the man of negotiation and compromise, made last-ditch efforts to avoid the coming war. It is not remarkable that these efforts were unsuccessful, Buchanan's firmly held view being that while the Southern states had no constitutional right to secede, he as president, on the other hand (should they secede), had no constitutional authority to prevent that secession. Retiring, from a Washington all but under siege, to Wheatland, his Pennsylvania estate, on March 4, 1861, Buchanan was to write a defense of his White House years, *Mr. Buchanan's Administration on the Eve of the Rebellion*, published in 1866. Living to see the Civil War ended and the Union preserved, Buchanan died at Lancaster, Pennsylvania on June 1, 1868. *See*: ELECTIONS: 1856.

References: Philip S. Klein, *President James Buchanan, A Biography* (University Park: Pennsylvania State University Press, 1962); Elbert B. Smith, *The Presidency of James Buchanan* (Lawrence: University Press of Kansas, 1975).

***BUCKLEY* v. *VALEO*,** 424 U.S. 1 (1976) was a seminal case in which the U.S. Supreme Court concluded that political contributions and expenditures were forms of expression protected by the First Amendment. There have been several recent proposals to amend the Constitution to allow for legislation that might significantly limit the amount of money flowing into political campaigns. Clearly, these proposals are aimed at overturning the Supreme Court's decision in *Buckley* v. *Valeo*. In fact, any contemporary campaign finance reform must confront the constitutional obstacles established by the Court's decision in this case.

Buckley v. *Valeo* arose out of a challenge to the 1971 Federal Election Campaign Act (FECA) brought by a number of individuals including Eugene McCarthy, a candidate for the presidency; James Buckley, who was seeking reelection as a senator from New York; and the New York Civil Liberties Union.

As amended in 1974, FECA can be divided into at least five parts. First, FECA limits the amount the money that individuals or groups are allowed to contribute to federal election campaigns. Next, the Act limits expenditures which may be made by either candidates themselves or by individuals and groups who are expending funds "relative to a clearly identifiable candidate." Third, FECA mandates the disclosure and reporting of most campaign contributions. All of the above provisions were to be enforced by a newly formed board called the Federal Election Commission (FEC). Finally, the Internal Revenue Code of 1954 was amended to provide for the public financing of presidential campaigns and elections.

In a per curium opinion representing the views of the eight participating Supreme Court Justices, the Court announced that both donating and spending money (contributions and expenditures) were forms of political expression and association deserving of protection under the First Amendment to the Constitution. In the words of the Court,

A restriction on the amount of money a person or group can spend on political communication during a campaign necessarily reduces the quantity of expression by restricting the number of issues discussed, the depth of their exploration, and the size of the audience reached.

The justices then moved to strike down FECA's limitations on candidate contributions and expenditures, arguing that the government's interest in cleansing the political system of both corruption and the appearance of corruption was not sufficiently advanced by the limitations to justify the heavy burden placed on First Amendment liberties. The Court reasoned that since candidates could not bribe themselves, it was difficult to understand how candidate contributions and expenditures could appear corrupting.

Relying on the same reasoning, the Court upheld the Act's reporting requirements as well FECA's caps on contributions by private citizens. In both of these situations the Court accepted what it admitted were burdens on speech based on the justification that these guidelines were closely linked to the compelling government interest of reducing both corruption and the appearance of corruption within the political system.

The Court failed to accept a similar justification for limitations on expenditures made "relative to a clearly identified candidate." In order to avoid the constitutional infirmity of vagueness, the Court construed the limitation so that it only reached "communications containing express words of advocacy of election or defeat." Although this began what would later be an important distinction between issue advocacy and express advocacy, the Court found that even the regulation of expenditures which urged the election of a specific candidate ran afoul of the Constitution. Unlike contributions, expressions of support which are not controlled by candidates "may well provide little assistance to the candidate's campaign and indeed may prove counterproductive." Moreover, any ban on express advocacy will likely be ineffective since (as we have seen) it is rather easy to indirectly advocate the election of a candidate without directly referring to the candidate.

Although *Buckley* v. *Valeo* is primarily known for its impact on campaign finance law, also challenged in this case was the constitutionality of the Federal Election Commission and the public financing of presidential campaigns and elections. Although the Court found that Congress had the power to provide publicly financed elections and a Federal Election Commission, the Court found that since members of the Federal Election Commission functioned as "Officers of the United States" their method of appointment had to be consistent with the provisions of Article II, section 2 of the Constitution. This section of the Constitution does not allow for appointments by officers of the U.S. Senate and House of Representatives while, according to FECA the members of the Commission were to be appointed by the President Pro Tempore of the Senate, and the Speaker of the House. The Congress responded to the Court's decision by having the president appoint all the members of the Federal Election Commission.

As a final note, it bears mentioning that the constitutional protections announced by the Supreme Court in this case are considered to be voluntarily surrendered by those choosing to accept federal matching funds. Wealthy candidates who do not need federal dollars to compete are free to spend as much of their own money as they see fit in pursuit of elective office. *See*: FEDERAL ELECTION CAMPAIGN ACT OF 1971; *FEDERAL ELECTION COMMISSION* v. *NATIONAL CONSERVATIVE PAC* (1985); MATCHING FUNDS; SOFT MONEY.

References: Robert E. Mutch, *Campaigns, Congress, and the Courts* (New York: Praeger, 1988); Daniel D. Polsby, "*Buckley* v. *Valeo*: The Special Nature of Political Speech," *Supreme Court Review* (1976); J. Skelly Wright, "Politics and the Constitution, Is Money Speech?" *Yale Law Journal*, Vol. 85 (1976).

BULL MOOSE PARTY is the unofficial name given to the Progressive Party of 1912, when Theodore Roosevelt was the party's presidential candidate. This party was formed as a bolt from the Republican Party which renominated William Howard Taft. The Progressive Party platform called for women's suffrage, direct election of U.S. Senators, support for a constitutional amendment for a federal income tax, and recall of judicial decisions. In the election of 1912, Roosevelt finished second with 27% of the popular vote, the best showing of any third-party candidate. *See*: ELECTIONS: 1912.

Reference: William H. Harbaugh, *The Life and Times of Theodore Roosevelt* (New York: Oxford University Press, 1975).

BULLOCK v. CARTER, 405 U.S. 134 (1972) declared that a Texas law requiring the payment of a filing fee in order to be placed on the primary election ballot was in violation of the Equal Protection Clause of the Fourteenth Amendment.

Chief Justice Burger, who authored the majority opinion, began by explaining that there was a relationship between ballot access and individual voting rights. Therefore, in denying ballot access to those unable to pay what the Court thought was an exorbitant filing fee, Texas was also denying to voters the opportunity to vote for these candidates. This amounted to a denial of equal protection rights to those voters who might want to vote for a candidate who was unable to afford the filing fee. The chief justice then insisted that a denial of equal protection of the laws could be held constitutional only if the state could prove that the discriminatory practices were necessary to forwarding some legitimate state objective. Burger concluded that, although Texas had a legitimate interest in regulating the number of people on a ballot, other methods were available to the state. Since Texas could advance its interest in other less arbitrary ways, the law failed the first prong of the test, and was therefore declared to be in violation of the Equal Protection Clause of the Fourteenth Amendment. *See*: FILING.

BUNDLING is the practice of combining individual contributions from members of the same interest group into one bundle of separate checks and presenting those checks to a particular candidate or political party. In theory, bundling meets the letter of the campaign finance law, but not the spirit of the law, because campaign finance contribution limits are designed to reduce the influence of large amounts of money coming from one source. Bundling is a strategy designed to circumvent the intent of the law.

BUSH, GEORGE HERBERT WALKER (1924–   ) was the forty-first president of the United States. He was born in Milton, Massachusetts and grew up in Greenwich, Connecticut. His father Prescott Bush, an investment banker, served as a U.S. Senator from Connecticut. George Bush served as a navy pilot during World War II, and was awarded the Distinguished Flying Cross for bravery. After the war, he earned a B.A. degree in economics from Yale University (1948). At Yale, he was Phi Beta Kappa and captain of the baseball team. After graduation, Bush went to Texas to learn the oil business. He started an oil and gas business in Midland, Texas, and later moved the business to Houston.

Bush was active in Texas Republican politics, and ran for a U.S. Senate seat in 1964, but was defeated by the incumbent Democratic Senator Ralph Yarborough. In 1966, Bush was elected to the U.S. House of Representatives and was reelected in 1968. In 1970 he ran again for the U.S. Senate and was defeated by Lloyd Bentsen. Presidents Nixon and Ford appointed Bush to a number of federal positions, including U.S. Representative to the UN; chairman of the Republican National Committee (1973–1974); Chief, U.S. Liaison to China; and director of the CIA (1976–1977). He was loyal to the president who appointed him; for example, as RNC Chairman, Bush remained loyal to President Nixon throughout the Watergate ordeal.

After he left the federal government in 1977, George Bush began his campaign for the 1980 Republican presidential nomination. Bush won the Iowa caucus, but was then defeated in a number of primaries by Ronald Reagan; Bush left the field of battle in May. Ronald Reagan selected Bush to serve as his running mate in 1980. Bush served as a loyal vice-president to President Reagan. The Reagan-Bush ticket was reelected in 1984. Bush finally received his party's presidential nomination at the GOP Convention in New Orleans in 1988. Bush selected Indiana Senator Dan Quayle as his running mate, and they easily defeated Democratic nominee Michael Dukakis in the general election.

President Bush assembled a respected and professional cabinet. He had to deal with a Democratic Congress; Bush attempted to be more conciliatory than President Reagan had been with the opposition party. In the 1988 presidential campaign Bush ran on the slogan: "Read my lips, no new taxes." Despite that pledge, in the fall of 1990 Bush agreed to a deficit reduction program which included a tax increase. One of President Bush's greatest successes was the Gulf War. In 1991, the United States took military action against Iraqi troops which had invaded the oil-rich country of Kuwait. This military action became known as "Operation Desert Storm." President Bush assembled a coalition of troops from many countries and launched air strikes against Iraq. The war ended quickly with few U.S. casualties. Immediately after the war, Bush enjoyed an unprecedented 91% approval rating.

President Bush's popularity was short-lived. In the 1992 presidential election, because of a perceived weak economy, Bush was defeated by William Clinton. Bush returned to Texas after his defeat. His oldest son George W. Bush was elected governor of Texas in 1994. *See*: ELECTIONS: 1988, 1992.

References: Herbert S. Parmet, *George Bush: The Life of a Lone Star Yankee* (New York: Scribner, 1997); Charles Tiefer, *The Semi-Sovereign Presidency: The Bush Administration Strategy for Governing without Congress* (Boulder, Colo.: Westview Press, 1995).

BUSH, GEORGE W. (1946–   ) was elected governor of Texas in 1994. He is the son of former president George Bush and Barbara Bush. He was born in New Haven, Connecticut, graduated from Yale University in 1968, and earned an M.B.A. from Harvard in 1975. He served in the Air National Guard from 1969 to 1973.

George Bush was raised in Midland, Texas. He ran for Congress in Texas in 1978 and lost. He served as an advisor to his father's presidential campaign in 1988, and became a partner in the Texas Rangers baseball team. In 1994 he challenged incumbent Governor Ann Richards for the governorship of Texas and defeated her by a margin of 53% to 46%. He, like many governors around the country, struggled with court-mandated school finance issues resulting from inequitable school funding. Bush was reelected in 1998 with 70% of the vote. *See*: BUSH, GEORGE HERBERT WALKER.

C

CADRE PARTY. A cadre type of party is one that is characterized by a small core group of activists who recruit candidates, raise money to maintain the party, and provide services to the candidates. American political parties are generally considered cadre parties in contrast to the mass membership parties that existed in Europe. *See*: MASS MEMBERSHIP PARTIES.

Reference: Leon D. Epstein, *Political Parties in the American Mold* (Madison: University of Wisconsin Press, 1986).

CAMPAIGN is an organized effort to persuade voters to vote for or against a particular candidate, party, or ballot issue. A campaign usually has a structured organization reflecting highly technical skills and specialization, such as polling, research, volunteer coordination, fund-raising, press relations, and media development. The political campaigns of the late twentieth century are candidate-centered and emphasize electronic media, which requires a tremendous amount of money. Political campaigns in the United States last for months, and presidential campaigns often last years. Because it is so expensive to hire qualified campaign specialists and fund an electronic media campaign, the contemporary candidates spend most of their time fund-raising. *See*: CAMPAIGN MANAGER.

Reference: Gerald M. Pomper, "Campaigning: The Art and Science of Politics," *Polity*, Vol. 2 (Summer 1970).

CAMPAIGN LITERATURE is all of the material printed for a political campaign. It usually highlights the qualities of the candidate. If it is party literature it will highlight a number of candidates. The literature gives information about the candidate's history, platform, and groups that support the candidate. The literature might give negative information about the opponent. Campaign literature can range from xeroxed materials to expensive, professionally developed campaign brochures. Campaign literature is frequently mailed out to the voters. In local elections it is often distributed door-to-door.

Reference: Dick Simpson, *Winning Elections: A Handbook of Modern Participatory Politics* (New York: HarperCollins, 1996).

CAMPAIGN MANAGER is responsible for managing a candidate's campaign. In the modern campaign the manager coordinates the campaign's finances, candidate scheduling, polling, and press events. The campaign manager designs the strategy for the campaign. After the strategy is adopted, the campaign manager is responsible to see that the strategy is implemented. In a local campaign, the manager is often a friend or supporter of the candidate. In state and national campaigns, the manager is a full-time paid professional.

Bob Dole's presidential campaign was often disorganized because Dole could not settle on a manager. Shake-ups in campaign staff are often a sign of a troubled campaign. *See*: CAMPAIGN; POLITICAL CONSULTANTS.

Reference: Dick Simpson, *Winning Elections: A Handbook of Modern Participatory Politics* (New York: HarperCollins, 1996).

CANDIDATE is a person seeking election to public office. In ancient Rome, a candidate seeking office wore a white toga, indicating the person did not have any stain on his character. The Latin root of the word is *candidus*, which means "shining white."

In modern political campaigns, the candidate has become the central part of the election process and the campaign. Today, modern campaigns are termed "candidate-centered," which means that the candidate, not the party, determines the voters' choice.

Reference: William Safire, *Safire's New Political Dictionary* (New York: Random House, 1993).

CARTER, JAMES EARL (JIMMY) (1924–   ) was the thirty-ninth president of the U.S. He was born in Plains, Georgia. In 1946 he graduated from the U.S. Naval Academy in Annapolis. While in the Navy, Carter served as a nuclear submarine officer under Admiral Hyman Rickover. He left the Navy in 1953 to manage the family's peanut business.

When he returned to Plains, Georgia, Carter became a leader in the Plains Baptist Church, served on the county school board, and in 1962 was elected to the Georgia State Senate. He was progressive on race relations in the South. In 1967 he lost a bid for the Democratic gubernatorial nomination, and after that loss he became a "born again" Christian. In 1970 he made a second effort to win the governor's office, and he was elected. He was a very innovative governor, and led the reorganization and modernization of the antiquated Georgia state government. As governor, Carter introduced Zero-Base Budgeting (ZBB), which required every state agency to justify its entire budget. He gained national recognition for his achievements as governor. Carter was not permitted to seek a second term as governor under the Georgia state constitution. After leaving office he started to actively pursue the Democratic Party's presidential nomination. One of his top aides, Hamilton Jordan, wrote an extensive memorandum on how to win the presidential nomination.

At the outset of the 1976 presidential campaign, Carter had very low name identification in polls listing presidential aspirants. Following Jordan's memo, Carter carefully worked to build support in the state of Iowa, which conducted its presidential caucuses in January 1976. Carter's efforts proved successful. He finished first in Iowa; this led, as Jordan predicted, to national press attention, and gave Carter the momentum he needed to win the New Hampshire primary and ultimately the party nomination. In order to offset the view that he was inexperienced, Carter selected Minnesota Senator Walter Mondale as his running mate. After Watergate, Carter sensed that the public wanted a change, and he offered himself as a Washington outsider. In the general election, Jimmy Carter defeated Gerald Ford in a close election. On inauguration day, Jimmy Carter and his wife Rosalyn walked down Pennsylvania Avenue to demonstrate that they were common people.

Carter's inexperience in national politics, which helped him in the election, became a liability while he was president. Despite large Democratic majorities in Congress, Carter was unable to successfully advance significant legislation. Carter inherited an economy suffering from unemployment and inflation, and it did not improve under his presidency. In the area of foreign policy, he gave a great deal of attention to the issue of human rights. Carter's mishandling of the overthrow of the Shah of Iran and the taking of 52 American hostages by Iranian terrorists made him appear weak and incompetent in foreign affairs. In 1980, Carter had to fend off a challenge for the Democratic presidential nomination by Massachusetts Senator Ted Kennedy. In the general election, Carter was decisively defeated by the Republican nominee for president, the former governor of California, Ronald Reagan.

After his defeat, Jimmy Carter retired to Plains, Georgia. He has been a role-model citizen, promoting such worthy causes as Habitat for Humanity. In foreign policy, he has promoted human rights policies in world affairs. *See*: ELECTIONS: 1976, 1980.

References: Jimmy Carter, *Keeping Faith: Memoirs of a President* (New York: Bantam Books, 1982); Jack W. Germond and Jules Witcover, *Blue Smoke and Mirrors: How Reagan Won and How Carter Lost the Election of 1980* (New York: Viking Press, 1981).

CASEWORK is the name for the services provided to constituents by an elected official or their staff. Casework is an effort by a national or state legislator to assist a citizen in resolving a problem with a government agency. Some examples include: a problem with a Worker's Compensation claim, a Social Security or Medicare payment. The legislator's staff also provides information and assistance to constituents about pending legislation. Members of Congress and some state legislators have district offices and staff to assist constituents. This is a valuable resource for incumbents and helps to build support for their reelection. This is one of the benefits of incumbency and contributes to the high rate of reelection of incumbents.

Reference: John R. Johanes, *To Serve the People: Congress and Constituency Service* (Lincoln: University of Nebraska Press, 1984).

CASS, LEWIS (1782–1866) was born in Exeter, New Hampshire on October 9, 1782. Educated at Phillips Academy, Cass, after a brief sojourn in Delaware, migrated to Ohio in 1800, claiming a land grant near Zanesville to which his family was entitled, based on his father's military service in the Revolutionary War. After studying law in Marietta, Cass was admitted to the bar in 1802. Serving as Muskingum County prosecutor from 1804 to 1806, Cass was in the latter year elected to the state legislature. Rewarded for both his party and personal loyalty to President Jefferson, Cass was appointed U.S. Marshall for Ohio in 1807, holding that office until taking leave five years later to bear arms against the British and their Indian allies in the War of 1812.

Commissioned as brigadier general in the U.S. Army in March of 1813, Cass, on October 29 of that same year, was appointed by President Madison to the civilian governorship of the Michigan Territory, a post he was to hold until 1831. His tenure as governor was marked by numerous treaties and agreements reached with Indian tribes within those parts of the old Northwest Territory over which Cass was given jurisdiction. Attempting to act as ''a humane man,'' but with all the prejudices of his age and race, Cass nonetheless came to be regarded by both tribes and settlers as an honest broker. Impressed with his administrative abilities and record, as well as by his keen partisanship, Cass was appointed secretary of war by President Jackson in 1831. Ironically, given Cass's largely benign relationship with the Indian tribes of the Michigan Territory, it fell upon him to plan for the forced migration of Cherokees and other Indian tribes from their lands in the southeastern states under the Jackson administration's Indian Removal Act of 1830. In 1836, Cass resigned from the War Department to accept appointment as U.S. Minister to France. His differences with the Whig administration which came to power in March of 1841, particularly disagreement with Secretary of State Daniel Webster over the Webster-Ashburton Treaty, led to his resignation in 1842. Cass's major criticism of the treaty was that it did not resolve the ''right-of-search'' issue; that the Royal Navy would continue its discretionary practice of stopping American ships on the high seas, conducting searches, and impressing sailors on board claimed to be of British citizenship. With his opposition made public, Cass returned to the United States. Twisting the British lion's tail, always popular sport in nineteenth-century America, Cass suddenly found himself, for the first time in his career, to be a recognized national figure. As such he became, along with the frontrunner, former president Martin Van Buren, a major contender for the Democratic presidential nomination of 1844. Unfortunately for Cass, he and Van Buren deadlocked the convention with neither candidate being able to secure the required two-thirds vote from the assembled delegates. Party leaders turned to a compromise ''dark horse'' candidate, the relatively obscure James K. Polk of Tennessee who, known to have Andrew Jackson's endorsement, was nominated on the ninth ballot. Cass, denied this opportunity to go to the White House in March of 1845, nonetheless arrived in the nation's capital that same year and month, elected by the Michigan legislature to the U.S. Senate. In that chamber Cass became an ardent advocate of territorial expansionism, of ''manifest destiny.'' He urged settlement with the British of the question of control of the Oregon Territory, peacefully if possible, by war if necessary. He supported Texas annexation and the further acquisition of territory from Mexico by the same formula, peacefully if possible, but by war if necessary. While peace prevailed in the former instance, it did not in the latter, and Cass became fully supportive of the war effort in the years 1846–1848. The war presented, however, a political question that proved to be Cass's nemesis: the possible extension of slavery into the territories which would be acquired by the United States as a result of any peace settlement with Mexico. Personally opposed to slavery, but unwilling to endorse the Wilmot Proviso of 1846 (proposed legislation that would prohibit slavery in the newly acquired territories), Cass became one of the foremost advocates of ''popular sovereignty,'' the practice whereby settlers in the respective territories would decide for themselves whether to allow or prohibit slavery. Abolitionists, of course, were appalled by such a stance. With President Polk holding himself to his one-term pledge, and with Cass's position on both the question of Texas annexation and that of slavery's possible extension into the territories not unlike that of the retiring president, Cass was able to capture his party's presidential nomination in May of 1848. The Whigs again, as in 1840, nominated a popular military figure, General Zachary Taylor of Louisiana, the hero of the battle of Buena Vista. In a relatively close election, Cass and his running mate, William O. Butler of Kentucky, carried 15 states with 127 votes in the Electoral College; General Taylor and the Whig vice-presidential nominee, Millard Fillmore of New York, also carried 15 states, but with 163 Electoral College ballots, a clear majority. In the popular vote count Taylor also outdistanced Cass, with a plurality over the Democrats of nearly 140,000 votes. Analysts, however, point to the fact that Martin Van Buren and Charles Francis Adams, the national ticket of the anti-slavery, Free-Soil Party, drew 292,000 popular votes; while carrying neither a state nor a single Electoral College ballot, this popular vote total was double that of the Whig plurality and was sizeable enough in both Massachusetts and New York to deny those states to the Democrats and, thereby, to deny Cass the presidency. Cass, returned by the Michigan legislature to his seat in the U.S.

Senate, from which he had resigned in May of 1848, was to serve in that body until 1857. With the election of James Buchanan to the presidency, Cass, age 74, accepted appointment as secretary of state. In that position Cass was to have the satisfaction of reaching agreement with Great Britain effectively ending the Royal Navy's "right to search" American ships on the high seas, the issue over which he and Daniel Webster had engaged in bitter confrontation more than a decade earlier. In December of 1860, Cass demanded of Buchanan, now a lame-duck president, that he strengthen the federal military presence in those southern states threatening secession. Buchanan, turning aside the demand, did, however, accept the secretary of state's resignation. Cass, living to see the Civil War ended and the Union preserved, died on June 16, 1866. *See*: ELECTIONS: 1848.

Reference: Willard C. Klunder, *Lewis Cass and the Politics of Moderation* (Kent, Ohio: Kent State University Press, 1996).

CATHOLIC VOTE. The Catholic voters have traditionally favored the Democratic Party. The Democratic Party's nomination of New York's Catholic governor Al Smith for president in 1928 brought the Democrats a great deal of support from the urban Catholic population. They were a key element of the New Deal coalition forged by Franklin D. Roosevelt. The nomination and election of President John F. Kennedy also led Catholics to favor the Democrats. Catholics began to break away from the Democrats in the 1980 election when 50% of Catholic voters voted for Ronald Reagan. In 1992, Catholics voted 44% for Clinton, 36% for Bush and 20% for Perot. In the 1994 congressional election, a majority of Catholics voted for the Republican candidates. In 1998, Catholics favored the Democrats 53% to 47% for the Republicans.

Catholics were considered a key swing voting block in the 1996 presidential election, and were courted by both of the major parties' presidential candidates. The Republican national party leadership promoted the idea of selecting one of the many midwestern Catholic governors for the vice-presidential nomination to attract this key voting block. The Catholic vote swung back to the Democrats in the 1996 election; 54% of Catholic voters cast their ballots for Democratic party nominee Bill Clinton, only 38% of Catholics voted for Republican Bob Dole, and 9% voted for Ross Perot. The Catholic vote was key to Clinton's victory in the midwestern states.

References: David C. Leege and Lyman Kellstedt, eds., *Rediscovering the Religious Factor in American Politics* (Armonk, N.Y.: M. E. Sharpe, 1993); John R. Petrocik, *Party Coalitions: Realignments and the Decline of the New Deal Party System* (Chicago: University of Chicago Press, 1981).

CAUCUS is a private meeting of political party members to determine policy direction, select convention delegates, or conduct other party-related business. The word caucus is used in a variety of ways, including:

    1. State party caucuses and conventions were the principal means used to

select delegates to national party conventions until 1972. Since 1972 caucuses are used much less frequently. The caucus continues to be used in Iowa to select presidential delegates. A caucus is a meeting of party activists who are motivated to attend party meetings and state conventions. The participants in a caucus involve a very small percentage of the electorate. The turnout at a caucus may involve less than 5% of the electorate. In caucus/convention states there are a series of meetings organized as a pyramid which begins at the local level; those selected at the local level go on to a meeting at the county or congressional district level; those who are selected at that level go on to the state party convention. At each level, members are selected who are committed to particular national candidates in proportion to the candidate's proportion of support. It is at the state convention where the national convention delegates are finally selected in proportion to the vote cast at the precinct levels in the particular state. The Iowa caucus has been one of the first major events in the presidential nomination calendar. For a candidate to have success in a caucus system, he/she needs dedicated supporters and a strong grassroots organization in the state where a caucus is being held. Beginning in 1972, most states went to the open primary and the caucus method fell into disuse for selecting national party convention delegates. National party rules, state law, and state party rules determine the procedures for delegate selection.

2. In the early history of the United States, legislative caucuses were used to nominate candidates. For example, the members of a party in Congress met to nominate their respective parties' presidential candidates. James Chase argues that the legislative caucus for the nomination of presidential candidates was neither well attended nor widely accepted. Andrew Jackson, who was denied the nomination by this form of legislative caucus, campaigned against "King Caucus" and in 1828 it disappeared as the method for nominating presidential candidates.

3. The use of the word caucus, in the state legislature today, refers to a closed meeting of members of the state legislature who are in the same party to select leaders, develop a legislative agenda, and often prepare for the upcoming election by giving attention to raising money and recruiting candidates.

4. Caucus also refers to a meeting of the members of a particular political party in the U.S. Congress to select leaders or determine policy. There are groups in the national legislature who organize based on common characteristics or interests such as the Black Caucus or the Women's Caucus. These groups select leaders and develop an agenda. *See*: BLACK CAUCUS; IOWA CAUCUS.

References: James Chase, *Emergence of the Presidential Nominating Convention 1789–1832* (Urbana: University of Illinois Press, 1973); Susan Webb Hammond, Daniel P. Mulhollan, and Arthur Stevens, Jr., "Informal Congressional Caucuses and Agenda Setting," *Western Political Quarterly*, Vol. 38 (December 1985).

CHALLENGE is a procedure in state election law that permits an authorized poll watcher to assert that someone who is trying to vote is not qualified to vote at that voting location. The challenged voter is not permitted to vote until the issue has been resolved. Some states authorize parties to issue challenger papers to their poll watchers, which gives the poll watchers access to the polling place. This is designed as a safeguard against illegal voting and repeaters, which were more common in the days of political machines. *See*: MACHINE POLITICS.

CHRISTIAN COALITION. The Christian Coalition is an influential political organization that grew out of the 1988 "Pat Robertson for President" campaign. Robertson was a well-known television evangelist. The goal of the organization is to raise awareness about certain moral issues and give conservative Christians a voice in government. In 1996 the organization had an annual budget of $27 million. They claimed to have a membership of 1.9 million members. The Coalition promoted constitutional amendments to ban abortion and permit prayer in public schools. The Christian Coalition has become very active and very influential in Republican Party politics. They are also very active in local politics, where they often support candidates for school board positions. The executive director from its inception was Ralph Reed, who resigned in 1996. He was replaced by Donald Hodel, the president, and Randy Tate, who is the current executive director. The organization has attempted to recruit Catholics into their organization by promoting a Catholic Alliance, which has not been very successful.

The organization is recognized for its effective grassroots campaigns. It has focused on registering voters and getting out their vote. The coalition distributed 45 million voter guides before the 1996 general election. As a result of its political activities the tax exempt status of the organization has been challenged in federal court.

The Christian Coalition was not pleased that Republican nominee Bob Dole ignored many of their social issues in his 1996 presidential campaign. The leaders of the Christian Coalition have said they will select a candidate for the Republican nomination early for the presidential election of 2000 to insure that their issues are addressed. *See*: INTEREST GROUP; MORAL MAJORITY.

Reference: John C. Green, "The Christian Right and the 1994 Elections: A View from the States," *PS: Political Science & Politics*, Vol. 28 (March 1995).

CLAY, HENRY (1777–1852) was Speaker of the U.S. House of Representatives, U.S. Senator from Kentucky, secretary of state, and three times nominated for the presidency. He was in each of the latter instances to suffer disappointing defeat. Born on April 12, 1777, in that section of Hanover County, Virginia known as "the Slashes," Clay, when his family migrated to Kentucky in 1791, was sent to Richmond at the age of fourteen to begin his preparation for a career in law. Studying with Chancellor George Wythe, among others, Clay was to be admitted to practice first in Virginia in 1797, then in Kentucky in 1798, where he joined his family, now settled in the Lexington area. Soon becoming involved in frontier politics, Clay was elected to the Kentucky legislature in 1803. Three years later, filling an unexpired term, that body sent the 29-year-old Clay to the U.S. Senate. By age constitutionally ineligible to serve, Clay nonetheless took his seat, completing his brief three-month term unchallenged. Upon returning to Kentucky he was almost immediately reelected to the state legislature. A rising force in state politics, he served there until 1810 when once again he was chosen to complete an unexpired Senate term. Leaving the Senate for a second time, in March of 1811, he now claimed the seat in the U.S. House of Representatives to which Kentucky voters had elected him the previous August. New to the House, but recognized as a skillful orator, possessing a sharply honed wit, and with a reputation for political savvy, the yet youthful Clay found himself elected Speaker. As a "War Hawk," hoping militarily to secure the western frontiers and, possibly, the annexation of Canada, Clay became one of the leading proponents of the War of 1812 with Great Britain. Soon sobered, however, by the inconclusive course of the war, Clay resigned from the House in 1814 to accept President Madison's appointment to membership on the American Peace Commission, a body which by December of that year had negotiated the Treaty of Ghent, ending the increasingly unpopular war. Returning from Europe, Clay resumed his House career and was reelected to the Speakership in December of 1815. For nearly a decade, other than for a brief respite in 1821–1822, Clay, was to remain in the House, most often as its Speaker. There his nationalistic views came to be promoted as the "American System:" support of a high tariff protecting and encouraging national economic growth; support of federal funding for an extensive program of internal improvements such as road and canal construction, the latter argued as necessary instruments for economic expansion. It was at this time as well that Clay became a champion of the Bank of the United States. Having opposed rechartering of that institution in 1811, Clay, five years later, now convinced of its necessity in terms of economic stability, supported legislation establishing a second Bank of the United States. Indeed, it would be Clay's attempt to prematurely recharter the Bank in 1832 that would become a pivotal issue in that year's presidential campaign, an issue that, as exploited by President Jackson, would lead to Clay's overwhelming defeat. That defeat marked the second of Clay's failures in presidential politics, the first having come in 1824. Nominated for the presidency by the Kentucky legislature in 1823, Clay was joined in that crowded race by three other major candidates: Secretary of the Treasury William H. Crawford of Georgia, nominee of the Republican congressional caucus; Secretary of State John Quincy Adams of Massachusetts; and, the hero of the battle of New Orleans, Andrew Jackson of Tennessee. The election results poorly rewarded Clay for his advocacy of the "American System," the Kentuckian finishing last among the four contenders with but 37 Electoral College votes from three states. As no one of the four nominees secured an Electoral College majority, the presidential election, as provided by the Constitution, was transferred to the U.S. House of Representatives where each state delegation would cast its vote in support of one of the three candidates with the greatest number of Electoral College ballots. Thus was Clay eliminated from consideration by the House. As that chamber's most influential member, however, his support, given to Secretary of State Adams, was crucial in the latter's election to the executive office on February 9, 1825. Jackson, Clay's competitor from the West, was outraged: "Old Hickory" had gathered more popular votes than any other candidate, he had carried more states (11) with more Electoral College votes (99) than any other candidate, yet the House had chosen Adams. Soon Jackson's supporters had even more cause about which to cry "foul." Adams, once inaugurated, appointed Henry Clay secretary of state, a "corrupt bargain" in the eyes of the Jacksonians who immediately began to organize for the campaign ahead, forming a new party (the Democratic Party) to thwart the ambitions and policies of Adams and Clay. Jacksonian revenge over Adams came with Jackson's victory in the presidential election of 1828; for Clay, Jackson and his party had to wait until 1832. In December of 1831 at the Baltimore convention of the National Republican Party, Clay became its presidential nominee, with John Sergeant of Pennsylvania as his vice-presidential running mate. Trying to maneuver President Jackson into what Clay thought would be a politically unpopular position, Clay had legislation proposed in Congress to recharter the Bank of the United States, four years in advance of the existing charter's termination; legislation which Jackson vetoed on July 10, 1832. Clay's tactic badly misfired. Jackson, making a virtue of his veto, campaigned against the Bank and the vested interests he saw it representing, taking up the cause of the farmer and worker, and of the emerging middle class; interests he argued that were ignored or, at best, poorly served by the elitist Bank. It was a powerful argument. Clay and Sergeant were inundated by a flood of Jackson votes, the Democratic ticket of Jackson and vice-presidential nominee Martin Van Buren of New York, carrying 16 of the 24 states with 219 Electoral College ballots. Clay and Sergeant, polling 200,000 fewer popular votes than the Democrats, carried but 6 states with 49 votes in the Electoral College. (William Wirt, former attorney general of the United States, as the presidential candidate of the Anti-Masonic Party gathered more than 100,000 popular votes, carried Vermont, and gained seven Electoral College ballots). Clay's third failure to secure the executive office came in the election of 1844. Driving John Tyler out of the Whig Party (Tyler having succeeded to the presidency with William Henry Harrison's death on April 4, 1841, and having then vetoed National Bank legislation in August of that year), Clay cleared the way for his own nomination by unanimous resolution at the Whig convention of 1844, and was joined on the national ticket by Theodore Freylinghuysen of New Jersey as vice-presidential candidate. Democrats, rejecting the comeback bid of Martin Van Buren, nominated the relatively obscure James K. Polk of Tennessee, most recently the twice-defeated gubernatorial candidate of his party in that state. George M. Dallas of Pennsylvania was named as Polk's vice-presidential running mate. Clay anticipated victory and had it not been for the controversy of the Alabama letters, perhaps that would have been the result.

The question of Texas annexation, and of slavery's extension, had moved to the fore. While himself a slave holder, Clay had long argued against its extension and for the existing slave states gradually to move toward emancipation, providing financial compensation to slave owners. Clay, attempting to appeal to both North and South, now tried to finesse the issue. Writing to an Alabama newspaper editor in July of 1844, Clay equivocated, holding that while he personally favored Texas annexation he did so only if differences on the issue could be resolved so as to present no threat to the Union. Clay's elusive and ambiguous position outraged abolitionists. He then compounded his difficulties by issuing a second letter: he would be "glad" to have Texas annexed, provided it could be accomplished "without dishonor—without war, with common consent of the Union, and upon just and fair terms." The long-held view that the "Great Compromiser" was unprincipled, too clever by half, was now strongly reinforced, spelling disaster for Clay and his campaign. The obscure but more forthright Polk prevailed, narrowly: the Democratic ticket secured a thin popular vote plurality of 40,000 over Clay and Freylinghuysen, carried 15 states and 170 Electoral College votes, to the Whig's 11 states with 105 Electoral College ballots. Some analysts have argued that the 60,000 votes given to moderate abolitionist James G. Birney, candidate of the Liberty Party, denied Clay his expected victory; that had but a third of Birney's popular vote in New York gone to Clay, Whigs would have carried that state and thereby the election. Stunned, deeply disappointed, Clay, who had resigned his Senate seat in February of 1842, did not return to that chamber until 1849. There he was to engage, for him and for the nation, in one last effort to "harmonize" sectional differences and ward off the crisis of disunion. With the Missouri Compromise of 1820, which he had in significant part fashioned, now eroding, he joined with others in crafting the ill-fated Compromise of 1850: California to be admitted to the Union as a free state; other of the territories acquired as a result of the war with Mexico to engage in self-determination of the slavery issue; enactment of an enforceable federal fugitive slave law. For Clay it was the last hurrah; in failing health for more than a decade, having offered his resignation from the Senate effective in September, he died in his Washington hotel room on June 29, 1852. *See*: ELECTIONS: 1824, 1832, 1844.

References: Robert V. Remini, *Henry Clay, Statesman for the Union* (New York: Norton, 1991); Carl Schurz, *Life of Henry Clay*, 2 vols. (Boston: Houghton Mifflin, 1887).

CLEVELAND, GROVER (1837–1908), the only American president to serve non-consecutive terms in the executive office, was born on March 18, 1837 in Caldwell, New Jersey, the son of a Presbyterian clergyman. While living with family relatives in Buffalo, New York, Cleveland, age 18, became employed as a law clerk and subsequently "reading" the law, he was admitted to the bar in 1859. Cleveland was soon found dividing his time between his practice and political activity with the local Democratic organization. It was the latter that led to his appointment as an assistant district attorney for Erie County in 1863, and his election bid, unsuccessful, for the district attorney's office in 1865. Returning to private practice, Cleveland was not again to be on the ballot until 1870 when he was elected Erie County sheriff. Serving but one term, popularly regarded as an able and honest sheriff, Cleveland did not find the office particularly appealing. Perhaps this reaction stemmed from his participating in the execution by hanging of two sentenced convicts with Cleveland himself twice "springing the trap," not wishing to pass on to a deputy a gruesome duty that he himself was unwilling to perform. In 1881, again after a hiatus in practicing the law, Cleveland was elected mayor of Buffalo. His term was to set a familiar pattern: an emphasis on competent and honest administration; use of the patronage system as long as the employee was capable of performing adequately in his job; and exercise of the veto power as a means for imposing the will of the executive, as when, in disapproving of a suspiciously lucrative street-cleaning contract awarded by the Board of Aldermen, Cleveland lashed out: "I withhold my assent . . . because I regard it [i.e., the contract] as the culmination of a most barefaced, impudent, and shameless scheme to betray the interests of the people and . . . squander the public money." Cleveland thus came to build a reputation, extending beyond the city into the state, as an incorruptible, honest steward of the public interest. But months into his term as mayor, promoted by those party leaders who wanted a gubernatorial candidate free of ties to boss and machine, and to better contrast with the Republican nominee, Cleveland was made (to the suspicion of Tammany Hall) the Democratic Party nominee. On election day, New York voters rewarded those party leaders by giving Cleveland a solid victory. Inaugurated on January 3, 1883, Cleveland as governor reprised his performance as mayor: use of "rotation-in-office" as long as the party activist performed his public duties honestly and competently, and, again, use of the veto power to check against legislative transgressions. Joining with reform-minded legislators such as the young Theodore Roosevelt, Republican of New York City, Cleveland assisted in the enactment of measures to restructure and reform the government of New York City, an undertaking which further distanced the independent governor and Tammany Hall. In 1884, Democratic leaders in the nation were searching for the same type of candidate as had been the object of the search in New York in 1882; a candidate of unimpeachable honesty and proven executive ability who would offer a clear alternative to the likely GOP presidential nominee, Senator James G. Blaine, a legislator perceived to be of easy civic virtue; as Democrats chanted it, "Blaine, Blaine, that continental liar from the state of Maine." Giving a second ballot nomination to the New York governor, convention delegates nominated, as his vice-presidential running mate, Thomas A. Hendricks of Indiana. Probably few men other than Cleveland have come to a major party's presidential nomination so quickly on so few credentials: one term as county sheriff, one term as city mayor, but a year and a half into his first gubernatorial term. But Cleveland was, as is a commonly recognized prerequisite for success in politics, the right man, in the right place, at the right time. The ensuing campaign was one that was more directed toward the personal character of the two candidates than to substantive issues. Democrats, intending to score off the contrast between the reputation of Cleveland and that of Blaine, received a severe jolt when, in late July, it was alleged in a number of newspaper articles that Cleveland, a bachelor, had fathered an illegitimate child for whom he accepted responsibility. Cleveland, however, turned the disclosure to his political advantage; while himself uncertain as to the child's paternity, he acknowledged his assumed responsibility, instructing his campaign aids and advisors to simply "tell the truth." The November election result proved to be one of the closest in presidential history: out of a total popular vote cast of slightly more than ten million ballots, Cleveland's margin over Blaine was a mere 26,000 votes; the Cleveland-Hendricks ticket carrying 20 states and 219 Electoral College votes to 18 states with 182 ballots in the Electoral College for Blaine and his vice-presidential running mate, Senator John A. Logan of Illinois. Many analysts have pointed to the cruciality of the vote in New York. There Cleveland's plurality over Blaine was but 1,200 votes, and it is argued that had not a last-minute blunder been committed, Blaine would have carried the state, its Electoral College votes, and, thereby, the election. At a meeting with New York City clergymen on October 29, the Rev. Samuel D. Burchard, a Presbyterian minister, referred to the Democrats as the party of "Rum, Romanism, and Rebellion." While it is unclear whether Blaine actually heard the slander, it was not by him, or any one of his aids, immediately repudiated. By the time the senator did disavow the remark the damage among Catholic voters was done, and in sufficient numbers, it is argued, to have cost the Republicans New York State, and, thereby the presidency. Inaugurated on March 4, 1885, Cleveland's first term was marked by vigorous implementation of the Pendleton Civil Service Act of 1883 whereby thousands of positions in the federal bureaucracy were shifted from the patronage to the merit system. Continuing to use, as he had done both as mayor and governor, the executive veto as a means for enforcing his will, Cleveland put his negative to hundreds of private bills authorizing veteran pensions; bills which Cleveland argued constituted an unconscionable congressional raid upon the federal treasury. Cleveland's major disappointment of his first term was the failure to secure from Congress reform legislation instituting tariff reduction, a failure in part at the hands of the "protectionist" congressional wing of his own party. Renominated by the Democrats in 1888, Cleveland and vice-presidential candidate Allen G. Thurman of Ohio faced the Republican ticket of Benjamin Harrison, former U.S. Senator from Indiana, and Levi P. Morton of New York. While Cleveland's popular vote plurality was considerably greater than the razor-thin margin of four years earlier, by an unusual twist of political fate, election day brought defeat to the Democratic national ticket. Outpolling the Republicans by more than 90,000 votes, Cleveland-Thurman, in carrying 18 states with 168 Electoral College votes, lost the presidency to Harrison who, with Morton, carried 20 states including New York, for an Electoral College total of 233 ballots, a clear majority. President Cleveland, the popular choice, in gentlemanly fashion accepted his Electoral College defeat, giving the transition to Harrison's presidency a sorely needed, but for all Cleveland's generosity a never fully achieved, legitimacy. Returning to the practice of law in New York City, Cleveland remained politically active, receiving in 1892, on the first ballot, his third presidential nomination from the Democratic Party. Joining him on the national ticket as vice-presidential candidate was Adlai E. Stevenson of Illinois. The Democrats were now to avenge their loss of 1888. The Cleveland-Stevenson ticket outdistanced President Harrison and his running mate, U.S. minister to France Whitelaw Reid of New York, by nearly 400,000 votes and, on this occasion, secured the needed Electoral College majority, having 277 ballots from 23 states. The Republicans carried but 16 states with 145 Electoral College votes. A third-party ticket, that of the Populists, with presidential candidate (former Greenbacker) James B. Weaver of Iowa and running mate James G. Field of Virginia, made an impressive showing, capturing one million popular votes, 4 states, and 22 ballots in the Electoral College. Inaugurated for a second time on March 4, 1893, Cleveland was almost immediately faced with the great Panic of 1893 and the severe economic depression that followed. The president (an economic conservative), firmly believing that the way out of the deepening depression was by restoring business confidence in a sound money, led Congress by the fall of 1893 to a repeal of the Sherman Silver Purchase Act of 1890. The following year, to buttress the gold reserves of the United States, Cleveland, with legislative authorization, directed the Treasury Department to sell government bonds for gold to a syndicate headed by New York financier J. P. Morgan; the resulting transaction, administration critics argued, greatly favored the syndicate at the expense of the government of the United States. For all of the efforts of Cleveland and his key aids and advisors, the depression, with its hardships visited on farmers and laborers, continued, and as it continued popular support for administration policies as well as the personal popularity of the president dramatically eroded. A further event was to cause Cleveland distress; by June of 1894, a strike begun in late 1893 at the Pullman Car Company in Chicago had spread into a more generalized railroad strike. Cleveland, to insure public order in Chicago and, to safeguard the delivery of the mails and of freight in interstate commerce, ordered federal troops into Chicago on July 4th, 1894. With the subsequent indictment of strike leaders, and the continuing presence of overwhelming federal force on Chicago streets, the strike collapsed on July 10th. Cleveland's handling of the situation, while generally approved, was met with disappointment and anger on the part of many who constituted working-class America. Leaving office in 1897, the depression yet lingering, Cleveland, as unpopular as he had been popular when inaugurated in 1893, retired to his home in Princeton, New Jersey. Joining the Board of Trustees of Princeton University in 1901, he became the Board's chairman in 1904. As such, Cleveland was to have frequent contact with Princeton's first secular president, academician, future governor of New Jersey, and president of the United States, Woodrow Wilson. The author of numerous magazine articles, Cleveland in retirement also frequently appeared on the national lecture circuit. His public standing restored, Cleveland died of a heart attack at his Princeton home on January 24, 1908. *See*: ELECTIONS: 1884, 1888, 1892.

References: Allan Nevins, *Grover Cleveland, A Study in Courage* (New York: Dodd, Mead, 1933); Richard E. Welch, Jr., *The Presidencies of Grover Cleveland* (Lawrence: University Press of Kansas, 1988).

CLINTON, DeWITT (1769–1828), Jeffersonian Republican, who paradoxically became the presidential nominee of the Federalist Party in 1812, was born at Little Britain, New York on March 2, 1769. Of a prominent New York family, Clinton was graduated from Columbia College in 1786. Admitted to the bar in 1789, Clinton, however, was to prefer a career in politics rather than in the practice of law, and became private secretary to his uncle, Governor George Clinton in 1790. Except for two brief excursions into national politics, DeWitt Clinton's life was spent in the rough-and-tumble of a much-factionalized state politics. His skill in, and fascination with, that politics were balanced by a private side marked by an abiding, virtually professional interest in history, the arts, and the natural sciences. Before election to his first term as governor in 1817, Clinton had already acquired vast experience in state government: he had served in both houses of the state legislature, as mayor of New York City (an appointive position), as member of the state canal commission, and as the state's lieutenant governor, 1811–1813. In all of these positions Clinton had demonstrated unusual energy and ability. As mayor of New York City, his administration was progressive, with establishment of a free public school system, and of humanely operated institutions for the care of orphans and the insane. The great project of Clinton's life, however, was his advocacy of construction of a statewide canal system, the key link of which would be the Erie Canal. The latter waterway, when completed, would connect New York harbor and the Hudson River to Lake Erie, opening relatively inexpensive lines of transportation and commerce with the West. Clinton, the guiding force behind this project, served without compensation on the canal commission for nearly fifteen years, being dismissed in 1824 through efforts of the Van Buren faction within the state Republican Party. Clinton, however, had his revenge. He was in that year returned to the governorship, in time to preside with great public ceremony over the opening of the Erie Canal in 1825. Clinton's two forays into national politics were neither lengthy nor particularly rewarding. Appointed to fill an unexpired term, he served briefly in the U.S. Senate, 1802–1803, resigning in order to accept appointment to the first of his several terms as mayor of New York City. In 1812, as an anti-war Republican (a position that he would later reverse) and disgruntled that his uncle, George Clinton (the former governor, Jefferson's second and Madison's first and current vice-president), had been denied the

from two to four years in 1984, and Clinton was reelected in 1984 and 1988. Clinton introduced the testing of teachers, and eighth-grade students were required to pass a high school entrance exam. He raised the state sales tax by 1% to finance his educational reforms. Clinton gained national attention by serving as the chair of: the Democratic Leadership Council, the Democratic Governor's Association, and the National Association of Governors. In 1988, Clinton considered running for the Democratic nomination for president, but instead gave the nominating speech for Michael Dukakis at the Democratic National Convention.

Clinton entered the presidential sweepstakes in 1992. The field of declared Democratic candidates was not formidable because of President Bush's high approval rating, a result of Bush's success in the Gulf War. During the primaries, Clinton was almost sidelined by revelations of an affair with Gennifer Flowers. He faced the allegations head on, and finished second to Paul Tsongas in the New Hampshire primary declaring himself the "Comeback Kid." He went on to win the southern primaries and his party's nomination. Clinton won the general election by defeating George Bush, whose reelection chances suffered from a weak economy.

In his first term as president, Clinton concentrated on domestic issues. He assigned his wife Hillary the task of reforming the national health care system. The issue of health care reform turned sour; it reminded the public of big government solutions; and the 1994 election produced Republican majorities in the House and the Senate. Clinton had success in the area of foreign affairs: he brought peace to war-torn Bosnia. In 1996, Clinton's poll numbers improved, the economy continued to expand, and he easily defeated Republican nominee Bob Dole in 1996. In his second term, Clinton attempted to be more cooperative with the Republican Congress. He continued to be dogged by investigations into Whitewater, questionable campaign fund-raising practices in the 1996 election, and a liaison with a White House intern named Monica Lewinsky. *See:* ELECTIONS: 1992, 1996.

Reference: John Hohenberg, *The Bill Clinton Story: Winning the Presidency* (Syracuse, N.Y.: Syracuse University Press, 1994).

COALITION is a temporary alliance or fusion of various individuals, groups, parties, or regions that unite to achieve a common goal. The American political parties are coalitions. One of the most durable coalitions in the twentieth century was the New Deal coalition. The Democratic Party of Franklin Roosevelt was made up of union members, blacks, Catholics, Jews, city residents, and southern whites. This coalition has begun to break up in recent decades, with southern whites shifting their allegiance to the Republican Party. In recent years, the Republican party has been made up of a coalition of economic conservatives who often hold libertarian views on social issues, and social conservatives who want government to restrict abortion and permit prayer in school. There is tension between these groups within the Republican Party.

The goal of a political campaign is to put together a majority coalition. Voters are seen as belonging to groups such as: blacks, Catholics, elderly, union members, farmers, women, and Hispanics. In 1996 the successful campaign of President Clinton focused its attention on the elderly, young voters, and women to put together a winning coalition of voters.

Coalitions can also be formed in the legislature. President Clinton needed to put together a coalition of Democrats and Republicans to pass NAFTA. In 1980, President Ronald Reagan crafted a coalition of Republicans and conservative southern Democrats to pass tax reforms. In multiparty systems, coalitions of parties are created to form governments.

Reference: John R. Petrocik, *Party Coalitions: Realignment and the Decline of the New Deal Party System* (Chicago: University of Chicago Press, 1981).

COATTAILS refers to the influence of the top of a party ticket on the outcome of lower ballot offices in the same election. The pull of Franklin Roosevelt's candidacy in 1932 and 1936 led to significant Democratic Party gains in the House of Representatives and the Senate. In 1964, Lyndon Johnson's landslide win over Barry Goldwater brought large Democratic majorities to the House of Representatives. The top of the ticket also influences the outcome of state and local races. The influence of successful national candidates has been weaker in recent presidential elections. Richard Nixon's reelection in 1972 and Jimmy Carter's election in 1976 did not result in significant gains in the national legislature for their respective parties. Reagan's candidacy in 1980 did have some coattail effect resulting in a Republican majority in the Senate with a gain of twelve seats. Reagan's pull in 1980 and 1984 did not lead to significant gains for the Republicans in the House of Representatives. In 1980 the GOP picked up 33 seats in the House. In 1984, Reagan's eighteen-point landslide over Mondale resulted in a paltry gain of fourteen seats in the House and a loss of two Senate seats for the GOP. The most significant shift in the House was in 1949 when Harry Truman squeaked by Republican candidate Tom Dewey, and the Democrats picked up 75 seats. That year, Truman campaigned against the "do-nothing" Republican Congress.

The importance of coattails has diminished since the 1960s because of the rise of split-ticket voting and candidate-centered campaigns. In 1996, President Clinton did not overtly campaign for a Democratic Congress. Clinton visited states and congressional districts where the Democratic candidates were in a close race. At those sites Clinton did ask the voters to vote for a particular candidate, but he never asked the voters for a Democratic Congress. Likewise, many incumbent Republican congressional candidates wanted neither Republican presidential candidate Bob Dole nor Speaker Newt Gingrich campaigning for them in their district. They preferred to run their campaigns independently, hoping that the voters would split their ticket, which many voters did. *See*: SPLIT-TICKET VOTING.

Reference: Richard Born, "Reassessing the Decline of Presidential Coattails: U.S. House Elections 1952–1980," *Journal of Politics*, Vol. 46 (February 1984).

COLEGROVE **v.** *GREEN,* 328 U.S. 549 (1946) is a case in which the U.S. Supreme Court relied on the "political questions" doctrine to reject a challenge to a 1901 Illinois apportionment statute. Several citizens of the state of Illinois had brought suit alleging that population shifts within the state of Illinois rendered the apportioning statute in violation of various sections of the Constitution as well as the Reapportionment Act of 1911. The Supreme Court failed to rule on the merits of the case, instead arguing that the division of a state into electoral districts is a political rather than a judicial matter. According to the Court, it would be "hostile to a democratic system to involve the judiciary in the politics of the people." Furthermore, the Court asserted that if a state was found to be malapportioned, judges would be incompetent to reapportion states so as to remedy the constitutional infirmity. For a time, it appeared that this case would serve as a roadblock to those who sought judicial review of apportionment statutes. *See: BAKER* v. *CARR* (1962); POLITICAL QUESTIONS DOCTRINE; REAPPORTIONMENT.

COLORADO REPUBLICAN FEDERAL CAMPAIGN COMMITTEE **v.** *FEDERAL ELECTION COMMISSION,* 518 U.S. 604 (1996). In this case the U.S. Supreme Court rejected a claim that the Colorado Republican Party had violated expenditure limits established by the Federal Election Campaign Act of 1971 when the party paid for radio advertisements critical of a potential Democratic candidate. Writing for a divided Court, Justice Breyer argued that the money spent on the commercials was to be considered an independent expenditure, and not a campaign contribution. Relying on the Court's prior decision in *Buckley* v. *Valeo* (1976), Breyer concluded that any attempt to limit this type of independent contribution would run afoul of the First Amendment's protection of free speech. The case appears to open the floodgates for unregulated campaign spending by political parties. *See: BUCKLEY* v. *VALEO* (1976); FEDERAL ELECTION CAMPAIGN ACT OF 1971; SOFT MONEY.

COMMITTEE ON POLITICAL EDUCATION (COPE) is the political arm of the AFL-CIO. This organization was created to encourage and assist affiliated unions to register their members to vote, and get out the vote on election day for candidates favorable to union policies. When the labor federations merged in 1955, the newly formed AFL-CIO created the Committee on Political Education to raise money and support candidates favorable to the unions' policies. COPE is viewed as the forerunner of the modern-day PAC. The influence of the unions has waned in American politics because of the erosion of their membership. The AFL-CIO made a major effort to defeat the Republican majority in Congress in 1996. Organized labor spent $35 million airing negative advertising in an unsuccessful effort to defeat the Republican Congress. *See*: LABOR ORGANIZATIONS; POLITICAL ACTION COMMITTEE.

COMMON CAUSE is a public interest group founded in the 1970s by John Gardner to promote good government in the reform tradition. Common Cause has organized chapters at the national and state levels. It persistently lobbies to bring about changes in government ethics and campaign finance reform. Common Cause strives to achieve the goals of "open, accountable government and the right of all citizens to be involved in helping to shape our nation's public policies." It has promoted sunshine laws in federal and state law because it believes the public has the right to know. It has pushed for financial disclosure by public officials. It lobbied to restrict outside honoraria earned by public officials. It is the premier nonpartisan watchdog interest group in the United States on the issues of ethics, campaign finance reform, and public disclosure. The organization does not support particular candidates and uses earned media to bring public attention to the issues and concerns Common Cause is addressing. In 1997, Common Cause was very active in promoting campaign finance reform at the federal level.

Reference: Jeffrey Berry, *Lobbying for the People: The Political Behavior of Public Interest Groups* (Princeton, N.J.: Princeton University Press, 1977).

COMPACTNESS is a measure used to evaluate legislative districts. It is the least distance between all the parts of a constituency. A district should reflect compactness. Redistricting legislation often stipulates compactness to avoid gerrymandering of a district. A compactness requirement limits oddly shaped legislative districts. Compactness also implies that the district is to be contiguous, that is, all parts are connected. *See*: GERRYMANDERING; REAPPORTIONMENT; REDISTRICTING.

Reference: David Butler and Bruce Cain, *Congressional Redistricting* (New York: Macmillan, 1992).

COMPETITIVE ELECTION is an election where the outcome is in doubt, and both parties have an opportunity to win the election. Presidential elections in the United States since World War II have been competitive. Of the thirteen presidential elections in the postwar period, the Republicans have won seven times and the Democrats six times. For decades after the Civil War, elections in the South were not competitive because the South was overwhelmingly Democratic and the Republican Party was not competitive. Many congressional districts in the United States are not competitive because one of the two parties is dominant. Incumbency also reduces the competitiveness of many congressional and state legislative districts in the United States. *See*: TARGETING.

Reference: Austin Ranney, "Parties in State Politics," in *Politics in the American States: A Comparative Analysis.* 3rd ed., Herbert Jacobs and Kenneth Vines, eds. (Boston: Little, Brown, 1976).

CONGRESSIONAL CAMPAIGN COMMITTEES. In Congress each political party has a congressional campaign committee, often referred to as Hill Committees, that provide assistance to candidates seeking election to Congress. There are four committees: the Democratic Congressional Campaign Committee (DCCC) to assist Democratic candidates running for seats in the House of Representatives; the Democratic Senatorial Campaign Committee (DSCC); the National Republican Congressional Committee (NRCC); and the National Republican Senatorial Committee (NRSC). These committees have a chair, which is an important position for a member of Congress aspiring to a leadership position. In the 1994 election cycle, the size of the staff of these committees ranged from 25 to 104. All of these committees perform the same functions: they recruit candidates for both open seats and as challengers to incumbents of the opposition party; they provide campaign training for the candidates and the candidates' campaign managers. They provide in-kind support such as staff and polling. They provide significant financial support, especially to targeted candidates.

The amount of the contribution the congressional campaign committees can make to candidates is limited by federal campaign finance law. The FECA limits party committees to $5,000 per election cycle. The FECA has a special provision which permits party committees to spend money on behalf of candidates, called coordinated spending. For House campaigns, the adjusted ceiling was $29,300, for Senate campaigns this cap on coordinated expenditures varies with population size. In the 1996 election, as a result of the federal court decision in *Colorado Republican Federal Campaign Committee* v. *Federal Election Commission* (1996), the campaign committees, particularly the Republicans, raised and spent millions of dollars on behalf of their targeted candidates.

The Hill Committees provide access to major donor groups and PAC leaders. The committees spend a great deal of time raising millions of dollars to carry out these functions. *See: COLORADO REPUBLICAN FEDERAL CAMPAIGN COMMITTEE* v. *FEDERAL ELECTION COMMISSION* (1996); TARGETING.

References: Paul S. Herrnson, *Congressional Elections: Campaigning at Home and in Washington*, 2nd ed. (Washington D.C.: Congressional Quarterly Press, 1998); Gary C. Jacobson, *The Politics of Congressional Elections*, 4th ed. (New York: Longman, 1997).

CONGRESSIONAL DISTRICT is a geographic division of a state, from which one member of the House of Representatives is elected. The boundaries are drawn by the respective state legislature. The boundaries are frequently drawn to the benefit of the party in the majority in that state legislature. The number of districts in a state are determined after the national census is conducted, every ten years. A few states (Alaska, Delaware, Montana, North Dakota, South Dakota, Vermont, and Wyoming) have only one congressional district, hence the boundaries of the state are the boundaries of the district.

Congress has not specified criteria for drawing up districts. The U.S. Supreme Court ruled in *Wesberry* v. *Sanders* (1964), that congressional districts had to be equal in population size. In the early 1990s, a number of states, in an effort to meet the requirements of the Voting Rights Act, created majority-minority districts. In 1995, the Supreme Court, in *Miller* v. *Johnson* (1995), decided that race could not be the determining factor in the boundaries of a district. The federal courts have ordered many states, that had drawn congressional districts based on race, to redistrict the boundaries of their congressional districts. *See*: COMPACTNESS; *MILLER* v. *JOHNSON* (1995); REAPPORTIONMENT; REDISTRICTING; VOTING RIGHTS ACT; *WESBERRY* v. *SANDERS* (1964).

References: David Butler and Bruce Cain, *Congressional Redistricting: Comparative and Theoretical Perspectives* (New York: Macmillan, 1992); Richard K. Scher, Jon L. Mills, and John J. Hotaling, *Voting Rights and Democracy: The Law and Politics of Districting* (Chicago: Nelson-Hall, 1997).

CONGRESSIONAL ELECTIONS. The national legislative elections in the United States are candidate-centered. All of the elections are held in single-member districts, and most are plurality elections, which contributes to the maintenance of the two-party character of the legislative elections. Most legislative candidates are self-recruited and have to win a primary to become a party nominee. The primary campaign requires the candidates to build their own organizations separate from the party. The development of modern campaign technology, offered by professional campaign consultants, such as: direct mail, television advertising, and polling, have made the party organizations less important to congressional candidates.

There are 435 separate House elections. Most of them are not true contests. Many incumbent House members, who hold safe seats, are not seriously challenged by the opposition party. The focus of Republican and Democratic national party organizations is on open seats, where the incumbent has decided not to seek reelection. Those open districts draw the most able candidates and the attention of party committees and PACs, and these open districts determine where the gains and losses of the parties will be. Frequently, there is an effort to challenge recently elected incumbents. In 1996 the labor movement and the Democratic legislative campaign committees targeted a number of the Republican freshmen who won in 1994, a key part of the first Republican takeover of the House of Representatives in 40 years.

The reelection rate of incumbent House members has remained over 90%, even in the anti-incumbent, check overdraft, mini-scandal House election of 1992, and the surprising Republican takeover of the House of Representatives in 1994. Incumbents enjoy reelection because of their high name identification, and they are well financed in comparison to their underfinanced challengers.

PACs prefer incumbents and are reluctant to donate to challengers. Incumbents are active in their districts attending events and enjoying publicity. They often vote in accord with their constituents wishes, and they have well-financed and well-staffed offices that perform constituent services.

The outcome of the presidential election has some effect on the national legislative elections. The party that wins the White House usually gains seats in the legislature. This coattail effect has weakened in recent elections and in 1992, when Clinton won, the Democrats lost ten House seats primarily because of reapportionment, which occurs every ten years. The party in the White House usually suffers legislative losses in the midterm election. The Republicans captured the majority of the House in the midterm election of 1994, with a Democrat in the White House. The regional bases of the parties have changed in recent decades. The Republicans have made significant gains in the South in recent years, while losing ground in the East and Midwest. Of course, Democratic gains and losses are the reverse. The growing strength in the South of the Republican Party is reflected in the leadership of both the House and the Senate: Speaker Newt Gingrich, House Majority Leader Dick Armey, and the Senate Majority Leader Trent Lott, are all from southern states.

U.S. Senate elections, similar to House elections, are candidate-centered. In Senate elections the focus of the parties is on the open seats where most of the party gains and losses occur. Senate incumbents are not as secure as House incumbents. From 1960 to 1994 the reelection rate of Senate incumbents was 80%. The reasons for the more competitive Senate races are: first, they are statewide races and reflect the degree of interparty competition in the state; second, the candidates that are recruited are usually well-known and well financed; and third, the Senate races are much more visible than House races. The composition of the Senate membership, like that of the House, reflects the growing strength of the Republicans in the South. *See*: HILL COMMITTEES; MARGINAL SEAT; OPEN-SEAT RACES; POLITICAL ACTION COMMITTEE.

References: Paul R. Abramson, John H. Aldrich, and David W. Rhode, *Change and Continuity in the 1992 Elections*, rev. ed. (Washington, D.C.: Congressional Quarterly Press, 1995); Paul S. Herrnson, *Congressional Elections: Campaigning at Home and in Washington*, 2nd ed. (Washington, D.C.: Congressional Quarterly Press, 1998); Gary C. Jacobson, *The Politics of Congressional Elections*, 4th ed. (New York: Longman, 1998).

CONSERVATISM. Modern conservatism is a variant of seventeenth- and eighteenth-century liberalism. Edmund Burke (1729–1797), often identified as the founder of modern conservatism, was engaged in an effort to conserve older liberal principles against the onslaught of radical democratic (and arguably illiberal) theories popularized by the French Revolution. This relationship between liberalism and conservatism is most obvious if one brings the liberal principle first articulated by the philosopher John Stuart Mill (1806–1873) to one's examination of both ideologies. John Stuart Mill argued that government ought to regulate only those behaviors which injured other people. Self-regarding actions and ideas were to be immune from governmental and social regulation.

Mill's liberating principle guides both liberalism and conservatism. Both ideologies promise human freedom and limited government. Moreover, both liberalism and conservatism allow for government action when a harm needs to remedied. Thus the real argument between these two ideologies involves defining harms. Conservativism advocates the conservation of traditional definitions of that which is harmful and therefore subject to government action. It follows that conservatives are willing to recognize things such as promiscuity as harmful. To the conservative, loose morality has traditionally been viewed as injurious to society. Modern data on the plight of unwed mothers merely reinforces this opinion. On the other hand, conservatism does not recognize the economic and environmental injuries which have served to stimulate modern liberalism's most ambitions programs (for example, the New Deal and Great Society programs). After all, aggressive economic activity has traditionally been viewed as a right which creates beneficial (rather than harmful) by-products for society. *See*: LIBERAL; LIBERALISM.

References: Edmund Burke, *Reflections on the Revolution in France* (Indianapolis, Ind.: Hackett Publishing, 1987); Patrick Devlin, *The Enforcement of Morals* (London: Oxford University Press, 1965); Russell Kirk, *The Conservative Mind, from Burke to Santayana* (Chicago: Regnery, 1953); John Stuart Mill, *On Liberty* (New York: W. W. Norton, 1975).

CONSERVATIVE. As the root of the word indicates, conservatives are interested in preserving a particular mode of political thought. As currently used, a conservative is generally one who promotes the traditional idea that government has a very limited role to play in the economic lives of citizens. Most conservatives also argue, however, that the government has an affirmative magisterial role in instructing and regulating the moral behavior of citizens. Often these two prongs of conservative activity are referred to respectively as "economic" and "social" conservatism. Nevertheless, there are really not two forms of conservatism. The economic and social ideas that conservatives promote are merely two aspects of the overall political theory which conservatives seek to "conserve." *See*: CONSERVATISM.

CONSERVATIVE PARTY OF NEW YORK is a third party founded in the state of New York in 1962 to promote conservative ideas. It is not affiliated with any national party, but it is affiliated with the American Conservative Union. The party usually nominates the Republican Party candidate. The election law of the state of New York permits cross-endorsement, and in 1994, the Conservative Party of New York supported Republican gubernatorial candidate George E. Pataki, who won by 173,798 votes. The Conservative Party line, with

Pataki's name on it, captured 328,605 votes. The Conservative Party claimed it made the difference in his election. The Conservative Party did not support Republican New York City Mayor Rudolph Giuliani in 1993, preferring to run their own candidate. In 1994, the Conservative Party of New York promoted a Contract with New York similar to the Contract with America, promising to cut taxes, reduce spending, support term limits, school vouchers, and eliminate rent control. The current party chairman is Michael R. Long. *See*: CROSS-ENDORSEMENT; CROSS-FILING; LIBERAL PARTY OF NEW YORK; THIRD PARTIES.

Reference: Howard Scarrow, ''Cross-Endorsement and Cross-Filing in Plurality Partisan Elections,'' in *Electoral Laws and Their Political Consequences*, Bernard Grofman and Arend Lijphart, eds. (New York: Agathon Press, 1986).

CONSTITUENT is a resident of a represented district. The district as a whole is often referred to as the member's constituency.

A major part of a legislator's time is spent on constituent service. The legislator acts as a liaison between the constituent and the government bureaucracy. Constituents request help with all sorts of problems ranging from passports to Medicare benefits. The legislator and the staff spend time answering letters, requests, and providing tours of government offices to their constituents. Constituent service is one explanation for the high reelection rate of incumbents. *See*: CASEWORK.

References: Gary C. Jacobson, *The Politics of Congressional Elections*, 4th ed. (New York: Longman, 1997); Malcolm E. Jewell, ''Legislator-Constituency Relations and the Representative Process,'' *Legislative Studies Quarterly*, Vol. 8 (August 1983).

CONTRACT WITH AMERICA was a platform of legislative proposals put together by the Republican House leadership led by Newt Gingrich and Dick Armey, which they used to nationalize the 1994 congressional elections. In 1994 the Republicans won control of the House of Representatives for the first time in 40 years. The Contract with America has been given credit for this surprising victory.

In September 1994, the Contract with America was unveiled at the Capital, and most Republican congressional candidates signed the Contract. The Contract was made up of ten items. The items in the Contract had been market-tested with focus groups before they were offered to the public. GOP Pollster Frank Luntz was especially interested in the response of former Perot voters to the proposals, since they were one of the target populations of the Republican campaign in 1994. The Republicans did not promise that the items would pass, only that they would be voted on in the first 100 days of the next Congress, if the GOP gained a majority in the election. There was some debate on the merits of this approach for a congressional election since House elections are viewed as candidate-centered and are usually focused on local issues. The candidates emphasized the parts of the Contract that were most attractive in the districts they were seeking election.

The main elements of the Contract with America included: a balanced budget amendment, a line item veto, a change in tax policy, an anti-crime package with block grants, welfare reform, tax credits for children, a stronger national defense and no U.S. troops under UN command, legal reform, an end to unfunded mandates, regulatory reform, and term limits. Most of these items were voted on, and many of them were enacted into law in the 104th Congress.

The Republicans pushed very hard to reduce the budget in the 104th Congress, and they had a number of confrontations with President Clinton. This conflict between the legislature and the president over the budget led to a number of government shutdowns which hurt the Republicans more than President Clinton. The elements of the Contract with America that had not been enacted were not promoted by the Republicans in 1996, and there were no national themes offered by the Congressional GOP, except that they should be reelected to check President Clinton. The Republican majority, elected in 1994, was reelected in 1996. This was the first time that the GOP had had a majority elected in two consecutive congressional elections since 1928. The Republican congressional candidates ran traditional, candidate-centered and local-issue-focused campaigns in 1996. *See*: CONGRESSIONAL ELECTIONS; GINGRICH, NEWT(ON).

Reference: James G. Gimpel, *Fulfilling the Contract: The First 100 Days* (Needham Heights, Mass.: Allyn and Bacon, 1996).

CONVENTION is a meeting of party delegates to select or endorse a party nominee for office and adopt a platform and party rules. The national party conventions are held every four years. Some state party conventions only adopt platforms and amend rules. The political parties in the state of Virginia are able to select either the convention or the primary to nominate their statewide candidates. In 1994 the Virginia Republican Party used the convention method to nominate Oliver North for the U.S. Senate. In 1996 the Virginia Republicans opted to use the primary system to renominate incumbent Senator John W. Warner. The convention method of nomination in states has fallen into disuse. The national party conventions have evolved from deliberating bodies to the ratification of primary results. The friction at the national party conventions is now restricted to platform language. *See*: NATIONAL PARTY CONVENTION.

COOLIDGE, CALVIN (1872–1933), governor of the state of Massachusetts from 1919 to 1921, vice-president of the United States succeeding to the presidency at the death of President Harding in 1923, parsimonious with words, "Silent Cal," ironically, held the White House during the most frenzied years of "the roaring twenties," leading journalist William Allen White to assign him the sobriquet "puritan in Babylon." Born in Plymouth, Vermont on July 4, 1872, where his great-great-grandfather had settled in 1777, Coolidge attended

Amherst College in Massachusetts, graduating in 1895. Not choosing to return to rural Vermont, Coolidge took up residence in Northampton, Massachusetts, where he studied law and was admitted to the bar in 1897. Establishing his practice there, he soon became active in Northampton politics, being elected as a Republican to city council and, in 1910, to the mayor's office. Having served in the lower house of the Massachusetts legislature from 1907 to 1909, he was elected to the state senate in 1911, to the office of lieutenant-governor in 1915, and, by a narrow margin, to the governorship in 1918. His route to the governorship was marked by the capable, if unexciting, performance of routine duty and the methodical climbing of the party organizational ladder. Little in Coolidge's political career before coming to national attention in 1919 suggests deep ideological or issue commitment; a pragmatic utilitarian, his creed was summed up in the terse admonition, "do the day's work." It was the Boston police strike in September of 1919 that brought this taciturn Yankee to national attention. At first seeing the strike as a matter for city authorities, the governor was slow to respond to calls for his intervention to stem the ensuing wave of crime and public disorder. However, as the situation seemed to worsen, Coolidge yielded and issued an executive order bringing the full force of the state militia onto the city's streets. Subsequently, in an exchange of telegrams between the governor's office and that of Samuel Gompers, president of the American Federation of Labor, Coolidge set out words that were to give him immediate fame: "There is no right to strike against the public safety by anybody, anywhere, any time." Not only did the fifteen words, with the press coverage they received, lead to Coolidge's landslide reelection victory in Massachusetts that November, but, as well, they placed him firmly in the minds of delegates assembled in Chicago at the Republican National Convention less than a year later. Those delegates, led by party leaders to the nomination of Senator Warren G. Harding of Ohio as their presidential candidate, balked at the attempt of those same leaders to dictate the selection of Senator Irvine L. Lenroot of Wisconsin as vice-presidential nominee. Someone in the vast hall, calling out the name "Coolidge," set the rebellious delegates on their way to a first ballot nomination of the Massachusetts governor as Harding's 1920 running mate. A war-weary electorate, responding to Harding's call for "a return to normalcy," created a Republican tide of historic proportions. The Harding-Coolidge ticket was swept into office with a plurality of nearly seven million popular votes over the Democratic national ticket of Governor James M. Cox of Ohio and Assistant Secretary of the Navy Franklin D. Roosevelt of New York. As with most vice-presidents to that point in time, Coolidge presided over the Senate, performing his constitutional responsibility, but declined to be further drawn into the administration's policy processes, even as the opportunity presented itself in that President Harding provided his vice-president a seat at cabinet sessions. Coolidge, however, chose to be a spectator rather than a participant. All this was to change in August of 1923. President Harding, returning from Alaska as part of an extended western tour, fell ill in Seattle, presumably suffering a heart attack. Continuing to California, he died in San Francisco the evening of August 2. Vice-president Coolidge, on vacation in Vermont, by the light of an oil lamp, took the presidential oath administered to him by his father, a certified notary. The most immediate problem for the new president was to distance himself from the swirl of scandal rumors circulating that summer in Washington. As rumor turned into fact within months of Harding's death, Coolidge skillfully moved to de-politicize the issue, announcing, on January 26, 1924, his intention to appoint "special counsel," emphasizing that "it is the function of the courts," not the president or congressional investigating committees, "to determine criminal guilt or render judgment in civil cases." Also soon gone from official Washington were Secretary of the Interior Albert Fall who had resigned the previous January and who would eventually serve a jail sentence, Attorney General Harry M. Daugherty, Secretary of the Navy Edwin Denby, and numerous others of the so-called "Ohio gang." Coolidge devoted every effort, successfully, to showing himself to the American people as a bluntly honest steward of their interests, above the scandals, determined to remove every last trace of corruption from the executive branch. The 1924 Republican nomination of Calvin Coolidge for the presidency, and his subsequent election bid, which had once seemed so problematic, proved by mid-summer 1924 to be absolutely secure. Facing a deeply divided Democratic Party, and with that party further weakened by the Progressive Party presidential candidacy of Senator Robert M. LaFollette of Wisconsin, Coolidge and his running mate, Charles G. Dawes of Illinois, won an easy election-day victory. The Republican ticket polled nearly sixteen million votes with a plurality of more than seven million over Democrats John W. Davis of West Virginia and Governor Charles W. Bryan of Nebraska. Cutting deeply into the Democratic vote, LaFollette and Progressive Party vice-presidential candidate Senator Burton K. Wheeler of Montana garnered nearly five million votes. The Electoral College count gave 382 ballots from 35 states to the Republicans, with 136 votes from 12 states going to the Democrats. LaFollette carried his home state of Wisconsin with 13 Electoral College votes. Coolidge's presidency was marked by a national prosperity unrivaled in the American experience. Day-by-day as the stock market soared, Americans from Wall Street to Main Street, anxious for quick wealth, poured their savings, and then their borrowed monies, into the acquisition of stock certificates. Administration-promoted tax cuts, orchestrated by Secretary of the Treasury Andrew Mellon, further fueled the exercise in speculation. Coolidge's own laissez-faire notions as to economic enterprise prevented any additional attempts, beyond enforcement of laws already enacted, to further regulate or control either the security markets or the nation's banks. The wild ride was left to run its course. In August of 1927, on the fourth anniversary of his coming to the presidency, Coolidge, widely expected to be a candidate for reelection in 1928, issued a characteristically terse disclaimer, "I do not choose to run." The president's wife, Grace Goodhue Coolidge, was subsequently to remark, "Poppa says there's a depression coming." Certainly accurate in that forecast, Coolidge expediently departed from the presidency before the great stock market crash of October 1929, escaping immediate responsibility for the economic devastation the ensuing depression brought to the American people and the political devastation it brought to his party. In retirement, suffering an eroding reputation for having done so little to prevent, or even to have warned against, the crisis, an unruffled Coolidge wrote his autobiography, which was published in 1929, and in 1930–1931 authored a series of newspaper and magazine articles. The former president died at Northampton, Massachusetts on January 5, 1933, but two months before the presidential inauguration of Democrat Franklin D. Roosevelt, and the coming of the New Deal. *See*: ELECTIONS: 1920, 1924.

References: Calvin Coolidge, *Autobiography of Calvin Coolidge* (New York: Cosmopolitan, 1929); Robert H. Ferrell, The Presidency of Calvin Coolidge (Lawrence: University Press of Kansas, 1998); Donald R. McCoy, *Calvin Coolidge, the Quiet President* (New York: Macmillan, 1967).

COORDINATED EXPENDITURES are permitted party expenditures on behalf of federal candidates. These expenditures are made in coordination with a candidate's campaign, and are usually for some kind of campaign service such as a poll, staff support, television commercials, or direct mail. This type of spending can only occur for a general election. The Federal Election Campaign Act imposes limits on the party for this type of spending. There is an established formula for each federal office. In 1996, it was $12 million for each of the presidential candidates, $30,910 for congressional candidates, and the Senate cap is determined by each state's population. California was the highest capped at $1.4 million. These amounts are adjusted by inflation and population changes. State party committees are allowed to spend the same amounts in House and Senate races. The state party often lacks the necessary funds, so "agency agreements" are made with national parties who can then double their expenditures for candidates in those states. *See*: CONGRESSIONAL CAMPAIGN COMMITTEES; FEDERAL ELECTION CAMPAIGN ACT OF 1971 AND AMENDMENTS.

Reference: Anthony Corrado, "Party Soft Money," in *Campaign Finance Reform: A Sourcebook*, Anthony Corrado, Thomas E. Mann, Daniel R. Oritz, Trevor Potter, and Frank J. Sorauf, eds. (Washington, D.C.: Brookings Institution, 1997).

COPPERHEAD was the peace faction of the Democratic Party during the Civil War. This faction was led by Congressman Clement L. Vallandigham of Ohio. He advocated constitutional sectionalism in which a majority of electors from each section of the country were required to elect the president. In his plan, secession was a right of a state only when the legislatures of each state in the section voted for it. These proposals were designed to meet the concerns of the South. Vallandigham was defeated in his reelection bid for Congress. During the Civil War he was arrested for disloyalty; he was tried and convicted. President Lincoln commuted his sentence. The Ohio Democrats defiantly nominated Vallandigham for governor in 1863. He conducted his Ohio gubernatorial campaign from Canada, and he lost the election by 247,000 to 185,000.

References: Ralph M. Goldman, *The National Party Chairmen and Committees: Factionalism at the Top* (Armonk, N.Y.: M. E. Sharpe, 1990); Eugene H. Roseboom, *A History of Presidential Elections* (New York: Macmillan, 1957).

COUNTY CHAIRMAN/COUNTY CHAIRWOMAN are the leaders of a local county party organization. The party leader and a few activists make decisions in the name of the party. County party leaders of minority parties literally beg party members to "fill the ticket." In most counties in the United States the position of chair is a voluntary one, and activity occurs only during election time. In large urban counties the county party may have a year-round office and some paid staff. The strength of local parties varies by region of the country. *See:* LOCAL PARTY ORGANIZATIONS; PRECINCT COMMITTEEMAN/ COMMITTEEWOMAN.

Reference: Cornelius P. Cotter, James L. Gibson, John F. Bibby, and Robert J. Huckshorn, *Party Organization in American Politics* (New York: Praeger, 1984).

COUNTY UNIT VOTING is a winner-take-all electoral system (similar to that which is employed by most states to determine the awarding of presidential electors) which was once used in primary elections in Georgia. Under this system the candidate obtaining a plurality of the votes cast in each county was awarded all of the "county unit votes." Two different formulas were used for allocating these county votes. Originally, each county was allocated two votes for every member that it was entitled to in the state assembly. County representation in the state assembly was not proportional to the relative populations within each county; obviously, the county unit votes were similarly skewed. The county unit system was later modified so that county unit votes were related to the population. Nevertheless, a decreasing increment of votes was granted as population increased. The result was that a county with a population of 60,000 would get six county unit votes, while a county twice as large received only ten county unit votes. The U.S. Supreme Court found that both types of county unit systems fell outside of the "one person, one vote" requirement of the Equal Protection Clause of the Fourteenth Amendment. *See: GRAY* v. *SANDERS* (1963).

COUSINS **v.** *WIGODA,* 419 U.S. 477 (1975) is one of the earliest cases asserting the essentially private nature of national political parties. This case resulted from a dispute within the Democratic Party over which delegates from Chicago were to be "seated" at the 1972 Democratic National Convention in Miami, Florida. Fifty-nine "Wigoda" delegates were elected during the March primary in Illinois. An equal number of "Cousins" delegates challenged the credentials of the Wigoda delegates before the Democratic National Committee. The party's Credentials Committee ruled in favor of the Cousins delegates, but the party's action was enjoined by the Illinois Circuit Court. The U.S. Supreme Court overturned the decision of the Illinois court, arguing that the state court's action infringed upon the freedom that party members have to associate with whomever they want at their national conventions. In order to limit freedom of association a state must show that such an action is necessary to forwarding a compelling state interest. In this case, the Illinois circuit court, representing the state of Illinois, failed to provide the required justification. *See*: CREDENTIALS COMMITTEE; DELEGATE; *DEMOCRATIC PARTY OF U.S.* v. *WISCONSIN* (1981).

COX, JAMES M. (1870–1957), journalist and publisher, three times governor of the state of Ohio, defeated presidential candidate of the Democratic Party in the "return to normalcy" election of 1920. Cox was born on March 31, 1870 in rural Jacksonburg, Ohio. Largely self-educated, certificated as a teacher, Cox began his career as a newspaperman in the 1890s working for his uncle, publisher of the *Middleton Weekly Signal*, subsequently being hired as a cub reporter with the *Cincinnati Enquirer*. Developing a keen interest in politics, Cox left the *Enquirer* in 1893 to become secretary to Democratic congressman Paul J. Sorg. When Sorg retired from the House in 1897, he assisted Cox in purchasing the moribund *Dayton Evening News*, a paper which Cox would restore to health and which would (as the *Dayton Daily News*) eventually become the cornerstone first of a state and much later of a highly successful national newspaper chain, the latter with major market publications in Atlanta, Georgia, and Miami, Florida. With his Ohio papers firmly established by 1908, Cox felt sufficiently secure to indulge both his sense of civic responsibility and his continuing passion for politics. Elected in that year to the U.S. House of Representatives, he served there as a progressive Democrat until 1913, leaving the House to be inaugurated governor of Ohio, an office to which he had been elected the previous November. In that year of a factionalized Republican Party, Cox, with slightly more than 40% of the total vote cast in a three-candidate contest, won a solid victory over Republican and Progressive, "Bull Moose" opposition. Cox, a Wilsonian, immediately embarked on a crusade of reform, targeting in particular administrative reorganization of state government, reorganization and strengthening of the public school system, reorganization and modernization of the state penal system with emphasis on prisoner "education, reform, and probation." Labor legislation, including maximum hour and health and safety measures, was introduced and passed by "Boss Cox's" Democratic majority in the Ohio legislature. By election year 1914, however, the activist governor had both exhausted and outdistanced his Ohio constituency; by a relatively narrow margin Cox was defeated in his reelection bid. Moderating his agenda, playing down the need for additional reform, Cox recaptured the governorship in 1916 and retained that office for the Democrats in the Republican sweep of 1918. With U.S. entry into World War I, Cox's latter two terms, 1917–1921, were essentially given over to wartime administration; attempting to solve the related problems associated with manpower, production, and transportation needs. At this time the governor also became deeply concerned with the potentially damaging effect of sabotage (should it occur) of the war effort, and with the harm done, as he saw it, by unpatriotic statements and behavior. Cox subsequently initiated, or endorsed, a wide variety of jingoistic, anti-German measures including loyalty tests and the banning of German language instruction in Ohio schools. As the 1920 presidential election approached, Cox, while not a preconvention frontrunner, was nonetheless given considerable attention as a major state governor who had, as a Democrat, survived the Republican high tide of 1918. When the San Francisco convention deadlocked, Cox became an increasingly appealing compromise candidate. On the forty-fourth ballot weary delegates named the Ohio governor their party's presidential nominee, joined on the national ticket with vice-presidential candidate Assistant Secretary of the Navy Franklin D. Roosevelt, young, handsome, and of prominent name. The 1920 election turned into a national referendum on the Wilson administration; its conduct of the war, its negotiation of the Paris peace treaties, its endorsement of U.S. participation in the League of Nations, and its plans for the economic transition from wartime to peace. For the most part an ardent defender of Wilson, his progressive record and his war leadership, Cox did, however, attempt to finesse the League of Nations issue. While personally committed to U.S. membership in the League, Cox felt that lengthy campaign discussion of the issue would result in fatal damage to the Democratic Party cause. Avoiding the issue, however, served only to alienate Wilsonians and anger the president, recovering at the White House from his massive stroke of October 1919. It was a war-weary American electorate that went to the polls in November of 1920, an electorate greatly expanded by women voters exercising their franchise for the first time under provisions of the Nineteenth Amendment to the Constitution, ratified on August 18, 1920. It was also an electorate that was to find the call for a "return to normalcy," issued by Republican presidential candidate Senator Warren G. Harding of Ohio, overwhelmingly appealing. Cox and the Democrats were to suffer a loss of historic proportions. The Republican ticket of Harding and vice-presidential candidate Governor Calvin Coolidge of Massachusetts rolled up a plurality of nearly seven million votes over Cox and Roosevelt, carrying 37 of the 48 states, with an Electoral College total of 404 votes to 127 for the Democrats. Cox, despite temporary disappointment, returned with energy and skill to the field of journalism, enlarging over the next three decades a chain of newspapers into a publishing empire. He did not, however, wholly abandon politics, becoming in the 1920s, and now that election pressures were removed, a forceful advocate of the League of Nations and of U.S. membership in that international organization. In 1933 his running mate of 1920, Franklin D. Roosevelt, now president of the United States, appointed Cox vice-chairman of the American delegation to the World Monetary and Economic Conference in London, a meeting that ended inconclusively as to recommendations for world economic recovery. As the 1930s progressed, Roosevelt and Cox drifted apart, Cox becoming selectively critical of New Deal policies. Living into the Eisenhower era, Cox, age 87, died at his estate, "Trailsend" near Dayton, Ohio on July 15, 1957. *See*: ELECTIONS: 1920.

References: Wesley M. Bagby, *The Road to Normalcy: The Presidential Campaign and Election of 1920* (Baltimore: Johns Hopkins University Press, 1962); James M. Cox, *Journey through My Years* (New York: Simon and Schuster, 1946).

CREDENTIALS COMMITTEE is a key committee of the national party conventions. This committee meets before the convention and determines the qualifications of delegates and alternates that will be recognized to vote at the conventions. Some of the fiercest convention fights have been over which delegates will be seated. There have not been challenges to the seating of state delegations at national party conventions since the 1970s.

Challenges to the seating of delegates has occurred when a contest for the nomination exists at the convention. At the 1952 Republican National Convention, the supporters of Dwight D. Eisenhower were able to have the convention overturn a decision of the credentials committee to seat 68 delegates (from three southern states), who supported Robert A. Taft, and seat the Eisenhower delegates. The seating of Eisenhower's supporters contributed to the outcome of the nomination battle. At the 1972 Democratic National Convention, there were disputes over whether states had complied with the McGovern-Fraser Commission guidelines. There were 80 challenges involving more than 1,300 delegates. *See:* COUSINS v. WIGODA (1975); *DEMOCRATIC PARTY OF U.S.* v. *WISCONSIN* (1981); NATIONAL PARTY CONVENTION.

References: Paul Allen Beck, *Party Politics in America*, 8th ed. (New York: Longman, 1997); James W. Davis, *National Conventions in the Age of Party Reform* (Westport, Conn.: Greenwood Press, 1983).

CRITICAL ELECTION is an election during which a new partisan voting alignment occurs. For the election to be viewed as critical the new voting pattern must persist in subsequent national elections. The critical election portends a lasting shift in the popular coalition supporting the new majority political party. If this shift in voting persists, then realignment is determined to have occurred. Political scientists have determined that there were at least three such shifts in American electoral history. The last one to occur was the election of Franklin D. Roosevelt and the Democratic Party in 1932, which was a response to the economic conditions during the Great Depression. The coalition that supported the 1932 realignment has weakened, particularly with the rise of the Republican Party in the South. A new permanent coalition has not yet emerged to replace the New Deal coalition. The most accurate description of elections in recent decades is dealignment. *See:* DEALIGNMENT; REALIGNMENT.

References: Walter Dean Burnham, *Critical Elections and the Mainsprings of American Politics* (New York: W W Norton, 1970); Angus Campbell, Philip Converse, Warren E. Miller, and Donald E. Stokes, *The American Voter* (New York: Wiley, 1960); Warren E. Miller and J. Merrill Shanks, *The New American Voter* (Cambridge, Mass.: Harvard University Press, 1996).

CROSS-ENDORSEMENT is a candidate running for an office as the candidate of more than one party. This was a common practice in the United States in the late nineteenth and early twentieth centuries. Since 1960 this procedure is only permitted in three states. Cross-endorsement is permitted in the state of New York. Two or more parties can nominate and support the same candidate for office. Governor George Pataki of New York was the nominee of both the Republican Party and the Conservative Party of New York State. The votes he received for each party listing on the ballot were combined for his total vote. This law encourages and sustains the existence of third parties in the state of New York. Third parties in New York State occasionally impact on the outcome of an election. In 1980, Alfonse D'Amato was the nominee of both the Republican and Conservative Parties of New York State for the U.S. Senate. The Liberal Party of New York supported Jacob Javits, who was the Republican incumbent and had been defeated in the GOP primary by D'Amato. Many observers saw Javits's Liberal Party candidacy in the general election as draining votes away from the Democratic nominee and aiding in D'Amato's victory.

In 1981, Koch was both the Republican Party and Democratic Party candidate for mayor of New York. Rudolph Giuliani was the candidate of the Liberal Party and the Republican Party in New York City in 1993. Under New York law, a non-member is not permitted to file in a party primary unless the party executive committee permits it. *See*: CONSERVATIVE PARTY OF NEW YORK; CROSS-FILING; FUSION TICKET; LIBERAL PARTY OF NEW YORK.

Reference: Howard A. Scarrow, "Cross-Endorsement and Cross-Filing in Plurality Partisan Elections," in *Electoral Laws and Their Political Consequences*, Bernard Grofman and Arend Lijphart, eds. (New York: Agathon Press, 1986).

CROSS-FILING occurs where state election law permits a candidate to seek the nomination of more than one party for the same office in the same primary. The term "cross-filing" originated with an amendment to the California Constitution in 1913. Prior to that California had a closed primary system. The amendment was put forward by the Progressives, who believed that partisanship should not matter and that parties should nominate the best candidate. Republican and Democratic office-seekers began to run in the primaries of both parties. In the mid-1950s, 75% of all candidates for state and national office in California were cross-filing. This was a great advantage to incumbents who benefited from name identification. Cross-filing was repealed in California in 1959. Cross-filing is still permitted in New York State where it has significant electoral consequences. The U.S. Supreme Court recently ruled that cross-filing was a prerogative of the particular state and not a right of the party or the candidate. *See*: CONSERVATIVE PARTY OF NEW YORK; CROSS-ENDORSEMENT; FUSION TICKET; LIBERAL PARTY OF NEW YORK; *TIMMONS* v. *RAMSEY* (1997).

Reference: Howard A. Scarrow, "Cross-Endorsement and Cross-Filing," in *Electoral Laws and Their Political Consequences*, Bernard Grofman and Arend Lijphart, eds. (New York: Agathon Press, 1986).

CUMULATIVE VOTING is an election system that uses multi-seat districts and permits a voter to cast more than one vote for a particular candidate. For example, if a city used the cumulative voting system to elect seven council members; the voter would be able to cast seven votes, and the voter is able to cast all seven votes for one candidate. Of course, the voter could distribute his seven votes among the candidates in a variety of ways, including one vote for seven candidates.

This system of voting was used to elect the Illinois House of Representatives from 1870 until 1980. The Illinois method allowed voters to indicate support for up to as many candidates as there are seats. In Illinois, the voter's choices were allocated equally among the candidates he/she supported. As an example, in a five-seat race, if you vote for one, that candidate gets five votes. If you vote for two, those candidates receive two and one-half votes, and so on. The Illinois cumulative voting system had a 25% threshold requirement, and difficult ballot access laws. According to Robert Richie of the Center for Voting and Democracy, these restraints contributed to bipartisan representation and impeded the development of third parties in Illinois, when this system was in use.

The cumulative voting system empowers minor parties to gain representation. It also allows a minority group greater opportunity to elect their first choice. This election system has been offered as a means of achieving greater representation of minorities on city councils in order to meet the goals of the Voting Rights Act of 1965. Over 40 localities in Texas; Alamogordo, NM; Sisseton, SD; Peoria, IL; and four towns is Alabama use cumulative voting. The city of Cincinnati, Ohio rejected cumulative voting as a means to address minority representation when it was offered as a referendum. *See*: AT-LARGE ELECTION SYSTEM; LIMITED VOTING; VOTING RIGHTS ACT.

References: Douglas Amy, *Proportional Representation: The Case for a Better Election System* (Northampton, Mass.: Crescent Street Press, 1997); Edward Still, "Cumulative Voting and Limited Voting in Alabama," in *United States Electoral Systems: Their Impact on Women and Minorities*, Wilma Rule and Joseph F. Zimmerman, eds. (Westport, Conn.: Greenwood Press, 1992).

D

DALEY, RICHARD J. (1902–1976) served as mayor of Chicago and chairman of the Cook County Democratic Central Committee. Richard Daley was born in the Bridgeport section of Chicago. He worked in the stockyards while attending DePaul University Law School. He was admitted to the Illinois bar in 1933. He worked his way up in the local Democratic Party, and was elected chairman of the party in 1953. In 1955, he was elected mayor of Chicago. He retained both positions.

As a political leader, Daley was very influential in Illinois state politics and national politics. He is credited with John F. Kennedy's close victory in Illinois over Richard Nixon in the presidential election of 1960. At the 1968 Democratic National Convention, he was criticized for the treatment of protestors by the Chicago police. As mayor of Chicago, Daley was credited with good management, and the revitalization of the central business district. In a recent survey, he was recognized as one of best mayors in the United States. His son, Richard M. Daley, was elected mayor of Chicago in 1989.

Reference: Milton Rakove, *Don't Make No Waves—Don't Back No Losers* (Bloomington: Indiana University Press, 1975).

DARK HORSE. A dark horse candidate is not favored to win at the beginning of the nomination process. The dark horse candidate is nominated as a result of a compromise after the national convention delegates have deadlocked over the frontrunners. The first dark horse candidate nominated was James Polk of Tennessee at the Democratic Convention of 1844. He was selected after an impasse developed between the supporters of former president Martin Van Buren of New York and the supporters of Lewis Cass of Michigan. After eight ballots the convention delegates turned to the dark horse candidate, James Polk, who was nominated on the ninth ballot. Franklin Pierce was a dark horse in 1852. He was not a candidate until the thirty-fifth ballot, and he was nominated on the forty-ninth ballot. Both Warren G. Harding in 1920 and Wendel Willkie in 1940 were considered dark horse candidates. They became presidential nominees because their parties could not agree on the better-known candidates of the day. Dark horse nominations are less likely today because of the current system of delegate selection, where delegates are pledged to particular candidates and are selected in primaries. *See*: NATIONAL PARTY CONVENTION.

Reference: A. James Reichley, *The Life of the Parties: A History of American Political Parties* (New York: The Free Press, 1992).

DASCHLE, THOMAS A. (1947–   ) was elected Senate minority leader of the Democrats in 1995. He is the senior Senator from South Dakota. Daschle grew up in Aberdeen and graduated from South Dakota State in 1969. He served in the Air Force, and in 1972 he became a staffer for Senator James Abourezk. In 1978, Daschle was elected to what was then South Dakota's eastern House district. In 1982 he had to run for South Dakota's one at-large house seat.

In 1986, Daschle challenged incumbent Republican Jim Abdnor, who had a tough primary. Daschle defeated Abdnor with 52% of the vote to 48%. In 1989, Senate Majority Leader George Mitchell named Senator Daschle co-chair of the Senate Democratic Policy Committee. In 1994, Mitchell announced his retirement as Senate majority leader, and Daschle announced his candidacy for the leadership position. The early frontrunner for the leadership post was Tennessee Senator Jim Sasser, but he lost his seat in the 1994 election. After the 1994 election, Daschle sought the position of minority leader because the Democrats had lost the majority in the Senate. Daschle faced Connecticut Senator Christopher Dodd, who was the preference of the more senior Democratic senators; Daschle defeated Dodd narrowly by a vote of 24 to 23.

Daschle is soft-spoken, and has a liberal voting record in the Senate. He has developed a working relationship with Senate Majority Leader Trent Lott. Daschle is up for reelection in 1998. *See*: LOTT, TRENT.

DAVIS, JOHN W. (1873–1955) was one of the preeminent lawyers of the first half of the twentieth century, one of the most respected advocates ever to argue before the Supreme Court of the United States. Davis was born, the son of a lawyer and two-term congressman, in Clarksburg, West Virginia on April 13, 1873. Educated in Lexington, Virginia at Washington and Lee, the college and the law school, Davis was admitted to the bar in 1895. After a year of small-town practice, Davis accepted an assistant professorship of law at his alma mater. While he valued the teaching experience, Davis concluded that his true interest was in the "rough and tumble" of routine practice. Returning to Clarksburg in 1897, Davis established over the next decade a successful practice in the environment of a booming economy stimulated by expansion in the coal, oil, and natural gas fields, an expansion which produced a wide variety of highly diversified litigation. For most men drawn into the political arena, and eventually to presidential politics, though educated in the law, their ruling passion and vocation becomes politics. For John W. Davis, however, it was the exact opposite; politics became an avocation, his life's commitment to the law always remaining steadfast. Thus, as a reluctant candidate, this Democrat with Jeffersonian principles was elected to the West Virginia legislature, 1898–1900, and later to the U.S. House of Representatives, 1911–1913, where his reputation as a gifted lawyer preceded him and resulted in his assignment to the House Judiciary Committee. So quickly did the freshman legislator gain the reputation as "the ablest lawyer in Congress" that, in August of 1913, Davis resigned his House seat, accepting President Wilson's appointment to the Justice Department as the nation's chief lawyer, Solicitor General of the United States. Davis, in his five-year tenure as solicitor general, argued the government's cases (more specifically the Wilson administration's cases,) before the high court, often defending progressive policies to which he did not personally subscribe. His own political philosophy remained, as he defined it, "Jeffersonian," with an emphasis on states' rights underscored by a keen skepticism as to the exercise of national government power. In September of 1918, President Wilson asked the solicitor general to accept appointment as U.S. ambassador to Great Britain, the president perhaps attempting to avoid pressure that, in the interests of a bipartisan foreign policy, he offer the sensitive position to a prominent Republican such as former president Taft or former secretary of war and of state, Elihu Root. While untrained and inexperienced in formal diplomacy, Davis left Great Britain in March of 1921, with high marks for having protected, even in the cold draft of Woodrow Wilson's personal austerity, the fabric of Anglo-American friendship and cooperation. Returning to the United States, Davis joined the prestigious New York City law firm of Stetson, Jennings and Russell, among whose clients was J. P. Morgan and Company, the latter an association that would prove something of a political liability to Davis but three years later. As delegates assembled in New York City's Madison Square Garden to nominate the Democratic Party's national ticket of 1924, two prominent frontrunners squared off, their differences as much ones of political culture as of ideology or issue: one contender, the former secretary of the treasury William G. McAdoo, Georgia-born, urbane, corporation lawyer, son-in-law of Woodrow Wilson; the other presidential hopeful, governor of the state of New York Alfred E. Smith, grandson of Irish immigrants, "up from the streets" of New York City, Catholic, and educated with the degree, as he quipped, F.F.M., awarded by the Fulton Fish Market, where he had worked as a teenager. As the temperature within Madison Square Garden rose from the heatwave outside, as radio microphones broadcast for the first time a national convention's proceedings; as hours, then days, passed, so did the mounting number of convention ballots. As the 103rd ballot approached on the convention's fifteenth day, with many delegates already returning home, exhausted McAdoo and Smith forces surrendered to a compromise candidate, John W. Davis. Seen as a representative of the party's conservative wing, the vice-presidential nomination, at Davis's instruction, was given to populist governor Charles W. Bryan of Nebraska, "Brother Charlie" to William Jennings Bryan, and with known sympathies toward the Ku Klux Klan. All in all, it was a highly inauspicious beginning to a presidential campaign; one which never managed to hit stride and ended in embarrassing defeat: Davis and Bryan fell more than seven million votes behind the Republican ticket of Calvin Coolidge, now succeeded to the presidency, and vice-presidential candidate Charles G. Dawes of Illinois, the Republicans carrying 35 states with 382 Electoral College ballots to 12 states for the Democrats with 136 votes in the Electoral College. Senator Robert M. LaFollette of Wisconsin, with his running mate Senator Burton K. Wheeler of Montana, nominees of the Progressive Party, gathered, with the assistance of disenchanted liberal Democrats, an astonishing third-party vote of nearly five million ballots, carrying the state of Wisconsin and its 13 Electoral College votes. LaFollette and Wheeler cut so deeply into the normal Democratic vote, particularly beyond the Mississippi, that in some western states the Davis-Bryan vote dipped to below 10% of the total presidential vote cast. The wholly anticipated defeat behind him, Davis, relieved and enthusiastic, returned to his New York City law practice, establishing himself over the next three decades as the preeminent lawyer of his era. In the period 1924–1955, Davis provided oral argument in some 60 cases before the bench of the U.S. Supreme Court including, in the very last years of his life, two landmark decisions, Davis prevailing in one case and failing to do so in the other. In *Youngstown Sheet and Tube Co.* v. *Sawyer* (1952), Davis argued that President Truman's authorization of federal government seizure of the nation's steel mills threatened by strike, while the nation was at war in Korea, was, notwithstanding, an unconstitutional exercise of presidential power. A much divided court majority agreed. In *Briggs* v. *Elliott* (1954), one of five public school racial desegregation cases (the most famous being *Brown* v. *Board of Education of Topeka*), Davis argued for the state of South Carolina in support of a racially segregated public school system, asking the court to uphold as precedent the applicable "separate-but-equal" doctrine of *Plessy* v. *Ferguson* (1896). A unanimous court disagreed. While after 1924 the law was Davis's consummate interest, he continued a modest political activity, growing more conservative as his nature and law practice seemed to dictate. Davis became, as he put it, "a Democrat in exile," leaving his party in the 1930s in opposition to the liberal, and by his definition collectivist, tendencies of the New Deal. At the level of presidential politics he endorsed, uninterruptedly, a string of Republican candidates from Landon in 1936 to Eisenhower in 1952. In failing health, troubled and disappointed that he had not prevailed in the public school racial desegregation cases of 1954; comforted, however, by the virtually unqualified esteem shown by his profession, John W. Davis, the lawyer's lawyer, died at age 89 in Charleston, South Carolina on March 24, 1955. *See*: ELECTIONS: 1924.

Reference: William H. Harbaugh, *Lawyer's Lawyer, The Life of John W. Davis* (New York: Oxford University Press, 1973).

DAVIS v. *BANDEMER,* 478 U.S. 109 (1986) is a case that was initiated by Indiana Democrats who alleged that the Republicans in control of the Indiana state legislature were guilty of political gerrymandering when they reapportioned the state in 1981. The significance of the case lies in the U.S. Supreme Court's willingness to review a charge of political gerrymandering under the equal protection clause of the Fourteenth Amendment. The Court had already established the justiciability of cases involving racial gerrymandering, and where the principle of "one person, one vote" had been violated. In *Davis,* however, it was a political party rather than a racial group which claimed that it was being discriminated against. Furthermore, the Indiana legislature had managed to apportion the vote equally relative to population. The Court's prior holdings with regard to similar claims of political gerrymandering had led some to conclude that such claims represented non-justiciable political questions. A majority of the justices in this case disregarded these prior holdings, and stated that claims of political gerrymandering might properly be brought before a court. Nevertheless, a different majority decided that the district court had erred when it declared the actions of the Indiana legislature to be a violation of the Equal Protection Clause. Ironically, several members of this latter majority thought the lower court was wrong because the case was non-justiciable. *See: BAKER* v. *CARR* (1962); GERRYMANDERING; POLITICAL QUESTIONS DOCTRINE.

DEALIGNMENT is the weakening of voter attachment to the major national political parties. In a period of dealignment, the relevance of party in the voters' choices is less significant. Since the 1960s, voters have become increasingly independent. It has been the youngest members of the electorate who are the least attached to the parties. Voters are casting their votes more for the candidate and less for the party. The impressive 19% vote for independent Ross Perot in 1992 is evidence of the loss of appeal of the two major parties to the voters. A period of dealignment is also characterized by volatility. The 1992 victory of Democratic president Bill Clinton followed by the 1994 election of the Republican majority in the House is evidence of a volatile electorate in the 1990s.

The last realignment was the New Deal coalition of Franklin D. Roosevelt. Evidence of that coalition deteriorating is the recent sectional realignment of the South toward the Republicans, and the occasional swing of the Catholic vote and working-class whites in the North to the Republicans and then back to the Democrats. The number of voters identifying themselves as independents has increased since the mid-1960s and is also evidence of dealignment. Some scholars argue that dealignment precedes a realignment of voters. *See*: REALIGNMENT.

References: William H. Flanigan and Nancy H. Zingale, *Political Behavior of the American Electorate*, 8th ed. (Washington, D.C.: Congressional Quarterly Press, 1994); Warren E. Miller and J. Merrill Shanks, *The New American Voter* (Cambridge, Mass.: Harvard University Press, 1996); Martin Wattenberg, *The Decline of American Political Parties, 1952–1988.* (Cambridge, Mass.: Harvard University Press, 1990.)

DEBS, EUGENE V. (1855–1926) was the Social Democratic Party's presidential candidate five times. Debs was born in Terre Haute, Indiana. At the age of fourteen, he began to work for the Vandalia railroad as a paint scraper, and moved up to become an engineer. He joined the Brotherhood of Locomotive Firemen and became active in that union. He participated in the Pullman strike of 1894 and served six months in jail as a result of his activities during that strike.

He was elected city clerk of Terre Haute in 1879, and later to the state legislature. In 1897 he announced his conversion to Socialism. He helped to found the Social Democratic Party in 1898. In 1900 he ran as the party's presidential candidate. In 1904 he ran again, collecting 400,000 votes, four times his 1900 vote total. In 1908 his vote total was a disappointing 420,793, a negligible increase over his second attempt. In 1912 he had his most successful campaign, collecting 897,011 votes, 6% of the total vote cast. He did not run in 1916. In 1918 he spoke out against World War I and was arrested, tried, and convicted under the Sedition Act. He was sentenced to ten years in prison. While in prison, he was nominated as the Socialist presidential candidate for the 1920 election, and garnered 919,000 votes. With women voting for the first time, this was only 3.5% of the votes cast. He was set free from prison by President Warren G. Harding in 1921.

Debs was recognized as a skilled orator and for his optimism. He was an ardent Socialist and ran for president to educate the workers of their class interest. During his career, Debs was at odds with Samuel Gompers, leader of the American Federation of Labor. *See: ELECTIONS*: 1920.

References: Harold W. Currie, *Eugene V. Debs* (Boston: Twayne, 1976); Nick Salvatore, *Eugene V. Debs: Citizen and Socialist* (Urbana: University of Illinois Press, 1982).

DELEGATE is a credentialed voting member of a major national party convention. There are three methods of delegate selection: (1) the presidential primary; (2) the party caucus/convention process; (3) for Democrats, there is automatic delegate status conferred on certain elected officials, called PLEOs (Party Leaders and Elected Officials) or superdelegates. Delegates are apportioned to the states under national party rules. The method of delegate selection is determined by state party by-laws and state statutes, which must conform to national party rules. The National Democratic Party rules are more directive to the state Democratic parties than the National Republican Party, which is more confederal in its relationship to state parties. The Democratic Party's McGovern-Fraser Commission Report, in the 1970s, led to the adoption of the primary as the principal means of delegate selection. The authority of national party rules over state parties and state legislatures was confirmed in the U.S. Supreme Court decision *Democratic Party of the United States* v. *Wisconsin* (1980).

Delegates to national party conventions are more extreme in their positions on issues related to the voters in their particular party. That is, Democratic Convention delegates are more liberal than Democratic voters, and Republican Convention delegates are more conservative than Republican voters. This is evident in the following *New York Times*/CBS NEWS poll results of 1996 national party convention delegates:

Percentage of . . .	Dem. Delegates	Dem. Voters	All Voters	GOP Voters	GOP Delegates
SCOPE OF GOVERNMENT					
Government should do more to . . .					
solve the nation's problems	76	53	36	20	4
regulate the environment and safety practices of businesses	60	66	53	37	4
promote traditional values	27	41	42	44	56
SOCIAL ISSUES					
abortion should be permitted in all cases	61	30	27	20	4
affirmative action programs should be continued	81	59	45	28	9
POLITICAL IDEOLOGY IS . . .					
very liberal	15	7	4	1	0
somewhat liberal	28	20	12	6	0
moderate	48	54	47	39	27
somewhat conservative	4	14	24	36	31
very conservative	1	3	8	17	35

See: CONVENTION; DELEGATE APPORTIONMENT; *DEMOCRATIC PARTY OF U.S.* v. *WISCONSIN* (1981); NATIONAL PARTY CONVENTION; SUPERDELEGATE.

References: John F. Bibby, *Politics, Parties, and Elections in America*, 3rd ed. (Chicago: Nelson-Hall, 1996); Nelson W. Polsby and Aaron Wildavsky, *Presidential Elections: Strategies and Structures in American Politics*, 9th ed. (Chatham, N.J.: Chatham House, 1996); the *New York Times*/CBS News Poll in the *New York Times NATIONAL*, August 26, 1996, p. A12.

DELEGATE APPORTIONMENT. Party rules determine the allocation of delegates to the various states. The two parties use very different formulae for distributing delegates.

The Democratic Party allocates 50% of each state's delegation based on the state's population, and 50% on the basis of the state's Democratic vote in the last three presidential elections. This rule has been challenged, because it does not follow "one man, one vote." The federal court has upheld the Democratic Party's formula. In 1996 the Democrats had 4,298 delegates at their national convention in Chicago. In 1996, 777 were superdelegates.

The Republican Party allots delegates based on: (1) statehood, every state receives six delegates; (2) congressional districts, three delegates for each district; (3) election of Republican officeholders, one each for governor and U.S. Senators; (4) if the Republican candidate for president carried the state in the last presidential election, then that state is awarded four and one-half delegates plus a number equal to 60% of the number of Electoral College votes of that state; (5) if one-half of the Representatives from a state are Republican, the state is awarded one delegate; (6) Republican majorities, or a 25% gain in Republican membership in any chamber of a state legislature, is awarded one delegate for each chamber and a delegate, if both chambers have Republican majorities. In 1996 there were 1,981 delegates at the Republican National Convention in San Diego. The formula clearly favors the smaller and more Republican-leaning states. The Republican formula was unsuccessfully challenged in federal court by the moderate Republican Ripon Society.

During the nineteenth century, the parties allocated delegates based on electoral college votes. The Republicans, after the divisive 1912 convention between Taft and Roosevelt, moved to reduce the number of delegates apportioned to the southern states. At their 1924 convention, the Republicans introduced the first bonus system as a reward to the state for voting for the GOP ticket. The Democrats adopted this practice in 1944.

In 1996 the Republicans were not satisfied with the front-loaded primary schedule first used that year. The GOP will award states that move their primaries back later in the spring of the year 2000 bonus delegates. *See*: DELEGATE; NATIONAL PARTY CONVENTION; SUPERDELEGATE.

References: *The Rules of the Republican Party*, adopted by the 1996 Republican National Convention, August 12, 1996; Stephen J. Wayne, *The Road to the White House 1996: The Politics of Presidential Elections* (New York: St. Martin's Press, 1996).

DEMAGOGUE is a political leader who gains power and influence by arousing the public's emotions. A demagogue is a spellbinding speaker who appeals to fear and hatred. Appealing to class divisions is also a tactic of a demagogue. Recent American political figures who were called demagogues include Governor Huey Long of Louisiana and Senator Joseph McCarthy of Wisconsin. There are no contemporary demagogues who have had success in attracting the nation's attention. Demagogues may be products of difficult times such as a poor economy or serious global tensions.

DEMOCRAT, YELLOW DOG refers to a very loyal Democrat who would vote for a yellow dog, if the dog was running for office as a Democrat. The term "Yellow Dog Democrat" is a phrase more commonly used in the South. Recently, the more conservative Democrats have been referred to as the Blue Dog Democrats, which infers that they are somewhat independent of the party. These more independent-minded conservative Democrats are often from the South. *See*: BLUE DOG COALITION.

Reference: William Safire, *Safire's New Political Dictionary* (New York: Random House, 1993).

DEMOCRATIC LEADERSHIP COUNCIL (DLC) is a moderate policy organization, made up of Democrats, which is not formally connected to the Democratic National Committee. It was founded in 1985 by Al From, a southern Democratic House staff member. Many Democrats, particularly southern Democrats, were concerned about the liberal agenda and direction of the National Democratic Party. They believed that Walter Mondale and Michael Dukakis had led a party that was too liberal to be elected, and it was a burden on the Democratic candidates seeking state and local office, particularly in the South. The DLC was created to move the Democratic Party to the political center. The organization was led by party leaders such as Representative Richard Gephardt, Senator Sam Nunn, and Senator Albert Gore. It developed a think tank, the Progressive Policy Institute, that generated many of the ideas that Bill Clinton based his campaign on in 1992. The DLC created the notion of a New Democrat, a more moderate Democrat. In 1991, Clinton was selected as the chair of the DLC. Clinton was able to use the DLC to gain exposure throughout the country, promote the new ideas of the DLC, and advance his candidacy.

Reference: Jon F. Hale, "The Democratic Leadership Council: Institutionalizing a Party Faction," in *The State of the Parties: The Changing Role of Contemporary American Parties*, Daniel M. Shea and John C. Green, eds. (Lanham, Md.: Rowman & Littlefield, 1994).

DEMOCRATIC NATIONAL COMMITTEE (DNC) was formed at the 1848 Democratic National Convention to issue the next convention call and direct the national campaign. This was the first national party committee. The committee was made up of one representative from each state, selected by the convention delegates from each state. The first Democratic National chairman was Benjamin Hallett from Massachusetts. The National Democratic Party did not have a permanent headquarters until 1928. The DNC governs the party between the national party conventions.

The confederal character of state representation on the DNC was changed by the McGovern-Fraser Commission in the 1970s, when the party based DNC membership on state population and electoral characteristics. The size of the committee was expanded. The DNC currently has a membership of 431. The members are apportioned among the states the same way convention delegates are distributed: on the basis of population and past voting for Democratic candidates; this accounts for 212 members. Under this system, California selects 20 members and Alaska selects four members. There is also representation of each state party chair and the highest ranking official of the opposite sex. There are also numerous groups of Democratic elected officials represented, including the Democratic leadership in the House and the Senate, governors, county officials, state legislatures, and mayors. The size of the committee is unwieldy and decisions are made by the chair and the executive committee of the party.

The full committee meets twice a year, and the executive committee, consisting of 54 members, meets four times a year. The executive committee is composed of nine party officers, twenty regional representatives, ten ''at-large'' members elected by the DNC, and fifteen others representing various affiliates. Since 1984, the Democrats have owned their office in Washington, D.C. They reported a staff size of 80 in 1996.

The DNC has asserted its authority by mandating that states follow the national committee rules for delegate selection. The U.S. Supreme Court supported the authority of the national committee, when it upheld the argument that national party rules take precedence over state party rules and state statutes in delegate selection. *See*: DEMOCRATIC PARTY; *DEMOCRATIC PARTY OF U.S.* v. *WISCONSIN* (1981); McGOVERN-FRASER COMMISSION.

References: Paul Allen Beck, *Party Politics in America*, 8th ed. (New York: Longman, 1997); Democratic National Committee, 430 S. Capital St. S.E., Washington, D.C. 20003; http://www.democrats.org; Ralph M. Goldman, *The National Party Chairman and Committees: Factionalism at the Top* (Armonk, N.Y.: M. E. Sharpe, 1990); Philip A. Klinker, *The Losing Parties: Out-Party National Committees, 1956–1993* (New Haven, Conn.: Yale University Press, 1994).

DEMOCRATIC PARTY is one of the two major political parties in the United States. It is the oldest political party in the United States. It has its origins in the Democratic-Republican Party of Thomas Jefferson. After the election of the egalitarian Andrew Jackson, in 1828, members of the party increasingly referred to themselves as Democrats. At the 1840 national convention, the name was formally changed to the Democratic Party. This party was the dominant party during the early history of the Republic until it was fractured over the issue of slavery. After the Civil War, the Democratic Party became a sectional party of the South. It reemerged in 1932 as the majority party in the United States under Franklin D. Roosevelt and the New Deal realignment.

The New Deal coalition of organized labor, cities, ethnics, minorities, Catholics, Jews, and the South has weakened in recent decades. The loss of Southern whites, in particular, has significantly weakened the Democratic Party. In recent presidential elections, the South has voted Republican. In the congressional election of 1994, for the first time since the Civil War, a majority of the congressional delegation was Republican in the states of the Old Confederacy. In the presidential elections of 1992 and 1996, the Democrats developed a bicoastal alliance of East and West Coast states to elect President William Clinton. California is key to this successful Electoral College formula.

The Democratic Party has benefited from the emerging gender gap in the American electorate. In 1996, Democratic presidential nominee Bill Clinton enjoyed 54% of the votes of women to 38% for Bob Dole. The Democrats have benefited from overwhelming support from African Americans, Clinton garnering 84% of that voting cohort. In 1996 the Democrats also enjoyed gains with Hispanic voters, collecting 72% of that vote, which will help in future presidential contests in California. *See*: DEMOCRATIC NATIONAL COMMITTEE; GENDER GAP; NEW DEAL COALITION; SOUTHERN STRATEGY.

References: Jeff Faux, *The Party's Not Over* (New York: Basic Books, 1996); William G. Mayer, *The Divided Democrats: Ideological Unity, Party Reform, and Presidential Democrats* (Boulder, Colo.: Westview Press, 1996).

DEMOCRATIC PARTY OF U.S. v. WISCONSIN, 450 U.S. 107 (1981) is a case in which the Supreme Court reaffirmed its position that political parties are private organizations entitled to use their internal rules to exclude those with whom they do not wish to associate. The specific question in this case was whether the National Democratic Party could refuse to seat Wisconsin's delegates at the party's national convention because that state's electoral laws violated Democratic Party rules.

Wisconsin election law called for open primaries. Under this open primary system, those who had not publicly declared their affiliation with the National Democratic Party were still allowed to participate in the Democratic Party of Wisconsin's primary preference election. Although the final selection of delegates who would go to the Democratic National Convention was made by state party caucuses consisting only of Democrats, state law required that the votes of these delegates be consistent with the results of the primary election. The result was that the votes of non-Democrats influenced the behavior of delegates to the Democratic National Convention. The National Democratic Party concluded that this violated party rules which stated that only party members could participate in the selection of delegates to the national convention. Because of this violation, the National Democratic Party said that delegates chosen according to Wisconsin's primary laws would not be seated at the national convention. Wisconsin argued that the party had to seat the delegates.

The Supreme Court decided in favor of the National Democratic Party, arguing the state of Wisconsin could not force a political party to seat delegates elected in violation of party rules. The Court reasoned that, although the state of Wisconsin had a right to regulate elections, it was a violation of First Amendment associational rights to force a political party to accept delegates chosen through that method. *See: COUSINS* v. *WIGODA* (1975); CREDENTIALS COMMITTEE; DELEGATE; DEMOCRATIC NATIONAL COMMITTEE.

DEVIATING ELECTION is an election outcome that is a departure from the underlying strength of the two parties in the electorate. The election of the president from the minority party, while the partisan alignment remains intact, is an example of a deviating election. This was the case when Dwight D. Eisenhower won in 1952 and 1956; and when Richard M. Nixon was elected president in 1968 and 1972. In these elections the Democratic alignment was still intact; however, the quality of the candidates and/or divisions in the dominant party created circumstances for the minority party to win. This type of election is a temporary deviation from the normal distribution of party loyalty. This type of election does not signal a change in the existing party alignment in the electorate. *See*: REALIGNMENT.

References: Angus Campbell, "A Classification of Presidential Elections," in *Elections and the Political Order*, Angus Campbell et al, eds. (New York: John Wiley & Sons, 1966); William H. Flanagan and Nancy H. Zingale, *Political Behavior of the American Electorate*, 8th ed. (Washington, D.C.: Congressional Quarterly Press, 1994).

DEWEY, THOMAS E. (1902–1971), three times elected governor of the state of New York, twice failing to be elected president of the United States, Thomas E. Dewey shaped the image of the mid-twentieth-century Republican Party as the carrier of what he and later Dwight D. Eisenhower were to promote as progressive or "modern" Republicanism. Born in Michigan on March 24, 1902, Dewey took his undergraduate degree from the University of Michigan. Following graduation from Columbia University School of Law in 1925, Dewey chose not to return to the midwest but to pursue a career in law in New York City. In the 1930s he gained a national reputation for his successful prosecutions of some of the most notorious of New York and national crime figures, foremost among them that of mobster Lucky Luciano in May of 1936. Dewey gained such widespread recognition that even with his limited track record at the polls he became a serious contender in 1940 for the Republican presidential nomination, a nomination that ultimately would go to Wendell Willkie. Dewey's first bid for public office had come in 1937 when he secured a landslide victory as Republican candidate for district attorney of New York County. A year later, as GOP nominee for governor, he lost by a surprisingly narrow margin to the respected and highly favored Democratic incumbent Herbert Lehman. Dewey captured the first of his gubernatorial victories in 1942, beginning an ironclad control of the state Republican Party which was to last until the arrival of Nelson A. Rockefeller on the New York political stage in 1958. Dewey was not merely the dominant force within the state Republican Party but also in large measure within the presidential wing of the national Republican Party; twice securing (1944 and 1948) the party's presidential nomination, twice influencing (1952 and 1956) its nomination of Dwight D. Eisenhower. As architect of what came to be known as modern Republicanism, Dewey defined its major features: a conservative fiscal policy which through streamlined management would allow for popular New Deal domestic initiatives such as social security and federally supported welfare programs to remain in place or even be expanded. On the foreign policy front modern Republicanism rejected isolationism, advocating instead an activist postwar leadership role for the United States so as to safeguard non-communist nations from advances initiated by the Soviet Union or, as it was viewed in Republican circles, the renegade regime on mainland China. Dewey's modern Republicanism was also to stand in support of government's role in promoting opportunity and, albeit cautiously, advances in the field of civil rights. His twelve years in the New York governorship manifested many of these positions: management efficiency resulting in state budgetary surpluses; expansion of state unemployment compensation and welfare programs; legislation prohibiting racial or religious discrimination in public housing, education, or the workplace; construction of a modern state highway network; the opening of opportunities in higher education through development of the State University of New York system. Dewey's definition of the Republican message and program, while largely unchallenged in the New York political arena, did not go unchallenged across the nation. Throughout his career he did constant battle with a conservative, essentially mid-western Republicanism whose most effective political voice was Senator Robert A. Taft of Ohio, unsuccessful contender for his party's presidential nomination through several election cycles (1940–1952), and whose influential, often strident media voice was Colonel Robert McCormick's *Chicago Tribune*. Much to Dewey's dismay, conservative Republican forces long unsuccessful within the presidential wing of their party were gradually expanding in constituency and effectiveness, ultimately paving the way for the victory in the 1980s of Reagan Republicanism over modern Republicanism. As political history is written Dewey's successes both in policy and personal terms are likely to be forever overshadowed by the recounting of his stunning defeat in the presidential election of 1948. While no one expected Dewey to win the presidency in 1944 when he and vice-presidential nominee Governor John W. Bricker of Ohio ran against the nation's wartime leader Franklin D. Roosevelt, it was largely on the basis of that credible showing that he had become the widely proclaimed preelection favorite in 1948. Harry S. Truman, who had succeeded to the presidency upon Roosevelt's death in April of 1945, found himself three years later the nominee of a divided Democratic Party from which both left-wing and Southern conservative forces had bolted, in the former instance leading to the Progressive Party candidacy of Henry A. Wallace, and in the latter case to the Dixiecrat challenge of Governor Strom Thurmond of South Carolina. Against such a splintered opposition Dewey and his running mate, California governor Earl Warren, were expected by journalists and broadcasters, professional politicians and pollsters, to sweep to a decisive election-day victory. Attempting to protect this assumed lead, Dewey waged both a ''safe'' campaign, treating issues in highly generalized fashion, and a ''decorous'' campaign, ignoring the street-smart tactics and rhetoric of a determined, feisty Truman. In October, as some economic indicators turned downward, memories of Herbert Hoover and the Great Depression were rekindled. Voters, particularly in the midwest, surged to Truman and the Democrats. Dewey's astonishing defeat was perhaps less a factor of Truman's colorful whistlestop speeches in support of his proclaimed "Fair Deal" than of emerging voter fear of a GOP victory and a presumed Republican insensitivity to the plight of farmers and industrial workers should the nation again be plunged into depression. Following his 1948 defeat Dewey chose never again to consider national office, even as invitations were extended to join the Eisenhower cabinet and as twice (first in 1953 and again in 1969) discussion surfaced as to Dewey being nominated for the chief justiceship of the U.S. Supreme Court. Thomas E. Dewey did not long outlive the demise of that progressive Republicanism which he had advocated for more than three decades to party and nation. In Florida for vacation and medical tests, but a few days before his sixty-ninth birthday, Dewey suffered a fatal heart attack on March 16, 1971. *See*: ELECTIONS: 1944, 1948.

References: Barry K. Beyer, *Thomas E. Dewey, A Study in Political Leadership* (New York: Garland, 1979); Richard Norton Smith, *Thomas E. Dewey and His Times* (New York: Simon and Schuster, 1982).

DIRECT DEMOCRACY is a type of government in which policy decisions are made directly by the citizens. This type of democracy is in contrast to a representative democracy, where the citizens select representatives to make decisions. Direct democracy was used in ancient Greece and Rome. In the United States, direct democracy is used in the New England town meetings, where the citizens in the town meet to vote directly on budgets and policies for their town. A number of American states have a form of direct democracy where the citizens are provided the right of initiative, referendum, and recall. The voters may vote directly on citizen-initiated state statutes and constitutional amendments. A number of the most sensitive and controversial issues of the day have been addressed through this form of direct democracy. In 1996 the voters in California voted an initiative proposal to abolish affirmative action in that state. The U.S. Constitution does not provide for direct democracy at the national level. *See*: INITIATIVE; RECALL; REFERENDUM.

DIRECT MAIL is used extensively for fund-raising by candidates and parties. The Republican National Committee was one of the first party organizations to use direct mail for successful fund-raising. Direct mail fund-raising has become a major source of funds for national and state party organizations. The advent of the computer has made large donor lists manageable for the parties. Direct mail is also used for campaign purposes. This campaign method is used to persuade and mobilize voters. Computerized direct mail allows campaigns to target particular groups of voters with their message. The U.S. Post Office offers political parties a special bulk rate charge for their mailings.

Reference: Barbara G. Salmore and Stephen A. Salmore, *Candidates, Parties, and Campaigns: Electoral Politics in America*, 2nd ed. (Washington, D.C.: Congressional Quarterly Press, 1989).

DISFRANCHISE is to take away or deny the privilege of voting. Loss of citizenship or conviction of a felony are reasons to remove someone's right to vote. More frequently, citizens are denied the right to vote because they failed to register to vote or re-register to vote. Citizens who move are often unable to vote because they have not met the state's residency requirement. Women were granted the right to vote in 1920 with the passage of the Nineteenth Amendment. African Americans were granted the right to vote in 1870 with the Fifteenth Amendment. Discrimination in the South against African Americans voting did not cease until the Voting Rights Act was passed in 1965.

In 1993, Congress attempted to address the problem of low voter turnout by passing the Motor Voter Law. This law required states to offer voter registration when citizens applied for a driver's license. This law enabled nine million citizens to register to vote. However, in the presidential election of 1996, the turnout rate dropped below 50% for the first time since 1924. *See:* FIFTEENTH AMENDMENT; MOTOR VOTER LAW; NINETEENTH AMENDMENT; VOTING RIGHTS ACT.

DISTRICT, PACKING. One party is able to draw the boundaries of legislative districts and packs as many voters of the opposition party into one district as possible. This limits the opportunity for that party to win legislative districts since their votes are concentrated in a few districts. If an electoral group's strength is excessively dispersed, that is called "cracking." *See:* GERRYMANDERING; REDISTRICTING.

Reference: David Butler and Bruce Cain, *Congressional Redistricting: Comparative and Theoretical Perspectives* (New York: Macmillan, 1992).

DOLE, ROBERT J. (BOB) (1923–) served as majority leader of the Republicans in the U.S. Senate, and was the Republican presidential nominee in 1996. Robert Dole was born in Russell, Kansas. As a young man he was an outstanding athlete. He was involved in college athletics at the University of Kansas. Dole was severely wounded in combat during World War II. He spent three years in V.A. hospitals and he lost the use of his right hand.

After he recovered from his war wounds, Dole attended Washburn University, and in 1952 earned a law degree. He was elected to the Kansas state legislature in 1951, county attorney in 1953, and in 1960 was elected to the U.S. House of Representatives. He was elected to the U.S. Senate in 1969, and was reelected four times. He usually won by large margins, but almost lost his Senate seat in 1974 under the cloud of Watergate.

Bob Dole was known for his sharp wit and his ability to compromise. Recognized for his legislative skills, he was elected majority leader in 1984. He resigned from the Senate in May 1996 to boost his floundering presidential campaign. He served the Republican Party in a number of other roles: he was selected by Richard Nixon to serve as Chairman of the Republican National Committee from 1971 to 1973; and he was selected by Gerald Ford to serve as the vice-presidential candidate for the Republican ticket in 1976.

Dole was divorced from his first wife in 1972, and in 1975 he married Elizabeth Hanford, who served various roles, including cabinet member, in the Reagan, Nixon, and Bush administrations. She currently is the president of the national Red Cross.

Bob Dole's legislative experience and skills did not serve him well in his quest for the presidency. In 1980, Dole lost his first bid for the GOP presidential nomination to Ronald Reagan. In 1988 he lost in his bid to challenge George Bush for the nomination. In 1996 he finally won his party's nomination. In that election he gave up on his traditional, midwestern conservative balanced budget values, and accepted the supply-side program of his running mate and longtime adversary Jack Kemp. Dole's 1996 promise of a tax cut did not ring true. Bob Dole restrained his quick wit during the presidential campaign of 1996, and he never connected with the voters. His poor performance, coupled with a strong economy, gave incumbent President Bill Clinton an easy victory. After his defeat Bob Dole retired from public life. There continues to be speculation that his wife Elizabeth, who gave a strong performance at the 1996 Republican National Convention, might seek the Republican presidential nomination in 2000. *See*: ELECTIONS: 1996.

Reference: Robert Dole, Elizabeth Dole, and Richard Norton Smith, *The Doles: Unlimited Partners* (New York: Simon and Schuster, 1988).

DONKEY is the symbol of the Democratic Party. It was first used by cartoonist Thomas Nast in 1874 in *Harper's Weekly*. Nast developed a series of cartoons that gave attention to a critical statement by Ignatius Donnelly, who said: "The Democratic Party is like a mule—without pride of ancestry nor hope of posterity." *See*: ELEPHANT.

Reference: William Safire, *Safire's New Political Dictionary* (New York: Random House, 1993).

DOUGLAS, STEPHEN A. (1813–1861), the "Little Giant" of the U.S. Senate and of Illinois politics, was born on April 23, 1813, in Brandon, Vermont. Moving to New York, westward to Missouri, and finally to Jacksonville, Illinois, the 21-year-old Douglas, having "read" the law, was certificated to practice as an attorney in 1834. Almost immediately becoming involved in local politics as a Jacksonian Democrat, Douglas was appointed state's attorney in 1835 and, subsequently, elected to the state legislature in 1836, where he was to meet another freshman, a Whig serving on the other side of the aisle, Abraham Lincoln. Narrowly losing by 36 votes a bid for a seat in the U.S. House of Representatives in 1837, Douglas was subsequently appointed Illinois secretary of state in 1840–1841, and then to a seat on the state's supreme court in 1841–1842. In the following year, Douglas again attempted to be elected to Congress, and this time successful, he served in the House until 1847. Generally adhering to the Democratic Party line, Douglas became a supporter of President Polk's commitment to "manifest destiny," and, more specifically, to the president's objectives of territorial control both in Oregon and in Texas and the Southwest, the latter, of course, leading to war with Mexico in 1846–1848, a war effort fully endorsed by Douglas. The congressman, by vote of the Illinois legislature, was to move from House to Senate in December of 1847. The remainder of Douglas's career, with ever-increasing influence, was to be spent in the latter chamber where he was to chair the Committee on Territories until the coming of the Republican majority in 1861. Territorial legislation, including that for the governance of New Mexico and Utah Territories, became Douglas's area of specialized expertise. Essentially an ardent nationalist intent on territorial expansion which would provide land for farms and cities, for railroads and commerce, it was only incidentally that Douglas became involved with the slavery issue; an issue which would, however, come to define his career and ultimately destroy his chance for the presidency. It was in the necessity to find answers to the slavery question, so that his objectives in territorial policy could be realized, that Douglas acquired his reputation as a master of the art and practice of compromise politics. In 1850 it was Douglas who, from the failing hands of Henry Clay, finalized the Compromise of 1850: legislation which allowed California to be admitted to the Union as a free state; allowed New Mexico Territory, and the states which should come to be carved from it, to be organized free or slave, to be determined by those within the territory on the basis of "popular sovereignty"; and, allowed Southern interests to be further mollified by adoption of an enforceable federal fugitive slave law. By this compromise package, Douglas, as with many in his party, concluded that they had bought peace in their time; made remote the possibility of civil war over the slavery issue; cleared the way for unimpeded development in the territories; and, politically, insured for the foreseeable future the sway of the Democratic Party. These great expectations were to be shattered as early as 1854, ironically, at the hands of Stephen A. Douglas who, wholly captured by the notion of "popular sovereignty," perhaps seeing the possibility of further advancing his own presidential ambitions, promoted the Kansas-Nebraska Act as a logical extension of this democratic formula for resolving the slavery issue. Provisions of the Act would discard the last remnants of the Compromise of 1820, which prohibited slavery north of 36° 30', and allow the determination for Kansas, as slave or free, to be made by the votes of the people themselves; surely a practice, so Douglas believed, which all could accept, whether they be abolitionists or slavery's "ultras." With the passage of the Act, Douglas was to be astonished at what occurred: the rush into Kansas by those who, in support of their cause, meant to prevail at any cost, however violent; turning the exercise of "popular sovereignty" into the reality of "Bleeding Kansas." Perhaps it was the attempt made in 1857 by pro-slavery forces to have Kansas admitted as a slave state through submission of the jerry-rigged Lecompton Constitution that was for Douglas the beginning of his transformation from one who believed that a compromise could be fashioned to avert the crisis to someone who, while still seeking that compromise, was no longer confident in the possibilities of the politics which he had practiced all of his life. Douglas had now decided that when the inevitable crisis came he would stand opposed to the secessionists, for the Constitution and preservation of the Union. Occurring at the beginning of this transformation was Douglas's bid in 1858 to be reelected by the Illinois legislature to the U.S. Senate, his opponent being the former Whig, Abraham Lincoln, now a member of the newly organized, anti-slavery Republican Party. Douglas and Lincoln were to wage a vigorous campaign, the high point of which was the seven (now historic) debates which they conducted across Illinois from August 21 through October 15, 1858; debates widely attended and, by reports of the press, capturing national attention. Perhaps for each competitor the most significant of the debates was that in Freeport on August 27. Lincoln reconfirmed his claim that a nation "can not permanently exist half slave and half free," and Douglas countered with what would come to be known as his "Freeport Doctrine," a last attempt to argue that, notwithstanding "Bleeding Kansas," and the 1857 decision of the U.S. Supreme Court in the Dred Scott case, *legitimate* exercises in "popular sovereignty" could yet be used to determine the extension of slavery into territories, or within new states proposed to enter the Union. Whatever the popular judgment as to the debates, Douglas was to emerge the winner of the decision made by the Illinois legislature, being returned to the U.S. Senate by the narrow vote of 54 to 46. Douglas and Lincoln, however, were fated to meet again two years later in the muddled political environment of the 1860 presidential contest. Douglas, who had unsuccessfully sought his party's nomination in 1852 and 1856 when Democrats were yet able to finesse the slavery issue and, thereby, capture presidential election victories, was now given the nomination of a divided party, no longer able to finesse and no longer able to win. Meeting in Charleston, South Carolina in the spring of 1860, the convention stalemated; adjourning to a later date and reconvening in Baltimore, Southern Democrats bolted the party, leaving the rump convention to give its nomination to Douglas, joining with him as vice-presidential candidate anti-secessionist Senator Benjamin Fitzpatrick of Alabama. Fitzpatrick, thinking better of it, was subsequently to decline the nomination, leaving to the Democratic National Committee the naming of former Georgia governor Herschel V. Johnson, also an anti-secessionist, as Senator Douglas's running mate. Southern Democrats, at their separate Baltimore convention, advanced a national ticket of Vice-President John C. Breckinridge of Kentucky and Senator Joseph Lane of Oregon. A third party, the Constitutional Union Party, also emerged. Committed to finding a compromise solution to ward off the pending crisis, but without disclosing one clue as to what that compromise might be, the Constitutional Unionists offered former Whig John Bell of Tennessee as their presidential candidate and as his running mate, Edward Everett of Massachusetts. These three parties, in turn, were to face the challenge of a unified, anti-slavery Republican Party which at the Wigwam in Chicago nominated Abraham Lincoln for president and Senator Hannibal Hamlin of Maine for vice-president. As the campaign wore into the fall, and as Douglas sensed his almost certain defeat and Lincoln's almost certain victory, the senator decided on an uncommon course for a mid-nineteenth-century presidential candidate, a campaign tour through the Southern and border states. On this extended campaign swing, Douglas argued not his own cause so much as the unionist cause, attacking secessionist claims, and, warming to his argument, at one point, labeling secession as treason. The election result was as Douglas anticipated: in a four-way race, with the Democratic vote splintered, the Republican ticket led the way with 39.8% of the total presidential vote cast and with 180 Electoral College ballots from 18 states; Douglas-Johnson with 29.5% of the vote carried but one state and its 12 Electoral College votes; Breckinridge-Lane took 18.1% of the vote and gained 11 states with 72 ballots in the Electoral College; Bell-Everett with 12.6% of the total presidential vote cast, claimed 39 Electoral College votes from 3 states. With Lincoln's election the country moved rapidly toward civil war; South Carolina seceded from the Union on December 20, 1860, and was followed by six other states of the deep South by Inauguration Day, March 4, 1861. In this period Senator Douglas sought desperately, but unsuccessfully, for that one last compromise that would avert war. When, however, war came, Douglas gave his unqualified endorsement to the Union cause, becoming both a supporter of, and a friend to, the beleaguered president in the White House, his erstwhile rival, Abraham Lincoln. At Lincoln's urging, Douglas set out in April of 1861 on a speaking tour aimed at building support for the war effort and for administration policies. The cooperation between the two former competitors, now joined in a common cause, was, however, to be short-lived. On June 3, 1861, within three months of Lincoln's inauguration, Douglas, never in robust health, died at age 48 in Chicago, Illinois. *See*: ELECTIONS: 1860.

Reference: Robert W. Johannsen, *Stephen A. Douglas* (New York: Oxford University Press, 1973).

DUKAKIS, MICHAEL S. (1933–) served as the governor of Massachusetts, and in 1988 he was the Democratic Party presidential nominee. Michael Dukakis was born in Boston, Massachusetts, the son of Greek immigrants. He graduated from the Harvard Law School in 1960. In 1975 he was elected governor of Massachusetts. As governor, he was often at odds with the Massachusetts state legislature, and in 1979 he was defeated in the Democratic Party primary. In 1982 he made a surprising political comeback, winning the Democratic gubernatorial primary and the general election. He was more conciliatory toward the state legislature in his next term. In 1986 he was reelected governor. Federal contracts brought into the state by Speaker Tip O'Neil and Senator Ted Kennedy led to a strong economy termed the ''Massachusetts Miracle,'' for which Governor Dukakis was given credit. Dukakis was widely regarded as an effective public manager.

In 1988 he successfully sought the Democratic Party nomination for president. Dukakis did well in the early primaries in the Northeast, and he was able to raise a great deal of money from Greek-Americans. He was nominated on the first ballot at the National Democratic Convention. Dukakis was not able to mount an effective general election campaign, and his efforts were no match for the effective campaign of Bush-Quayle. *See*: ATWATER, LEE; BUSH, GEORGE HERBERT WALKER; ELECTIONS: 1988.

Reference: Charles Kenny, *Dukakis: An American Odyssey* (Boston: Houghton Mifflin, 1988).

DUVERGER'S LAW. Maurice Duverger, in his 1951 work *Political Parties: Their Organization and Activity in the Modern State*, argued that plurality systems that use single member districts encourage and sustain a two-party system, while the proportional representation electoral system favors multi-partyism. The single-member district plurality election system is frequently used as one of the explanations for the two-party system in the United States. Duverger also argued that two-partyism contributes to a more stable political system, particularly in parliamentary systems.

Duverger's thesis is frequently tested and debated by political scientists. Critics of Duverger argue that single districts promote two strong parties in particular districts, but they may not be the same two parties across a nation. India and Canada are cited as examples of this weakness in Duverger's thesis. In recent years there has been renewed interest in proportional representation systems in the United States. *See*: MULTIMEMBER DISTRICT; PROPORTIONAL REPRESENTATION; SINGLE-MEMBER DISTRICT.

References: Maurice Duverger, *Political Parties: Their Organization and Activity in the Modern State* (New York: John Wiley & Sons, 1963); Bernard Grofman and Arend Lijphart, eds., *Electoral Laws and Their Consequences* (New York: Agathon Press, 1986); Douglas W. Rae, *The Political Consequences of Electoral Laws* (New Haven, Conn.: Yale University Press, 1967).

E

EARLY VOTING, which is offered in some states, permits voters to go to a designated site and vote during a specified period prior to the election. In Texas, early voting is permitted for twelve days before election day. States that permit early voting include: Arizona, Nevada, New Mexico, Tennessee, and Texas. Early votes make up one-fifth of Texas votes. Early voting differs from absentee voting for which some reason must be given for not voting at the polls on election day. *See*: ABSENTEE BALLOT; VOTE-BY-MAIL.

Reference: "Early Voting in the States," *Party Developments*, Vol. 2 (December 1996).

EARNED MEDIA is an effort by a campaign to gain favorable attention by the electronic or written press. Stories created by press releases, staged events, and editorials at little cost, are a vital part of the modern political campaign. Earned media is not necessarily free, but is usually cheaper than paid advertisements. Also, positive reports about a candidate from the press are seen by the reader or the viewer as having more credibility than paid media, since they are coming from a neutral source. Incumbents have an easier time getting attention from the media. Earned media is not always positive for the candidate. The press will focus on scandals and stories that are generated by conflict. *See*: MEDIA EVENT.

Reference: Daniel M. Shea, *Campaign Craft: The Strategies, Tactics, and Art of Political Campaign Management* (Westport, Conn.: Praeger, 1996).

EISENHOWER, DWIGHT D. (1890–1969), professional soldier, president of the United States from 1953 to 1961, "Ike" was Texas-born, Kansas-raised. Eisenhower was born in Dennison, Texas on October 14, 1890, and grew up in

Abilene, Kansas. Gaining admission to the U.S. Military Academy, Eisenhower graduated from West Point in 1915. The next 33 years of his life were spent in various army assignments: during World War I at Camp Colt, Gettysburg, Pennsylvania, a training center for the army's newly organized tank corps; a tour of duty in the canal zone in Panama, 1922–1924; staff officer to General Douglas MacArthur in the 1930s, first in Washington then in Manila, 1935–1939, where, in 1936, Eisenhower achieved the rank of lieutenant colonel. Eisenhower graduated from the Command and General Staff School at Fort Leavenworth in 1926, and the Army War College in Washington in 1929. It was, however, with the coming of World War II that Eisenhower's reputation was to be established; a reputation grounded in his ability to think in terms of broad strategy, identifying and planning the tactical support required for that strategy, and in his uncommon ability to get individuals of diverse backgrounds and opinion to work effectively together, joined in a common cause. At the outbreak of World War II he was a brigadier general in command of the Third Army, headquartered in San Antonio, Texas, and was ordered to Washington on December 12, 1941. Eisenhower was assigned to the War Plans Division, reporting directly to Chief of Staff, General George C. Marshall; Eisenhower was soon to direct this division as chief of operations. Roughly six months later, Eisenhower was appointed commanding general of American forces, European theater, with responsibility for the planned invasion of North Africa in the fall of 1942 and the subsequent invasions of Sicily and Italy in 1943. With the successful allied operation in North Africa, and with full British approval, Eisenhower became supreme commander of all allied forces in Europe in December of 1943, with particular responsibility for the planning and execution of Operation Overlord, the cross-channel invasion of Nazi-occupied France, an operation which was to result in the massive amphibious assault staged on June 6, 1944. The invasion was successful and Eisenhower was to accept at Reims, eleven months later, the unconditional surrender of Nazi Germany on May 7, 1945. Having been made a five-star general in December of 1944, and with allied occupation of Germany established, Eisenhower returned to the United States, and was appointed Army Chief of Staff in November of 1945. His work done, his duty met, Eisenhower, rejecting presidential overtures from both the Democratic and Republican Parties, retired from active military service in February of 1948, accepting the presidency of Columbia University. Eisenhower's years on Morningside Drive, the location of the home of Columbia's president, were to be relatively few. With the outbreak of the Korean War, fearing a Russian invasion of western Europe, President Truman, in the fall of 1950, asked Eisenhower to become supreme commander of NATO forces in Europe. Taking a leave of absence from Columbia, Eisenhower returned to Paris on January 1, 1951. The general's immediate objective was to quickly accomplish a build-up of the fledgling organization's military arm by seeking greater troop commitments from the member states. With the United States leading the way, the build-up was successfully realized and NATO forces came within months to constitute an emerging counterdeterrent to the Soviet Union's Red Army. As the presidential election of 1952 approached, backed by influential party leaders such as Senator Henry Cabot Lodge, Jr. of Massachusetts and Governor Thomas E. Dewey of New York, encouraged by highly favorable coverage in *Time* and other of the Henry R. Luce publications, with public support demonstrated at rallies such as that at New York City's Madison Square Garden in February of 1952, the Republican "Draft Eisenhower" movement gained ever-increasing momentum. That momentum was further fueled on March 11, 1952, when Eisenhower forces secured victory over supporters of Senator Robert A. Taft of Ohio, in the nation's first-of-the-season presidential primary election in New Hampshire. Given his deeply held conviction that in a polarized world strong American leadership was essential, perhaps with an awakening of presidential ambition, Eisenhower now for the first time publicly declared himself a Republican, resigned his post, and retiring from active duty on June 1, 1952, returned to the United States, a soldier about to enter the unfamiliar battleground of domestic political warfare. In this he was to prevail. Slightly more than a month after his "return to Abilene" on June 4, he was the first-ballot presidential nominee of Republican delegates at the party's Chicago convention. Joined with him on the national ticket was the 39-year-old U.S. Senator from California, Richard M. Nixon. On the campaign trail Eisenhower's themes were simple, frequently repeated, and highly generalized: Washington would be cleared of the corruption and scandals of the Truman administration; the concentration of power in Washington would be decentralized, with power being returned to the states and to the people; reckless federal government spending would be eliminated, the budget balanced and inflation controlled; also to be controlled, if not rolled back, would be the spread of international communism; and, pledging, "I shall go to Korea," the war there would be ended on honorable terms, without communist victory. The Democratic Party found itself for the first time since the campaign of 1928 on the defensive. The party's presidential candidate, Governor Adlai E. Stevenson of Illinois, was placed in the difficult position of trying, while defending and further promoting New Deal programs, to distance himself from the New Deal administration of President Harry Truman, an administration that had become increasingly unpopular with the American people. Perhaps because the electorate simply felt that after 20 years of uninterrupted Democratic rule it was time for a change; perhaps because they succumbed to the famous Eisenhower grin as much as to the force of his message, election day produced a decisive Republican victory: the Eisenhower-Nixon ticket rolled up a 6.5 million vote plurality over Stevenson and Democratic vice-presidential candidate U.S. Senator John Sparkman of Alabama. Breaking into the Democratic "Solid South," the Republicans carried 39 states and 442 Electoral College ballots to 9 states and 89 Electoral College votes for Stevenson-Sparkman. His fact-finding trip to Korea behind him, Eisenhower was inaugurated on January 20, 1953. For the entirety of what was to become Eisenhower's eight-year tenure in the White House, the constant challenge was to maintain the peace: preventing nuclear war among the superpowers in an international environment of cold war which could, on the slightest miscalculation, emerge as World War III. The great accomplishment of the Eisenhower presidency was that this fragile peace was kept, war averted, and to some small degree international tensions lessened, particularly with realization of the Korean War armistice of July 1953. The domestic policy accomplishments of the administration were far more modest. Eisenhower budgets, balanced on three occasions, set conservative agendas designed primarily for the control of inflation. Critics argued that the latter objective was at the expense of government stimulated growth, thereby contributing to, if not causing, the economic recessions of 1954 and 1957–1958. New Deal social welfare programs were generally left in place, but, other than for social security coverage, not expanded. Two pieces of civil rights legislation (1957 and 1960) were signed into law by the president, more the product of Democratic congressional majorities than of administration initiative. When faced with questions surrounding implementation of the U.S. Supreme Court's public school racial desegregation decisions of 1954–1955, Eisenhower would go no further than to make clear that he accepted the Court rulings and would, as president, see that federal law and federal court mandates were faithfully executed, as was his constitutional duty. His commitment was to ''acceptance of'' not ''agreement with'' the Court decisions. As such, in the fall of 1957 he ordered federal authorities, later federal troops, into Little Rock, Arkansas, to enforce a court-approved desegregation plan for that city's Central High School. Two major public works projects, both of considerable scale, were supported by the administration: the building of the St. Lawrence Seaway and authorization for the construction of the vast network of roads that was to become the nation's interstate highway system. Perhaps Eisenhower's two most innovative initiatives, both in the field of international politics, were his ''Atoms for Peace'' proposal before the United Nations on December 8, 1953, and his ''Open Skies'' plan in July of 1955, presented at the four powers Geneva summit conference of that year. ''Atoms for Peace'' was aimed at encouraging, through an International Atomic Energy Authority, the constructive use of fissionable materials; ''Open Skies'' proposed that the United States and the Soviet Union should both allow aerial inspection of their territories, thereby revealing military installations and armaments, a first step toward a more comprehensive disarmament accord. For Eisenhower, renominated in 1956, even though having suffered a serious heart attack in September of 1955, the campaign and election of that year reprised themes, and results, from 1952: Eisenhower-Nixon improved on their popular vote plurality of four years earlier, defeating Stevenson and his 1956 running mate, U.S. Senator Estes Kefauver of Tennessee, by some 9.5 million votes. The Republicans carried 41 states with 457 Electoral College ballots to 7 states and 73 Electoral College votes for the Democratic national ticket. The administration record, in the second term, continued to be one of controlled vigilance in the field of foreign affairs and cautious initiatives in domestic policy. The latter faded, however, after the congressional elections of 1958 which greatly increased Democratic majorities in House and Senate, with the new approach becoming one of containing proposed programs and spending endorsed by congressional Democrats through Eisenhower's vigorous use of the executive veto. Deeply disappointed that the Republican ticket of Vice-President Richard M. Nixon and UN ambassador Henry Cabot Lodge, Jr., did not prevail in the elections of 1960; Eisenhower, upon the inauguration of his Democratic successor, U.S. Senator John F. Kennedy of Massachusetts on January 20, 1961, retired to his Gettysburg farm. Writing his presidential memoirs, (published in 1963–1965), sustained by the continuing affection of the American people, but suffering ever more threatening heart problems, Eisenhower died at age 79 at Washington's Walter Reed Hospital on March 28, 1969. *See*: ELECTIONS: 1952, 1956.

References: Stephen E. Ambrose, *Eisenhower*, 2 vols. (New York: Simon and Schuster, 1983–1984); Robert F. Burk, *Dwight D. Eisenhower: Hero and Politician* (Boston: Twayne, 1986); Dwight D. Eisenhower, *The White House Years*, 2 vols. (Garden City: Doubleday, 1963–1965); Chester J. Pach, Jr. and Elmo Richardson, *The Presidency of Dwight D. Eisenhower*, rev. ed. (Lawrence: University Press of Kansas, 1991).

ELECTION is a procedure where the citizens select public officeholders. Elections also provide voters an opportunity to decide state and local ballot issues. The conduct of elections in the United States is a function of state government. The franchise rules, determined by both federal and state law, define who is eligible to vote in an election. The state defines ballot access rules for parties, candidates, and issues. The introduction of the Australian ballot in the United States provided the voters with a secret ballot. An election should offer the voters a choice of a government. In some parts of the United States, where one party is dominant, the weaker party frequently does not offer voters a viable choice in the general election and the voter choice occurs in the primary. According to V. O. Key, the one-partyism of the South led to the introduction of the primary to provide voters a choice.

Elections are a procedure that insures legal succession to office and provides legitimacy to the elected government. The United States has more elections than any other country in the world. The United States also has one of the lowest voter participation rates of all of the democracies in the world. *See*: VOTER TURNOUT.

Reference: W. J. M. MacKenzie and Stein Rokkan, "Elections," in *International Encyclopedia of the Social Sciences*, Vol. 5, David L. Sills, ed. (New York: Macmillan and The Free Press, 1968).

ELECTION DAY. In the United States, the general election is scheduled for the first Tuesday after the first Monday in November. The date of the primary election is scheduled by the particular state and there is a great deal of variation. In Article II, Section I of the U.S. Constitution, Congress is empowered to determine when the college electors will meet. The Second Continental Congress directed states to select their electors 34 days preceding the first Wednesday in December. In the 1840 election, voters cast ballots for electors from October 30 in Ohio and finished voting November 12 in North Carolina. In 1845, Congress established the first Tuesday after the first Monday in November for selecting college electors. In 1872, Congress established the first Tuesday after the first Monday in November for selecting members of Congress, and the same language was later used for the election of U.S. Senators, after the adoption of the Seventeenth Amendment in 1914, which provided for direct election of senators. In 1934, Congress passed a law requiring the presidential electors to meet on the first Wednesday after the first Monday in December, and that law is still in effect.

Currently, there are advocates of Sunday elections, who argue the change will increase voter turnout. Sunday elections were rejected in earlier times for religious reasons. Election day may soon become outdated. The state of Oregon has started to use vote-by-mail for the conduct of their elections. Ballots are mailed out to registered voters and many are returned weeks before election day. *See*: PRIMARY; VOTE-BY-MAIL.

Reference: John L. Moore, *Congressional Quarterly's Guide to U.S. Elections* (Washington, D.C.: Congressional Quarterly Press, 1985).

ELECTIONS

1789

The first elections held under the new constitution were organized by the outgoing Articles of Confederation Congress. On September 13, 1788, almost three months after New Hampshire provided the requisite ninth vote for ratification of the Constitution, the Articles of Confederation Congress decided that electors would be chosen on the first Wednesday in January 1789. The electors were to cast their presidential ballots on February 4 of that year.

There was no formal campaign in 1788. It was considered inappropriate for candidates to indicate a desire for higher office, and George Washington was the obvious choice for the position. After all, Washington's prestige had helped to secure passage of the new constitution, and only Benjamin Franklin could boast of a similar national reputation. A year earlier, Washington had expressed profound reservations about leaving behind his retirement at Mount Vernon to participate as a delegate (and eventual chair) at the Constitutional Convention in Philadelphia. By 1788, however, excitement about the new government and a feeling of responsibility toward the new nation (and perhaps some financial difficulties) made a quiet retreat from public affairs less enticing to the former general. Once it was clear that Washington would accept the presidency, the only competition in the election of 1789 involved the vice-presidency.

To give the appearance of balanced representation, it was thought that Washington, who was from a Southern state, ought to be paired in office with a

Northerner. John Hancock was considered, but his support for the ratification of the Constitution had been lukewarm, and besides, he was already serving as governor of Massachusetts. John Adams was a better choice, even though he and Washington had not been on good terms during the Revolutionary War. Washington indicated that he would not object to Adams's selection.

Three of the thirteen states did not cast electoral votes in February of 1789. North Carolina and Rhode Island had yet to ratify the Constitution and so were not, as yet, formal parties to the new constitution. The state of New York, though having ratified the Constitution, was unable to overcome the divisions which had made the New York ratifying convention so contentious. The two houses of the New York legislature stalemated over the appointment of electors. The result was that New York cast no electoral votes in the election of 1789.

Of the ten states casting their electoral votes in early 1789, only Maryland, Pennsylvania, and Virginia allowed for the direct election of electors. New Hampshire and Massachusetts allowed for public participation, but the ultimate choice devolved upon the legislature. The remaining five states (Connecticut, Delaware, Georgia, New Jersey, and South Carolina) relied on direct legislative selection.

Because of a delay in achieving a quorum in the newly established U.S. Senate, the electoral votes were not counted until April 6, 1789. In the end, George Washington received the votes of all of the 69 electors. Under the terms of Article II of the Constitution, each elector also cast a second ballot which, in this election, would determine who would become the first vice-president of the United States. The voting went as expected, with John Adams receiving 34 votes, followed by John Jay with nine votes. No other individual received more than six votes. *See*: ADAMS, JOHN; WASHINGTON, GEORGE.

1792

By 1792 all of the original thirteen states had ratified the Constitution. In addition, Vermont and Kentucky had been formally admitted to the Union, bringing the total number of states to fifteen. Once George Washington agreed to seek a second term, it was clear that he would be unanimously reelected. The vice-president, John Adams, did not share Washington's security in office. A two-party system had already begun to develop within Washington's cabinet. Secretary of State Jefferson and Secretary of the Treasury Hamilton were on opposite sides of the major economic and foreign policy disputes of the day. Those who supported Hamilton's economic reforms and were sympathetic to Great Britain inherited the Federalist label. The former Anti-Federalists, who were suspicious of Hamilton's domestic proposals and who championed the cause of the revolutionaries in France, gradually assumed the name ''republican'' to advertise their anti-monarchical stance (and thereby implicitly question the leanings of the Federalists). Since it was politically unwise to attack Washington, the Republicans aimed their criticisms at Vice-President Adams. Adams was clearly a Federalist; as vice-president, he had broken several ties in the Senate in favor of Hamilton's legislative proposals.

After some flirtations with Aaron Burr, the Republicans decided that Burr's fellow New Yorker, Governor George Clinton, would receive the support of Republican electors. This would at least temporarily remove Clinton from New York politics (where his manipulation of the 1792 gubernatorial election had damaged his reputation), and had the additional benefit of providing a Republican heir to Washington. Despite the plans of the Republicans, and with the expected exception of New York, none of the Northern states gave any significant support to Clinton. Adams was therefore reelected by a comfortable margin, receiving the support of 77 of the 132 electors. The electors were once again unanimously in favor of Washington continuing in office. *See*: WASHINGTON, GEORGE.

1796

Federalist Party nominee: John Adams

Republican (Jeffersonian) Party nominee: Thomas Jefferson

The election of 1796 was significant in that it represented the first formal transfer of power under the new constitution. Many suspected—and his closest advisors knew—that George Washington would not seek a third term, but he did not make his intention clear until the end of the summer of 1796. It was only then that a real campaign for the presidency could begin. The actual campaign, though brief by modern standards, was vicious.

This was the beginning of what would become known as King Caucus, where prominent congressional leaders determined the standard-bearers for each party. The Federalists in Congress decided that Vice-President Adams would be their presidential candidate. Of course, Jefferson was the unquestioned leader of the Republicans, and therefore the only possible presidential choice. Thomas Pinckney, a South Carolinian, was to be Adams's running mate, while most Republicans in Congress favored Aaron Burr of New York.

The Jay Treaty served as a dividing line between the Federalists and the Republicans. To the Republicans, the treaty was unduly favorable toward Great Britain, and was evidence of the pro-British (and monarchical) sympathies of the Federalist Party. The Federalists thought Jefferson an atheist revolutionary who would bring to America the horrors of the French Revolution.

Perhaps the most interesting character in the election of 1796 was Alexander Hamilton. Although not able to be the candidate for the Federalist Party, Hamilton was clearly that party's leader. Historians disagree about the precise role that Hamilton played in the election of 1796. That Hamilton opposed the election of Jefferson is clear. Yet he was also not comfortable with having Adams elevated to the presidency. One solution to this dilemma would have been to somehow arrange to have Thomas Pinckney, the Federalist candidate for vice-president, garner more votes than Adams. This was possible since, prior to the ratification of the Twelfth Amendment, electors simply cast two votes, and had no opportunity to distinguish between presidential and vice-presidential choices.

Whatever his motives, Hamilton urged Federalist electors in the North to give equal support to both Adams and Pinckney. Since Pinckney and Jefferson were both from the South, Hamilton might have assumed that some electors from that region would give their votes to Pinckney but not Adams. The result would be the election of Pinckney. This was not, however, what happened.

The people were allowed to vote for presidential electors in six of the sixteen states that were then part of the Union. In the remaining ten states, the legislature named the electors. The electors divided their votes, with thirteen individuals receiving at least one vote for president, six of those collecting more than ten votes. The final tally was very close, with Adams receiving 71 electoral votes to Jefferson's 68. Unfortunately for Hamilton and the Federalists, Pinckney managed to secure only 59 votes, nine less than Jefferson. The result was that the Federalist Adams had to serve the next four years with the leader of the Republican Party, Thomas Jefferson, as his vice-president. *See*: ADAMS, JOHN; FEDERALIST PARTY; JEFFERSON, THOMAS; TWELFTH AMENDMENT.

1800

Federalist Party nominee: John Adams

Republican (Jeffersonian) Party nominee: Thomas Jefferson

The 1800 election was one of the most important national elections ever held, the results contributing to the demise of a political party and the amending of the Constitution.

During his four years in office, John Adams had become increasingly unpopular. The Alien and Sedition acts, passed at his request, had rallied opinion against both Adams and the Federalist Party that he represented. Furthermore, Adams's one major triumph, averting war with France, divided the Federalists, and robbed them of what might have been a key issue during the election. As in 1796, Adams faced Thomas Jefferson, a formidable opponent. Ultimately, however, it was neither Jefferson nor Adams's own policy choices that brought down the first Federalist administration. The blame for Adams's defeat falls squarely in the lap of fellow Federalist Alexander Hamilton.

Hamilton relished the power that he had been able to exert during the Washington administration. When it became apparent that Adams would not allow Hamilton to have a similar influence within his administration, Hamilton set himself up as a rival to the president. Their disagreement over the nation's policy toward France was a mere symptom of this larger conflict. This schism within the Federalist Party was skillfully exploited by Jefferson's supporters. For example, Aaron Burr, a Republican from New York who would eventually serve as Jefferson's vice-president, managed to lay his hands on an allegedly confidential pamphlet entitled *Letter from Alexander Hamilton Concerning the Public*

Conduct and Character of John Adams. In the letter—apparently intended by Hamilton to encourage Federalist electors to withhold votes from Adams and thus grant victory to the Federalist candidate for vice-president, Charles Pinckney—Hamilton ravaged Adams. Burr promptly published some of the more damning remarks, thereby forcing Hamilton to make public the entire letter.

It is significant that both Burr and Hamilton were from the state of New York, because New York was an important swing state in the election of 1800. As was the practice in eleven of the sixteen states, the state legislature in New York was charged with selecting that state's electors. Therefore, the vote in April of 1800 for the state legislature was really a form of presidential election. And here again the Republicans showed their skill by presenting the superior slate of legislative candidates to the people.

In the end, the Federalists suffered a devastating loss from which they would never really recover. The Federalists decided upon Charles Cotesworth Pinckney as Adams's running mate. As already noted, Jefferson's Republicans decided that Burr would have their support for the position of vice-president. Burr had also been the Republican candidate for vice-president in 1796 when, to his embarrassment, a number of Republican electors had withheld their votes from him. Burr's acceptance in 1800 was conditioned upon Republican electors pledging their support. Unfortunately for the Republicans, the electors kept their word, and Jefferson and Burr each received 73 votes. This created a serious constitutional crisis because, at the time, the Constitution did not call for a clear distinction between votes for president and votes for vice-president. Therefore, although the Republican electors clearly thought that they were casting votes for Jefferson as president and Burr as vice-president, all votes were, strictly speaking, cast for president. Under the provisions of Article II of the Constitution, a tie vote was to be resolved by the House of Representatives. The Federalists in the House considered for a time electing Burr as president. Indeed, there is some evidence indicating that Burr could have actually been elected had he agreed to govern as a Federalist.

As the House began to ballot, Jefferson enjoyed the support of a majority of House members. Nevertheless, under Article II, individual members did not vote; rather, each state had one vote, with a majority of representatives from each state determining which candidate would win that state's support. Sixteen states were then in the Union, and the support of a majority of nine states was therefore necessary. Initially, the House was not able to decide because delegates from Maryland and New Hampshire were equally divided. These states were therefore unable to cast a vote for either candidate. Through 35 ballots, Jefferson was never able to garner more than eight states, one short of a majority. Finally, on the thirty-sixth ballot, most of the Federalists withheld their votes (not being able to bring themselves to vote for Jefferson). The result was that Jefferson was able to secure a majority of delegates voting in ten states.

In response to the crisis precipitated by the electoral tie in 1800, the Twelfth Amendment was added to the Constitution. Under this amendment, electors are

required to cast separate ballots for president and vice-president. *See*: ELEC-
TORS; JEFFERSON, THOMAS; TWELFTH AMENDMENT.

1804

Federalist Party nominee: Charles Cotesworth Pinckney
Republican (Jeffersonian) Party nominee: Thomas Jefferson
The contrast between the election of 1804 and the presidential contest held
four years earlier is remarkable. Of course the Twelfth Amendment, ratified just
months before presidential electors were selected in 1804 and calling for separate
ballots for presidential and vice-presidential candidates, made a direct repeat of
the controversy of 1800 impossible. In addition, the incumbent president, Thomas Jefferson, faced little competition from the Federalists. Jefferson's first term
was filled with successes. His policies were popular, and he managed to greatly
enlarge the territory controlled by the United States through the Louisiana Purchase. It was a foregone conclusion that the Republican leaders in Congress
would renominate Jefferson when they met in caucus in February of 1804. The
only question, and indeed the only balloting that took place during the Republican caucus, involved the choice for vice-president. Aaron Burr had become
despised within the party and was not even considered as a candidate for the
seat which he continued to hold. Instead, the party selected another prominent
New Yorker, George Clinton. Clinton's only serious competition was John
Breckinridge from Kentucky.
The Federalists, sensing defeat, did not even bother to hold a formal caucus
in 1804. In fact, there is some dispute among historians as to what process led
to the selection of Charles Cotesworth Pinckney, a South Carolinian who had
run with Adams in 1800, as the Federalist presidential candidate. Rufus King,
who like Burr and Clinton hailed from New York, was selected as the vice-
presidential candidate.
Consistent with the democratic ideal espoused by the Jeffersonians, 1804 witnessed the first presidential election in which a majority of the states allowed
the people to vote directly for electors. The result was an overwhelming victory
for Jefferson and Clinton. One hundred sixty-two of the one hundred seventy-
six electors who participated in the 1804 election gave their votes to the Republican candidates. *See*: JEFFERSON, THOMAS; PINCKNEY, CHARLES
COTESWORTH.

1808

Federalist Party nominee: Charles Cotesworth Pinckney
Republican (Jeffersonian) Party nominee: James Madison
Thomas Jefferson's Republican Party faced a difficult challenge in 1808. Jefferson's second term in office had been filled with difficulties. The most vexing
national issue during Jefferson's last years in office involved what was known
as ''impressment.'' This term refers to the British practice of forcibly removing

sailors from American ships who were thought to be British citizens. Jefferson's ultimate response to this problem was the passage of the Embargo Act of 1807. The Embargo Act forbade American ships from trading with foreign countries. Eventually, the Embargo Act, because of its negative impact on American commercial enterprises, became extremely unpopular and was repealed by Congress on Jefferson's last day in office.

Jefferson had made it clear from the beginning of his second term that he would not seek a third term in office. Therefore, the Republicans, for the first time in their history, had to find a new leader. This was the age of "King Caucus," and the Republicans in Congress met in late January of 1808 to nominate candidates for the presidency and the vice-presidency. Most Republicans supported James Madison. James Monroe, however, had significant support in his (and Madison's) home state of Virginia. Still other Republicans felt that the sitting vice-president, George Clinton, ought to be the presumed successor to Jefferson. In the end, Madison was the choice of the Republican caucus. Clinton received almost as much support as Madison, but for the position of vice-president rather than president.

The Federalists did not choose their candidates until late August of 1808, eight months after the Jeffersonians had selected Madison and Clinton. The Federalists once again selected Charles Cotesworth Pinckney of South Carolina as their presidential candidate, and Rufus King of New York as their vice-presidential nominee.

As in 1804, ten (arguably nine since the popular vote in New Jersey was, for technical reasons, superseded by the legislature) of the seventeen states allowed for the popular election of electors. The Republicans won by a landslide, with Madison capturing 122 of the 175 votes cast for president. The election was even more lopsided than these figures show, since six of the votes not given to Madison were given to his running mate George Clinton. *See*: JEFFERSON, THOMAS; MADISON, JAMES; PINCKNEY, CHARLES COTESWORTH.

1812

Federalist Party nominee: Dewitt Clinton
Republican Party nominee: James Madison

The election of 1812 took place against the background of war with Britain. Madison, though originally opposed to war, had allowed himself to be seduced by Napoleon's duplicity, and pressured by the so-called "war hawks" in Congress (including the new Speaker of the House, Henry Clay) into declaring war in June of 1812. The war itself divided the nation. The Federalists had always been more distrustful of France than Britain, and suspected that President Madison had declared war on the wrong party. Moreover, the real aims of the war—unfettered access to the northern and western parts of the continent—were of more interest to the Southern and western states that already leaned in a Republican direction.

Congressional Republicans, meeting in caucus, supported James Madison for a second term as president. Madison's vice-president, George Clinton, had died in office. In his place, the Republicans first nominated John Langdon of New Hampshire. Langdon declined the position, and was replaced by Elbridge Gerry of Massachusetts.

The Federalists, meeting in New York City, decided upon the nephew of the late (Republican) George Clinton to represent their party. Dewitt Clinton, who had earlier been in favor of war, was willing to champion the cause of peace for the Federalists (particularly since the Republican nomination was out of his reach). Jared Ingersoll of Pennsylvania was chosen as Clinton's running mate.

The selection of electors was actually less "democratic" in 1812 than it had been in 1808. Only eight of the eighteen states allowed for the popular vote to determine who would serve as an elector. The final vote mirrored the war divisions within the country. With the exception of Vermont, all of the New England states gave their votes to Clinton. The South went solidly for Madison. The result was a very close victory for Madison, who received 128 electoral votes to Clinton's 89. *See*: CLINTON, DeWITT; MADISON, JAMES.

1816

Federalist Party nominee: Rufus King
Republican Party nominee: James Monroe
This election formally inaugurated what became known as the "era of good feelings." The term refers to the end of party rivalry triggered by the demise of the Federalist Party. In truth, the Federalist Party was more terminally ill than dead in 1816. In fact, Rufus King—Federalist candidate for vice-president in 1804 and 1808—received the presidential electoral votes of three states. Nevertheless, support for the party was so weak that several states did not even bother to field a slate of Federalist electors. In Maryland and Delaware some of the Federalist electors did not even bother to cast their votes.

Two factors contributed to the collapse of the Federalists. First there was the infamous "Hartford Convention" of December 1814. The convention was attended by New England Federalists, some of whom were sympathetic to secessionist arguments. Although the final report of the convention fell short of actually advocating secession, the Federalists were not able to escape charges (of which they were not entirely innocent) that they were not firmly committed to the Union. Perhaps more devastating to the Federalist Party was the willingness of the Republicans to adopt Federalist policies and programs. This left the Federalists as a party without issues.

In the end, James Monroe had a more difficult time securing the nomination of the Republican Party (or Democratic-Republican Party) than he did winning a majority of electoral votes for president. Monroe's major rivals for the nomination were Daniel Tompkins of New York and William Crawford of Georgia. Although the practice of allowing members of Congress to nominate presidential candidates was coming under attack, the Republicans in Congress met twice in March of 1816 to select their party's standard bearer. At their second meeting, Monroe received eleven more votes than Crawford and thus became the party's nominee. Tompkins was named as the Republican candidate for vice-president.

As already noted, Monroe and Tompkins faced no significant opposition. The Federalist Rufus King received only 34 of the 217 votes cast. This left Monroe with the remaining 183 electoral votes. *See*: KING, RUFUS; MONROE, JAMES.

1820

Republican Party nominee: James Monroe

The Federalist Party, though still represented in Congress, played no role at all in the presidential election of 1820. Although the controversy over the admission of Missouri to the Union as a slave state had created an issue that the Federalists might have been able to use to rebuild their support, the Republicans managed to arrange an agreement—the "Missouri Compromise"—between slave and free states that temporarily diffused the debate before the Federalists could take full advantage of any rifts in the Republican camp.

In an indirect way, the results of the Missouri Compromise produced the only drama attending the election of 1820. Under the terms of the famous (or infamous) compromise, Missouri was allowed to be admitted as a slave state. As a precondition for being fully admitted as a new state, however, Missouri had to pledge that it would not refuse to allow free blacks into the state, despite what was otherwise implied in the state's constitution. Since Missouri had failed to make this pledge when the state's electors cast their votes, there was some question as to whether Missouri's three electoral votes ought to count.

Although Congress eventually agreed to allow Missouri's votes to be registered, the decision had no real impact on the election results. President James Monroe and his vice-president, Daniel Tompkins, although not formally nominated, were virtually the unanimous choice of the electors. Monroe, in fact, received all but one of the 232 votes cast for president. A legend, more apocryphal than true, holds that William Plummer, the New Hampshire elector who voted for John Quincy Adams rather than Monroe for president, did so in order to insure that George Washington would remain the only president to be unanimously elected. *See*: MONROE, JAMES.

1824

No formal party nominations

This election signaled the end of the both the King Caucus and the "era of good feelings." Four years earlier, in 1820, a congressional caucus meeting for the purpose of nominating a presidential candidate agreed instead to nominate no one. In part, this was because President Monroe had no opposition to his renomination. By 1824 there had developed an antagonism, even in Congress, to the notion of having caucuses determine the presidential candidates. When a caucus was called in February of 1824, only 66 Republicans (or, as they were sometimes called, Democratic-Republicans) attended. The caucus recommended Treasury Secretary William Crawford of Georgia as the presidential candidate, and Albert Gallatin of Pennsylvania as the vice-presidential candidate. The recommendations of the caucus, however, had little impact on the electors. This is because the Republican Party was beginning to disintegrate; the end of the "era of good feelings" was clearly in sight.

With no direction from Congress, states took it upon themselves to nominate presidential and vice-presidential candidates. In all but six of the states electors were chosen by popular vote. This was the first election, therefore, for which it was possible to use the popular vote for electors as a way of gauging popular support for presidential candidates. This method is not entirely accurate, however, since most of the states used incomplete ballots; that is, ballots which did not contain the names of all candidates seeking the presidency.

When the electors finally cast their votes, they divided their support among four individuals. Ninety-nine electors (representing 152,901 popular votes) voted for Andrew Jackson, a war hero and former member of Congress who had enormous support among the people. John Quincy Adams, who served as secretary of state under Monroe, received the support of 84 electors (114,023 popular votes). William Crawford, the candidate supported by the congressional caucus, was given 41 electoral votes (47,217 popular votes), of which 24 came from a single state, Virginia. Finally, the perennial Speaker of the House, Henry Clay, received a total of 37 votes (46,979 popular votes).

According to the provisions of the Twelfth Amendment, if, as happened in this election, no candidate manages to secure a majority of the electoral votes cast for president, the House of Representatives is given the responsibility of choosing the next president from among the top three candidates. The House met for that purpose on February 9, 1825. Since Henry Clay was not among the top three candidates to receive electoral votes, he could not be considered by the House over which he presided as Speaker. He threw his support to John Quincy Adams who was then elected president by a majority of the states on the first ballot. Since Adams had not received a plurality of the popular vote, and since he later named Clay to be his secretary of state, some suspected that a "corrupt bargain" had been made. This charge would later haunt Adams's bid for reelection.

Albert Gallatin, who had been nominated for vice-president by the congressional caucus, was forced to withdraw from the race because of questions about legal qualifications for office (Gallatin had arrived in the United States in 1780). John C. Calhoun of South Carolina received 182 electoral votes for vice-president, more than a majority of the 261 votes cast; therefore, his election did not require any congressional action. *See*: ADAMS, JOHN QUINCY; CLAY, HENRY; JACKSON, ANDREW; TWELFTH AMENDMENT.

1828

Democratic Party nominee: Andrew Jackson, 56%
National Republican Party nominee: John Quincy Adams, 44%

This election marked the formal return of two-party politics to the United States. The Republicans, who had also been known as the Democratic-Republicans, formally divided into the Democratic and the National Republicans. The alleged corrupt bargain that had placed the incumbent John Quincy Adams into office doomed his chances for reelection. The very notion that Adams could become president while Andrew Jackson had garnered a plurality of the popular votes cast for electors was seen as anti-democratic, and democracy was on the rise in 1828. Only two states (Delaware and South Carolina) did not allow for the popular election of presidential electors. Adams, as he had demonstrated in the election of 1824, was not a candidate who could appeal to the masses. Moreover, the National Republicans, unlike their rivals the Democrats, were not organized at the local level. Jackson's party understood how to appeal to the general public, an absolute necessity by the late 1820s.

The 1828 campaign was probably the longest (and arguably the nastiest) campaign that the United States has ever seen. The campaign began in 1825, when the Tennessee legislature nominated Andrew Jackson for president. There was never any serious doubt that John Quincy Adams would be once again the National Republicans' choice. In fact, at the National Republican Convention in Pennsylvania (the most prominent of several state conventions) Adams was not even formally nominated. Instead, the Pennsylvania convention selected Richard Rush as the party's vice-presidential candidate. It was necessary to select a new vice-presidential candidate inasmuch as the incumbent, John C. Calhoun, had joined forces with Jackson. Another National Republican, John Andrew Shulze of Pennsylvania, also received one state's nomination for vice-president.

Throughout the next three years, the parties traded shots at one another. In addition to the charge that Adams had stolen the election from the people in 1824, Adams was also accused of procuring a prostitute for the Russian czar and of spending lavishly on the White House. The National Republicans, of course, leveled their own charges in return. Jackson's behavior during the War of 1812 was questioned, along with the legitimacy of his marriage to his wife Rachel. Rachel had been previously married, and she incorrectly thought that her husband had obtained a divorce when she married Jackson. Although Jackson remarried his wife once her divorce became official, the charge of bigamy plagued Jackson throughout the campaign. It did not, however, hurt him with the voting public. Jackson garnered 56% of the more than one million votes cast in the election of 1828. The final electoral count was even more lopsided. Andrew Jackson received 178 (68%) electoral votes to Adams's 83. The vice-presidential results were similar with John C. Calhoun (now a Democrat) defeating Richard Rush 171 to 83. William Smith of South Carolina received the remaining seven electoral votes cast for vice-president. *See*: ADAMS, JOHN QUINCY; DEMOCRATIC PARTY; JACKSON, ANDREW.

1832

Democratic Party nominee: Andrew Jackson, 54.5%
National Republican Party nominee: Henry Clay, 37.5%
Anti-Masonic Party nominee: William Wirt, 8%

Andrew Jackson's ascension to the White House in 1824 had signaled a radical and democratic change in American politics. Although other presidents had been popular, Jackson was the first true "man of the people" to hold the nation's highest office. To most Americans he signaled a turn away from America's aristocratic roots and so-called "monied interests" toward a government that would represent the average American. The people expected change, and change was what Jackson gave them. Jackson came into office with a flurry, immediately bestowing political jobs (patronage)—the spoils of victory—on his loyal followers. There were at least two major issues which helped to define Jackson's first term. The first was his veto of congressional legislation rechartering the Bank of the United States. Despite the valuable role the Bank played in stabilizing the finances of the United States, the Bank was not popular. The states resented what they saw as unfair competition for their own, state-chartered banks. Also, the Bank had come to symbolize the power and influence that wealthy individuals (who of course owned stock in the Bank) had on the national government. The veto was therefore popular with the minions who supported Andrew Jackson.

The second major issue of Jackson's first term had its roots in the prior administration and was not resolved until shortly after Jackson's reelection. A tariff had been passed during the final months of John Quincy Adams's term. Southerners, and particularly South Carolina, had an intense dislike for the tariff, blaming it for their economic woes. The leader of the anti-tariff movement was John C. Calhoun, Jackson's (and Adams's) vice-president. This dispute took on greater importance in November of 1832 when South Carolina sought to "nullify" the tariff, claiming a superiority of states over the federal government. South Carolina's nullification ordinance contained a threat to secede from the Union if force was used against the state. Although the dispute was later settled by an agreement which allowed both South Carolina and the federal government to save face, it created an insurmountable rift between Andrew Jackson and John C. Calhoun.

The only question regarding Jackson's renomination in 1832 involved the president himself. He had suggested, early in his term, that he thought it inappropriate for a president to serve more than one term. By 1830, however, it was clear that Jackson would again run on the Democratic ticket. This was the first election in which the major party candidates were nominated at national conventions. The Democrats held their convention in Baltimore in May of 1832.

Every state except Missouri sent delegates to this convention, the purpose of which was not to formally nominate Andrew Jackson, since that was a foregone conclusion; rather, the convention was needed to nominate a vice-presidential candidate. The president's choice for vice-president was Martin Van Buren, who had recently resigned as secretary of state. Given Jackson's control over the convention, it is not surprising that Van Buren received overwhelming support, and secured the Democratic Party's nomination on the first ballot. Van Buren received the votes of 208 of the delegates. Van Buren's closest rival, Philip Barbour of Virginia, received only 49 votes.

The Democratic National Convention followed on the heels of two other national conventions. The first was held in May of 1831 by the Anti-Masonic Party, an organization that had entered the American political stage in the late 1820s in response to the alleged 1826 kidnaping by the Freemasons of William Morgan. Curiously enough, the Anti-Masonic Party nominated a former Freemason, William Wirt of Maryland, to be their presidential candidate. Justice John McClean of Ohio had been the Anti-Masons first choice, but by the time the convention met it was clear that he did not enjoy enough national support to win the presidency. After selecting Wirt, the Anti-Masons chose Amos Ellmaker of Pennsylvania as their vice-presidential candidate.

Seven months after the Anti-Masons held what was the first national political convention, the National Republicans (soon to become the Whigs) held their convention, also in Baltimore. The National Republicans were unanimous in their support of Henry Clay for president, and John Sergeant of Pennsylvania for vice-president.

All but one state (South Carolina) allowed for the popular election of presidential electors in 1832. As in 1828, Andrew Jackson did not face a serious challenge. In the final electoral count, Jackson garnered 219 of the 286 votes cast for president. Henry Clay, the National Republican candidate, received 49 votes, and the Anti-Mason William Wirt collected only 7 votes. South Carolina, which at the time was considering secession, gave all of its electoral votes to John Floyd of Virginia. The electoral vote for the vice-presidential office mirrored the presidential vote. The only exception came from the Pennsylvania delegation which cast its 30 vice-presidential electoral votes for a favorite-son candidate, William Wilkens. *See*: ANTI-MASONIC PARTY; JACKSON, ANDREW; PATRONAGE.

1836

Democratic Party nominee: Martin Van Buren, 50.8%

Whig Party nominees: William Henry Harrison, 36.7%; Daniel Webster, 2.7%; Hugh Lawson White, 9.7%

Although not a candidate, Andrew Jackson dominated the election of 1836. He remained an enormously popular politician, and his opposition to the Bank of the United States was a pivotal issue in the 1836 election.

Jackson's handpicked successor, former secretary of state Martin Van Buren, was the unanimous choice of the Democratic Party which once again chose Baltimore as the venue for its national convention (although this time a church, rather than a bar, served as the convention's meeting place). Richard Johnson of Kentucky received the party's nod as its vice-presidential candidate, although he did not receive unanimous support.

A new opposition party, the Whigs (borrowing their name from the British party opposing the executive prerogative), had replaced the National Republicans. The Whig Party was an amalgam of National Republicans and Anti-Masons joined together by their dislike of Andrew Jackson and his policies. The Whigs did not hold a national nominating convention. William Henry Harrison was the choice of most of the state party conventions held by the Whigs. Some state parties, however, decided to support favorite-son candidates instead. Apparently, the Whigs concluded that they were unlikely to outpoll Van Buren with one candidate. The strategy was to field several popular candidates in hopes of denying Van Buren a majority in the Electoral College; for example, the Alabama legislature nominated Hugh Lawson White, and the Whigs in Massachusetts selected Daniel Webster. The vice-presidential choice was similarly splintered, with Francis Granger of New York sharing support with John Tyler of Virginia and William Smith of Alabama.

As in 1832, only South Carolina denied its citizens the privilege of voting for presidential electors. When the votes were finally counted, Martin Van Buren had the support of a majority (170) of the 294 electors; however, for the first and only time in our history, no vice-presidential candidate was elected, as none received an electoral majority. Following the provisions of the Twelfth Amendment, the responsibility for choosing the next vice-president fell on the U.S. Senate. Under the provisions of the amendment, senators were allowed to consider only the two candidates who had received the most electoral votes, in this case the Democrat Richard Johnson and the Whig Francis Granger. The senators gave their votes to Johnson by more than a two-to-one margin. *See*: VAN BUREN, MARTIN; WHIG PARTY; HARRISON, WILLIAM HENRY.

1840

Whig Party nominee: William Henry Harrison, 52.9%

Democratic Party nominee: Martin Van Buren, 46.8%

Martin Van Buren essentially inherited the presidency from Andrew Jackson. Unfortunately for Van Buren, the presidency was not the only thing that Jackson bequeathed to him; what would become known as the ''Panic of 1837'' was also part of Jackson's legacy, brought on by his policies toward the Bank of the United States. The economic downturn that resulted did much to embolden the Whigs, and during the mid-term elections they almost took over the majority position in the House of Representatives. The stage was set for a Whig victory in the 1840 election, and it was with much anticipation that the Whigs assembled in Harrisburg, Pennsylvania at the end of 1839 to select their candidate for the presidency. By rights the nomination should have gone to Henry Clay, inasmuch as he was largely responsible for the success of the party. Clay, however, was a Freemason, and the Anti-Masonic presence in the party was strong. Rather than risk disunity within the party, it was safer to nominate a non-controversial candidate. On the third day of the convention, the Whigs finally nominated an elderly war hero, William Henry Harrison from Ohio. John Tyler, though not the first choice of the convention, eventually became the party's nominee for vice-president. This latter choice would come back to haunt the Whigs.

In May of 1840, the Democrats, meeting once again in Baltimore, unanimously supported Van Buren for a second term in office. The Democrats could not agree on a vice-presidential candidate, and so resolved to allow the state conventions to select suitable candidates.

Slavery was becoming an issue by 1840; in fact, one of the charges leveled at Harrison by the Democrats was that he was an abolitionist. Whether or not Harrison believed in the abolition of slavery, this was not the official position of the Whig Party. Abolitionists who felt abandoned by both major parties formed their own political party. Known as the Liberty Party, they met in upstate New York in December of 1839 and nominated James Gillespie Birney of New York for president, and Thomas Earle of Pennsylvania for vice-president.

During the campaign, the Whigs, borrowing a successful strategy from the Democrats, tried to show that Harrison was a common man. Much was made of the idea that Harrison, lacking the refined tastes of Van Buren, would be content drinking hard cider and living in a log cabin. This rustic image became central to Harrison's popularity. Ultimately, Harrison and the Whigs overwhelmed the Democrats, capturing not only the White House, but also Congress. The final electoral count showed Harrison defeating Van Buren 234 to 60. Overall, Van Buren won only seven states. John Tyler, the Whigs' vice-presidential candidate, also received 234 electoral votes. Richard Johnson, the incumbent Democratic vice-president, was able to garner the votes of only 48 electors.

The Whigs, and specifically President Harrison, were not given much time to enjoy their victory. Harrison died 31 days into his presidency, and was succeeded by Tyler. *See*: HARRISON, WILLIAM HENRY; LIBERTY PARTY; TYLER, JOHN; VAN BUREN, MARTIN.

1844

Democratic Party nominee: James K. Polk, 49.5%

Whig Party nominee: Henry Clay, 48.1%

Liberty Party nominee: James Gillespie Birney, 2.3%

The decision by the Whigs to name John Tyler as their vice-presidential candidate was fraught with risk. Tyler was by nature a Democrat, and it was only his animosity toward Jackson that drove him into the Whig camp. Once

Tyler succeeded to the presidency, his sympathies became clear. Within his first year in office he twice vetoed Whig legislation aimed at restoring a somewhat altered version of the Bank of the United States. So infuriated were the Whigs that they disassociated themselves from Tyler. All but one of Tyler's Whig cabinet members resigned, and Tyler replaced them with former Democrats.

Tyler's boldest move involved his negotiating of an annexation treaty with Texas in the spring of 1844. Van Buren had been reluctant to admit the Republic of Texas into the Union for fear that the balance of power between slave and free states would be disrupted by absorbing such a large slave-holding territory into the United States (since it was assumed that the territory might be divided up into several states). Furthermore, any formal annexation of Texas might easily lead to war with Mexico. Tyler, however, thought that the acquisition of such a large territory would assure his place in history. The Senate refused to consent to the treaty, however, and the entire matter became a major issue in the election of 1844.

In August of 1843, prior to the controversy over Texas, the Liberty Party held a national convention in Baltimore. Once again, James Gillespie Birney of New York was nominated as the party's presidential candidate. Thomas Morris of Ohio was selected as the Liberty Party's vice-presidential candidate.

In May of 1844 the Whigs again met in Baltimore. Henry Clay was unanimously selected as the Whigs' presidential candidate. The convention was more divided over their choice for vice-president. Eventually, however, the convention selected Theodore Frelinghuysen, a senator from New Jersey, for the position.

The conventions of the Liberty and the Whig parties were fairly mundane affairs compared with the Democratic convention. Tyler's only serious hope for a second term rested with the Democrats. The Democrats, however, seemed determined to renominate Van Buren. Approximately one month before the Democrats were to meet in Baltimore to nominate their candidates for the 1844 election, however, Van Buren published a letter opposing the annexation of Texas. The letter offended Southern Democrats (who favored annexation) and cost Van Buren support at the convention. Van Buren would, nonetheless, have been the Democrats' candidate had the convention not adopted their usual "two-thirds" rule—requiring the nominee to secure the votes of two-thirds of the delegates. Once the rule was adopted the lack of Southern support made it impossible for the convention to select Van Buren.

On the first four ballots taken at the convention, Van Buren received a majority of the 266 votes cast. Indeed, on the first ballot he was only 32 votes shy of the required two-thirds majority. By the fourth ballot, however, the deficit had nearly doubled. When the fifth ballot was taken, Lewis Cass of Michigan overtook Van Buren. Cass increased his lead over Van Buren on the sixth and seventh ballots, but remained far short of the two-thirds support that was needed. The convention adjourned at that point; when it reconvened the next day a "dark horse" candidate emerged from Tennessee. His name was James K. Polk, and he immediately received 44 votes. This placed him into third place behind the leader Cass, and Martin Van Buren. On the ninth and final ballot, a letter from Van Buren was read to the convention. The letter stated that Van Buren's name was to be withdrawn from consideration if such a move would be necessary to the success of the convention. A delegate from New York read the letter, and promptly cast his state's votes for Polk. Other states followed suit, and Polk, the "dark horse," charged to victory. The convention then nominated Senator Silas Wright of New York for vice-president. Wright, a friend and supporter of Van Buren, declined the nomination. Eventually, the Democrats settled on George Dallas of Pennsylvania.

As already noted, the issue of Texas loomed large in this election. The Democratic Party's platform endorsed annexation, and eventually even the Whig candidate, Henry Clay, was forced to give lukewarm support to the notion of adding Texas to the Union. Even though Clay's endorsement of annexation was cautious, it cost him support among anti-slavery Whigs. Particularly in New York, enough anti-slavery Whigs deserted Clay in favor of the abolitionist (Liberty Party candidate) Birney to throw the election to Polk and the Democrats, 170 to 105. *See*: CLAY, HENRY; DARK HORSE; LIBERTY PARTY; POLK, JAMES K.; TWO-THIRDS RULE.

1848

Whig Party nominee: Zachary Taylor, 47.3%
Democratic Party nominee: Lewis Cass, 42.5%
Free-Soil Party nominee: Martin Van Buren, 10.1%

Few presidents have had as much of an impact on the geography of the United States as James K. Polk. Under his leadership, successful negotiations were concluded with Great Britain giving the United States clear ownership of the Oregon Territory. A more significant acquisition had actually been initiated by President Tyler when, at the end of his term, he signed a joint congressional resolution annexing Texas. The border between Texas and Mexico was in dispute and following annexation, the United States took the side of Texas. The eventual result was a war with Mexico which ended with the triumph of U.S. forces. The Treaty of Guadalupe Hidalgo, signed in February of 1848, ended the fighting. Under the terms of the treaty Mexico ceded the territory that now contains Arizona, California, Colorado, New Mexico, Nevada, and Utah.

Despite the eventual benefits which accrued to the United States following the war with Mexico, the war itself was not popular in all of the states. The Whigs took advantage of this, and gained control of the House during the 1846 mid-term elections. There were many reasons to oppose the war with Mexico. Polk acted without a declaration of war from Congress. Moreover, many felt that the border claims of Texas lacked strong foundations and could have been resolved through negotiations. But disagreements caused by the war with Mexico went beyond simple disagreement over the military action. For behind the acquisition of any new territories lay the volatile issue of the extension of slavery.

As the Democrats gathered in Baltimore in May of 1848 to nominate their presidential and vice-presidential candidates, the issue of slavery quickly took center stage. Two delegations arrived from New York. One delegation, known as the "Barnburners," opposed the extension of slavery in the territories newly acquired from Mexico. A second delegation, the "Hunkers," did not want slavery prohibited. Rather than agree to split the state's vote, both delegations refused to attend. After a number of ballots, the Democrats finally agreed to nominate Lewis Cass, a leading candidate during the contentious convention of 1844, to head the ticket. William O. Butler of Kentucky was chosen as the vice-presidential candidate.

The Whigs met the next month in Philadelphia. Remembering their triumph under war hero William Henry Harrison back in 1840, they sought out Zachary Taylor, who had distinguished himself during the recent war with Mexico. Taylor's only significant competitor was Henry Clay. As in 1840, however, the Whigs chose victory over loyalty, nominating Taylor on the third ballot. Millard Fillmore of New York was selected as the party's vice-presidential candidate.

The fact that the Whigs' presidential candidate, Zachary Taylor, was a slave owner infuriated those in the party who opposed slavery. Many of these Whigs joined with disgruntled Northern Democrats to form a third political party, known as the Free-Soil Party. Although this party cannot with accuracy be called a single-issue party, it was united in its opposition to the extension of slavery to new territories (soil) that had been acquired by the United States. The Free-Soil Party gathered in August of 1848 in Buffalo. It nominated Martin Van Buren—the former Democrat—for president, and John Quincy Adams's son Charles for vice-president. Before the national elections were held, the Liberty Party had merged with the Free-Soil Party.

Although Van Buren received no electoral votes for the presidency, he did manage to outpoll Democratic candidate Lewis Cass, in New York. The result was that all 36 of New York's electoral votes went to Zachary Taylor. Coincidentally, Taylor's total of 163 electoral votes were exactly 36 more than Cass received. Taylor was therefore elected president. As in 1840, the Whig president died before completing his term. *See*: BARNBURNERS; CASS, LEWIS; FREE-SOIL PARTY; POLK, JAMES K.; TAYLOR, ZACHARY; VAN BUREN, MARTIN.

1852

Democratic Party nominee: Franklin Pierce, 50.7%
Whig Party nominee: Winfield Scott, 43.9%
Free-Soil Democratic Party nominee: John Parker Hale, 4.9%
This was the final election for the Whig party. A growing sectionalism—

where Northerners and Southerners disagreed more than Democrats and Whigs—had already been evident in the election of 1848. Disagreements about slavery were behind this split. By 1852 the debate over slavery dominated American politics and threatened to overshadow parties. The question of extending slavery to lands newly acquired from Mexico was made more immediate by the discovery of gold in California. As individuals flocked to California seeking wealth, the population grew to the point where statehood had to be considered. Of course, any discussion of the admission of a new state to the Union initiated a heated battle over whether the new state would be slave or free. Californians, when they drafted a state constitution, had voted to outlaw slavery. That prohibition became part of what is known as the Compromise of 1850. In return for a free California, the slave states received a guarantee that any other states admitted from the former Mexican territory could decide for themselves whether or not to allow slavery. Slave states also were granted stronger legislation enforcing the return of fugitive slaves. Millard Fillmore, who had by then succeeded to the presidency, signed the compromise legislation. Although some Southern Democrats opposed the compromise for having given away too much, the Democrats for the most part supported the legislation. The Whigs, however, were torn apart. Southern Whigs supported the compromise, while Northern Whigs were bitterly opposed.

When the Whigs met in Baltimore in June of 1852 to nominate a presidential candidate, the Compromise took center stage. There was no safe position for a potential candidate, since opinion among the delegates was starkly divided. It took more than 50 ballots before the delegates could agree on Winfield Scott, a former general, whose chief virtue was that he had taken no position on the Compromise of 1850. William Graham was rather quickly nominated as Scott's running mate. Unfortunately for the Whigs, the neutrality reflected in their choice of Scott did not extend to the party platform. As adopted, the platform gave grudging support to the fugitive slave legislation contained in the Compromise of 1850. The schism that this platform language created within the Whig Party would very quickly prove fatal.

The Democrats, as already noted, were much more united than the Whigs. The Democrats held their convention in June 1852. The application of the two-thirds rule for presidential nominations once again made it difficult for the Democrats to name a candidate. As in 1844, the Democrats voted again and again, with no candidate receiving more than 131 votes of the 291 votes available. Finally, and on the thirty-fifth ballot, the name of Franklin Pierce of New Hampshire was introduced. As had been previously orchestrated, Pierce gradually accumulated votes until, on the forty-ninth ballot, a rush of delegates gave him their support. On that ballot he received the votes of 282 of the delegates.

The Free-Soil Party once again nominated candidates for president and vice-president. John Hale of New Hampshire and George Julian of Indiana were the party's respective choices. Perhaps because their candidates were less well-known than in 1848, the Free-Soil Party did not have as much of an impact on this election.

Two other parties entered the fray in 1852. The Southern Rights Party, supporting states' rights and slavery, nominated George Troup of Georgia for president. The American Party, soon to be known as the Know-Nothing Party and advancing an anti-immigrant platform, also fielded a presidential ticket. The American candidates, Jacob Broom for president and Reynall Coates for vice-president, did not enjoy any significant national support in 1852. By 1856, however, this would change.

Ultimately, it was Democratic unity that carried what was by all accounts a fairly dismal campaign in 1852. When balloting concluded, the self-destructing Whigs captured a total of only 42 electoral votes, and the support of only 4 states. The Democratic candidate, Franklin Pierce, captured the remaining 254 electoral votes, winning by a landslide. *See*: FREE-SOIL PARTY; KNOW-NOTHING PARTY; PIERCE, FRANKLIN; SCOTT, WINFIELD; WHIG PARTY.

1856

Democratic Party nominee: James Buchanan, 45.3%
Republican Party nominee: John C. Frémont, 33.1%
American Party nominee: Millard Fillmore, 21.5%

The harmony promised by Democratic president Franklin Pierce in his inaugural address in 1853 was shattered by the introduction of the Kansas-Nebraska bill of 1854, offered by Illinois senator Stephen A. Douglas. The bill proposed dividing the Nebraska Territory into two states: Kansas and Nebraska. In an effort to collect Southern support, the bill proposed that the issue of slavery would be resolved by popular sovereignty, that is, by a vote of the residents in these new states. This breach of the Missouri Compromise set off a furor and led to the creation of the new Republican Party, and the break-up of the Whig Party.

The name "Republican" was adopted by a group of Conscience Whigs, Free-Soilers, and Anti-Slavery Democrats who met in Jackson, Michigan in 1854. They were assembled in protest to the Kansas-Nebraska bill. The focus of this new sectional party was to prevent the expansion of slavery into the territories; not to abolish slavery where it existed. The new party held its nominating convention in Philadelphia in June of 1856. The Republicans nominated John C. Frémont, the explorer of the Far West, who was 43 years old. They selected William L. Dayton, former Whig senator from New Jersey, as his running mate. In its platform, the new party demanded the admission of Kansas as a free state.

The Democrats met in Cincinnati in June, and passed up Pierce because of the Nebraska troubles. They nominated James Buchanan of Pennsylvania on the seventeenth ballot. John Breckenridge of Kentucky was selected as his running mate. The Democrats supported the Kansas-Nebraska bill, and popular sovereignty. They opposed the "agitation of [the] slavery question," and condemned the Know-Nothing movement.

A third force in this election was the American Party, which was also known as the Know-Nothing Party. This party was based on anti-immigrant and anti-Catholic bigotry. In its platform, it proposed that immigrants reside in the United States for 21 years before being granted citizenship. This party was popular on the East Coast, where immigrants had moved into the cities. The Know-Nothing Party had success in states like Massachusetts. This party nominated former president Millard Fillmore. The party was split over the Kansas-Nebraska bill. This allowed the emerging Republicans to become the new major party and absorb the support of Know-Nothing followers. A faction of Know-Nothings called the North Americans accepted Frémont as their nominee.

There was considerable activity in this campaign. The Democrats called their opponents "Black Republicans." The Republicans insisted they were only opposed to the expansion of slavery. The Democrats also accused Frémont of being a Roman Catholic. The Democrats enjoyed financial support from New York business leaders because of the fear of a break-up of the nation.

James Buchanan was elected with 1,838,169 votes. Frémont collected 1,341,264 votes and the American candidate Fillmore garnered 874,534 votes. In the Electoral College vote: Buchanan received 174 votes, Frémont 114, and Fillmore, who carried only Maryland, received 8 Electoral College votes. The Republicans had made an impressive showing in their first election. Almost all of their votes, however, came out of the North. This demonstrated the sectional appeal of their message. *See*: BUCHANAN, JAMES; FRÉMONT, JOHN CHARLES; KNOW-NOTHING PARTY; REPUBLICAN PARTY.

1860

Republican Party nominee: Abraham Lincoln, 39.8%
Democratic Party nominee: Stephen A. Douglas, 29.5%
Democratic Party nominee: John C. Breckinridge, 18%
Constitutional Union Party nominee: John Bell, 12.6%

After the 1856 election, Democratic president James Buchanan thought he could quiet the agitation over the slavery issue. He endorsed popular sovereignty in his inaugural address. Two days after his inauguration, the Supreme Court announced its Dred Scott decision; declaring that slavery was legal in the territories, and that neither Congress nor the territorial legislatures could interfere with the rights of slave owners. The Court decision divided the Democratic Party.

The bitter division in Kansas continued. In October of 1859, John Brown, in an attempt to stir a slave uprising, led his famous raid on the federal arsenal at Harpers Ferry, Virginia. He was arrested, prosecuted, and hung. Brown became a martyr for the abolitionists, and his violent raid created a sense of alarm about the future of the nation. In 1857 the economy went into a depression, but recovered before the 1860 election.

The Democrats met in Charleston, South Carolina in April, and split between the North and the South. The Southern Democrats demanded a platform that called for federal protection of slavery. The Northerners refused, and the delegates from eight Southern states walked out. They met again in June in Baltimore, and the Northern Democrats nominated Stephen A. Douglas on a popular sovereignty platform. Herschel V. Johnson of Georgia was selected as his running mate. The Southern Democrats, meeting in the same city at about the same time, nominated John C. Breckinridge of Kentucky and called for federal protection of slavery. This faction of the party selected Joseph Lane of Oregon as its vice-presidential nominee. President Buchanan supported Breckinridge.

The Republicans met in the Wigwam in Chicago. The Republican contenders included the following individuals: William Seward of New York, who had a number of enemies; Samuel Chase of Ohio, who did not enjoy the total support of his state; and Abraham Lincoln of Illinois, who had not been in politics as long as his rivals, and consequently had fewer enemies. Lincoln had positioned himself as a moderate on the slavery issue. He was opposed to the expansion of slavery. Lincoln was nominated on the fourth ballot. Hannibal Hamlin of Maine was selected as his running mate. The Republicans adopted a platform in opposition to the expansion of slavery. They called for admitting Kansas as a free state. In addition, they adopted a mild pro-tariff position to attract eastern business interests. They called for a homestead act, and a Pacific railroad to gain support in the West. They also condemned discriminatory legislation against naturalized citizens to appease the German immigrants. The old Whigs and the Know-Nothings joined forces and created a Constitutional Union Party with an eye to saving the Union, and they nominated John Bell of Tennessee.

There was considerable interest in the election because of the secession issue. The Republicans ran a very active campaign with torchlight parades and Wide Awake rallies. Lincoln did not actively campaign or speak about the issues. Douglas was the first presidential candidate to go on a nationwide speaking tour. Lincoln was not on the ballot in the South. His major competitor in the North was Douglas. The division of the Democrats insured Lincoln's election, he received 1,866,352 votes. Douglas drew 1,375,157 votes, Breckinridge 849,781 votes, and Bell was last with 589,581. Lincoln was elected with less than 40% of the popular vote. The electoral vote did not reflect the popular vote. Lincoln had an overwhelming tally of 180 electoral votes; Breckinridge was second with 72, Bell was third with 19, and Douglas had only 12. *See*: DOUGLAS, STEPHEN A.; LINCOLN, ABRAHAM; REPUBLICAN PARTY.

1864

Republican Party nominee: Abraham Lincoln, 55%
Democratic Party nominee: George B. McClellan, 45%

The bloody Civil War was the background for the presidential election of 1864. The war was not going well for the North in 1864. In the midterm election of 1862, the Republican majority in the House declined from 59% to 55%. The Radical Republicans, led by Senator Benjamin F. Wade and others, were not pleased with many of Lincoln's policies, and charged him with being too soft on the South.

The Republicans formed a coalition with Democrats who supported the war. They held their National Union Party Convention in Baltimore in June. At the convention the Radical Republicans sought out someone to replace Lincoln. Salmon Chase, Lincoln's secretary of the treasury, tested the waters, but lacked support in his native Ohio and withdrew. Lincoln was nominated on the first ballot. Hannibal Hamlin was denied the vice-presidential nomination in favor of Andrew Johnson of Tennessee; Johnson was the only Southern senator who had remained loyal to the Union. The National Union Party did not slight the radicals. They adopted a platform calling for a constitutional amendment to abolish slavery.

The Democrats met in Chicago in August and nominated General George B. McClellan on the first ballot. He had been removed from his command by Lincoln in 1862 for his inaction. In their platform, the Democrats offered a peace plank calling for a cessation of hostilities. George H. Pendleton, an Ohio congressman, was selected as McClellan's running mate.

Lincoln's electoral fortunes looked grim until September 3, 1864, when General Sherman captured Atlanta; Lincoln's popularity then rebounded. Frémont gave up his candidacy and the Radicals quickly moved to support Lincoln. The Democrats continued their peace campaign, and Lincoln was overwhelmingly reelected. Lincoln carried every state except Delaware, New Jersey, and Tennessee for an Electoral College vote of 212 to McClellan's 21. The popular vote was as follows: Lincoln garnered 2,213,665 votes to McClellan's 1,802,237 votes. The Republicans increased their congressional majority to an unprecedented 78%. *See*: LINCOLN, ABRAHAM; McCLELLAN, GEORGE B.; UNION PARTY.

1868

Republican Party nominee: Ulysses S. Grant, 52.7%

Democratic Party nominee: Horatio Seymour, 47.3%

The post–Civil War question, How should we treat the South? provided the background for the 1868 presidential election. President Abraham Lincoln had been assassinated soon after his 1864 reelection victory. Lincoln's successor, Andrew Johnson (a Democratic senator from Tennessee and loyal to the Union during the Civil War), was restrained in his treatment of the defeated Southern States. The Radical Republicans in Congress were very unhappy with Johnson, and asserted their will with harsh Reconstruction legislation, including military occupation of the South. They also granted the voting franchise to African

Americans in the South. The Radical Republicans attempted to impeach John-son, and lost in that effort by only one vote in the Senate. In the midterm election of 1886, the Republicans gained a two-thirds majority in the House.

The Democrats met in July in New York City's new Tammany Hall. After numerous ballots, the Democrats nominated former New York governor Horatio Seymour. The Democrats adopted the two-thirds rule for this convention. Gen-eral Francis Blair, Jr., was selected as Seymour's running mate. The Democratic platform declared that the Reconstruction Act was unconstitutional. The Repub-licans met in Chicago in May and they nominated the popular war hero General Ulysses S. Grant, who had been a Democrat, but supported the Radical Repub-licans' position on Reconstruction. Grant was nominated unanimously on the first ballot. There was a struggle for the vice-presidential nomination. Radical Ohioan Ben Wade, who had lost his Senate seat, sought the vice-presidential nomination. The Republican convention selected the Speaker of the House, Schuyler Colfax of Indiana.

Horatio Seymour, who accepted the nomination reluctantly, did not actively campaign. General Grant, who also did not campaign, refused to state his po-sition on a number of issues. He offered the theme "Let us have peace." The Republicans accused Seymour of being a traitor, and the Democrats accused Grant of drunkenness and stupidity. Grant easily won the Electoral College vote with 214 votes to Seymour's 80. The popular vote was much closer at 3,012,813 for Grant to 2,703,249 for Seymour.

The close popular vote demonstrated the importance of the black vote to the Republicans. Without the black vote in the South, Grant may have been denied a majority of the popular vote. In their platform, the Republicans had stated that the issue of black voting rights belonged to the states. However, as a result of the election results, the Republicans quickly moved to promote the Fifteenth Amendment. This Amendment stated that the right to vote could not be denied or abridged on account of race, color, or previous condition of servitude. *See*: FIFTEENTH AMENDMENT; GRANT, ULYSSES S.; JOHNSON, ANDREW; SEYMOUR, HORATIO.

1872

Republican Party nominee: Ulysses S. Grant, 55.6%

Liberal/Democratic Parties nominee: Horace M. Greeley, 43.9%

The setting for the 1872 election was the post–Civil War performance of the Grant administration. The nation enjoyed a strong economy which did not weaken until 1873. Grant had a cozy relationship with the emerging industrial class in America. The scandals which discredited the Grant administration were not revealed until the second term. Grant was criticized for cronyism in the selection of his cabinet, and there were calls for appointments based on merit. The treatment of the South remained controversial; the Grant administration pursued a hard-line policy.

One of the major political events in the 1872 election emerged in Missouri. In 1870 a group of disgruntled Missouri Republicans, calling themselves Liberals, broke from the party, and nominated their own candidate for governor. The candidate subsequently won the race for governor. This led to an 1872 convention of reform-minded Liberal Republicans that was held in Cincinnati in May. In a surprise move, the Liberals nominated Horace Greeley for president. Greeley had long been editor of the *New York Herald*, and had been instrumental in the founding of the Republican Party. Governor Brown of Missouri was selected as Greeley's running mate. This party of reformers called for the following: universal amnesty, local self-government, supremacy of civil order over military rule, civil service reform, and opposition to land grants for the railroads. They were oblique in their stand on the tariff issue, over which they were divided. The Democrats, who met in Baltimore in July, agreed to nominate Greeley and accept the platform of the Liberals. The regular Republicans met in Philadelphia in June, and nominated Grant without any opposition. The Republicans turned away from Vice-President Colfax, and selected Henry Wilson of Massachusetts as Grant's running mate. At the urging of Susan B. Anthony, who supported Grant, the Republicans made reference to their "obligations to the loyal women of America" in their platform.

The general election campaign was not very lively. Horace Greeley was demeaned by the press; he was presented as eccentric. Greeley had been a free thinker, and many of the ideas he promoted as an editor were revisited and ridiculed during the campaign. Grant was treated as a drunkard, and his administration was accused of corruption and incompetence. Nonetheless, Greeley's supporters lost heart, and Grant won easily, capturing 286 of the 349 electoral votes. The popular vote was overwhelmingly for Grant who garnered 3,597,132 votes to Greeley's 2,834,125 votes. Greeley's wife died during the campaign, and he died soon after the election. His Electoral College votes were dispersed, most of them going to Brown. The Republicans made gains in the congressional elections. The Liberals disappeared, but many of their ideas dominated the political agenda for the next quarter century. *See*: GRANT, ULYSSES S.; GREELEY, HORACE.

1876

Democratic Party nominee: Samuel J. Tilden, 51%

Republican Party nominee: Rutherford B. Hayes, 48%

The end of the Grant presidency, marked by scandal and economic hardship, set the stage for the election of 1876. The collapse of Jay Cooke's banking company in 1873 triggered an economic downturn. Corruption in the Grant administration was highlighted with the exposure of the Whiskey Ring scandal. In 1874, the Republicans lost the House for the first time in 20 years.

The early favorite for the nomination among the Republican faithful was Maine senator James G. Blaine. He had been damaged in the spring of 1876 by letters which revealed he had done favors for an Arkansas railroad. At their convention in Cincinnati in June, the Republicans turned to Ohio governor Rutherford B. Hayes, and nominated him on the seventh ballot. William A. Wheeler of New York was selected as Hayes's running mate. Their platform was vague. The Democrats met two weeks later in St. Louis, and nominated New York governor Samuel J. Tilden. He was popular with the reformers because, as state attorney general, he prosecuted boss William Tweed of Tammany Hall. The Democrats selected Thomas A. Hendricks, a greenbacker of Indiana, as their vice-presidential nominee. The Democrats adopted a platform that called for reform of government and the financial system.

The candidates agreed on most of the major issues including civil service reform, hard money, and the end of Reconstruction in the South. The campaigns hurled personal attacks against the candidates. Tilden won the popular vote with 4,300,00 votes to Hayes's 4,036,000. It also appeared that Tilden won the election in the Electoral College. There were, however, four states, with a total of twenty electoral votes, in which the outcome of the elections was in dispute. When the electoral votes were counted, Tilden was one short of a majority. The Republicans, under the leadership of their national party chairman Zachariah Chandler, made an effort to deny Tilden the election. Oregon's one disputed vote was resolved quickly for Hayes. The other challenged votes were centered in three Southern states: Louisiana, Florida, and South Carolina.

The national legislature was divided with the Democrats controlling the House, and the Republicans holding a majority in the Senate. In an effort to resolve the conflict, a bipartisan electoral commission was established with seven Democrats and seven Republicans. A Republican, Justice Joseph Bradley, served as the fifteenth member. The commission ruled by a vote of eight to seven in favor of Hayes, gave him all the challenged electoral votes, and he was elected president. There were loud accusations of corruption. The Hayes forces negotiated with Southern Democrats and offered them the withdrawal of the remaining federal troops in the South and cabinet appointments, to gain their acceptance of the disputed results. The final electoral vote was 185 for Hayes and 184 for Tilden. As a result of the election of 1876, Reconstruction came to an end in the South. *See*: ELECTORAL COLLEGE; HAYES, RUTHERFORD B.; TILDEN, SAMUEL J.

1880

Republican Party nominee: James A. Garfield, 48.3%
Democratic Party nominee: Winfield Scott Hancock, 48.3%
Greenback/Labor Party nominee: James B. Weaver, 3.3%

The setting of the 1880 election was the pledge by Rutherford B. Hayes that he would only serve one term and refused to seek his party's nomination. Hayes had supported civil service reform and completed his term with an unblemished record. Under Hayes, Reconstruction came to an end. In the 1878 midterm election, the Democrats captured both Houses of Congress. The economy, which had been in a recession since 1873, began to recover.

The stalwart Republicans attempted to bring Ulysses Grant back for a third term. Many of Grant's opponents initially rallied behind James G. Blaine, who failed to gain the nomination on the first ballot. After 35 ballots, the Republicans turned to dark horse James A. Garfield; a young Ohio congressman, who was Senator-elect. The Republicans met in Chicago in early June and selected Chester A. Arthur of New York as Garfield's running mate. The Democrats met in Cincinnati late in June, and they nominated General Winfield Scott Hancock of Pennsylvania without a struggle. They selected William H. English of Indiana as his running mate. The Democrats adopted ''tariff for revenue only'' as a key part of their platform.

The candidates were not very exciting, and with very few exceptions the parties held to very similar positions. Fearful of the Democrats' stand on the tariff, business interests fueled the Republicans' war chest. The Republicans advocated a more protectionist position. The South was now solidly Democratic. The popular vote was very close: Garfield drew 4,454,416 to Hancock's 4,444,952. The Greenback Party presidential candidate, James B. Weaver, collected 308,578 votes. The Electoral College margin was much wider with Garfield collecting 214 votes to Hancock's 155. *See*: GARFIELD, JAMES A.; GREENBACK PARTY; HANCOCK, WINFIELD SCOTT.

1884

Democratic Party nominee: Grover Cleveland, 48.5%
Republican Party nominee: James G. Blaine, 48.2%
The election of 1884 was set by the assassination of President James Garfield a few months after his inauguration in 1881. He was succeeded by Vice-President Chester Arthur, who was regarded as an able administrator. President Arthur supported government reform. The Pendleton Act, which instituted the Civil Service Commission, was passed during his tenure in office. The Republican Party was beset by factions, and the GOP lost the House in the midterm election of 1882. The economy went into a slump in 1883, and the downturn lasted through the 1884 presidential election. The economic difficulties contributed to the election of Grover Cleveland, who returned the White House to the Democrats for the first time in a quarter of a century.

The Republicans met in Chicago in June and nominated James G. Blaine of Maine. Blaine had served as Speaker, as a U.S. Senator, and as secretary of state. He had failed to capture the GOP nomination in 1876 and 1880 because he had been implicated in a railroad scandal. Chester Arthur also sought the nomination, but was unable to appease the various party factions. He also suffered from poor health. Blaine was nominated on the fourth ballot, and John Logan of Illinois was selected as his running mate. A number of reform-minded Republicans refused to support Blaine, and gave their support to the Democratic presidential nominee Grover Cleveland. These Republican deserters were named the "Mugwumps" by the press.

The Democrats nominated New York governor Grover Cleveland. After overcoming some Tammany Hall efforts to block his selection, Cleveland was nominated on the third ballot at the Democratic National Convention in Chicago in July. He had gained a reputation as a reformer as a result of his opposition to Tammany Hall. Thomas A. Hendricks of Indiana was selected as Cleveland's running mate.

There were few policy differences between the two major parties in this election. Cleveland campaigned very little, giving only a few speeches. Blaine was a more vigorous candidate, giving over 400 speeches in the 1884 campaign. This presidential campaign was noted for its mudslinging. During the campaign, it was revealed that Grover Cleveland had taken up with a Buffalo widow and fathered a son. He provided financial support for both of them. The Republicans enjoyed chanting: "Ma! Ma! Where's my pa?" After the election the Democrats responded with: "Gone to the White House. Ha! Ha! Ha!"

Blaine had problems of his own. Letters tying Blaine to the railroad scandals were printed in the Boston and New York newspapers with some new revelations about the story. On October 29, Blaine attended a meeting of pro-Blaine Protestant clergy, and the Reverend Samuel D. Burchard, in giving the welcoming address, closed with the words: "We are Republicans and don't propose to leave our party and identify with the party whose antecedents have been Rum, Romanism, and Rebellion." Blaine did not respond, and the Democrats saw that these remarks were printed in all of the newspapers. The result of these bigoted remarks, without Blaine's renunciation of them, drove the Catholic vote to Cleveland. This hurt Blaine, particularly in New York State which he lost by 1,149 votes.

The election results were very close. Cleveland pulled 4,874,986 votes to Blaine's total of 4,851,981 votes. Cleveland took 219 Electoral College votes to Blaine's 182. The Democrats retained their majority in the House and the GOP continued to hold the Senate. *See*: BLAINE, JAMES G.; CLEVELAND, GROVER; TAMMANY HALL.

1888

Democratic Party nominee: Grover Cleveland, 48.6%

Republican Party nominee: Benjamin Harrison, 47.8%

The setting for the 1888 election was defined by the election of Grover Cleveland in 1884, the first Democratic president elected in 25 years. As president, Cleveland ran afoul of the Democratic Party regulars by not exploiting patronage opportunities to the degree that the party regulars expected. Cleveland's patronage opportunities were restrained by the Pendleton Act, which was passed during the Arthur administration.

The most notable piece of legislation passed during Cleveland's first term was the Interstate Commerce Act in 1887. This law created the Interstate Commerce Commission, the first independent regulatory commission. This was not a Cleveland initiative. Cleveland gave his attention to the protective tariff system, which he opposed. Cleveland introduced the Mills bill, which would have lowered the tariff rates. The Mills bill became deadlocked in Congress. It passed in the House, which was under the control of the Democrats, but was blocked in the Republican Senate. The tariff became the central issue in the 1888 election. Cleveland's first term was generally one of prosperity. The Democrats lost only twelve seats and retained their majority in the House in the midterm election of 1886.

The Democratic Party held its national convention in St. Louis in the month of June 1888. It nominated Grover Cleveland by acclamation, and adopted a "tariff plank." A resolution supporting passage of the Mills bill to lower the tariff was accepted from the floor. The convention also approved a resolution urging statehood for four western territories, and expressed sympathy for home rule in Ireland; this was clearly a bid for the Irish vote. The Democrats selected former Ohio senator Allen G. Thurman as Cleveland's running mate.

The Republicans held their national convention in Chicago in June. Before the convention, the popular James G. Blaine wrote a letter declining the nomination. That left John Sherman of Ohio, whose manager was the skillful Mark Hanna, as the frontrunner. Sherman was not able to capture the nomination on the first ballot, and on the eighth ballot, former frontrunner Indiana senator Benjamin Harrison was nominated. Harrison was the grandson of President William Henry Harrison, and a Civil War hero. Levi Morton, a wealthy businessman from New York, was selected as Harrison's running mate. The Republicans adopted a pro-tariff plank.

President Cleveland did not actively campaign in 1888. Harrison conducted a successful campaign from the front porch of his Indianapolis home. The Republicans were very well financed by the pro-tariff manufacturers. Protectionist champion William McKinley and popular James G. Blaine actively campaigned for the GOP ticket in 1888.

Benjamin Harrison was elected with fewer popular votes than Cleveland received. Harrison drew 5,439,853 votes collecting 233 Electoral College votes. Cleveland garnered 5,540,329 votes and 168 electoral votes. Harrison won very close contests in New York and Indiana. The Republicans gained 22 seats and the majority in the House in 1888. *See*: CLEVELAND, GROVER; HARRISON, BENJAMIN.

1892

Democratic Party candidate: Grover Cleveland, 46%
Republican Party candidate: Benjamin Harrison, 43%
Populist Party candidate: James B. Weaver, 8.5%
The return of the Republicans in 1888 with the election of President Benjamin

Harrison set the stage for a rematch with Grover Cleveland in 1892. President Benjamin Harrison and the Republicans undertook an ambitious legislative agenda. The House was led by Speaker Thomas "Czar" Reed, who instituted strong party rule. Congress passed the McKinley Tariff of 1890, fulfilling their major campaign pledge. The Republicans also passed the Dependent Pension bill, which had been vetoed by Cleveland. The bill provided pensions to disabled Union veterans as well as the widows and orphans of the veterans. This was the largest social welfare program introduced until the onset of the New Deal. They also passed the Sherman Antitrust Act. During Harrison's term the country was hit by a recession and the Republicans lost 85 seats and their congressional majority in 1890. The economic downturn, which hit the midwest particularly hard, and the 1890 election results appeared to repudiate the Republican program of protectionism.

The Republicans met in Minneapolis in June. The professional politicians in the Republican Party were unhappy with Harrison for ignoring their patronage requests, and they attempted to push James G. Blaine for the GOP nomination in 1892. Blaine resigned as secretary of state three days before the convention started, and with the support of a number of important party leaders, challenged Harrison for the nomination. Harrison rebuffed Blaine's challenge, and was nominated on the first ballot. In their platform, the Republicans reaffirmed their belief in the tariffs. Whitelaw Reid of the *New York Tribune* was selected as Harrison's running mate.

The Democrats met in Chicago in June, and once again nominated Grover Cleveland. The Democrats selected Adlai Stevenson as Cleveland's running mate. Cleveland benefited from the discontent with protectionism, and remained a strong advocate of lower tariffs. Cleveland opposed free silver which ingratiated his candidacy with the financial interests in the East. The eastern financial interests were concerned about the free coinage of silver advocated by the growing agrarian Populist movement in the West and the South. The emerging Populist Party held its convention in Omaha, Nebraska in July. They nominated James B. Weaver as their presidential nominee, and James Field as his running mate. In addition to free silver, the Populists advocated a reform program, which included the popular election of senators, and a graduated income tax.

The two major party candidates were not active. Harrison did not campaign because his wife was quite ill. Cleveland did not campaign out of respect for Harrison's wife. In this campaign, the Republicans were not able to raise the campaign funds as successfully as they had in 1888. The eastern financial interests were not strongly opposed to Cleveland. The Republicans' argument that the workers benefited from their tariff policies rang hollow. During the campaign there was a great strike at the Carnegie Works in Homestead, Pennsylvania. The strike failed. Labor's view was that protectionism benefited the profits of the owners, but did not benefit workers; therefore, Labor did not join with the Populists.

Grover Cleveland won the 1892 election with 5,556,543 votes. Harrison garnered 5,175,582 and the Populist Weaver had an impressive showing of 1,004,886 votes. In the Electoral College Cleveland captured 227 votes, Harrison 145, and Weaver 22. Weaver carried Colorado, Idaho, Kansas, and Nebraska. He received one electoral vote from North Dakota and one from Oregon. The Democrats lost eleven seats, but retained their majorities in the House and the Senate. *See*: CLEVELAND, GROVER; HARRISON, BENJAMIN; PEOPLE'S PARTY.

1896

Republican Party nominee: William McKinley, 51%
Democratic Party nominee: William Jennings Bryan, 47%
The setting for the 1896 presidential election was held against the backdrop of the economic panic of 1893, which brought social unrest and high unemployment. Democratic president Grover Cleveland was unwilling to respond to the growing popular demand for the free coinage of silver, and other progressive demands like a graduated income tax. His administration was repudiated by his divided party. The Democrats lost 112 House seats in the midterm election.

The major Republican contenders were William Allison of Iowa, House Speaker Thomas Reed of Maine, and William McKinley of Ohio. William McKinley, the governor of Ohio, had established a national reputation as a proponent of high tariffs. His major ally in his bid for the presidency was the skillful, wealthy, Ohio industrialist Mark Hanna. Through the able organizational ability of Mark Hanna, William McKinley was nominated on the first ballot at the St. Louis GOP Convention in June 1896. The Republican platform stated that "the existing gold standard must be preserved." Garret Hobart was selected to be McKinley's running mate.

The Democrats had a more contentious convention. They repudiated much of the Cleveland administration and nominated the brilliant orator, Nebraskan William Jennings Bryan. Bryan had campaigned on the silver plank. He was only 36 years old, and gave his famous "Cross of Gold" speech in Chicago at the Democratic convention in July. The speech moved the delegates and he was nominated on the fifth ballot.

Democratic nominee Bryan created a fusion ticket with the emerging Populist Party. The Populist Party nominated Bryan, and their nominee for vice-president was Thomas E. Watson. There was some tension in this fusion ticket, because the Democrats did not replace their vice-presidential nominee, Arthur Sewall, with Watson, as the Populists expected. By Bryan's account, he traveled over 18,000 miles and gave 600 speeches. Republican McKinley, recognizing that he could not match Bryan's oratorical ability, conducted a front porch campaign from his home in Canton, Ohio, where he received an estimated 750,000 visitors. The Republican campaign was well organized and very well financed due in great part to the efforts of Republican Party chairman Mark Hanna. The major newspapers supported McKinley, and Bryan was treated as a radical. McKinley emphasized law and order.

There were over fourteen million votes cast in the 1896 election. A record 79% of the eligible voters cast ballots. McKinley received 7,102,246 votes. Bryan garnered 6,492,559 votes. The division of the Electoral College was 271 for McKinley to 176 for Bryan. The monetary debate was a sectional clash which was reflected in the election results. The agrarian South and West supported the silverite Bryan, and the East and midwest supported the "goldbug" and protectionist McKinley. The industrial workers in the urban areas of the midwest went for McKinley, and the struggling farmers of the South and West gave their support to Bryan. Despite their presidential victory the Republicans lost 40 seats in the House of Representatives. *See*: BRYAN, WILLIAM JENNINGS; McKINLEY, WILLIAM.

1900

Republican Party nominee: William McKinley, 51.7%
Democratic Party nominee: William Jennings Bryan, 45.5%

The background for the election of 1900 was a prosperous economy that started in McKinley's first term. The other major development that evolved since the election of 1896, was the active foreign policy of McKinley. In 1898, the United States had gone to war against Spain over Cuba. The war ended with the Treaty of Paris, ratified in 1899, that gave the Philippine Islands to the United States.

The Democrats met in July 1900 in Kansas City. The Democrats' choice was their 1886 nominee, silverite William Jennings Bryan of Nebraska. He did not face serious opposition for his party's nomination in his second try for the White House. The vice-presidential nomination was given to Adlai Stevenson, who had served as vice-president under President Grover Cleveland.

The Republicans met in Philadelphia in June of 1900, and renominated their popular incumbent president William McKinley. The drama for the GOP was over the vice-presidential nomination. McKinley's 1886 running mate, Hobart, had died. The influential Republican state party bosses; Thomas Platt of New York and Mathew Quay of Pennsylvania, wanted to move New York governor Theodore Roosevelt out of the governor's office, so they promoted him for the vice-presidential nomination. The influential Mark Hanna resisted Roosevelt's selection, but the convention delegates were taken by Roosevelt, and he was nominated to be the Republican vice-presidential candidate in 1900.

This election did not offer the same excitement that this same match-up had in 1896. Bryan continued to be wedded to the silver issue, but the issue had less voter appeal than it had in 1886. Bryan attempted to make an issue out of imperialism because there was controversy over the occupation of the Philippines. Like silver, imperialism did not attract many voters, so Bryan also focused on the issue of trusts. McKinley was more reluctant to campaign in 1900 than he had been in 1896. The campaign was left to the efforts of Ohio senator Mark Hanna, who raised the money and built the campaign organization, as he had in 1896. Theodore Roosevelt was an energetic campaigner, and he traveled extensively delivering speeches in defense of the incumbent administration's economic and foreign policies. Good economic conditions led to "the full dinner pail" becoming the GOP slogan.

The Republican victory in 1900 was more impressive than it was in 1896. The GOP ticket of McKinley-Roosevelt took 292 Electoral College votes with a popular vote total of 7,318,491. The Democrats collected 176 Electoral College votes, and 6,356,734 popular votes. The Republicans made significant gains in the western states. See: BRYAN, WILLIAM JENNINGS; McKINLEY, WILLIAM; ROOSEVELT, THEODORE.

1904

Republican Party nominee: Theodore Roosevelt, 56.4%
Democratic Party nominee: Alton B. Parker, 37.6%
Socialist Party nominee: Eugene V. Debs, 3%

The setting for the 1904 presidential election was the candidacy of incumbent president Theodore Roosevelt, who succeeded to the office after the assassination of William McKinley. McKinley was assassinated in September 1901, soon after he took the oath of office. This gave Roosevelt the opportunity to put his mark on the administration, and capture control of the Republican Party organization. With the exception of a mild recession in 1903, the country continued to enjoy prosperity under the new president. Roosevelt pursued progressive policies during his first term. He was the first president to use federal power to regulate the growing trusts in the American economy.

The Republicans met in Chicago in June, and nominated Theodore Roosevelt on the first ballot. He had wrested control of the party machinery from Mark Hanna, and had the convention well under his control. The Republicans nominated Charles Fairbanks from Indiana as his running mate. The Democrats met in St Louis in July, and turned away from silverite William Jennings Bryan. The more conservative "reorganizers" took control of the party, and nominated Alton P. Parker, who was a chief justice on the New York State Court of Appeals bench. Parker was nominated on the first ballot. His closest rival was William Randolph Hearst. They selected wealthy, 82-year-old West Virginian Henry G. Davis as Parker's running mate. Parker announced that he was in favor of the gold standard.

In the 1904 presidential election neither Roosevelt nor Parker actively campaigned. Roosevelt stuck to the tradition that an incumbent president does not campaign. The Socialists emerged as the dominant third party, with Eugene Debs as their nominee. Democratic Party presidential nominee Parker was unable to gain momentum, and his campaign collapsed everywhere except in the South. The GOP chairman was George B. Cortelyou, Roosevelt's secretary of commerce, and he collected a war chest four times the size of the Democrats. Parker made an issue out of the campaign contributions collected from big business by the Republicans.

Teddy Roosevelt enjoyed a smashing landslide; he won 7,628,785 popular votes and 336 Electoral College votes, to Parker's total vote of 5,084,442 and 140 electoral votes. Debs and his Socialists collected only 3% of the vote. See: PARKER, ALTON B.; ROOSEVELT, THEODORE.

1908

Republican Party nominee: William Howard Taft, 51.6%
Democratic Party nominee: William Jennings Bryan, 43%
Socialist Party nominee: Eugene V. Debs, 2.8%

Theodore Roosevelt made himself a lame duck soon after his 1904 election by declaring that he would not seek reelection. He had pursued a number of progressive policies in his second term. Roosevelt led the effort to create the Interstate Commerce Commission, which regulated railroad rates. He also secured legislation that prohibited corporate contributions to national political campaigns. The economy slumped in 1907, the first significant economic downturn since the GOP came to power in 1896. The GOP lost 28 seats in the midterm election. The economy began to recover in 1908.

After the Democrats' crushing defeat in 1904 under Alton Parker, the Democrats returned one final time to the more progressive leadership of William Jennings Bryan. In 1906, Bryan, after an international tour, returned to the United States and outlined the issues of the 1908 campaign. He gave up on the soft money issue, and focused on the anti-trust issue. Bryan's forces took control of the Democratic Party, and in July 1908 he was nominated on the first ballot in Denver. Bryan's running mate for the 1908 election was John W. Kern of Indiana.

Theodore Roosevelt was in control of the Republican Party and after some deliberation determined that his secretary of war, William Howard Taft, would be his successor. Taft preferred an appointment to the Supreme Court, but at the urging of others, including family members, he accepted Roosevelt's call to succeed him. In June, Taft was nominated on the first ballot at the Republican National Convention in Chicago. James S. Sherman of New York was selected as his running mate. The influence of Theodore Roosevelt was very strong at this party's convention.

The 1908 campaign got off to a slow start. Bryan published his list of contributors and challenged Roosevelt to disclose who the Republicans received their contributions from. William Randolph Hearst, in an effort to embarrass Bryan, published files from Standard Oil which revealed that Oklahoma governor Charles Haskall had dealings with the oil trust. Haskall was Bryan's campaign treasurer, and was forced to resign. Roosevelt was very active in the campaign, occasionally engaging Bryan, and he urged Taft not to answer Bryan but to "attack" him, which Taft did.

Republican presidential nominee Taft easily defeated the Democrat Bryan. Taft garnered 7,679,006 popular votes to Bryan's total vote of 6,409,106. Taft won 321 Electoral College votes to Bryan's 162. Bryan's Electoral College votes came from the solid South and the states of Kentucky, Oklahoma, Nebraska, Colorado, and Nevada. The GOP lost three seats in the House. *See:* BRYAN, WILLIAM JENNINGS; TAFT, WILLIAM HOWARD.

1912

Democratic Party nominee: Woodrow Wilson, 41.8%

Progressive Party nominee: Theodore Roosevelt, 27.4%

Republican Party nominee: William Howard Taft, 23.2%

Socialist Party nominee: Eugene V. Debs, 6%

The background for the 1912 presidential election was increased public support for progressive ideas such as the income tax, the initiative, recall, and the direct election of senators. The Democrats, who had made gains in 1908, captured a majority in the House in the midterm election of 1910. The economy was strong going into the election of 1912. The most significant event was the return of former president Theodore Roosevelt to the national political stage. In 1908, he had selected President William Howard Taft to be his successor, participated in the election of Taft, and then left for Africa and Europe. On his return, the progressives in the party tried to recruit him to challenge Taft.

Theodore Roosevelt answered the call in February of 1912 by declaring: "My hat is in the ring." He would challenge William Howard Taft for the 1912 Republican nomination. Robert LaFollette had also decided to oppose Taft, but Roosevelt became the major opponent. Roosevelt challenged Taft in the new primary system. Roosevelt won nine primaries, including Ohio's. Taft won only one primary. Most delegates were selected in party caucuses and conventions and Taft held the support of the party professionals. The Taft-controlled Republican National Committee ruled in favor of the Taft delegates in all disputes. Taft was nominated on the first ballot at the Republican National Convention in Chicago, which was held in June. Roosevelt and his supporters bolted the convention and declared that they would start a new party. James S. Sherman was renominated as Taft's running mate. Sherman died in October, and the RNC selected Nicholas Murray Butler, president of Columbia University, as the vice-presidential nominee.

The newly formed Progressive Party of Theodore Roosevelt met in Chicago in August of 1912. They nominated Roosevelt for president, and Senator Hiram Johnson of California as his running mate. The new party adopted a radical platform, embracing most of the progressive ideas of the day. The party's program was called the "New Nationalism." This party was also referred to as the

"Bull Moose Party." Many of the progressive Republicans who had supported Roosevelt in the Republican nomination battle did not join the new party.

The divisions in the Republican Party provided the Democrats a good opportunity to win the office of president. The Democrats lacked a clear frontrunner to be their nominee. The Democrats met in Baltimore in June 1912. William Jennings Bryan, who had dominated the Democratic Party in past conventions, was not a candidate at this convention. Bryan did play a significant role by refusing to support the frontrunner, House Speaker Champ Clark, because he was supported by New York's Tammany Hall. On the forty-sixth ballot, Woodrow Wilson, the governor of New Jersey, was nominated. The party selected Thomas R. Marshall of Indiana as his running mate.

The general election was not a pitched battle. Taft refused to campaign. Wilson preferred a dignified and intellectual style. He offered a program called the "New Freedom." Bryan actively campaigned for Wilson in the West. However, Roosevelt was vigorous in his campaign; shot by a madman on October 14 in Milwaukee, Roosevelt insisted on giving his speech.

The election returns were not a surprise. The results reflected the sharp divisions in the Republican Party. Woodrow Wilson drew 6,293,120 votes, Roosevelt was second with 4,119,582, and Taft trailed with 3,485,082 votes. Eugene V. Debs, the Socialist Party nominee, led the third parties with a total vote of 900,672. The Electoral College vote was even more dramatic: Wilson garnered 435 Electoral College votes, Roosevelt 88, and Taft 8. The Democrats captured solid majorities in the House and the Senate for the first time since the Civil War. *See*: ROOSEVELT, THEODORE; TAFT, WILLIAM HOWARD; WILSON, WOODROW.

1916

Democratic Party nominee: Woodrow Wilson, 49.2%
Republican Party nominee: Charles Evans Hughes, 46.1%

The background for the 1916 election was the growing importance of international affairs in American politics. The war in Europe had started in 1914. The United States was attempting to avoid conflict and protect the rights and property of its citizens. On the domestic front, the economy had slumped during Wilson's first term, but had rebounded in 1916 with the demands created by the European war. Wilson had taken very progressive positions, expanding the role of the federal government, particularly in labor relations, with the Adamson bill, which created an eight-hour day.

The Republicans were still divided from the 1912 split between Taft and Roosevelt. The party sought a candidate who would reunite the factions. Roosevelt had made an unsuccessful effort to gain the nomination in the spring of 1916. Roosevelt rejected Eliah Root as an acceptable candidate. Root had served as Roosevelt's secretary of state, but had played a role in renominating Taft. The party turned to Associate Justice of the Supreme Court Charles Evans

Hughes of New York State, nominating him on the third ballot. The GOP convention was held in Chicago in June. It was a mild affair as the party made every effort to reunite the factions from 1912. The party nominated Charles Fairbanks, who had been Roosevelt's running mate in 1904, to serve as Hughes's running mate in 1916.

The Democrats met in St. Louis in June, and renominated Woodrow Wilson on the first ballot. The major theme of the 1916 Democratic convention was peace and an international position of neutrality. Wilson eased out William McCombs as head of the DNC and replaced him with Vance McCormick. Wilson had moved to a much more progressive domestic agenda.

Wilson campaigned very little. Hughes was not a particularly skillful politician and his campaign manager William R. Willcox was inept. Hughes offended Hiram Johnson, who was running for the Senate in California, by not meeting with him when they were staying in the same hotel in California. Johnson won his election and Hughes lost California by about 5,000 votes.

The 1916 presidential election was close. Wilson received 9,129,606 popular votes collecting 277 Electoral College votes. Charles Evans Hughes garnered 8,538,221 popular votes and 254 Electoral College votes. The East went strongly for Hughes. Wilson had successfully constructed an alliance of the South and the West for his victory, an alliance that had long alluded William Jennings Bryan. The Democrats lost fourteen seats in the House in the election of 1916. *See*: HUGHES, CHARLES EVANS; WILSON, WOODROW.

1920

Republican Party nominee: Warren G. Harding, 60%
Democratic Party nominee: James M. Cox, 34%
Socialist Party nominee: Eugene V. Debs, 3%

The setting for the 1920 presidential election was the end of the second term of the Democratic administration of President Woodrow Wilson. World War I had ended and Wilson advocated the League of Nations, which the Republican Senate did not ratify. The postwar economy had gone into a tailspin, experiencing both inflation and unemployment. The Republicans gained a majority in the congressional election of 1918.

The Republicans faced the 1920 election without a clear party leader. Theodore Roosevelt had died and William H. Taft was not seen as a viable candidate. The Republicans met in Chicago in June and nominated Ohio senator Warren G. Harding on the tenth ballot after the frontrunners, one of whom was General Leonard Wood, an ally and close friend of Theodore Roosevelt, failed to capture the nomination. The Republicans nominated Massachusetts governor Calvin Coolidge as Harding's running mate. The Republicans adopted a conservative platform.

The Democrats met in San Francisco in late June, and like the Republicans, lacked a clear frontrunner. On the forty-fourth ballot they nominated the third-term governor of Ohio James M. Cox, and selected Assistant Secretary of the Navy Franklin D. Roosevelt as Cox's running mate.

The general election: Warren G. Harding preferred a front porch campaign, and he did little campaigning. As a formal newspaper editor, he enjoyed good relations with the press. Will Hayes, the Republican National chairman, raised a great deal of money for the campaign, and organized a very effective campaign for the Republicans. Democratic nominees Cox and Roosevelt were very active candidates. The Democrats made an issue out of the Republicans' fund-raising activities. The Democratic ticket tried to make the defeat of the League of Nations the central issue in the campaign. Harding was evasive about his stand on the League because the Republicans were very divided on the issue.

In 1920 the Republicans won by a landslide. The Republican ticket garnered 16,152,200 votes to the Democrats' total of 9,147,353. The Socialist Debs took over 900,000 votes. Harding received 404 Electoral College votes to Cox's 127. The Republicans won every state outside the deep South. The Republicans also gained 61 seats in the House. *See*: COX, JAMES M.; HARDING, WARREN G.

1924

Republican Party nominee: Calvin Coolidge, 54%
Democratic Party nominee: John W. Davis, 28.8%
Progressive Party nominee: Robert M. LaFollette, 16.6%

The setting for the 1924 election included the death of Republican president Warren G. Harding in August of 1923, amidst the growing Teapot Dome scandals, and the succession of Vice-President Calvin Coolidge to the presidency. Coolidge was not touched by the scandals, and he took action to remove members of the administration who were implicated. Coolidge set a conservative direction for the Republican administration. The Republicans had lost 78 congressional seats in the 1922 midterm election.

Coolidge took control of the party machinery, and he was able to fend off a challenge for the nomination by Senator Hiram Johnson of California. Johnson was able to win only the South Dakota primary. Coolidge defeated Johnson in California, and by the use of patronage, was able to control the Republican delegates from the South. Coolidge was nominated unanimously on the first ballot at the June Republican National Convention in Cleveland. Charles Dawes was selected as the Republican vice-presidential nominee over Herbert Hoover.

The Democrats had a much more contentious convention in New York City. The early leader for the nomination was William Gibbs McAdoo, who was Woodrow Wilson's son-in-law. He was damaged by his financial association with some of the Teapot Dome figures. The other candidate, who emerged as a frontrunner, was the popular Catholic governor of New York, Al Smith. There was conflict at the Democratic convention over the issue of condemning the anti-Catholic, racist, and bigoted Ku Klux Klan in the platform. A direct condemnation of the Klan was not included. Because of the two-thirds rule, the convention deadlocked for nine days over McAdoo and Smith. On the 103rd ballot the convention nominated compromise candidate John W. Davis, a Wall Street lawyer and West Virginia native. The convention selected Charles W. Bryan, governor of Nebraska and brother of William Jennings Bryan, as the vice-presidential nominee. Both of the major party candidates were conservative; that led to an effort by the Progressive Party, which was rooted in the Teddy Roosevelt campaign of 1912, to challenge the two major parties. The Progressive Party met in Cleveland and nominated Wisconsin senator Robert LaFollette as its presidential nominee. Senator Burton K. Wheeler of Montana was selected as LaFollette's running mate.

Calvin Coolidge was known to be taciturn, and did not actively campaign. Dawes was an active vice-presidential candidate. Davis campaigned, but his candidacy was damaged by the divisive Democratic convention, and the Democratic National Party chairman Clement L. Shaver was inexperienced and ineffective. LaFollette's campaign was competitive in the early weeks of the campaign, but he finished a disappointing third, winning only his home state of Wisconsin. LaFollette did very well in the cities, pulling the ethnic vote away from the GOP. The Republicans gained only 21 seats in the House in 1924.

The Republican Coolidge won 382 Electoral College votes with 15,719,921 popular votes. Democratic nominee Davis collected 136 Electoral College votes with his 8,385,586 popular votes. LaFollette collected a disappointing 4,826,471 votes and only Wisconsin's thirteen Electoral College votes. *See*: COOLIDGE, CALVIN; DAVIS, JOHN W.; TWO-THIRDS RULE.

1928

Republican Party nominee: Herbert Hoover, 58.2%
Democratic Party nominee: Al Smith, 40.8%
President Calvin Coolidge set the stage for the 1928 election when he announced on August 3, 1927 that: "I do not choose to run for President in 1928." There was continued prosperity in the nation under the long reign of the Republicans, and there were no disruptive international issues. There were notable changes in society, including more freedom for women, widespread smoking of cigarettes, and rapid urbanization. The Eighteenth Amendment, which banned alcohol, continued to be a controversial issue.

Herbert Hoover, a son of Iowa, successful engineer, and Coolidge's secretary of commerce, moved quickly to claim the GOP nomination. President Coolidge did not intervene in the nomination process. Hoover did not have any major opponents, except a few favorite sons, and he captured the nomination on the first ballot at the Republican convention in Kansas City in June of 1928. The Republicans selected Charles Curtis of Kansas as Hoover's running mate. In the platform the GOP pledged "observance and vigorous enforcement of the Eighteenth Amendment."

The Democrats turned to popular New York governor Alfred E. Smith as their nominee. Party leaders were concerned about his being a Catholic and his ties to Tammany Hall, a metaphor for political corruption. Al Smith was nominated on the first ballot without significant opposition. The Democrats finally accepted the Republicans' position on high tariffs in their platform. The Democrats offered to make an honest effort to enforce the Eighteenth Amendment in their platform, but Smith, in a telegram on the last night of the convention, wrote that there should be "fundamental changes in the present provisions for national prohibition." He clearly signaled a wet position. The Democrats met in Houston, Texas and selected Senator Joseph T. Robinson of Arkansas as Smith's running mate; a dry Southerner and a Protestant.

Herbert Hoover campaigned as if he were above politics. He used the radio quite effectively compared to Smith, whose city accent made him sound less than presidential. Smith was a very vigorous and colorful candidate. Al Smith's religion was a central issue in the campaign. Protestant church leaders warned of the threat of rum and romanism. A son of Irish immigrants, raised in New York City, Smith represented the changes that were coming to America that were resented and resisted by the offspring of those who had settled earlier.

The ugly issue of religious bigotry was the salient issue of the 1928 election, but it did not determine the outcome of the election—prosperity did. The Democrats could not overcome the political benefit of a growing economy to the incumbent party. Republican Herbert Hoover garnered 21,437,277 popular votes, and Al Smith drew 15,007,698 votes. Hoover captured 444 Electoral College votes while Smith took only 88. Hoover made inroads in the South because of the religious issue, and Smith did very well in the eastern cities. There was a large turnout in this election, reaching 67% of the voting age population. The GOP added 30 seats to its majority. *See*: HOOVER, HERBERT C.; SMITH, ALFRED E.; TAMMANY HALL.

1932

Democratic Party nominee: Franklin D. Roosevelt, 57.4%
Republican Party nominee: Herbert Hoover, 39.6%
Socialist Party nominee: Norman Thomas, 2.2%

The setting for the 1932 election was the collapse of the national economy. The stock market crash of 1929 was followed by the Great Depression. The Democrats gained a slim majority in the congressional election of 1930. President Herbert Hoover responded to the economic conditions with a number aggressive programs, including the Reconstruction Finance Corporation, which provided loans to banks, railroads, and businesses.

The Republicans held their convention in Chicago in June, and renominated Herbert Hoover for president and Charles Curtis for vice-president. The GOP convention was dispirited. There was an effort to dump Curtis and replace him with a fresh face, but the effort failed. The Republicans sent mixed signals on the Eighteenth Amendment (Prohibition), offering continuing support for it, but also permitting states to determine how spirits were to be regulated. There was a motion to support outright repeal, but it failed in a close vote at the convention.

The Democrats met later in the month of June in Chicago. They recognized they had a good chance to win because of the poor economic conditions. The frontrunner was New York governor Franklin D. Roosevelt, who had won the important governorship of New York in the Republican landslide of 1928, and was reelected by a wider margin in 1930. Al Smith, the 1928 nominee, wanted another chance at the presidential election. John Nance Garner of Texas, the Speaker of the House, was an active candidate who enjoyed the support of newspaperman William Randolph Hearst. Roosevelt's advisors plotted to eliminate the two-thirds convention rule, but met strong opposition from the South. After a number of ballots, the frontrunner Roosevelt made a deal with Garner, offering him the vice-presidential nomination. Roosevelt was nominated on the fourth ballot, and Garner was then selected as his running mate. The Democrats came out for repeal of the Eighteenth Amendment. They promised to reduce federal spending and promised a balanced budget. Roosevelt broke with tradition and made an appearance at the 1932 convention. In his acceptance speech he pledged ''a new deal for the American people.'' Cartoonist Rollin Kirby picked up on that phrase and showed a cartoon with a farmer looking up at an airplane with NEW DEAL emblazoned on the wings.

Democratic nominee Franklin D. Roosevelt conducted a very energetic campaign. He traveled widely and offered a variety of positions. He hit hard on the farm problems and on the regulation of utilities. He was equivocal on the tariff issue. He was well served by his skillful advisor James Farley, who had become the Democratic National chairman. Roosevelt was particularly effective on the radio, which was widely used in this campaign. Hoover was also active in the campaign. He blamed World War I and the Democrats for the economic conditions, and he argued that the economy was improving, which it was; but those improvements were not being felt by average American households.

The outcome of this election was never in doubt. The prosperous economy which had kept the Republicans in office for so many years had collapsed, and the Democrats won by a landslide in 1932. Roosevelt garnered 22,821,857 popular votes to Hoover's 15,761,841. The Electoral College vote was even more lopsided: Roosevelt collected 472 Electoral College votes to Hoover's 59. Roosevelt carried 42 of the 48 states. Roosevelt was especially strong in the South and the West. The Democrats took large majorities in both the House and the Senate. *See*: HOOVER, HERBERT C.; NEW DEAL; ROOSEVELT, FRANKLIN D.

1936

Democratic Party nominee: Franklin D. Roosevelt, 60.8%
Republican Party nominee: Alfred M. Landon, 36.5%

The setting for the 1936 election was the record of the Roosevelt administration in addressing the conditions of the national economy. The 1932 election was a vote against Hoover and the Republicans because of the bad economic conditions. The Democrats gained seats in the 1934 election, a rare occurrence in a midterm election for the party in the White House. The 1936 election was about the economic programs and policies of Roosevelt. Roosevelt had created a large and active national government to address the economic conditions of the country. The administration created the Agricultural Adjustment Administration (AAA) to help farmers, the Works Progress Administration (WPA) to hire the unemployed, and Public Works Administration (PWA) to assist states and local governments build highways and bridges.

As a result of their devastating electoral losses, the Republicans lacked candidates of national stature. The GOP met in Cleveland in early June, and settled on Alfred E. Landon, governor of Kansas, who was elected in 1932 and reelected in 1934. Landon, a former Bull Mooser, was nominated on the first ballot. The GOP selected Colonel Frank Knox, publisher of the *Chicago Daily News*, as his running mate. The Republicans were ambivalent about how to address the popular New Deal. They criticized the unbalanced budget, but gave support to many of Roosevelt's programs in their platform.

The Democrats met in Philadelphia in late June and enthusiastically renominated Roosevelt and John Garner. The Democrats played on class divisions in their platform, which was written in the White House. The Democrats did away with the two-thirds rule at this convention.

Alf Landon was uncertain how to proceed in the campaign. In the early part of the campaign he was complimentary toward many aspects of the New Deal. By the end of the campaign, Landon was charging Roosevelt with acting outside the Constitution. The GOP used professionally developed radio ads in this campaign. They tried to arouse the voters' fears over the social security tax. Roosevelt took to the campaign trail late, but he was a masterful campaigner, and a much better speaker than Landon. The Democrats' campaign was well funded by organized labor. The Roosevelt campaign made an overt and successful effort to attract Ethnic-Catholic and African-American votes in 1936. The Republicans had hoped that the newly formed Union Party made up of radical elements would draw votes from Roosevelt. This did not occur.

Roosevelt won the 1936 election by a landslide. Roosevelt collected 27,751,597 popular votes to Landon's 16,679,583. In Electoral College votes Roosevelt collected 523 to Landon's 8. Landon won only Maine and Vermont. The Democrats gained seats in the House in 1936. *See*: LANDON, ALFRED M.; NEW DEAL COALITION; REALIGNMENT; ROOSEVELT, FRANKLIN D.; TWO-THIRDS RULE; UNION PARTY.

1940

Democratic Party nominee: Franklin D. Roosevelt, 54.7%
Republican Party nominee: Wendell L. Willkie, 44.8%

The setting for the 1940 election was the U.S. involvement in the war in Europe. The Nazis invaded Norway and Denmark in early 1940. In June, France fell to the Nazis. There was a debate in the United States over aid to Britain. After a modest recovery, the national economy fell back in 1937. Roosevelt was rebuked in his effort to pack the Supreme Court. In the midterm election of 1938 the Democrats lost 71 seats. Roosevelt had pursued traditional policies of restricting spending to balance the budget. In 1938, Roosevelt was persuaded that he needed to prime the pump; he returned to deficit spending, and an expansion of the money supply. These policies and the increased demand for munitions turned the economy around. The interesting political question was whether Roosevelt would seek an unprecedented third term.

The Republican convention was held in Philadelphia in June. The leading Republican candidates were the district attorney of New York, Thomas E. Dewey, and Ohio senator Robert Taft. A political outsider, Wendell Willkie, a Wall Street lawyer and utility company president, orchestrated a brilliant draft movement for himself. At the convention, Willkie came from behind and captured the nomination on the sixth ballot. The GOP selected Oregon senator Charles L. McNary as Willkie's running mate. The GOP offered a compromise platform on the war in Europe between the positions of those who favored a U.S. role and those who advocated continued neutrality.

The Democrats met in Chicago in July. Roosevelt kept his intentions to himself. Two former allies of Roosevelt, the skillful Democratic National chairman James A. Farley, and Roosevelt's vice-president, John Nance Garner, both challenged Roosevelt's bid for a third term. Roosevelt was nominated by the Democrats for the third time on the first ballot. After some arm twisting at the convention by the Roosevelt forces, Secretary of Agriculture Henry Wallace was nominated as his running mate. In their platform the Democrats disavowed any intention to "participate in foreign wars," adding the phrase "except in case of attack."

Both candidates conducted vigorous campaigns. Willkie was accommodating at the outset, but became more critical of Roosevelt's foreign policy toward the end of the campaign. Willkie claimed he was the real peace candidate. Willkie seemed to gain strength in the closing weeks of the campaign, but to no avail. Roosevelt garnered 27,243,466 popular votes, with 449 Electoral College votes, to Willkie's total of 22,304,744 votes and 82 Electoral College votes. The Democrats gained only seven seats in the House in the 1940 election. *See*: ROOSEVELT, FRANKLIN D.; WILLKIE, WENDELL L.

1944

Democratic Party nominee: Franklin D. Roosevelt, 53.4%

Republican Party nominee: Thomas E. Dewey, 45.9%

The setting for the 1944 election was the continuation of the war in Europe and Asia. The war effort for the United States had not gone well in 1942. Roosevelt had created a series of new government agencies to mobilize the nation's economy for the war. The domestic economy suffered from shortages and inflation. There were also labor problems. In the midterm election the Democrats lost 47 House seats. In 1943, Roosevelt spent a lot of his time meeting with Allied leaders on war plans. He played the role of commander-in-chief very well, and that increased his stature in the nation. There was growing concern in the nation over Roosevelt's health.

The 1940 GOP nominee, Wendell Willkie, was an early frontrunner for the GOP nomination. He promoted internationalist ideas. Willkie had never held an elective office; consequently he was not popular with the party regulars. Willkie entered the primaries. He showed some strength in New Hampshire, but was soundly defeated by the state party organization in Wisconsin, and he withdrew as a candidate in April. There was a boomlet for General Douglas MacArthur which was short-lived. The Republicans met in Chicago in late June, and nominated New York governor Thomas E. Dewey on the first ballot. The GOP selected Ohio governor John Bricker as his running mate. In their platform the GOP condemned New Deal government centralization, but supported most New Deal programs, including old age and unemployment insurance.

The Democrats met in mid-July in Chicago and renominated their war president, Franklin D. Roosevelt, for an unprecedented fourth time. There was strong party opposition to retaining Vice-President Henry Wallace on the ticket. Wallace was viewed as too liberal and added little to the ticket. Roosevelt did not encourage Wallace to step aside. The Democrats finally focused on Missouri senator Harry S. Truman as their choice, and he was nominated on the second ballot. It was reported that Roosevelt, on the vice-presidential choice, told his aides: "And clear everything with Sidney." It was a reference to Sidney Hillman, head of the CIO-PAC, and radical labor leader. The GOP picked up on this quote and used it in the general election.

Roosevelt, as war leader, decided not to campaign in the usual way, and stayed off the campaign trail until late in the campaign. The American war effort had improved. The Americans had driven into Germany; and MacArthur made his return to the Philippines. Dewey tried to make the case that the Roosevelt administration had been in office too long, was inefficient, and was not adequately planning for demobilization. The campaign turned nasty at the end, and Roosevelt began his campaign. One of his most cited campaign speeches was one that had nothing to do with policy; it was a tongue-in-cheek defense of his dog, Fala, against attacks by the Republicans. The results of the election were quite similar to the 1940 results. Roosevelt captured 432 Electoral College votes to Dewey's 99. The popular vote total dropped by almost two million votes. Roosevelt garnered 25,602,504 to Dewey's 22,006,285. Americans retained their war leader. The Democrats gained 22 seats in the House. *See*: DEWEY, THOMAS E.; ROOSEVELT, FRANKLIN D.; TRUMAN, HARRY S.

1948

Democratic Party nominee: Harry S. Truman, 49.5%
Republican Party nominee: Thomas E. Dewey, 45.1%

States' Rights Party nominee: J. Strom Thurmond, 2.4%

Progressive Party nominee: Henry A. Wallace, 2.4%

The setting for the 1948 election was the end of World War II and the succession of Vice-President Harry S. Truman to the presidency after the death of Franklin D. Roosevelt in April 1945. The economy slumped after the end of the war, and the Republicans gained 54 seats in the House in the 1946 midterm election, taking the majority for the first time since the Depression. The economy rebounded in 1948. Truman had set a new direction with an active foreign policy with the Marshall Plan aid for war-torn Europe, and worldwide containment of the growing threat of the Soviet Union.

After their long drought during the Roosevelt years, the Republicans saw an opportunity for victory in 1948, and a number of candidates stepped forward. The early frontrunner was Harold Stassen, the former governor of Minnesota. The other leading candidate, the 1944 GOP presidential nominee, New York governor Thomas E. Dewey, defeated Stassen in the Oregon primary. Ohio senator Robert Taft, who also sought the nomination, and Stassen tried to stop Dewey at the 1948 Republican convention in Philadelphia in June, but Dewey was nominated on the third ballot. The GOP selected California governor Earl Warren as his running mate.

There was an effort by some Democrats to draft General Dwight D. Eisenhower, but he rebuffed their overtures. Truman's problems were not opponents, but bolters. Truman had proposed a series of measures to Congress guaranteeing the rights of black Americans. At the 1948 Democratic National Convention, the delegates voted to adopt a resolution praising Truman for these efforts. This provoked 35 Southern delegates to walk out, including all of Mississippi's delegates, and half of the Alabama delegation. Later, these bolters organized the States' Rights Democratic Party. They held a convention in Montgomery, Alabama where they nominated the governor of South Carolina, J. Strom Thurmond, as their presidential candidate.

At the Democratic convention, Harry Truman delivered a fiery acceptance speech and made the surprise announcement that he was calling the 80th Congress back in session to consider his proposed legislation. The Republican Congress did not act on his proposals and Truman conducted his presidential campaign against the do-nothing Republican Congress. The Democrats nominated Kentucky senator Alben W. Barkley for vice-president. Truman faced trouble on the left, as Progressive Citizens of America nominated Henry A. Wallace for president.

With skillful assistance from the Democratic National Committee, Truman conducted a very well-organized and aggressive campaign. Dewey ignored Truman and ran a dull campaign. Dewey offered himself as a high-minded, public-spirited candidate, confident of victory. The Wallace campaign, which blamed Truman for the cold war, was discredited when the Soviet Union invaded Czechoslovakia. The threat of the Thurmond campaign was confined to four states and the Dixiecrats took 39 electoral votes in the South.

The nation's pollsters and pundits had all predicted a Dewey victory, and the nation was surprised by Truman's come-from-behind win. In a low turnout election, Truman garnered 24,105,812 popular votes to Dewey's 21,970,065. Truman carried 28 states, which yielded 303 electoral votes to Dewey's 16 states and 189 electoral votes. *See*: DEWEY, THOMAS E.; SOUTHERN STRATEGY; STATES' RIGHTS DEMOCRATIC PARTY; THURMOND, J. STROM; TRUMAN, HARRY S.

1952

Republican Party nominee: Dwight D. Eisenhower, 55.1%
Democratic Party nominee: Adlai E. Stevenson, 42%
The setting for the 1952 election was America's active postwar role in the world. Truman, who would not seek the 1952 Democratic nomination, had been successful in developing a containment policy in Europe, but was less successful in Asia. China had become communist, and the Korean War was not settled at the end of his term. On the domestic front, the Democrats held a slim majority in the House; consequently, Truman was unable to advance his Fair Deal agenda. The economy was growing, but not at a rapid rate, and there was inflation.

The Republicans were divided into two factions. The liberal, internationalist, eastern wing of the party had controlled the recent Republican nominations. The conservative, isolationist wing of the Republican Party was led by Ohio senator Robert Taft. To block Taft from the nomination, the eastern wing of the party recruited General Dwight D. Eisenhower for the 1952 Republican nomination. Eisenhower allowed Henry Cabot Lodge to place his name on the New Hampshire primary ballot, and he defeated Taft by a healthy margin. The GOP met in Chicago in July. The Eisenhower forces appeared to be better organized. They were able to get the Republican National Convention to adopt a "fair play" amendment to the GOP rules. This rule stated that contested delegations that did not receive a two-thirds vote of the National Committee could not vote on the credentials of others. Eisenhower, who also enjoyed the support of the national press, was nominated on the first ballot. The Eisenhower forces selected the junior senator from California, Richard M. Nixon, as the vice-presidential nominee. He had attracted national attention for his pursuit of Alger Hiss on charges of espionage. The GOP platform called for the "liberation" of the captive people of Eastern Europe.

The early leader for the Democratic nomination was Estes Kefauver, who defeated Truman in the New Hampshire primary. Truman had not intended to run, but this defeat hastened his withdrawal. Tennessee senator Kefauver had gained national attention by heading up a Senate Crime Investigation committee. He exposed ties between urban Democratic Party organizations and organized crime; this alienated many party leaders. The party leaders turned to Illinois governor Adlai E. Stevenson, and drafted him to be their candidate. Stevenson gave a rousing welcoming speech at the Democratic National Convention in Chicago in late July, and by the fourth day of the convention he was a candidate. He was nominated on the fourth ballot. The Democrats imposed a loyalty oath on the delegates fearing a repeat of the Southern bolt of 1948. The civil rights plank in the platform was quite vague. The Democrats selected Alabama senator John Sparkman as Stevenson's running mate.

Eisenhower was determined to run an aggressive campaign and draw out those who stayed at home in 1948. Eisenhower made peace with Taft by accepting many of Taft's positions. Eisenhower's early campaign, however, was lackluster. Richard Nixon was caught up in a minor scandal, when it was revealed that he had a slush fund of $16,000, provided to him to cover expenses. Nixon successfully defended himself on national television with his famous "Checkers" speech. Nixon spoke of his humble origins, the sparse lifestyle he and his wife Pat led, and said he would not give up the family cocker spaniel, Checkers, who was given to the family as a gift. Eisenhower made the war in Korea and the stalled peace negotiations the central issue in the campaign; he promised that he would go to Korea if elected. The Eisenhower campaign saturated the airwaves in the last three weeks of the campaign with paid TV advertising.

Eisenhower won by a landslide. Eisenhower took 33,824,351 popular votes and 442 Electoral College votes to Stevenson's 27,314,987 popular vote total, and 89 electoral votes. Stevenson did not win a state outside the South. The GOP gained a majority in Congress, but most observers view this election as a personal victory for Eisenhower. *See*: EISENHOWER, DWIGHT D.; NIXON, RICHARD MILHOUS; STEVENSON, ADLAI E.

1956

Republican Party nominee: Dwight D. Eisenhower, 57.4%

Democratic Party nominee: Adlai E. Stevenson, 42%

The setting for the 1956 election was the popularity of incumbent president Dwight D. Eisenhower. At the beginning of the election season, it was not clear that Eisenhower would seek reelection, since he had suffered a heart attack in 1955. The Republicans lost eighteen seats and their slim majority in the midterm election of 1954. Eisenhower had successfully negotiated a peace in Korea, and the economy was recovering from a recession in 1955.

In 1953, Adlai Stevenson went on a world tour; in Europe, he was treated as the leader of the opposition party. He campaigned for the Democrats in the midterm election of 1954, and in 1955, he announced he was a candidate for the Democratic presidential nomination. His major opponent was Estes Kefauver. Kefauver defeated Stevenson in the Minnesota primary. Averell Harriman also entered the race, with the backing of former president Harry Truman.

Stevenson had an impressive win in the Oregon primary, and enjoyed a two-to-one margin over Kefauver in the California primary. Kefauver withdrew from the race on August 1, and endorsed Stevenson. Truman held firm for Harriman.

Stevenson was nominated on the first ballot at the Democratic convention in Chicago in early August. Stevenson yielded the selection of his running mate to the convention. Massachusetts senator John F. Kennedy was the leader on the second ballot. Tennessee senator Albert Gore, Sr., who ran third, withdrew, and gave his support to Kefauver. Kefauver was selected as Stevenson's running mate on the third ballot.

The Republicans were anxious about President Eisenhower's health. He had suffered a heart attack in 1955, and had an ileitis operation in June 1956. Ike made a good recovery from his health problems and decided to run for reelection. There was a question as to whether he would keep Nixon on the ticket. Nixon had a number of critics who were trying to persuade Eisenhower to dump him. Harold Stassen was one of those trying to have Nixon replaced. On July 12, Leonard Hall, Republican National Committee chairman, announced that Eisenhower would run with Nixon. The GOP met at the end of August in San Francisco and nominated ''Ike and Dick.''

Eisenhower took the high road in this election. Stevenson attacked the administration and accused Eisenhower of being a part-time leader. He also questioned Eisenhower's health in an indirect attempt to make Nixon, who would be in line to succeed Eisenhower, the issue. There were no significant issues in this campaign. Stevenson did propose a nuclear test ban treaty and an end to the military draft. He also promoted an expansion of New Deal programs, but was equivocal on civil rights. There were two foreign policy crises at the end of the campaign: the Soviets invaded Hungary to crush a revolt; France, Britain, and Israel invaded Egypt over the Suez Canal. These crises favored the steady, experienced Eisenhower in the election.

To no one's surprise, Eisenhower won a landslide election. Eisenhower garnered 35,581,003 popular votes to Stevenson's 26,031,322 votes. Eisenhower had 457 Electoral College votes to Stevenson's 73. Stevenson won only seven states, all of them in the South. Eisenhower captured four southern states including Virginia, Florida, Texas, and Louisiana. This election was a personal victory for the war hero Eisenhower, yet despite his huge margin of victory, the Democrats retained both Houses of Congress. *See*: EISENHOWER, DWIGHT D.; NIXON, RICHARD MILHOUS; STEVENSON, ADLAI E.

1960

Democratic Party nominee: John F. Kennedy, 49.7%
Republican Party nominee: Richard Milhous Nixon, 49.6%

The setting for the 1960 presidential election was the end of the popular Eisenhower administration. Dwight D. Eisenhower was the first Republican president elected since Herbert Hoover in 1928. Eisenhower was more popular than his Republican Party. The GOP was unable to regain Congress in Eisenhower's 1956 landslide, and they lost 48 seats in the House in the midterm election of 1958. The economy was beginning to slump in 1960. The United

States appeared to be falling behind the Soviets in technology because the Russians had launched their Sputnik satellite. Rebel Fidel Castro had taken Cuba into the Soviet orbit.

Vice-President Richard M. Nixon was the clear favorite for the GOP nomination. New York governor Nelson A. Rockefeller, elected in 1958, considered challenging Nixon and orchestrated an unsuccessful draft movement late in the campaign. Rockefeller was able to draw Nixon into a secret meeting to discuss the platform. After the meeting, Nixon accepted many of Rockefeller's more liberal positions, which infuriated the conservatives in the party. The Republicans met in Chicago in late July, and nominated Richard Nixon. This made Nixon the first sitting vice-president to be nominated by a party since Martin Van Buren. UN Ambassador Henry Cabot Lodge was selected as Nixon's running mate.

The Democratic Party did not have a frontrunner when the nomination campaign started. Many of the leading contenders were members of the U.S. Senate, including the majority leader, Texas senator Lyndon B. Johnson, liberal Minnesota senator Hubert H. Humphrey, Missouri senator Stuart Symington, and the young, Catholic senator from Massachusetts, John F. Kennedy. Johnson avoided the primaries. Kennedy and Humphrey realized that they had to prove their electability, and they went head to head in the primaries. The first key primary was Wisconsin's, a neighboring state of Minnesota's senator Humphrey, which Kennedy won. The Minnesota victory, however, was not interpreted by the press as a knockout for Kennedy. The critical test, therefore, occurred in West Virginia, a state which was 95% Protestant. Kennedy took the religious issue head on, spent a great deal of family money, and won 61% to 39%. Humphrey then withdrew from the campaign. There was an unsuccessful "stop Kennedy" movement by the remaining candidates. Kennedy was nominated on the first ballot with very limited support from the southern states. Despite early statements that he was not interested, Lyndon B. Johnson accepted the offer to be Kennedy's running mate. Kennedy defined the "New Frontier" in his acceptance speech.

The campaign got off to a slow start. Nixon suffered from a knee infection, and Kennedy was detained in Washington with a late session of Congress. Nixon promised a 50-state campaign, which was very difficult to accomplish. Kennedy focused on the large industrial states, hoping that Johnson would hold the South. Television had become the most important medium in this campaign. The candidates agreed to four televised presidential debates, which most experts agree benefited Kennedy. On the campaign trail, Nixon talked about his experience. Eisenhower campaigned late in the campaign and criticized Kennedy's inexperience. Civil Rights leader Martin Luther King was jailed in Georgia, and candidate Kennedy took the opportunity to phone King's wife. Kennedy took on the Catholic issue with an address to the Houston Minister's Association, where he made a pledge of support for the separation of church and state.

The election was extremely close. Kennedy had a popular vote total of

34,227,096 to Nixon's 34,107,646. The Electoral College vote was 303 to 219. Evidence of vote fraud in Illinois and Texas was not pursued by Nixon. *See*: KENNEDY, JOHN FITZGERALD; NIXON, RICHARD MILHOUS; PRESIDENTIAL DEBATES.

1964

Democratic Party nominee: Lyndon B. Johnson, 61.1%
Republican Party nominee: Barry Goldwater, 38.5%
The setting for the 1964 presidential election was the assassination of John F. Kennedy on November 22, 1963. Kennedy was succeeded by Vice-President Lyndon B. Johnson. Johnson pursued the agenda of the Kennedy administration. The Democrats lost only five House seats in the midterm election of 1962. In 1964, Congress passed a tax cut which boosted the economy. The most pressing domestic issue was racial justice. Martin Luther King, Jr. had led marches in the South, and in August 1963 led a March on Washington. In June 1964, Congress passed the Civil Rights Act. Senator Barry Goldwater, the eventual Republican nominee, opposed the Civil Rights Act. President Johnson led an attack on poverty with his Great Society legislative initiatives.

The Republican Party did not have a frontrunner for the nomination in 1964. Many leading Republicans thought the cause was hopeless because of the good economic conditions, and the popularity of the incumbent Democrats. Conservative Republicans, frustrated by Republican nominees who accepted the premises of the New Deal, wanted to nominate a conservative candidate. A number of conservatives, led by F. Clifton White, former national chairman of the Young Republicans, met in Chicago in 1961 to plot the nomination of a conservative candidate. Their choice was Arizona senator Barry Goldwater. In 1963, a group led by Texas state party chairman Peter O'Donnell announced the formation of a National Draft Goldwater Committee. The leading candidate of the moderate eastern Republicans, who had long controlled the party, was Governor Nelson A. Rockefeller. Rockefeller was damaged by his divorce and second marriage to a recently divorced woman. In the 1964 New Hampshire primary, the voters spurned both Goldwater and Rockefeller and wrote in Henry Cabot Lodge. Later, Rockefeller outpolled Lodge in Oregon. Lodge gave his support to Rockefeller for the California primary, which Goldwater won with 51% of the vote. Clifton White had developed a brilliant grassroots campaign for state party caucuses and conventions, and captured most of the delegates. A late effort by Pennsylvania governor Scranton to stop Goldwater was unsuccessful. Goldwater was nominated on the first ballot at the Republican National Convention in July in San Francisco. William E. Miller, a congressman from upstate New York, was selected as Goldwater's running mate. Charges of extremism by his Republican opponents damaged Goldwater before the general election began. Goldwater set the tone of the general election in his often-quoted remark in his acceptance speech: "extremism in the defense of liberty is no vice."

In an effort to create interest in the Democratic convention, Johnson had refused to make public his choice for a running mate. At the convention, Johnson announced that he had selected Minnesota senator Hubert Humphrey.

There was never any doubt that Johnson would win the general election. Goldwater's effort to offer ''a choice, not an echo'' did not resonate with the American people and Goldwater was reckless in some of his remarks. For example, he talked about the use of tactical nuclear weapons, and breaking off relations with the Soviet Union. The Johnson campaign exploited this image by running the famous ''Daisy'' commercial where a young girl is seen picking daisies, with a nuclear mushroom cloud in the background. The commercial was canceled, but Goldwater was put on the defensive. Many Republican party leaders and candidates deserted Goldwater.

Johnson was elected in a landslide; he garnered 43,126,218 popular votes to Goldwater's 27,174,898 votes. Johnson collected 486 Electoral College votes. Goldwater won only 6 states including his home state of Arizona, and 5 southern states, for a total of 52 Electoral College votes. Goldwater's southern strategy, however, would serve as a road map for future GOP campaigns. The Democrats gained 38 seats in the House, many of them in the North. This would enable President Johnson to pass a number of landmark pieces of legislation. *See*: GOLDWATER, BARRY M.; HUMPHREY, HUBERT HORATIO, JR.; JOHNSON, LYNDON BAINES.

1968

Republican Party nominee: Richard Milhous Nixon, 43.4%
Democratic Party nominee: Hubert H. Humphrey, 42.7%
American Independent Party nominee: George C. Wallace, 13.5%

The setting for the 1968 presidential election was the unpopular war in Vietnam. President Johnson went against his 1964 campaign pledge and sent half a million American soldiers to Vietnam. He also initiated a bombing assault against North Vietnam. On the domestic front, Johnson launched the Great Society, which expanded social welfare spending. Those expenditures, combined with the spending on the war, contributed to inflation. Nevertheless, the economy remained robust. There was growing opposition to the war. In the midterm election of 1966, the Republicans gained 47 seats in the House. Despite the Civil Rights Act and the War on Poverty, race relations worsened, and became inflamed when Rev. Dr. Martin Luther King, Jr. was assassinated on April 5, 1968.

The leading Republican candidate in 1968 was Richard Nixon, who had orchestrated an amazing political comeback. Nixon had campaigned hard for Republicans in the midterm election of 1966 and persuaded party leaders that he could unite the conservative and liberal factions in the party. His challengers for the nomination included George Romney, Nelson Rockefeller, and Ronald

Reagan. Michigan governor George Romney was the early leader. His position on Vietnam was muddled, however, and at one point he said he was "brainwashed." That washed him up and he withdrew before the first primary. At the GOP convention in Miami Beach, which was held in August, Nixon was the frontrunner. Rockefeller and Reagan attempted to stop Nixon but he was nominated on the first ballot with only 25 convention votes to spare. Nixon selected unknown Maryland governor Spiro T. Agnew as his running mate. The Republicans, under the deft leadership of RNC chairman Ray Bliss, adopted a platform without any public squabbling.

The Democrats had a much more difficult time nominating a candidate. Minnesota senator Eugene McCarthy announced he would run against President Johnson, in opposition to the Vietnam War policy. College students flocked to the McCarthy campaign, and McCarthy did surprisingly well against Johnson, collecting 42% of the Democratic vote in the New Hampshire primary. Robert Kennedy announced he was a candidate three days later. On March 31, on the eve of the Wisconsin primary, Johnson announced he would not seek reelection. Vice-President Hubert Humphrey then announced his candidacy. Humphrey, however, was too late to enter any of the remaining primaries. McCarthy and Kennedy contested the remaining primaries. Kennedy outpolled McCarthy in Indiana, while McCarthy out polled Kennedy in Oregon. The June California primary became the showdown between these two anti-war candidates. In California, Kennedy garnered 46% to McCarthy's 42%. Tragically, Robert Kennedy was assassinated election night and died on June 6.

The Democrats met in Chicago in late August. The nomination was never in doubt. Hubert Humphrey, who did not run in a primary and had the support of organized labor and party regulars, was nominated on the first ballot. Maine senator Edmund Muskie was selected as Humphrey's running mate. The McCarthy forces criticized many of the party rules. In response the Democrats abolished what was known as the unit rule, and set up a commission to reform delegate selection procedures. Eventually, this commission would profoundly alter the nomination process. The convention itself was a public relations disaster. There were thousands of anti-war protesters in Chicago that clashed with police on television. There was disagreement between the factions over the platform language on ending the bombing of North Vietnam. Humphrey did not leave the convention with the usual convention bounce.

George Wallace was able to get his American Independent Party on the ballot in all 50 states. The Wallace candidacy threatened to deadlock the Electoral College. Nixon refused to debate Humphrey if Wallace was included, and so no presidential debates were held. Nixon held a sizable lead in the polls early in the campaign. Humphrey's campaign started badly. Humphrey gained momentum in late September when he broke with Johnson on a halt to the bombing of North Vietnam. The unions successfully beat back the Wallace threat in the industrial North. The leaking Wallace vote broke to Humphrey, something the

Nixon campaign did not expect. In the closing days of the campaign, the peace talks in Paris produced a halt to the bombing. Nixon won by a narrow margin. The Republicans gained only five seats in the House.

The popular vote was quite close. Nixon received 31,783,783 votes to Humphrey's total of 31,266,006. Wallace captured 9,906,473 votes. The Electoral College vote was not as close. Nixon received a total of 302 Electoral College votes to Humphrey's 191. George Wallace won 5 states with 45 Electoral College votes. *See*: AMERICAN INDEPENDENT PARTY; HUMPHREY, HUBERT HORATIO, JR.; McGOVERN-FRASER COMMISSION; NIXON, RICHARD MILHOUS; UNIT RULE; WALLACE, GEORGE CORLEY.

1972

Republican Party nominee: Richard M. Nixon, 60.7%
Democratic Party nominee: George McGovern, 37.5%
The setting for the 1972 election was the long and unpopular war in Vietnam. President Nixon tried to defuse the war issue, which he had promised to end during the 1968 campaign, by reducing the commitment of American troops, and having the South Vietnamese take up more of the war effort. The United States restricted its war activity to bombing raids. On the domestic policy side, Nixon's domestic policy advisor, Daniel Patrick Moynihan, proposed a far-reaching welfare reform with a guaranteed income; the Democratic Congress refused to enact it. In his first term, Nixon provided the leadership for the creation of the Environmental Protection Agency. The Nixon administration imposed wage and price controls in 1971, and the sluggish economy recovered in 1972. In the 1970 midterm election the Republicans lost twelve seats.

In 1972 the Democrats imposed the McGovern-Fraser Commission rules for the nomination of its presidential candidate. Senator Edward Kennedy was knocked out of the presidential race by the 1969 Chappaquiddick incident. The early leader was Senator Edmund Muskie. His campaign collapsed after he failed to capture 50% of the vote in his neighboring state of New Hampshire, and he appeared to cry in front of the *Manchester Union Leader* over a story about his wife. Muskie withdrew after he was defeated by George McGovern in the Massachusetts primary. George Wallace, who ran as a Democrat in 1972, did very well in the southern and border states, but was severely wounded by an assassin in May. The two remaining contenders were Senator George McGovern and Hubert Humphrey. The new party rules favored McGovern's campaign, with its army of committed anti-war activists. These issue-motivated activists were reliable voters in the Democratic Party's new primary and caucus delegate selection system. At the July Democratic National Convention in Miami, there was a struggle over the seating of the California delegation, which McGovern won. The McGovern forces then unseated the Illinois delegation of Mayor Richard Daley for not meeting the diversity requirements of the new rules. All of these party struggles played badly on television. The Democrats selected Missouri senator Thomas Eagleton as McGovern's running mate. Eagleton would later be replaced by Sargent Shriver, when it was revealed that Eagleton had been treated for depression. The Democrats' central platform was an immediate end to the war.

Richard Nixon faced primary opposition from Congressman Pete McClosky, who ran as a dove on Nixon's left, and Congressman John Ashbrook, who ran as a conservative objecting to Nixon's overtures to China. Neither of these candidates was a serious threat, and Nixon and Agnew were renominated at the August GOP convention in Miami.

The Democrats' nomination contest and convention, coupled with the mishandling of the Eagleton vice-presidential nomination, doomed their campaign. Nixon acted presidential during the campaign and he enjoyed a number of foreign policy achievements. He had opened relations with China and he improved relations with the Soviet Union, negotiating two major agreements: the ABM and SALT treaties. Nixon's well-financed Committee to Reelect the President operated outside the RNC and did little to help other Republicans. Some of Nixon's campaign staff broke into Democratic headquarters in the Watergate building in Washington, D.C. This incident, which would have profound consequences for Nixon, had no impact on the 1972 election. Nixon won with a landslide. Americans gave Nixon 47,165,235 votes to McGovern's 29,170,774. Nixon carried 49 states collecting 521 electoral votes. McGovern carried only Massachusetts and the District of Columbia for a total of 17 electoral votes. The Republicans gained only twelve House seats in this presidential landslide. *See*: KENNEDY, EDWARD M.; McGOVERN-FRASER COMMISSION; McGOVERN, GEORGE; NIXON, RICHARD MILHOUS; WALLACE, GEORGE CORLEY.

1976

Democratic Party nominee: James Earl (Jimmy) Carter, 50.1%
Republican Party nominee: Gerald R. Ford, 48%

The political fallout from Watergate set the stage for the 1976 presidential election. President Richard Nixon had resigned in August of 1974, amidst the growing Watergate investigation. In 1973, Nixon had nominated Gerald R. Ford to replace Spiro Agnew as the vice-president. Agnew had resigned to avoid sentencing on extortion charges unrelated to Watergate. Ford, after acceding to the presidency, selected and had confirmed Nelson A. Rockefeller as the vice-president. As president, Ford pardoned Richard Nixon. The economy was suffering from stagflation. Real growth had declined and inflation was in the double-digit range. The inflation was driven by an oil embargo by oil-producing nations. In the midterm election of 1974, the Republicans lost 48 seats.

Despite all the problems faced by the incumbent Republicans, the Democrats entered the 1976 nomination period without a clear frontrunner. Walter Mondale, who had explored the possibility of running for two years, bowed out before the process began. Ted Kennedy, haunted by the Chappaquiddick incident, did not run. A virtual unknown, former governor of Georgia James Earl Carter, emerged as a formidable candidate. He did well in Iowa, won the New Hampshire primary, and received a great deal of favorable press attention. In New Hampshire, he defeated Birch Bayh of Indiana, Morris Udall of Arizona, and Fred Harris of Oklahoma. He went on to defeat George Wallace in Florida, which ended Wallace's presidential career. In Pennsylvania, Carter defeated Henry "Scoop" Jackson who had the support of the party regulars and organized labor. Carter ran as the outsider. He was proud to proclaim that: "I'm not a lawyer, I'm not a member of Congress and I've never served in Washington." Carter won more than one-half of the 30 primaries and was nominated on the first ballot at the Democratic National Convention in New York in July. Carter, the outsider, selected a political insider, Senator Walter Mondale, as his running mate.

President Ford was unable to avoid a challenge for his party's nomination. Another outsider, Governor Ronald Reagan of California, representing the conservative wing of the party, gave Ford a stiff challenge for the GOP nomination. Ford narrowly defeated Reagan in the New Hampshire primary, but Reagan won primaries in the South and West. Prior to the July GOP convention in Atlantic City, Reagan had tried to woo delegates by announcing that his running mate would be the liberal Republican senator from Pennsylvania, Richard Schwieker. That did not move enough delegates to secure his nomination. The primary had forced President Ford to dump Rockefeller and select the more conservative senator from Kansas, Robert Dole, as his running mate.

Gerald Ford, behind in the polls, challenged Carter to debate. They agreed to three debates. Gerald Ford gained in the polls after the first debate. In the second debate, Ford erred when he said that there was "no Soviet domination of Eastern Europe" and did not correct the error when he faced further questioning on his remark during the debate. Ford improved in the third debate. Carter, a born-again evangelical Christian, in an interview published by *Playboy* during the campaign, created a furor when he said he looked at other women with lust. The press made a great deal out of this campaign blunder. Ford tried to run as the president, but the voters saw little difference between the two party nominees. The Ford campaign was very well run, and surprisingly, given all the obstacles Ford had to overcome, it was a close election. Carter won with 40,828,929 popular votes to Ford's total vote of 39,148,940. The Electoral College vote was 297 for Carter and 240 for Ford. *See*: CARTER, JIMMY; FORD, GERALD R., JR.

1980

Republican Party nominee: Ronald Reagan, 50.7%
Democratic Party nominee: James Earl (Jimmy) Carter, 41%
Independent: John Anderson, 6.6%

The background for the 1980 election was the long hostage crisis in Iran, coupled with the rise in oil prices, which reignited double-digit inflation in the American economy. President Jimmy Carter had difficulty connecting with his party's majority in Congress. Economic productivity in the economy was down, inflation was up, and President Carter spoke of the "malaise" in the nation. The job growth in the economy went unrecognized. The president did not seem to be in control of events. Carter's greatest accomplishment in foreign policy was the Camp David Accord, which was a breakthrough peace agreement between Egypt and Israel. A signal of Americans' changing attitudes toward government occurred in California in 1978 with the passage of Proposition 13, which rolled back property taxes.

President Carter was unable to deter challengers for the Democratic nomination. Carter's most worrisome opponent was Massachusetts senator Ted Kennedy. Kennedy had the misfortune to announce his candidacy three days after the hostage crisis in Iran began. Kennedy had a large lead in the polls before his announcement, but Americans rallied in support of their president in the face of the international crisis. Kennedy lost the early Iowa and New Hampshire contests. Kennedy eventually won a few primaries, but Carter had enough delegates to gain a first ballot nomination at the Democratic convention in New York City in August. Carter did accept some of the Kennedy platform proposals, including a call for wage and price controls.

The Republicans did not have a frontrunner when the 1980 nomination process started. Former California governor Ronald Reagan, representing the conservative wing of the party, had not stopped campaigning since the 1976 GOP convention, when he lost to President Ford by a mere 117 delegate votes. Other aspirants for the 1980 GOP nomination included John Connally, Howard Baker, John Anderson, and George Bush. Most of the field dropped out early. Bush gave Reagan the most trouble by winning the Iowa caucus in January 1980. Reagan staged a come-from-behind victory in the New Hampshire primary, and went on to win the nomination on the first ballot at the Republican convention in Detroit in July. Reagan engaged Gerald Ford in discussions about possibly being the vice-presidential nominee, but settled on George Bush. John Anderson, a liberal Republican congressman from Illinois, launched an independent campaign for president and received the support of the Liberal Party in New York State. He was on the ballot in all 50 states with his National Unity campaign.

Reagan rejected the notion that there was a crisis of confidence in America, and projected a confident cheerful attitude. Reagan made a number of verbal gaffes in the campaign, but was masterful in his use of the media, a result of his many years as a performer on radio and television. President Carter attacked Reagan and attempted to portray him as an extremist. In using this tactic, Carter displayed a mean streak in his public personality. There were a number of debates sponsored by the League of Women Voters. Anderson, because of his standing in the polls, was invited to the first debate. Carter refused to debate if Anderson was present. Both Reagan and Anderson fared well in this first debate.

There was a final debate in late October between Carter and Reagan. Reagan, in his peroration, asked the TV audience: "Are you better off today than you were four years ago?" The voters responded by electing Reagan by a landslide. Ronald Reagan garnered 43,899,248 popular votes to Carter's 35,481,435. Anderson collected only 5,719,437 popular votes and no Electoral College votes. Reagan took 489 Electoral College votes to Carter's 49. Carter carried only five states and the District of Columbia. Unexpectedly, the Republicans won thirteen Senate races and took the majority in the Senate for the first time since 1952. The GOP also gained 33 seats in the House. The long and troublesome hostage crisis ended the day Ronald Reagan was inaugurated. *See*: CARTER, JAMES EARL (JIMMY); REAGAN, RONALD WILSON.

1984

Republican Party nominee: Ronald Reagan, 58.8%

Democratic Party nominee: Walter Mondale, 40.5%

The setting for the 1984 presidential election was an economy growing out of a recession. The slow economy in the early 1980s had cost the Republicans 27 House seats in the 1982 midterm election. President Reagan, unlike his immediate Republican predecessors, challenged the policy assumptions of the New Deal, successfully reduced the growth in the rate of government spending, and lowered federal tax rates. At the same time, he pushed for higher defense spending. Reagan was assertive in foreign policy. In 1984 a majority of Americans believed the country was moving in the right direction.

The frontrunner for the Democratic nomination was Walter Mondale, who had served as vice-president under President Jimmy Carter. Mondale had the support of the large labor organizations such as the National Education Association and the AFL-CIO. Mondale's support by the traditional forces in the Democratic Party was not sufficient to deter a number of other candidates from seeking the 1984 Democratic presidential nomination. The two major challengers that remained in the fight were Rev. Jesse Jackson and Colorado senator Gary Hart. Early in the campaign, Jackson hurt his chances by referring to New York as "Hymietown" and by his association with the controversial Rev. Louis Farrakhan. Gary Hart, the more moderate and contemporary Democratic candidate, defeated Mondale in New Hampshire. Mondale regained his momentum in the South on Super Tuesday. Mondale went on to win enough delegates to be nominated on the first ballot at the July Democratic National Convention in San Francisco. Mondale selected New York congresswoman Geraldine Ferraro as his running mate. This was the first woman nominee on a national party ticket. The Republicans met in Dallas in August, and renominated Ronald Reagan and George Bush. At their convention the Republicans talked a great deal about church, home, and family.

President Reagan's poll numbers improved as the economy improved in 1984. Reagan set the tone of the campaign by an emotionally moving, nationally televised commemoration of the landing of the troops on the beaches at Normandy. Mondale attempted to raise a number of issues in the campaign. He tried emphasizing the need for the separation of church and state, since Reagan had blasted "modern day secularism." Mondale also tried to raise concerns about the growing deficit, and, in an attempt to show candor, called for a tax increase. None of these efforts to attract voters worked, and some of them backfired. One issue that the Reagan camp needed to manage was the age issue. Reagan was 73. In the first televised debate, Reagan fared poorly in comparison to Mondale's performance. However, Reagan recovered in the second debate, and managed the age issue himself with the remark that he would not "exploit for political purposes my opponents youth and inexperience." The quip worked; everyone chuckled, and Reagan won a second term with a landslide. President Reagan received 54,450,603 popular votes to Mondale's 37,573,671 votes. Reagan's Electoral College vote total was 525 to Mondale's 13. Mondale only won his home state of Minnesota and the District of Columbia. *See*: BUSH, GEORGE HERBERT WALKER; JACKSON, JESSE L.; MONDALE, WALTER FREDERICK; REAGAN, RONALD WILSON.

1988

Republican Party nominee: George Bush, 53.4%

Democratic Party nominee: Michael Dukakis, 45.6%

The end of the popular and successful presidency of Ronald Reagan set the stage for the presidential election of 1988. The economy continued to recover and grow out of the recession of the early 1980s. The GOP had lost only five seats in the 1986 midterm election. The slump in the stock market in October 1987 did not affect economic growth. Overall, there was peace in the world. U.S. relations with the Soviet Union improved as the new Soviet leader, Michael Gorbachev, promoted democracy and economic reform. The only dark cloud was the Iran-Contra scandal. It was revealed that monies from arms sales to Iran were diverted to the Contra rebels in Nicaragua. This scandal reached to the inner circle of the White House.

The early leading candidate for the Democratic nomination was Gary Hart, who had offered a formidable challenge to Walter Mondale in 1984. There were lingering questions about Hart's womanizing, and in 1987 the *Miami Herald* conducted a surveillance of his home; then they found him hosting model Donna Rice for the weekend, while his wife was in Colorado. That revelation drove Hart out of the race in 1987. His departure left a field of seven candidates. Senator Biden of Maryland soon quit the race on charges that he plagiarized his speeches. Michael Dukakis, the governor of Massachusetts, emerged as the frontrunner by winning the New Hampshire primary by a wide margin. He then split Super Tuesday's primary states with Senator Albert Gore and Jesse Jackson. Later, Jackson won the caucus in Michigan, which made him, for a short time, a legitimate candidate. Dukakis went on to defeat Jackson in Wisconsin,

New York, and Pennsylvania. By the end of the primary season, Dukakis had enough delegates to claim a first ballot nomination at the Democratic National Convention in Atlanta. The Dukakis forces made concessions on the platform to gain the support of Jackson. Dukakis selected Texas senator Lloyd Bentsen as his running mate, evoking memories of the Massachusetts-Texas axis of the victorious 1960 Democratic campaign.

Vice-President George Bush emerged as the early frontrunner for the GOP nomination. There were a number of challengers to Bush. Televangelist Pat Robertson tried to mobilize the influential religious right to his cause. The most serious challenge to Bush was mounted by Senator Robert Dole, who defeated Bush handily in Iowa. Bush won a very close primary battle against Dole in New Hampshire, and went on to win South Carolina and then the Super Tuesday primaries. Bush benefited greatly from has association with the popular Ronald Reagan. George Bush was nominated on the first ballot at the GOP convention in New Orleans in August. Bush selected the junior senator from Indiana, Dan Quayle, as his running mate. In his acceptance speech, Bush made his ''No new taxes'' pledge.

Despite the baggage of eight years in office, the Republicans were quite formidable in this election. The experienced Bush campaign team was led by James Baker, Lee Atwater, and media consultant Roger Ailes. The Bush team quickly launched a negative campaign. The campaign's most remembered and most negative ad was the ''Willy Horton ad,'' which depicted Dukakis as soft on crime because of the weekend furlough program Massachusetts ran for prisoners. One of those released for a weekend was a black prisoner named Willy Horton, who raped and terrorized a woman in Maryland while on leave. The Dukakis campaign did not respond effectively and permitted the Bush campaign to define the campaign. Dukakis maintained that ''This election is not about ideology, it is about competence.'' He did not want to be seen as a liberal but as a competent manager. In the second debate, when Dukakis was asked if he would continue to oppose the death penalty if his wife Kitty was raped and murdered, Dukakis showed no emotion and was severely criticized for his bland response. In the vice-presidential debate, Senator Lloyd Bentsen delivered one of the best lines of the campaign when he said to Dan Quayle that he knew President Kennedy and ''Senator, you are no Jack Kennedy.'' George Bush, running as the heir to the popular Reagan, tried to soften some of the Reagan administration edges by calling for ''a kindler and gentler nation.'' President Ronald Reagan actively stumped for his party's presidential candidate. George Bush regained the lead in the polls with the bounce he received from the New Orleans convention, and he never relinquished it. He garnered 48,881,278 popular votes to Dukakis's total of 41,805,375. The Electoral College margin was wider, with Bush collecting 426 to Dukakis's total of 112. Bush had no coattails in 1988; the GOP actually lost House seats in this election. *See*: BUSH, GEORGE HERBERT WALKER; DUKAKIS, MICHAEL S.

1992

Democratic Party nominee: William Jefferson (Bill) Clinton, 43%
Republican Party nominee: George Bush, 38%
Independent candidate: Ross Perot, 19%
The setting for the 1992 presidential election was a 1990 downturn in the national economy. In 1991, the U.S. Gross Domestic Product dropped, and unemployment rose to over 6%. In 1990, President Bush entered a budget deal with the congressional Democrats with a mix of tax increases and spending cuts. By doing this, Bush broke his 1988 campaign pledge of "Read my Lips, No New Taxes." In foreign policy, President Bush enjoyed great success: East and West Germany were now united; the Soviet Union abandoned communism; and the United States enjoyed a great military victory over Iraq in the Gulf War. In March 1991 the polls showed President Bush with an extraordinary 88% approval rating.

In the view of many observers, Bush's high approval rating kept some of the Democrats' top tier candidates out of the race. The Democrats who did seek their party's nomination included Senator Tom Harkin of Iowa, Senator Bob Kerrey of Nebraska, Governor William Clinton of Arkansas, Governor Douglas Wilder of Virginia, and former governor Jerry Brown of California. Arkansas governor Bill Clinton entered the race with the best organization and the most money. He was almost derailed by an early 1992 tabloid revelation of marital infidelity; however, Bill Clinton and his wife Hillary appeared on *60 Minutes* to limit the damage of this story. Clinton finished second in New Hampshire to Massachusetts native Paul Tsongas; yet Clinton, based on his runner-up finish, proclaimed himself the "Comeback Kid." Clinton regained significant momentum by sweeping the South on Super Tuesday. In mid-March, Clinton demonstrated voter appeal outside the South by winning Illinois and Michigan. Paul Tsongas's campaign faltered, ran out of money, and Tsongas suspended his campaign in March. Jerry Brown stayed in the race and won Connecticut, but Clinton captured the remaining primaries. Clinton selected fellow southerner and baby-boomer Albert Gore as his running mate to emphasize change. These were the young, moderate "New Democrats." In July, the Democrats orchestrated a very good convention in New York City, and Clinton received a significant bounce in the polls.

President Bush was not able to deter a challenge for his party's nomination; he faced conservative columnist Patrick Buchanan in the primaries. Buchanan gave the Bush campaign a scare in New Hampshire, but, in terms of popular support, Buchanan was unable to climb out of the 30% range. Buchanan's candidacy revealed Bush's vulnerability on the economic issues, and also forced Bush to move to the right. George Bush and Dan Quayle were renominated in Houston in August. The Republican convention scheduled Patrick Buchanan and televangelist Pat Robertson to speak during prime time. In his speech, Buchanan called for a "culture war." This made the party appear dogmatic and mean-spirited. The volatility of this election was made evident when billionaire Ross Perot announced that he would be a presidential candidate if volunteers made an effort to get his name on the ballot in all 50 states, which they did. In May of 1992 polls showed Independent Perot ahead of the two major party nominees.

The Bush campaign tried to define their opponent using the same negative advertising that had worked successfully for them in 1988. Bush attempted to paint Clinton as a tax and spend liberal; Bush also tried to focus attention on the character issue. The Clinton campaign, under the deft leadership of James Carville, responded immediately to every Bush campaign charge. The Clinton campaign was disciplined and pitched their message of change to voters, who were dissatisfied with the state of the economy. There were three presidential debates and Perot was included in all of them. All of the candidates managed to do well in these debates. The Perot campaign was damaged by the poor performance of its vice-presidential candidate James Stockdale. The second presidential debate was conducted with an audience of undecided voters, and Clinton displayed his skill in using electronic media. Bush finally started to close the gap in the polls in the final weeks of the campaign. However, in the last days of the campaign, Independent Counsel Lawrence Walsh, who had been investigating Iran-Contra, released a copy of a memo showing Bush at a meeting he said he did not attend. The Clinton campaign turned the trust issue against Bush.

In 1992, after twelve years, the Republicans lost the White House. Sparked by Perot's candidacy, voter turnout was the highest since 1960. Clinton received 44,908,233 popular votes, Bush garnered 39,102,282 votes and Perot had an impressive total of 19,741,048. Clinton collected 370 Electoral College votes to Bush's total of 168. Perot, despite his impressive showing—the best for a third-party candidate since Teddy Roosevelt—did not receive one Electoral College vote. Despite losing the presidency, the GOP picked up ten seats in the House. *See*: BUSH, GEORGE HERBERT WALKER; CLINTON, WILLIAM JEFFERSON (BILL); PEROT, ROSS.

1996

Democratic Party nominee: William Jefferson (Bill) Clinton, 49%
Republican Party nominee: Robert J. (Bob) Dole, 41%
Reform Party nominee: Ross Perot, 8%
The 1996 presidential election was set in 1992 when Bill Clinton captured the White House for the Democrats for the first time in twelve years. American presidential politics was dramatically altered by the ending of the cold war. Foreign policy played a very small role in the 1992 election, and had only a negligible impact on the presidential election of 1996.

In 1992 the Democrats had gained control of both the executive and legislative branches of government, bringing to an end a long period of divided government. In his first two years, President Clinton pursued a liberal agenda. Early in his administration, he got entangled in a public relations fiasco by advocating for gays in the military. Clinton compounded his problems by raising taxes as part of his first budget. President Clinton's main thrust in his first years was a proposed government reform of the health care system, developed under the leadership of his wife Hillary Clinton. This effort failed, but defined Clinton as a big government Democrat. Clinton's missteps in the first two years led to the shattering election of 1994, in which the Republicans captured both houses of Congress.

The newly elected Republican 104th Congress, under the leadership of Speaker Newt Gingrich, misread their mandate and overreached in 1995. The Republican Congress confronted Clinton on the budget, which led to a shutdown of the federal government in late 1995 and 1996. The public was not impressed, and blamed the Republicans rather than Clinton for the immature behavior of their national government. Clinton was able to strike a presidential image when he responded to the shocking bombing of a federal building in Oklahoma. He demonstrated leadership when he went against public opinion, and sent troops to troubled and war-torn Bosnia. Under the deft guidance of political consultant Dick Morris, who had been summoned to save a White House in political disarray, Clinton adopted a tactic of triangulation. Clinton would finish his first term by holding a position between the liberal Democrats and the conservative Republicans. His agenda in the second half of his presidency was much more modest than his agenda in the first two years. Most significantly, President Clinton enjoyed a growing economy and few notable global problems, which made him a formidable candidate in the 1996 election.

President Clinton was able to successfully deter any Democrat from challenging him for the nomination. This was the first time the Democrats had not had a contest for their presidential nomination since 1964.

The Republicans had a number of presidential aspirants. Robert Dole, long-time party warhorse and senate majority leader from Kansas, led from the starting gate in both polls and fund-raising, and he eventually captured the nomination. The more credible, younger Republican challengers, such as former vice-president Dan Quayle and Jack Kemp, were either unwilling or unable to generate the support and money necessary to challenge Dole, and did not enter the contest. The Republicans who did enter included Texas senator Phil Gramm, columnist Patrick Buchanan, Lamar Alexander, Alan Keyes, Indiana senator Richard Lugar, California governor Pete Wilson (who withdrew early), Congressman Robert Dornan, moderate Pennsylvania senator Arlen Specter, and the very wealthy Steve Forbes.

Steve Forbes, who inherited a large fortune, did not accept matching federal funds for his candidacy; consequently his spending was not limited by the caps imposed on the other Republicans. Forbes's excessive spending in New Hampshire, much of it on negative attacks against frontrunner Bob Dole, created the opportunity for Patrick Buchanan, who had a dedicated level of support, to win the New Hampshire primary. Forbes' well-financed vanity candidacy also made it difficult for one of the more credible candidates to break out of the pack and challenge Dole. As a result of his win in South Carolina on March 2, Dole was able to regain his footing. With his superior organization and large campaign account, Dole was able to capture the rest of the front-loaded primaries, many of them winner-take-all events, and capture the nomination by late March.

Signs of weakness in Dole's candidacy were exposed in the primary. His age and his inability to articulate a clear purpose for his candidacy led to doubts about the presumptive GOP nominee. In an effort to jump-start his campaign Dole resigned from the Senate on May 15, 1996.

Still, Dole continued to have serious problems. He had reached the spending limit under the federal campaign law during the primary. President Clinton, who had also raised the maximum, but had not spent his money, was able to finance a negative campaign against Dole in the late spring and summer of 1996. In their advertising, the Clinton campaign tied Dole to the unpopular Newt Gingrich, and to cuts in Medicare, education, and the environment. Dole was unable to respond because of the imposed spending cap. The Clinton campaign also relied on soft money raised by the Democratic National Committee to finance ''issue advocacy'' ads to maintain their negative barrage against Dole in battleground states. Frightened by the 1994 results, the Clinton campaign was urged by Dick Morris to maintain their lead in the polls by continuous media spending.

At the mid-August 1996 Republican National Convention, Dole was able to energize the convention by selecting Jack Kemp as his running mate. Dole also announced that he now favored a 15% tax cut, abandoning his long-held opposition to supply-side economics. Apart from a squabble over Dole's proposed tolerance language as part of the GOP's plank of abortion, the Republicans produced a very successful convention, and Dole's convention bounce in the polls had him almost even with Clinton.

The Democratic convention in late August in Chicago was very well produced and uneventful, with the exception of the revelation that the guru of the Clinton political comeback, Dick Morris, was forced to resign from the campaign because a tabloid revealed he had been having a dalliance with a Washington prostitute. In his acceptance speech, Clinton took advantage of Dole's bridge to the past metaphor by offering his candidacy as a bridge to the next century.

Ross Perot, who had demonstrated significant voter appeal in 1992, entered the 1996 contest by creating a new party—the Reform Party. At first Perot was unwilling to claim the nomination of this new party for himself, and provoked a challenge from former Colorado governor Richard Lamm. The Reform Party held a two-weekend convention with mail and electronic voting and, predictably, Perot was nominated. He was eligible for a federal subsidy of $30 million based on his 1992 vote. As in 1996, Perot was unable to recruit a national figure for his new party's vice-presidential nomination and had to settle for protectionist advocate, economist Pat Choate.

President Clinton started the general election campaign with a double-digit lead over his challengers, Republican Bob Dole and Reform Party nominee Ross Perot. Perot did not have the impact on the 1996 election that he had in 1992. In fact, Perot was not allowed to participate in the two presidential debates because the Commission on Presidential Debates determined that Perot did not have a "realistic chance of election." In those debates the candidates were cautious. Dole was reluctant to attack Clinton because his advisors determined from focus groups that females reacted badly to attacks by politicians in the debates, and Dole was already faring poorly with female voters.

In the campaign, Clinton maintained the high road by continuing to act presidential and refusing to directly engage Dole. The Clinton campaign continued its negative media barrage against Dole. Dole struggled for a theme, and finally focused on Clinton's lack of character. Dole argued that Clinton could not be trusted. Polls showed that many voters agreed with Dole's assessment of Clinton, but approved of Clinton's handling of the economy and preferred to keep him in office. The election turned in Dole's favor in the closing weeks of the campaign when the press began to reveal the questionable fund-raising practices of the national Democrats, particularly accepting donations from Indonesian and other foreign economic interests. Clinton won with less than 50% of the vote, and the turnout dropped below 50%, the lowest turnout since 1924.

Clinton garnered 47,401,054 votes to Dole's 39,197,350 and Perot collected 8,085,285 votes. Clinton's Electoral College vote was 379 to Dole's 159. Clinton retained his electoral alliance of the East- and West-Coast states. Dole held the Republican base states in the West and the South. Clinton was able to capture Florida, usually a GOP stronghold.

The 1996 election produced a divided government. The Republicans lost nine House seats but retained their majority. In the Senate the GOP gained two seats, adding to their majority. *See*: CLINTON, WILLIAM JEFFERSON; DOLE, ROBERT J.; ISSUE ADS; PEROT, ROSS; PRESIDENTIAL DEBATES; PRESIDENTIAL NOMINATING CAMPAIGNS; SOFT MONEY.

References: Ellsworth Barnard, *Wendell Willkie: Fighter for Freedom* (Marquette: Northern Michigan University Press, 1966); Michael Barone, *Our Country: The Shaping of America from Roosevelt to Reagan* (New York: The Free Press, 1990); Paul H. Bergeron, *The Presidency of James K. Polk* (Lawrence: University Press of Kansas, 1987); Paul F. Boller, Jr., *Presidential Campaigns*, rev. ed. (New York: Oxford University Press, 1996); Ralph Adams Brown, *The Presidency of John Adams* (Lawrence: University Press of Kansas, 1975); James McGregor Burns, *Roosevelt, The Soldier of Freedom 1940–1945* (New York: Harcourt, Brace, & Jovanovich, 1970); James Ceaser and Andrew Busch, *Upside Down and Inside Out: The 1992 Elections and American Politics* (Lanham, Md.: Rowman & Littlefield, 1993); Donald B. Cole, *The Presidency of Andrew Jackson* (Lawrence: University Press of Kansas, 1993); Noble E. Cunningham,

Jr., *The Presidency of James Monroe* (Lawrence: University Press of Kansas, 1996); Justus D. Doenecke, *The Presidencies of James A. Garfield and Chester A. Arthur* (Lawrence: Regents Press of Kansas, 1981); James Thomas Flexner, *George Washington and the New Nation, 1783–1793* (Boston: Little, Brown, 1970); Douglass Southall Freeman, *George Washington: A Biography*, vol. 6 (New York: Charles Scribner's Sons, 1954); Jack W. Germond and Jules Witcover, *Blue Smoke and Mirrors: How Reagan Won and Why Jimmy Carter Lost the Election of 1980* (New York: Viking Penguin, 1981); William E. Giennap, *The Origins of the Republican Party, 1852–1856* (New York: Oxford University Press, 1987); Paul W. Glad, *McKinley, Bryan and the People* (Philadelphia: Lippincott, 1964); *The Trumpet Soundeth: William Jennings Bryan and His Democracy, 1896–1912* (Lincoln: University of Nebraska Press, 1960); Ulysses S. Grant, *Ulysses S. Grant: Warrior and Statesman* (New York: Morrow, 1969); Oscar Handlin, *Al Smith and His America* (Boston: Little, Brown, 1958); James T. Havel, *U.S. Presidential Candidates and Elections: A Biographical and Historical Guide* (New York: Macmillan, 1996); Melvin L. Hayes, *Mr. Lincoln Runs for President* (New York: Citadel Press, 1960); Sidney Kraus, ed., *The Great Debates: Carter v. Ford* (Bloomington: Indiana University Press, 1979); Allan J. Lichtman, *The Keys to the White House, 1996* (Lanham, Md.: Madison Books, 1996); Arthur S. Link, *Wilson* (Princeton, N.J.: Princeton University Press, 1947); Milton Lomask, *Aaron Burr: The Years from Princeton to Vice-President, 1756–1805* (New York: Farrar, Straus, Giroux, 1979; Horace S. Merrill, *Bourbon Leader: Grover Cleveland and the Democratic Party* (Boston: Little, Brown, 1957); Samuel Eliot Morrison and Henry Steele Commager, *The Growth of the American Republic*, vol. 1, 4th ed. (New York: Oxford University Press, 1956); Michael Nelson, ed., *The Elections of 1988* (Washington, D.C.: Congressional Quarterly Press, 1989); *The Elections of 1992* (Washington, D.C.: Congressional Quarterly Press, 1993); *The Elections of 1996* (Washington, D.C.: Congressional Quarterly Press, 1997); Norma Lois Peterson, *The Presidencies of William Henry Harrison and John Tyler* (Lawrence: University Press of Kansas, 1989); Keith Ian Polakoff, *The Politics of Inertia: The Election of 1876 and the End of Reconstruction* (Baton Rouge: Louisiana State University Press, 1973); Gerald M. Pomper, ed., *The Election of 1996: Reports and Interpretations* (Chatham, N.J.: Chatham House, 1997); Henry F. Pringle, *The Life and Times of William Howard Taft* (Boston: Little, Brown, 1958); Eugene H. Roseboom, *A History of Presidential Elections*, 3rd ed. (New York: Macmillan, 1970); Robert Allen Rutland, *The Presidency of James Madison* (Lawrence: University Press of Kansas, 1990); Larry J. Sabato, ed., *Toward the Millennium: The Elections of 1996* (Needham Heights, Mass.: Allyn & Bacon, 1997); Arthur M. Schlesinger, ed., *History of U.S. Political Parties*, vol. 2 (New York: Chelsea House, 1973); Arthur M. Schlesinger, Jr., and Fred L. Israel, eds., *History of American Presidential Elections* (New York: Chelsea House, 1971); Elbert B. Smith, *The Presidencies of Zachary Taylor and Millard Fillmore* (Lawrence: University Press of Kansas, 1988); Richard Norton Smith, *Thomas E. Dewey and His Times* (New York: Simon and Schuster, 1982); Homer E. Socolofsky and Allan B. Spetter, *The Presidency of Benjamin Harrison* (Lawrence: University Press of Kansas, 1987); Edward Stanwood, *A History of the Presidency from 1788 to 1897* (Boston: Houghton Mifflin, 1898); Glyndon Van Deusen, *Horace Greeley: Nineteenth Century Crusader* (Philadelphia: University of Pennsylvania Press, 1953); Richard E. Welch, *The Presidencies of Grover Cleveland* (Lawrence: University Press of Kansas, 1988); Theodore H. White, *The Making of the President, 1960* (New York: Mentor, 1967); *The Making of the President, 1972* (New York: Bantam Books, 1973).

ELECTORAL COLLEGE. This term refers to the 51 separate delegations of electors who meet in their respective state capitals (and in the District of Columbia) to cast separate ballots for the president and the vice-president. Since the electors do not meet in a central location, the word "college" refers only to their shared task. *See*: ELECTORS.

ELECTORS. Every four years when the American people show up at the polls to vote for president, most are unaware that they are not actually voting for the presidential candidate of their choice. Rather, they are selecting from among various slates of electors, nominated by each party running a presidential candidate. Article II, Section 1, empowers certain individuals, known as electors, to choose the president and vice-president of the United States. Prior to 1804 a majority of states did not allow their citizens to directly participate in this appointment of electors. Under the Constitution, the only requirement is that electors, however chosen, be apportioned according to the number of representatives that a state has in the Congress.

This complex and somewhat undemocratic system for selecting the leaders of the executive branch was the result of months of debate at the Constitutional Convention during which several plans were considered and rejected. The most frequently discussed proposal called for the legislature to elect the president. Legislative election was ultimately rejected, however, because of fears that the executive branch would then become beholden to the Congress. An alternative plan calling for the popular election of the president was also dismissed, in no small part because of the fear that a state with a large population would dominate the election. The resulting compromise was offered near the end of the Philadelphia Convention by the Committee for Unfinished Business. Under the plan, each state was to choose (according to procedures devised by the individual state legislatures) one elector for each member that it had in the House and Senate (although electors were forbidden to actually hold federal office). This guaranteed even the smallest state at least three electors (regardless of size, every state has at least one house member and two senators). As an additional protection for the smaller states, each elector was required to vote for two candidates, one of whom could not be from their own state. This prevented a single large state from always choosing its "favorite-son" candidate as president. *See*: ELECTORAL COLLEGE; ELECTIONS: 1789.

References: Shlomo Slonim, "The Electoral College at Philadelphia: The Evolution of an Ad Hoc Congress for the Selection of the President," *Journal of American History*, Vol. 73 (June 1986); Edward Stanwood, *A History of the Presidency from 1788 to 1897* (Boston: Houghton Mifflin, 1898).

ELEPHANT is the symbol of the Republican Party. The symbol was first used by cartoonist Thomas Nast in a cartoon published in *Harper's Weekly* on November 7, 1874. The cartoon was designed in the context of the 1874 midterm election, in which the Republicans did poorly. The elephant remains as a symbol of the Republican Party. Nast was depicting the Republicans running as if they were deserting their party, because of phony charges of caesarism—based on the rumor that President Grant would seek a third term. *See*: DONKEY.

References: John C. Batchelor, *"Ain't You Glad You Joined the Republicans?" A Short History of the GOP* (New York: Henry Holt, 1996); William Safire, *Safire's New Political Dictionary* (New York: Random House, 1993).

EMILY'S LIST is a political action committee (PAC) that contributes to the campaigns of female candidates. The PAC targets Democratic female candidates who promote its agenda, especially its pro-choice position. This PAC was created in 1985, when it became clear that women candidates for major offices were not winning because they were not able to raise money. EMILY's List has become quite successful in raising money. EMILY is an acronym for Early Money Is Like Yeast (it makes the dough rise). It is also of assistance to women candidates that the PAC selects to support, because it is a signal that the candidate has an opportunity to win, and that will draw money from other contributors.

EMILY's List is a good example of bundling, because the PAC encourages its supporters to direct their contributions to specific candidates and mail their checks to EMILY's List which "bundles" or collects all of the checks and sends them to the individual candidates. In 1996, EMILY's List directly gave $400,000 to 204 state and local candidates, and its members gave a total of $6.7 million. There are about 45,000 members. The president of EMILY's List is Ellen R. Malcolm. The WISH list (Women in the House and Senate), formed in 1992, assists Republican women candidates that support abortion rights. It raised $380,000 in 1996. *See*: BUNDLING; POLITICAL ACTION COMMITTEE; WOMEN'S SUFFRAGE.

Reference: Gary C. Jacobson, *The Politics of Congressional Elections*, 4th ed. (New York: Longman, 1997); http://www.emilylist.org.

EQUAL-TIME RULE is a regulation of the Federal Communications Commission which states that licensed television and radio broadcasters are not required to sell air time to non-federal candidates. If, however, they do sell time to a candidate, they must make equal time available to opposing candidates on equal terms. The same conditions apply if free air time is provided to a candidate by television or radio. The rule does not apply to news coverage. *See*: FAIRNESS DOCTRINE.

ETHNIC POLITICS describes a distinctive immigrant group, or the children of immigrants, who vote and engage in politics as a block in American elections and politics. In order to receive their support, office seekers and political parties must satisfy the demands of these ethnic groups. Office seekers may engage in ethnic politics, by promoting policies that appeal to specific ethnic groups in the United States. For example, both President Clinton and the Republicans designed their foreign policy toward Cuba in a way that appealed to the Cuban-American community in Miami, Florida, a very significant voting block in Florida elections. The American-Jewish community supports candidates that espouse favorable policies toward Israel.

In older, urban machine politics, the various ethnic groups were recognized on the party's balanced slate of candidates. This was important to the maintenance of the urban party's coalition. Catholic ethnics made up an important part of the New Deal Coalition, but in recent elections they have broken away from that coalition. Catholic ethnics gave their support to Reagan and voted for the 1994 Republican takeover of Congress. They were a target group of both the Clinton and Dole campaigns in 1996. Other ethnic groups, such as African Americans, have remained very loyal to the Democratic Party. Hispanic-Americans increased their participation rate in 1996, and voted heavily for President Clinton. They were reacting to immigrant bashing by some of the candidates in the Republican primary. *See*: BLACK VOTING; CATHOLIC VOTE; HISPANIC VOTE.

References: John A. Kromkowsi, "The Politics of Inclusion: Ethnics in the 1996 Election," in *America's Choice: The Election of 1996*, William Crotty and Jerome M. Mileur, eds. (Guilford, Conn.: Dushkin/McGraw-Hill, 1997); Mark T. Levy and Michael Kramer, *The Ethnic Factor* (New York: Simon and Schuster, 1972).

EU **v.** *SAN FRANCISCO DEMOCRATIC COMMITTEE,* 489 U.S. 214 (1989) is a case in which the Supreme Court found unconstitutional various provisions of the California election code regulating party endorsements and party organization. The Court decided that the state of California did not provide sufficient justification for the heavy burden that these provisions placed on fundamental rights guaranteed by the First and Fourteenth Amendments to the U.S. Constitution.

The first provision analyzed by the Court forbade the governing bodies of political parties to endorse or oppose candidates in primary elections. The Court concluded that this regulation hampered the free speech rights of party leaders, subjecting them to what amounted to a gag order when it came to discussing candidates in primary elections. The Court recognized that associational rights also had been abridged, since party leaders only suffered under this regulation when engaged in joint (party) activity with other members. Finally, the Court found that the regulation touched on associational rights in another, slightly less direct, way by preventing parties from working against a candidate whose views were contrary to those held by the party. The result might be that in a subsequent general election, party members would be forced to associate themselves with an inappropriate candidate. This had in fact happened in 1980 when Tom Metzger, a Grand Dragon with the Ku Klux Klan, won the democratic primary for a position in the state legislature.

Since freedom of speech and freedom of association are both fundamental rights, the Court applied the strict scrutiny test. Under this test, the state's actions were presumed unconstitutional unless found to be a narrowly tailored effort to advance a compelling state interest. California offered as justification its compelling interests in preventing intraparty disputes (which would presumably be provoked by those who failed to receive an endorsement), and in protecting primary voters from confusion and the influence of party leaders. The Court found neither argument persuasive, arguing that the state had no real interest in disagreements that may go on within a political party, or in preventing the communication of party opinion to party members.

California had also sought, under its election laws, to place term limits on the chairs of the state parties, and to require that the parties alternate between chairs from the southern and northern regions of the state. The Court saw this as a highly intrusive regulation which violated the associational rights enjoyed by political parties. The Court noted that the justification offered by the state, its "interest in the democratic management of the political partys' internal affairs," would only be considered compelling if, absent the regulation, it could be shown that the voting rights of party members would be abridged. Since California was not likely to be able to make such an assertion, these regulations on party organization, like the regulations on party endorsements, were declared in violation of the First and Fourteenth Amendments. *See: COUSINS* v. *WIGODA* (1975); *DEMOCRATIC PARTY OF U.S.* v. *WISCONSIN* (1981); PREPRIMARY ENDORSEMENT; PRIMARY; STRICT SCRUTINY; *TASHJIAN* v. *REPUBLICAN PARTY OF CONNECTICUT* (1986).

EXIT POLLS are conducted at selected polling places around the country. A pollster is sent to a polling place and asks a sample of voters to complete a survey. The poll asks the respondents which candidates they voted for, and also seeks demographic information about the voters. The most prominent exit poll is conducted by the network-sponsored research firm, Voter News Service (VNS). The sites selected are sample precincts that represent certain voter characteristics; some of the sites used are swing precincts. The data is collected before the polls are closed and is analyzed at a central location for each state. The data is used to predict election results by the television networks. There is some controversy surrounding these predictions, since predictions of state election outcomes, especially in presidential elections, may influence voter choice and turnout, particularly in states where the polls have not closed. The exit poll data is also used to create demographic profiles of voters and relate that to their choices.

In the general election of 1996, NBC erred by predicting the defeat of New Hampshire Senator Smith based on exit poll data. Smith was reelected. *See:* POLL.

EXIT POLLS 165

References: Kenneth M. Goldstein, "Public Opinion Polls and Public Opinion in the 1996 Election," in *America's Choice: The Election of 1996*, William Crotty and Jerome M. Mileur, eds. (Guilford, Conn: Duskin/McGraw-Hill, 1997); Seymour Sudman, "Do Exit Polls Influence Voting Behavior?" *Public Opinion Quarterly*, vol. 50 (Fall 1986); Michael W. Traugott and Paul J. Lavrakas, *The Voter's Guide to Election Polls* (Chatham, N.J.: Chatham House, 1996).

F

FAIRNESS COMMISSION was one of the last of a long series of Democratic Party reform commissions, beginning with the McGovern-Fraser Commission, created to revise the rules for the Democratic Party's presidential nominations. The Fairness Commission was created after the defeat of Walter Mondale in 1984. Jesse Jackson and Gary Hart, the losing candidates in the Democratic Party nomination contest of 1984, called for further reforms. They were upset over the fact that the superdelegates, created by the Hunt Commission, favored Mondale. Jackson complained about the effects of the 20% threshold requirement for the awarding of delegates. In response to these complaints, the Democratic Party chair, Paul Kirk, created the Fairness Commission under the leadership of Donald L. Fowler, who served as chairman. Fowler was a moderate, white Southerner, who would later become DNC chair under President Bill Clinton.

The Fairness Commission, under Fowler, did not want to give the appearance that it was buckling to Jackson, because the Democratic Party had developed an image of being a captive to special interests. Nonetheless, the Fairness Commission did lower the threshold requirement from 20% to 15%. The Fairness Commission, however, held firm to the concept of superdelegates, and actually increased the number of superdelegates for future party conventions to 16% of the delegates. It also relaxed the rule restricting participation in Democratic primaries and caucuses to Democrats only, so that open primaries could be held in Wisconsin and Montana with national party approval.

After the 1988 election, the Democrats required all states to divide their elected delegates proportionally among candidates that received 15% of the vote. After 1988, the party also expanded the number of superdelegates to 18% of the convention delegates. *See*: FOWLER, DONALD; HUNT COMMISSION; McGOVERN-FRASER COMMISSION; MIKULSKI COMMISSION.

Reference: Philip A. Klinker, *The Losing Parties: Out-Party National Committees, 1956–1993* (New Haven, Conn.: Yale University Press, 1994).

FAIRNESS DOCTRINE was a policy established in 1949 by the Federal Communications Commission (FCC), which provided that television and radio present all sides of significant public issues. The law was administered by the FCC, a seven-member independent regulatory commission that grants licenses to broadcasters. This law has now been abandoned by the FCC.

The FCC has also attempted to regulate content of political advertising. In 1996, the U.S. Circuit Court of Appeals for the District of Columbia struck down an FCC order that permitted broadcasters to restrict graphic political advertisements during the time children would probably be watching TV. At issue was the graphic depiction of aborted fetuses. The Court ruled that the FCC could not restrict the ability of the candidate to "fully and completely" inform the voters, nor could it inhibit the unrestricted discussion of the issues by legally qualified candidates. *See*: EQUAL-TIME RULE.

FAVORITE SON/FAVORITE DAUGHTER is a leading state party figure who is supported by his/her state party's delegation for the presidential nomination. The leading party figure in a particular state is nominated by the party's state convention. Frequently, the favorite-son candidate is not a serious candidate for the presidential nomination. The candidacy is advanced as a way for the state party leaders to broker the state's delegation at the national party convention. At the convention, the favorite-son candidate is nominated on the first ballot in order to hold the state's votes for the first round of balloting. Then, the votes are traded for special treatment of the particular state by the more serious contenders. This practice has fallen into disuse for two reasons: First, the National Democratic Party rules require that, for a name to be placed in nomination, a petition must be submitted indicating support for the nominee from at least 300 delegates, and not more than 50 of those signatures can come from the same state delegation. A delegate cannot sign more than one petition. Second, and more significantly, there are no longer favorite-son candidacies because the major candidates compete in all of the primaries to accumulate enough delegates to gain the nomination on the first ballot. Those serious national candidates will not defer to a state political figure who is running as a favorite son in a state's presidential primary. The type of nomination system that encouraged favorite sons and brokered conventions has disappeared with the introduction of the party nomination reforms of the 1970s. The term "favorite son" is similar in meaning to the term "native son." *See*: McGOVERN-FRASER COMMISSION; NATIONAL PARTY CONVENTION.

References: National Democratic Party, *Procedural Rules of the 1996 Democratic National Convention*; Nelson W. Polsby and Aaron Wildavsky, *Presidential Elections: Strategies and Structures in American Politics*, 9th ed. (Chatham, N.J.: Chatham House, 1996).

FEDERAL CORRUPT PRACTICES ACT OF 1910 AND 1911 was the first campaign finance disclosure law in American politics. This law was also called the Publicity Act of 1910. The 1910 law required post-election disclosure of contributions and expenditures of national party committees and campaigns that operated in two or more states. In 1911 the law was amended to require disclosure for House and Senate campaigns for primaries and general elections. Campaign committees were required to report their finances before and after an election. This was the first law to impose campaign spending limits. In 1921 the Supreme Court ruled, in *Newberry* v. *United States* (1921), that spending limits could not be imposed in primaries, and struck down the limits. Spending limits were reimposed for general election campaigns in the Federal Corrupt Practices Act of 1925. *See*: FEDERAL CORRUPT PRACTICES ACT OF 1925; TILLMAN ACT OF 1907.

Reference: Herbert E. Alexander, *Financing Politics: Money, Elections, and Political Reform*, 4th ed. (Washington, D.C.: Congressional Quarterly Press, 1992).

FEDERAL CORRUPT PRACTICES ACT OF 1925 governed federal election campaign financing until the Federal Election Campaign Act of 1971. The Corrupt Practices Act was the result of the U.S. Supreme Court decision in *Newberry* v. *United States* (1921). Truman Newberry had been convicted of excessive campaign spending in his campaign against Henry Ford in a 1918 U.S. Senate election in Michigan. Newberry's conviction was overturned by the Supreme Court because much of his spending was in the primary. The Court ruled that congressional authority to regulate campaign spending did not extend to primaries. The 1925 Federal Corrupt Practices Act deleted the restrictions on primaries which had been contained in the Federal Corrupt Pratices Act of 1910 and 1911. The new law required that all multi-state committees, as well as House and Senate candidates, disclose all contributions over $100, even in non-election years. This disclosure was to occur quarterly. The Act also raised the spending limits imposed by the Publicity Act of 1910 as amended in 1911. The 1925 law set the limits at $25,000 for Senate campaigns, and $5,000 for House candidates. This campaign finance regime was ineffective because the law did not create an effective regulatory mechanism. Only two people were ever excluded from office for violating this act.

The Corrupt Practices Act of 1925, as is the case of most campaign finance laws, was a response to scandal. In this instance, it was a reaction to the Teapot Dome scandal of the Harding administration. *See*: FEDERAL CORRUPT PRACTICES ACT OF 1910 AND 1911; FEDERAL ELECTION CAMPAIGN

ACT OF 1971 AND AMENDMENTS; HATCH ACT; TILLMAN ACT OF 1907.

References: Herbert E. Alexander, *Financing Politics: Money, Elections, and Political Reform*, 4th ed. (Washington, D.C.: Congressional Quarterly Press, 1992); Anthony Corrado, Thomas E. Mann, Daniel R. Ortiz, Trevor Potter, Frank J. Sorauf, eds., *Campaign Finance Reform: A Sourcebook* (Washington, D.C.: Brookings Institution, 1997); Robert E. Match, *Campaigns, Congress, and the Courts: The Making of Federal Campaign Finance Law* (New York: Praeger, 1988).

FEDERAL ELECTION CAMPAIGN ACT OF 1971 was the first major revision of campaign finance law to follow the Corrupt Practices Act of 1925. This 1971 law, signed by President Nixon in 1972, established campaign spending limits, limited the amount of money that could be donated to federal campaigns, required disclosure of all contributions, established limits for media spending, and limited how much of their own money the candidates could spend. The new regulations applied to both primaries and general elections. The finance reports were to be filed with the secretary of state in the state where the election was conducted, and with the clerk of the House for House campaigns, and the secretary of the senate for Senate campaigns. This was a significant reform, for it required disclosure, limited contributions, and imposed spending limits. The limits placed on the campaign spending would eventually be ruled unconstitutional in *Buckley* v. *Valeo* (1976). President Richard Nixon supported this law with the understanding that the new law would not apply to his presidential campaign of 1972. *See: BUCKLEY* v. *VALEO* (1976); FEDERAL CORRUPT PRACTICES ACT OF 1925; FEDERAL ELECTION CAMPAIGN ACT AMENDMENTS OF 1974; TILLMAN ACT OF 1907.

References: Herbert E. Alexander, *Financing Politics: Money, Elections, and Political Reform*, 4th ed. (Washington, D.C.: Congressional Quarterly Press, 1992); Anthony Corrado, Thomas E. Mann, Daniel R. Ortiz, Trevor Potter, and Frank J. Sorauf, eds., *Campaign Finance Reform: A Sourcebook* (Washington, D.C.: Brookings Institution, 1997).

FEDERAL ELECTION CAMPAIGN ACT AMENDMENTS OF 1974 were sweeping amendments to the Federal Election Campaign Act of 1971, signed by President Gerald Ford in 1974. The impetus for campaign finance reform was spurred by the campaign finance abuses of President Nixon's Committee to Reelect the President in 1972. These amendments radically altered the Federal Election Campaign Act of 1971, which they amended. The specific media spending limits of the Federal Election Campaign Act of 1971 were deleted, and strict limits on campaign spending were imposed with this law. Limits were imposed on primary and general election spending for all federal candidates. The spending limits were to be adjusted by the population size of each state. These spending limits were later found to be unconstitutional in *Buckley* v. *Valeo* (1976).

Under the amendments, a limit of $1,000 was placed on individual contributions to federal candidates for primary, general, and runoff elections. Donations by political action committees were restricted to $5,000. These contribution limits are still in effect and have not been adjusted for inflation. Contribution limits were imposed on candidates and their immediate families. These limits were later struck down by *Buckley* v. *Valeo* (1976).

The law restricted the amount of money national party committees could spend on behalf of federal candidates. The law also provided a subsidy to the major national parties (defined as parties that received 25% of the vote in the last presidential election) for their national conventions. Minor parties would receive lesser amounts. Finally, the law restricted the amount that could be spent on a national convention.

For the first time public financing was provided for major national party presidential candidates. The general election campaign of presidential candidates was fully funded by a large grant on condition that the candidate agree not to accept private donations. In 1996 that amount of the public subsidy exceeded $60 million for the general election campaigns of Democratic nominee Bill Clinton and Republican nominee Bob Dole. Minor party candidates may also qualify for this subsidy depending on the vote they received. Ross Perot received almost $30 million. The amount was calculated based on his 1992 vote. The subsidy goes directly to the candidates and not to the parties.

In the presidential primary, there is also a federal subsidy in the form of matching money (after meeting the requirement that they raise a minimum of $5,000 and have contributions from at least 20 states). Candidates are eligible to receive matching federal money for donations of $250 or less. If they accept these matching public funds, the candidates are subject to calculated spending limits for each state's primary. There is also an overall spending cap, which restricted Bob Dole's campaign in the 1996 post-primary period. Pat Robertson, in his 1984 presidential primary campaign, and Steve Forbes in his 1996 bid, did not take the matching funds, and were free to spend whatever they could raise. In the case of Forbes, he spent an estimated $40 million of his inherited fortune.

This law also created the Federal Election Commission (FEC), an independent regulatory agency to enforce and implement the campaign finance laws. Disclosure and reporting requirements were tightened by this law. *See: BUCKLEY* v. *VALEO* (1976); FEDERAL ELECTION CAMPAIGN ACT OF 1971 AND AMENDMENTS; FEDERAL ELECTION COMMISSION; POLITICAL ACTION COMMITTEE; SOFT MONEY.

References: Herbert E. Alexander, *Financing Politics: Money, Elections, and Political Reform*, 4th ed. (Washington, D.C.: Congressional Quarterly Press, 1992); Herbert Alexander and Anthony Corrado, *Financing the 1992 Election* (Armonk, N.Y.: M. E. Sharpe, 1995); Frank J. Sorauf, *Money in American Elections* (Glenview, Ill.: Scott, Foresman, 1988).

FEDERAL ELECTION CAMPAIGN ACT AMENDMENTS OF 1976 were in response to the portions of the previous Federal Election Campaign Act law declared unconstitutional by the U.S. Supreme Court decision in *Buckley* v. *Valeo* (1976). The Court struck down the spending limits imposed in the Federal Election Campaign Act Amendments of 1974 as an unconstitutional restriction on free speech. The Court did uphold spending limits as a requirement of public financing of campaigns, if the money and the limits are accepted voluntarily by the recipient candidate. If a presidential candidate refuses the public matching money, the candidate is free to spend whatever he can raise. The contribution limits in the 1974 FECA law were upheld by the Court, but contribution limits could not be imposed on the spending of the candidate's own money, unless the candidate accepted public funds. If they accept the matching money, presidential candidates' own contributions are restricted to $50,000. Of course, this has resulted in a great advantage to wealthy candidates. Michael Huffington broke all campaign spending records in his unsuccessful 1994 U.S. Senate campaign in California by spending approximately $26 million, and Steve Forbes spent $40 million of his money on his failed 1996 presidential bid.

This law limited an individual's contribution to a PAC to $5,000 per year, and individual contributions to national party committees was limited to $20,000. It also included a number of disclosure requirements on independent expenditures, and a required declaration that the expenditures did not occur in collusion with a candidate.

The Supreme Court ruled, in *Buckley* v. *Valeo* (1976), that the 1974 FECA-designed structure of the Federal Election Commission was unconstitutional on the principle of separation-of-powers. The 1974 law had given the Speaker of the House, the president pro tem of the Senate, and the president the right to appoint two members, one from each party, subject to congressional approval. In response to the Court's decision, the 1976 amendment to FECA provided that all six members be appointed by the president, subject to Senate confirmation. No more than three members could be from the same political party, and a vote of four was required to issue regulations or initiate civil action. The legal authority of the Federal Election Commission was enhanced by this amendment to the Federal Election Campaign Act. *See*: FEDERAL ELECTION CAMPAIGN ACT OF 1971 AND AMENDMENTS; FEDERAL ELECTION COMMISSION; INDEPENDENT EXPENDITURES; SOFT MONEY.

References: Herbert E. Alexander, *Financing Politics: Money, Elections, and Political Reform*, 4th ed. (Washington, D.C.: Congressional Quarterly Press, 1992); Anthony Corrado, Thomas E. Mann, Daniel R. Ortiz, Trevor Potter, and Frank J. Sorauf, eds., *Campaign Finance Reform: A Sourcebook* (Washington, D.C.: Brookings Institution, 1997).

FEDERAL ELECTION CAMPAIGN ACT AMENDMENTS OF 1979 were designed to deal with various criticisms that had been leveled against the FECA laws since they were introduced in 1971. This law attempted to reduce the burdensome paperwork requirements, which was a common complaint of candidates. Also, federal candidates would no longer be permitted to convert excess campaign funds for personal use.

The federal campaign finance reform effort, which began in 1971, directed that all campaign funds for federal candidates be placed under the control of the candidate. The contributions and the expenditures by political parties on behalf of candidates were very restricted. Prior to 1979 the only attention given to the national parties by the Federal Election Campaign Act as amended was a public subsidy to the parties to hold their national conventions. Party leaders and party scholars expressed concern about the diminished role of parties fostered by these campaign finance reforms. To enhance the role of parties, the 1979 amendments to the Federal Election Campaign Act allowed that certain types of party-related campaign spending were exempt from the spending limits imposed on federal candidates. Party committees were now allowed to spend monies for grassroots activity and party building.

The 1979 law stated the types of state and local party activities that would not count against the party's limit in supporting federal candidates. These included grassroots campaign materials such as slate cards, which must list at least three candidates. Voter registration and get-out-the-vote drives were also permitted. This type of spending was not considered to be a form of direct assistance to a specific candidate.

The intent of these reforms was to encourage civic participation. These reforms did not create "soft money." They allowed parties to use hard dollars for party building without having those expenditures count against the party's contribution limits to federal candidates. It was the Federal Election Commission's Advisory Opinions and Supreme Court decisions that created the opportunity for "soft money," not this law. *See: BUCKLEY* v. *VALEO* (1976); FEDERAL ELECTION CAMPAIGN ACT OF 1971 AND AMENDMENTS; FEDERAL ELECTION COMMISSION; SOFT MONEY.

References: Herbert E. Alexander, *Financing Politics: Money, Elections, and Political Reform*, 4th ed. (Washington, D.C.: Congressional Quarterly Press, 1992); Frank J. Sorauf, *Money in American Elections* (Glenview, Ill.: Scott, Foresman, 1988).

FEDERAL ELECTION COMMISSION was created in 1974 to administer and enforce the campaign finance laws passed in the 1970s. In the original legislation, two of the six members were to be appointed by the president, two by leaders of the House, and two by the leadership of the Senate. There were to be three Republicans and three Democrats. The Supreme Court, in *Buckley* v. *Valeo* (1976), ruled that the role of Congress in the appointment of members was unconstitutional. In response to the Court, Congress revised the appointing process; the six members are now nominated by the president, and confirmed by the Senate. In the revised law, a provision was added that required a vote of four out of the six members for the Commission to take any action.

The Federal Election Commission has the responsibility for insuring that federal candidates and political committees comply with the limitations, prohibitions, and disclosure requirements of the federal election law. The Commission provides information and advice to candidates and committees through publications and workshops. More formal legally binding advice is given through Advisory Opinions which serve as a future guide and legal precedence.

The Federal Election Commission also administers the public funding of presidential elections. It oversees and certifies matching funds for presidential primary candidates, public funding for major party presidential candidates, and public grants for major party national party conventions. The Commission audits the use of these funds.

The Commission has very limited authority to sanction violators. In the view of many reform groups, the Federal Election Commission is underfunded and has weak enforcement authority. *See*: FEDERAL ELECTION CAMPAIGN ACT OF 1971 AND AMENDMENTS; ISSUE ADS; REVENUE ACT OF 1971; REVENUE ACT OF 1978; SOFT MONEY.

References: Thomas E. Mann, ''The Federal Election Commission: Implementing and Enforcing Federal Campaign Finance Law,'' in *Campaign Finance Reform: A Source Book*, Anthony Corrado, Thomas E. Mann, Daniel R. Ortiz, Trevor Potter, and Frank J. Sorauf, eds. (Washington, D.C.: Brookings Institution, 1997); Address: Federal Election Commission, 999 E Street N.W., Washington, D.C. 20463; http://www.fec.gov.

FEDERAL ELECTION COMMISSION (FEC) v. NATIONAL CONSERVATIVE PAC,

470 U.S. 480 (1985). In this case, the Supreme Court declared unconstitutional a provision of the Presidential Election Campaign Fund Act which made it illegal for independent political committees to spend more than $1,000 for the purpose of electing a particular presidential or vice-presidential candidate. The Act only applied to presidential and vice-presidential candidates who had accepted public financing for their campaigns. The Federal Election Commission (FEC) had asked the Court to rule on the constitutionality of the Act.

In his majority opinion, Justice Rehnquist reaffirmed the Court's holding in *Buckley* v. *Valeo* (1976) that political expenditures which lead to speech are protected by the First Amendment. Because the expenditures of organizations like the National Conservative PAC fall within the purview of the First Amendment, the burden is on Congress to justify the regulation. Rehnquist acknowledged that the threat of corruption or the appearance of corruption would be sufficient to allow the Congress to intrude on First Amendment freedoms; nevertheless, Rehnquist reasoned that since PACs do not coordinate their activities with candidates, and do not (in this case) directly give money to candidates, there was no obvious opportunity for corruption or bribery. Therefore, Congress's interest was not compelling enough to allow what the Court saw as a substantial burden on First Amendment rights. As a result of this case, it is nearly impossible for Congress to limit the amount of money spent by PACs

on presidential elections. *See: BUCKLEY* v. *VALEO* (1976); POLITICAL AC-
TION COMMITTEE.

FEDERALIST PARTY was an early American party led by Alexander Hamilton and John Adams. This is considered the first American political party. This
party advocated a strong national government. This group was successful in
promoting the adoption of the U.S. Constitution. The Federalists were generally
anti-party in their sentiments, thus they were reluctant to engage in grassroots
party building. This eventually contributed to their decline as a viable political
party. The First Congress was entirely Federalist. By the Third Congress, however, the membership was divided between the Hamiltonians and the Jeffersonians, that is, between the Federalists and the Republicans. The Federalists
received their support from commercial and financial interests, and citizens with
higher occupational status and formal education. The Federalists did not hold
to very egalitarian views. They believed that government should be led by the
aristocracy. This early party advocated the creation of a national bank and the
imposition of a protective tariff.

The Republicans were opposed to a strong national government. The Federalists suffered an overwhelming defeat in the election of 1800 at the hands of
the Republicans. That election is viewed as the first realigning election. The
Federalist Party virtually disappeared as a national party after the election of
1816. The absence of the Federalists led to increasing factionalism within the
Republican Party. By 1824 two-party politics had returned to the United States.
See: DEMOCRATIC PARTY; ELECTIONS: 1800; WHIG PARTY.

References: Noble E. Cunningham, *The Jeffersonian Republicans: The Formation of
Party Organization, 1789–1801* (Chapel Hill: University of North Carolina Press, 1957);
Gerald Strouzh, *Alexander Hamilton and the Idea of Republican Government* (Stanford,
Calif.: Stanford University Press, 1970).

FIFTEENTH AMENDMENT. This post–Civil War amendment was ratified
in 1870. This amendment to the U.S. Constitution guarantees all citizens the
right to vote regardless of "race, color, or previous condition of servitude."
Despite the passage of this amendment, blacks were denied the opportunity to
vote in the South after the Civil War. The post-reconstruction white Southerners
instituted the white primary, the literacy test, and the poll tax to discourage
African-American voting. African Americans in the South did not vote in significant numbers until after the Voting Rights Act of 1965. The Fifteenth
Amendment provides constitutional justification for the Voting Rights Act. *See*:
BLACK VOTING; POLL TAX; PRIMARY, WHITE; VOTING RIGHTS ACT.

Reference: William Gillette, *The Right to Vote: Politics and Passage of the Fifteenth
Amendment* (Baltimore: Johns Hopkins University Press, 1969).

FILING is the legal act of declaring that one is a candidate for public office.
State statutes stipulate the filing regulations. Usually, there is a state or city

charter specified residency requirement. The petitions that a candidate has to file require a certain number of signatures. If it is a partisan nomination, the signatures must be from members of that particular party. The petitions are filed with the appropriate government officer. Depending on the state, that officer could be the secretary of state, or the county or city clerk. There is often a filing fee. The petition requirements and the fee must be significant enough to deter nuisance candidates; however, the barrier should not be so severe as to restrict citizens from seeking office. New York State has significant barriers to ballot access. In *Bullock* v. *Carter* (1972) the U.S. Supreme Court ruled that filing fees must be reasonable. *See: BULLOCK* v. *CARTER* (1972).

FILLMORE, MILLARD (1800–1874) was born into an extremely poor farm family on January 7, 1800, in what is now Summerhill, New York. He was to become the second Whig vice-president within a decade to succeed to the executive office at the death of an incumbent president (July 10, 1850). Apprenticed at age fourteen, Fillmore was largely self-educated. With hard-earned savings he bought himself out of apprenticeship, acquired a school teaching job, and as time permitted read the law, being admitted to the bar in 1823. Beginning his political career as an Anti-Mason and as something of the protégé of Thurlow Weed, Fillmore served several terms in the New York Assembly before being elected to the U.S. House of Representatives in 1833. As with Weed, Fillmore joined the Whig Party and in Congress became an ardent supporter of Henry Clay and his "American System," with its emphasis on protective tariffs and internal improvements. Returning to New York State politics, Fillmore waged, and narrowly lost, a bid for the governorship in 1844; three years later he was to be successful in a statewide campaign for the comptroller's office. It was from this position, with Clay's endorsement, and as a "Northern" Whig, that Fillmore was chosen to "balance" the party's ticket of 1848, becoming the vice-presidential running mate of the politically inexperienced, if not naive, military hero, General Zachary Taylor of Louisiana. This ticket was to secure a relatively narrow victory both in the popular and Electoral College balloting. With Taylor's death but sixteen months after inauguration, Fillmore assumed the presidency at a critical juncture. In Congress, Henry Clay and others had been fashioning a complex set of legislative proposals aimed at securing "compromise" on the issue of slavery's extension into territories acquired as the result of the war with Mexico, 1846–1848: among other provisions, Utah and New Mexico territories were to be organized without determination of the slavery question; California was to be admitted to the Union as a non-slave state; and a fugitive slave law was to be enforced by national authority. President Taylor, anxious to have California acquire statehood, and for reasons unrelated to the slavery question, otherwise vigorously opposed the remainder of the package and threatened its veto. Death stilled his opposition. Fillmore's long-standing friendship with Clay, perhaps his conclusion that the legislation would "buy time," led the new president to support its adoption. But two months after

Taylor's death Fillmore signed into law the "Compromise of 1850." Ironically, while the legislation bought a decade of time for the nation, it bought virtually no time for Millard Fillmore. Holding firmly to his constitutional duty to see that the laws be faithfully executed, Fillmore attempted to give even-handed enforcement to the fugitive slave statute. Thereby he angered anti-slavery, "conscience" Whigs, and in sufficient numbers to deny to himself renomination at the party's convention of 1852. Upon leaving office in March of 1853, Fillmore returned to New York. In 1856, however, he engaged in one political "last hurrah," accepting the presidential nomination of the American Party, the "Know-Nothings," a third party opposed to immigration and immigrants, particularly Catholics. It is ironic that Fillmore, who began his political career as an Anti-Mason, should end it as a Know-Nothing, securing nearly 900,000 popular votes, carrying the state of Maryland with its eight Electoral College ballots, but having no appreciable effect on the outcome, the election of Democrat James Buchanan, to the presidency. Fillmore now largely withdrew from politics, continuing with his law practice and enjoying his role as leading citizen of Buffalo, he died there on March 8, 1874. *See*: ELECTIONS: 1848, 1856; TAYLOR, ZACHARY.

References: Robert J. Rayback, *Millard Fillmore: Biography of a President* (Buffalo: Buffalo Historical Society, 1959); Elbert B. Smith, *The Presidencies of Zachary Taylor and Millard Fillmore* (Lawrence: University Press of Kansas, 1988).

FLOOR FIGHT. A dispute at a party's national nominating convention that cannot be resolved in one of the committees. The dispute is often over a credentials or a platform issue, and must go to the full convention for resolution. At the Democratic convention of 1968, the forces of Eugene McCarthy engaged Hubert Humphrey's supporters in a three-hour debate over Vietnam policy. At the Democratic convention of 1980, the supporters of Ted Kennedy debated economic policy for seventeen hours as they challenged the renomination of President Jimmy Carter. In 1996 the Republicans avoided a floor fight over the abortion language in their platform. However, the presumptive presidential nominee, Bob Dole, was unable to get his proposed tolerance language in the platform. The tolerance language was placed in the appendix. A bitter floor fight, for the televised convention of today, is very damaging to the party's image and its electoral fortunes. *See*: CREDENTIALS COMMITTEE; NATIONAL PARTY CONVENTION.

Reference: Paul T. David, Ralph M. Goldman, and Richard C. Bain, *The Politics of National Party Conventions* (Washington, D.C.: Brookings Institution, 1960).

FOCUS GROUP. The use of focus groups in political campaigns was introduced in the 1980s. They are now as common in campaigns as public opinion polls. The technique had been used in market research for 40 years. A focus group is a small discussion group of twelve to fifteen members guided by a moderator. The members of the focus group are not randomly selected populations as are sample populations for surveys. The composition of the group depends on the needs of the campaign. They may recruit a group of married women, Catholic voters, or whatever target group they would like to influence to attract more voters. The value of focus groups is that the campaigns are able to delve more deeply into the opinions of voters about the candidates and the issues. The focus group may yield significant insights. George Bush's pollster Bob Teeter discovered from a focus group that no one knew what George Bush was talking about when he used the phase "a thousand points of light." The success of the focus group in yielding valuable information for a campaign depends on the skill of the focus group moderator. Focus groups are used in campaigns to test themes, messages, and political advertisements that are being evaluated for use in the campaign.

The Clinton campaign relied heavily on focus groups in its "Manhattan Project," which was designed to restore Clinton's poor image after the bruising 1992 primary. Clinton was seen as untrustworthy, as just a typical politician. The focus groups that the Clinton campaign used consisted of members of the white middle class. The campaign discovered from the focus groups that providing additional information about Clinton would enable the campaign to overcome his negative image. This convinced Clinton to talk about his childhood, his widowed mother, and his struggle to put himself through college. That led to one of the major themes of the successful 1996 Democratic National Convention and restored Clinton's ratings in the polls.

Focus groups were used by GOP pollster Frank Luntz when the Contract with America was being developed. Luntz was very interested in having the Contract attract Perot voters. The findings of focus groups persuaded the 1996 Dole presidential campaign not to attack Clinton in the presidential debates because of the adverse effect that such an attack might have on women voters. *See*: CONTRACT WITH AMERICA; POLL.

Reference: Michael W. Traugott and Paul J. Lavrakas, *The Voter's Guide to Election Polls* (Chatham, N.J.: Chatham House, 1996).

FOLEY, THOMAS S. (1929–   ) served as Speaker of the House of Representatives from 1989 until 1994. Foley was born in Spokane, Washington. He earned his B.A. degree in 1951, and his law degree in 1957 from the University of Washington. He served as a Washington legislative staffer, and he was elected to the House in 1964 by defeating a 22-year incumbent Republican. In the House, Foley favored liberal issues. He was elected majority leader in the House in 1987. Two years later he was elected Speaker after Jim Wright was forced to resign. As Speaker, Foley was respected for his fairness and integrity.

In 1994, Foley was defeated in the state of Washington's Fifth Congressional District by Republican George Nethercutt in a very close election. Foley was the first Speaker defeated since 1862 when Galusha Grow of Pennsylvania lost his seat.

FORD, GERALD R., JR. (1913–) was the thirty-eighth president of the United States. Ford was appointed vice-president by Richard Nixon, after Vice-President Spiro Agnew was forced to resign. As vice-president, Gerald Ford succeeded President Richard Nixon, who resigned in August 1974. Ford grew up in Grand Rapids, Michigan. He graduated from the University of Michigan in 1935, and earned his law degree from Yale. During World War II, Ford served as a gunnery officer on a light aircraft carrier, which was engaged in every major battle in the South Pacific.

In 1948, Ford ran for Congress, and defeated the incumbent to win the Fifth Congressional District in Michigan. In 1951 he was appointed to the House Appropriations Committee and was influential in the area of defense funding issues. He supported Harry Truman on foreign policy: Ford supported the Marshall Plan for Europe, the Point Four program to aid underdeveloped countries, and increased funding for the military. Ford did not support Truman on most domestic issues. Ford was an early supporter of Dwight D. Eisenhower for president, and was a close friend of Richard Nixon from their service in the House together.

In 1963, Ford was elevated to the position of chairman of the House Republican Conference. He served on the Warren Commission. In the 1960s Ford opposed most of the domestic programs promoted by President Lyndon Johnson. In 1965 he was elected minority leader of the Republicans in the House. He was a very strong supporter of President Richard Nixon's legislation.

In 1973, Spiro Agnew resigned as vice-president, and President Richard Nixon selected Gerald R. Ford to serve as his vice-president. Ford's appointment was very well received in Congress and in the nation. He offered a calm and deliberative temperament in a period of turmoil. Ford defended Nixon throughout the Watergate ordeal. When Nixon resigned in August 1974, Ford became president. In September 1974, Ford granted Nixon "a full, free and absolute pardon" for all of his Watergate wrongdoing.

As president, Ford was confronted with an economy beset with both inflation and unemployment. He was defeated in his bid to be elected president in 1976 by former Georgia governor Jimmy Carter. Ford retired in California. *See*: CARTER, JIMMY; ELECTIONS: 1976; NIXON, RICHARD MILHOUS.

Reference: Gerald Ford, *A Time to Heal* (New York: Harper and Row, 1979).

FOWLER, DONALD (1935–) served as chairperson of the Democratic National Committee with Senator Christopher Dodd, who served as party general chairperson. Donald Fowler was selected chair of the National Democratic Party in 1995, after the 1994 smashing defeat of the Democrats in the midterm election. Fowler was selected by President Clinton to lead the party as the Democratic Party prepared for his reelection. After the 1996 election, Fowler was a central figure in the investigations of federal campaign finance abuses.

Donald Fowler has a long history as a Democratic Party activist and leader.

He served for many years as a national committee member from the state of South Carolina. He had served as chairperson of the National Democratic Party's Fairness Commission, which was created after the 1984 Democratic National Convention. That commission redefined the rules for delegate selection to the 1988 Democratic National Convention. Fowler oversaw the day-to-day operation of the national party headquarters while Senator Dodd served as the party's general chairman and as the spokesperson for the party. President Ronald Reagan, like Bill Clinton, had also chosen to split the duties of his national party's chairperson. Reagan had Senator Paul Laxalt as the RNC's spokesperson. After Fowler and Dodd left their positions in 1996, President Clinton split the leadership of national chairman again in 1997 when he recruited Governor Roy Romer of Colorado to serve as general chairman, and Steve Grossman of Massachusetts to oversee the daily operations of the committee. *See*: DEMOCRATIC NATIONAL COMMITTEE; FAIRNESS COMMISSION; ROMER, ROY.

Reference: Paul Allen Beck, *Party Politics in America*, 8th ed. (New York: Longman, 1997).

FREE-SOIL PARTY. This party was organized in 1848 specifically to oppose the extension of slavery. The party nominated Martin Van Buren for president, and it adopted a platform opposed to the extension of slavery. Many of the Free-Soilers had been Democrats, but left the party because, in 1848, the Democratic Party was silent on the slavery issue. The motto of the Free-Soilers was: "Free Soil, Free Speech, Free Labor, and Free Men." The campaign of the Free-Soilers in 1848 garnered 291,263 votes. Van Buren received half of his votes in the state of New York, where the Democratic Party was torn by the slavery issue. The Whig presidential candidate, Zachary Taylor, carried the state of New York, which he needed to be elected president. The party elected fourteen House members and two Senators. The base of the Free-Soil Party was too narrow to enjoy a major victory, and the party declined; it was absorbed into the Republican party in 1854. *See*: ELECTIONS: 1848.

Reference: Eric Foner, *Free Soil, Free Labor, Free Men: The Ideology of the Republican Party before the Civil War* (New York: Oxford University Press, 1964).

FRÉMONT, JOHN CHARLES (1813–1890) surveyor and explorer, was given recognition as the "pathfinder" of the West; in 1850 was the first U.S. Senator from the new state of California; in 1856 was the first presidential nominee of the newly formed Republican Party; was a controversial Civil War general. Frémont was born out of wedlock in Savannah, Georgia on January 13, 1813, a son of a French émigré artist and schoolteacher named Frémon and Anne Beverly Whiting, who was the daughter of a prominent Virginia family, married to Major John Pryor of Richmond, 45 years her senior. After Frémon's death in 1818, the family moved to Charleston, South Carolina, where, under the patronage of several influential Charlestonians, Frémont's education and career were advanced. Expelled from Charleston College in 1831 for his continual absence from classes, the 20-year-old Frémont was, nonetheless, able to secure appointment as a tutor in mathematics aboard the navy warship *Natchez*, 1833–1835. Over the next several years, Frémont joined several surveying and exploratory expeditions, some private, most under federal government sponsorship, often with U.S. Army direction, the latter leading to Frémont's commission as a second lieutenant in the topographical corp in 1838. Returning to Washington, D.C. from the Nicollet exploration of Minnesota and the Dakotas in 1841, Frémont was to meet Jesse Benton, daughter of Senator Thomas Hart Benton of Missouri, Democratic floor leader of that chamber. Secretly marrying Jesse over her family's strong objections on October 19, 1841, Frémont was to acquire not only a wife who deeply loved him but a spouse who was ever anxious to promote his ambition and cause among her and (once reconciled with her family) her father's powerful friends and acquaintances in Missouri and the nation's capital. Jesse Frémont's appeals, while well-intentioned, were not always helpful to her husband and often exasperating for those whom she solicited, as when in 1862 Vice-President Hannibal Hamlin despairingly asked of her, "what can I do. . . ." In May of 1842, Frémont was to make the first of his five major exploratory expeditions through the West, ultimately to California, 1842–1854, including the ill-fated fourth expedition when eleven members of the Frémont party died in the snows of the Wagon-Wheel pass in the San Juan mountains of New Mexico Territory. Each of these expeditions gave Frémont national attention, out of which grew his reputation as "pathfinder of the West." Perhaps, however, none of the expeditions more so than the third (1845–1847), set Frémont on a course that would eventually lead him to the U.S. Senate as a Democrat and to a presidential nomination as a Republican. In California in 1846 at the beginning of the war with Mexico, Lieutenant Colonel Frémont, with a battalion under his command, occupied Los Angeles on August 13, 1846, ending, in effect, Mexican control of California. Appointed military governor of California on January 16, 1847, Frémont was to become a victim in the battle for jurisdiction in California between navy commodore Robert F. Stockton, who issued Frémont's appointment, and army general Stephen Watts Kearny who, arriving from Santa Fe and outranking Frémont, claimed the governorship for himself. Reluctant to accept Kearny's claim, which was soon officially authorized, Frémont was ordered by Kearny to return east, where, at Fort Leavenworth in August of 1847, Kearny had Frémont put under arrest and made subject to court-martial, charged with failure to obey a superior officer, conduct prejudicial to military order and discipline, and mutiny. The three-month-long trial, conducted in Washington, drew national attention and even as the panel of military judges found Frémont guilty, public sympathy overwhelmingly supported him. Sentenced on January 31, 1848 to dismissal from the army, six of the thirteen judges, noting the ambiguity of the California situation, recommended full presidential pardon for Frémont. Following lengthy deliberation by the cabinet, President Polk announced his decision endorsing the verdict (except for the mutiny charge). The president, however, set aside the recommended punishment: "Lieutenant Colonel Frémont will accordingly be released from arrest, will resume his sword, and report for duty." Frémont declined the offer to return to duty, instead resigning his army commission. Returning to California, Frémont was to acquire "Los Mariposas," a ranch upon which gold was to be discovered and by which Frémont became a wealthy man; a fortune which, over the next four decades of his life, would melt away under absentee management and eventual loss of "Los Mariposas," and the burden of Frémont's failed business and railroad ventures in the post–Civil War period. With his return to California in 1849, and with his newly found wealth, Frémont was to make his longest foray into the world of politics. Elected in 1850 by the new state's legislature to a seat in the U.S. Senate, Frémont, a Democrat, having by lot drawn the short term, was defeated for reelection in 1851, largely on the basis of his strongly expressed, anti-slavery views. Frémont was to prove but five years later, however, to be just the kind of national candidate for which the newly formed Republican Party was looking: young, age 43, and energetic, with a reputation as a charismatic explorer and soldier, "free-of-politics," but with pronounced anti-slavery views. Accepting identification with the party, Frémont became, on the first ballot, the presidential choice of delegates at the Philadelphia convention in June 1856. Rounding out the national ticket, delegates selected as vice-presidential nominee former senator William L. Dayton of New Jersey, preferring Dayton to the candidacy of the less well-known Abraham Lincoln of Illinois. The election-day choices of 1856 were clear: the anti-slavery ticket of Frémont and Dayton, the Democratic status-quo ticket of James Buchanan of Pennsylvania and John C. Breckinridge of Kentucky or, a "wasted vote" to be given to the "Know-Nothings," the American Party nominees, former president Millard Fillmore and his running mate, Andrew Jackson Donelson of Tennessee. Not yet accepting the inevitability of civil war, voters preferred the known Democrats to the unknown Republicans or the know-nothing American Party ticket. Buchanan secured a popular vote plurality of nearly 500,000 votes over Frémont-Dayton who gathered, in a highly respectable first showing for the Republican Party, a total of 1,340,000 popular votes. In the Electoral College count, Democrats carried 19 states with 174 ballots to 11 states and 114 votes for the Republicans. The "Know-Nothings," while polling nearly 900,000 popular votes, carried only the state of Maryland with its 8 votes in the Electoral College. Four years later, with the Republican presidential victory of 1860, Lincoln now in the White House, and hostilities commenced between Union and Confederacy, Frémont resumed his military career, appointed as commander of the multi-state Department of the West with headquarters in St. Louis, and with rank of major general. The command was both politically and militarily sensitive as President Lincoln attempted to keep Missouri and Kentucky, both states with strong Confederate leanings, within the Union. Frémont proved rather more adept at military operations than political ones. Without securing Lincoln's approval, the major general issued, on August 30, 1861, an emancipation order that would free within his jurisdiction all slaves determined to be held by known Confederate sympathizers. Ignoring the president's "suggestion" that the language of the order be modified, Lincoln was forced to countermand the emancipation decree. Relieved of his post in St. Louis later in the fall of 1861, Frémont was reassigned in March of 1862 to command of the Mountain Department headquartered in Wheeling. Here, just the opposite of his last appointment, Frémont proved rather more adept at political operations than military ones; Union forces, superior in number, were out-maneuvered in the Shenadoah Valley by the troops of Confederate cavalry officer Stonewall Jackson. Again Lincoln moved, this time consolidating commands and making Frémont, much to his displeasure, subordinate to General John Pope. Frémont, disgruntled, requested to be relieved of his new assignment; Lincoln complied. As a result of the continuing friction between the two men, Frémont accepted, in May of 1864, the presidential nomination of a group of insurgent Republican radicals meeting in convention in Cleveland. The convention's adopted platform called for the immediate constitutional prohibition of slavery, successful prosecution of the war, and, with the war's end, congressionally mandated reconstruction of the South. By fall, however, fearing that his candidacy would only lead to the election of Democrat General George B. McClellan as president, Frémont, on September 22, aborted his presidential bid and, while having nothing of favor to say of the president, suggested that Lincoln, notwithstanding, was clearly the lesser of the two evils. The postwar years proved exceptionally difficult ones for Frémont, having lost his fortune in speculative business and railroad ventures, he and Jesse were driven to actual poverty. In 1878 he accepted appointment by President Hayes as governor of Arizona Territory. In retirement after 1883, Frémont wrote his *Memoirs*, published in 1887; he and Jesse subsequently took up residence in Los Angeles. Returning to New York City to settle certain business matters in 1889, Frémont died (Jesse having remained in California) in the sparse room of a Manhattan boarding house on July 13, 1890, just three months after Congress had voted to restore his military rank and award him a pension. *See*: ELECTIONS: 1856.

References: Allan Nevins, *Frémont, Pathmarker of the West*, rev. ed. (New York: Longman, Green, 1955); R. J. Bartlett, *John C. Frémont and the Republican Party* (Columbus: Ohio State University Press, 1930).

FRONT-LOADED PRIMARY. In 1988 the Southern states, in an effort to influence the Democratic presidential nomination, created Super Tuesday by moving their primaries to the same date in early March. In 1996 many other states moved their primaries into March, including California, New York, and Ohio. By the end of March 1996, two-thirds of the delegates had been selected with this new primary schedule. The states moved their primaries to the beginning of the primary calendar to gain the attention of the candidates and influence the selection of the respective parties' nominees. Early money became very important in this front-loaded primary system for the candidates.

In the 1996 presidential primaries the incumbent Democratic president, Bill Clinton, ran unopposed. That left only the Republicans to test out this new front-loaded presidential primary calendar. The Republicans were very unhappy with this compressed calendar, and RNC chairman Haley Barbour appointed a committee to study the possibility of reforming the system. The committee found that voters had insufficient time to evaluate the candidates between the primaries, and that turnout was dampened in the later primaries with this front-loaded schedule. As a result, the Republicans offered bonus delegates to the states that move their primaries back to the spring for the nomination contest in the year 2000. *See*: BARBOUR, HALEY; DELEGATE APPORTIONMENT; SUPER TUESDAY.

References: Paul Allen Beck, *Party Politics in America*, 8th ed. (New York: Longman, 1997); Harold W. Stanley, "The Nominations: Republican Doldrums, and Democratic Revival," in *The Elections of 1996*, Michael Nelson, ed. (Washington, D.C.: Congressional Quarterly Press, 1997).

FUSION TICKET exists when the name of a candidate is offered by more than one party. Fusion tickets are permitted in Arkansas, Connecticut, Delaware, Idaho, Mississippi, New York, South Carolina, South Dakota, Utah, and Vermont. The Liberal and Conservative parties of New York often play a significant role in determining the outcome of an election when they cross-endorse. Many states do not permit cross-filing and the Supreme Court recently upheld the right of the state to decide this issue in *Timmons* v. *Ramsey* (1997). The term "fusion" is used in New York City politics to describe the joining together of reform groups behind one candidate. There was a Fusion party in New York City in the 1940s that supported reform mayor Fiorello La Guardia, who was elected three times. *See*: CONSERVATIVE PARTY OF NEW YORK; CROSS-ENDORSEMENT; CROSS-FILING; LIBERAL PARTY OF NEW YORK; *TIMMONS* v. *RAMSEY* (1997).

G

GARFIELD, JAMES A. (1831–1881) was born on a northeastern Ohio farm on November 19, 1831, and died a half century later on September 19, 1881, as a result of an assassin's bullets fired at the president on July 2 of that year. Born into rural poverty, raised by a widowed mother, Garfield worked his way through various schools, ultimately graduating in 1856 from Williams College in Massachusetts, having first attended what is now Hiram College in Ohio. Garfield returned to the Ohio school, at age 25, as principal of its small faculty. In 1859, on the eve of the Civil War, Garfield was elected to the Ohio Senate. With the outbreak of hostilities in 1861, he organized and with rank of lieutenant colonel took command of a regiment of Ohio volunteers. Following engagement in the battles of Middle Creek, Shiloh, and Chickamauga, Garfield resigned his commission as major general in December of 1863 to take a seat in the U.S. House of Representatives, to which Ohio voters had elected him more than a year earlier. Garfield, a skilled orator and rising parliamentarian, a supporter of the radical Republican position on reconstruction, quickly joined his party's leadership ranks within the House. As such he was instrumental, as a member of the Election Commission, in negotiating the compromise that resolved the disputed presidential election of 1876, whereby Republicans were able to maintain control of the presidency while committing themselves to a termination of military occupation in the South. During the Hayes administration, 1877–1881, while Democrats held a House majority, Garfield served his party as its minority leader. In 1880 the Ohio legislature elected Garfield to the U.S. Senate, a seat which he was never to occupy because of his election to the presidency. Garfield, and Chester A. Arthur of New York, became the respective presidential and vice-presidential nominees of the Republican Party after the convention of 1880 deadlocked between its competing factions: "stalwarts" who urged delegates to give a third nomination to former president Grant, and "half breeds" who promoted the candidacy of Senator James G. Blaine of Maine. With Republicans again waving the "bloody shirt," the fall campaign, while resulting in a comfortable Electoral College majority, produced a razor-thin popular vote plurality for Garfield and Arthur. In the first days of his administration Garfield's decisions as to the making of appointments, and in the distribution of patronage, angered the "stalwart" faction, particularly its leader Senator Roscoe Conkling of New York. Both New York senators, Conkling and Thomas C. Platt, resigned their seats in protest (both were astonished when the New York legislature subsequently declined to reappoint them as they had readily anticipated). Amidst these heated intraparty disputes which were much attended by the press, Garfield, about to board a train in Washington, D.C., was shot by a disgruntled and mentally deranged "stalwart" office seeker on July 2, 1881. Lingering for some two months, Garfield died on September 19, 1881, from infection caused by surgical attempts to remove the assassin's bullets. Perhaps the greatest legacy of Garfield's brief, six-month administration was passage, two years following his death, of the civil service reform measure, the Pendleton Act of 1883. *See*: ELECTIONS: 1880.

References: Justus D. Doenecke, *The Presidencies of James A. Garfield and Chester A. Arthur* (Lawrence: University Press of Kansas, 1981); Allan Peskin, *Garfield: A Biography* (Kent: Kent State University Press, 1978).

GENDER GAP. In current usage this refers to the persistent difference in political preferences between men and women over political candidates, parties, and issues. In the early 1996 polls, Clinton had much greater support from women than he did from men. In a September 1996 *New York Times/CBS NEWS Poll*, white married women supported Clinton over Dole 49% to 39%. White men preferred Dole over Clinton 49% to 33%. Forty-three percent of women identified as Democrats, and 28% of women favored the Republicans. While 36% of men favored the Republican Party, 30% of men identified themselves as Democrats. Women also differed from men on level of support for affirmative action. A majority of women favored continuing it, while a majority of men wanted it abolished. Women were more supportive than men on the question of whether the government should do more to solve problems, but neither gender cohort favored the government doing more.

The exit polls from the November 1996 general election showed that 54% of women voted for Clinton and 38% voted for Dole; 44% of men voted for Dole; and 43% of men voted for Clinton. The gender gap has widened from previous presidential elections, which was first noticed in the election of 1980. It is also worth noting that women were 52% of the electorate in 1996.

The Republican Party was uncertain how to address the gender gap in the presidential election of 1996. The Democrats took full advantage of it. The gender gap cut across all class lines. Bill Clinton portrayed himself as the candidate of compassion. He scored high on caring about people. These are characteristics that rank high with women. Clinton gave attention to breast cancer and frequently referred to the Family and Medical Leave Act, which he had proposed and the Republicans voted against. Haley Barbour, when he left the chairmanship of the Republican National Committee, warned the Republicans that they needed to address this growing gender problem for the Republican Party.

Polling data after the 1996 general election indicates that little has changed: Men between the ages of 35 and 59 favor a Republican candidate for Congress by a margin of 51% to 33%. Women in the same age group favor a Democratic candidate for Congress 53% to 33%. Women favor government action for education, health care, and the environment.

References: Carey Goldberg, "Soccer Moms Step Onto the Political Playing Field," *New York Times*, October 6, 1996; Gerald F. Sieb, "Failure to Close the Gender Gap Continues to Puzzle Republicans," *Wall Street Journal*, November 7, 1996; "Women and the Vote," *Party Developments*, Vol. 3 (November 1997).

GENERAL ELECTION is an election held to select from among the candidates that were nominated in a primary. This is the end of a long process for candidates seeking office. The winner of this election will take the office. The general election is always held on the first Monday after the first Tuesday in November. Presidential elections and congressional elections are held in even years. General elections are conducted by states and governed by state statutes. Many local governments hold their elections in the odd years to avoid the partisan influence of the national election, and to insure that their local officials are selected based on their credentials and programs. *See*: ELECTION DAY; PRIMARY, RUNOFF.

GEPHARDT, RICHARD (1941–) serves as minority leader in the U.S. House of Representatives. Richard Gephardt was born in St. Louis, Missouri. His father was a milk truck driver. Gephardt graduated from Northwestern University in 1962, and earned his law degree from the University of Missouri in 1965.

After law school, Gephardt went to work for a large St. Louis law firm. He had a strong interest in politics, and in 1971 was elected St. Louis City Alderman. In 1976 congresswoman Leonor Sullivan announced she would not seek reelection. Richard Gephardt sought the seat she vacated, and was elected. As a freshman, Gephardt was able to gain a seat on the influential House Ways and Means Committee.

Early in his career, Gephardt was moderate in his positions. He was pro-life, supported Reagan's early tax cuts, and was one of the founders of the moderate Democratic Leadership Council. In 1988, Gephardt ran for the Democratic nomination for president. He moved to the political left, reversing his position on abortion and on other issues. Gephardt won the Iowa caucus in 1988, but lost to Michael Dukakis in New Hampshire, and lost in every state except Missouri on Super Tuesday. He withdrew from the presidential race, and did not seek his party's nomination in 1988.

Gephardt did advance his political fortunes in the House. In 1989, Speaker Jim Wright and Democratic Whip Tony Coelho resigned. Tom Foley was elected Speaker, and Richard Gephardt was elected majority leader, defeating Ed Jenkins by a vote of 181 to 76. As a leader of the House Democrats, Gephardt gave strong support to the first-term Clinton administration. Gephardt opposed NAFTA, supported GATT, and was a strong promoter of the Clinton health reform plan.

In the 1994 election, the Democrats suffered a stunning defeat. They lost 52 seats, the majority, and Speaker Tom Foley was defeated in his district. Richard Gephardt sought the position of minority leader and he was elected 150 to 58, defeating Charlie Rose of North Carolina. In June 1996, Gephardt and Senate Minority Leader Tom Daschle promoted a "Families First" agenda as an alternative to the Republicans' "Contract with America." Clinton gave little support to the House Democrats in the 1996 election, and despite Gingrich's unpopularity and the $35 million spent by organized labor, the Democrats were not able to regain the majority and give Gephardt the Speaker's gavel.

In 1997, Gephardt tried to distance himself from Clinton, and especially Vice-President Albert Gore. It appears that Gephardt will challenge Gore for the nomination in 2000. At the 1997 AFL-CIO National Convention, Gephardt, who spoke after Gore, denounced NAFTA, in an effort to point out Gore's lack of support for labor's issues.

Gephardt has not been able to take his Third District in Missouri for granted. He won his last two elections with less than 60% of the vote. In 1996 he spent over $3 million to hold his seat.

GERRYMANDERING is the drawing of legislative district boundaries to secure the advantage for one particular party. Gerrymandering ignores the redistricting principles of compactness and natural boundaries to gain partisan political advantage. For example, congressional district boundaries are drawn by state legislatures after the census. If the state government has one-party control, then that party will frequently draw the boundaries to benefit the majority party. The political party drawing the boundaries will concentrate the opposition party's support in a few districts, and spread its own support among many districts. The goal is to waste the votes of opponents by packing the opposition's voters into one district, and spread the favored party's vote to create comfortable but not wasteful majorities for the party in favor.

Gerrymandering may be done to achieve goals other than partisan advantage. In 1990, after the census, the state of North Carolina drew a ribbon-like district to create a majority-minority district. In *Shaw* v. *Reno* (1993), the U.S. Supreme Court ruled that racial gerrymandering was unconstitutional. This decision created a need to redraw a number of congressional districts in southern states. In *Wesberry* v. *Sanders* (1964), the Supreme Court ruled that congressional districts had to be equal in population size. Many states had favored rural areas in congressional redistricting. Today, the most pervasive manipulation of district lines is to protect incumbents regardless of party.

The term, "gerrymandering," arose in 1811 when Governor Eldridge Gerry signed a bill creating a district that resembled a salamander, hence the word gerrymander. *See*: COMPACTNESS; *DAVIS* v. *BANDEMER* (1986); REAPPORTIONMENT; REDISTRICTING; *SHAW* v. *RENO* (1993); *WESBERRY* v. *SANDERS* (1964).

References: David Butler and Bruce Cain, *Congressional Redistricting: Comparative and Theoretical Perspectives* (New York: Macmillan, 1992); Alan Rosenthal, *The Decline of Representative Democracy: Process, Participation and Power in State Legislatures* (Washington, D.C.: Congressional Quarterly Press, 1998).

GINGRICH, NEWT(ON) (1943–) became Speaker of the House in 1995. Newt Gingrich was born in Harrisburg, Pennsylvania on June 17, 1943 to Kathleen (Daugherty) McPherson. He was adopted by his mother's second husband Robert Gingrich, who was a career army officer. The family moved frequently. Newt graduated from Emory University in Atlanta in 1965. He earned a Ph.D. in History in 1971.

In 1970, Newt Gingrich joined the faculty of West Georgia College in Carrollton, Georgia. In 1974 he ran for Congress in the Sixth Congressional District. He challenged the Democratic incumbent Jack Flynt and lost by 2,800 votes. Gingrich ran again in 1976. The presidential candidacy of Georgia native Jimmy Carter helped Flynt stave off Gingrich's second challenge. In 1978, Flynt did not seek reelection, and Gingrich defeated Democrat Virginia Shepard by over 7,000 votes. At that time, he was Georgia's only Republican congressman. In 1990 and 1992, Gingrich was reelected by less than 1,000 votes. In 1996, he was reelected with a comfortable 58% of the vote, after spending a record $5.5 million.

As a congressman, Newt Gingrich advocated challenging, rather than accommodating, the Democratic agenda. He organized younger, like-minded GOP congressmen into the Conservative Opportunity Society. In 1987, Gingrich brought forward ethics charges against Speaker Jim Wright, who was forced to resign in 1989. In 1989, Gingrich challenged Edward Madigan, the candidate favored by Minority Leader Robert Michael, for minority whip. Gingrich won by a vote of 87 to 85. In October 1993, Michael announced he would step down, and Gingrich assumed the leadership of the 1994 Republican House campaign. He promoted the "Contract with America," a platform of ten ideas to which almost all of the GOP House candidates pledged their support. In his first two years, President Clinton led the Democrats into a debacle with his health care plan. Under the leadership of Newt Gingrich, who became Speaker, the Republicans took full advantage of the opportunity and gained 52 seats, capturing a majority in the House for the first time in 40 years. In the 1996 election, the GOP lost nine seats, but retained their majority in the House.

Newt Gingrich is a paradoxical figure for the Republicans. Without his vision and energy the Republicans would not have gained their majorities in Congress. On the other hand, Gingrich's style and leadership is not well received by the American people. He has a very high negative rating in public opinion polls. Republican concerns about their future under Newt Gingrich's continued leadership led to a failed plot against him in the summer of 1997. A few days after the Republicans lost five seats in the 1998 election, Gingrich announced his resignation as Speaker and as a member of the House. *See*: ARMEY, RICHARD K.

Reference: Newt Gingrich, *Lessons Learned the Hard Way* (New York: HarperCollins, 1998).

GOLDWATER, BARRY M. (1909–1998) was a U.S. Senator from Arizona, and the defeated Republican presidential candidate in 1964. He was born in Phoenix, Arizona. In 1928 he graduated from the Stauton Military Academy in Virginia. He dropped out of the University of Arizona after one year to work in his family's department store. He was active in the National Guard and flew non-combat missions in the U.S. Army Air Force during World War II.

In 1952, Goldwater was elected to the U.S. Senate. As a senator, and as the GOP presidential candidate, he was known as ''Mr. Conservative.'' In 1960 his book, *The Conscience of a Conservative*, was published. In it, he criticized big government and promoted states' rights. The book sold more than four million copies and propelled Goldwater into the national spotlight. It also generated a Draft Goldwater Committee for the 1964 GOP presidential nomination, which led to a conservative takeover of the Republican Party. At the National Republican Convention in San Francisco, he was nominated over the more moderate Republican New York governor Nelson Rockefeller. Goldwater said in his acceptance speech: ''extremism in the defense of liberty is no vice.'' The Democrats cast him as an extremist, and he was defeated in a Democratic landslide by incumbent Lyndon B. Johnson. Goldwater carried only six states, most of them in the deep South. Goldwater returned to the Senate in 1968 and retired in 1987. *See*: ELECTIONS: 1964; JOHNSON, LYNDON BAINES; ROCKEFELLER, NELSON A.

Reference: Barry Goldwater, *The Conscience of a Conservative* (Shephardsville, Ky.: Victor, 1960).

***GOMILLION* v. *LIGHTFOOT*,** 364 U.S. 339 (1960). The only issue in this case was whether a court was competent to entertain a challenge under the Fifteenth Amendment to a state's redrawing of its municipal boundaries. The Alabama legislature had changed the boundaries of the city of Tuskegee in such a way as to exclude virtually all African Americans from the city. The question before the Supreme Court was whether the District Court had erred when it dismissed a case brought by several African Americans claiming that the state of Alabama had denied them the right to vote in Tuskegee municipal elections based on their race.

Justice Felix Frankfurter, who fourteen years earlier had written the opinion in *Colegrove* v. *Green* (1946) which foreclosed for a time the review of legislative apportionments, argued that, in this case, Alabama's actions were too blatantly discriminatory to be ignored by a court. Therefore, the District Court was ordered to hear the case and to decide whether or not the state had violated the Fifteenth Amendment. Ironically, some recent cases involving the constitutionality of racial-gerrymandered majority-minority voting districts have relied on Gomillion as a precedent. *See: COLEGROVE* v. *GREEN* (1946); GERRYMANDERING; POLITICAL QUESTIONS DOCTRINE.

Reference: Bernard Taper, *Gomillion versus Lightfoot* (New York: McGraw-Hill, 1962).

GOP is an acronym for Grand Old Party. It is a nickname for the Republican Party. It is derived from the Grand Army of the Republic, an organization of Civil War veterans from the Union side which worked to aid veterans and their families. This organization of veterans was closely affiliated with the Republican Party, hence the party became identified as the Grand Old Party. The term "GOP" was first used at the national level in the election of 1880. *See*: REPUBLICAN PARTY.

Reference: Eugene H. Roseboom, *A History of Presidential Elections* (New York: Macmillan, 1957).

GOPAC is a political action committee developed by Delaware governor Pierre S.(Pete) duPont IV and nineteen other Republican governors in 1978 to recruit, develop, and support the election of Republican candidates. The goal was to build a Republican "farm team" at the state and local levels and build the future national candidates for the Republican Party. GOPAC focused on training Republican candidates in campaign techniques. In 1986, GOPAC was chaired by Newt Gingrich, and his dynamic leadership of GOPAC contributed to the election of the Republican congressional majority in 1994. Nearly one-half of the elected Republican freshmen in 1994 had received training and assistance from GOPAC. GOPAC was entangled in the 1997 ethics problems of House Speaker Newt Gingrich, for which he was reprimanded and fined $300,000. *See*: GINGRICH, NEWT(ON); POLITICAL ACTION COMMITTEE.

Reference: Paul S. Herrnson, *Congressional Elections: Campaigning at Home and in Washington*, 2nd ed. (Washington, D.C.: Congressional Quarterly Press, 1998).

GORE, ALBERT A., JR. (AL) (1948–   ) was elected vice-president of the United States in 1992. He was elected on the Democratic ticket with William Clinton.

Albert Gore Jr. was born in Washington, D.C., where his father served as a member of the House of Representatives from Tennessee. In 1969, Gore graduated from Harvard College with a degree in government. In 1970, he was drafted into the U.S. Army for service in Vietnam. In Vietnam, Gore served as an army reporter. He sent some of his writings to the Nashville *Tennessean*, which offered him a job in 1971, after he finished his tour of duty. In addition to his work as a newspaper reporter, Gore became a home builder, and a livestock and tobacco farmer. Unsure of his career goals, Gore studied religion and law at Vanderbilt University. His career goals became focused in 1976, when Democratic Representative Joe. L. Evins announced he would not seek reelection. Gore immediately announced he would run for that House seat. Gore had a battle in the primary. He defeated Democrat Stanley Rogers, the majority leader in the Tennessee House of Representatives, by only 3,559 votes. After that primary battle, Gore was never seriously challenged for his House seat. In the House, Gore focused on environmental issues. He was the architect of the ''Superfund'' bill designed to clean up toxic sites.

In 1983, Tennessee U.S. Senator and majority leader Howard H. Baker announced he would not seek reelection. Gore announced that he would run for Baker's seat. The Republicans squabbled over their nominee, and Gore won easily with a two-to-one margin. Gore took a moderate position in the Senate, focusing on nuclear weapons policies and disarmament issues.

In 1988, Gore sought the Democratic nomination for president. Gore had success on Super Tuesday, winning five southern primaries. In 1992, Gore announced he would not seek the Democratic presidential nomination. Democratic presidential nominee Bill Clinton surprised many by selecting Gore as his running mate in July of 1992. It was a surprise because Gore, like Clinton, was from the South and they were the same age. Gore did add to the ticket. Unlike Clinton, Gore served in Vietnam. Gore was identified with environmental issues; his book *Earth in the Balance: Ecology and the Human Spirit* was published in 1992. Also, Gore had served in Congress, which Clinton had not. Gore's selection was well received and he boosted the fortunes of the winning ticket. Gore played a significant role in the administration. He headed up the reinventing government study for the administration in 1993. Albert Gore is expected to seek, and is favored to be, the Democratic presidential nominee in 2000. *See*: CLINTON, WILLIAM JEFFERSON (BILL); ELECTIONS: 1992, 1996.

Reference: Betty M. Burford, *Al Gore: United States Vice-President* (Springfield, Ill.: Enslow, 1994).

GOTV is an acronym for Get-out-the-vote. As a result of the low turnout of voters in the United States, the party and candidate that successfully gets its potential voters to the polls enhances its opportunity to win an election. GOTV drives concentrate on those voters that are most likely to vote for your candidate. Getting out the vote involves many types of activities. The most common, and the one frequently invested in by candidates and parties, is a phone bank. Phone banks are used to identify supporters, and then to continue to call those identified supporters to make sure they vote. Phone banks are usually centralized in an office and staffed by both paid workers and volunteers. A voter registration program, door-to-door canvassing, and direct mail are also common GOTV activities.

Another GOTV activity is an absentee ballot application mail program. The party or the candidate frequently mails absentee ballot application forms and instructions to all previous absentee voters or to all registered voters. These GOTV activities are often funded by soft money, and in presidential campaigns, these activities are targeted for particular states where the election is close. *See*: SOFT MONEY.

References: Daniel M. Shea, *Campaign Craft: The Strategies, Tactics, and Art of Political Campaign Management* (Westport, Conn.: Praeger 1996); Dick Simpson, *Winning Elections: A Handbook of Modern Participatory Politics* (New York: HarperCollins, 1996).

GRANT, ULYSSES S. (1822–1885), the most successful Union army general of the Civil War (1861–1865), a failed Republican president of the Reconstruction period (1869–1877), Grant was born at Point Pleasant, Ohio on April 27, 1822. Educated at the U.S. Military Academy at West Point, Grant graduated in 1843 with the rank of second lieutenant. Assigned to the command of General Zachary Taylor, first in Louisiana, then in Texas, Grant was, under General Winfield Scott, to see combat in the most important battles of the war with Mexico (1846–1848), including those of Verracruz, Cerro Gorde and the assault on Chapultepec fortress in Mexico City in 1847. Following the war's end, promoted to first lieutenant, Grant was to serve in Oregon and later at Fort Humboldt in California. There in 1854, Grant resigned his commission and returned to his wife and children then living in Missouri. The next several years were difficult ones for Grant, moving his family to Galena, Illinois in 1860, he became at age 38 a clerk in his father's store, trading in hides and selling harnesses and other leather goods. With the outbreak of the Civil War, Grant joined, with rank of colonel, the volunteer infantry regiment that was the 21st Illinois. Promoted to brigadier general in August of 1861, Grant was to command union troops in Tennessee and Mississippi through the years 1862–1863. Securing the North's first significant victory, the capture of Fort Donelson on the Cumberland River on February 16, 1862, Grant gained the attention both of the Lincoln administration in Washington and of the public throughout the North. With the siege and capture, on July 4, 1863, of Vicksburg on the Mississippi River, Grant accomplished a major Union objective, separating the western Confederate states from the heart of the Confederacy to the east. Brought to Washington by President Lincoln in March of 1864, promoted to lieutenant general and made chief of the army, Grant was to wage the casualty-heavy war of attrition in 1864–

1865, which would ultimately lead, to Lee's surrender at Appomattox Court House on April 9, 1865. Having made a tour of the occupied South, and initially committed to President Andrew Johnson's intended policy of moderate Reconstruction, Grant in 1867 was to serve briefly as secretary of war. Caught as something of a pawn in the struggle between President Johnson and congressional radical Republicans, Grant calculated, correctly, the likely dominance of the latter over the former; the General became a hard-liner, a supporter of radical Republican plans for an extended military Reconstruction in the South directed not by presidential but by congressional policy determinations. As the Union's greatest war hero, Grant found himself attractive to a Republican Party looking for a successor to the martyred Lincoln, a replacement for the "accidental" Johnson. Receiving the party's presidential nomination by a unanimous first ballot vote of delegates at the Chicago convention in May of 1868, Grant was joined on the national ticket by the Speaker of the House, Congressman Schuyler Colfax of Indiana. Grant and Colfax were to secure a solid election-day victory, carrying 26 of the 34 states with 214 votes in the Electoral College. The Democratic ticket of former governor Horatio Seymour of New York and Francis P. Blair Jr., of Missouri received but 80 Electoral College ballots from 8 states. Four years later, Grant, renominated, and with a new vice-presidential running mate, U.S. Senator Henry Wilson of Massachusetts, improved moderately over the Republican election-day performance of 1868, achieving a popular vote plurality of more than 750,000 votes over the joined Democratic and Liberal Republican ticket of New York City newspaperman Horace Greeley and Missouri governor B. Gratz Brown. The Republican ticket carried 29 states with 286 Electoral College ballots to but 6 states and 66 votes in the Electoral College for the Democrats. Grant's two terms in the White House were to be dominated by Reconstruction policy and by virtually unending scandal. As to the former, having learned his lesson in politics from the example of Andrew Johnson, Grant gave way, entirely and willingly, to congressional initiative. Congress could make policy, the executive branch would see to its implementation. If radical Republicans should lose their ardor for a severe Reconstruction, or should they lose their congressional majorities, then the president-general would reconnoiter and make the appropriate adjustments. Personally honest but naive, Grant, in seeing to the implementation of the law, did not recognize the possibilities for corruption in an expanding postwar economy, one in which the federal government maintained military occupation through a vast region of the country. The scandals came, one upon the other: Crédit Mobilier, the Whiskey Ring, the Belknap Affair. Grant, shaken, acknowledged in his final State-of-the-Union message to Congress in 1876, his personal responsibility for leadership failures which were, as he put it, "errors of judgment, not of intent." Leaving office in March of 1877, Grant and his wife Julia were to make a world tour from May of 1877 to December of 1879. Relying heavily upon his personal popularity, hoping that the actual record of his presidency would not be resurrected, Grant looked to a third Republican presidential nomination in 1880. Only after the

Chicago convention found itself hopelessly deadlocked, ballot after ballot, between Grant's "stalwart" forces and James G. Blaine's "half-breeds," did Grant supporters concede to the dark horse nomination of compromise candidate James A. Garfield of Ohio. With the failure of the "stalwarts," Grant now retired from active politics and to his home in New York City. Made all but destitute in the spring of 1884 by the failure of a brokerage firm in which he was a partner, a bankrupt Grant turned to writing as a means of support. His plight became all the more desperate in that year as his health suddenly collapsed. Diagnosed early in 1885 as suffering from "the disease of epithelioma," cancer of the throat, Grant worked doggedly on the completion of his memoirs, the second volume of which he concluded but four days before his death on July 23, 1885, at Mount McGregor, New York. Posthumous publication of the *Personal Memoirs of U.S. Grant*, covering not his presidential but only his army years, proved both a commercial and critical success. The *Memoirs* continue to be read today, appreciated for their literary quality both as military history and biography. *See*: ELECTIONS: 1868; 1872.

References: Ulysses S. Grant, *Memoirs and Selected Letters* (New York: Library of America, 1990); William S. McFeely, *Grant, A Biography* (New York: Norton, 1981).

GRASSROOTS is a type of campaign activity that is organized and focused at the local level, and is almost always conducted by volunteers. A formal campaign will attempt to build a grassroots organization by using geographic units, usually political subdivisions and precincts. Volunteers will be recruited for every unit and the volunteers are to campaign for the candidate in their neighborhoods and among their family and friends. A grassroots campaign is organized hierarchically and the leaders are to recruit, communicate with, and coordinate the volunteers they supervise. Volunteers are often provided with voter lists and campaign materials. Prior to the advent of electronic media, this was the principal means for a party or a candidate to deliver their message to the voters, but it has fallen into disuse with the emphasis on electronic media in the modern campaign.

A grassroots campaign by a candidate means that the candidate intends to go out and meet the voters. A grassroots movement is one that has emerged up-from-the-people.

Reference: William Safire, *Safire's New Political Dictionary* (New York: Random House, 1993).

***GRAY* v. *SANDERS*,** 372 U.S. 368 (1963) is a U.S. Supreme Court decision in which the principle "one person, one vote" was first announced. The case involved a challenge to the Georgia Democratic Party's use of what was called "county unit voting" during primary elections. Under the system of county unit voting, the popular vote in an individual county was translated into a single set of county votes. The county vote was then tabulated to determine the primary election victor.

The Court first determined that the Georgia legislature had so carefully regulated party primaries that the electoral procedures were essentially the result of state action. This is an important conclusion, because private organizations do not have to live up to the demands of the Equal Protection Clause. After answering this threshold question, the Court could then move to the substantive issue of county unit voting. The problem with the county voting system was that the actual votes allocated to each county were not proportional to that county's population. The result was that the votes of those individuals dwelling in populous (and mainly urban) counties were "diluted" relative to voters in counties with smaller populations. The Supreme Court dismissed Georgia's argument that its county voting system mirrored the Electoral College and, furthermore, that the votes of Georgians were no more malapportioned than votes for U.S. Senators. The Court ruled instead that the system denied some residents of the state of Georgia equal protection of the law, in violation of the Fourteenth Amendment to the Constitution. *See*: COUNTY UNIT VOTING; *REYNOLDS* v. *SIMS* (1964); *WESBERRY* v. *SANDERS* (1964).

GREELEY, HORACE (1811–1872), journalist and editor; advocate of numerous, sometimes contradictory, causes; a true American eccentric; Greeley was born in Amherst, New Hampshire on February 3, 1811. Of a desperately poor family, apprenticed at age fifteen to a rural newspaperman in East Poultney, Vermont, the precocious Greeley at this early age committed himself to a career in journalism, rising to be (within a decade of the founding of the *New York Tribune* in 1841) the most influential newspaperman of his generation. Drawn to support of the Whig Party because of its advocacy of high protective tariffs, a policy to which the often otherwise erratic Greeley would consistently hold, his early political associations were with Thurlow Weed and William Seward, both men eventually becoming political enemies. Denied a seat by Weed in the New York delegation to the 1860 Republican convention, a party which he had helped to organize in the 1850s, Greeley maneuvered himself into the Oregon delegation, taking considerable satisfaction in the convention's rejection of Seward's presidential bid. Eventually turning to Lincoln, Greeley was to have an uneasy relationship with Lincoln, both as candidate and as president. An ardent opponent of slavery, Greeley at first favored allowing the Southern states to secede, free to go their separate way. Once war came, the editor became a frequent critic of Lincoln for, as Greeley saw it, the president's procrastination in proclaiming emancipation and in his failure to pursue a negotiated peace. In an effort to mitigate Greeley's criticism on the latter score, Lincoln permitted the editor in 1864 to meet in Canada with Confederate representatives presumed to have authority to open the way to negotiation of a peace settlement. Such authority did not exist and Greeley returned deeply disappointed, but only slightly less critical of Lincoln, whose reelection candidacy he waited until September to reluctantly endorse. With Lee's surrender at Appomattox in April of 1865, Greeley became an advocate of a general amnesty to be extended to all those who had taken up the Confederate cause; he, himself, in 1867 signed bail bond for the captured Jefferson Davis. In addition to his advocacy of national reconciliation, Greeley's causes, both before and after the Civil War, were legion: the right of workers to unionize; women's rights; temperance; "impartial suffrage" extended to the poor, and once freed, to the blackman; homestead opportunity, and yet more. On a more personal level, he became fascinated with Fourierism, supporting in the United States some several experiments in cooperative and communal living, including that in Colorado to which his name became attached. Whether in the political arena or on the editorial pages of the *Tribune*, Greeley, while often unpredictable, never bored those who were his audience. Nurturing some of the best writers of the day, the *Tribune* achieved an excellence heretofore unknown in American journalism. (An irony of history should be noted: for more than a decade, from 1852 to 1862, writing from London as the *Tribune*'s European correspondent was the author of *Das Capital*, Karl Marx). The influence of the anti-slavery *Tribune*'s weekly edition on readers in the North and midwest in the decade before the Civil War was enormous, leading one observer to comment that it stood in those homes, "next to the Bible." Greeley, not always wholly satisfied with his newspaperman's role, would be lured throughout his life by the possibility of holding high office. Having served a brief three month stint in the U.S. House of Representatives, (1848–1849), he would on several occasions seek support, always unsuccessfully, for election by the New York legislature to the U.S. Senate. While initially supporting the candidacy of Ulysses S. Grant, Greeley soon became disenchanted with the general's presidency, its policies, and its spoils system corruption. When it became apparent that Grant would not be denied renomination in 1872 within the regular Republican Party, Greeley joined others in organizing the reform, Liberal Republican Party. At the new party's Cincinnati convention in May of 1872, Greeley was given its presidential nomination, with Governor B. Gratz Brown of Missouri chosen as his vice-presidential candidate. Two months later, Democrats in convention, urged on by prominent party leaders, unenthusiastically endorsed the Liberal Republican slate as their nominees. Resigning his editorship, Greeley conducted a strenuous campaign in which he argued for civil service reform and strongly appealed for national reconciliation between North and South, contending that citizens were "eager to clasp hands across the bloody chasm." Grant and the Republicans simply reminded voters of Greeley's lukewarm support, indeed criticism, of the martyred Lincoln, and of the "friendship" extended to Jefferson Davis. For most voters that sealed Greeley's fate. Grant and his running mate, Senator Henry Wilson of Massachusetts, gained a decisive popular vote victory, carrying 29 of the 35 states with 286 Electoral College votes. Physically and emotionally drained, suffering his wife's death but five days before the national balloting, devastated by the overwhelming vote given to Grant, Greeley fell into illness and severe depression and died on November 29, 1872, but three weeks after his presidential defeat. *See*: ELECTIONS: 1872.

Reference: Glyndon G. Van Deusen, *Horace Greeley, Nineteenth Century Crusader* (Philadelphia: University of Pennsylvania Press, 1953).

GREENBACK PARTY was also known as the National Independent Party. The political base of support for this party was farmers, upset with the rates the railroads were charging for shipping their goods. The poor economic conditions of the 1870s drew labor support to this party because the Greenbacks advocated printing money that was not backed by gold. The Greenbacks demanded the unlimited issuance of U.S. legal tender notes.

The Greenback or National Independent Party was formally organized at a national convention in Cleveland, Ohio in March of 1875. The bitter railroad strikes in the late 1870s drew labor support to the Greenback Party.

This was a period of fusion politics, and the Greenbacks participated in the election of three state governors. In 1878 there were fourteen Greenbackers in the House of Representatives. The party did not fare as well in presidential elections: In 1876 the Greenbacks nominated Peter Cooper for president, who drew only 82,000 votes. In 1880 their nominee, James Weaver, collected 300,000 votes, and in 1884 they nominated the Greenback governor of Massachusetts, Ben Butler. Butler received 175,000 votes. When the economy recovered, the Greenback Party disappeared.

References: J. David Gillespie, *Politics at the Periphery: Third Parties in Two-Party America* (Columbia: University of South Carolina Press, 1993); Paul Kleppner, ''The Greenback and Prohibition Parties,'' in *History of U.S. Political Parties*, vol. 2, Arthur M. Schlesinger, Jr., ed. (New York: Chelsea House, 1973).

GROSS RATING POINTS is an important measure of campaign advertising on television. It identifies the number of targeted people reached by advertising. Gross Rating Points are determined by multiplying reach by frequency. Reach is the number of people who receive the message, and frequency is the number of times they are exposed to the advertisement.

GUBERNATORIAL ELECTIONS. The elections of most state governors occur every four years. Only two states continue to have two-year terms: New Hampshire and Vermont. When states extended the terms of their governors from two years to four years, they usually adopted the midterm election year for the election of their state officials to decouple the election from the partisan influence of the national presidential election. Thirty-four states with four-year terms use the midterm election year. Twelve states elect governors in presidential election years. Two states, New Jersey and Virginia, elect their governors in odd years.

Gubernatorial elections have taken on the candidate-centered characteristics of national campaigns. The style of the campaign focuses on the candidate rather than the party. The campaigns rely on expensive electronic media to deliver their message. Candidates for governor rely on their own fund-raising ability, rather than the party, to finance their campaigns. In 1994 combined spending for gubernatorial races in the large states of California, Florida, and Texas averaged over $20 million. Campaign spending is higher if there is an open seat. Gubernatorial candidates often campaign apart from their fellow partisans. Split-ticket voting has become significant in gubernatorial elections.

Two factors that significantly influence gubernatorial elections are incumbency and the political party in the White House. Incumbent governors are slightly more vulnerable than incumbent U.S. Senators and members of the House. Since the 1950s, governors have been reelected at the rate of 70%. Governors are more vulnerable because they become engaged in every issue in the state, and are held accountable for the conditions in the state. Midterm gubernatorial elections are sensitive to national mood swings, usually away from the party in the White House. In every midterm election between 1950 and 1994, the party in the White House lost governorships, except in 1962 and 1986. The 1994 election brought a tremendous swing, giving the Republicans a majority of the states' governorships for the first time since 1968.

References: Council of State Governments, *Book of the States 1994–95*, vol. 30 (Lexington, Ky.: Council of State Governments, 1994); Stephen A. Salmore and Barbara G. Salmore, ''The Transformation of State Electoral Politics,'' in *The State of the States*, 3rd ed., Carl E. Van Horn, ed. (Washington, D.C.: Congressional Quarterly Press, 1996).

H

HACK is a pejorative term that refers to a worn-out or inferior party worker or government official. It refers to one who only goes through the motions in carrying out his or her duties. Hack is derived from a hackney horse, a horse that is broken down and let out for hire.

Reference: William Safire, *Safire's New Political Dictionary* (New York: Random House, 1993).

HANCOCK, WINFIELD SCOTT (1824–1886) was born at Montgomery Square, Pennsylvania on February 14, 1824. Educated at the U.S. Military Academy at West Point, (1840–1844), his entire adult life was spent in military service; even his presidential nomination by the Democratic Party in 1880 did not bring his resignation nor interrupt his army career, a career that was by all measures a distinguished one. While commended for bravery in battle during the Mexican War (1846–1848), it was the Civil War that was to establish Hancock's national reputation, particularly his field command of Union troops under General George G. Meade at the battle of Gettysburg, where Hancock was to suffer a serious wound painful to him for the remainder of his life. Returning to the field eight months later, March of 1864, Hancock served under Ulysses S. Grant during the Wilderness campaign. In writing his war *Memoirs* in the last years of his life, Grant was to credit highly Hancock's command abilities, yet personal animosity had earlier existed between the two men, Hancock believing that President Grant and Republican congressional leaders had consistently denied him the assignments and promotions that were his due. Hancock, essentially apolitical, but known to regard himself as a Democrat, held that it was this latter affiliation that caused his perceived ill treatment. Perhaps no small part of Hancock's disfavor among post–Civil War radical Republicans stemmed from his tenure as military governor for Louisiana and Texas (1867–1868), where he exercised authority with a moderation which infuriated those in Washington who supported more harsh Reconstruction measures. Hancock's "General Order No. 40" became the particular target of Republican anger, an order which largely restored civilian authority in the two states of the Fifth Military District. Ironically, congressional criticism of Hancock was primarily led by Representative James A. Garfield of Ohio, the man to whom General Hancock would narrowly lose the presidential election of 1880. At his request, relieved of the Southern command in March of 1868, Hancock was to serve in the Department of the Dakotas before being given command in 1872 of the Division of the Atlantic, headquartered in New York City. With Democratic Party leaders searching for a presidential nominee against whom the "Bloody Shirt" could not be waved advantageously, Hancock, with his exemplary war record in the unionist cause, a self-identified Democrat as well, seemed a logical choice for the party's 1880 nomination. Joined on the national ticket with Indiana Democrat William H. English as vice-presidential candidate, Hancock campaigned from his home on Governor's Island. Largely unfamiliar with non-military policy, Hancock, when asked in a newspaper interview what his position would be on the tariff, responded that it was something to be settled as "a local question." Republicans, and many of the nation's newspapers, heaped ridicule on the seemingly naive candidate. For all that, the election was astonishingly close: a dead heat in the popular vote, with each party carrying nineteen states; in the Electoral College balloting, however, the Republican victory was decisive, 214 votes for Garfield and his running mate Chester A. Arthur of New York; 155 ballots for Hancock and English. Graceful in defeat, Hancock continued his army career. Still in command of the Division of the Atlantic, General Hancock died on Governor's Island, New York City on February 9, 1886. *See*: ELECTIONS: 1880.

Reference: Glenn Tucker, *Hancock the Superb* (Indianapolis, Ind.: Bobbs-Merrill, 1960).

HARD MONEY. This phrase refers to campaign funds that are raised and spent under the rules of the Federal Election Campaign Laws and the Federal Election Commission. This federal campaign finance law places limits on contributions. Individuals are restricted to contributions of $1,000 per candidate for each election, and are limited to a total of $25,000 per year. PACS are limited to contributions of $5,000 per candidate each election. There is no total contribution limit imposed on PACS. Federal candidates must declare contributions on their reports to the Federal Election Commission. The term "hard money" is best understood in relation to the term "soft money." *See*: FEDERAL ELECTION CAMPAIGN ACT OF 1971 AND AMENDMENTS; FEDERAL ELECTION COMMISSION; POLITICAL ACTION COMMITTEE; SOFT MONEY.

HARDING, WARREN G. (1865–1923). Born of a farm family in Blooming Grove, Ohio on November 2, 1865, Harding graduated in 1882 from Iberia (Ohio Central) College. Early on, as one of the editors of the school's first newspaper, Harding was attracted to the possibility of a newspaperman's career. Following a brief, unsatisfying stint as a teacher in Marion, Ohio, Harding at age nineteen joined with two other partners in the $300 purchase of a local newspaper precariously close to its last barrel of ink. Through hard work and the energetic commitment of his wife Florence Kling DeWolfe, whom Harding dubbed, "the Duchess," Harding was able to buy out his partners and turn the *Marion Daily Star* into a solid publishing venture. Acquiring a Republican identification, the newspaper emerged as a political influence in Democratic Marion County and beyond. With the *Daily Star* firmly established, Harding himself turned to politics in 1899, his first serious political candidacy, running successfully for the Ohio Senate, a seat to which he was reelected in 1901. Quickly rising in influence within a state Republican organization dominated by George Cox, the "Black" Boss from Cincinnati, and Senator Mark Hanna, the "Red" Boss from Cleveland, Harding was placed on the party's statewide ticket of 1903 as candidate for lieutenant-governor, an office which he won. But what the bosses could bestow they could also deny and in 1905 Harding, for no reason other than political expediency, found himself replaced as the GOP nominee for lieutenant-governor. Fully understanding how the system worked, Harding retired to Marion and the *Daily Star*; but now with an acquired ambition for the governorship, Harding hoped his stock would recover and, in time, a gubernatorial nomination would come his way. Unfortunately, the editor had to wait until 1910, a year in which the Ohio Republican organization, already dividing between Taft "regulars" and Roosevelt "insurgents," was unable to deliver victory. By political disposition, reinforced by organizational loyalty, Harding sided with the "regulars," giving, at the fractious Republican National Convention of 1912, the nominating speech for a beleaguered President William Howard Taft. Harding's orthodoxy was to be rewarded two years later, first with the Republican primary nomination for the U.S. Senate, followed in November by the first popular election of a U.S. Senator conducted in Ohio under provisions of the recently ratified Seventeenth Amendment to the U.S. Constitution, an election in which Harding rolled up a 100,000 vote plurality over his Democratic rival. In the Senate, again by reason of his own political inclinations and his deep sense of organizational loyalty, Harding followed the party line, casting votes in favor of pro-business measures and in support of congressional proposal of the Prohibition and Women's Suffrage amendments. He also, as a member of the Senate Foreign Relations Committee, voiced "reservations" with regard to the peace treaties negotiated in Paris by President Wilson, including provision for U.S. membership in a League of Nations. As the 1920 presidential election approached, Harding, while certainly not a frontrunner, was one among many who were given more than casual attention for the GOP presidential nomination.

Far from rejecting such attention, Harding and his supporters, chief among whom was Ohio politico Harry M. Daugherty, worked assiduously to advance the Ohio Senator as the Chicago convention's best choice should a deadlock develop. The Harding scenario emerged; none of the leading contenders could gather enough delegate votes for nomination; and on the convention's tenth ballot, compromise candidate Warren G. Harding became the party's presidential nominee, a decision, as the popular story goes, dictated by party leaders from a "smoke filled room" in the Blackstone Hotel. Presumably, this same party cabal preferred the vice-presidential candidacy of Senator Irvine L. Lenroot of Wisconsin, but delegates, rebelling, nominated instead the Massachusetts governor (of Boston police strike fame) Calvin Coolidge. The election results of 1920 were something of a foregone conclusion. American voters, with women casting ballots for the first time under provisions of the recently adopted Nineteenth Amendment, expressed their weariness with war and its aftermath, overwhelmingly accepting Warren Harding's front porch campaign pledge of "a return to normalcy." Governor James M. Cox of Ohio and his Democratic running mate, Assistant Secretary of the Navy Franklin D. Roosevelt of New York, were buried beneath an avalanche of Republican ballots, Harding and Coolidge running up a popular vote plurality of nearly seven million votes, carrying 37 of the 48 states with 404 Electoral College ballots to 11 states and 124 votes in the Electoral College for the Democrats. For Warren Harding, inaugurated on March 4, 1921, the jubilation of so great a victory turned to political nightmare and death by August of 1923. Engulfed in a rising flood of corruption and scandal yet unknown to the public, President Harding embarked on a tour across the country to the West and to Alaska presumably to build support both for his argument in behalf of American participation in the World Court and in behalf of his own reelection effort that would come the following year. Returning from Alaska the president became ill in Seattle. Suspected of having had a heart attack, he went on to San Francisco where, attempting to convalesce at the Palace Hotel, he died, as the medical bulletin described, of a "brain evolvement," the evening of August 2, 1923. The great Teapot Dome (naval oil deposit) scandal, which would eventually lead to the criminal conviction on conspiracy and bribery charges of Secretary of the Interior Albert B. Fall, would not fully unfold until 1924–1925. Other scandals surfaced implicating no small number of Harding friends and appointees, including his longtime Ohio associate Harry Daugherty, whom he had brought into his cabinet as Attorney General. History has not proved kind to Harding or to his administration. Yet he made good appointments as well as very bad ones. Few would question the ability brought to the cabinet by Charles Evans Hughes as secretary of state or Herbert Hoover as secretary of commerce. Nor was the administration without its accomplishments: the transition from a war economy to that of peacetime was reasonably well managed; the Budget and Accounting Act of 1921 established responsibility for the drafting of the federal government budget with the president of the United States assisted by a professional Bureau of the

Budget; on the foreign policy front, treaties of peace with the former enemy states of World War I were negotiated and secured Senate approval; further, the Washington Naval Conference of December 1921 resulted in an agreement reached by five of the world's major powers (Great Britain, the United States, France, Italy, and Japan) on a scheme of naval disarmament. Whatever these accomplishments, they did not prevent or outweigh the negative reassessment of Harding and his administration that came soon after his death. The body of the deceased president was brought by funeral train from California to Washington, where it lay in state at the White House, then returned to Ohio and Marion for burial there on August 10, 1923. *See*: ELECTIONS: 1920.

References: Robert K. Murray, *The Harding Era: Warren G. Harding and His Administration* (Minneapolis: University of Minnesota Press, 1969); Eugene P. Trani and David L. Wilson, *The Presidency of Warren G. Harding* (Lawrence: University Press of Kansas, 1977).

HARRISON, BENJAMIN (1833–1901). Grandson of President William Henry Harrison, U.S. Senator from Indiana, President of the United States, 1889–1893, "Little Ben" was born at his grandfather's home at North Bend, Ohio on August 20, 1833. Educated at Ohio's Miami University, he graduated in 1852. Studying the law, Harrison was admitted to the bar in 1853, subsequently establishing his practice in Indianapolis. Becoming active in the Republican Party, then being organized in Indiana, he was elected city attorney in 1857 and later to two terms as reporter for the Supreme Court of Indiana, the first term being interrupted by his taking command of the Seventieth Indiana Volunteer Regiment, which he had assisted in raising at the outbreak of the Civil War in 1861. At first guarding railway lines in Kentucky, the Seventieth Indiana was to participate in the siege of Atlanta in the summer of 1864. Known to his troops as a stern disciplinarian, and because of his height as "Little Ben," Harrison left the Union army in 1865 with the rank of brevet brigadier general. Defeated for the Indiana governorship in 1876, he was elected in 1881 by the state legislature to a six-year term in the U.S. Senate where he chaired the Committee on Territories. A vigorous proponent of veterans' rights and benefits, he opposed President Cleveland's repeated vetoes of private bill veteran pensions. Harrison's ambition to be reelected to the Senate was thwarted in 1886, Democrats having come into the majority in the Indiana legislature in 1884. Not long removed from the Senate, Harrison was to find himself in 1888 the nominee of the Republican Party for president of the United States, having emerging from a crowded field to become the party choice on the convention's eighth ballot. To balance the national ticket, delegates chose New Yorker Levi P. Morton as Harrison's running mate. In a campaign largely dominated by the tariff issue, Harrison, an advocate of protectionism, prevailed over his Democratic opponent, President Grover Cleveland, who had in his first term directed considerable energy to the unsuccessful attempt to have Congress adopt "reform and reduction" tariff legislation. Harrison's election victory, however, was clouded. Clearly and unquestionably the constitutional winner by the fact that he and Morton had secured an Electoral College majority, carrying 20 of the 38 states with 233 Electoral College ballots to 18 states and 168 votes in the Electoral College for the Democratic ticket of Cleveland and Allen G. Thurman of Ohio, Harrison had failed to win the popular vote; out of more than eleven million votes cast he trailed President Cleveland by more than 90,000 ballots. Whatever the constitutional argument, the democratic argument rested with Cleveland; Harrison's presidency was shadowed throughout his four-year tenure by the popular vote result. On the domestic policy front, the Harrison presidency was marked by Congress's adoption in 1890 of three major pieces of legislation, the highly protective McKinley Tariff Act, the moderately inflationary Sherman Silver Purchase Act, and the Sherman Anti-Trust Act, the latter prohibiting the operation of trusts or monopolies found to be in restraint of interstate trade. Administration foreign policy initiatives involved the attempt made by the president and Secretary of State James G. Blaine to improve U.S. relationships with Latin American states, the emphasis being placed on reciprocal trade agreements and on formalized mechanisms for the discussion of mutual hemispheric interests, the latter leading to meetings in 1889 and 1890 out of which was formed the Pan American Union. Questions of annexation or territorial expansion, as with Hawaii, were usually considered in light of President Harrison's strong preference for realizing U.S. objectives, and establishing its influence, through economic rather than military means. Renominated in 1892, Harrison was joined on the Republican national ticket by New Yorker Whitelaw Reid, most recently U.S. minister to France. The campaign and election, fought almost exclusively on economic issues, provided an opportunity for Democrats to avenge the loss of 1888. Former president Grover Cleveland once again headed the Democratic ticket, with Adlai E. Stevenson of Illinois as his running mate. The election results were to return Cleveland to the White House. He and Stevenson outpolled Harrison-Reid by more than 350,000 votes, carrying 23 states with 277 Electoral College ballots to 16 states and 145 votes in the Electoral College for the Republicans. The Populist Party ticket of former Greenback congressman James G. Weaver of Iowa and running mate James G. Field of Virginia captured an unusually large economic protest vote of more than one million ballots, allowing the Populists to carry 4 states with 22 Electoral College votes. With Cleveland's inauguration on March 4, 1893, Harrison returned to his home in Indianapolis, and to his law practice. Perhaps the most significant case subsequently taken by the former president was his representation of Venezuela in a border dispute with Great Britain involving British Guiana. Traveling to Paris in 1899 to present his brief before a specially constituted arbitral court, Harrison was to have the satisfaction of a decision supporting the majority of the Venezuelan claim. Highly respected within the legal profession, leading citizen of the city, Harrison died in Indianapolis at age 68 on March 13, 1901. *See*: ELECTIONS: 1888, 1892.

References: Harry J. Sievers, *Benjamin Harrison*, 3 vols. (Chicago: Regnery, 1952–1968); Homer E. Socolofsky and Allan B. Spetter, *The Presidency of Benjamin Harrison* (Lawrence: University Press of Kansas, 1987).

HARRISON, WILLIAM HENRY (1773–1841), first Whig elected to the presidency, delivered the longest inaugural address on record and, ironically, served the shortest period of time in office, from March 4 to his death one month later on April 4, 1841. Harrison was born in Berkeley, Virginia on February 9, 1773, of a distinguished family; his father, Benjamin Harrison, was one of the signers of the Declaration of Independence, and later governor of Virginia. Harrison was educated at Hampden-Sydney College, studied medicine with Dr. Benjamin Rush in Philadelphia, but, in 1791 chose to pursue an army career. Assigned to the Northwest Territory, Harrison established his military reputation in encounters with the Indian confederation under the leadership of the Shawnee chief Tecumseh. While Harrison derived his nickname and first national attention from the battle at Tippecanoe Creek in 1811, it was the American victory at Thames River, Ontario, during the War of 1812, that firmly set Harrison's military reputation and popular standing. Following the war, Harrison settled at North Bend in Ohio, turning from the fields of battle to the pursuits of politics. In 1816, Ohio voters elected him to the U.S. House of Representatives, and subsequently to the Ohio Senate. In turn, in 1825 the Ohio legislature elected Harrison U.S. Senator. At the appointment of President John Quincy Adams, Harrison was to serve a brief stint as American minister to Columbia from 1828 to 1829. Returning from Bogota to North Bend, he became clerk of courts, a not particularly elevated position for someone who had come to have presidential ambitions. Harrison became, nonetheless, an increasingly appealing figure to the leadership of the newly formed Whig Party. Uncertain as to a unified strategy for opposing the Democrats in 1836, the Whigs instead adopted the tactic of offering a number of regional nominees, of whom William Henry Harrison was to prove the most successful. Harrison, in losing to the Democratic ticket, received 550,000 popular votes to Van Buren's 750,000; carried 7 states with 73 Electoral College votes to Van Buren's 170 ballots from 15 states. If combined, the Whig popular vote scattered among the several regional nominees all but equaled that given to Van Buren. This lesson was not lost on Whig leaders, particularly as Van Buren and the Democrats approached the 1840 contest politically weakened by the ongoing economic depression. Harrison became in that year the single Whig nominee, with John Tyler of Virginia, former U.S. Senator, as the vice-presidential candidate. 1840 was to usher in the first modern presidential campaign in terms of party emphasis on the making of a broad-based popular appeal. The Whig campaign emphasized image over issue: Harrison portrayed as the candidate of the common man; mass meetings with the war hero speaking to assembled thousands; torchlight parades; and the extensive use of gimmicks, songs, and slogans ("Tippecanoe and Tyler too"). For this onslaught, Van Buren's conventionally organized machine was ill-prepared. The election, while reasonably competitive in the popular vote, was in the Electoral College balloting a rout: 19 states and 234 votes for the Whigs, 7 states and 60 ballots for the Democrats. This great party and personal victory, however, was to be short-lived. Inaugurated on March 4, 1841, in a driving rainstorm, Harrison, age 68, died of pneumonia one month later. Vice-President John Tyler, Jeffersonian Republican turned Whig, assumed the executive office. Unlike that which had been widely anticipated of Harrison, Tyler was neither disposed by temperament nor politics to defer to a collegial Whig leadership. Thereby, and without fair trial, the touted Whig model of government, balanced as to policy-making between cooperative, not competing, executive and legislative branches, died a stillbirth. *See*: ELECTIONS: 1836, 1840.

References: Dorothy B. Goebel, *William Henry Harrison, A Political Biography* (Indianapolis: Historical Bureau of the Indiana Library, 1926); Norma L. Peterson, *The Presidencies of William Henry Harrison and John Tyler* (Lawrence: University Press of Kansas, 1989).

HATCH ACT. This federal law, the Political Activities Act of 1939 (Hatch Act) as amended in 1940, 1966, and 1993, was enacted to protect federal employees from political pressure, and limit political contributions and spending. The law sought to protect federal employees from being pressured by political officeholders and political parties to engage in partisan political activities. Classified federal employees were prohibited from engaging in political campaigns. Government employees were prohibited from serving as party officials, circulating petitions, soliciting campaign donations, and they could not run for a partisan office. It was intended to clean up the remaining effects of the spoils system. The law specifically prohibits federal employees from soliciting campaign contributions.

Although the Hatch Act restrictions on federal employees have been upheld by the Supreme Court as constitutional, many believed the restrictions abridged the First Amendment rights of the employees. In 1973, the U.S. Supreme Court, in *United States Civil Service Commission* v. *National Association of Letter Carriers* (1973), upheld the restrictions of the Hatch Act.

The Hatch Act of 1939 also imposed a limit of $5,000 per year on individual contributions to federal candidates or national party committees, and a $3 million limit on the total that could be received or spent by a party committee operating in two or more states. These regulations were ineffective, and were repealed by the new limits set by the Federal Election Campaign Act of 1971.

The last revision of the Hatch Act occurred in 1993, and some of the political activity restrictions on classified federal employees were removed. The revised law maintained the rule that federal employees cannot run for a partisan office or solicit campaign donations from the general public. A number of states copied the federal Hatch Act and limit the political activities of classified public employees. *See*: FEDERAL ELECTION CAMPAIGN ACT OF 1971 AND AMENDMENTS.

References: Ralph C. Chandler and Jack C. Plano, *The Public Administration Dictionary* (New York: John Wiley & Sons, 1982); George J. Gordon and Michael E. Milakovich, *Public Administration in America*, 5th ed. (New York: St. Martin's Press, 1995).

HAYES, RUTHERFORD B. (1822–1893) was born in Delaware, Ohio on October 4, 1822, graduated from Kenyon College, and in 1845 from Harvard Law School. Before military duty during the Civil War, Hayes practiced law in Cincinnati. Leaving the army in the spring of 1865 with a record of personal bravery, and the rank of brigadier general, Hayes immediately entered the U.S. House of Representatives, to which he had been elected the previous fall by Ohio voters, without campaigning and while yet on active duty. Hayes subsequently served three two-year terms as Ohio governor, 1867–1871 and 1875–1877. In 1876, Republican convention delegates seeking candidates untarnished by Grant administration scandals nominated Hayes for the presidency, and William A. Wheeler, congressman from New York, as vice-presidential candidate. Hayes was inaugurated on March 4, 1877, following resolution of the disputed election result of the previous November. In that election Democrat Samuel J. Tilden, governor of New York, seemingly had secured both a solid popular and Electoral College vote majority over Hayes. Republican leaders, however, challenged the election results from three Southern states in which they claimed widespread fraud and the intimidation of blacks who otherwise might have voted for the Republican ticket. A fifteen-member electoral commission created by a divided Congress (Democratic House, Republican Senate) ultimately voted, in each instance 8–7, preferring Hayes electors over those of Tilden. Thus, by an Electoral College margin of one vote, 185 to 184, Republicans retained control of the presidency. The compromise by which this was accomplished was a verbal pledge by Republican leaders that a Hayes administration would remove the last of federal troops from the South, thereby ending military reconstruction and allowing for the full restoration of white Democratic political supremacy. Hayes, personally honest and not a party to the negotiations leading to the compromise, nonetheless strictly abided by the agreement. Military reconstruction effectively ended within days of the Hayes inaugural. The Hayes administration, however, was never fully to recover from the stigma placed on it by this ''compromise'' resolution of the disputed election. Hayes's political difficulties were made greater in that he faced a Democratic House throughout his term. In particular he and Congress sparred over monetary policy and civil service reform. Often abandoned in Congress by conservative members of his own party, Hayes secured few legislative victories. Not timid, however, in the use of purely executive power, Hayes intervened in the great railroad strike of 1877, ordering the deployment of federal troops to protect property and maintain social order. As his term ended Hayes found his personal popularity, as well as public confidence in the integrity of the presidency, considerably enhanced. He nonetheless held to his earlier pledge not to seek reelection. Leaving the presidency in 1881, Hayes retired to his farms near Fremont, Ohio. Much of his energy in retirement was devoted to service on the boards of trustees for the Peabody and Slater Funds, organizations which supported educational opportunities for the disadvantaged, particularly among Southern blacks. Hayes died at Spiegel Grove, his home near Fremont, on January 17, 1893. *See*: ELECTIONS: 1876.

References: Paul J. Haworth, *The Hayes-Tilden Disputed Presidential Election of 1876* (Cleveland: Burrows, 1906); Rutherford B. Hayes, *Hayes, The Diary of a President, 1875–1881*, T. Harry Williams, ed. (New York: McKay, 1964); Ari Hoogenboom, *Rutherford B. Hayes, Warrior and President* (Lawrence: University Press of Kansas, 1995); Ari Hoogenboom, *The Presidency of Rutherford B. Hayes* (Lawerence: University Press of Kansas, 1988).

HILL COMMITTEES is a name that refers to the four congressional campaign committees. *See*: CONGRESSIONAL CAMPAIGN COMMITTEES.

HISPANIC VOTE. Hispanic Americans have become a major force in American politics. Hispanics constitute 5% of the U.S. population. They enjoy political influence in the states where they are concentrated. The Cuban Americans in Florida, because of their large numbers, have been very influential in determining U.S. policy toward Cuba. Cuban Americans have traditionally voted Republican because of that party's strong anti-communist position. However, in 1996 the Hispanic vote in Florida became more Democratic because of the anti-immigration positions of the GOP. In other states where there is a significant Hispanic population they have gained a significant role in determining the outcome of national elections. The Hispanic vote in populous Orange County, California, once a strong Republican county, now 25% Hispanic, turned the county toward the Democrats. Their votes for Hispanic House candidate Loretta Sanchez toppled outspoken Republican House member Robert K. Dornan. Hispanics also helped President Clinton enjoy an easy win in California over Bob Dole in 1996.

Historically, the Hispanic turnout rate has been very low, compared to the rate of voting of the population as a whole. In 1996 the participation rate of Hispanics increased significantly. In Texas, Hispanic voting increased almost 60%. In 1980, Hispanics voted 59% for Carter and 33% for Reagan. In 1996, Hispanics voted 72% for Clinton and 21% for Dole.

Reference: B. Drummund Ayres, Jr., "The Expanding Hispanic Vote Shakes Republican Strongholds," *New York Times*, November 10, 1996.

HOOVER, HERBERT C. (1874–1964), internationally successful as a mining engineer, recognized for his humanitarian efforts during World War I and its aftermath, highly regarded among the newly emerging governing class of technocrats and scientific managers, he experienced at the hands of the Great Depression the frustration and disappointment of a failed presidency, 1929–1933. Born of Quaker parents in West Branch, Iowa on August 10, 1874, Hoover was left an orphan at age eight. Raised by relatives in Salem, Oregon, Hoover gained admission to Stanford University's inaugural freshman class in 1891, taking his degree from the newly opened engineering school in 1895. By the beginning of World War I in 1914, Hoover, living in London, had established an international reputation as a skilled mining engineer, having successfully undertaken projects on five continents, and acquiring in the process a substantial fortune. It was at this juncture that Hoover's humanitarian efforts began. He became chairman of the Commission for Relief in Belgium, a private charity to provide food and other supplies to Belgians suffering dislocation and deprivation as a result of the German invasion and occupation of their country in August–September 1914. With American entry into the war on April 6, 1917, Hoover returned to the United States and accepted President Wilson's appointment as head of the Food Administration Board, under provisions of the Lever Act of August 1917. The Board had broad jurisdiction in terms of agricultural production, transportation, and distribution, including food conservation and commodity price-fixing. By the time of the Armistice in November of 1918, Wilson, impressed with his appointee's organizational and management skills, had made Hoover chairman of a wide variety of wartime boards and commissions, including the American Relief Administration. Not a member of the official party accompanying President Wilson to the Paris treaty negotiations, Hoover nonetheless served the president while there as a special economic adviser. As the decade ended Hoover found himself in governmental circles possessed of both a national and international reputation as a talented technocrat able to cut through and across established governmental bureaucracies to get the job done, and in the popular arena regarded as the man who had saved countless thousands of lives from starvation and death in war-ravaged Europe. This reputation and popular standing were carefully nurtured both by Hoover himself, and by many of those who had worked with him and were ardent in their esteem and support of the ''Chief.'' While talked of as early as 1919–1920, in terms of high office, there was a question about Hoover's party identification, if any. Hoover answered the question in 1920; despite close association with the Wilson administration, he declared himself a Republican. Brought to the cabinet by President Harding as secretary of commerce, Hoover served in that position until 1928. In that role the Department gave support to establishment of the eight-hour workday standard and to regulation of child labor. The secretary also urged on American business the formation of trade associations both for the exchange of information and the promotion of common interests, advocating as well the development by those same businesses of more aggressively competitive postures in world markets. By 1928, and with President Coolidge declining to seek reelection, Hoover was positioned as the leading candidate for the Republican presidential nomination. Delegates at the party's Kansas City convention in June of 1928 gave the secretary of commerce a first-ballot nomination, adding to the ticket as Republican vice-presidential candidate Senator Charles Curtis of Kansas. One analyst has labeled the 1928 campaign as "a contest without issues"; Hoover simply relying upon the booming national economy and his reputation as one of prosperity's "engineers" as sufficient to carry the Republicans to victory. Tempting fate, as time would prove, Hoover, in his August acceptance speech, confidently asserted, "we in America today are nearer to the final triumph over poverty than ever before . . . we shall soon with the help of God be in sight of the day when poverty will be banished from this nation." In election year 1928, Hoover's optimism struck a highly responsive chord; he and Senator Curtis secured a plurality of more than six million votes over Democrats Governor Alfred E. Smith of New York and U.S. Senator from Arkansas Joseph T. Robinson. The Republican ticket even carried, with "Hoovercrat" support, 5 states of the Old Confederacy, a total of 40 states with 444 Electoral College ballots to but 8 states and 87 votes in the Electoral College for the Democrats. Hoover's breakthrough in the heretofore Democratic "Solid South" was in all probability a function of three Smith characteristics; the governor was "wet," Catholic, and up from the streets of New York City's lower east side. Significantly enough however, a much better trade-off for the future success of the Democratic Party was Smith's remarkable showing among urban voters of strong ethnic identification, a voting bloc attracted to him for the same aforementioned set of characteristics and one which would remain with the Democratic Party, forming in the 1930s a key component of the New Deal coalition that dominated American politics for the next half century. Inaugurated on March 4, 1929, with great expectations, Hoover was to see his presidency shattered but seven months later by the unprecedented stock market crash of October 1929, ushering in what would be a nearly decade-long period of economic depression of unusual depth and severity. Contrary to much of conventional wisdom, Hoover fought valiantly, sometimes even creatively, to stem the tide of collapse; perhaps the most innovative weapon was the establishment in January of 1932 of the Reconstruction Finance Corporation, designed primarily but not exclusively, to assist, and thereby stabilize, the economic integrity of the nation's railroads, insurance companies, and banks. It was, however, on the crucial question of the development of a systematic program of federally funded relief for unemployed workers and bankrupt farmers that Hoover remained handcuffed, tied to his long-standing and deeply held notions as to the values of volunteerism and individual initiative. One event more than any other came to fix indelibly in the public mind the perception of Hoover's intransigence and insensitivity to the plight of the desperate. In the spring and summer of 1932 a large number of World War I veterans and their supporters formed a "Bonus Army," marching on Washington to demonstrate in behalf of an early payment of bonuses, under the existing law not scheduled to be distributed until 1945. Temporary camp had been set up at Anacostia Flats in nearby Maryland, from which veterans and others would move downtown to the White House or Capitol or to other government buildings designated as the site of that day's particular demonstration. Seeking to clear the downtown area after a small number of violent incidents and the death of one veteran, army troops, at the president's decision and under the command of General Douglas MacArthur, were called in. Securing the area at bayonet point and with the use of tear gas, MacArthur, at his own initiative and contrary to clear presidential orders, moved his troops to Anacostia Flats where the encamped veterans were routed from their tents and shacks, most of which were then burned. Subsequently, different accounts surfaced as to who started the fires, whether the veterans themselves or MacArthur's troops. Whatever the case, for Hoover it was a catastrophic public relations disaster, one from which the president, even to his death more than three decades later, was never fully to recover. As this event was unfolding, the Republican National Convention convened in Philadelphia in June of 1932. Four years earlier delegates had gone to their convention sure of victory; this year they assembled equally sure of defeat. Renominating Hoover and Curtis, and given the most fundamental law in politics,—prosperity's incumbents win elections, depression's incumbents do not,—the Republican national ticket went down to overwhelming defeat. Democratic Party nominees Governor Franklin D. Roosevelt of New York and Speaker of the U.S. House John Nance Garner of Texas, out-polled Hoover-Curtis by a seven million vote plurality, carrying 42 states with 472 Electoral College ballots to but 6 states and 59 Electoral College votes for the Republicans. The long interregnum separating election and inauguration days proved particularly difficult; the president attempting to commit Roosevelt to administration-dictated economic policies, the president-elect equally adamant in avoiding such commitments so as to safeguard his own policy options. (To eliminate such prolonged interregnums, and the associated political problems, the Twentieth Amendment to the Constitution was ratified on February 6, 1933, moving the presidential inauguration to January 20, the change to begin with the next presidential election, that of 1936.) Herbert Hoover left the White House on March 4, 1933, with perhaps greater ill-will directed toward him by the American people than for any departing president before or since. Hoover was, however, to live long enough to see, given generational changes, and by his record of post–World War II public service, the erosion of that ill-will replaced by the kind of distanced respect accorded a historic figure. In the short run, the remaining years of the 1930s and those of the early 1940s, Hoover continued in his role as the Republican Party's most consistent critic of the New Deal, attacking its domestic policies as socialistic, undermining the free enterprise system and its foreign policy as too indiscriminately internationalist, particularly during the war years, in the alliance made with the Soviet Union. In 1946, setting partisanship aside, President Truman appointed Hoover, based on his relief work of the World War I period, chairman of the Famine Emergency Commission, the former president being asked once again to turn his organizational and managerial skills to the problems of relief for those in war-torn Europe. Subsequently, and again at President Truman's request, Hoover was to chair the Commission on the Organization of the Executive Branch of Government, 1947–1949. The "Hoover Commission" made recommendations, based on its study of the presidency, for structural reorganization aimed at modernization, the fuller realization of administrative efficiency, and the strengthening of the presidential advisory system. A second "Hoover Commission," again chaired by the former president, was established by President Eisenhower in 1953, presenting its final report in 1955. The last decade of Hoover's long life was spent in the role of party and presidential elder statesman. He died at age 90 in New York City on October 20, 1964. *See*: ELECTIONS: 1928, 1932.

References: David Burner, *Herbert Hoover, A Public Life* (New York: Knopf, 1979); Martin L. Fausold, *The Presidency of Herbert Hoover* (Lawrence: University Press of Kansas, 1985); Herbert Hoover, *The Memoirs of Herbert Hoover*, 3 vols. (New York: Macmillan, 1951–1952); George H. Nash, *The Life of Herbert Hoover*, 3 vols. to date (New York: Norton, 1983–1996).

HORSERACE JOURNALISM. The press, particularly the electronic media, treat political campaigns as if they were a game or a contest. The tendency of the media is to focus on which candidate is ahead in the public opinion polls, and which candidate has the most money. Television networks enlist campaign consultants and pundits to speculate on the various strengths and weaknesses of the candidates. The media often use the language of a game to describe elections. One reason the media prefer horserace coverage is that it is relatively easy to do. Placing elections in a horserace contest makes the election more entertaining. Candidates respond to this press interest by providing information on their campaigns that fit the horserace venue. The amount of press coverage of the policy positions offered by the candidates has dwindled. The media are criticized by many observers for not giving more attention to the substantive policy positions of the candidates.

Reference: Stephen Ansolabehere, Roy Behr, and Shanto Iyengar, *The Media Game: American Politics in the Television Age* (New York: Macmillan, 1993).

HUGHES, CHARLES EVANS (1862–1948). Possessor of one of the most distinguished records in American public service, Hughes, son of an abolitionist Baptist clergyman, was born in Glens Falls, New York on April 11, 1862. After attending what is now Colgate University (1876–1878), Hughes transferred to Brown from which he graduated in 1881. Admitted to the bar in 1884, Hughes had attended Columbia Law School (1882–1884). Practicing in New York City for several years in 1891 Hughes accepted a professorship at Cornell Law School. Requiring a more substantial income, Hughes reluctantly gave up academic life in 1893. Much later in life, reflecting on the period of his professorship, Hughes was to regard it with particular satisfaction. Returning to practice in New York City, Hughes served as legal counsel for state investigations of gas and electric rates charged by utility companies in New York City and of alleged corruption involving New York–based life insurance companies. Hughes's role in the two investigations made him attractive to Republican leaders, including the New Yorker in the White House, Theodore Roosevelt, as a gubernatorial candidate in 1906. Elected, subsequently reelected in 1908, Hughes's governorship was progressive, with particular accomplishments in the fields of labor law, social welfare legislation and, based on his earlier investigative experience, utility and insurance regulation. In October of 1910, Hughes left Albany, having resigned the governorship to accept appointment by President Taft to a seat on the U.S. Supreme Court. In his years as justice of the Court (1910–1916), Hughes was to set his reputation as a gifted jurist. Not a captive of a particular ideology, he has been described by some Court analysts as a "moderate," by others as a "non-doctrinaire pragmatist." Perhaps above all else, Hughes demonstrated an exceptionally high level of legal craftsmanship, his written opinions marked by thoroughness and clarity. As the presidential election of 1916 approached, Republican leaders, both in the party's conservative and progressive wings, searched for a candidate who could reunite the party, one who was not involved in the Taft-Roosevelt fratricide of 1912. Hughes, isolated on the Court, above the battle of 1912, struck many as the ideal candidate. Neither encouraging nor opposing the effort being made to bring him the nomination, Hughes remained on the Court, aloof, allowing politics to run its course. The result was a second ballot presidential nomination for the Supreme Court justice who, in accepting that nomination, immediately submitted his resignation from the Court on June 10, 1916. The Hughes campaign, weakly organized, the candidate never seeming to quite hit his stride, was something of a disaster. In criticizing President Wilson for the lack of U.S. military preparedness, Hughes appeared to be arguing for American entry into World War I. Democrats were quick to ask, "Hughes and war or Wilson and peace?" putting additional emphasis on their much-used slogan "He kept us out of war." The vote in the Electoral College was remarkably close. The Democratic ticket of Wilson and Marshall polled 49.2% of the total presidential vote cast, carrying 30 states with 277 Electoral College ballots. The Republican ticket of Hughes and running mate Charles W. Fairbanks of Indiana, the former vice-president of the United States (1905–1909), gathered 46.1% of the vote and 254 ballots in the Electoral College from 18 states. Some analysts have attributed the Hughes defeat to his failure to carry California and its Electoral College votes, a state which Hughes lost by less than 4,000 votes. It is contended by these analysts that had Hughes, while campaigning in California, not "snubbed" Hiram W. Johnson, the Republican governor and U.S. Senate candidate, thereby irritating Johnson supporters, Hughes would have won the state, secured an Electoral College majority, and, thereby, been elected president of the United States. Following his election defeat, Hughes returned to the practice of law in New York City. With the coming of the Harding administration in 1921, Hughes accepted the president's appointment to the cabinet as secretary of state. Perhaps the greatest achievement of his tenure (1921–1925), was the Washington Naval Conference of December 1921 which resulted in an agreement among the representatives of Great Britain, France, Italy, Japan, and the United States as to a scheme of naval disarmament. Leaving the State Department in March of 1925, Hughes was to accept, three years later, a judicial appointment to the Permanent Court of International Justice at the Hague in the Netherlands. Early in 1930, faced with the resignation of William Howard Taft as chief justice of the U.S. Supreme Court, President Hoover turned to Hughes, whose nomination was subsequently confirmed in the U.S. Senate by a vote of 52 to 26 on February 13, 1930. Hughes returned to the Court, as its Chief, during a crucial decade. Court membership was virtually evenly divided; four justices of conservative persuasion, four justices of liberal persuasion. It was presumed that Chief Justice Hughes, a moderate, would come to hold the decisive swing vote in the Court's decision-making. With the coming of the New Deal in 1933, as would be expected, many of its bold and innovative initiatives, particularly those associated with economic regulation or redistribution, were challenged in the courts, some cases rising on appeal or on *certiorari* to the high court. And there, on occasion, the piece of New Deal legislation in question failed of Court approval on a 5 to 4 vote, Hughes joining the conservative bloc. Following his landslide victory of 1936, presuming a mandate, President Roosevelt, on February 5, 1937, proposed "reform" of the Court which would allow an expansion of its membership in the interest, as the president argued it, of Court efficiency, the added justices permitting the Court to more expeditiously handle its workload. The "reform" if adopted would, of course, also allow the president to appoint to the Court New Deal justices who would provide votes in sufficient numbers to uphold challenged administration policy. With Chief Justice Hughes, on the basis of his presentation of Court workload statistics, quickly knocking down the efficiency argument, the "reform" proposal stood exposed as the bald power play that it was. Attacked by much of the press, criticized by many in Congress within his own party, Roosevelt allowed the proposal to die a quiet death. The great confrontation between Roosevelt and the Court and Chief Justice Hughes ended, as one observer paraphrased, "not with a bang but a whimper." Four years later, the Court secure in its historic role, its membership changed by natural attrition and now more favorably disposed toward the New Deal, Chief Justice Hughes submitted his resignation effective July 1, 1941. In retirement, continuing with a wide variety of intellectual pursuits, spending time with his family, Hughes's final years were both productive and satisfying. In failing health, he was to make one last trip to his daughter's summer cottage on Cape Cod, and there, on August 27, 1948, he died at age 86. *See*: ELECTIONS: 1916.

References: Dexter Perkins, *Charles Evans Hughes and American Democratic Statesmanship* (Boston: Little, Brown, 1956); Merlo J. Pusey, *Charles Evans Hughes*, 2 vols. (New York: Macmillan, 1952).

HUMPHREY, HUBERT HORATIO, JR. (1911–1978) served as vice-president of the United States from 1965 to 1969, and was a leading voice for liberal causes in the U.S. Senate. He was the Democratic Party nominee for president in 1968. Humphrey graduated from the University of Minnesota in 1939, and received an M.A. from Louisiana University in 1940. After college, Humphrey worked for the Works Progress Administration. He promoted the merger of the Minnesota Democrats and the Farmer-Labor Party; he was able to unite that party for the 1944 election. In 1945, he was elected mayor of Minneapolis. As mayor, he worked against discrimination. At the Democratic National Convention in 1948, Humphrey spoke on behalf of the minority Civil Rights plank. He told the delegates to: "get out of the shadow of states' rights and walk forthrightly into the sunshine of human rights." The minority plank he proposed was adopted by the 1948 convention, and prompted the delegates of four Southern states to walk out of the convention and nominate Strom Thurmond as the Dixiecrat candidate. Humphrey was elected to the U.S. Senate in 1948, and served until 1964, when he was elected vice-president with Democratic presidential candidate Lyndon B. Johnson.

Hubert Humphrey was a liberal Democrat. As majority whip in the Senate, he was instrumental in the passage of the historic Civil Rights Act of 1964. Humphrey considered that his greatest achievement.

When President Lyndon B. Johnson declared he would not seek reelection in 1968, Humphrey sought the 1968 Democratic Party presidential nomination, and became the favorite of the Democratic Party leaders. Humphrey did not enter any primaries. The primary season was marred by the assassination of Robert Kennedy. The backdrop of the Vietnam War, which Humphrey supported, and the protests at the Democratic convention in Chicago made it difficult for Humphrey to start his campaign. He was defeated by Richard Nixon in a close election. Humphrey returned to the Senate in 1970 and served there until his death in 1978. *See:* ELECTIONS: 1968; MINNESOTA FARMER-LABOR PARTY.

Reference: Carl Solberg, *Hubert Humphrey, A Biography* (New York: Norton, 1984).

HUNT COMMISSION. This was a commission established by the Democratic National Committee as a result of the crushing defeat of President Jimmy Carter in 1980. Also, Democratic Party leaders were disgruntled with the independent stance of the Carter administration toward the Democratic Party in Congress. Carter had been nominated and elected as an outsider, and had a difficult time relating to the leadership of the Democratic Congress. This was blamed on the existing nomination system used by the Democrats, which excluded state party and governmental officials. To rectify this problem, South Carolina Governor James B. Hunt was appointed to head a commission to reform the rules for the 1984 nomination. Most significantly, this commission recommended a new category of delegates, soon called superdelegates or PL/EOs (Party Leaders and Elected Officials). There were to be 550 unpledged Democratic National Convention delegates selected by Senate and House Democratic caucuses, and the remainder appointed by state party chairs. There were already a few appointed delegates under the old rules. These reforms were to give existing party leaders a stake and a role in the selection of the Democratic nominee, create a true party nominee, and give more attention to party building.

The Hunt Commission also unbound the delegates; that is, they could vote on good conscience, rather than be bound to the candidate they were pledged to when elected. This was a demand of the Kennedy campaign at the 1980 convention. The Commission also urged greater diversity in the national delegates. They extended the language on convention delegate discrimination to include sexual orientation. Sexual orientation along with race, gender, age, religion, and other characteristics could not be used to exclude a person from serving as a delegate. In addition, the Commission strengthened the language on affirmative action to specify that groups should be recognized to reflect their size in the Democratic electorate.

The Hunt Commission also relaxed the proportional representation requirement on state primaries and caucuses, which had been mandated in 1980. It established the winner-take-more system which permitted a state to award the top vote-getter in each district one extra delegate. This was to put an end to the type of long divisive battle that developed between Kennedy and Carter. The Hunt Commission wanted to enable a candidate to seal the nomination early and avoid a long bitter battle. They also permitted a return to the ''loophole'' primary which was outlawed in 1980. In the ''loophole'' primary, the voter was able to cast a vote for individual delegates identified by presidential preference. This often allowed for a sweep by the frontrunner of district delegates and enabled a candidate to gain momentum. *See*: DEMOCRATIC NATIONAL COMMITTEE; FAIRNESS COMMISSION; McGOVERN-FRASER COMMISSION; SUPERDELEGATE.

References: Philip A. Klinker, *The Losing Parties: Out-Party National Committees, 1956–1993* (New Haven, Conn.: Yale University Press, 1994); Nelson W. Polsby and Aaron Wildavsky, *Presidential Elections: Strategies and Structures in American Politics*, 9th ed. (Chatham, N.J.: Chatham House, 1996).

HUSTINGS is a place from which a campaign speech is made. It is often used today to refer to the campaign trail. In British usage it is the platform from which a speech is made.

Reference: William Safire, *Safire's New Political Dictionary* (New York: Random House, 1993).

I

IDEOLOGY is a set of interrelated values and beliefs about the nature of man and society held by an individual, group, or society. An ideology helps to interpret reality and is often a guide to action. The ideology of the United States is often referred to as capitalism. This ideology places an emphasis on free markets and individualism. The ideology of the delegates to the Republican National Convention is determined by the delegates' overall position on issues. Some delegates are more conservative than others, determined by their positions on social issues such as abortion and prayer in school. Throughout their history American political parties have not been very ideological when compared to European parties. *See*: CONSERVATISM; LIBERALISM.

References: Roy C. Macrides, *Contemporary Political Ideologies: Movements and Regimes*, 2nd ed. (Boston: Little, Brown, 1983); Iain McLean, *The Concise Oxford Dictionary of Politics* (New York: Oxford University Press, 1996).

INCUMBENT is an individual who holds an office. Incumbents enjoy an electoral advantage because they are able to provide services to constituents. Incumbents are also able to receive press and media attention, which builds up their name identification with the voters. Their opponents are usually less well-known and are unable to seriously challenge the incumbent. Incumbents are able to raise more campaign money, usually from PACs, which prefer to restrict their contributions to incumbents. Incumbent members of the House of Representatives are reelected at the rate of 90%. Incumbents who hold the highest offices, such as governors and U.S. Senators, are slightly more vulnerable because their challengers are often well-known, and are able to raise campaign funds and gain media attention. In some states the incumbent is given the top position on the ballot, which is a significant advantage. *See*: CASEWORK; POLITICAL AC-TION COMMITTEE.

Reference: Paul Allen Beck, *Party Politics in America*, 8th ed. (New York: Longman, 1997).

INDEPENDENT. An independent is a voter who does not identify with a particular political party. They cast their vote for the person and not the party. The number of independents has increased in the American electorate. Independents account for more than one-third of the American electorate. The number of self-identified independents is almost 50% among younger voters. The rise in the number of independent voters explains the decline in voter turnout since strong partisans are very dedicated voters. Independents are often a source of support for third-party candidates. In 1996, 26% of the voters claimed they were independent, and 17% of them said they voted for Ross Perot.

There are also independent candidates who seek office without a party label. John Anderson ran as an independent in 1980. State law usually permits ballot access for individuals seeking office as independents. There are signature requirements on petitions and established filing dates for independent candidates. The number of signatures required for independent candidates is usually higher than the number required for a party nomination. There are also sore loser restrictions, that is, someone who lost as a partisan candidate is usually not allowed to run as an independent for the same office in that year. *See*: BALLOT ACCESS; INDEPENDENT CANDIDATE.

Reference: William H. Flanigan and Nancy H. Zingale, *Political Behavior of the American Electorate*, 8th ed. (Washington, D.C.: Congressional Quarterly Press, 1994).

INDEPENDENT CANDIDATE is someone who seeks political office who is not affiliated with a party. Independent candidates are not nominated in a primary. State law permits independent candidates access to the general election ballot if they collect a required number of signatures. Some of the recent more notable independent presidential candidacies include: John Anderson's bid for president in 1980 and Ross Perot's candidacy in 1992. Maine and Connecticut have elected independent candidates to the office of governor in recent elections. The sole independent in the U.S. House of Representatives is Bernie Sanders of Vermont. *See*: BALLOT ACCESS.

Reference: Alan Ehrenhalt, "The Man without a Party," in *State Government*, Thad L. Beyle, ed. (Washington, D.C.: Congressional Quarterly Press, 1997).

INDEPENDENT EXPENDITURES are expenditures by individuals and committees involving elections for federal offices that are not coordinated with the candidate seeking office. It is money spent for advertisements advocating the election or defeat of a candidate for federal office by an individual or a group. The spending cannot be made with the cooperation or consultation of the candidate they are trying to elect. There are no limits on the amount spent by the independent individual or committee. The spending must be reported to the Federal Election Commission. In *Buckley* v. *Valeo* (1976), the Supreme Court held that independent expenditures are a form of protected speech. Groups that engage in independent expenditures campaigns often use very negative advertisements.

Until recently, the Federal Election Commission presumed that party committees were not capable of making independent expenditures because the party and the candidate were so intertwined. However, the U.S. Supreme Court, in *Colorado Republican Federal Campaign Committee* v. *Federal Election Commission* (1996), ruled that party committees have the same right to make independent expenditures as any other committee, provided that they act independently of the candidate.

Restrictions on independent expenditures was part of a recent campaign finance reform proposal that was not adopted by Congress. *See: BUCKLEY* v. *VALEO* (1976); *COLORADO REPUBLICAN FEDERAL CAMPAIGN COMMITTEE* v. *FEDERAL ELECTION COMMISSION* (1996); INTEREST GROUP; POLITICAL ACTION COMMITTEE; SOFT MONEY.

References: Herbert E. Alexander, *Financing Politics: Money, Elections, and Political Reform*, 4th ed. (Washington, D.C.: Congressional Quarterly Press, 1992); Anthony Corrado, Thomas E. Mann, Daniel R. Ortiz, Trevor Potter, and Frank J. Sorauf, eds., *Campaign Finance Reform: A Sourcebook* (Washington, D.C.: Brookings Institution, 1997).

INFOMERCIAL is the name given to the type of campaign commercial used by Ross Perot in his 1992 presidential campaign. These commercials were one-half hour in length and focused on the budget deficit and other national economic issues. Perot used a pointer and graphs to make his argument. In 1992 the ads drew large audiences. The infomercials Perot used in his 1996 campaign were not as successful in drawing an audience. In 1992, Perot was able to raise the balanced budget issue to the top of the political agenda. In 1996, Perot was unable to find an issue to set the agenda. He attempted to focus on campaign finance reform which did not resonate with voters until the final weeks of the campaign. *See*: PEROT, ROSS.

INITIATIVE is a process permitted in 24 states where citizens are empowered to place statutory and constitutional proposals, which the citizens develop, directly before the people for approval. The proponents of the initiative must submit their petition with an exacting number of required signatures in order to have their proposal voted on. There are two forms of initiative proposals: the indirect and the direct. The indirect initiative must be submitted to the legislature, after the required number of signatures is gathered, for action by the legislature. If the legislature fails to enact the citizen-initiated legislation, then it is placed on the ballot. The direct initiative is placed on the ballot after the required number of signatures has been collected by the proponents of the proposal. For constitutional changes, sixteen states permit the direct initiative, and two states allow the indirect initiative. For statutory proposals, seventeen states permit the direct initiative and nine states allow the indirect initiative.

States have varying signature requirements for initiatives. The petition initiatives require signatures ranging from 2% to 15% of various defined state populations, ranging from the number of residents in North Dakota, to the votes cast for governor in the last election in Ohio. Some states require a higher number of signatures for constitutional amendment proposals than they require for statutory proposals. Some states have geographic distribution requirements for the signatures. Some states limit the period when petitions are allowed to be circulated. A number of states require circulators to witness the signatures, and some states require circulators to declare if they are being paid.

The initiative was promoted by the Progressive movement to counter the influence of money in state government. It is ironic that many initiatives on state ballots today are promoted by well-financed special interest groups. One of the best-known initiatives was the successful Proposition 13 in California, which froze property taxes at their existing level. The most popular initiative in recent years has been term limits, which has been imposed in almost every state that permits the use of the initiative. Some of the most sensitive social issues of the day, including the repeal of gay rights in Colorado, abortion issues, school choice, Proposition 187 in California, which passed in 1994, barred illegal immigrants from receiving social welfare benefits. In 1996, Arizona and California voted to legalize the use of marijuana for medical purposes. Those proposals were placed before the voters by initiative petition. California voted in favor of Proposition 209 in 1996, which did away with affirmative action. Promotion of legalized gambling by special interest groups reached the ballot in many states that permit the use of the initiative petition. In November 1996, there were 94 initiatives on the ballot in the United States.

Initiatives have led to a minor industry. There are political consultants and firms that specialize in initiative campaigns. Millions of dollars are spent qualifying the initiative and promoting it by television advertising in large states like California. There are continuing debates about the merits of the initiative. A number of worthwhile government reforms have resulted from the initiative process, as well as many very controversial and ill-conceived state statutes and constitutional amendments. The concept of the initiative can be traced to a 1715 Massachusetts law and to an 1898 amendment to the South Dakota State Constitution. Most initiatives are binding. There are also non-binding initiatives which reflect the sentiment of the public on an issue, and it is assumed the public officials will heed the view expressed by the initiative. *See*: RECALL; REFERENDUM.

References: David Butler and Austin Ranney, *Referendums: A Comparative Study of Practice and Theory* (Washington, D.C.: American Enterprise Institute for Public Policy Research, 1978); Council of State Governments, *The Book of the States: 1996–97*, vol. 31 (Lexington, Ky.: 1996); David B. Magleby, *Direct Legislation: Voting in Ballot Propositions in the United States* (Baltimore,: Johns Hopkins University Press, 1984); Alan Rosenthal, *The Decline of Representative Democracy: Process, Participation, and Power in State Legislatures* (Washington, D.C.: Congressional Quarterly Press, 1998); Joseph F. Zimmerman, "Civic Strategies for Community Empowerment," *National Civic Review* (May/June 1988).

INSTANT RUNOFF (IRV) is an election method for a single-member district election. Without requiring a second-round election, this voting method leads to a majority decision by a ballot count that simulates a series of runoffs. Voters are permitted to rank candidates in order of preference. If no candidate wins a majority of first choice votes, the last place candidate is eliminated, and ballots cast for that candidate are redistributed to each voter's next choice. This process of elimination of candidates continues until a candidate wins a majority.

Australia uses this system for the election of its parliament and Ireland uses it for the election of its president. It is a single-transferable-vote method that leads to a majority decision. It is also commonly referred to as the alternative vote. The Center for Voting and Democracy created the following simulation of "instant runoff" for the 1992 presidential election in the United States:

Final Tally (First Choice % Ballots Redistributed to 2nd Choice)

George Bush	38% + 10% = 48%
Bill Clinton	43% + 9% = 52%
Ross Perot	19% – 19%

Assume that of the 19% who voted for Perot, slightly more than half of the 19% preferred Bush as their second choice, and slightly less than half preferred Clinton as their second choice. With Perot eliminated and those votes redistributed, Clinton ends up with 52% of the vote and a clear majority. This system eliminates the need for runoff elections. *See*: SINGLE-MEMBER DISTRICT; PLURALITY; RUNOFF.

Reference: Center for Voting and Democracy, P.O. Box 60037, Washington, D.C. 20039.

INTEREST GROUP is an organized group with common interests that attempts to achieve its goals by influencing government officials. Interest groups lobby government officials, and they donate campaign funds to political campaigns, often through their PACs. They may become influential in a particular political party, as the Christian Coalition is in the Republican Party and the labor unions are in the Democratic Party. Interest groups may engage in propaganda by using free or paid media to advocate or oppose a policy. The "Harry and Louise" advertisements were paid for by the insurance industry to defeat Clinton's health reform plan in 1993. Interest groups may recruit candidates to run for office. EMILY's List encourages women to seek public office. In the states that allow the initiative, interest groups may advance ballot propositions. Interest groups also litigate. As an example, the NAACP (National Association for the Advancement of Colored People) advanced many of its goals in the federal court system. Groups may demonstrate, strike, boycott, or engage in violence. *See*: LOBBYIST; POLITICAL ACTION COMMITTEE; SINGLE-ISSUE GROUPS.

References: Paul S. Herrnson, Ronald G. Shaiko, and Clyde Wilcox, eds., *The Interest Group Connection: Electioneering, Lobbying, and Policymaking in Washington* (Chatham, N.J.: Chatham House, 1998); Philip A. Mundo, *Interest Groups: Cases and Characteristics* (Chicago: Nelson-Hall, 1992); Kay Lehman Schlozman and John T. Tierney, *Organized Interests and American Democracy* (New York: Harper and Row, 1986).

IOWA CAUCUS. The Iowa caucus is the first major electoral test for a presidential campaign. It is the first electoral event in the year of the presidential nomination. Iowa's position as the first step in the delegate selection process was unsuccessfully challenged by a few other states in 1996. Most of the Republican candidates refused to participate in pre-Iowa events, and those events were not recognized by the media as a true test of the Republican candidates' ballot strength.

The Iowa caucus has had a significant impact on the fortunes of presidential aspirants. In 1996, Bob Dole, who was considered to be very strong in Iowa, won by only a slim margin. This energized his opponents to challenge him for the nomination, and Dole had to fight it out against a relatively weak field to regain his frontrunner status. Traditionally, candidates running in Iowa have emphasized organization and retail politics. Steve Forbes, with his personal fortune, spent approximately $4 million for a media blitz in Iowa that resulted in what was seen as a strong showing for an unknown. Forbes did not invest in building an organization, which may alter the way candidates campaign in Iowa in the future. In 1996 the well-financed Senator Phil Gramm finished a poor fifth and his campaign never gained momentum.

A strong showing in Iowa may propel an unknown candidate to the forefront of the pack. In 1976, Jimmy Carter, who was relatively unknown, won Iowa, and this gave a major boost to his campaign. In 1980, Ronald Reagan lost to George Bush in Iowa, and Reagan had to fight hard in New Hampshire to regain his position. In 1984, Gary Hart's second place showing in Iowa knocked Ohio Senator John Glenn out of the race and propelled Hart to a New Hampshire victory over Mondale. Because it is first, the Iowa caucus has a significant impact on the presidential nominating process. It receives a tremendous amount of news coverage. *See*: CAUCUS; PRIMARY.

References: Nelson W. Polsby and Aaron Wildavsky, *Presidential Elections: Strategies and Structures in American Politics*, 9th ed. (Chatham, N.J.: Chatham House, 1996); Peverill Squire, ed., *The Iowa Caucuses and the Presidential Nominating Process* (Boulder, Colo.: Westview, 1989); Stephen J. Wayne, *The Road to the White House 1996: The Politics of Presidential Elections* (New York: St. Martin's Press, 1996).

ISSUE ADS are used to present or criticize a candidate's position on an issue, but do not advocate the election or defeat of a particular candidate. This type of political advertisement was used extensively in the 1996 congressional and presidential elections by the national party committees, organized labor, and other interest groups. "Issue advocacy" is outside the regulation of the federal election laws according to the standards set by the Supreme Court when it restricted the reach of federal election law in *Buckley* v. *Valeo* (1976). Trevor Potter, a former chairman of the Federal Election Commission, wrote that issue advocacy, "is a communication that does not 'expressly advocate' the election or defeat of a clearly identified federal candidate." The ad cannot use words or phrases such as "vote for," "support" or "vote against" a particular candidate.

Common Cause estimated that the Democratic Party committees spent $22 million from July 1995 to June 1996, much of it soft money, promoting Clinton's candidacy with issue advocacy advertising in targeted states. The Republican Party used soft money for issue advocacy ads to keep Bob Dole's candidacy alive after his campaign reached the spending cap at the end of the presidential primary period. The AFL-CIO spent $35 million of union treasury funds on issue advocacy ads in dozens of congressional districts. They would end the ad with a message such as "Our Congressman voted to block a minimum wage increase, after he voted to cut Medicare and cut college loans—all to give a big tax break to the rich. Let's tell Congressman Christensen—raise the minimum wage. And start working for America's working families." This ad is considered "issue advocacy" and not "express advocacy." Business interests responded with their own issue advocacy campaigns.

Tax exempt groups also engaged in issue advocacy spending to promote causes which may be associated with candidates. These groups do not have to disclose their donors, and are not limited in the amounts they can collect. *See: BUCKLEY* v. *VALEO* (1976); *COLORADO REPUBLICAN FEDERAL CAMPAIGN COMMITTEE* v. *FEDERAL ELECTION COMMISSION* (1996); ELECTIONS: 1996; FEDERAL ELECTION CAMPAIGN ACT OF 1971 AND AMENDMENTS; HARD MONEY; SOFT MONEY.

References: Anthony Corrado, "Financing the 1996 Elections," in *The Elections of 1996*, Gerald Pomper, ed. (Chatham, N.J.: Chatham House, 1997); Trevor Potter, "Issue Advocacy and Express Advocacy," in *Campaign Finance Reform: A Sourcebook*, Anthony Corrado, Thomas E. Mann, Daniel R. Ortiz, Trevor Potter, and Frank J. Sorauf, eds. (Washington, D.C.: Brookings Institution, 1997).

ISSUE VOTING. Many voters respond to the issue positions of candidates based on the voter's own particular policy preferences. Many believe that voters should vote on the basis of the candidates' positions on the issues. This requires voters to know what the candidates' views are on particular issues. Voters frequently think that their (the voter's) policy preferences are held by the candidate or the party which they prefer, regardless of whether or not that is true. John Bibby points out that for issue voting to occur there needs to be a number of conditions present: (a) the voter has to be concerned about certain issues; (b) the candidates need to have clear and different positions on issues; (c) the voters must see these differences in relationship to their positions on the issues. In many elections these conditions are not met.

There are many single-issue voters and single-issue groups. The National Rifle Association, the Christian Coalition, and the National Organization for Women are examples of organizations that track the statements and voting records of candidates and keep their membership informed. The more ardent members of these organizations vote on the basis of the candidates' position on a particular single issue.

At times, highly salient issues may capture the attention of the American voter. The poor economic conditions during the Great Depression became a concern to most Americans and led to a significant shift in partisan alignment. *See*: SINGLE-ISSUE GROUPS.

References: Paul R. Abramson, John H. Aldrich, and David W. Rhode, *Change and Continuity in the 1992 Elections*, rev. ed. (Washington, D.C.: Congressional Quarterly Press, 1994); John F. Bibby, *Politics, Parties, and Elections in America*, 3rd ed. (Chicago: Nelson-Hall, 1996).

J

JACKSON, ANDREW (1767–1845) was born at Waxhall settlement on the border between North and South Carolina on March 15, 1767, but a few days following his father's death. There he grew to manhood, attending frontier schools, but largely self-educated. That education took place within a frontier culture, harsh and frequently violent; a culture in which for males a code of behavior often turned differences of opinion or perceived slights into brawls, perceived insults into duels. As boy and man, Jackson subscribed to this code, brawled, and fought his duels, perhaps the most famous being the one in 1806 with Charles Dickenson whom he killed, fought over an alleged insult in which Dickenson presumably questioned the legitimacy of Jackson's marriage. Jackson's attachment to military life began during the Revolutionary War when, in 1781 at age fourteen, he and his brother volunteered for militia duty (an older brother having already died in the patriot cause). Captured by the British at Hanging Rock, the two brothers were taken as prisoners of war to Camden, South Carolina. Subsequently released, his brother dying of smallpox, followed by his mother's death that same year (1781), Jackson found himself a fourteen-year-old orphan. Teaching school in Waxhall, eventually coming to read the law, he opened his law office in Martinsville, North Carolina in 1787. Jackson was to move westward in 1788, ultimately settling in Nashville where he was, over the next several years, to serve in the appointive position of district attorney general, join the militia, begin his enterprise in land speculation, and marry Rachel Donelson Robards. As Tennessee moved toward statehood, Jackson served as a delegate to the convention which drafted the new state's first constitution in 1795–1796. With Tennessee admitted to the Union, Jackson became its first and, at that juncture, only member of the U.S. House of Representatives. His brief tenure in the House was followed in 1797 by an almost equally brief tenure in the U.S. Senate, a seat from which he resigned in 1798. For the next decade Jackson was to be actively involved in the buying and selling of land, eventually establishing himself as a slave-holding planter; also in this period, Jackson was elected to the state superior court, and, in 1802, to the rank of major general in the Tennessee militia. It was in this latter capacity that Jackson was drawn into the War of 1812, a war which would give him national fame as "Old Hickory," the hero of the battle of New Orleans, a battle fought, unknown to either Jackson or the opposing British, more than a week after a negotiated settlement to the war had been reached by the American Peace Commission at Ghent. The victory on January 8, 1815 was, nonetheless, significant in that it lifted national morale at a time when it was at low ebb, many seeing the war, at best, as a stalemate, at worst, as an American defeat. Jackson, now commissioned as a major general in the U.S. Army, remained in New Orleans as commander of the Southern District. In 1817–1818, Jackson was to become involved in the most controversial undertaking of his military career; at his initiative, given ambiguous orders, he engaged troops under his command in what would become known as the Seminole War, pursuing Indian forces across the border into Spanish Florida, capturing Pensacola and several other military outposts. Angering Spain, Jackson went yet a step further, summarily executing two British subjects on the grounds that he believed them guilty of inciting certain of the Seminole border attacks. With both Spain and Great Britain lodging protests, Congress in 1819 debated a vote of censure against Jackson who, considering the Seminole War ended, had now returned to Nashville, occupying himself in construction of his plantation home, "the Hermitage." Monroe administration support for Jackson, except for Secretary of State John Quincy Adams, was lukewarm at best. Adams, however, felt that Jackson's invasion had strengthened his hand in negotiations with Spain to cede the Floridas to the United States, an agreement realized later in 1819 with the Adams-Onis Treaty. Jackson now returned to Florida as the new territory's first governor in 1821. Increasingly, the national hero was discussed in terms of the presidency. To promote that cause the Tennessee legislature in 1823 returned Jackson to the U.S. Senate, and in 1824, endorsing Tennessee's favorite son, Pennsylvania, by convention in Harrisburg, advanced Jackson's name as a presidential nominee. The election of that year, however, was a muddled affair. With the demise of the Federalist Party and the disintegration of the Jeffersonian Republican coalition, an additional number of sectional and factional presidential nominations were to be advanced: Secretary of the Treasury William H. Crawford of Georgia, the choice of the Republican congressional caucus; Henry Clay of Kentucky, Speaker of the U.S. House, and from Massachusetts, secretary of state John Quincy Adams. In such a crowded field, even though he gained the largest popular vote and carried more states than any other candidate, Jackson failed of an Electoral College majority. As provided by the Constitution the presidential election was now transferred to the House, where each state delegation would cast one ballot in support of one of the three candidates having received the greatest number of Electoral College ballots: Jackson with 99 votes from 11 states; Adams with 84 ballots from 7 states; Crawford with 41 Electoral College votes from 3 states. Clay, as the fourth candidate, with but 37 votes from 3 states, was eliminated from House consideration. He would, however, play a crucial role in determining the outcome; opposed to Jackson, his competitor from the West, Clay delivered support to John Quincy Adams who on the first ballot of the House, on February 9, 1825, was elected president of the United States with thirteen state delegations voting for Adams, seven for Jackson, and four for Crawford. Irate, Jackson supporters were soon given further reason to call "foul" and claim "a corrupt bargain": Adams named Clay as secretary of state, thereby placing the Kentuckian high on the ladder of presidential succession. Forming a new, popularly based political party out of remnants of the old Jeffersonian Republican coalition, and as joined with frontier democrats, the new Democratic Party immediately focused on the election of 1828, the earliest opportunity to retire Adams from the White House. In the first presidential election significantly driven by the popular vote, the new party scored a decisive victory: the Democratic ticket of Jackson and vice-presidential nominee, the incumbent vice president of the United States John C. Calhoun of South Carolina, was given nearly 650,000 votes, carrying 15 states with 178 Electoral College ballots to the 500,000 votes gathered by the National Republicans; Adams and Richard Rush carried 9 states and 83 votes in the Electoral College. Inaugurated on March 4, 1829, two great controversies, both surfacing in Jackson's first term and both resolved in his second, came to define the Jackson presidency. The nullification crisis, slowly emerging, reached its crest in 1832–1833. The theory that in a federal system a state could legitimately declare a national law to which it was opposed to be null and void, unenforceable, within its jurisdiction, had long been debated. Indeed, both Jefferson and Madison, as they prepared drafts of what would become the Kentucky and Virginia resolutions in opposition to the Alien and Sedition Acts of 1798, had considered, but ultimately rejected, outright advocacy of the theory. In the 1830s, among the most prominent advocates of the argument were Vice-President John C. Calhoun and his fellow South Carolinian, Senator Robert Y. Hayne, both of whom viewed the theory, if applied, as a means of protection for the South, its agrarian interests, and its peculiar institution, slavery. Presuming that Jackson, as a Southern planter and a slave holder, would endorse their argument, nullificationists were first astonished, then angered, to find early on that the president was, in thought and deed, a committed nationalist willing to use force to preserve the Union and to see that the laws of the United States were faithfully executed. In July of 1832, Jackson signed into law tariff legislation seen by many in the South as inimical to Southern interests. Almost immediately, South Carolina raised the threat of nullification. Jackson, making a reasoned argument against nullification, and clearly indicating that he would use the military to put down a theory which, if practiced, would "lead directly to civil war and bloodshed," secured congressional authorization for such a response in the Force Bill of

March 1833. In the face of Jackson's clear determination, cooler heads prevailed. Congress, while passing the Force Bill, also enacted new, and more moderate tariff legislation. South Carolina passions, fueled by Calhoun's resignation from the vice-presidency in December of 1832 and Hayne's departure from the Senate, now receded and the state, for the time being, moved away from nullification. The second great controversy of the Jackson presidency was that over renewing the charter of the Bank of the United States. Jackson, seeing the Bank as a self-serving tool for an elite of wealth and privilege, poorly serving the interests of farmers, workers, and of a rising middle class, made known his absolute opposition to such a renewal. Henry Clay, wishing to manufacture an issue in support of his presidential candidacy of that year, steered through Congress in 1832 legislation to recharter the Bank, even though the institution's existing charter did not expire until 1836. Jackson, on July 10, 1832, vetoed such legislation, took his argument against the portrayed temple of the rich to the common man, and turned the issue to his great advantage. The success of this tactic was demonstrated in the election returns of 1832, a landslide Democratic Party victory: Jackson, with his running mate Martin Van Buren of New York, scored a popular plurality of more than 200,000 votes, carrying 16 of the 24 states with 219 Electoral College ballots. Clay and John Sergeant of Pennsylvania carried but 6 states for the National Republican ticket, 49 votes in the Electoral College. Adding interest to the election of 1832 was the third-party presidential candidacy of William Wirt, former attorney general of the United States, and nominee of the Anti-Masonic Party. Wirt, with a popular vote in excess of 100,000, carried Vermont and seven Electoral College ballots. In addition to the latter state, Wirt, surprisingly, secured significant popular support in Massachusetts, Connecticut, New York, and Pennsylvania. With the impetus of his landslide endorsement, Jackson was greatly strengthened in what would be his successful battles against both nullificationists in 1833 and the Bank of the United States and its now discredited supporters. Beginning the withdrawal of federal government deposits from the Bank in October of 1833, Jackson was, with unconcealed satisfaction, to witness the Bank's demise and collapse. Having successfully endorsed Vice-President Martin Van Buren as his successor, Jackson retired from the White House to the Hermitage in March of 1837, dying there on June 8, 1845. *See*: ELECTIONS: 1824, 1828, 1832.

References: Donald B. Cole, *The Presidency of Andrew Jackson* (Lawrence: University Press of Kansas, 1993); Robert V. Remini, *Andrew Jackson*, 3 vols. (New York: Harper and Row, 1977–1984); Arthur M. Schlesinger, Jr., *The Age of Jackson* (Boston: Little, Brown, 1945).

JACKSON, JESSE L. (1941–   ) emerged as the dominant black leader in the United States by seeking the Democratic Party presidential nomination in the 1980s. Jesse Jackson was born in Greenville, South Carolina. In 1964 he graduated from North Carolina Agricultural and Technical College in Greensboro, where he played football and served as student body president.

In 1963 he became active in the campus civil rights movement. He attended the Chicago Theological Seminary but left after two years to work full-time for Martin Luther King's Atlanta-based Southern Christian Leadership Conference (SCLC). He headed up the Chicago Operation Breadbasket, which used boycotts and pickets to bring about the hiring of more blacks.

He was appointed national coordinator in 1967, and was with King when he was assassinated in Memphis in 1968. He was not selected to succeed King; instead, Charles Abernathy was chosen. Jackson founded Operation Push, which was to push for a greater share of economic and political power for poor people in America. He received philanthropic and government grants to fund PUSH-Excel which focused on problems of inner city youth.

In 1983 he started his quest for the Democratic presidential nomination. During the campaign he negotiated with Syria for the release of a navy pilot whose plane had been shot down. It was reported during the campaign in New York that he referred to Jews as "Hymies," and New York as "Hymietown." He was also plagued by his ties to Louis Farrakhan, head of the Black Muslims, who was viewed as anti-Semitic.

In the March 13 Super Tuesday primary in the South, Jackson drew a heavy African-American vote. In the New York primary, he garnered 25% of the vote. He won the District of Columbia and Louisiana primaries. Overall, in 1984, he won 18% of the primary vote and 12% of the delegates.

In 1986 he founded his multiracial National Rainbow Coalition for his 1988 presidential bid. In the 1988 campaign he moved closer to the political center. He stunned the political establishment by winning 54% of the vote in Michigan. He could not sustain the momentum, however, and finished the 1988 nomination season with an impressive 29% of the primary vote, 29% of the delegates, and as the winner of seven primaries. At the convention, he pushed for changes in the Democratic Party rules on the distribution of delegates and a reduction in the number of superdelegates.

Jackson did not run in 1992. He kept his distance from Clinton but later developed close ties to the president. His son, Jesse Jackson Jr., was elected to Congress from a Chicago district. His presidential campaigns have been credited with mobilizing the African-American vote, and he has become the preeminent black leader in the United States.

JEFFERSON, THOMAS (1743–1826), author of the Declaration of Independence, first American secretary of state, third president of the United States, and, as he so dictated the final line of his epitaph, "father of the University of Virginia," was born at Shadwell plantation in the Virginia piedmont of an established landowning and slave holding family on April 13, 1743. Regarded by many as the most intellectual of the founding fathers, tutored in mathematics, philosophy, and languages, Jefferson was, after two years at the College of William and Mary, to read the law in the Williamsburg offices of George Wythe and be admitted to the bar in 1767 at age 24. As would become a type in

American political culture, the young lawyer also became the youthful politician, entering the Virginia House of Burgesses in 1769 where his skill with language and in writing came to be recognized and valued. Identifying early on with the emerging patriot cause, Jefferson was sent by the Virginia assembly as a delegate to the Second Continental Congress in 1775, filling the seat vacated by Peyton Randolph. Returning to Philadelphia in May of 1776, Jefferson, along with several of his colleagues, among them John Adams and Benjamin Franklin, was assigned the task of drafting a declaration announcing and justifying the resolution for independence which the Congress was expected to adopt. Seemingly by common consent, Jefferson became the primary author, even as other committee members, and indeed the Congress, were later to make certain changes in Jefferson's original draft. Even allowing for such modifications, there can be no doubt that the powerful language and argument, the style and substance of what was adopted on July 4, 1776 as the Declaration of Independence was the product of Jefferson's pen. Grounded in familiar natural law argument, particularly as derived from John Locke, the Declaration shouts to the ages,

> We hold these truths to be self-evident: that all men are created equal;
> that they are endowed by their creator with certain and inalienable rights;
> that among these are life, liberty & the pursuit of happiness:
> that to secure these rights, governments are instituted among men,
> deriving their just powers from the consent of the governed.

The Declaration was to be Jefferson's contribution to the American nation of which he was most proud, and to which he devoted the first line of his aforementioned epitaph, "Author of the Declaration of American Independence." His work on the Declaration completed, Jefferson returned from Philadelphia to a seat in the Virginia House of Delegates where he authored his second state document of that year, the Virginia statute on religious freedom, not to be adopted, however, until a decade later. In June of 1779, Jefferson was elected by vote of the Virginia legislature to the governorship, a tenure marked by the difficulties of war administration. Indeed Jefferson, as well as other executive and legislative authorities, was forced by British advances to abandon the capital at Richmond, retreat to Charlottesville, and then retreat yet again into the mountains and beyond; Governor Jefferson, himself, narrowly escaped capture as he made his departure from Monticello. It was this adventure that subsequently led to an embarrassing inquiry by the legislature into the conduct of the executive. With Jefferson personally answering the charges made, the inquiry was closed and ultimately a resolution passed by both houses of the Assembly commending the former governor upon his "Ability, Rectitude and Integrity as chief Magistrate" of the Commonwealth. It was perhaps the unpleasant aftertaste of Jefferson's experience in wartime governance, coupled with the sorrow which accompanied his wife's death in 1782, that led Jefferson to return to Philadelphia as part of his state's delegation to Congress and to accept in May of 1784 that body's appointment as U.S. minister to France, one of three ministers plenipotentiary in Europe (Franklin and Adams being the other two). While Jefferson did not neglect his diplomatic duties in Paris and at Versailles, he did devote much of his time to observation of all facets of French and European society, economic and agricultural, social and political. His study provided an interesting comparison with similar observations he had already made of his native Virginia, leading to publication in Paris in 1785 (followed by a London edition in 1787), of what was to be Jefferson's only book, *Notes on the State of Virginia*, in which, among much else, he provided an account of slavery as found in Virginia, concluding with an argument for eventual emancipation. Returning from France in 1789, Jefferson missed the opportunity to have been part of the convention in Philadelphia called to propose amendments to the Articles of Confederation but which ended in offering to the American people that document known today as the Constitution of 1787. While deeply committed to the value of decentralized governance, Jefferson nonetheless recognized, in 1787–1788, the need to augment national authority. While concerned that the proposed Constitution did not contain a Bill of Rights, he supported ratification and looked forward to quick amendment of the new Constitution so as to provide for the former. With that ratification and the unanimous vote in the Electoral College bringing George Washington to the presidency, Jefferson accepted the new president's invitation to become, as secretary of state, part of an emerging cabinet system. With Washington looking to his cabinet secretaries not simply for advice and execution of policy within their assigned fields but, as well, for more wide-ranging counsel, it is not surprising that those two strong personalities, Jefferson and Secretary of the Treasury Alexander Hamilton, would soon collide in their competition for Washington's endorsement of their rival proposals. Jefferson intruded his views upon Hamilton to urge the cause of agrarian interests relative to those of commerce and manufacturing. Hamilton intruded his opinions upon Jefferson to urge a foreign policy more pro-British than pro-French. And in their mutual interventions both saw conspiracy: Jefferson loathed Hamilton's attempts to strengthen national, and particularly executive authority, relative to that of the states, seeing this as nothing more than a prelude to the establishment of an American monarchy. Hamilton, in turn, scorned the attempts of Jefferson, as he saw it, at counterrevolution, wishing to restore to the states powers which had come to the national government under the new Constitution, thereby attempting to reestablish the old confederacy with powers so decentralized as to bring about mob democracy. Small wonder that such policy divisions within the executive branch spilled over to the Congress and to the nation. As each side attempted to gather popular support in order to control decision and policy making, there emerged in the 1790 decade the first American party system: a two-party system with Federalists like Hamilton, John Adams, Fisher Ames, and John Marshall facing Republicans such as Jefferson, James Madison, Albert Gallatin, and, publicist of the Republican cause, Philip Freneau. With clear signs that Hamilton was winning the battle for Washington's allegiance, Jefferson resigned his cabinet post at the end of 1794. With Washington adamantly opposed to all efforts to be recruited to a third term, Jefferson was advanced in 1796 by the nascent Republican Party to oppose John Adams, the sitting vice-president, now championed by the Federalist Party as Washington's successor. The Electoral College balloting resulted in an extremely close vote, 71 ballots given to Adams and 68 to Jefferson. The oddity which emerged from the Electoral College balloting in 1796 was that the existing constitutional language (later amended) did not provide electors an opportunity to vote separately for the presidential and vice-presidential offices, or to vote for a party ticket, the result being that Jefferson, with the second highest vote total to Adams, was elected to the vice-presidency. For the next four years the nation was to experience the peculiar circumstance of having a president and vice-president of different political parties. The consequence was what would have been predicted: Adams was unwilling to bring Jefferson, as leader of the opposition, into the policy processes of a Federalist administration; Jefferson, as that opposition leader and thus divorced from administration policies, was therefore free to become the administration's most severe critic. Jefferson's opposition, sometimes open, was more often covert, as with his anonymous authorship of the Kentucky resolutions in opposition to passage by the Federalist Congress of the Alien and Sedition Acts in the summer of 1798. Jefferson's contention, as originally drafted, was that if the national government should come to exercise powers not constitutionally granted, the states had "a natural right . . . to nullify of their own authority all [such] assumptions of powers," an argument claimed more than a quarter century later by John C. Calhoun and other states' rights advocates as the nation slowly moved toward civil war. The continuing controversy during the Adams administration between Republicans and Federalists as to states' rights versus national authority, the virtues of republican governance versus a more elitist regime, made the election of 1796 simply the predicate to that of 1800 when Adams and Jefferson were again competitors for the presidential office. The peculiar results of the Electoral College balloting in 1796 became yet more bizarre in 1800. Jefferson and the presumptive Republican vice-presidential candidate Aaron Burr tied in the balloting, each with 73 votes to 65 for Adams and one less for Charles Cotesworth Pinckney, the Federalist vice-presidential candidate. The election was thus thrown into the U.S. House of Representatives where Federalists, holding a lame-duck majority until the new House should be convened, had the unusual opportunity of making one of the two Republicans, as the tied Electoral College vote-getters, president of the United States. Aaron Burr, ever ambitious, failed to give way to Jefferson, as he had indicated he would do in the event of a tie vote, and it was not until the thirty-sixth ballot in the House that Jefferson, on February 17, 1801, emerged the victor, with ten state delegations voting for the Virginian, four for Burr, and two state delegations, their members unable to agree, abstaining. Aaron Burr, his party loyalty now highly suspect not only to Jefferson but to most of the Republican leadership as well, assumed, as the constitutional law then provided, the vice-presidency in which office he was be as roundly ignored by Jefferson as Jefferson had been ignored by Adams. Such unanticipated misfirings of the Electoral College proceedings both in 1796 and again in the election of 1800 led, before Jefferson's first term had ended, to adoption of the Twelfth Amendment. Jefferson's first term was otherwise remarkable for its degree of policy change, expansion of presidential power, and for the personal popularity which Jefferson came to enjoy. The Hamiltonian economic program in place for a decade was, if not wholly rescinded, greatly modified: agrarian interests were now promoted over those of manufacturing and commerce, federal taxation reduced or abolished, and the national debt, seen by Hamilton as benign, scheduled for extinction. But the most extraordinary feature, enlarging the dimensions of presidential power and bringing high approval to Jefferson, was the one undertaking about which Jefferson, himself, had greatest reservation: the acquisition through treaty with France of a vast, uncharted, western territory which would more than double the size of the United States. Philosophically committed to the theory of decentralized governance and to the practice of strict observance of the limitations of power felt to be imposed by the Constitution, Jefferson initially concluded that territorial expansion of this magnitude would require constitutional authorization through adoption of an appropriate amendment. Becoming convinced, however, that neither time, his own party in Congress, nor France would await the slow process of constitutional adjustment, Jefferson acted to expand, as he put it, ''the empire of liberty''; the Louisiana Purchase was made, the treaty being ratified by the U.S. Senate on October 20, 1803. The purchase marked not simply the birth of a more activist presidency but, even more significantly, the emerging expansion of national power. In a less dramatic way the latter had been demonstrated one year earlier when the U.S. Supreme Court had handed down its decision in the now historic case, *Marbury* v. *Madison* (1802). Writing an opinion for a unanimous court, Jefferson's distant but Federalist cousin, Chief Justice John Marshall, had reiterated, while giving the technical decision to Jefferson and Secretary of State Madison, the Federalist principle of the Constitution as ''high law'' to which all other law was subordinate, it being the role of Supreme Court (i.e., national authority) to interpret that law and to prefer that law to any other law in conflict with it, such conflicting law to be declared by the Court null and void. The Republicans, delightedly accepting the decision on the narrow point, were furious, as they saw it, at Marshall's wholesale manufacture of the larger doctrine of judicial review. This decision, joined by those others that would come from the Marshall Court over the next two decades, would further fuel the continuing debate between Republicans as advocates of states' rights and Federalists as exponents of national authority. If, however, Federalists were to take their satisfaction in John Marshall's constitutional law it was to be small comfort, for the electoral arena was increasingly and overwhelmingly dominated by the Jeffersonian Republicans as the Electoral College balloting of 1804 was to demonstrate. Jefferson, joined by New York governor George Clinton as vice-presidential candidate, replacing the discredited and controversial Aaron Burr, carried the Electoral College ballots of 15 states with only Connecticut and Delaware in the Federalist camp of Charles Cotesworth Pinckney and Rufus King. As with Washington, Jefferson was to find his second term, relative to his first, far more problematic in terms of policy, and far less rewarding in terms of personal satisfaction. Much of the president's energy was turned to putting down the Burr conspiracy on the western frontier and in attempting to prevent the United States from being drawn into the Napoleonic wars raging in Europe, particularly as Great Britain continued its policy of interdiction of U.S. ships on the high seas. Successful in meeting the former challenge, Jefferson found it far more difficult, short of war, to resolve the difficulties with Great Britain. The chosen instrument of the administration came to be embodied in the Embargo Act of 1807 whereby, in an effort to insure respect by all belligerents for U.S neutrality, the export of American goods was prohibited. Abroad the embargo seemed to have little impact; at home it proved difficult to enforce and aroused in many quarters deep resentment and vigorous opposition. Not only did Federalists, the established representatives of commercial interests, react, but so did a number of Republicans, some on philosophic grounds objecting to what seemed to them an excessive, perhaps unconstitutional, exercise of national government power, and others in more purely economic terms, protesting the damage being done to agrarian interests by prohibiting the export of farm products. While most of the nation, even as economic problems mounted, gave support, albeit grudgingly, to the administration, Jefferson, unaccustomed to such dissent, and with his White House days drawing to a close, increasingly removed himself from decision making and the exercise of presidential leadership. Secure in knowing that his party had retained control of the national government, Jefferson left the presidency on March 4, 1809, returning to his Virginia estate at Monticello; returning as well to his family, to farming, to his books and intellectual pursuits, and, in his estimation, most importantly, to creating (1816–1819) the University of Virginia, an institution which he guided in all phases of its development until his death on July 4, 1826. The date was, appropriately enough, the fiftieth anniversary of the adoption of the Declaration of Independence. *See*: ELECTIONS: 1796, 1800, 1804.

References: Noble E. Cunningham, Jr., *In Pursuit of Reason: The Life of Thomas Jefferson* (Baton Rouge: Louisiana State University Press, 1987); Dumas Malone, *Jefferson and His Time*, 6 vols. (Boston: Little, Brown, 1948–1981); Forrest McDonald, *The Presidency of Thomas Jefferson* (Lawrence: University Press of Kansas, 1976).

JEWISH VOTE. In national elections the Jewish vote has been overwhelmingly Democratic since the New Deal. Despite economic success, the Jewish experience with anti-Semitism and discrimination has led them to be supportive of social welfare policies and civil rights. The Republican courting of the Christian Right has pushed the Jewish voters even further toward the Democratic Party.

In 1992, 80% of the Jewish vote went to Clinton. In 1996 the Jewish vote was 3% of the total vote, and 78% voted for Democrat Bill Clinton.

There is a large concentration of Jews in New York City, and in 1993 they supported the Republican mayoral candidate Rudolph Guliani. Despite their liberalism, the American Jewish community has occasionally had tense relations with African Americans in urban areas. The anti-Semitism of Muslim leader Louis Farrakhan has added to this tension. *See*: NEW DEAL COALITION.

References: John A. Kromkowski, ''The Politics of Inclusion: Ethnics in the 1996 Election,'' in *America's Choice: The Election of 1996*, William Crotty and Jerome M. Mileur, eds. (Guilford, Conn.: Dushkin/McGraw-Hill, 1997); Mark R. Levy and Michael G. Kramer, *The Ethnic Factor* (New York: Simon and Schuster, 1972).

JOHNSON, ANDREW (1808–1875) was born of a desperately poor family in Raleigh, North Carolina on December 29, 1808. His family unable to provide him with even the rudiments of a school education, Johnson, illiterate, was apprenticed to tailor James Selby at age thirteen. Taught by friends to read and write, Johnson ran away from his apprenticeship in 1824. Two years later, taking his mother and stepfather with him, Johnson resettled in Greeneville, Tennessee, where he opened his own tailor's shop. Taking an interest in local politics, Johnson, at age 22, and after a term as alderman, was elected Greeneville mayor in 1830. For the remainder of Johnson's life, the Jacksonian Democrat was to be found either holding or seeking public office. Elected in 1835 to the Tennessee legislature, he would be defeated in 1837, but reelected in 1839, subsequently to move from the lower chamber to the Tennessee Senate in 1841. For the next decade, Johnson would hold a seat in the U.S. House of Representatives (1843–1853). Returning to Tennessee in 1853, the now experienced politician was to be elected, and subsequently reelected, to the governorship (1853–1857). In 1857 the state legislature elected Johnson to the U.S. Senate where he was to continue to serve even following Tennessee's decision in 1861 to withdraw from the Union and join the Confederacy. Aware of the building secessionist sentiment, Senator Johnson, a staunch unionist, had returned to his home state in the spring of that year to vigorously make the anti-secessionist argument. Following the popular vote on June 8, 1861, endorsing the legislature's decision to secede, Johnson had literally to escape the state with his life. Returning to Washington, he was the only member of the U.S. Senate from the seceded states to remain in that chamber, preferring Union over Confederacy. With Union armies largely in control of Tennessee by the spring of 1862, President Lincoln appointed Johnson as military governor of the state on March 4. The most interesting feature of Johnson's relatively harsh tenure (harsh in terms of his treatment of secessionists and confederate sympathizers), was the governor's endorsement of emancipation. His acceptance of emancipation was not a result of any personal, deeply felt opposition to slavery, but rather a pragmatic calculation as to what would be politically necessary for the full restoration of

Tennessee to its prewar status in the Union. Johnson's popularity in the North, as a Union Democrat and military governor, was such that Republican leaders in 1864, hoping to attract Democratic votes to Lincoln's reelection cause, engineered the substitution of Andrew Johnson for the sitting vice-president Hannibal Hamlin as Lincoln's running mate. Thus, the election of 1864 resulted in the victory of an incumbent Republican president and a newly chosen Democratic vice-president, both inaugurated on March 4, 1865. Within six weeks of that inauguration the unionist Democrat was president of the United States, Lincoln having succumbed to an assassin's bullet on April 15, 1865. As the war ended Johnson, in a calculation of diverse political interests, committed himself to a period of brief, moderate reconstruction, marked by little regard for either the definition, or once defined, the protection of basic citizenship rights for the newly freed black man. The president, clearly, had placed himself on a collision course with congressional Radical Republicans, who had quite different notions as to the length and severity of reconstruction and who planned on the use of constitutional amendment as a means for defining both the newfound rights of blacks and the new authority and power of the national government. While something of a stalemate initially developed between president and Congress, the midterm elections of 1866 dramatically strengthened the hand of the Radical Republicans, Johnson then finding his executive vetoes routinely overridden. Two key pieces of Radical Republican legislation, both becoming law over Johnson's vetoes on March 2, 1867, were ultimately to move the House toward impeachment of the president nearly a year later on February 24, 1868: The Reconstruction Act divided the Confederate South into five military districts each under martial law, enfranchised newly freed black males, and disfranchised ex-Confederates; the Tenure of Office Act prohibited a president from removing from office without Senate consent any appointee, including cabinet officers, whose initial appointment had been subject to Senate confirmation. (The Tenure of Office Act was significantly amended during the Grant administration and all but repealed in 1887. The U.S. Supreme Court, in 1926, held such limitations on the presidential appointment power to be unconstitutional in *Meyers* v. *United States*). Johnson, by attempting on several occasions to unilaterally dismiss Edwin Stanton, the secretary of war, who would have major responsibility for implementing the Reconstruction Act of 1867, thereby signaled his defiance to Congress. The impeachment trial before the U.S. Senate, with the chief justice of the Supreme Court presiding, opened on March 30, 1868. After five weeks, argument ended on May 7; Washington and an absorbed nation awaited the verdict nine days later on May 16, 1868. In a solemn moment of high political theater, each Senator in alphabetical turn responded to Chief Justice Salmon P. Chase's question as to the first article of impeachment, "Mr. Senator, how say you?" Thirty-five senators responded "guilty," nineteen senators answered the chief justice with two words, "not guilty." By the constitutional requirement of a two-thirds vote needed for conviction, on that day (completed as to other articles of impeachment on May 26) Andrew Johnson, president of the United

States, stood acquitted by one vote. Among the nineteen senators saving for Johnson the presidential office were all twelve of the chamber's Democrats, joined by seven Republicans. Johnson, spared being driven from office, was, however, left as a virtually powerless figurehead for the remainder of his term. Disappointed not to be considered for the Democratic Party's presidential nomination in July of 1868, Johnson, not attending General Ulysses S. Grant's inauguration, on March 4, 1869 returned to Tennessee, there to continue his career in seeking and holding public office. Defeated in an attempt to return to the U.S. Senate in 1869, he was also to fail of election to the U.S. House of Representatives in 1872. In 1874, however, the Tennessee legislature did what it failed to do in 1869; it sent Andrew Johnson back to the U.S. Senate. Returning to Tennessee in the summer of 1875 for vacation, Johnson died at his daughter's farm near Carter's Station on July 31, 1875. *See*: ELECTIONS: 1864; LINCOLN, ABRAHAM.

References: Albert Castel, *The Presidency of Andrew Johnson* (Lawrence: University Press of Kansas, 1979). David M. Dewitt, *The Impeachment and Trial of Andrew Jackson* (New York: Macmillan, 1903); Hans L. Trefousse, *Andrew Johnson, A Biography* (New York: Norton, 1989);

JOHNSON, LYNDON BAINES (1908–1973) was the thirty-sixth president of the United States. Johnson was born near Stonewall, Texas. His father Samuel E. Johnson was a businessman who experienced both economic success and failure, and was also a state legislator. The family moved to Johnson City, Texas in 1913. Johnson graduated from Southwest Texas State Teachers College in 1930. After graduation, Johnson taught school in Houston. He then became an aide to Democratic Congressman Richard Kleberg, and went to Washington, D.C. in 1931. Johnson worked in the House during the early years of the New Deal. In 1934 he married Claudia Alta (Lady Bird) Taylor, who came from a prosperous family.

In 1935, Johnson was appointed state director of the National Youth Administration, to assist young people during the Depression. In 1937, Congressman James Buchanan of the Tenth Congressional District died and Johnson was elected to the vacant seat. In the House, Johnson became a close ally of House Speaker Sam Rayburn. In 1941, Johnson entered a special senatorial election and lost to the governor of the state, W. Lee O'Daniel. Johnson lost the election by his poor showing in east Texas.

Lyndon Johnson enlisted in the Navy in 1942, and served in the Pacific theater. In 1943 the Johnsons purchased a radio station in Austin, Texas. This was the beginning of a substantial media empire; later they would purchase a television station in Austin. In 1948 another opportunity for a U.S. Senate seat occurred with O'Daniel's retirement. This time Johnson faced former governor Coke Stevenson. In a runoff election, Johnson won by only 87 votes. Stevenson's forces charged that the election was stolen in east Texas. Johnson was able to withstand the allegations and held onto the Senate seat. From that election, he became known as "Landslide Lyndon." This challenged election victory contributed to Johnson's reputation as a wheeler-dealer.

Johnson's style and personality were a good fit for the postwar Congress. He quickly rose in the ranks of the Democrats, and in 1953 was elected minority leader; in 1954 he became majority leader. He pursued a bipartisan approach on foreign policy with the Eisenhower administration. In 1956 he made his first serious bid for the presidential nomination, but failed to block the renomination of Adlai Stevenson. In 1960, Johnson overrated his national prominence as a legislative leader, and started his active campaign too late to stop the young Massachusetts senator John F. Kennedy, who had taken his campaign into the state primaries. At the Democratic convention in July, Kennedy offered Johnson the vice-presidential nomination which he accepted. Johnson proved to be a major asset to the ticket, carrying Texas for Kennedy by a narrow margin. Johnson was marginalized in the Kennedy administration. On November 22, 1963, Kennedy was assassinated in Dallas, Texas. Johnson quickly reassured the nation of his commitment to the Kennedy agenda.

In his first term, President Johnson had remarkable legislative accomplishments. In 1964 the Civil Rights Act was passed. In May 1964 he called for the "Great Society." This proposed agenda would eliminate poverty, provide security of the elderly, and rebuild American cities. All of this was to be done without redistributing wealth. After his landslide reelection over the very conservative Republican nominee Barry Goldwater, Johnson pushed for his Great Society agenda. Medicare and Medicaid were passed in 1965. Also, funding for poverty programs was adopted, including money for Head Start and the community action programs. The Voting Rights Act was passed in 1965. In the area of domestic policy, Johnson was the most influential president in the twentieth century, except for Franklin Roosevelt. In foreign policy his legacy is not significant, and his Achilles heel—the Vietnam War—overshadowed his administration.

In 1965, Johnson authorized the bombing of North Vietnam to force negotiations. He gradually intensified military pressure on North Vietnam with little success. This sparked protest in the United States. The remainder of his term was overshadowed by this war which he could not win, and his popularity plummeted. On March 31, 1965, after almost losing the New Hampshire primary to Eugene McCarthy, Johnson told the nation that: "I shall not seek, and I will not accept the nomination of my party for another term as your president." Johnson retired to his ranch in Texas. *See*: ELECTION; ELECTIONS: 1960, 1964; GOLDWATER, BARRY M.; KENNEDY, JOHN FITZGERALD; RUN-OFF.

Reference: Robert A. Caro, *Lyndon Johnson: Means of Ascent* (New York: Knopf, 1990).

JUDICIAL ELECTIONS. Four states empower the state legislature to select state court judges. In the remaining states, various systems are used to elect judges. Ten states use partisan elections. Thirteen states use nonpartisan elections. There are a number of variations of these types of judicial elections. In Ohio, for example, judges are nominated in partisan primaries to run as nonpartisan candidates in the general election. Many states that use a merit plan or select judges by gubernatorial appointment then require the appointee to run in a retention election, where a majority of the voters must vote "yes" for the appointed judge to retain the seat. One of the most controversial retention elections was the challenge to California chief justice Rose Bird, a liberal judge, who was ousted by an expensive campaign financed by California conservatives. In 1996 a Tennessee intermediate appellate court judge, Penny White, was rejected by 55% of the vote for being perceived as soft on crime.

The districts that are used for judicial elections have been challenged in recent years. African Americans have not been successful in getting elected to the bench in statewide and in at-large local districts. Some of these districts have been challenged under the Voting Rights Act of 1965. In a number of states, sweeping at-large districts, where each judicial seat was elected separately, have been divided into smaller districts. In some jurisdictions, such as Cook County, Illinois, electoral subdistricts were created with the intention of electing African Americans to the bench. *See*: MISSOURI PLAN.

References: Richard L. Engstrom, "Alternative Judicial Election Systems: Solving the Minority Vote Dilution Problem," in *United States Electoral Systems: Their Impact on Women and Minorities*, Wilma Rule and Joseph F. Zimmerman, eds. (Westport, Conn.: Greenwood Press, 1992); John J. Harrigan, *Politics and Policy in States and Communities*, 5th ed. (New York: HarperCollins, 1994); Herbert Jacob, "Courts: The Least Visible Branch," in *Politics in the American States: A Comparative Analysis*, 6th ed., Virginia Gray and Herbert Jacob, eds. (Washington, D.C.: Congressional Quarterly Press, 1996).

JUNGLE PRIMARY was the name used to describe the primary system adopted by California voters, which was proposed as an initiative in the California primary of 1996. The initiative passed despite opposition from the Republican and Democratic state party organizations. The jungle primary is formally known as a Blanket Primary, which is used in Alaska and Washington.

The argument put forward by the proponents of the jungle primary for California was that this type of primary would lead to the nomination of more moderate candidates. They argued that closed party primaries were dominated by extremist voters. The California initiative creating the jungle primary was upheld by the federal court. *See*: PRIMARY, BLANKET.

JUNIOR TUESDAY was held on the first Tuesday in March of 1996, a week before Super Tuesday. It was regional in that five New England states scheduled their primaries on that day, called by some the Yankee Primary. These New England primaries were scheduled along with primaries in Georgia, Maryland, and Colorado. Minnesota and Washington also scheduled caucuses that day. In 1996, Dole finished first in all ten contests, capturing 185 of the 208 Republican

National Convention delegates. *See*: FRONT-LOADED PRIMARY; PRI-MARY, REGIONAL; SUPER TUESDAY.

Reference: Larry J. Sabato, ''Presidential Nominations, the Front-loaded Frenzy of '96,'' in *Toward the Millennium: The Elections of 1996*, Larry J. Sabato, ed. (Needham Heights, Mass.: Allyn and Bacon, 1997).

K

KANSAS-NEBRASKA ACT OF 1854. This bill was introduced by Senator Stephen A. Douglas, Democrat of Illinois, to bring the territory of Nebraska into the Union as two states, Kansas and Nebraska. The proposal did not stipulate whether they would be free or slave states. The bill proposed that the settlers would decide the status of slavery in the respective states. With the support of the Southern members of Congress, this bill became law in the spring of 1854. The Missouri Compromise of 1820 was broken by this law, and slavery would be permitted in the West and Northwest. This brought slavery to the forefront of American politics. The Democratic Party was split by this issue, and the Republican Party was born in 1854 at various meetings in the North of anti-Nebraska Free-Soilers. The name ''Republican'' was first used in February 1854 in Ripon, Wisconsin. A noted mass meeting of Republicans was held in Jackson, Michigan on June 6, 1854, which many view as the founding of the Republican Party. *See*: REPUBLICAN PARTY.

References: William E. Gienapp, *The Origins of the Republican Party, 1852–1856* (New York: Oxford University Press, 1987); Malcolm Moos, The Republicans: *A History of Their Party* (New York: Random House, 1956).

KENNEDY, EDWARD M. (TED) (1932–   ) has served as the Democratic Senator from the state of Massachusetts since 1962. In the U.S. Senate, he is third in seniority. He was born in Boston to the prominent political family of Joseph and Rose Kennedy. He received a B.A. degree from Harvard and a law degree from the University of Virginia in 1959. Ted Kennedy became a national spokesman for the liberal causes after his brother Robert was assassinated.

Ted Kennedy's presidential aspirations suffered a fatal setback by the July

1969 Chappaquiddick incident, in which a young woman drowned. He sought the Democratic presidential nomination in 1980; after a hopeful start, Kennedy was easily defeated by incumbent President Jimmy Carter.

Ted Kennedy has been a strong and consistent voice for liberal causes. For years, he advocated a Canadian-style single-payer national health care program. As a Senate leader, he gave strong support to President Clinton's failed National Health Security Act. He was a promoter of the Family and Medical Leave Act, which was signed by President Clinton in 1993.

In 1994, Kennedy faced a stiff challenge for his seat by wealthy businessman Mitt Romney, son of former governor George Romney of Michigan. Kennedy was criticized in the press for raising questions about Romney's Mormon faith, after John Kennedy faced religious bigotry in his 1960 presidential election. The early polls showed Kennedy running behind. After a nasty and expensive race, Kennedy won with 58% of the vote. He serves as the ranking minority member of the Senate Labor Committee.

KENNEDY, JOHN FITZGERALD (1917–1963) was the thirty-fifth president of the United States. John Kennedy was born in Brookline, Massachusetts. His father, Joseph Patrick Kennedy, was a successful Wall Street financier who had served in a number of positions in the administration of Franklin D. Roosevelt. John Kennedy graduated from Harvard in 1940. His senior honors thesis was published under the title *Why England Slept* (1940). He suffered from a bad back but was able to enter the U.S. Navy during World War II, and he was assigned to command a PT boat in the South Pacific. His boat was rammed by a Japanese destroyer, and Kennedy acted in a heroic manner.

In 1946, Kennedy was elected to Congress from the Eleventh Congressional District in Massachusetts. In 1952 he ran for the U.S. Senate against incumbent Henry Cabot Lodge; he won that election by a narrow margin. In 1953 he married Jacqueline Lee Bouvier. In 1954 he underwent back surgery, and in his long recovery wrote *Profiles in Courage* (1956), which won a Pulitzer Prize for biography in 1957. He was viewed as a distant and an aloof figure in the Senate. In 1956 he sought the Democratic vice-presidential nomination, but lost to Estes Kefauver. In 1958 he was reelected to the Senate by a large margin, and he started his quest for the 1960 Democratic presidential nomination.

Well financed by his family's fortune, Kennedy defeated Hubert Humphrey in the Wisconsin and West Virginia primaries, proving that he was a potent vote-getter and that his Catholicism was not an electoral liability. He was nominated on the first ballot at the 1960 Democratic National Convention in Los Angeles. He offered the vice-presidential nomination to Texas senator and majority leader Lyndon Johnson. The 1960 presidential campaign was the first one to have televised presidential debates. In contrast to the Republican nominee, Richard M. Nixon, Kennedy appeared poised on television. There was a very large turnout in the 1960 election—64%. Kennedy won by a very narrow margin and there were charges of vote fraud in a number of states, including Illinois.

Nixon refused to press the vote fraud issue and Kennedy was elected. He was the youngest person ever elected president, and the first Roman Catholic.

In his inaugural address, Kennedy offered this memorable statement: "And so, my fellow Americans, ask not what your country can do for you; ask what you can do for your country." Kennedy pursued an activist foreign policy. In an effort to strengthen Latin America against the threat of communism, Kennedy formed the Alliance for Progress and created the Peace Corps to assist in the development of those nations. Kennedy also approved a CIA plan to arm Cuban exiles to overthrow the communist government of Fidel Castro. In April 1961 the invading exiles were crushed by the Castro forces. In 1962, after it was discovered that the Soviet Union was building missile bases in Cuba, Kennedy ordered the U.S. Navy to stop all Soviet vessels destined for Cuba and search them for "offensive weapons" and then turn them back. Soviet leader Nikita Khrushchev backed down from challenging the blockade, avoiding a potential nuclear war. Kennedy's progressive domestic proposals were blocked by Congress. On November 22, 1963, Kennedy was assassinated by Lee Harvey Oswald in Dallas, Texas. He was succeeded by Vice-President Lyndon Johnson. *See*: ELECTIONS: 1960; NIXON, RICHARD MILHOUS.

Reference: Theodore H. White, *The Making of the President, 1960* (New York: Atheneum, 1961).

KEYNOTE ADDRESS is the second most important political speech at a national political convention, after the nominee's acceptance speech. In contemporary national conventions, the keynoter is scheduled for prime-time television. This speech sets the tone of the fall presidential campaign. In 1996 it was given on the second night of the convention. Republican nominee Bob Dole selected youthful, pro-choice, Staten Island congresswoman Susan Molinari to be the Republican National Convention keynoter. She was selected to improve the image of the party with women and to demonstrate that the party was open to pro-choice voters. Democratic nominee President Bill Clinton had popular Indiana governor Evan Bayh give the keynote address at the 1996 Democratic National Convention in Chicago.

The keynote address is expected to unify the delegates. The keynoter often invokes memories of the great party leaders of the past. If the party is out of power, then the keynoter directs his or her remarks at the shortcomings of the party in office. In 1992 the Democrats offered three keynoters. One of the most memorable recent keynote addresses was given by Mario Cuomo in 1984. The keynoter is looked upon as a future leader to the party. *See*: NATIONAL PARTY CONVENTION.

Reference: Stephen J. Wayne, *The Road to the White House 1996: The Politics of Presidential Elections* (New York: St. Martin's Press, 1996).

KING, MARTIN LUTHER, JR. (1929–1968) was the preeminent U.S. civil rights leader of the twentieth century. He was a Baptist minister who used nonviolent tactics to desegregate the South. In 1955, Rosa Parks refused to give up her seat on a bus to a white man in Montgomery, Alabama and was arrested. Martin Luther King organized and led a boycott of the Montgomery bus system. In 1956, Montgomery buses were integrated, and King gained national prominence as a civil rights leader. He led the famous March on Washington on August 28, 1965. At the Lincoln Memorial, he gave his famous "I have a dream" speech. His movement led to the civil rights legislation of the 1960s. He was assassinated in Memphis, Tennessee on April 4, 1968. His assassination led to further expansion of the Civil Rights Act and increased interest in gun control. His birthday was proclaimed a national holiday in 1983. *See*: VOTING RIGHTS ACT.

Reference: David J. Garrow, *Bearing the Cross: Martin Luther King Jr. and the Southern Christian Leadership Conference* (New York: Morrow, 1986).

KING, RUFUS (1755–1827), the last presidential candidate of the Federalist Party, was born in what is now Scarborough, Maine on March 24, 1755. Enrolled at Harvard at the outbreak of the Revolutionary War, King was to graduate in 1777. King subsequently "read" the law, being admitted to the Massachusetts bar in 1780. He began his lifelong career in national politics as one of his state's representatives to Congress under the Articles of Confederation, 1784–1787. In that body King was a staunch advocate of New England commercial and maritime interests, and on politico-economic grounds an opponent of slavery, the extension of which to the northwest territories he vigorously and successfully opposed. In 1787, King was selected to be one of his state's delegates to the Philadelphia constitutional convention. Influenced by Shay's Rebellion in his home state, King became one of the convention's ultra-nationalists, going so far as to suggest the possible elimination of the states as separate political entities, to be replaced by a strong unitary national government capable of protecting property rights. He continued his opposition to slavery and was responsible for certain of the compromise provisions on that issue included in the proposed constitution. With ratification of that document, King transferred his political career from Massachusetts to New York where, in 1789, he was elected by the state legislature to a seat in the U.S. Senate. A close friend and political ally of Alexander Hamilton, King gave active support to Senate approval of the treasury secretary's economic program and to ratification of the Jay Treaty in 1794. Resigning from the Senate in 1796, King accepted President Washington's appointment as ambassador to Great Britain, a position that he retained through the Adams administration and, for a short period of time, the administration of that president so anathema to Federalists, Thomas Jefferson. Returning to the United States in 1803, King allowed himself to become the Federalist candidate for vice-president in 1804, and again in 1808. Both were token, and unsuccessful, candidacies for King. Overwhelmed by Hamilton's death in 1804, and the unyielding sway of Jeffersonian republicanism, for nearly a decade King all but retired from active politics, not returning to the arena until his election to the U.S. Senate in 1813. Opposed to the War of 1812, King, once hostilities commenced, strongly supported funding of the war effort and legislative proposals to strengthen the national defense. King stood, as he always had, for the survival of the federal Union against its enemies, whether foreign or domestic. When in 1814 certain disgruntled Federalists opposed to "Mr. Madison's War" talked of New England secession, organizing the ill-conceived, ill-fated Hartford convention, King refused to lend his reputation or support to the disunionist cause. In 1816, King had the unusual distinction of being both Federalist candidate for the New York governorship and his party's presidential nominee. In the spring of 1816, while gathering a respectable popular vote, he narrowly lost the gubernatorial contest; autumn, however, was less kind, bringing overlwhelming defeat in the presidential election: King and the Federalists gained but 34 Electoral College ballots from 3 states to James Monroe's 183 votes from 16 states. For the Federalist Party it was the last hurrah. Not so for King. He continued to serve in the Senate until 1825, remaining a spokesman for the propertied interests of New York and New England; maintaining his opposition to slavery to which he now added a moral, as well as a politico-economic, objection. This latter opposition led King to reject the Missouri Compromise of 1820. Appointed to his former post of ambassador to Great Britain by President John Quincy Adams in May of 1825, failing health required his resignation but a year later. Returning to his home in New York, King died there on April 29, 1827. *See*: ELECTIONS: 1816.

References: Robert Ernst, *Rufus King, American Federalist* (Chapel Hill: University of North Carolina Press for the Institute of Early American History and Culture, 1968); Charles R. King, ed., *The Life and Correspondence of Rufus King*, 6 vols. (New York: Putnam's, 1894–1900).

KIRKPATRICK **v.** *PREISLER,* 394 U.S. 526 (1969) is a case which interpreted the principle "one person, one vote," to mean that states had to show that they had made a "good faith effort to achieve precise mathematical equality" when apportioning the vote in congressional districts. The case arose out of Missouri's attempts to respond to the U.S. Supreme Court's decision in *Wesberry* v. *Sanders* (1964) ordering state legislatures to follow the standard of "one person, one vote" when drawing congressional districts. Missouri's 1967 apportionment statute would have resulted in voting districts that varied approximately 3% above and below the mathematical ideal of 431,981 people per district. Justice Brennan's majority opinion insisted that even this slight variation among districts, absent a justification acceptable to the Court, violated the Constitution. *See*: CONGRESSIONAL DISTRICT; *GRAY* v. *SANDERS* (1963); MALAPPORTIONMENT; REAPPORTIONMENT; REDISTRICTING; *REYNOLDS* v. *SIMS* (1964); *WESBERRY* v. *SANDERS* (1964).

Reference: David Miller and Bruce Cain, *Congressional Redistricting* (New York: Macmillan, 1992).

KNOW-NOTHING PARTY (AMERICAN PARTY). The formal name of this party was the American Party. This party was made up of secretive societies, one of which was named the Supreme Order of the Star Spangled Banner. These were clandestine, far-right-wing societies in the 1840s that were extremely anti-Catholic. These nativist forces, in order to advance their political agenda, developed the American Party. They did not want immigrant Catholics to vote or hold political office. They proposed that the immigrants wait 21 years to vote, and that they should never be allowed to hold office. This party concealed its identity and also the candidates it was supporting. This secretive behavior led to the name "know-nothing." When members were asked about the party they answered "I don't know." This name was given to them by newspaperman Horace Greeley. This party also promoted abolition of slavery, free public schools, and the prohibition of alcohol.

In the 1850s the Know-Nothings controlled state legislatures and governorships in a half dozen states. In 1854 the party won 63% of the vote in Massachusetts, taking every state senate seat. In the Thirty-Fourth Congress, it was estimated that at least 20% were members of the Know-Nothing Party. It appeared that this party would fill the vacuum left by the collapse of the Whigs over the slavery issue; but the Republican Party rose to become the new major party. The American Party nominated pro-slavery Millard Fillmore in 1856, and the Northern anti-slavery delegates bolted and joined up with the Republicans. The American Party collapsed over slavery after the 1856 election. The term "Know-Nothing" is still used to describe someone who is a bigot and a nativist. *See*: ELECTIONS: 1856; REPUBLICAN PARTY.

References: J. David Gillespie, *Politics at the Periphery: Third Parties in Two-Party America* (Columbia: University of South Carolina Press, 1993); David Potter, *The Impending Crisis, 1848–1861* (New York: Harper and Row, 1976); A. James Reichley, *The Life of the Parties: A History of American Political Parties* (New York: The Free Press, 1992).

L

LABOR ORGANIZATIONS. Workers organize into unions to improve their compensation and working conditions. Unions attempt to achieve most of their objectives through collective bargaining. However, public policy is also very important to unions, and in order to achieve their objectives unions are very involved in politics. Labor unions played a key role in the New Deal coalition, and they are a central element of the Democratic Party. The major umbrella labor organization in the United States is the American Federation of Labor-Congress of Industrial Organizations (AFL-CIO), which is a federation of most of the unions in the United States. The percentage of American workers that belong to unions has declined because of the change in the nature of work brought on by the development of the service economy, and the decline of the industrial economy. In 1997 the AFL-CIO claimed a membership of thirteen million. The percentage of the work force that belongs to a union has declined in recent decades. Today, only 10% of the private work force is unionized, and 14.5% of the total work force belongs to unions.

Labor support for Democratic candidates has also weakened in recent decades. President Reagan enjoyed considerable support from unionized blue-collar workers. The AFL-CIO, under its new president John J. Sweeney, vowed to conduct a major campaign to defeat the Republican Congress in 1996. It assigned 70 field representatives in key congressional districts, and assessed their members $1.80 per member to help support a $35 million media campaign directed against the Republican Congress. This campaign fund was beyond what the unions usually spend on elections. Unions donated $42.3 million from their PACs in 1994.

The major effort by the unions to defeat the Republican congress failed in 1996. Of the thirty-one freshman that labor targeted, only eleven were defeated.

The U.S. Chamber of Commerce and other business groups spent $8 million countering labor's negative media campaign. The unions were more successful in persuading their members to vote Democratic. In 1994, when the GOP took control of Congress, 40% of union households voted Republican. Exit polls of the 1996 electorate showed that only 35% of union households voted Republican. *See*: COMMITTEE ON POLITICAL EDUCATION.

Reference: Michael Byrne, "Union Campaign Puts Spotlight on Workers," *AFL-CIO News*, May 16, 1996.

LANDON, ALFRED M. (1887–1987). Suffering in 1936 one of the great losses in modern presidential politics, Landon was, however, to retain considerable influence within the Kansas Republican Party and enjoy a long career in national politics, in which he addressed issues pragmatically and often, as seen by some within his party, unpredictably. In advanced years, he became increasingly critical of positions taken by Goldwater and Reagan forces, occasionally threatening to leave the Republican Party he had once led. Born in West Middlesex, Pennsylvania on September 9, 1887, Landon was raised in Ohio. In 1904, the family moved to Kansas and Landon entered the University of Kansas, from which he earned a law degree in 1908. While admitted to the bar, Landon opted for a career not in law but in business, becoming a successful entrepreneur in the oil fields and much later in communications, acquiring a number of Kansas and Colorado radio stations. Early on Landon became politically active in the Kansas GOP, identifying himself with the party's progressive wing, and particularly with the gubernatorial career of Governor Clyde Reed (1929–1931), during whose administration Landon served as state party chairman. Throughout the 1920s, with the Democrats offering only token opposition to the entrenched Republicans, political competition was restricted to Republican primary elections where conservative and progressive forces alternated almost evenly in their control of both the party organization and of state government. The Great Depression, however, energized the Democrats and in 1932 Republicans faced an anomaly, an incumbent Democratic administration and the need to unify the party to regain state control, all this in a national political environment which promised to be one of great advantage to the Democrats. Landon, largely successful in achieving party harmony, won a narrow victory in a three-candidate race. His victory in the face of that year's Democratic surge was remarkable, the only Republican west of the Mississippi to be elected to a governor's office. Two years later, with the New Deal still at high tide, Landon was the *only* Republican nationwide to have a gubernatorial victory. It is not astonishing that, as a demoralized party turned to its 1936 convention, Landon became, almost inevitably, its leading contender for the presidential nomination. While Landon's strength was in large part based on the stark fact that he was one of a very few elected Republicans left in prominent office across the nation, his record in that office was not inconsequential. While governing Kansas could not be compared in the scope of its problems with those of New York or Pennsylvania, Landon had, nonetheless, met the severe challenges of the Great Depression within his state with some success: bank collapse was averted; taxes were lowered; governmental efficiency stressed; and budget surpluses realized. Across the country Landon's reputation became that of a no-nonsense, plain-spoken, "tax-reducing, budget-balancing governor." Such an image was fostered by coverage in major newspapers and magazines, particularly those of William Randolph Hearst. Although former president Herbert Hoover hoped that his enthusiastically received address at the Cleveland convention would turn into a draft, and even as Landon faced competitors in Senator William E. Borah of Idaho and Chicago publisher Frank Knox, such competition melted away by the convention's first ballot, which brought the Kansas governor's all but unanimous nomination, Knox joining the ticket as the vice-presidential candidate. From the beginning the Landon campaign was plagued by major difficulties; not only did he oppose an exceptionally popular incumbent in Franklin D. Roosevelt, but he also faced the dilemma of how to satisfy both the progressive and conservative wings of his own party. Through the campaign, Landon, a cautious progressive by temperament, a pragmatist in terms of decision making, awkwardly walked a tightrope strung between the two separate poles of the Republican Party. His message often struck American voters as contradictory: on the one hand, he not only endorsed major New Deal welfare and farm relief policies, but promised an extensive, more prudently managed expansion of such programs; on the other hand, he greatly belabored the growth of big government, reckless spending, and the centralization of decision-making power in Washington, particularly in the hands of the nation's chief executive. Despite some national polls, such as that of the *Literary Digest*, which suggested a Landon victory, the result was one of the great defeats in the annals of presidential politics. Roosevelt and Vice-President John Nance Garner ran up a plurality over the Landon-Knox ticket of more than 11 million popular votes out of a total of nearly 45 million cast, with only the 8 Electoral College ballots of 2 states, Maine and Vermont, going to the Republicans. Republican fortunes across the country had reached their nadir for the New Deal period. Landon suffered the further embarrassment of not only failing to carry his home state but also a Democratic gubernatorial victory there, requiring him to turn over the statehouse to the opposition as his term expired in January of 1937. Landon, returning with marked success to the world of business, was never again to seek political office. He remained in the short run, however, an influential voice within the national Republican Party and for more than a decade after his presidential defeat the controlling voice of the Kansas Republican Party. After 1950, and as his long life played out, his role became increasingly that of a party elder statesman whose views were given a courteous hearing before being subsequently dismissed or ignored. In 1978, Landon had the satisfaction of seeing his daughter, Nancy Landon Kassebaum, successfully embark on what was to be a sixteen-year career in the U.S. Senate where her voice, as with her father's, was that of a moderate, pragmatic Kansas

Republican. Alf Landon became one of the longest lived of American presidential candidates, dying at age 100 at his Kansas home in 1987. *See*: ELECTIONS: 1936.

Reference: Donald R. McCoy, *Landon of Kansas* (Lincoln: University of Nebraska Press, 1966).

LANDSLIDE is a term to describe a lopsided election result. The term usually refers to a victory of 10% or more. In 1984, President Ronald Reagan received 59% of the vote to Walter Mondale's 41%. In a landslide, the opposition is buried. The Electoral College can give victorious winners the appearance of a landslide. In 1996, Bill Clinton received 49% of the popular vote but garnered 70% of the Electoral College vote.

Reference: William Safire, *Safire's New Political Dictionary* (New York: Random House, 1993).

LEADERSHIP PAC is a Political Action Committee formed by a prospective presidential candidate who has not formally announced his/her candidacy. The prospective candidate raises funds to support his/her travel and other related campaign expenditures. The candidate has the opportunity to build up a mailing list for fund-raising. The prospective candidate will also use the PAC funds to make donations to candidates for federal office, to build up goodwill and ''IOUs'' for their anticipated campaign. Stephen Wayne estimated that leadership PACs spent $25 million in the 1988 election cycle.

Bob Dole's leadership PAC was called Campaign America. Between 1985 and 1995, Campaign America raised over $19 million. Dole used the funds to support Republican candidates, particularly candidates in New Hampshire. Dole handed control of this PAC over to Dan Qualye. In addition to PACs, presidential candidates will often form foundations that enjoy non-profit, tax exempt status. The purpose of these foundations is to develop policy position papers and engage in other educational activities that promote the views of the prospective candidate.

Leadership PACs are also used by congressional leaders to assist candidates from their party running for office. In 1996, Senator Trent Lott, majority leader, collected $1.7 million for his PAC, the New Republican Majority Fund. Lott donated $1.3 million from this fund to other Republicans running for office in 1996. The largest leadership PAC in 1996 was GOPAC, which raised $4.5 million in 1995–1996. GOPAC is headed up by Representative John Shadegg of Arizona. GOPAC had been directed by Speaker Newt Gingrich.

The advantages of Leadership PACs to legislative leaders are twofold. First, the committee may qualify as a ''multi-candidate'' committee and qualify to accept individual contributions up to $5,000 (instead of the normal individual limit of $1,000). Second, leadership PACs are not viewed as affiliated with the individual member's account so they can collect contributions from the same sources for both accounts. *See*: CONGRESSIONAL ELECTIONS; FEDERAL ELECTION CAMPAIGN ACT OF 1971 AND AMENDMENTS; GOPAC; PO- LITICAL ACTION COMMITTEE; PRESIDENTIAL ELECTION CAM- PAIGN.

References: Anthony Corrado, Thomas E. Mann, Daniel R. Ortiz, Trevor Potter, and Frank J. Sorauf, eds., *Campaign Finance Reform: A Sourcebook* (Washington, D.C.: Brookings Institution, 1997); Leslie Wayne, "Congress Uses Leadership PACs to Wield Power," *New York Times, NATIONAL,* March 13, 1997; Stephen J. Wayne, *The Road to the White House 1996: The Politics of Presidential Elections* (New York: St. Martin's Press, 1996).

LEAGUE OF WOMEN VOTERS is a nonpartisan political organization that attempts to educate the electorate on issues and encourage voting. It was founded in 1920 as a successor to National American Woman Suffrage Association (NAWSA) at the urging of its president, Carrie Chapman Catt. The organization was created after the ratification of the Nineteenth Amendment. The goals of the organization were to assist women with their newly won suffrage rights.

Today, the League advocates open and honest government through citizen participation. The League remains outside of partisan political activity, and it will not endorse candidates for public office. It does take positions on issues after the members do extensive research and consensus building. It has a com- ponent part, the League of Women Voters Educational Fund, which has spon- sored presidential debates in the past. There are a number of local affiliates throughout the country that often serve as watchdogs on local and state govern- ments. The issues that the League supports are not limited to issues directly affecting women in the United States. The League has taken strong stands on environmental issues and welfare reform at the national level. On the state and local levels, many chapters have focused on election law and land-use planning.

Reference: Naomi Black, "The Politics of the League of Women Voters," *International Social Science Journal,* Vol. 35 (1983); Address: League of Women Voters, 1730 M Street, N.W., Washington, D.C. 20036.

LIBERAL. As commonly used, the term refers to individuals who believe that government should play an active role in protecting those who cannot protect themselves. This means that liberals generally support programs that aid the poor. Liberals, however, do not limit their concern to the poor. Liberals are also sympathetic to those who, for whatever reason (race, religion, or simply uncon- ventional beliefs), may fall victim to a majoritarian political system in which they cannot effectively compete. This often leads liberals to vigilantly defend the rights of women, members of racial or ethnic minorities, and those whose activities and beliefs place them outside of the mainstream. Liberals are often accused of encouraging growth in government. While this is true if one is dis- cussing social programs such as welfare or Social Security, it is important to recognize that liberals also tend to resist the government actions that are intolerant toward minority groups. *See*: LIBERALISM.

LIBERAL PARTY OF NEW YORK is a third party founded in New York State in 1946 as a splintered faction of the American Labor Party. It was led by Alex Rose of the Millinery Workers. The party has enjoyed the support of garment workers and Jewish voters in New York City. It has been a strong advocate of political reform and progressive social welfare policies. The party is able to survive because of the cross-filing provisions in New York State electoral law. The Liberal Party is able to nominate one of the candidates offered by the major parties as its candidate. The Liberal Party generally nominates Democratic Party candidates for local and state office.

Occasionally, the Liberal Party will support a Republican. In 1980 the Liberal Party nominated incumbent Senator Jacob Javits, who had been defeated by Alfonse D'Amato in the Republican primary. The Liberal Party drained votes away from the Democratic candidate and unintentionally aided D'Amato's victory in the general election. The Liberal Party supported Republican John Lindsey in 1965, who won; in 1969, Lindsey, who was defeated in the Republican primary, was reelected mayor of New York on the Liberal line. This was probably the Liberal's finest hour in New York City politics. In 1993 the party endorsed Mayor Rudolf Giuliani who ran on both the Republican and Liberal Party lines. The Liberal Party bargains with the candidates on policy positions and appointments prior to endorsing a candidate. The Liberal Party is able to affect the outcome of a New York City and State election because of the New York State cross-endorsement law. *See*: CROSS-ENDORSEMENT; CROSS-FILING.

Reference: Jewel Bellush and Dick Netzer, eds., *Urban Politics New York Style* (Armonk, N.Y.: M. E. Sharpe, 1990).

LIBERALISM. Liberalism was originally conceived as an ideology which focused on maximizing human freedom. Initially, it was thought that this could be achieved by limiting the power of government. Early liberal theorists such as John Locke relied on popular consent and limited delegation (both of which could be achieved through a social contract) to control government. By the nineteenth century, theorists such as John Stuart Mill (1806–1873) and Alexis de Tocqueville (1805–1859) worried that democratic consent, even when coupled with rhetoric about natural rights, might not be sufficient to protect the freedoms of those in the minority. What was needed was a principle, less abstract than natural rights, that could be applied to test whether or not the actions of the majority were legitimate. What Mill came up with is commonly referred to as the ''harm to others'' principle. Mill would only allow the government to act in areas where specific, identifiable injuries either had or would occur to an individual other than oneself. Although Mill clearly believed that government could play a positive role in society, self-regarding actions—that is, actions which had no effect on, and so could not harm, others—were to be immune from government control.

In a sense, Mill's principle continues to guide modern liberalism in the United States. By the early twentieth century, however, definitions of "harms" began to change. The Great Depression of the 1920s presented in its starkest form the reality of economic harms (about which Mill had not been unaware). By mid-century, the damaging effects of racism and prejudice entered the heretofore limited class of acts that were deemed harmful to others and thus regulable. With these additions, however, liberalism began to dovetail into two distinct ideologies, one of which became known as economic conservatism.

Once liberalism began to expand its list of cognizable harms, particularly with the identification of economic harms as demanding remedial action, liberalism took upon itself a pro-active perspective. In short, liberalism began to recognize that in order to avoid harms, help was often necessary. For example, perhaps the only way to protect people from the harms of poverty was to help them achieve some means. It also became clear that only the government (and often only the federal government) possessed the resources necessary to aid those in need. One notices, however, that liberalism's basic attitude toward government had to be recast. Concerns about the potentially oppressive nature of government became subordinate to the perceived need for state action. Henceforth, at least one theme of modern liberalism was distributive justice. One must be careful not to overstate the positive relationship between liberalism and strong government, for where liberalism finds no harm, it continues its historic opposition to government power. *See*: LIBERAL.

References: Louis Hartz, *The Liberal Tradition in America* (New York: Harcourt, 1955); John Locke, *Two Treatises of Government* (New York, Cambridge University Press, 1960); John Locke, *A Letter Concerning Toleration* (Englewood Cliffs, N.J.: Prentice-Hall, 1950); John Stuart Mill, *On Liberty* (Indianapolis, Ind.: Bobbs-Merrill, 1963); John Rawls, *A Theory of Justice* (Cambridge, Mass.: Harvard University Press, 1971); Alexis de Tocqueville, *Democracy in America* (New York: Knopf, 1972).

LIBERTARIAN PARTY is a contemporary third party in the United States that promotes the libertarian philosophy. This party promotes the idea of extremely limited government. The party proposes to substantially reduce the size and intrusiveness of government. The Libertarian Party favors cutting all taxes. It promotes the philosophical ideas of writers such as Ayn Rand. It wants to eliminate most government restrictions on behavior and most government regulations. For example, it opposes government imposition of curfews on teenagers. It favors the legalization of drugs and same-sex marriages. It favors U.S. withdrawal from the UN.

The party has a national executive committee, holds national conventions, and has a number of state and local chapters. One of its major concerns is ballot access. The party has nominated a candidate for president in every election since

1972. The candidate in 1996 was Harry Browne; the vice-presidential candidate was Jo Jorgensen. The Libertarian Party nominees were excluded from presidential debates and virtually ignored by the media. In 1996, the Libertarian presidential ticket received a disappointing 485,120 votes. In 1996, it was on the ballot in all 50 states. *See*: THIRD PARTIES.

Reference: J. David Gillespie, *Politics at the Periphery: Third Parties in Two-Party America* (Columbia: University of South Carolina Press, 1993); Address: Libertarian Party, 2600 Virginia Ave. N.W., Suite 100, Washington, D.C. 20037.

LIBERTY PARTY was a party founded in the late 1830s with a single issue— abolish slavery. The party was very limited in its appeal since it would not adopt any secondary issues. Abolitionists were not drawn to the party since many of them did not believe in political action. The party nominated James Birney as its presidential nominee in 1840 and 1844. He was decisively defeated in both elections. In the election of 1844, Birney garnered over 15,000 votes in New York State, and allowed Democrat James Polk to outpoll the Whig Party candidate, Henry Clay, by 5,000 votes in New York. The Liberty Party took credit for Clay's defeat. It was uncompromising and did not persist after the 1844 election.

Reference: J. David Gillespie, *Politics at the Periphery: Third Parties in Two-Party America* (Columbia: University of South Carolina Press, 1993).

LIKELY VOTER is a respondent to a poll who has been identified by the pollster as likely to vote. The determination is made through a series of questions on voter registration and past voting history. Likely voters are very important to pollsters since a sampling of their opinion is a good predictor of the outcome of an election.

John Zogby, president of John Zogby Group International, a national polling firm, argues that the key to successful polling is identification of "likely voters." He contends that a sampling based only on registered voters will give results that are skewed toward the Democratic candidates. He also maintains that pushing undecided voters to make a choice can also lead to false results since they will tend to go against the incumbent. Zogby argues that it is necessary to weigh the sample to gain good results. Zogby Group/Reuters had the best results of all of the final preelection polls for the November 1996 election. *See*: SAMPLE.

References: Michael W. Traugott and Paul J. Lavrakas, *The Voter's Guide to Election Polls* (Chatham, N.J.: Chatham House, 1996); John Zogby, "The Perils of Polling: A Look at Why Our Polls are Different," *The Polling Report*, Vol. 12 (November 18, 1996).

LIMITED VOTING is an electoral system with multi-member districts, that is, districts that elect more than one member, and in which the voter can cast more than one vote but has fewer votes than the number of seats available. This is used in the South in a few local government electoral systems. According to

Joseph Zimmerman, it was introduced in parts of the South after the Civil War to address the problem of representation of the minority party in a one-party dominated system. Limited voting does not permit the voter to express a preference for the candidates by ranking them.

Limited voting is required by law to be used for any multi-seat district local election in Connecticut. Some places use it in combination with "limited nomination," where a party must nominate fewer candidates than seats. Limited nomination is used in the District of Columbia for at-large city council seats.

Limited voting was accepted by the federal courts to resolve Voting Rights cases in Alabama, North Carolina, and Georgia. As a result of these cases, limited voting is used as a remedy to enhance the opportunity for electing African Americans in local government elections. *See*: MULTI-MEMBER DISTRICT.

References: Bernard Grofman and Arend Lijphart, eds., *Electoral Laws and Their Political Consequences* (New York: Agathon Press, 1986); Wilma Rule and Joseph F. Zimmerman, eds., *United States Electoral Systems: Their Impact on Women and Minorities* (Westport, Conn.: Greenwood Press, 1992).

LINCOLN, ABRAHAM (1809–1865). First Republican elected to the presidency, leader of the Union during the nation's darkest days of civil war, first president to die in office at the hands of an assassin, Lincoln, "the Great Emancipator," was born in the humble setting of a one-room Kentucky log cabin on February 12, 1809. As the family moved from Hardin County, first to Indiana then to Illinois, Lincoln, largely self-educated, developed an appreciation for, and a command of, the English language that was to remain with him throughout his life, producing in its maturity some of the most elegant and powerful words ever used by an American politician. From the debate at Freeport, Illinois in 1858, to the Gettysburg Address in 1863, to the second inaugural address of March 4, 1865, as the nation looked to reconstruction and reconciliation, Lincoln's words mattered:

With malice toward none; with charity for all; with firmness in the right, as God gives us to see the right, let us strive on to finish the work we are in; to bind up the nation's wounds; to care for him who shall have borne the battle, and for his widow, and his orphan—to do all which may achieve and cherish a just, and a lasting peace, among ourselves, and with all nations.

Lincoln's early years were spent in a variety of jobs: farmer's fieldhand, deckhand working on the Mississippi flatboats, storekeeper, postmaster, and, as with Washington, surveyor. Perhaps it was the storekeeper's role, with it opportunities for village talk and debate, that led the young Lincoln to politics. Elected to the Illinois legislature as a Whig in 1834, Lincoln was twice reelected. It was at this time that Lincoln began to "read" the law, was subsequently admitted to the bar in 1836, and in the following year opened his practice in Springfield,

Illinois, with partner William H. Herndon. Lincoln first appeared on the national scene in 1847, having been elected to the U.S. House of Representatives the previous year. Largely holding to the Whig Party line, the freshman congressman opposed war with Mexico and argued against the extension of slavery into existing or newly acquired territories, stopping short, however, of advocacy of the wholesale abolition of slavery, the latter being a position to which Lincoln would long adhere even as he came to the presidency, and from which he would not depart until promulgation of the Emancipation Proclamation on January 1, 1863. Actively campaigning for Zachary Taylor's election as president in 1848, Lincoln did not seek reelection to the House. Returning, as he put it, "assiduously," to the practice of law in Springfield in 1848, aborting a campaign for the U.S. Senate in 1854, Lincoln was not again to become a serious candidate for office until 1858, when, with the demise of the Whigs, he became a candidate for the U.S. Senate of the new Republican Party, an anti-slavery party which he had actively helped to organize in Illinois. It was, of course, this bid for election by the Illinois legislature to a seat in the Senate that established Lincoln's national reputation; the result of a widely followed, (now historic) set of debates with incumbent Democrat Senator Stephen A. Douglas. "The Little Giant," was prominent in the Democratic Party's national leadership, often discussed as a possible presidential candidate, and known in the U.S. Senate and in Illinois as a master of skillful compromise. Recently, however, Douglas had fallen on hard times. As one of the authors of the Kansas-Nebraska Act of 1854, which, in destroying the last remnants of the Compromise of 1820, opened Kansas Territory on the basis of "popular sovereignty" to the possibility of slavery, the senator had been charged by his critics with responsibility for "Bleeding Kansas" and, thereby, for raising the slavery issue to new heights of confrontation. Perhaps the most famous of the seven Lincoln-Douglas debates was that at Freeport on August 27, 1858, in which Lincoln, responding to Douglas's criticism, reaffirmed what was for him a fundamental truth, "I repeat that I do not believe that government *can* endure permanently half slave and half free." Lincoln was always careful, however, to qualify his position on slavery; as he did two weeks after the Freeport debate in a campaign speech at Edwardsville, Illinois, where he reassured his audience that while he and his party saw "slavery as a moral, social and political wrong," "an unqualified evil," neither he nor others of his party would "molest" that evil "in the States where it exists; they [i.e., the Republicans] will not overlook the constitutional guards which our forefathers have placed around it; they will do nothing which can give proper offense to those who hold slaves by legal sanction; but they will use every constitutional method to protect the evil from becoming larger and involving more negroes, more white men, more soil, and more States in its deplorable consequences." For all the popular attention given to the debates— the huge crowds which listened, and the press which reported to the state and to the nation—it would not be the people who would decide for Lincoln or Douglas but the Illinois legislature, and there the decision would be for Douglas by a vote of 54 to 46, the Democrats having retained legislative control in the fall elections. While Douglas was to return to the U.S. Senate and Lincoln to his law practice, in but two years they would compete again, this time as candidates for the presidency of the United States. For Douglas, however, it was as the nominee of a deeply divided Democratic Party which in 1860 was to produce, from two separate conventions, two separate national tickets: Douglas the presidential candidate of Northern Democrats, was given as his vice-presidential running mate, at the decision of the Democratic National Committee, anti-secessionist Herschel V. Johnson, recently governor of Georgia; Southern Democrats named incumbent vice-president John C. Breckinridge of Kentucky to head their ticket, with Senator Joseph Lane of Oregon as vice-presidential nominee. Further muddying the political waters was the national ticket of former Whig, John Bell of Tennessee, and Edward Everett of Massachusetts, running as Constitutional Unionists, a new party desperately committed to some compromise resolution of the slavery crisis, a resolution which, however, the Constitutional Unionists could neither find nor articulate. In a political environment so otherwise confused, Lincoln and his Republican running mate, Senator Hannibal Hamlin of Maine, as candidates of a unified, anti-slavery party, with a relatively unambiguous, albeit controversial message, emerged winners. The Republican ticket gained 39.8% of the total presidential vote cast; Douglas-Johnson, 29.5%; Breckinridge-Lane, 18.1%, and Bell-Everett, 12.6%. The Electoral College result, however, provided a more substantial Republican victory with Lincoln-Hamlin carrying 18 states and 180 votes, to 11 states and 72 votes for Breckinridge-Lane, 3 states and 39 votes for Bell-Everett, and but one state and 12 votes for Douglas-Johnson. The Republican victory was achieved strictly along regional, North-South, lines, establishing a pattern of voter behavior and party division that was to be discernible in American presidential politics well into the next century. During the course of the interregnum from election day in November to inauguration day in March the situation further deteriorated; South Carolina, as a reaction to Lincoln's election, seceded from the Union on December 20, 1860, followed by six additional states of the deep South in the first months of 1861. In the White House, still seeking a last minute acceptable compromise, President Buchanan equivocated as to ordering the reinforcement of federal military posts in the South, believing that such an act on his part would only further antagonize and thereby prevent negotiation with the secessionists, real and potential. Lincoln's position was not equivocal; failing to recognize any constitutional right of secession, he vowed to preserve the Union. His inaugural address of March 4, 1861, made clear who bore responsibility, ''in your hands, my dissatisfied fellow countrymen, and not in *mine*, is the momentous issue of civil war.'' Within days his countrymen resolved the issue in favor of war. The Lincoln administration thus became, for the entire span of its days, a war administration, its efforts concentrated on the raising and supply of armies and navies; funding the costs of war; maintaining popular support for the war effort, particularly through days of delay and defeat; and the conduct of a foreign diplomacy so as to preserve European neutrality. By scale and tragedy, the Civil War was something unknown in the American experience. In the North it led to governmental activity of unprecedented dimension, with the president and those in the administration extending their exercise of power to, or as critics argued, dangerously beyond heretofore recognized constitutional limits; particularly as the president, primarily but not exclusively through suspension of the writ of habeas corpus, would cause, in the words of one of his modern biographers, "greater infringements on individual liberties than in any other period in American history." By the spring of 1865, however, as the long and bloody war drew to a close, Lincoln looked forward to a relatively brief period of non-vindictive reconstruction, to be followed by a gradual national reconciliation. It was this that he signaled in his second inaugural address on March 4, 1865, having been reelected to the presidential office the previous November. In that election Lincoln had been challenged by one of his dismissed generals, "War Democrat" George B. McClellan. Besieged during the campaign by Democrats of both the "war" and "peace" variety for his inept war leadership, his wholesale violation of individual civil liberties, his failure to pursue a negotiated restoration of peace, Lincoln still prevailed. Joined on the national ticket by Democrat "unionist" Andrew Johnson of Tennessee, Lincoln secured a 400,000 popular vote plurality over McClellan and his vice-presidential running mate Congressman George H. Pendleton of Ohio. In a Union reduced in size by secession, Lincoln carried 22 states with 212 Electoral College votes to 3 states and 21 Electoral College ballots for the Democrats. Even allowing for the probability of some fraud in the taking, in the field, of the "soldier vote," the Lincoln victory was decisive. As election day stretched toward inauguration day, and with the war's end in sight, Lincoln had begun systematic planning of his program for a non-revengeful reconstruction of the Union. Whether his argument for moderate reconstruction would have prevailed over Radical Republican demands in Congress for a more harsh, prolonged military reconstruction is of course a question left unanswered by dint of an assassin's bullet. Attending a performance of "Our American Cousin" at Ford's Theatre on Good Friday, April 14, Lincoln became the victim of John Wilkes Booth. Carried from his theater box to a nearby house, never regaining consciousness, Lincoln died the morning of April 15, 1865. Following a period of national mourning the body was returned to Springfield, Illinois, for burial there. *See*: ELECTIONS: 1860, 1864.

References: David H. Donald, *Lincoln* (New York: Simon and Schuster, 1995); Phillip S. Paludan, *The Presidency of Abraham Lincoln* (Lawrence: University Press of Kansas, 1994); J. G. Randall with Richard N. Current, *Lincoln the President*, 4 vols. (New York: Dodd, Mead, 1945–1955).

LIST SYSTEM is the most widely used form of proportional representation. The voter casts a vote for one party and the list of candidates offered by that party. Party lists can be "open" or "closed." A closed list means that the party determines the order of its candidates to be elected. An open list permits the voters to determine a party's list of candidates by indicating preferences for individual candidates. If a party wins 30% of the votes, it wins approximately 30% of the seats. *See: OREGON* v. *MITCHELL* (1970); MIXED MEMBER PROPORTIONAL; PROPORTIONAL REPRESENTATION.

References: Douglas Amy, *Real Choices, New Voices: The Case for Proportional Representation Elections in the United States* (New York: Columbia University Press, 1993); Institute for Democracy and Electoral Assistance: http://www.int-idea.se.; Rein Taagepera and Matthew Shugart, *Seats and Votes: The Effects and Determinants of Electoral Systems* (New Haven, Conn.: Yale University Press, 1989).

LITERACY TESTS were introduced in the South to circumvent the post–Civil War Fifteenth Amendment to the U.S. Constitution, which banned denial of the right to vote based on "race, color or previous condition of servitude." Literacy tests were used as a qualification for voting. It was a reading test. They were frequently used to deny blacks in the South the right to vote. The examining official had wide discretion, since the tests were usually administered orally. The 1970 amendments to the Voting Rights Act barred all literacy tests as a requirement for voting. The U.S. Supreme Court upheld the ban in *Oregon* v. *Mitchell* (1970). *See*: PRIMARY, WHITE; VOTING RIGHTS ACT.

LIVINGSTON, ROBERT L. (1943–   ) was named Speaker-elect of the House in 1998. Robert Livingston was born in Colorado Springs, Colorado. He recieved a B. A. degree and a J.D. degree from Tulane University. He served as a prosecutor before being elected to Congress in 1977. He represents Louisiana's First Congressional District, which includes much of the newer, upscale metropolitan area of New Orleans. It is one of the state's most Republican districts. Livingston was noted as a tough opponent of government spending when he served as minority member of the Appropriations Committee. He was tapped by Gingrich to serve as the chairman of that committee in the 104th Congress. A few days after the November 1998 election, in which the Republicans lost five seats, Livingston announced he would oppose Gingrich for Speaker of the House. On November 6, Gingrich announced his resignation, and on November 18, 1998, Livingston was selected without opposition. In an unexpected turn of events, during the House of Representatives' Clinton impeachment debate on December 19, 1998, Livingston announced that he would step down as Speaker-elect. House Republicans then chose J. Dennis Hastert of Illinois as Speaker-elect. *See*: GINGRICH, NEWT(ON).

Reference: Jeffrey L. Katz, "Shakeup in the House," *Congressional Quarterly Weekly*, Vol. 56 (November 7, 1998), 2989–2992.

LOBBYIST is one who represents an interest group, and attempts to influence public officials to rule or vote the way the group prefers the public official to act. Lobbyists work to pass or defeat proposed legislation that affects the group they represent. Lobbyists will often testify before legislative committees that are hearing a bill that affects their group. According to John Tierney and Kay Schlozman, 70% of lobbyists represent business interests. Organized labor is another important part of the lobbying community. Lobbyists present valuable information to legislators. Tactics of lobbyists include: gaining direct access to officials, making campaign contributions, endorsing particular candidates, mobilizing a grassroots letter, fax, or phone campaign, and influencing public opinion through paid advertising. A number of states and the federal government require lobbyists to disclose the amount they spend to influence legislation. Efforts to restrict lobbyists are restrained by the First Amendment right to petition the government. See: INTEREST GROUP; SINGLE-ISSUE GROUPS.

References: Paul S. Herrnson, Ronald G. Shaiko, and Clyde Wilcox, eds., *The Interest Group Connection: Electioneering, Lobbying, and Policymaking in Washington* (Chatham, N.J.: Chatham House, 1998); Philip A. Mundo, *Interest Groups: Cases and Characteristics* (Chicago: Nelson-Hall, 1992); John T. Tierney and Kay Lehman Schlozman, "Congress and Organized Interests," in *Congressional Politics*, Christopher J. Deering, ed. (Chicago, Ill.: The Dorsey Press, 1989).

LOCAL OPTION ELECTIONS. A local option election is allowed in certain states to control the sale of intoxicating liquors. The question is placed before the voters in a precinct as a result of a petition submitted by an interested party. The petition must be signed by voters who reside in the affected precincts. The petition may request permission to expand the sale of alcohol or restrict the sale of alcohol. Only the voters in the affected precinct can vote on the issue, and it takes a majority to change the existing law.

Reference: Sherrod Brown, Secretary of State, *Ohio Election Laws Annotated* (Columbus, Ohio: Banks-Baldwin Law Publishing Company, 1986).

LOCAL PARTY ORGANIZATIONS. The local party organization is the basic unit of American political party organizations. Local party organizations are usually organized by county. The basic organizational structure of the local party is often defined in state statute. The basic unit of a county party is the party precinct committee person, who is elected by the members of a particular party in the precinct, in a primary or caucus. A precinct is a geographic unit designed to organize voting, and usually has a voting roll of less than 1,000 voters. After they are elected, the precinct committee members meet to select local county party officers. In some states, the committee persons select the members of the state party committees.

The national and state parties do not have direct authority over the local party committees. The higher party committees must persuade the local parties to move in the direction they would like them to go. This is often accomplished by providing the local party with funds. For example, the national and state committees will provide the local parties with funds to operate phone banks to get out the vote. Frequently, those funds are soft money donations to the national party that are passed down to the state party, and then to the local parties. Local parties vary in their level of influence and the amount of campaign activity they generate. The most notable party-in-control style, local parties such as the Cook County Democratic Party Organization under Mayor Richard Daley, which successfully controlled the nomination of candidates, are disappearing from the contemporary political scene. There are a number of well-financed, effective local party organizations, with permanent headquarters and full-time paid staffs, but they are the exception. A national survey of local county parties, conducted in 1980, found that 10% of county party organizations had full- or part-time paid staff, and only slightly more reported a year-round headquarters. Many local party committees are led by volunteers, have limited financial resources, and are only active during the campaign season. The local party that is in the minority has a difficult time recruiting a full slate of candidates and a full complement of county committee members. The local party committees emphasize grassroots campaigning: voter registration, door-to-door literature distribution, yard signs, absentee voting, and get-out-the-vote on election day. There is some evidence that local county parties are more active today than they were a few decades ago. There is a great deal of variation in local party strength by region. *See*: MACHINE POLITICS; PRECINCT; TAMMANY HALL.

References: Cornelius P. Cotter, James L. Gibson, John F. Bibby, and Robert J. Huckshorn, *Party Organizations in American Politics* (New York: Praeger, 1984); John Frendreis, Alan R. Gitelson, Gregory Flemming, and Anne Layzell, "Local Political Parties and Legislative Races in 1992," in *The State of the Parties: The Changing Role of Contemporary American Parties*, Daniel Shea and John C. Green, eds. (Lanham, Md.: Rowman & Littlefield, 1994).

LOTT, TRENT (1941–   ) is the Senate majority leader. He was born on October 9, 1941 in Grenada, Mississippi. His father, Chester Paul Lott, was a shipyard worker, and his mother, Iona, was a schoolteacher. He grew up in the working-class town of Pascagoula, Mississippi on the Gulf Coast. In 1963 he graduated from the University of Mississippi with a degree in public administration, and in 1967 he graduated from the University of Mississippi's law school.

After graduation, Lott was appointed to the staff of Democratic congressman William M. Colmer of the Fifth Congressional District of Mississippi, which was located on the Gulf Coast. When Colmer announced that he would not seek reelection in 1972, Lott announced he would run as a Republican for the vacant seat. Lott was elected with 55% of the vote over Democratic state senator Ben Stone. Colmer endorsed Lott in the election. Lott was aided in his 1972 election by the popularity of Richard Nixon. Lott's election was an augur of the future GOP gains in the South.

In his first term in the House, as a member of the Judiciary Committee, Lott was confronted with the impeachment proceedings against President Richard Nixon. Lott was a very strong defender of the president. Lott served eight terms in the House; he was reelected by large margins. In 1980, Lott was elected minority whip by his Republican colleagues in the House. In that contest, he defeated Congressman E. G. Shuster of Pennsylvania by a vote of 96 to 90. In the House, he was instrumental in passing President Reagan's first budget. He served as chairman of the Republican National Convention's platform committee in 1980 and 1984.

In 1988, Mississippi Democratic senator John C. Stennis announced he would not run for reelection, after 40 years of service. Congressman Trent Lott announced he would seek Stennis's vacated seat. In this Mississippi Senate election, Lott collected 54% of the vote, defeating Democratic congressman Wayne Dowdy. Lott was reelected to his Senate seat in 1994, with 69% of the vote. In 1992, Lott was elected secretary of the Senate Republican Conference, defeating two senators, both senior to him in service. In December 1994, Lott was elected majority whip, ousting Senator Alan K. Simpson by one vote. In his ousting of Simpson, Lott enjoyed the support of junior senators with whom he had served in the House. Despite early misgivings, Lott served Senate majority leader Bob Dole with loyalty, and gained recognition for his organizational skills.

In the summer of 1996, Bob Dole resigned to campaign for president. Trent Lott was elected Senate majority leader with 44 votes. Eight votes were cast for the senior senator from Mississippi, Thad Cochran, and there was one abstention. The Senate Republicans added seats to their majority in the 1996 election despite President Clinton's reelection.

As the new Senate majority leader, Trent Lott has become less ideological, and has displayed a willingness to compromise with members of the Senate and with the Clinton administration. Lott is very conscious of his constituency, and has been criticized for supporting subsidies for the Mississippi shipbuilding industry. Senator Lott is the national leader of the Republican Party. There is speculation that he will seek his party's nomination for president in 2000.

M

MACHINE POLITICS describes a type of political organization which was common in early twentieth-century urban America. The local party was organized hierarchically, with a boss at the top, and below the boss, a layer of ward leaders very loyal to the boss. The ward leaders had a number of precinct workers loyal to them. The loyalty was based on material incentives, such as patronage jobs and contracts. The organization also provided an array of social benefits; for example, many of the early urban party organizations had baseball teams.

The party machines attempted to control the nomination and election of officeholders and, in return, expected the officeholders to render material benefits to the machine for distribution to its supporters. The machines were viewed as corrupt, and many of the reforms of the Progressive Era, such as the open primary and civil service reform, were promoted to break the grip of the machines on local and state politics. *See*: LOCAL PARTY ORGANIZATIONS.

References: Anne Freedman, *Patronage: An American Tradition* (Chicago: Nelson-Hall, 1994); Harold F. Gosnell, *Machine Politics: Chicago Model*, 2nd ed. (Chicago: University of Chicago Press, 1968).

MADISON, JAMES (1751–1836), father of the Constitution of 1787, was born at Port Conway, Virginia on March 16, 1751, just 50 miles from Montpelier, the family plantation that Madison was to regard as his home throughout his long life in public service. Educated at Princeton, then the College of New Jersey, from which he graduated in 1771, the scholarly Madison was undecided as to a career in law or the ministry. Early on, drawn to the patriot cause, he chose law and government over religion and the church. Madison's study of law and political systems placed emphasis on history and theory; as such he never sought admission to the bar nor chose to pursue the practice of law. A member of the Virginia Constitutional Convention of 1776, Madison was to argue there, as later, for religious freedom and disestablishment of the Anglican Church. As part of the advisory Governor's Council, Madison served two of Virginia's revolutionary war governors, Patrick Henry, who was to become a political opponent, and Thomas Jefferson, who was to become a lifelong ally and valued friend. In the years immediately before the constitutional convention at Philadelphia in 1787, Madison served separate terms in both the Continental Congress (1780–1783) and in the Virginia legislature. Convinced of the weaknesses of the Articles of Confederation and of the need to greatly strengthen the existing national government, Madison became part of the Virginia delegation to the Philadelphia convention. There, by his recognized talent, he assumed the role of floor leader for the nationalist cause, arguing for a system to replace the confederation that would be democratic, but not *too* democratic, with a strong national government sharing the political terrain with strong state governments; and within that national government three separate branches respectively assigned executive, legislative, and judicial functions. Each branch was to have both independent and shared powers: a force-counter-force system in which the exercise of power was to be cooperative, balanced, and thereby restrained. When the convention adjourned in September of 1787, Madison threw himself into the battle for ratification of the proposed constitution. It was in this context that he joined with New Yorkers Alexander Hamilton and John Jay in the writing of the *Federalist Papers*, 85 essays designed to both explain and convince; in effect, to build support for ratification of the Constitution. The actual contribution of the essays to the success of ratification is difficult to assess. What is not debatable is the permanent value of the essays as the single greatest exposition of the U.S. Constitution, and of the intent of the drafters. Upon ratification, Madison immediately became part of the new national government, elected to the U.S. House of Representatives, he was, again by his ability, to assume the role of floor leader; in 1789 steering Congress to proposal of that set of constitutional amendments, subsequently adopted by the states, which has come to be known as the national Bill of Rights. Madison's floor leadership role soon evolved, however, into that of opposition leader as he and colleagues objected to the comprehensive economic plan developed by Secretary of the Treasury Alexander Hamilton, a plan, in their estimation, unduly emphasizing commercial and manufacturing interests over agrarian ones. These initial differences over administration economic policy, combined eventually with disagreement in other policy areas, led to the development in the 1790 decade of the first American party system; a two-party system of Federalists, then dominant, and opposition Republicans, a party largely formed around Jefferson and, in Congress, organized by Madison. Retiring from the House in 1797, Madison, allied with Jefferson, was to take a leading role in opposition to Federalist enactment of the Alien and Sedition Acts of 1798, opposition which led them to anonymously author what became, upon adoption by the respective state legislatures, the Kentucky and Virginia Resolutions. With the Republican election victory of 1800, Madison was appointed to the cabinet by President Jefferson, serving as secretary of state throughout the Jefferson presidency (1801–1809). Despite the success of the negotiation of the Louisiana Purchase in 1803, the secretary's major task became that of trying to maintain American neutrality in the face of Europe's Napoleonic wars. Particularly difficult was the attempt to protect American shipping and trade from intercession by either of the two major belligerents, Great Britain and France. It was these efforts which led to Congress's enactment of the Embargo Act of 1807, which in its enforcement was unpopular at home and ineffective abroad. In 1808, Madison became by inheritance the Republican presidential candidate. With his running mate, Jefferson's second-term vice-president, former New York governor George Clinton, an easy victory was secured over token Federalist opposition. Even more so than with his tenure at the State Department, Madison's presidency was consumed by the issue of war and peace. Urged on by the congressional "War Hawks," Madison sought, and received on June 18, 1812, a declaration of war against Great Britain. While "War Hawk" hopes were high for annexation of Canada and for defeat on the western frontier of Indian forces allied with the British, the United States was ill prepared for the war. With his war leadership yet untested, Madison and the Republican vice-presidential nominee Elbridge Gerry of Massachusetts were able in the autumn of 1812 to defeat the Federalist ticket of DeWitt Clinton and Jared Ingersoll. The Electoral College balloting was, however, closer than in any presidential contest since 1800: 11 states and 128 Electoral College votes for the Jeffersonian Republicans, 7 states and 89 Electoral College votes for the Federalists. As Madison's second term unfolded, his war leadership proved increasingly ineffective. Despite some victories, most initial objectives, and certainly many of the "War Hawk" expectations, went unfulfilled. British capture of Washington, D.C., and the burning of the White House and the Capitol in August of 1814, made a negotiated peace politically incumbent on Madison. The Treaty of Ghent, formally ending the war, was signed on December 24, 1814. American morale, and Madison's popular standing, were boosted, however, by an ironic twist of fate some two weeks later. On January 8, 1815, with the war's termination unknown to them, American troops under General Andrew Jackson won a remarkable victory over the British in the Battle of New Orleans, turning what had seemed to many Americans as a lost war into a victorious one. Now able in the last two years of his second term to address domestic rather than war policy, Madison, borrowing from the Federalist program, led Republicans in Congress to reestablishment of the Bank of the United States and to adoption of a moderately protective tariff. Leaving office in March of 1817, Madison was to return to Virginia, and to Montpelier. Significant in his nearly two decades of retirement were a number of intellectual pursuits, foremost among them the editing of what would become his famous *Notes*, a day-by-day, secretly kept record of the proceedings of the Constitutional Convention of 1787.

The *Notes*, invaluable to historians, was published posthumously in 1840, four years after Madison's death at Montpelier on June 28, 1836. *See*: ELECTIONS: 1808, 1812.

References: Irving Brant, *James Madison*, 6 vols. (Indianapolis: Bobbs-Merrill, 1941–1961); Ralph Ketcham, *James Madison, A Biography* (New York: Macmillan, 1971); Robert Allen Rutland, *The Presidency of James Madison* (Lawrence: University Press of Kansas, 1990).

MAINTAINING ELECTION is an election in which the existing alignment of voter preferences is not disturbed. In these elections, the candidate from the largest party wins. Usually, the majority party retains control of the presidency and the Congress. One of the two major parties establishes control of the government for a considerable period of time, until there is a critical election and realignment occurs. The critical election of 1932 established the New Deal and realignment occurred. The elections that followed the 1932 election were maintaining elections. The Democrats won the next four presidential elections and controlled the Congress. A maintaining election continues the prevailing pattern of partisan alignment. *See*: CRITICAL ELECTION; REALIGNMENT.

Reference: William H. Flanagan and Nancy H. Zingale, *Political Behavior of the American Electorate*, 8th ed. (Washington, D.C.: Congressional Quarterly Press, 1994).

MAJORITY-MINORITY DISTRICT is a district that is drawn to insure that there is a majority of a minority population to enhance the opportunity of a minority to be elected. Sometimes this is called affirmative-action redistricting. It was assumed by state legislatures that this was the intent of the Voting Rights Act. In a recent Supreme Court decision, *Shaw v. Reno* (1993), it was determined that redistricting based solely on race was unconstitutional. *See: MILLER* v. *JOHNSON* (1995); *SHAW v. RENO* (1993).

Reference: Holly Idelson, "Court Takes a Harder Line on Minority Voting Blocs," *Congressional Quarterly Weekly Report*, July 1, 1995.

MALAPPORTIONMENT is an uneven distribution of voters in congressional and state legislative districts. Before the mid-1960s, many of the congressional and the legislative districts of the states favored the less populated rural areas, which gave those areas undue influence in national and state legislatures. In the early 1960s, the Supreme Court ruled in favor of "one person, one vote"; that is, legislative districts must be equal in population size. The Court based its decision on the equal protection clause in the Fourteenth Amendment.

The first malapportionment case was *Baker* v. *Carr* (1962), in which the Supreme Court determined that it had jurisdiction over state legislative districts and apportionment issues. In *Wesberry* v. *Sanders* (1964) the Supreme Court ruled that congressional districts had to be substantially equal in population size.

In *Reynolds* v. *Sims* (1964) the Supreme Court rejected the argument that one state legislative body could be apportioned on a criterion other than population.

These court rulings, supporting "one person, one vote," increased the influence of urban areas in state legislatures, which had previously been underrepresented, and in some states enhanced the opportunity for Democrats to make gains in state legislatures. *See: BAKER* v. *CARR* (1962); REAPPORTIONMENT; REDISTRICTING; *REYNOLDS* v. *SIMS* (1964); *WESBERRY* v. *SANDERS* (1964).

References: Paul Allen Beck, *Party Politics in America*, 8th ed. (New York: Longman, 1997); David Butler and Bruce Cain, *Congressional Redistricting: Comparative and Theoretical Perspectives* (New York: Macmillan, 1992).

MANDATE is a vote for a candidate or a party in an election, that is interpreted as a vote for a policy or set of policies. Mandates are difficult to determine from elections in the United States. President Clinton assumed he had a mandate for health care reform when he was elected. He put forth specific proposals to reform the health care system, and they were rejected by Congress. The loss suffered by the Democrats in the midterm congressional elections in 1994 was interpreted to be a rejection of Clinton's health care proposals.

The Republicans gained a majority in the House of Representatives in 1994, for the first time in 40 years. The 104th Congress, with a Republican majority led by Speaker Newt Gingrich, assumed they had a mandate to implement the Contract with America, which they had proposed in their effort to nationalize the congressional election of 1994. Some elements of the Republicans' Contract proved to be unpopular, and they suffered a loss of seats in the 1996 election. It is often difficult to discern a specific policy mandate from election results in the United States. *See*: CONTRACT WITH AMERICA.

Reference: Everett C. Ladd, "On Mandates, Realignments, and the 1984 Presidential Election," *Political Science Quarterly*, Vol. 100 (Spring 1985).

MARGINAL SEAT. A marginal seat is a legislative district where the incumbent is vulnerable because the party registration and voting pattern of the district do not match the party affiliation of the incumbent. For example, in 1994, Michael Patrick Flanagan, a Republican, defeated Democratic congressman Rostenkowski, who had been involved in a number of scandals. Rostenkowski's district in Chicago had a heavy Democratic registration. In 1996 the Democrats easily won the seat back from the Republicans.

A marginal seat can also be one where the district is competitive in party registration, and/or the incumbent's last election victory was less than 55%. A number of the incumbent Democrats, defeated in 1994, were in districts that Reagan or Bush had carried in previous presidential elections. Redistricting, following the decennial census, frequently contributes to vulnerable incumbents, because they are not as well-known in the newly drawn district, or they are not a good match for the new district. Hence, they have a tenuous hold on their seat and become targets of the opposing party. There are no longer many sections of the country where one party is dominant. *See*: SAFE SEATS; TARGETING.

Reference: Paul R. Abramson, John H. Aldrich, and David W. Rhode, *Change and Continuity in the 1992 Elections*, rev. ed. (Washington, D.C.: Congressional Quarterly Press, 1995).

MASS MEDIA refers to the means of communication that are technologically capable of reaching most people and affordable to almost everyone. The term "mass media" usually includes television, radio, newspapers, and magazines. Government officials communicate with millions of people through the mass media, which they do not control. The media stand between the politicians and their constituents. The media can filter, distort, or ignore what the political leaders are trying to communicate.

The media can significantly influence the course of a campaign by focusing on certain issues and exposing scandals and weaknesses of the candidates. Political candidates use both free media, ranging from appearances on radio talk shows, to press conferences, and paid media, where the candidates spend most of their campaign war chest for campaign advertising, creating an image of themselves and attempting to create a negative image of their opponent. There is growing concern with the concentration of ownership of all forms of media in the United States.

References: W. Lance Bennett, *News: The Politics of Illusion*, 3rd ed. (White Plains, N.Y.: Longman, 1996); Doris A. Graber, *The Mass Media and American Politics*, 5th ed. (Washington, D.C.: Congressional Quarterly Press, 1997).

MASS MEMBERSHIP PARTIES are parties with large numbers of very active dues-paying members. This type of party is not found in the United States. The term "mass membership party" was used to describe the political parties on the left in Europe. *See*: CADRE PARTY.

MATCHING FUNDS. Presidential candidates seeking a party nomination are the only federal candidates eligible to receive federal matching funds. The matching funds are available for the presidential nomination campaigns. This method of financing presidential elections is defined by the Federal Election Campaign Act of 1971 (FECA), the Revenue Act of 1971, and the FECA amendments of 1974, 1976, and 1979. The intent of the federal matching funds is to reduce the influence of large contributors and create a level playing field for the candidates. The law also imposes spending limits for the campaigns in each state. The spending cap is based on the voting age population in each state. If the candidates accept the matching funds, they must also accept the spending limits. In addition to the individual state limits, there is also a cap on total spending. The cap on total spending restricted the 1996 Dole campaign from matching Clinton's spending in the summer of 1996. In 1996, Steve Forbes did not accept the matching funds and was able to outspend the other candidates in the primaries he contested. Also, presidential candidates who accept matching funds are limited to a $50,000 personal contribution to their own campaigns. If a presidential candidate does not accept the matching funds, then there is no personal contribution limit.

For presidential candidates to receive matching funds, they must raise $5,000 in 20 states, in contributions of $250 or less, and raise a total of $100,000. Only the first $250 of each contribution is matched. In 1996 the government provided $55.9 million in matching funds to presidential candidates. Funds cannot be released until January 1 of the year of the election, but candidates can solicit money to be matched in the preceding year. The funds are derived from the tax check-off on the federal tax return. It is expected that the voluntary check-off funds will not be sufficient to match the candidates' contributions in 2000.

Almost one-half of the states provide some type of state financing of elections. In some states, the money goes to the candidates; in other states, the funds are given to the parties. *See*: FEDERAL ELECTION CAMPAIGN ACT OF 1971 AND AMENDMENTS; REVENUE ACT OF 1971.

References: Herbert E. Alexander and Anthony Corrado, *Financing the 1992 Election* (Armonk, N.Y.: M. E. Sharpe, 1995); Brooks Jackson, "Financing the 1996 Election: The Law of the Jungle," in *Toward the Millennium: The Elections of 1996*, Larry J. Sabato, ed. (Boston: Allyn and Bacon, 1997); Harold W. Stanley, "The Nominations: The Republican Doldrums, the Democratic Revival," in *The Elections of 1996*, Michael Nelson, ed. (Washington, D.C.: Congressional Quarterly Press, 1997).

McCLELLAN, GEORGE B. (1826–1885). Professional soldier and engineer, sometime politician, McClellan, son of a prominent Philadelphia physician, was born in that city on December 3, 1826. An exceptionally precocious child, McClellan entered the University of Pennsylvania at age thirteen, and, by special permission, the U.S. Military Academy at West Point at sixteen. He graduated from the Academy with the rank of brevet second lieutenant in 1846, choosing assignment with the corps of engineers. By the time he was 22, McClellan had a distinguished record in the war with Mexico (1846–1848), participating in the battles of Contreras, Churubusco, and the assault on Chapultepec fortress in Mexico City, leaving the war with the rank of captain. Returning to West Point, McClellan served as an instructor in engineering from 1847 to 1851, subsequently being assigned to an exploratory mission on the Red River border separating Texas and Indian Territory. In 1855, McClellan became part of a small contingent of officers sent to Europe to observe military operations associated with the Crimean War, McClellan's assignment being with the Russian Army. Upon his return from Europe, McClellan resigned his army commission to accept the civilian post of chief engineer for the Illinois Central Railroad, soon being promoted to vice-president. His career as a railroad man continued when he moved from Chicago to Cincinnati in 1860 to assume the presidency of the

Ohio and Mississippi Railroad, later of the St. Louis, Missouri, and Cincinnati Railroad. With the outbreak of the Civil War, McClellan accepted, on April 23, 1861, appointment by the governor of Ohio as major general of that state's volunteers. A week later, McClellan rejoined the U.S. Army, retaining the rank of major general and given command of the multi-state Department of Ohio. One of McClellan's major responsibilities, and one in whose performance he had a particular genius, was the molding of a volunteer force, in relatively short time, into a well-organized, disciplined army; an undertaking which he was to reprise with even greater success when he assumed command of the Division of the Potomac in July of 1861. McClellan came to the latter position on the strength of his success in the western counties of Virginia in the spring of 1861, where troops under his command cleared the region of Confederate forces, paving the way for those unionist counties to themselves secede from Virginia, becoming the new state of West Virginia in 1863. McClellan's subsequent record with the Army of the Potomac in the Washington-Richmond theater was mixed. He again received high marks for his ability to organize and train a vast army of soldiers who as volunteers and conscripts were wholly inexperienced in military life. He proved, however, much less effective in terms of battlefield command, hesitating to commit those armies he had so well organized to battle and to the decimation that would result. McClellan was removed from command by President Lincoln following the failure of the Peninsular Campaign in the spring of 1862. Returned to command in the fall of that year, McClellan was again removed by Lincoln after the Union victory at the battle of Antietam when Lee's Army of Northern Virginia was allowed to retreat, regroup, and survive to continue the hostilities. In this instance, McClellan, in November of 1862, was sent to Trenton, New Jersey to await reassignment, orders which never came. While a man of extraordinary ability, McClellan was also a man of enormous ego, coming, when he was first summoned to Washington in the summer of 1861, to see his role as Napoleonic. Writing to his wife, he reflected, "who would have thought, when we were married, that I should so soon be called upon to save the country . . . the people call on me to save the country . . . I would cheerfully take the dictatorship and agree to lay down my life when the country is saved." Further, it was a Napoleon who saw himself as constantly harassed and deprived of needed resources by an inept political administration headed by a president uneducated and incompetent. Hardly astonishing that Lincoln should have sent McClellan, for all his ability, into exile in New Jersey, particularly as the president also suspected presidential ambitions of the "Democrat" general. Those ambitions were to surface in the election year of 1864. Nominated for the presidency by a Democratic Party deeply factionalized, McClellan found himself, a "War Democrat," running on a "Peace Democrat" platform; his own position being that the war should be successfully waged to the conclusion that the seceded Southern states were brought back into the Union, given conciliatory terms, with the question of slavery left to state determination. The general did not accept the platform resolution written by the

"Peace Democrats" calling for "immediate efforts to be made for a cessation of hostilities . . . to the end that, at the earliest practicable moment, peace may be restored on the basis of the Federal Union of the States." Waging no active campaign (McClellan had not resigned from the army when he accepted the presidential nomination), he did make known his opposition to Lincoln and his administration, pointing to the wartime economic dislocations of soaring inflation and high interest rates, the result of a hugely mounting war debt. Critical attention was also called, as McClellan saw it, to Lincoln's repeated violations of constitutionally protected civil liberties. The election result was a victory for Lincoln and his running mate, Tennessee unionist, Democrat Andrew Johnson. Lincoln's popular vote plurality over McClellan was slightly more than 400,000 votes; of the 25 states then comprising the Union, Lincoln carried 22 states with 212 Electoral College ballots to 3 states and 21 Electoral College votes for McClellan and Democratic vice-presidential candidate, Congressman George H. Pendleton of Ohio. Political historians have pointed to the probability that McClellan's popular vote was undercounted on the basis of election corruption and fraud, particularly with regard to the soldier vote taken in the field. McClellan, choosing not to raise that issue, accepted the election result. Having resigned from the army on election day, McClellan, a month shy of his thirty-ninth birthday, spent the next several years, 1865–1868, on an extensive European tour. Returning, he served a brief period as chief engineer for New York City's Department of Docks (1870–1872). McClellan was also to make one last foray into the field of politics, elected governor of New Jersey in 1878 with his term ending in 1881. Four years later, at his home in Orange, New Jersey, McClellan, age 59, died on October 29, 1885. *See*: ELECTIONS: 1864.

Reference: Warren W. Hassler, *General George B. McClellan, Shield of the Union* (Baton Rouge: Louisiana State University Press, 1957).

McGOVERN, GEORGE (1922–   ) was the Democratic Party's presidential nominee in 1972. McGovern was born and raised in South Dakota. His father was a Methodist preacher. McGovern received his A.B. degree from Dakota Wesleyan. During World War II, McGovern served as a B-24 pilot, and was awarded the Distinguished Service Flying Cross. After the war, he earned a Ph.D. in History at Northwestern University, and he returned to South Dakota to teach at Dakota Wesleyan.

In 1957 he was elected to the U.S. House of Representatives. In 1962 he was elected to the U.S. Senate and he served as a member of the Senate Agricultural Committee. In the late 1960s he became an opponent of the war in Vietnam. After the 1968 election, he headed up the McGovern-Fraser Commission, which reformed the delegate selection process for the Democratic National Convention. In 1972 he became a candidate for the Democratic presidential nomination and had the support of the anti-war and liberal forces in the Democratic Party. He was nominated as the Democratic presidential candidate in that year. He lost that election to Richard Nixon by one of the largest margins in U.S. presidential election history. *See*: ELECTIONS: 1972; McGOVERN-FRASER COMMIS-SION; NIXON, RICHARD MILHOUS.

Reference: George McGovern, *Grassroots* (New York: Random House, 1972).

McGOVERN-FRASER COMMISSION. This commission of the Democratic National Committee created in 1968 transformed the method of nominating presidential candidates. This commission was appointed by DNC chair Fred Harris to study and make recommendations to reform the procedures for the selection of delegates after the public relations fiasco of the 1968 National Democratic Convention in Chicago. At that convention, Hubert Humphrey had been nominated without entering a primary contest. Senator George McGovern (D.-S.D.) was appointed chair of the Commission on Party Structure and Delegate Selection. McGovern later resigned to seek the Democratic nomination for president, and Congressman Donald Fraser (Minn.) was appointed to succeed him.

There were 28 members on the McGovern-Fraser Commission. The Commission was composed of elected officials and party leaders. They recommended that the state parties be required to follow the procedures set out by the National Committee for delegate selection.

The Commission recommended a nominating process that was to be open, timely, representative, and encourage greater participation. State parties were required to use primaries or caucuses (using procedures defined by the Commission) to select delegates. The delegates were to be distributed based on proportional representation. Winner-take-all primaries were banned. They also recommended demographic representation of delegates, particularly women and minorities. Delegates were also to reflect geographic representation in each state. Three-fourths of the delegates were to be selected at the congressional district level.

These rules have been criticized by many for creating a nominating system that has damaged the Democratic Party's ability to nominate a winning ticket, and for weakening political parties. Numerous reforms have been introduced by subsequent Democratic Party commissions to address some of these perceived problems.

The McGovern-Fraser Commission rules profoundly affected the way presidential nomination politics is conducted in the United States. The influence of state parties and state leaders has been diminished by these reforms, and a candidate-centered political world for presidential nominations has been created. There are no longer state delegations, handpicked by party leaders and led by favorite sons, characteristics of the system prior to 1972. The Democratic reforms, particularly the use of the primary, influenced the Republican Party procedures as well. The Republicans followed the Democrats in adopting the primary as the principal method for delegate selection. *See: COUSINS* v. *WIGODA* (1975); FAIRNESS COMMISSION; HUNT COMMISSION; MIKULSKI COMMISSION; PRIMARY, OPEN.

References: Denise L. Baer and David A. Bositis, *Elite Cadres and Party Coalitions* (Westport, Conn.: Greenwood Press, 1988); Philip A. Klinker, *The Losing Parties: Out-Party National Committees, 1956–1993* (New Haven, Conn: Yale University Press, 1994); Nelson W. Polsby, *Consequences of Party Reform* (New York: Oxford University Press, 1983).

McKINLEY, WILLIAM (1843–1901) was born at Niles in northeastern Ohio on January 29, 1843. Attending Allegheny College in Meadville, Pennsylvania (1859–1860), McKinley returned after one year of study to Poland, Ohio, where his family had moved in 1852. With the outbreak of the Civil War, the 18-year-old McKinley, a private, joined the Twenty-third Ohio Volunteers, an infantry regiment later commanded by Rutherford B. Hayes. Having participated in a number of battles, including that of Antietam in September of 1862, McKinley was subsequently cited for bravery and left Union army ranks in 1865 as a 22-year-old major. Returning to Ohio, McKinley studied law with local attorneys in Youngstown, followed by a more formal education at New York's Albany School of Law in 1866–1867. Admitted to the bar in the latter year McKinley established his practice in Canton, Ohio, where the youthful Republican was elected Stark County Prosecutor in 1869, only to be defeated in his reelection bid two years later. Building his law practice until the time of his election to the U.S. House of Representatives in 1876, McKinley was to serve there, with rising influence (but for one brief interruption in 1884), until his reelection defeat in 1890. Having become chairman of the powerful House Ways and Means Committee, he put his name to the McKinley Tariff Act of 1890, a strongly protectionist measure which, to its date, established the highest tariff rates ever enacted by Congress. Subject to much criticism from the Democrats, with implementation of the act being seen by the public as the cause of rapidly rising consumer prices, McKinley and the House Republican majority were turned out of office in the midterm congressional elections of 1890. McKinley's absence from office was brief; with the guidance of his friend and political supporter Mark Hanna, Cleveland industrialist and one of the two powerful bosses of the Ohio Republican organization, McKinley was successful in nomination for, and election to, the Ohio governorship in 1891, an office to which he was reelected in 1893. The legislative initiative of which the governor was most proud was that adopted in his first term establishing a state general arbitration board for the settlement of labor disputes and strikes. Ironically, it was a strike in Ohio's coal mines, called by the United Mine Workers (UMW) in April of 1894, that led to McKinley's most decisive action as governor, the calling out of the Ohio National Guard to end strike-related violence and restore public order; a decision which, while castigated by UMW leadership, was generally applauded. While McKinley's name had been placed in nomination at the 1892 Republican national convention, the governor did not become a serious presidential contender until 1896. So well had Mark Hanna and other McKinley supporters prepared the way for the Ohio governor in that year that he received a first ballot nom-

ination at the St. Louis convention, delegates giving the vice-presidential nomination to businessman and party activist Garret A. Hobart of New Jersey. The
1896 presidential campaign provided a sharp contrast between the two major
parties, not only in terms of issue differences but, as well, in terms of the
personalities and electioneering styles of the respective candidates. In the "battle
of the metals," McKinley, a high tariff protectionist, now wholly committed to
gold, spoke to thousands brought by railroad excursion, day-after-day, to the
front porch of his Canton, Ohio, home. The Democratic Party nominee, William
Jennings Bryan of Nebraska, age 36, committed to silver and to tariff reform
and reduction, toured the nation by train, logging more than 18,000 miles as he
displayed his formidable oratorical skills before mass crowds. In an election
politically dividing the American people more deeply along economic class lines
than ever before, McKinley and the Republicans emerged the winners over
Bryan's substantial challenge. Out of a total presidential vote of nearly 14 million, the GOP plurality was but 600,000. McKinley-Hobart carried 23 states and
271 Electoral College ballots to 22 states with 176 votes in the Electoral College
for Bryan and his Democratic vice-presidential running mate, Arthur Sewall of
Maine. Inaugurated on March 4, 1897, McKinley's first term saw congressional
passage of the highly protectionist Dingley Tariff Act of 1897 and the subsequent Gold Currency Act of 1900. On the foreign policy front, Hawaiian annexation was approved in 1898 and agreement was reached with European
powers in 1900 assuring an "Open Door" policy protecting American trading
rights in China. The major foreign and military policy determinations of the
McKinley administration were, however, those which led to the declaration of
war with Spain on April 25, 1898; a war prompted by alleged Spanish abuses
perpetrated in Cuba, reluctantly entered into by President McKinley, and with
hostilities lasting but four months. The American victory, recognized in the
Treaty of Paris (December 10, 1898), left the United States with possessions
stretching from Puerto Rico in the Caribbean to the islands of Guam and the
Philippines in the far Pacific. McKinley, not imperialistic by temperament or
politics, but a man of deep Christian faith, accepted for the nation "the white
man's burden," particularly as to the Philippines, there to strengthen Christianity
and bring forward civilization's benefits. Renominated in 1900, McKinley was
again to face his opponent of four years earlier, Democrat William Jennings
Bryan. Prosperity restored, a victorious war concluded, the "battle of the metals" all but forgotten, a Republican election-day victory was secure. The president, with the party's new vice-presidential candidate, Governor Theodore
Roosevelt of New York, modestly extending the Republican plurality of four
years earlier to some 800,000 votes, carried 28 states with 292 ballots in the
Electoral College. Bryan with his running mate, the former vice-president of the
United States, Adlai E. Stevenson of Illinois, carried 17 states and 155 Electoral
College votes. Returned to the presidency, McKinley's days in that office were
numbered. Traveling to Buffalo, New York, to attend the Pan-American Ex-
position, McKinley became the victim of an assassin's bullet on September 6,

1901. Remaining with his doctors in Buffalo, hopeful of recovery, McKinley was to die as the result of infection one week later on September 14. What many Republican conservatives had greatly feared took place: the presidential oath of office was taken by the independent and often unpredictable Theodore Roosevelt, as Mark Hanna put it, that "damned cowboy" now in the White House. *See*: ELECTIONS: 1896, 1900.

References: Lewis L. Gould, *The Presidency of William McKinley* (Lawrence: University Press of Kansas, 1980); H. Wayne Morgan, *William McKinley and His America* (Syracuse, N.Y.: Syracuse University Press, 1963).

MEDIA EVENT. In statewide and national campaigns, candidates stage events to attract the attention of the mass media. Appearances by candidates are staged for a good photo-opportunity for newspapers or a good backdrop for television. The remarks of the candidate are written and delivered to provide a sound bite for the evening television news. The scheduling of the event is done to meet the deadlines of the media.

The Clinton presidential campaigns displayed an aptitude for media events. After the 1992 Democratic National Convention, the bus caravan attracted a great deal of favorable media coverage, because it was novel and provided good visuals for television. In 1996, Clinton took the train to Chicago for the Democratic National Convention. That gave some vitality to what would have been a lackluster convention. The 1996 "Dole for President" campaign appeared to lack imagination for effective use of earned media. The exception was Dole's 96-hour marathon campaign at the end of the election. *See*: CAMPAIGN; EARNED MEDIA; MASS MEDIA.

Reference: F. Christopher Arterton, "Campaign '92: Strategies and Tactics of the Candidates," in *The Election of 1992*, Gerald Pomper, F. Christopher Arterton, Ross Baker, and Walter Dean Burnham, et al. (Chatham, N.J.: Chatham House, 1993).

MICHELS, ROBERT (1876–1936) was known for his iron law of oligarchy theory. Michels' classic hypothesis was that organizations, particularly parties and unions that are committed to democratic ideals, have oligarchical tendencies. According to Michels, to say organization is to say oligarchy. He studied German working-class parties and found that the elected leaders of the party became an oligarchy and, eventually, were unwilling to subject their leadership and their decisions to democratic rules. Michels saw oligarchy as having the following characteristics: stable leadership, emergence of a bureaucracy (that is, paid staff with regular duties), centralized authority, goal displacement(a shift from the ideological goals to the goal of perpetuating the organization), and a reduction in the members' opportunity to participate in decision making. According to Michels' famous monograph, *Political Parties*, it is organization that creates the oligarchic tendency.

Reference: Juan J. Linz, ''Robert Michels,'' in *International Encyclopedia of the Social Sciences*, vol. 10, David L. Sills, ed. (New York: Crowell Collier and Macmillan 1968).

MIDTERM ELECTION is the election in the even year between the presidential elections, the middle of a president's term. The entire House of Representatives, one-third of the Senate, and most state governorships are elected in the midterm election. The party in the White House has suffered losses in the House in every midterm election since the Civil War, except in 1934. Economic conditions and a decline in presidential popularity are contributing factors to the midterm losses of the president's party. The composition of the electorate is also quite different. In the midterm election, there is a much lower turnout rate. In 1992, a presidential election year, the turnout rate for congress was 51%. In 1994, a midterm election year, when the Republicans captured control of Congress, the turnout rate was 38%. Surprisingly, the Democrats gained five seats in 1998.

Reference: Harold W. Stanley and Richard G. Niemi, *Vital Statistics on American Politics*, 5th ed. (Washington, D.C.: Congressional Quarterly Press, 1995).

Congressional Midterm Election

Year	President	Party	Number of Seats Gained or Lost by the President in the House
1934	Roosevelt	Democratic	+ 9
1938	Roosevelt	Democratic	− 71
1942	Roosevelt	Democratic	− 55
1946	Truman	Democratic	− 55
1950	Truman	Democratic	− 29
1954	Eisenhower	Republican	− 18
1958	Eisenhower	Republican	− 47
1962	Kennedy	Democratic	− 5
1966	Johnson	Democratic	− 47
1970	Nixon	Republican	− 12
1974	Ford	Republican	− 48
1978	Carter	Democratic	− 15
1982	Reagan	Republican	− 26
1986	Reagan	Republican	− 5
1990	Bush	Republican	− 8
1994	Clinton	Democratic	− 53
1998	Clinton	Democratic	+ 5

MIKULSKI COMMISSION was a Commission appointed by the Democratic Party to address the shortcomings of the McGovern-Fraser Commission. It was appointed by the Democratic chair Robert Strauss to address the concerns of organized labor about the conditions of the party after the 1972 election defeat. The original chair of this Commission was Leonard Woodcock of the United

Auto Workers, who resigned. The vice-chair was Barbara Mikulski of Baltimore, at that time a member of the Baltimore City Council, who took the chairmanship.

After the crushing defeat of McGovern in 1972, Democratic Party regulars believed it was time to revise the nomination rules and this Commission was created. The major recommendation of this Commission was to require that participation in the primaries be restricted to Democrats only. This rule made open primaries unacceptable. Also, the Commission required that delegates be allocated proportionally to all contenders that met a 15% threshold. The quota requirement of McGovern-Fraser was abolished, while affirmative action in delegate selection was still promoted. The Commission permitted slate-making for delegates, which had been outlawed by the McGovern-Fraser rules. Finally, the Mikulski Commission recommended the creation of a Compliance Review Commission to monitor compliance of the rules by state parties. The attempt to overturn the thrust of the McGovern-Fraser Commission that the party regulars had hoped for was not achieved. *See: COUSINS* v. *WIGODA* (1975); FAIRNESS COMMISSION; HUNT COMMISSION; McGOVERN-FRASER COMMISSION; WINOGRAD COMMISSION.

References: Philip A. Klinker, *The Losing Parties: Out-Party National Committees, 1956–1993* (New Haven, Conn.: Yale University Press, 1994); L. Sandy Maisel, Parties and Elections in America, 2nd ed. (New York: McGraw-Hill, 1993).

MILLER v. *JOHNSON*, 515 U.S. 900 (1995). In *Shaw* v. *Reno* (1993) the U.S. Supreme Court had determined that race-conscious redistricting plans, even when benefiting racial minorities, were potentially in violation of the Equal Protection Clause of the Fourteenth Amendment. In order to be found constitutional, such plans would have to pass the legal test known as ''strict scrutiny.'' In *Miller*, the Supreme Court for the first time applied this stringent test to a race-conscious redistricting plan.

The redistricting scheme examined in *Miller* had been proposed by the Georgia legislature following the 1990 census. In response to pressure from the Justice Department (Georgia was forced to seek ''preclearance'' from the Justice Department under the terms of the Voting Rights Act), the Georgia legislature had created three majority-minority congressional districts within the state. One of the those districts, the Eleventh, connected areas that were more than 250 miles apart. White voters within the Eleventh District claimed that the Georgia legislature had engaged in racial gerrymandering when the state created the Eleventh District. The voters argued that, under *Shaw* v. *Reno* (1993), Georgia was therefore in violation of the Equal Protection Clause unless the state could show that the redistricting plan was narrowly tailored to advance a compelling state interest.

The Supreme Court decided that compliance with the Justice Department's understanding of the Voting Rights Act did not provide a compelling reason for Georgia's use of a racial classification. Since the state was unable to provide any other compelling justification for its redistricting plan, the Court found in favor of the white voters, and declared Georgia's plan unconstitutional. *See*: GERRYMANDERING; MAJORITY-MINORITY DISTRICT; PRECLEARANCE; REAPPORTIONMENT; REDISTRICTING; *SHAW* v. *RENO* (1993); STRICT SCRUTINY; VOTING RIGHTS ACT.

MINNESOTA FARMER-LABOR PARTY was a very influential populist third party in Minnesota in the 1920s and 1930s. It was the most successful third party at the state level in the United States. It was the major opposition party to the Republicans, and the main governing party in Minnesota in the 1930s. The party was a coalition of farmers and urban workers. It was one of the few successful class-based parties in the United States. The party began in 1918 and was very influential by 1924. The major force in its early development was William Mahoney, editor of the *St. Paul Union Advocate*. It was successful in electing twelve members to the U.S. House of Representatives and three members of the U.S. Senate. One of the influential governors of Minnesota, elected by the Farmer Labor Party, was Floyd B. Olson, who led the enactment of a progressive state income tax in 1933. It advocated very strong Socialist positions during the Great Depression. As the Depression eased the party began to weaken, and in 1944 the Minnesota Farmer-Labor Party merged with the Minnesota Democratic Party, forming the Minnesota Democratic-Farmer-Labor Party, the most liberal Democratic state party in the United States. *See*: HUMPHREY, HUBERT HORATIO, JR.; MONDALE, WALTER FREDERICK.

Reference: Richard M. Valelly, *Radicalism in the States: The Minnesota Farmer-Labor Party and the American Political Economy* (Chicago: University of Chicago Press, 1989).

MISSOURI PLAN is a state judicial selection plan created by an amendment to the Missouri State Constitution in 1940. It has been adopted by fourteen other states. Under the Missouri Plan, a nonpartisan nominating board nominates three qualified candidates for each vacant judgeship, and the governor appoints the judge from those nominations. After a period of not less than a year, the appointed judge stands for election in an unopposed nonpartisan ratification vote by the electorate. The intent of the Missouri Plan is to create a more qualified and less political judiciary. It is also referred to as a form of merit judicial selection. Many states continue to have direct election of state court judges. *See*: ELECTION; JUDICIAL ELECTIONS.

Reference: Karen L. Tokarz, "Women Judges and Merit Selection under the Missouri Plan," *Washington University Law Quarterly*, Vol. 6 (1966).

MIXED MEMBER PROPORTIONAL (MMP) is an increasingly popular election system around the world. This is a hybrid system that elects some seats from single-seat, winner-take-all districts, and some from party lists using proportional representation. This mixed member proportional system combines geographic representation and representation of ideological interests. *See*: LIST SYSTEM; PROPORTIONAL REPRESENTATION; SINGLE-MEMBER DISTRICT.

Reference: Rein Taagepera and Matthew Shugart, *Seats and Votes: The Effects and Determinants of Electoral Systems* (New Haven, Conn.: Yale University Press, 1989).

MOBILE, CITY OF, **v.** *BOLDEN*, 446 U.S. 55 (1980) is a case in which the U.S. Supreme Court upheld the at-large electoral system used to select the three city commissioners who governed the city of Mobile, Alabama. Several appellants, representing all African Americans in Mobile, alleged that the electoral scheme resulted in the "dilution" of the African-American vote in violation of both the Equal Protection Clause of the Fourteenth Amendment and voting rights protected by the Fifteenth Amendment. A federal district court ruled against the city, and ordered the adoption of a mayor-council system, with council members being elected from single member districts. A federal court of appeals affirmed the district court's ruling.

Although six of the nine members of the Supreme Court voted to overturn the lower court decisions, there was no majority opinion. Justice Stewart, joined by three other members of the Court, declared that the city of Mobile had not violated the Constitution and therefore voted to overturn the decision of the district court. According to Stewart, in order to establish that either the Equal Protection Clause or the Fifteenth Amendment had been violated, it must first be shown that the state was "motivated by a discriminatory purpose" when it enacted the challenged legislation. For Justice Stewart, the mere absence of proportionate representation in Mobile did not establish the requisite discriminatory intent. Justice Stevens, although arguing that a more flexible legal standard should have been applied by the Court, agreed that the Constitution had not been violated

Justice Blackmun did not accept Justice Stewart's conclusion that there was no discriminatory purpose behind the at-large voting system. Nevertheless, Justice Blackmun disagreed with the remedy proposed by district court, and was therefore willing to vote to overturn that court's decision. The result of this fractured decision was the understanding that, absent a finding of discriminatory intent, the lack of proportional representation that may result from at-large voting systems is not prima facie evidence of an impermissible dilution of voting rights in violation of the Fourteenth and Fifteenth Amendments to the Constitution. In response to the Court's decision in this case, the Congress in 1982 amended Section 2 of the Voting Rights Act to make clear that this section of the Voting Rights Act could be violated even without a showing of discriminatory intent. *See*: AT-LARGE ELECTION SYSTEM; SINGLE-MEMBER DISTRICT.

MONDALE, WALTER FREDERICK (1928–) was the defeated Democratic presidential candidate in 1984. He was born in Ceylon, Minnesota. He graduated from the University of Minnesota in 1951, and after serving in the army, he earned a law degree from the University of Minnesota in 1956. While in college, Fritz Mondale was active in the Minnesota Democratic-Farmer-Labor party. In 1960 he managed the reelection campaign of Governor Orville Freeman and was then selected to complete the term of the state attorney general, who had resigned. Mondale was reelected attorney general two times, and in 1964 was appointed to serve out the U.S. Senate term of Hubert Humphrey, who had been elected vice-president.

As a U.S. Senator, Mondale had a liberal voting record on civil rights and labor issues. He was reelected to the Senate in 1966 and 1972. In 1976 he dropped out of the Democratic presidential nomination contest saying he did not have the necessary drive and determination. In that year, Mondale was selected by Democratic presidential nominee Jimmy Carter to serve as his running mate. Mondale served as vice-president under President Jimmy Carter from 1976 to 1980, when they were defeated by the Republican ticket of Ronald Reagan and George Bush. In 1984, with strong backing from organized labor, Mondale captured the Democratic Party nomination for president. Mondale selected as his running mate Geraldine Ferraro, the first woman vice-presidential candidate. The 1984 Democratic ticket of Mondale-Ferraro was easily defeated by the reelection campaign of Ronald Reagan. Mondale was later appointed ambassador to Japan by President Clinton. *See*: ELECTIONS: 1976, 1980, 1984.

Reference: Finlay Lewis, *Mondale: Portrait of an American Politician*, rev. ed. (New York: Harper and Row, 1984).

MONROE, JAMES (1758–1831), in leaving the White House in March of 1825, brought to an end the reign of the ''Virginia Dynasty,'' a group of patriots of that state who had held the executive office for all but 4 of the first 36 years of its history. Joining the Continental Army in 1776, after but two years at the College of William and Mary, Monroe (who had been born of a Westmoreland County planter family on April 28, 1758) rose to the rank of lieutenant colonel; wounded at the battle of Trenton, cited for bravery by General Washington, he left military service in 1780. Studying law with the war governor of Virginia, Thomas Jefferson, Monroe was subsequently to establish his practice in Fredericksburg, Virginia in 1786. Monroe's career, however, was to be more one of politics and diplomacy than of the routine practice of law. Service in both the Virginia legislature and the Continental Congress in the 1780 decade failed to convince Monroe, as contrasted with his friend James Madison who held similar offices, of the need to replace the Articles of Confederation with a system in which national power was significantly strengthened. As such, Monroe became an anti-federalist opposed to ratification of the proposed Constitution of 1787. Once ratification took place, however, Monroe accepted the new system and sought election to the U.S. House of Representatives. Ironically, he was to lose that contest to James Madison. In 1790, Monroe was to have that defeat avenged, the Virginia legislature appointing him to the U.S. Senate, a seat initially aspired to by Madison. This political rivalry was without "an atom of ill will" and soon he and Madison found themselves united in Congress in their common opposition to Secretary of the Treasury Alexander Hamilton's economic program, allied in the defense of agrarian interests, and joined in organization of the emerging Jeffersonian Republican Party. No rift in their friendship developed until 1808 when Monroe became a competitor of Madison's for the Republican presidential endorsement. Even this disagreement was soon healed and in 1811, President Madison turned to Monroe to become his secretary of state, subsequently and concurrently selecting him to be his secretary of war as well. Early on, Monroe had been recruited to a number of diplomatic missions. His record of success, however, was mixed. Resigning from the Senate in 1794 to accept appointment by President Washington as minister to France, he was recalled by the president but two years later, presumably for being so pro-French as to ill-represent Washington's policy of neutrality. In 1803, President Jefferson again sent Monroe to France, this time to assist in negotiation for the purchase of the city of New Orleans. He and Ambassador Robert Livingston conducted their assignment so successfully that the United States found itself acquiring by purchase not only the city but the vast Louisiana Territory as well. Continuing his diplomatic mission in Europe, Monroe and William Pinckney, minister to Great Britain, negotiated in London a treaty largely dealing with trade matters. Unfortunately, one of the non-trade issues left unresolved was that of the Royal Navy's interception and search of American ships, with the all-too-frequent impressment of sailors aboard those ships claimed to be of British citizenship. Without resolution of this sensitive issue, President Jefferson declined in 1807 to submit the negotiated treaty to the U.S. Senate. Monroe then resigned his European post, returned to Virginia and in 1811, as in 1799, was elected to the governorship. His tenure, however, was brief, as in that same year Monroe joined the cabinet as secretary of state. Pushed by congressional "War Hawks" into conflict with Great Britain, his and the secretary of war's leadership ineffectual, President Madison came to rely heavily on Monroe, appointing him (in September of 1814, following the British capture of Washington, D.C.) secretary of war, concurrent with his State Department duties. Monroe was to receive high marks for bringing order out of chaos; and with peace restored in 1815, while resigning his dual post, he continued as secretary of state. In 1816 the secretary inherited the Republican presidential nomination and, with vice-presidential candidate Governor Daniel D. Tompkins of New York, won the national contest with but token opposition, the last presidential campaign observed by the moribund Federalists. Reelected without competitors in 1820, Monroe and Tompkins presided over a brief period of one-party politics, "the Era of Good Feelings." Monroe in that year received all but one of the 232 Electoral College ballots cast, the single vote withheld so as to safeguard Washington's distinction as the only president to be unanimously elected. Monroe's two terms were characterized by several foreign policy initiatives: in 1817 the

Rush-Bagot Agreement with Great Britain stabilized the relationship between the United States and Canada as to the Great Lakes, eventually leading to realization of a fully demilitarized border; in 1819 the Adams-Onis Treaty with Spain ceded control of the Floridas to the United States; and in 1823 promulgation of the Monroe Doctrine declared Latin America to be closed to further foreign colonization or military intrusion. Monroe's successes in the foreign policy field were in no small part the result of his selection, despite his Federalist antecedents, of diplomat John Quincy Adams as secretary of state. The major domestic policy determination of the Monroe presidency was Congress's adoption of the Missouri Compromise of 1820, legislation about which Monroe had serious reservations but which he nonetheless accepted as a means for mitigating sectional rivalries and, particularly as to the slavery question, resolving differences for a foreseeable future. James Monroe's retirement was not a particularly satisfying one; plagued by debt, he was forced to sell certain of his Virginia land holdings. Making his home with his daughter in New York City, Monroe died there in 1831. As with the predeceased Jefferson and John Adams, Monroe's death came on Independence Day, July 4. *See*: ELECTIONS: 1816, 1820.

References: Harry Ammon, *James Monroe: The Quest for National Identity* (New York: McGraw-Hill, 1971); William Penn Cresson, *James Monroe* (Chapel Hill: University of North Carolina Press, 1946); Noble E. Cunningham, Jr., *The Presidency of James Monroe* (Lawrence: University Press of Kansas, 1996).

MORAL MAJORITY is a political organization of Christian fundamentalists, founded and led by television evangelist Jerry Falwell. The organization supported conservative candidates who promoted the social agenda of the organization which included the following: prayer in school, an anti-abortion constitutional amendment, vouchers for private schools, and opposition to gay rights. Falwell's purpose was to mobilize millions of Christians to defend religious practices and the family. He claimed that his organization registered 2.5 million voters for the 1980 election. In 1986, Falwell changed the name of his organization to the Liberty Federation. In 1989 it was disbanded. The leading conservative Christian political group in the 1990s is the Christian Coalition, which promotes many of the same issues as the Moral Majority and is quite influential in the Republican Party. *See*: CHRISTIAN COALITION.

Reference: Duane M. Oldfield, "The Christian Right in the Presidential Nominating Process," in *In Pursuit of the White House: How We Choose Our Presidential Nominees*, William G. Mayer, ed. (Chatham, N.J.: Chatham House, 1996).

MOTOR VOTER LAW is a popular name for the National Voter Registration Act, which was passed by the Democratic Congress in 1993. The law (PL103–31) requires states to permit citizens to register to vote when they apply for their driver's license. It also provides that states permit mail-in voter registration, which was already in use in 28 states. The law requires registration forms to be made available at state and federal offices that provide public assistance, such as unemployment and welfare agencies. The Democrats had tried to pass this during the Bush administration, but President Bush vetoed it, and the Democrats were unable to override his veto. The Democrats were successful in passing the bill with President Clinton in the White House. The Republicans had feared that easing registration would aid the Democrats. There is no evidence that there has been a boost for the Democrats from the enactment of the law. The rise in registration has principally been among independents, and the law has boosted Republican registration in the South.

A number of states unsuccessfully challenged the law in federal court. The law went into effect in January 1995, and almost nine million Americans registered to vote when they received or renewed their driver's licenses under the new law. The League of Women Voters estimated that another six million will register under the motor voter law by the end of 1996, making it the greatest increase in voter registration in any two-year period in the history of the nation. Despite that fact, the 1996 presidential election had a record low turnout, with only 48.8% of the eligible population voting.

The Federal Election Commission's 1997 annual report on the National Voter Registration Act reported that the most popular place for people to register to vote in 1995 and 1996 was at their local motor vehicle registration offices, accounting for 33.1% of voter registrations. The report also pointed out that 72.8% of the voting age population is currently registered to vote. *See*: REGISTRATION, VOTER; VOTER TURNOUT.

References: Richard Sammon, " 'Motor Voter' Rides a Fast Track through the House," *Congressional Quarterly*, Vol. 51 (February 6, 1993); " 'Motor Voter' Report Sent to President and Congress," in Federal Election Commission, *RECORD* (August 1997).

MUGWUMPS are those who desert their party's nominee and support another party's candidate. The term is also used to characterize someone who straddles the fence, since they have their mug on one side and their rump on the other side. It is also used to describe bolters. The term was used to characterize those Republicans who deserted Republican James Blaine in the election of 1884, in order to support the Democratic nominee Grover Cleveland.

References: A. James Reichley, *The Life of the Parties: A History of American Political Parties* (New York: The Free Press, 1992); William Safire, *Safire's New Political Dictionary* (New York: Random House, 1993).

MULTI-MEMBER DISTRICT is a defined electoral geographic unit from which more than one candidate is elected. In the United States, multi-member districts are most frequently used for at-large city council elections, in which there is more than one candidate to elect. Multi-member districts were used for the election of state legislatures. This practice has fallen into disuse, and today most state and national legislatures in the United States are elected in single-member districts. A multi-member district distributes available offices based on either a plurality system or a proportional representation system. A multi-member district that uses plurality elects two or more legislatures from the district. The seats are distributed, according to the ranking of the candidates from the most votes received to the least votes received, until all the seats are distributed in a plurality or winner-take-all election system. The district is the boundaries of the political subdivision.

Multi-member districts is a requirement in an electoral system where proportional representation is used for the election of legislatures. This type of system is not used in the United States for the election of legislatures. It is used by the National Democratic Party, which requires the use of proportional representation where primaries and caucuses are used for the selection of delegates to the Democratic National Convention. In this system, seats are distributed to the candidates in proportion to the vote received in the primary. If a candidate receives 30% of the vote, he/she is to receive 30% of the delegates out of the pool of delegates available in the defined geographic unit, which could be a congressional district or a state.

Multi-seat districts are used in all European elections except the parliamentary elections in France, the United Kingdom, and mixed systems, like Germany's, where some candidates run in districts and some on lists. *See*: DISTRICT, PACKING; DUVERGER'S LAW; PROPORTIONAL REPRESENTATION; SINGLE-MEMBER DISTRICT.

References: Gordon E. Baker, ''Whatever Happened to the Reapportionment Revolution in the United States?'' in *Electoral Laws and Their Political Consequences*, Bernard Grofman and Arend Lijphart, eds. (New York: Agathon Press, 1986); M. Margaret Conway, ''Creative Multimember Redistricting and Representation of Women and Minorities in the Maryland Legislature,'' in *United States Electoral Systems: Their Impact on Women and Minorities*, Wilma Rule and Joseph F. Zimmerman, eds. (Westport, Conn.: Greenwood Press, 1992); Douglas W. Rae, *The Political Consequences of Electoral Laws* (New Haven, Conn.: Yale University Press, 1967).

N

**NATIONAL ASSOCIATION FOR THE ADVANCEMENT OF COL-
ORED PEOPLE (NAACP)** was founded in 1909 by W.E.B. Du Bois to advance the cause of African Americans in the United States. The organization
has played a significant role in the Civil Rights movement. It was committed
to the Niagara Movement platform, calling for equality and civil rights. It pursued its goals through legislation and in the legal system. The organization
successfully challenged the white primary in federal court. One of the organization's most notable accomplishments was its challenge of the "separate but
equal" language in *Plessy* v. *Ferguson* (1898) in the Supreme Court. It won a
great victory with the landmark Supreme Court decision, *Brown* v. *Board of
Education* (1954), which ruled that separate educational facilities were unconstitutional.

The NAACP has continued to be a major political voice for African Americans. After some organizational and financial problems in the early 1990s, it
reestablished its role in 1995, with the election of Kweisi Mfume as president
of the NAACP. Mfume was a member of the U.S. House of Representatives
from Baltimore, and had served as the leader of the Congressional Black Caucus.
It is expected that he will resolve the organization's financial problems and give
a sharper focus to the organization's mission. Mfume has put a voter empowerment program high on the NAACP's agenda. Voter empowerment is a three-
pronged effort of registration, education, and participation. The NAACP was
involved in a massive voter registration drive in 1996. Republican presidential
nominee Bob Dole created a controversy when he turned down an invitation to
speak to the NAACP's 1996 annual convention. *See*: BLACK VOTING.

Reference: Lucius J. Barker and Mack H. Jones, *African Americans and the American Political System*, 3rd ed. (Englewood Cliffs, N.J.: Prentice-Hall, 1994).

NATIONAL COMMITTEES of the Democratic and Republican parties play a significant role in national elections because they raise and spend a great deal of money, including "soft money," which they funnel to targeted states. In the presidential year of 1996, each committee received $12.4 million in federal money for GOTV. They also received $12.4 million to finance their conventions. The national committees have a large professional staff to provide services to party candidates. The out-party (out of the White House) national committee is often quite innovative and the chair is one of the national spokespersons for that party. The national committee of the party in the White House has become an extension of the president, who customarily selects the national chairperson.

The party national committees no longer direct the presidential campaigns, as they did when they were originally formed in the 1840s and 1850s. The presidential campaigns have become candidate-centered, rather than party-centered. The national committees have come to play a supporting role to the candidates' committee and political consultants. The importance of electronic media has contributed to this weakened role for the party, as well as the fact that the public funding of presidential campaigns goes to the candidates and not to the parties. *See*: DEMOCRATIC NATIONAL COMMITTEE; REPUBLICAN NATIONAL COMMITTEE.

References: Ralph M. Goldman, *The National Party Chairmen and Committees: Factionalism at the Top* (Armonk, N.Y.: M. E. Sharpe, 1990); Philip A. Klinker, *The Losing Parties: Out-Party National Committees, 1956–1993* (New Haven, Conn.: Yale University Press, 1994).

NATIONAL PARTY CONVENTION. The first national party convention was held in 1831 in Baltimore by the Anti-Masonic Party. It nominated William Wirt as its presidential candidate. The other parties soon followed the Anti-Masons in using conventions to nominate their presidential candidates. The Democratic Party held its first convention in 1832, and nominated Andrew Jackson. In 1880, the Republicans nominated their first dark horse candidate, James A. Garfield of Ohio, after 36 ballots. The last multi-ballot convention was in 1956, when Adlai Stevenson was nominated over Estes Kefauver at the Democratic National Convention.

National party conventions are no longer deliberative bodies when it comes to selecting presidential nominees. The national conventions of today ratify the decisions made by the primary voters. In 1996, 42 states held primaries to select delegates. The party conventions continue to adopt platforms almost always incorporating the language of the platform committee, which is influenced by the presumptive nominee. The national party conventions have become the kick-off for the parties' fall general election campaign. Today's conventions are designed for television, despite the fact that the national networks have reduced their coverage, and the ratings have declined significantly.

The national parties receive public funds to put on their conventions. In 1996 each national party received $12.4 million.

Site and Size of National Party Conventions, 1948–1996

DEMOCRATS			REPUBLICANS	
Year	Site	Delegates	Site	Delegates
1948	Philadelphia	1,234	Philadelphia	1,094
1952	Chicago	1,230	Chicago	1,206
1956	Chicago	1,372	San Francisco	1,322
1960	Los Angeles	1,521	Chicago	1,331
1964	Atlantic City	2,316	San Francisco	1,308
1968	Chicago	2,622	Miami Beach	1,333
1972	Miami Beach	3,016	Miami Beach	1,348
1976	New York	3,008	Kansas City	2,259
1980	New York	3,331	Detroit	1,994
1984	San Francisco	3,933	Dallas	2,235
1988	Atlanta	4,161	New Orleans	2,277
1992	New York	4,288	Houston	2,210
1996	Chicago	4,289	San Diego	1,990

See: DELEGATE.

References: James S. Chase, *Emergence of the Presidential Nominating Convention 1789–1832* (Urbana: University of Illinois Press, 1973); Congressional Quarterly, *Guide to the 1996 Democratic National Convention*, Vol. 54 (August 17, 1996); Congressional Quarterly, *Guide to the 1996 Republican National Convention*, Vol. 54 (August 13, 1996); Larry David Smith and Dan Nimmo, *Orchestrating National Party Conventions in the Telepolitical Age* (New York: Praeger, 1991).

NATIONAL REPUBLICANS were the supporters of John Quincy Adams in 1928; they also supported Henry Clay in the election of 1832. They opposed Andrew Jackson, the leader of the Democratic Party. The National Republicans enjoyed their greatest support in New England and the Middle Atlantic states. The party held a convention in 1831 (this was one of the first parties to hold a nominating convention) to nominate Henry Clay for president in the 1832 election, and they won 49 Electoral College votes. The National Republicans were absorbed into the Whig Party in 1834. This party is not considered a forerunner of the current Republican Party. *See*: WHIG PARTY.

Reference: Ralph M. Goldman, *The National Party Chairmen and Committees: Factionalism at the Top* (Armonk, N.Y.: M. E. Sharpe, 1990).

NATURAL LAW PARTY is a minor party, founded in 1992, at the Maharishi International University in Fairfield, Iowa. The party's presidential nominee in

1992 was John Hagelin. He received 40,000 votes, and was renominated in 1996 at the party's four-day convention at the Mayflower Hotel in Washington, D.C. In 1996 the party was on the ballot in 49 states, with close to 1,000 candidates for other offices. The party principles include the following: preventative health care, reliance on renewable energy, agriculture without the use of hazardous chemicals, and the use of transcendental meditation to reduce social stress and violence in prisons. The party claims its proposals have been scientifically proven. In 1996 the vote for the national ticket was above 110,000 votes, which was .1% of the vote. This was a poor showing for a party that claimed to be the fastest growing third party in the United States. The Natural Law Party trailed the Reform, Green, Libertarian, and Taxpayers parties in the 1996 election. The party did demonstrate organizational capacity in that it recruited and filed candidates in most congressional districts in the United States. That was a difficult task. The Natural Law Party leaders claimed that its campaign was ignored by the press and that it was not permitted to participate in the presidential debates.

NEGATIVE ADVERTISING is a form of political advertising by a campaign that attacks and criticizes the opponent with paid media. This type of campaigning has become more common in American politics. The 1964 "Daisy" commercial, which was used by the Lyndon Johnson campaign against Barry Goldwater, was one of the first notable negative advertisements. In this ad, a young girl is shown picking daisies, with the countdown for a nuclear explosion in the background, implying that Goldwater was trigger-happy and would lead the United States into a nuclear war. A more recent negative ad by a presidential campaign was the 1988 Willie Horton ad produced by the George Bush campaign. The Willie Horton ad focused on the weekend furlough program for inmates in Massachusetts correctional facilities. Willie Horton was an inmate on a weekend pass who kidnaped and raped a woman in Maryland. Horton was black and the woman was white. The ad used the visual of a revolving door, with prisoners going in and out of prison. The negative ad suggested that Michael Dukakis allowed criminals out on the street who then committed heinous crimes, suggesting that Dukakis was soft on crime

Independent campaigns conducted by PACs against candidates are often totally negative. The media campaign conducted by the AFL-CIO against targeted Republican members of Congress in 1996 was entirely negative. Negative advertising is used because studies have shown that it is effective in moving voters. Candidates who are behind in the polls are very likely to "go negative." Radio is a good medium for negative political advertising. Stephen Ansolabehere and Shanto Iyengar, in their recent study, argue persuasively that in 1992, negative advertising drove down the potential vote by over six million. They argue that the voters who are driven away from the election are independents. They also argue that negative ads are used by political campaigns because they are more effective than positive ads. Others speculate that negative advertising contributes to the growing distrust of politicians and government in the United States. *See*: CAMPAIGN; POLITICAL CONSULTANTS.

Reference: Stephen Ansolabehere and Shanto Iyengar, *Going Negative: How Political Advertisements Shrink & Polarize the Electorate* (New York: The Free Press, 1995).

NEW ALLIANCE PARTY was a minor party, based in New York City, that preached minority rights and redistribution of wealth. It ran candidates in a variety of elections. It was founded by Dr. Fred Newman in 1979. The party backed Lenora B. Fulani for president in 1988 and 1992. In 1988, Fulani was on the ballot as an independent in all 50 states. In 1992 perennial candidate Fulani was on the ballot in 37 states and the District of Columbia. She was on the ballot as the New Alliance Party's candidate in 24 states and D.C. In 1992 the party joined the Federation of Independent Parties which became the Patriot Party in April 1994. In 1996 the party backed Ross Perot's Reform Party and assisted Perot in gaining ballot access for the Reform Party by circulating petitions.

Reference: Frank Bruni, "Perot and Populist Group See Benefits in an Alliance," *New York Times*, August 21, 1996, p. 1.

NEW DEAL COALITION developed as a response to the economic collapse in the 1930s, which led to the Great Depression. The economic crisis precipitated the 1932 election of Democratic president Franklin D. Roosevelt. Roosevelt's Democratic coalition was a significant and lasting realignment of the electorate. The New Deal was the set of social welfare and economic policies introduced by Roosevelt and the Democrats to correct the nation's economic conditions. The policies that the Roosevelt Democrats introduced led to a much more active and extensive national government.

The New Deal coalition of voters consisted of the following groups: white southerners; Catholic urban workers, who had been attracted to the Democrats with the nomination of Al Smith in 1928 and were often aligned with urban machines; recent immigrants from eastern and southern Europe; blue collar workers attempting to unionize and adversely affected by the economic downturn; black voters turned away from the party of Lincoln because of their economic plight; and Jews, who were attracted to Roosevelt's opposition to Nazi Germany. This coalition of voters came to dominate American politics for decades. In fact, it is the last recognized realignment of the American electorate. In recent decades, the New Deal coalition has been breaking apart. The most significant break-up of the New Deal coalition was the defection of white southerners to the Republican Party, which began with Republican presidential voting in the 1960s, and has led to a majority of the Republican members of the 1994 Congress coming from the Old Confederate states. Union members and Catholics have also broken loose from the New Deal coalition and have become key swing voters in national elections. *See*: DEALIGNMENT; ELECTIONS: 1932; REALIGNMENT; ROOSEVELT, FRANKLIN D.

References: Michael Barone, *Our Country: The Shaping of America from Roosevelt to Reagan* (New York: The Free Press, 1990); John R. Petrocik, *Party Coalitions* (Chicago: University of Chicago Press, 1981); Harold W. Stanley and Richard G. Niemi, "The Demise of the New Deal Coalition: Partisanship and Group Support, 1952–1992," in *Democracy's Feast: Elections in America*, Herbert F. Weisberg, ed. (Chatham, N.J.: Chatham House, 1995).

NEW HAMPSHIRE PRIMARY has been the first presidential primary, and it has played a significant role in the nomination of presidential candidates. The New Hampshire primary became important after the New Hampshire legislature added a presidential preference line to its primary ballot in 1949. In 1952, Massachusetts senator Henry Cabot Lodge placed Dwight D. Eisenhower's name on the ballot without his permission. Eisenhower won the Republican primary in New Hampshire, defeating Ohio senator Robert Taft, and Eisenhower went on to win the struggle for the Republican Party nomination.

From 1952 until 1992, every elected president had won the New Hampshire primary. That streak was broken in 1992 when Arkansas governor Bill Clinton finished second to former Massachusetts senator Paul Tsongas. Clinton, struggling against allegations of marital infidelity, finished a strong second in New Hampshire and claimed to be the "comeback kid." In the 1996 Republican primary, Steve Forbes did not build an organization or pursue the retail style of politics that has become common in New Hampshire. Instead, Forbes spent much more money on media than the other candidates, because he was not subject to the spending limits imposed on those who took the federal matching funds. He ran a negative campaign against frontrunner Robert Dole, who had the support of then Republican governor Steve Merrill and the New Hampshire GOP establishment. Forbes's campaign changed the dynamics of the race, and Patrick Buchanan finished first in New Hampshire. This has placed the bellwether character of the New Hampshire primary in doubt for future elections. Also, Steve Forbes's campaign, which ignored grassroots organization and focused on a media blitz, has cast doubts on the value of the traditional retail character of the New Hampshire primary campaign.

New Hampshire may not be the first primary in the year 2000. The rules adopted by the 1996 Republican convention state that "no presidential primary, caucus, convention, or other meeting may be held for the purpose of voting for a presidential candidate and/or selecting delegates or alternate delegates to the national convention, prior to the first Monday of February or after the third Tuesday of June." This rule allows other states to select that date, and New Hampshire and Iowa will not be permitted to move their primaries back. *See*: BELLWETHER; ELECTIONS: 1996; IOWA CAUCUS; PRIMARY.

References: Gary R. Orren and Nelson W. Polsby, eds., *Media and Momentum: The New Hampshire Primary and Nomination Politics* (Chatham, N.J.: Chatham House, 1987); The 1996 Republican National Convention, *The Rules of the Republican Party* (August 12, 1996).

NICHOLSON, JAMES R. (1938–   ) is chairman of the Republican National Committee. He was elected on January 17, 1996, on the fifth ballot, as a compromise candidate.

James Nicholson, who was born on February 4, 1938, is married and the father of three children. Nicholson graduated from West Point in 1961, and earned his law degree from the University of Denver in 1972. He served as special assistant to the director of the Office of Emergency Preparedness, Executive Office of the White House, from 1960 to 1971. He was awarded a bronze star and a number of other military decorations for his service in Vietnam. After leaving the military, he became a successful Colorado homebuilder.

Nicholson was elected a member of the Republican National Committee from Colorado in 1986. In 1996 he was appointed to serve as the chairman of the committee that reviewed the front-loaded primary system. That committee recommended that the GOP move away from the front-loaded primary. Nicholson succeeds the very effective Haley Barbour, who stepped down as RNC chairman after the 1996 election. Nicholson is a pro-life Catholic. Ralph Reed of the Christian Coalition said "Jim Nicholson is not only someone we can work with, he's someone we look forward to working with." *See*: REPUBLICAN NATIONAL COMMITTEE.

Reference: Alan Greenblatt and Ronald D. Elving, "Nicholson, Romer Picked to Lead National Committees," *Congressional Quarterly Weekly Report*, Vol. 55 (January 25, 1997).

NINETEENTH AMENDMENT is the 1920 amendment to the U.S. Constitution, which gave women the right to vote. The women's suffrage movement began in the United States in 1849, at the Seneca Falls Convention, where Elizabeth Cady Stanton promoted the right to vote as part of the Declaration of Sentiments, which was a listing of the concerns of women. Susan B. Anthony argued for expansion of women's suffrage when the post–Civil War Fourteenth and Fifteenth Amendments were being proposed. Her arguments were rejected. Stanton organized the National Women's Suffrage Association in 1869. In 1890 various women's groups joined forces to create the National American Womens' Suffrage Association (NAWSA). In the early twentieth century this organization pressed for both state and federal suffrage law. Carrie Chapman Catt served as the president of NAWSA when the Nineteenth Amendment was finally ratified. The League of Women Voters became the official successor of NAWSA after ratification of the amendment. *See*: GENDER GAP; LEAGUE OF WOMEN VOTERS; NOW.

Reference: M. Margaret Conway, Gertrude A. Steuernagel, and David W. Ahern, *Women & Political Participation: Cultural Change in the Political Arena* (Washington, D.C.: Congressional Quarterly Press, 1997).

NIXON, RICHARD MILHOUS (1913–1994) was the thirty-seventh president of the United States. Nixon was born in Yorba Linda, California; his parents were Quakers of humble means. In 1934 he received his B.A. degree from Whittier College, and in 1937 he earned a law degree from Duke University. Nixon enlisted in the U.S. Navy during World War II, and served in the Pacific theater. After World War II, Nixon was elected to the U.S. House of Representatives from California, and served from 1947 to 1951. In his campaign for Congress, he cast his Democratic opponent as soft on communism. Nixon gained national attention as a member of the House Committee on Un-American Activities for his role in pursuing Alger Hiss for spying; Hiss was eventually convicted of perjury. In 1951, Nixon won a U.S. Senate seat from California by once again casting his Democratic opponent as soft on communism.

In 1952, Nixon was selected to serve as the vice-presidential running mate of Republican presidential nominee Dwight D. Eisenhower. In that campaign, Nixon went on television to refute charges that he personally benefited from a slush fund; his rebuttal to the charges is referred to as the "Checkers speech" because he made reference to the family dog named Checkers. The Republican ticket of "Ike and Dick" was elected in 1952, and reelected in 1956. Nixon was a very visible and active vice-president; he was particularly active in foreign affairs. In 1959 he had his famous "kitchen debate" with Khrushchev in Moscow. In 1960, Nixon received the Republican nomination for president and he was defeated in a close election by Democratic nominee John F. Kennedy. In an effort to restart his political career, Nixon ran for governor of California in 1962; he lost that race, expressed bitter disappointment, and it appeared that Nixon's political career was over.

Richard Nixon then moved to New York to practice law, and wrote his book *Six Crises* (1962). He continued to actively campaign for Republicans around the country, and was able to secure the Republican nomination for president in 1968. Nixon narrowly defeated Hubert Humphrey in that election. As president, Nixon had to deal with a Democratic Congress, and a very divided country. Nixon made his mark as president in foreign affairs: he successfully brought an end to the divisive Vietnam War, stabilized relations with the USSR, and opened up U.S. relations with Communist China. On the domestic front Nixon instituted wage and price controls in 1971. In 1972, Nixon was reelected by a landslide, easily defeating George McGovern.

During the 1972 election, Republican campaign operatives broke into Democratic Headquarters in the Watergate building in Washington, D.C. Revelations of efforts to cover up that activity, which surfaced after the election, eventually led to Nixon's resignation in August of 1974. Nixon's successor, Gerald Ford, pardoned President Nixon for any wrongdoing. Nixon spent the rest of his life writing influential books on public affairs. In his later years, Nixon's advice and counsel were sought by leaders of both political parties. *See*: ELECTIONS: 1952, 1956, 1968, 1972.

References: Stephen Ambrose, *Nixon*, 3 vols. (New York: Simon and Schuster, 1987–1991); Richard Nixon, *RN: The Memoirs of Richard Nixon* (New York: Grosset & Dunlap, 1978).

NOMINATION is an action by a party to designate a candidate to be its nominee for a particular office. There are a variety of methods employed for nominating candidates, including caucuses, conventions, and primaries. The selection of the party presidential nominees is lengthy, costly, and complex. The presidential nomination process includes state primaries, state caucuses, and culminates with a national party convention.

In the United States, the primary has become almost universal in the nomination of party candidates. The electorate in these primaries varies by state. In a 1996 referendum, California voters voted to open the parties' primaries to all voters by adopting a blanket primary.

The use of the primary for the nomination of candidates distinguishes the U.S. party system from all other democracies, where party organizations have greater control over the selection of their nominees. *See*: CAUCUS; CONVENTION; PRESIDENTIAL NOMINATING CAMPAIGNS; PRIMARY.

Reference: Paul Allen Beck, *Party Politics in America*, 8th ed. (New York: Longman, 1997).

NONPARTISAN ELECTION is often used for local elections in the United States where the party affiliation of the candidate does not appear on the ballot. Nonpartisan elections were part of the reform movement of the early twentieth century, designed to break the control of party machines, particularly in urban areas. Municipal reformers believed that there is neither a Republican nor Democratic way to manage a city. A number of cities use nonpartisan elections; for example, the city of Cleveland holds its first municipal election early in the fall, when all the candidates are listed on one ballot, without party identification, and the top two vote-getters have a runoff in the general election in November. The party of the candidates is not identified on the ballot.

The use of the nonpartisan ballot has not eliminated the influence of parties in elections where it has been adopted. Party organizations often recruit candidates to run in nonpartisan elections and mobilize their members to vote for a particular candidate. Some studies argue that nonpartisan municipal elections reduce turnout and favor candidates from the majority population. Local school board and judicial elections are usually nonpartisan. *See*: JUDICIAL ELECTIONS.

Reference: Susan Welch and Timothy Bledsoe, "The Partisan Consequences of Nonpartisan Elections and the Changing Nature of Urban Politics," *American Journal of Political Science*, Vol. 30 (February 1986).

NOW (NATIONAL ORGANIZATION FOR WOMEN) is the largest and most influential public interest group for women in the United States. The organization was founded in 1966 to lobby the Equal Employment Opportunity Commission to enforce the "sex" equality provision of the 1964 Civil Rights Act. Betty Friedan became NOW's first president. The organization is dedicated to using political action to pursue its agenda. Unlike the League of Women Voters, NOW endorses and opposes candidates. In 1996, NOW refused to support President Clinton, because he signed the welfare reform bill which NOW argued would harm poor children. For a number of years, the major goal of the organization was ratification of the Equal Rights Amendment (ERA), which failed. NOW is a national organization with local chapters. The president of NOW is Patricia Ireland. *See*: LEAGUE OF WOMEN VOTERS.

Reference: Jane J. Mansbridge, *Why We Lost the ERA* (Chicago: University of Chicago Press, 1986).

NRA (NATIONAL RIFLE ASSOCIATION) is one of the first and most influential single-interest groups in the United States. The organization was founded in 1871 to promote firearm possession, gun collecting, and hunting in the United States. It offers safety training in firearm use. It trains Olympic shooters and offers discounts and insurance to its members. The NRA opposes any form of gun control. To justify this position, the NRA invokes the Second Amendment, which states that, "A well regulated militia, being necessary to the security of a free state, the right of the people to keep and bear arms shall not be infringed." The organization has two important assets that contribute to its influence in American politics. First, it has a large membership which it mobilizes to lobby federal and state legislatures, and second, it has a well-funded NRA-Political Victory Fund PAC to help finance the campaigns of favored candidates.

The NRA lost a number of legislative battles in recent years. In 1993 the Brady bill was passed. The bill, named for James Brady, a former White House press secretary who was shot and seriously wounded in the 1981 assassination attempt on President Ronald Reagan, provides for a five-day waiting period and background check to purchase a handgun. The NRA also opposed a 1994 crime bill which banned nineteen assault weapons for sale in the United States. The NRA has tried to get this law repealed.

The NRA has been very influential in recent national elections. In 1994, President Clinton blamed the NRA for the loss of the Democratic majority in Congress. The NRA was able to use its influence in Congress to organize the Ruby Ridge hearings. The NRA's influence was also evident when the House voted to repeal the ban on assault rifles in 1996.

The NRA's influence has weakened since the 1994 election. The organization has suffered from internal divisions. It has also lost membership. In a letter to members, the NRA referred to federal agents as jack-booted thugs in their dealings with the militia movement. In response to that criticism of federal authorities, former President George Bush resigned as an NRA member. Bush's resignation was symptomatic of the organization's growing organizational problems. *See*: INTEREST GROUP; LOBBYIST; SINGLE-ISSUE GROUPS.

Reference: Clyde Wilcox, ''The Dynamics of Lobbying the Hill,'' in *The Interest Group Connection: Electioneering, Lobbying, and Policymaking in Washington*, Paul S. Herrnson, Ronald G. Shaiko, and Clyde Wilcox, eds. (Chatham, N.J.: Chatham House, 1998).

O

OFF-YEAR ELECTION refers to an election held in a non-presidential year. The midterm election occurs in the even year, between the presidential elections, when the Congress is elected. Most state governments elect their administrative officials in that year. State governments have selected the off-year to avoid the influence of the presidential election on the selection of their officials. The party in the White House is usually adversely affected in the midterm election. Turnout in the midterm election is lower than it is in the presidential election. Turnout in the midterm election of 1994 was 36%.

Off-year election also refers to the odd-numbered year elections, when local governments hold their elections. Turnout is usually very low in these odd-numbered election years. *See*: MIDTERM ELECTION.

O'NEILL, THOMAS P. (TIP), JR. (1912–1994) served as Speaker of the House from 1977 to 1987. Tip O'Neill was raised in Cambridge, Massachusetts, and in 1936 graduated from Boston College. Also, in 1936 he was elected to the Massachusetts legislature. In 1947 he was elected minority leader, and in 1949 O'Neill became the first Democratic Speaker of the Massachusetts House in more than a century.

In 1952, Tip O'Neill was elected to the U.S. House of Representatives from Massachusetts, in the seat vacated by John F. Kennedy, who had been elected to the U.S. Senate. In 1954, when the Democrats regained the majority in the House, O'Neill was appointed to the powerful House Rules Committee. He was a supporter of Speaker Sam Rayburn and Majority Leader John McCormack. During the Vietnam War, O'Neill broke with the House leadership and opposed the war.

In 1972, when Majority Leader Hale Boggs died in a plane crash, the Democrats unanimously elected O'Neill majority leader. In 1977, when Speaker Carl Albert retired, O'Neill was elected Speaker. It was expected that Speaker O'Neill would work closely with newly elected Democratic president Jimmy Carter. O'Neill was not given access to the White House, and he did not work well with the Carter administration. President Ronald Reagan, in his first two years in office, was able to collect the support of conservative southern Democrats in the House and work around O'Neill. In the 1982 midterm elections, the Democrats gained seats, and Tip O'Neill was then able to block many of Reagan's legislative proposals. O'Neill retired in 1987; he had the longest consecutive service as Speaker in congressional history. His most famous quote is: "All politics is local."

Reference: Thomas P. O'Neill, *Man of the House: The Life and Political Memoirs of Speaker Tip O'Neill* (New York: Random House, 1987).

OPEN-SEAT RACES are legislative districts in which there is no incumbent running. If the seat is considered safe for one of the parties, then the primary will be very competitive. If it is a competitive district, then the Hill Committees will target the open district, because the opportunity to win is enhanced with no incumbent advantage. Incumbents are difficult to defeat, since they enjoy high name identification, a history of service to their constituents, and a fund-raising advantage. Candidates in open-seat House races usually spend more than incumbents.

In 1996 there were 53 open-seat House districts. The Republicans won 29, ten of which had been held by Democrats. Those Republican gains in open-seat contests were located mostly in the South. The Democrats won 24 open-seat races. Only four of those had been held by Republicans. The Republican gains that resulted from winning open seats contributed to their retention of their majority in the House of Representatives in 1996. The Republicans also made gains in the 1996 U.S. Senate elections where there were a record 13 open seats.

State legislative campaign committees also focus their attention and resources on open seats. There will be an increasing number of open seats in state legislative elections as term limit amendments to state constitutions go into effect. *See*: MARGINAL SEAT; TARGETING.

References: Paul S. Herrnson, *Congressional Elections: Campaigning at Home and in Washington*, 2nd ed. (Washington, D.C.: Congressional Quarterly Press, 1998); Daniel M. Shea, *Transforming Democracy: Legislative Campaign Committees and Political Parties* (Albany: State University of New York Press, 1995).

OPPOSITION RESEARCH is a common practice of the modern campaign. Opposition research might focus on key votes of legislators which are unpopular, or "flip flops." Discovery of absenteeism, or a bad rating by an interest group, will also be used for negative messages about the opponent. Research may also turn up a "gaffe" by the opponent, who misspoke. Contradictions on positions can be highlighted. Exaggerated claims of military service or public service might be discovered with research. A review of the opponents' campaign contributions may turn up questionable associations or actual campaign violations. The campaign can use this information for its media ads or it might give the information to the press. *See*: CAMPAIGN.

Reference: Daniel M. Shea, *Campaign Craft: The Strategies, Tactics, and Art of Political Campaign Management* (Westport, Conn.: Praeger, 1996).

OREGON **v.** *MITCHELL*, 400 U.S. 112 (1970). In 1970 the Congress passed several amendments to the Voting Rights Act of 1965. Included in these amendments were provisions allowing 18-year-olds to vote (this case was decided before the Twenty-Sixth Amendment was proposed and ratified), and banning literacy tests in all states for a period of five years. The major question in this case was whether the Congress had the constitutional authority to interfere with state elections in this manner. A sharply divided Court declared that the federal government has "the final control of the elections of its own officers," and upheld all of the controversial provisions. Because literacy tests were often used to discriminate against non-whites, the Court found that Congress had the authority under Section Five of the Fourteenth Amendment to pursue an absolute ban on the practice. The states, however, retained the power to establish whatever minimum age requirements they saw fit in state and local contests. *See*: LITERACY TESTS; TWENTY-SIXTH AMENDMENT; VOTING RIGHTS ACT.

P

PAID MEDIA are the central part of the modern campaign. The lion's share of the modern campaign is spent on purchased media. An effective campaign develops a message based on polling. The media strategist designs an image that will communicate that message. If television is used, the message is best delivered visually. Paid media can also employ newspaper ads, radio ads, and direct mail. Polls are used not only to design the message, but test the delivery of the message. *See*: EARNED MEDIA; TRACKING POLLS.

Reference: Daniel M. Shea, *Campaign Craft: The Strategies, Tactics, and Art of Political Campaign Management* (Westport, Conn.: Praeger, 1996).

PARKER, ALTON B. (1852–1926). Lawyer and jurist, presidential nominee of the Democratic Party in 1904, Parker was born on a farm near Cortland, New York on May 14, 1852. First employed at age sixteen as a school teacher, Parker secured a clerkship with a Kingston law firm in preparation for a year of formal study at the Albany School of Law in 1872. Admitted to the bar the following year, Parker returned to Kingston to establish his practice. Taking an interest in county Democratic politics, Parker was elected surrogate in 1877. His organizational skills soon came to the attention of prominent state Democrats, including three men who had held, or were to hold, the New York governorship: Samuel J. Tilden, Democratic presidential nominee in 1876; Grover Cleveland, first Democrat since the Civil War to be elected president of the United States; and David B. Hill, elected to the governor's office in 1885, and for whom Parker served as campaign manager. With Hill's success, and when in that same year a vacancy on the New York Supreme Court occurred, Parker was rewarded with the governor's appointment. For nearly two decades Parker's life was to be spent in state judicial service, culminating in 1897 in his election as chief judge of the state's highest tribunal, the New York Court of Appeals. It was from this position that Parker resigned in August of 1904 to accept his party's presidential nomination. Following the two unsuccessful presidential campaigns of populist, "Free Silver" candidate William Jennings Bryan of Nebraska, many conservative and moderate leaders of the Democratic Party sought a nominee "safe," "sane," and "solid." They found that candidate in Judge Parker; capturing control of the 1904 St. Louis convention, an anti-Bryan coalition made the New Yorker the first ballot nominee of the Democratic Party. As his running mate, delegates chose "the grand old man" of West Virginia politics, 81-year-old Henry Gassaway Davis. Upon receiving word of his nomination, Parker issued a brief policy statement in which he pledged support of the established gold standard. He had not done so prior to the convention, believing it inappropriate for a judge to address such political issues from a position on the bench. Party leaders who had hoped to finesse the currency issue were stunned by Parker's telegram but, for reasons of political expediency, declined to ask the assembled delegates to reopen the nomination process. From his New York home Parker conducted a McKinleyesque, "front porch" campaign, dignified and unexciting. It was in its appeal no match for that of the flamboyant, unpredictable "cowboy" in the White House, Republican Theodore Roosevelt. To appeal to progressives, attention was called to Judge Parker's pro-labor court decisions: protection for a union's right to strike; the constitutional validity of state child labor laws and of laws limiting hours of work in environments with potential health hazards. Nothing resonated, however, in a campaign dominated by "TR." The election result produced a Republican landslide of historic proportions: Roosevelt and his running mate, Senator Charles W. Fairbanks of Indiana, secured a popular vote plurality of more than 2.5 million votes. Carrying only the Democratic "solid South," Parker and Davis were limited to 13 states with 140 Electoral College ballots; the Republican ticket claimed 336 ballots from 32 states. Journalistic opinion consoled Parker with the postmortem that no Democratic candidate in 1904 could have defeated Roosevelt. Returning to the law, Parker built over the next 20 years an exceptionally lucrative practice, establishing himself as one of the pre-eminent figures in his profession. Continuing his support of the labor cause, he represented the American Federation of Labor and its president, Samuel Gompers, in the famous Danbury Hatters' Case of 1908. Professional recognition led Parker to serve terms both as president of the New York State Bar Association and the American Bar Association. The noted attorney died in New York City on May 10, 1926. *See*: ELECTIONS: 1904.

Reference: Fred C. Shoemaker, "Alton B. Parker: The Images of a Gilded Age Statesman in an Era of Progressive Politics," unpublished M.A. Thesis, 1983, Ohio State University, Columbus, Ohio.

PARTISANSHIP is loyalty and support for one party. It is the feeling of affection or sympathy for, and loyalty to, one political party. This attachment is usually learned in childhood, and often lasts for a lifetime. Since the 1960s, partisanship in the United States has declined, as the number of independents has increased, particularly among younger voters. In 1992 the percentage of independents was at 38%, which was larger than the percentage of identified Democrats or Republicans. *See*: INDEPENDENT; NON-PARTISAN ELECTION; PARTY IDENTIFICATION; REALIGNMENT.

References: William H. Flanagan and Nancy H. Zingale, *Political Behavior of the American Electorate*, 8th ed. (Washington, D.C.: Congressional Quarterly Press, 1994); Warren E. Miller, "Party Identification and Political Belief Systems: Changes in Partisanship in the United States, 1980–1984," *Electoral Studies*, Vol. 5 (August 1986).

PARTY IDENTIFICATION is the sense of attachment a person feels to a political party. In the United States it is an attitude or sentiment. It is not a formal dues-paying relationship with a political organization. People acquire party identification as children, from their parents. The stronger the political attachment of the parent to a party, the stronger the attachment of the children to that party. It is often the first political attitude children acquire. The standard measure of partisan identification in the United States is the National Elections Studies information, collected by the Center for Political Studies at the University of Michigan. They ask the following questions in their survey: Generally speaking, do you consider yourself as a Democrat, a Republican, an Independent, or what? If they answer Republican or Democrat, the interviewer asks a strong Democrat [Republican] or not very strong Democrat [Republican]? If the answer is Independent the interviewer asks: Do you think of yourself as closer to the Republican Party or Democratic Party? These questions lead to a classification of respondents into eight categories: Strong Democrat, Weak Democrat, Independent Democrat [those who said they were Independent but were closer to the Democrats], Independent, Independent Republican [those who said they were Independent, but were closer to the Republicans], Weak Republicans, Strong Republicans and Other [belonged to another party or were apolitical]

Below is a table that displays some of the results of that study over a 30-year period: *See*: PARTISANSHIP; POLITICAL PARTY.

	DEMOCRAT		INDEPENDENT			REPUBLICAN	
			Ind.		Ind.		
Year	Strong	Weak	Dem.	Ind.	Rep.	Weak	Strong
1964	27	25	9	8	6	14	11
1966	18	28	9	12	7	15	10
1968	20	25	10	11	9	15	10

1970	20	24	10	13	8	15	9
1972	15	26	11	13	10	13	10
1974	17	21	13	15	9	14	8
1976	15	25	12	15	10	14	9
1978	15	24	14	14	10	13	8
1980	18	23	11	13	10	14	9
1982	20	24	11	11	8	14	10
1984	17	20	11	11	12	15	12
1986	18	22	10	12	11	15	10
1988	17	18	12	11	13	14	14
1990	20	19	12	11	12	15	10
1992	17	18	14	12	13	15	11
1994	15	19	13	10	12	15	16

References: American National Election Study, Center for Political Studies, University of Michigan at Ann Arbor; Bruce E. Keith, David B. Magleby, Candice J. Nelson, Elizabeth Orr, Mark C. Westlye, and Raymond E. Wolfinger, *The Myth of the Independent Voter* (Berkeley, Calif.: University of California Press, 1992).

PARTY IN GOVERNMENT refers to members of the same party who hold government offices. Partisan officeholders dominate their political party, structure partisan conflict, and create the public image of their party. American national and state legislatures are organized by party. As an example, the leadership in Congress is selected by the majority party. The majority party also determines the organizational procedure and the agenda of the legislature.

The term "party in government" is one of the three elements of party identified by V. O. Key, a political scientist who significantly influenced the way parties are studied in the United States. The other two elements of party, according to Key, include the party in the electorate and the party organization.

The term includes the party of the president and his/her cabinet. It also refers to the party in Congress, which is the means by which legislatures organize themselves through the selection of their leaders, committee members, and the way the legislature makes many policy decisions. In addition, the term suggests the relationships between the branches of the national government, and the national government's relationship with state governments, in those cases where party plays a role.

References: Paul Allen Beck, *Party Politics in America*, 8th ed. (New York: Longman, 1997); James W. Davis, *The President as Party Leader* (New York: Greenwood Press, 1992); V. O. Key, *Politics, Parties, and Pressure Groups*, 5th ed. (New York: Crowell, 1964); David R. Mayhew, *Divided We Govern: Party Control, Lawmaking, and Investigations, 1946–1990* (New Haven, Conn.: Yale University Press, 1991).

PARTY LINE is the position or doctrine of a party organization. It could be the official positions adopted by a party committee, to which the members are expected to adhere. It might be the party's answer to a controversial question:

for example, the party line answer to questions about Watergate, for Republican leaders, was that Nixon did nothing wrong. The party line answer to questions about the questionable fund-raising practices of the National Democratic Committee is that they have done nothing wrong. The term "party line" might also refer to a line on the ballot which displays the party nominees.

PARTY ORGANIZATION refers to the formal, often legal, structures of the American parties which include the national, state, and local party committees, the party officers of those committees, and paid staff and volunteers. Usually, the state and local party organizations are defined by state statutes. Some political scientists maintain that the national and state party organizations have become more important in recent decades, because they have access to more resources. They have become providers of services, such as polling, media development, and opposition research, and are very effective at fund-raising. They have become more valuable to candidates. For example, the national party committees have become the pass-through for enormous amounts of "soft money" used in campaigns. Party organization was identified by V. O. Key as one of the three elements of a political party. *See*: PARTY IN GOVERNMENT; SOFT MONEY.

Reference: Cornelius P. Cotter, James L. Gibson, John F. Bibby, and Robert J. Huckshorn, *Party Organizations in American Politics* (New York: Praeger, 1984).

PARTY UNITY SCORE refers to the degree to which members of the same party vote the same way in the legislature. Party unity scores have increased in recent years. In fact, in the first session of the 104th Congress, party unity scores reached an all-time high for the postwar years. According to *Congressional Quarterly*, in the House, a majority of Republicans voted against a majority of Democrats, a record 72.3% of the time; in the Senate, the figure was only slightly lower, at 68.8% for that same period. This is evidence of the increasing partisanship in the national legislature. Many political scientists see this as a result of the increasing ideological division of the two parties. It is also a reflection of the decline in the number of conservative Democrats in the South. It was Southern Democrats who frequently voted with the Republicans, and contributed to lower party unity scores in the legislature. The number of Southern Democrats has been declining in Congress as the Republicans have made gains in the South. The conservative Democrats have recently dropped their name "Boll Weevil," and have taken on the tag "Blue Dog Democrat." There is also a decline in the number of moderate and liberal Republicans in Congress, who in the past, frequently voted with the Democrats. *Congressional Quarterly Weekly Report* regularly gives the party unity score of individual members of Congress. *See*: BLUE DOG COALITION.

Reference: "As Hostilities Rage on the Hill Partisan-Vote Rate Soars," *Congressional Quarterly: Guide to Current American Government Fall, 1996* (Washington, D.C.: Congressional Quarterly Press, 1996).

PATRONAGE refers to the appointment of supporters to government jobs as a reward for political support. At one time, government jobs were the major material inducement for party activists. In return for a political appointment, the party activist would donate time, energy, and part of his/her salary to the party organization. Patronage has a rich and colorful history in American political parties. Andrew Jackson, who created the first mass-based party, used patronage to build up his party's membership and organization.

The urban political party organizations in eastern and midwestern cities (often referred to as machines), like Mayor Richard J. Daley's Cook County Democratic Party organization, were built on patronage. It was estimated that Daley controlled 35,000 patronage jobs. Many midwestern state party organizations were also patronage-based organizations. The state highway departments have been a favorite place to employ party workers. Civil service laws, public sector unions, and federal court cases have made patronage the exception in American politics. The most significant recent federal case on patronage was *Rutan* v. *Republican Party of Illinois* (1990), in which the Supreme Court ruled that politically based hiring, firing, and promotion was unconstitutional. *See*: ASSESSMENT; MACHINE POLITICS; *RUTAN* v. *REPUBLICAN PARTY OF ILLINOIS* (1990).

References: Paul Allen Beck, *Party Politics in America*, 8th ed. (New York: Longman, 1997); Anne Freedman, *Patronage: An American Tradition* (Chicago: Nelson-Hall, 1994).

PAY YOUR DUES. In older party organizations, a prospective candidate was to spend an unspecified period of time working for the party and serving in lower elected positions, before being elevated to a higher office. Office seekers had to pay their dues before they could advance up the political ladder. Some Republicans believed that Bob Dole deserved the Republican Party's presidential nomination because he had paid his dues, as a longtime Republican Party stalwart in the Senate. This idea was also quite common in old urban machines— one worked one's way up the ladder, and politics was considered a career. This notion has gone out of favor with the modern-day, media-defined, candidate-centered politics. Office seekers who are well financed can go right to the top. In states that have imposed term limits, it has become difficult for party organizations to persuade office seekers to wait their turn before seeking a higher office. Also, in the contemporary period, Americans look with disfavor on career politicians.

PENDLETON ACT OF 1883 was the Act to Regulate and Improve the Civil Service of the United States. It was passed by Congress in 1883 to improve the civil service and introduce merit into federal employment. Federal government hiring practices were to be based on open, competitive examinations, administered by the Civil Service Commission, which was also created by this law. The passage of this Act was spurred by the assassination of President James Garfield by a disappointed job seeker. This was the beginning of the end of patronage in the federal government and a weakening of political parties. Progressive reformers, who advocated merit employment and civil service, also tried to break the control of political machines in urban areas, whose base of strength was patronage. *See*: PATRONAGE.

References: Patricia Wallace Ingraham, *The Foundation of Merit: Public Service in American Democracy* (Baltimore: Johns Hopkins University Press, 1995); David H. Rosenbloom, ed., *Centenary Issues of the Pendleton Act of 1883: The Problematic Legacy of Civil Service Reform* (New York: Dekker, 1982).

PEOPLE'S PARTY (POPULIST PARTY). This party followed many of the ideas of the Greenback Party. It was founded in 1891 in Cincinnati, Ohio. The free coinage of silver was the major issue of this influential third party. In 1892 the People's Party nominated the 1880 Greenback presidential candidate, James Weaver. The platform they adopted included nationalization of railroads, civil service reform, a shorter work week, a graduated income tax, a secret ballot, the initiative, the referendum, the direct election of U.S. Senators, and of course the free coinage of silver.

In 1892, James Weaver won more than one million votes. He carried 5 states, garnering 22 Electoral College votes. Weaver ran first in Colorado, Idaho, Kansas, Nevada, and North Dakota. The People's Party showed considerable strength in the South where it outpolled the Republicans in four states. Twenty-two Populists were elected to the House, and two members were sent to the U.S. Senate.

In 1896, William Jennings Bryan and the Populist free silverites captured the Democratic party nomination. The People's Party also nominated Bryan as their standard bearer that year. By nominating Bryan, the Democrats co-opted many of the planks of the People's Party. The People's Party continued to nominate a presidential candidate until the 1908 election, but its influence withered away. *See*: ELECTIONS: 1896; GREENBACK PARTY.

Reference: Lawrence Goodwyn, *Democratic Promise: The Populist Movement in America* (New York: Oxford University Press, 1976).

PEROT, ROSS (1930–   ) was born in Texarkana, Texas in 1930. He graduated from the U.S. Naval Academy in 1953. He was honorably discharged from the navy as a lieutenant in 1957, and went to work for IBM as a salesman. He left IBM in 1962, to found Electronic Data Systems (EDS). He became a billionaire with his data processing company, which served Blue Cross/Blue Shield Medicaid billing. Perot sold EDS to General Motors in 1984 for $2.5 billion.

Beyond his vast fortune, Perot gained recognition for his interest in public issues. During the Vietnam War, Perot took up the cause of the POWs and the MIAs. In 1979 he orchestrated a daring rescue of two of his employees held captive in Iran. His success was in sharp contrast to the Carter administration's inability to rescue 52 American hostages held at the American Embassy in Tehran. At the request of the Texas governor, Perot headed up the state's war on drugs.

Perot was frequently urged to run for president, and on February 20, 1992, on *Larry King Live*, Perot announced that he would run as an independent candidate for president, if the citizens got his name on the ballot in the 50 states. His announcement drew a very favorable response, and by September 17 Perot was on the ballot in all 50 states. Perot's candidacy was well received by an electorate that was unhappy with the choice between Bill Clinton and George Bush. Perot dropped out of the race on July 18 and reentered it on October 1. He claimed he dropped out because Republican ''dirty tricksters'' were threatening to disrupt his daughter's wedding. This made Perot appear unstable. He participated in the presidential debates in 1992. Perot drew 19% of the vote, the best showing of an independent presidential candidate since Teddy Roosevelt's in 1912. During the campaign, Perot focused attention on the growing federal deficit. In many respects, he set the political agenda for the next four years, even though he did not win the election.

In 1996, Perot reemerged as a presidential candidate. This time he started by announcing the formation of the Reform Party, a new party, on *Larry King Live* on September 25, 1995. The initial response to a third party was very positive. The hope, at the time, was that General Colin Powell would take up the challenge. In November 1995, Powell announced that he would not run as a third-party candidate; the attention was then focused on the now less popular Ross Perot as the Reform Party nominee. The Reform Party held a two-part national convention in August 1996. Perot was challenged for the Reform Party nomination by Richard Lamm, the former governor of Colorado. Some believe that Lamm was not given a fair chance since he was not given the names of the members of the party. Perot was nominated. In the 1996 election, Perot was not allowed to participate in the presidential debates because he did not have a realistic chance of being elected. Perot tried to make campaign finance reform and opposition to free trade—specifically NAFTA—the central issues, but he, and those issues, lacked the appeal that the balanced budget issue did in 1992. Perot collected more than eight million votes, which was 8.4% of the votes cast. *See*: ELECTIONS: 1992, 1996; REFORM PARTY.

Reference: Gordon S. Black, *The Politics of American Discontent: How a New Party Can Make Democracy Work Again* (New York: Wiley, 1994).

PETITION is a state-issued form required for the following: placing a candidate on the ballot, initiating a referendum, placing a new party on the ballot, or recalling an elected official. There are stipulated deadlines for filing such petitions and a specified number of signatures are required. For candidates seeking a party nomination, the signatures in many states must be those of party members. In the case of initiatives and ballot access for new political parties, there is a burdensome number of signatures required. *See:* BALLOT ACCESS; INITIATIVE; RECALL; REFERENDUM.

Reference: Max Neiman and M. Gottdiener, "The Relevance of the Qualifying Stage of the Initiative Politics: The Case of Petition Signing," *Social Science Quarterly*, Vol. 63 (September 1982).

PIERCE, FRANKLIN (1804–1869), described by a historian as one of the "most gracefully attractive" yet "weakest" men to have come to the presidency, Pierce was born in Hillsboro, New Hampshire on November 23, 1804. Graduated at age 20 from Bowdoin College in Maine, Pierce studied the law, being admitted to the state bar in 1827. Two years later, as his father, General Benjamin Pierce, reclaimed the governorship, voters sent the son to the state legislature. In 1833 those same voters elected Pierce to the U.S. House of Representatives, a body which he left in 1837, the New Hampshire legislature having selected him to fill one of the state's two seats in the U.S. Senate. In both chambers Pierce proved himself to be a staunch Jacksonian Democrat, particularly supportive of the president as he waged war on internal improvement legislation and on the attempt to recharter the Bank of the United States. Pierce did, however, early in his congressional career, develop congenial ties, personal and political, with a number of Southern legislators· even, while rejecting the man, accepting, short of nullification, much of the theoretic argument of John C. Calhoun of South Carolina as to states' rights and the claim of constitutional protection afforded to slavery, the South's "peculiar institution." It was this sympathy with the Southern argument, maintained throughout his life, that led critics to regard Pierce as a "doughface," a Northern man with Southern principles. What is perhaps more accurate is that Pierce had come to develop a deeply rooted commitment to "original" constitutional principles which he interpreted as protecting "sacred from all touch of usurpation . . . the reserved rights and powers of the several States and of the people." Under extreme pressure from his wife, Jane Means Appleton, to remove himself from (as she saw it) Washington's debilitating social and political temptations, Pierce resigned his Senate seat in 1842, returning to Concord and the smaller stage of New Hampshire law and politics. Other than for his military service (1847–1848), at the time of the Mexican War and from which he gained the rank of brigadier general, Pierce was to remain in the Granite State, with but few excursions, until called to his presidential inauguration on March 4, 1853. That Franklin Pierce should have become the presidential nominee of the Democratic Party in 1852 is nothing short of astonishing. With neither high office nor national reputation, undistinguished as to battlefield heroics, with but a modest law practice and a role in state politics in which he repeatedly refused his party's offer of nomination to office, Pierce was nonetheless to emerge on the national scene in 1852 as his party's presidential candidate. With the convention deadlocked among four major rivals, Pierce's obscurity became a virtue. Prompted by party leaders the restless delegates made Pierce their nominee on the convention's forty-ninth ballot, adding to the national ticket as vice-presidential candidate Senator William R. King of Alabama. The Democratic platform, as did the Whig, endorsed the Compromise of 1850, but unlike the loquacious Winfield Scott, Pierce took the vow of silence, maintaining it throughout the campaign and remaining in New Hampshire, allowing the greater strength of the Democratic organization to prevail. The result was a landslide victory for the Democrats: Pierce and King rolled up better than a 200,000 popular vote plurality over the Whig ticket of Scott and William A. Graham of North Carolina, carrying 27 states with 254 Electoral College ballots to but 4 states and 42 votes in the Electoral College for the Whigs. Even though the Free Democrat (Free-Soil) ticket of Senator John P. Hale of New Hampshire and George W. Julian of Indiana gathered 150,000 popular votes, it carried neither a state nor an Electoral College ballot, failing in any appreciable way to diminish the extent of the Democratic Party victory. The satisfaction and confidence that the election results should have given to Pierce were, however, undermined by personal tragedy. Early in January 1853, the president-elect, his wife, and their sole surviving son "Bennie," age eleven, departed Andover, Massachusetts by train to return to Concord. A mile from Andover station their car derailed and their son, the sole victim, was killed in the wreckage. Pierce and his wife, physically unscathed, were to bear deep emotional scars for the rest of their lives. It was thus a shattered and mourning president that was inaugurated on March 4, 1853. The Pierce presidency, following his approval of the Kansas-Nebraska Act on May 30, 1854, was consumed by the increasingly polarized and violent struggle over the extension of slavery. The Kansas-Nebraska Act in effect destroyed the last remnants of the Missouri Compromise of 1820 whereby slavery had been prohibited north of 36° 30'. Kansas Territory would now be opened to the possibility of slavery, the question to be determined on the basis of "popular sovereignty," that is, the decision to rest with those settled in the territory. Slavery's advocates and rival abolitionists in, or moving into, the territory now did bloody battle for Kansas. Atrocities mounted, committed by both friends and foes of slavery, while the president and his administration stood by, unable to resolve the issue, unable or unwilling to authorize adequate federal force to restore order and prevent further factional warfare. As Kansas bled so did the political career of Franklin Pierce; unable to secure renomination by his party in June of 1856, the President played out his days in the White House hoping for the restoration of order in Kansas, hoping, should it not occur, that the violence would remain regionally isolated, hopes which the Pierce administration did little to encourage by way of policy. On retiring from the presidency, Pierce and his wife made a prolonged European tour (1857–1859). Upon his return, the former president, making but few public appearances, continued to urge a peaceful solution to the sectional divisions now moving the nation rapidly toward Civil War. When war came, Pierce became a severe critic of Lincoln administration policies, arguing, as in his July 4 speech in 1863, for a negotiated settlement which through "peaceful agencies" would end the "fearful, fruitless, fatal civil war." Among the vast majority of his Concord townsmen, and across the state and through the North, Pierce's reputation suffered yet further erosion. All but an outcast, Pierce died in Concord, New Hampshire on October 8, 1869. *See*: ELECTIONS: 1852.

References: Larry Gara, *The Presidency of Franklin Pierce* (Lawrence: University Press of Kansas, 1991); Roy F. Nichols, *Franklin Pierce, Young Hickory of the Granite Hills*, rev. ed. (Philadelphia: University of Pennsylvania Press, 1958).

PINCKNEY, CHARLES COTESWORTH (1746–1825) was born on February 25, 1746, into a colonial family of established position and wealth. Owners of plantations and of slaves, the family was part of the South Carolina coastal aristocracy. Educated in England at Christ Church College, Oxford, and in the law at Middle Temple of the Inns of Court, Pinckney was admitted to the English bar in 1769. Returning shortly thereafter to Charleston, Pinckney chose to practice both law and politics, early on joining the patriot cause. From 1775 to 1783 he served as an officer in the Continental Army, and in 1777 was part of Washington's general staff. Taken as a prisoner of war in 1780 at the time of the surrender of Charleston, Pinckney was to leave military service in 1783 with the rank of brigadier general. Pinckney's time over the next decade was spent in an effort to reestablish his law practice and rebuild the family fortune, which was much eroded by the war years and the British occupation. He did, however, leave Charleston in 1787 to serve as one of South Carolina's representatives to the Constitutional Convention at Philadelphia. While firmly convinced of the need to strengthen national government authority, Pinckney was at first reluctant to go beyond consideration of amendments to the Articles of Confederation. Subsequently joining the majority of delegates proposing to the states a wholly new constitution, Pinckney argued against what he considered excessive democratic arrangements, such as popular election of the U.S. House of Representatives, and for stronger language in support of slavery. Notwithstanding these reservations, Pinckney actively supported ratification of the proposed constitution and, once ratified, of Washington's election to the presidency. While a staunch supporter of the new president, Pinckney nonetheless remained so committed to his endeavors in South Carolina as to refuse a number of offers made by the president that he join the cabinet, also declining in 1791, nomination to the U.S. Supreme Court. In 1796, however, Pinckney felt himself able to accept Washington's proffered assignment of a diplomatic mission to France. This mission, continued by President Adams, ended in the infamous "XYZ Affair." Responding to the attempt by French minister Talleyrand's representatives to extract a bribe from the American government, Pinckney was to utter the words "no! not a sixpence," a line that would evolve into the more quotable and now legendary, "millions for defense, but not a cent for tribute." Upon returning to the United States, Pinckney was to stand on three successive occasions as Federalist nominee for national office; as the vice-presidential candidate in 1800 and subsequently as the party's presidential nominee in 1804 and 1808. Unsuccessful in each instance, Pinckney, after the election of 1800, was under no illusions as to Federalist Party revival. Philosophically opposed to the leveling tendencies of Jeffersonian republicanism, Pinckney stood for office simply as a performance of duty, gaining the Electoral College ballots of but two states in 1804 and of five states in 1808. More so than in partisan involvement, Pinckney's life was one devoted to civic, charitable, and religious activities. He died in Charleston on August 16, 1825. *See*: ELECTIONS: 1804, 1808.

Reference: Marvin R. Zahniser, *Charles Cotesworth Pinckney, Founding Father* (Chapel Hill: University of North Carolina Press for the Institute of Early American History and Culture, 1967).

PLATFORM, PARTY. A party platform is a statement of the principles of a political party adopted at a convention. The first platform was adopted by the Democrats in 1840.

At the quadrennial national party conventions, adoption of the platform has been the source of most of the recent controversies within parties. For example, Republican Party presidential nominee Bob Dole was unable to get his proposed tolerance language in the abortion plank in the 1996 party platform. The conservative delegates on the platform committee would not accept the language Dole recommended. Dole had to settle for tolerance language as part of the appendix of the platform. This was done to appease the outnumbered moderate Republicans, who threatened a disruptive floor fight, which the Dole forces wanted to avoid. Dole later claimed that he had not read the platform, suggesting he was not bound by the language. Nevertheless, Gerald Pomper, political scientist, makes a good case that platforms are a guide to many of the policies a party will pursue, if it gains office. Many state political parties also adopt platforms. For example, many of the state Republican Party committees adopted Contract with America platforms in 1994, at the urging of the Republican National Committee. Following is a table which compares the 1996 Democratic and Republican Party platforms on a number of issues.

Comparison of the 1996 National Party Platforms

Democrats	Republicans

The Economy

"The economy is stronger, the deficit is lower, and the government is smaller."

We cannot go on like this. For millions of families, the American dream is fading."

Taxes

"America cannot afford to return to the era of something-for-nothing tax cuts." Promote a $500 tax cut for children and a tax credit for college tuition.

Support a 15% reduction in the tax rate.

Abortion

"Respect the individual conscience of each American on this difficult issue."

"The unborn child has a fundamental individual right to life which cannot be infringed. We support a human life amendment to the Constitution. . . ."

Affirmative Action

"We should mend it, not end it."

We will attain our nation's goal of equal rights without quotas or other forms of preferential treatment."

Immigration

Permit the children of illegal immigrants to attend public schools and receive welfare benefits.

Prohibit the children of illegal immigrants from attending public schools and restrict benefits to illegal immigrants.

Balanced Budget

Promise to balance the budget by the year 2002.

Support a constitutional amendment requiring a balanced budget.

Gun Control

Support for a waiting period for buying handguns and a ban on the sale of certain assault weapons.

"Defend the constitutional right to keep and bear arms."

Star Wars

"The Democratic Party opposes the Republican National Missile Defense plan—spending up to $60 billion on a revival of the 'Star Wars' program. . . ."

"We therefore endorse the Defend America Act of 1996, introduced by Senator Bob Dole, which calls for a national missile defense system for all fifty states by the year 2003."

References: "Draft Democratic National Platform," *Congressional Quarterly: Guide to the 1996 Democratic National Convention*, Vol. 54 (August 17, 1996); Thomas H. Little, "An Experiment in Responsible Party Government: National Agenda Setting and the State Replicas of the Contract with America," *American Review of Politics*, Vol. 18 (Spring/Summer 1997); Gerald M. Pomper and Susan S. Lederman, *Elections in America* (New York: Longman, 1980); *The Republican Party Platform 1996*.

PLEBISCITE is a direct vote by the entire country on an issue of great importance. In the United States, it is not possible for a national vote on an issue. At the state level, there are opportunities for direct legislation by the people. Forty-nine states require a vote of the people on proposed constitutional amendments. A number of state constitutions permit the state legislature to place an issue before the people, and 23 states permit the citizens to place an issue on the ballot by petition for a vote of the people. In France, President Charles deGualle placed a number of important national constitutional amendments and legislative proposals before the people. He threatened to resign if they failed. His success at these efforts enhanced his authority to govern.

In 1994 the congressional Republicans claimed that their victory at the polls was a mandate for their proposed Contract with America. *See*: CONTRACT WITH AMERICA; INITIATIVE; MANDATE; REFERENDUM.

PLURALITY is an election system in which the candidate with the most votes (though not necessarily a majority) is nominated (if it is a primary) or elected to office (if it is a general election). It is the most widely used election system in the United States. The Electoral College uses a plurality system for the distribution of Electoral College votes in each state. Only one of the fifty states was won with a majority of the vote in the 1992 presidential election. Congressional elections, and most state and local elections, are also plurality elections. One variation of the plurality system that is used in the United States is the two-ballot plurality with a runoff provision. In that system, if a candidate does not reach a certain threshold, usually 50% (sometimes 40%, as in New York City's Democratic primary), then a runoff is held between the top two. There are plurality elections that use multi-seat/at-large districts.

In plurality systems, the voter is restricted to casting only one vote per candidate, and an opportunity to rank the choices is not offered. It is argued that the plurality election system contributes to a two-party system. Voters, who might prefer a minor party candidate, will often vote for the least objectionable, major party candidate, so that they do not waste their vote. *See*: PRIMARY; PROPORTIONAL REPRESENTATION; RUNOFF; SINGLE-MEMBER DISTRICT.

Reference: Peter C. Fishburn, "Social Choice and Plurality Like Electoral Systems," in *Electoral Laws and Their Political Consequences*, Bernard Grofman and Arend Lijphart, eds. (New York: Agathon Press, 1986).

POLITICAL ACTION COMMITTEE (PAC) is an organization designed to raise funds and then donate those funds to candidates seeking office. PACs are a major source of campaign funds for political campaigns. The first PAC in the United States was called the Political Action Committee; it was created by the Congress of Industrial Organizations (CIO) as a response to Congress in the Taft-Hartley Act, making it illegal for labor unions to use union treasury funds for political donations. Its purpose was to raise money through voluntary donations, and pursue its political interests by supporting candidates.

A large number of PACs were created in the 1970s, in response to the post-Watergate Federal Election Campaign Act, which limited individual contributions to $1,000 and allowed Political Action Committee donations of $5,000. PACs became the means through which interest groups could directly support candidates they favored. PACs also flourished in this period because of the growth of special interest groups in Washington.

There are two types of PACs. The first is the connected PAC, which is responsible only to its parent organization and may not solicit from the general public. Examples of this type are corporations, trade groups, and unions. The second type of PAC is the non-connected PAC, which raises money from the general public. There are also leadership PACs, which are created by legislative leaders and national candidates. The number of federally registered PACS in July 1997 was 3,875. Corporate PACs remain the largest category with 1,602 committees, followed by non-connected (956), trade/membership/health PACs (826), labor (332), corporations without stock (118), and cooperatives (41).

PACs play various roles. PACs can be accomodationists, that is, seek access to members of Congress by donations; PACs can be partisan, that is, favor candidates of one party; or a PAC can be adversarial, that is, spend money to defeat members opposed to the positions of the PAC.

In the 1995–1996 election cycle, PACs contributed $217.8 million to federal candidates. Incumbents received $146.4 million, and challengers received $31.6 million. Republicans received more than Democrats since they are in the majority. In addition to the contributions to candidates, PACs spent $106 million in independent expenditures for and against candidates. *See*: FEDERAL ELECTION CAMPAIGN ACT OF 1971 AND AMENDMENTS; FEDERAL ELECTION COMMISSION; LEADERSHIP PAC.

References: Paul S. Herrnson, Ronald G. Shaiko, and Clyde Wilcox, eds., *The Interest Group Connection: Electioneering, Lobbying, and Policymaking in Washington* (Chatham, N.J.: Chatham House, 1998); Larry Sabato, *PAC Power: Inside the World of Political Action Committees* (Washington, D.C.: Brookings Institution, 1985); Frank J. Sorauf, "Political Action Committees," in *Campaign Finance Reform*, Anthony Corrado, Thomas E. Mann, Daniel R. Ortiz, Trevor Potter, and Frank J. Sorauf, eds. (Washington, D.C.: Brookings Institution, 1997).

POLITICAL AMATEURS are political activists who support a candidate or a party because they believe in a cause, and their political activity is often short-lived. Political amateurs are often unwilling to compromise. When state and local party organizations were more formidable, there was tension between the professionals, who were party regulars, and the amateurs, who were motivated by ideals. They had little respect for the party organization members. James Q. Wilson wrote that: "An amateur is one who finds politics intrinsically interesting because it expresses a conception of the public interest." In contrast, a professional is one who is seeking some material benefit, such as a job, or whose major concern is winning the election. *See*: PATRONAGE; PROGRESSIVE MOVEMENT.

Reference: James Q. Wilson, *The Amateur Democrat: Club Politics in Three Cities* (Chicago: University of Chicago Press, 1962).

POLITICAL BASE is the voters who will predictably support a particular candidate. Every precinct, ward, county, and state has a reliable and predictable base vote for a particular party. The candidate's campaign does not focus a great deal of attention on persuading base voters. Mobilization of the base to vote is a key element of a successful political campaign. The political party is often responsible for mobilizing the base vote with GOTV efforts. *See*: GOTV.

Reference: Joel Bradshaw, "Who Will Vote for You and Why: Designing Strategy and Theme," in *Campaigns and Elections American Style*, James A. Thurber and Candice J. Nelson, eds. (Boulder, Colo.: Westview Press, 1995).

POLITICAL CONSULTANTS are advertising specialists who are hired to create an image of a candidate which is packaged and sold to the voters. When television advertising became the central element of the political campaign, hired political consultants replaced party leaders as central figures in modern political campaigns. In addition to television commercials, political consultants provide an array of other modern services including polling, direct mail, fund-raising techniques, opposition research, and overall campaign strategy. Political consultants work on campaigns at the local, state, and national levels. They are often hired by legislative campaign committees. Consultants usually have ties to, and work for, only one of the major political parties.

Political consultants have a professional organization, the American Association of Political Consultants (AAPC), and in 1996 the organization adopted a resolution condemning push polls. Despite their efforts to develop an ethos of professionalism, the image of consultants suffers from the behavior of some of their members. Ed Rollins, a noted Republican consultant who ran Ronald Reagan's 1984 campaign, embarrassed the gubernatorial campaign of Christy Todd Whitman, in New Jersey in 1994, by telling the press he gave money to black church leaders to dampen black turnout. His claim was never proven. In 1996, Dick Morris, who was credited with bringing President Clinton's political fortunes back after the Democrats' defeat in 1994, and who was the lead political consultant for Clinton's 1996 reelection campaign, had to resign in disgrace during the 1996 Democratic National Convention when it was revealed in a weekly tabloid that he was involved with a prostitute, with whom he was sharing campaign gossip and information. Morris was unique, because in addition to

Clinton, he had worked for a number of Republicans, including Louisiana U.S. Senator Trent Lott. There have been notable consultants who have garnered respect, including Roger Ailes, who headed CNBC, ran the Bush reelection in 1988, and said he left political consulting when the candidates began asking him what they should stand for. Another notable consultant was James Carville, who ran the Clinton campaign in 1992 and refused opportunities to become a lobbyist. One difference between the political handlers of the past and the modern political consultants in recent years is that the old handlers sought anonymity. *See*: NEGATIVE ADVERTISING; PUSH POLL.

Reference: Larry J. Sabato, *The Rise of Political Consultants: New Ways of Winning Elections* (New York: Basic Books, 1981).

POLITICAL CULTURE is the set of attitudes, beliefs, and expectations of the people in a nation or a state, about what government should do, and who should participate. It defines the accepted rules of politics. The political culture defines the extent and scope of government.

Daniel Elazar divides American political culture into three subcultures: the individualistic, the moralistic, and the traditional. The individualist culture maintains that politics is a means to improve oneself, economically and socially. The moralistic political culture sees politics as an activity that centers on some notion of the public good and advancement of the public interest. The traditionalistic political culture accepts a social hierarchy, and expects those at the top to have a dominant role in government.

The type of subculture that is dominant in a state affects the character of the politics in the state. A number of midwestern states, such as Ohio and Indiana, characterized as individualistic, have a history of strong party organizations based on patronage. States that have a moralistic political culture, like Minnesota and Wisconsin, have state politics and parties that focus on issues, have a low tolerance for corruption, and a preference for merit in public employment. The South is the only region of the country that has had traditionalistic political culture, according to Elazar.

These regional variations in political culture, identified by Elazar, have diminished. The electronic media have homogenized cultural values, and the politics of states has become more similar and less different in recent decades. *See*: POLITICAL SOCIALIZATION.

References: Daniel J. Elazar, *American Federalism: A View from the States*, 2nd ed. (New York: Crowell, 1972); Lucian Pye, ''Political Culture,'' *International Encyclopedia of the Social Sciences*, vol. 12, David L. Sills, ed. (New York: Macmillan, 1968).

POLITICAL PARTY is an organization that seeks to elect party members to public office, to achieve its policy goals. Those characteristics are what distinguishes a political party from other types of organizations, such as interest groups. One often-cited, classic definition of party was offered by seventeenth-century British philosopher Edmund Burke, who defined a party as "a body of men united, for promulgating by their joint endeavors the national interest, upon some particular principle in which they are all agreed." That quote does not capture the frequent, diverse opinions that reside within the two American political parties. A contemporary political scientist, Leon Epstein, best captures American parties when he defines parties as loosely organized groups "seeking to elect government officeholders under a given label."

V. O. Key and Ralph Goldman, noted students of political parties, argue that one could best understand political parties by recognizing their tripartite elements: the party in the electorate, those who identify with the party; the party organization, which includes the party committees and volunteers; and the party in government, who are those party members elected to office.

Political parties are critical to the functioning of a constitutional democracy. Parties are a link between the voters and the government. Parties structure the choices for the voters. See: INTEREST GROUP.

References: Paul Allen Beck, *Party Politics in America*, 8th ed. (New York: Longman, 1997); Ralph Goldman, *The National Party Chairman and Committees: Factionalism at the Top* (Armonk, N.Y.: M. E. Sharpe, 1990).

POLITICAL QUESTIONS DOCTRINE. A doctrine used by the U.S. Supreme Court to avoid involvement in cases that are "non-justiciable," that is, cases which involve issues or subjects that, for whatever reason, do not lend themselves to resolution by a court of law. Historically, the judicial branch has used this doctrine to avoid confrontations with the legislative and executive (i.e., "political branches") of government. The doctrine has not been consistently applied and is the subject of much controversy, particularly when the Court uses the political nature of a case to evade vexing constitutional issues. For example, for many years the Supreme Court refused to hear malapportionment cases, claiming that the drawing of voting districts involved choices that were blatantly political. Therefore, the obvious solution to malapportionment, the redrawing of electoral districts, would be an activity for which the courts were ill-suited. In the case of *Baker* v. *Carr* (1962), the Supreme Court reversed itself, and announced that the political questions doctrine would no longer serve as a bar to the judicial resolution of apportionment controversies. See: BAKER v. CARR (1962); COLEGROVE v. GREEN (1946); MALAPPORTIONMENT; REAPPORTIONMENT; REDISTRICTING.

References: Louis Henkin, "Is There a 'Political Questions' Doctrine?" *Yale Law Journal*, Vol. 85 (1976); Walter F. Murphy, James E. Fleming, and Sotirios A. Barber, *American Constitutional Interpretation*, 2nd ed. (Westbury, N.Y.: Foundation Press, 1995).

POLITICAL SOCIALIZATION is the process by which people develop their political attitudes and values. The family is a major agent of socialization, as values are transmitted from one generation to the next. Other significant agents of socialization are schools, churches, peer groups, and social organizations. Through political socialization, people learn to be citizens. Political socialization impacts on the types and the degree of political participation citizens engage in. Political socialization is a lifelong process, but much of it takes place at a young age. In the United States and other stable democracies, political socialization contributes to the development of support for the political system. *See*: PARTISANSHIP; POLITICAL CULTURE.

References: Fred I. Greenstein, *Children and Politics* (New Haven, Conn.: Yale University Press, 1965); M. Kent Jennings and Richard Niemi, *The Political Character of Adolescence: The Influence of Families and Schools* (Princeton. N.J.: Princeton University Press, 1974).

POLK, JAMES K. (1795–1849). First "dark horse" candidate to win a major party's presidential nomination, eleventh president of the United States, Polk was born on November 2, 1795, in Mecklenburg County, North Carolina. Migrating west in 1806, Polk's family settled in the Duck River valley of Tennessee. Polk attended the University of North Carolina from which he graduated in 1818. Subsequently studying the law, admitted to the bar, he began his practice in Nashville in 1820. Elected to the Tennessee legislature in 1823, he was two years later sent by district voters to the U.S. House of Representatives. Polk, becoming an ardent Jackson loyalist, was to serve in that chamber until 1839, rising in influence and power first as chairman of the Ways and Means Committee and later, in 1835, as Speaker. Courted by his party, Polk resigned his seat in 1839 to accept nomination by Tennessee Democrats as their gubernatorial candidate. Elected to the governorship that year, Polk was unable to hold that office against the Whig challenge in 1841, or to recapture the office in 1843. Given these election defeats, Polk was not among those given preconvention consideration for the Democratic presidential nomination of 1844. Early balloting at the Baltimore convention in May of 1844 resulted in a deadlock: Van Buren, the former president, seeking renomination as the frontrunner could not, however, reach the two-thirds delegate vote required; no more successful was his major rival, Lewis Cass of Michigan. To break the stalemate, party leaders advanced the name of the relatively obscure Polk; solid and uncontroversial, he became, on the convention's ninth ballot, the party's presidential nominee. After Van Buren supporter Senator Silas Wright of New York declined the vice-presidential nomination, delegates selected another little-known candidate to complete the national ticket, George M. Dallas of Pennsylvania. In an election thought to be all but won by Whigs Henry Clay and Theodore Frelinghuysen, Polk was to be the recipient of an unanticipated victory; a victory made possible by the strong endorsement given to Polk by the venerated Andrew Jackson; by Clay's self-inflicted campaign blunders, particularly his waffling on the issue of Texas annexation; and, by contrast, Polk's own forthright stance, favoring admission of Texas to the Union, and as a slave state. Others would credit the Polk victory to voters drawn from support of Clay by the Liberty Party and its presidential candidate, moderate abolitionist James G. Birney; pointing out that had Clay received but a share of Birney's popular vote in New York he would have carried that state, its Electoral College vote, and, thereby, the election. However viewed as to the cause, the election results provided a narrow victory to the Democratic Party: Polk and Dallas secured a popular vote plurality of less than 40,000 votes over Clay and Frelinghuysen, carried 15 states to 11 for the Whigs, with 170 Electoral College ballots to 105 for their opponents. While Birney gathered more than 60,000 popular votes in the Liberty Party cause, he carried no state and received no votes in the Electoral College. Polk's presidential tenure, 1845–1849, marked a period of American territorial expansion unmatched since the Jefferson administration's purchase of Louisiana Territory in 1803. To that expansionism, seen as an expression of "manifest destiny," Polk gave his full and enthusiastic support. Texas, as a slave state, was now admitted to the Union, annexation having been approved by joint resolution of Congress, signed into law by President Tyler on March 1, 1845; a decision known to be supported by president-elect Polk, who would be inaugurated but three days later. Avoiding war with Great Britain over possession of the Oregon Territory, setting aside the popular battle cry "54° 40' or fight," a compromise agreement was reached on April 23, 1846, fixing the Northern border at the forty-ninth parallel. Indulging in war with Mexico, the Slidell mission having failed, the Treaty of Guadalupe Hidalgo of 1848 restored peace, mandating, in return for $15 million, that Mexico cede to the United States the vast expanse of land that was California and New Mexico territory. While these acquisitions were generally popular, they fueled anew sectional rivalries with regard to the extension or prohibition of slavery in the new territories. Some would argue, thereby, that the war with Mexico (1846–1848), made inevitable the American Civil War that was to follow (1861–1865). On the domestic policy front, perhaps Polk's greatest achievement was congressional enactment of the moderate Walker Tariff Act of 1846, a measure which while greatly pleasing no one, deeply offended few; no small accomplishment in the history of tariff legislation. Satisfied that the goals for his presidency had been met, committed to the one-term pledge he had made when first inaugurated, Polk departed the executive office in March of 1849, to return to Nashville. Never in robust health, exhausted by the burdens of the presidential office, James Knox Polk died on June 15, 1849, less than four months after leaving the White House. *See*: ELECTIONS: 1844.

References: Paul H. Bergeron, *The Presidency of James K. Polk* (Lawrence: University Press of Kansas, 1987); Charles A. McCoy, *Polk and the Presidency* (Austin: University of Texas Press, 1960); James K. Polk, *Polk: The Diary of a President, 1845–1849*, Allan Nevin, ed. (New York: Longmans, Green, 1929); Charles G. Sellers, *James K. Polk*, 2 vols. (Princeton: Princeton University Press, 1957, 1966).

POLL means (1) a counting of heads; (2) a place where people vote; (3) today, a poll usually refers to a randomly selected, sample survey of the electorate that seeks to determine the public's political opinion. Polls are conducted frequently by the media and by candidates, during a political campaign. Preelection polls, designed to predict the outcome of an election, have a significant effect on political campaigns. The poll results affect the viability of a campaign, that is, the ability of the candidate to raise money, and the manner in which the campaign is treated by the press. Media attention to poll results is what has been termed ''horserace journalism,'' where the attention is focused on the polls and not on the issues raised by the candidates. The campaign is treated as a game.

The contemporary method of polling was first developed by George Gallup in the 1930s. He devised a method of gauging public opinion through the use of scientifically selected samples. He was quite successful in predicting election outcomes, except the 1948 Dewey-Truman election, where he, and others, predicted Dewey would win.

Recent preelection polls have accurately predicted the winner, but have not been successful in predicting the margin of victory. Pollsters have difficulty allocating the undecided vote in the closing days of the campaign. Polls should be viewed as snapshots of the electorate at the time they are taken. *See*: HORSE-RACE JOURNALISM; SAMPLE.

Reference: Michael W. Traugott and Paul J. Lavrakas, *The Voter's Guide to Election Polls* (Chatham, N.J.: Chatham House, 1996).

POLL BOOK is the list of eligible voters in a precinct with their voting records. It is used to determine voter eligibility in states that have voter registration. *See*: REGISTRATION, VOTER.

POLL TAX was originally used by state and local governments as a head tax, to collect revenue from those who did not own property. The tax rolls also served as the eligible voter lists. As white male suffrage increased in the nineteenth century, use of the poll tax waned. Poll taxes were reintroduced in the South after the Civil War and reconstruction, by the Southern Democrats who were threatened by African-American and poor whites voting Republican. The poll tax, coupled with literacy tests, discouraged Southern blacks, who were generally poor sharecroppers, from voting. The poll taxes lasted in the Southern states until 1964, when the Twenty-Fourth Amendment to the Constitution was adopted, which banned the use of poll taxes in federal elections. At that time, five states still used the poll tax: Alabama, Arkansas, Mississippi, Texas, and Virginia. The U.S. Supreme Court, in *Harper* v. *Virginia State Board of Elections* (1966), ruled that the use of poll taxes, in all elections, was unconstitutional under the equal protection clause of the Fourteenth Amendment. *See*: LITERACY TESTS; TWENTY-FOURTH AMENDMENT.

Reference: Morgan J. Kousser, *The Shaping of Southern Politics* (New Haven, Conn.: Yale University Press, 1974).

POOL REPORTER is a reporter that represents all of the press when it is not possible for more than a few reporters to attend an event or fly on an airplane with a candidate. In the current media age a pool feed may be a single camera crew, filming for all of the networks.

PRECINCT is the basic geographic unit for the conduct of an election. The precinct is the smallest subdivision of a county, in which there are located anywhere from 200 to 1,000 registered voters. There is an established location for those voters to cast their ballots on election day. Pollworkers are hired for the day to assist voters, protect the integrity of the election, and in some parts of the country, count the results. There are a variety of devices for recording and tabulating election results, including paper ballots, scanner-read ballots, punch cards, and voting machines. Some of these are counted at the precinct level.

Precincts are also the basic unit of the political parties. Many county parties in the United States have elected precinct committee men and women in every precinct. A number of precincts gain special attention during an election because they are determined to be swing precincts and are targets for special campaign efforts. Precincts are also the units sampled by exit polls to predict election outcomes. *See*: EXIT POLLS; GOTV; PRECINCT COMMITTEEMAN/COMMITTEEWOMAN.

Reference: Raymond Wolfinger, ''The Influence of Precinct Work on Voting Behavior,'' *Public Opinion Quarterly*, Vol. 27 (1963).

PRECINCT COMMITTEEMAN/COMMITTEEWOMAN is the basic unit of a party organization. The committee person is elected by party members at the precinct level in party primaries or local caucuses. These elected committee persons are members of the county central committee and they select the county party chairman. The committee person, frequently, has some statutory authority in the conduct of elections. They are issued challenger papers and are empowered to challenge voters that they view as ineligible to vote. In political campaigns, they are to register voters, and campaign for the party's slate in their neighborhoods. They are the grassroots members of their party. The members of party committees were central to the conduct of political campaigns before the rise of electronic media. They continue to be very important in GOTV efforts. *See*: GOTV; LOCAL PARTY ORGANIZATIONS; PRECINCT.

Reference: Paul Allen Beck, *Party Politics in America*, 8th ed. (New York: Longman, 1997).

PRECLEARANCE. Under the terms of Section 5 of the Voting Rights Act of 1965, certain political subdivisions within the United States must submit proposed changes in electoral laws (including the redrawing of electoral districts) to either the Federal District Court for the District of Columbia or to the attorney general of the United States. In order for the proposed change to go into effect, one of these agencies must declare or certify that the change "does not have the purpose or will not have the effect of denying or abridging the right to vote on account of race or color." The initial aim of preclearance was simply to make sure that areas with a history of voter discrimination were not able to bypass the Voting Rights Act by continually passing discriminatory legislation that would remain in force until a case was brought before a court. Over time, however, preclearance has become a tool used by the federal government to maximize minority representation. In some cases, the attorney general has placed significant pressure on a state covered by Section 5 to adopt an apportionment plan which maximizes the opportunity for African Americans to be elected to office. In recent years the Supreme Court has registered its displeasure with racially gerrymandered voting districts that have resulted from preclearance pressures. In 1976 the Supreme Court established what is known as the "non-retrogression" standard for preclearance review under Section 5. This is a relative standard under which preclearance is to be given to any changes in voting laws which, even if not maximizing or improving the position of minority voters, do not place those voters in a less advantageous position. *See: BEER* v. *U.S.* (1976); GERRYMANDERING; *MILLER* v. *JOHNSON* (1995); *RENO* v. *BOSSIER PARISH SCHOOL BOARD* (1997); *SHAW* v. *RENO* (1993); *SOUTH CAROLINA* v. *KATZENBACH* (1966); *UNITED JEWISH ORGANIZATIONS* v. *CAREY* (1977); VOTING RIGHTS ACT.

Reference: Richard K. Scher, Jon L. Mills, and John J. Hotaling, *Voting Rights and Democracy: The Law and Politics of Districting* (Chicago: Nelson-Hall, 1997).

PREFERENCE VOTE is called "choice voting" by the Center of Voting and Democracy. Academics usually refer to it as "single transferable vote." It is a system of proportional representation. It requires a multi-member district. Voters order their preferences on the ballot. If a candidate receives the minimum number of votes (called a threshold) on the first count, that candidate is elected. If all the seats are not filled on the first count then a ballot transfer occurs. The last-place candidate is eliminated, and the votes are transferred to the voters' second choice on the ballots cast for the eliminated candidate. That process continues until all of the seats are filled.

It has been the most common form of proportional representation used in former British colonies. It is used in Ireland, Australia (for senate elections), and in Cambridge, Massauchettes (for city council and school committee) and New York City (for local school boards). Earlier in this century it was used to elect city councils in New York, Cleveland, Cincinnati, and several other cities. *See*: PROPORTIONAL REPRESENTATION.

Reference: Douglas J. Amy, *Proportional Representation: The Case for a Better Election System* (Northampton, Mass.: Crescent Street Press, 1997).

PRE-PRIMARY ENDORSEMENT. State and local party organizations frequently vote to support a particular candidate in the primary. This is termed a pre-primary endorsement. The party organization does this to achieve a balanced ticket, reduce party divisions that result from a contested primary, and cue the party primary voters to the best qualified candidate or the most electable candidate. In the days of political machines, local party organizations frequently endorsed candidates in the primary, to maintain control over patronage and government contracts. Local party, pre-primary endorsements are waning.

State party organizations endorse, and some of them enjoy statutory authority for their endorsement activities. Seven states are required, by state statute, to hold pre-primary endorsements by state party convention, which enhances the role of the state party in an era of declining party influence. In Connecticut, ballot access is restricted to candidates who receive at least 20% of the state convention pre-primary endorsement vote. The endorsement, in these seven states, confers on the preferred candidate direct access to the ballot, and the endorsed candidate is often listed first on the primary ballot. In Colorado, a candidate who receives 50% of the party convention votes, is automatically the party's nominee without primary opposition. There are also extralegal, state party endorsements, which do not grant any legal benefit to the candidate. In an extralegal party endorsement, the resources of the party organization are committed in support of the endorsed slate of candidates. The National Party Committees and the Hill Committees almost never endorse candidates in contested primaries. *See*: BALLOT ACCESS; PRIMARY.

References: John F. Bibby, *Politics, Parties, and Elections in America*, 3rd ed. (Chicago: Nelson-Hall, 1996); *Eu* v. *San Francisco County Democratic Committee* (1989); Malcolm E. Jewell and David M. Olson, *Political Parties and Elections in American States* (Chicago: Dorsey, 1988).

PRESIDENTIAL DEBATES. The televised presidential debates have become an important and institutionalized part of the presidential campaign. The first televised debate was in 1960, between Republican presidential nominee, Vice-President Richard M. Nixon, and the Democratic nominee, Massachusetts senator John F. Kennedy. There were four televised presidential debates in 1960. One was a split screen, with the candidates in different cities. Hindsight suggests that Nixon made a mistake in accepting Kennedy's challenge to debate. The debate forum placed Senator Kennedy on an equal footing with Vice-President Nixon, giving Kennedy much-needed exposure, and allowing him to appear more poised than Nixon. In 1964, incumbent Lyndon B. Johnson refused to debate Republican nominee Barry Goldwater, and Johnson won a landslide election. In 1968, Nixon refused Humphrey's challenge to debate and won the election. In 1972, Nixon refused to debate Democratic nominee George McGovern, arguing that an incumbent president could not talk about everything that he knew, an excuse that was acceptable in the Cold War era, and Nixon crushed McGovern at the polls.

In 1976, trailing in the polls, incumbent Gerald Ford challenged Democratic presidential nominee Jimmy Carter to debate. The Ford-Carter debates made debates, once again, a central part of the presidential election. In 1976 there were three presidential debates and one vice-presidential debate. Ford was unable to gain ground by debating, and in one debate, left the impression that he thought Poland was not under Soviet domination. Ford's running mate, Senator Bob Dole, offended some with his caustic wit in the vice-presidential debate with Senator Walter Mondale. In 1980, Reagan and Carter disagreed over whether John Anderson should be included in the debate. Anderson was eventually excluded, and the debates helped Reagan, who may not have won on high school debating points, but projected his benign personality and reassured voters who did not know him well. In 1984 there were two presidential debates and one vice-presidential debate. Reagan did poorly in the first one. He was stronger in the second debate, in which he amused the audience by jokingly saying that he would not make the age and the inexperience of his opponent an issue in this campaign. Reagan successfully defused the age issue in this debate.

The first televised presidential debates were sponsored by the non-partisan League of Women Voters. In 1987 the two national political party committees announced the formation of a bipartisan Commission on Presidential Debates, made up equally of Democrats and Republicans, who would determine the format, the number, the ground rules, the location, and organize the debates. This made the debates a permanent part of the presidential campaign process. In 1988 the league sponsored the two debates between George Bush and Michael Dukakis. In one of those debates Dukakis was severely damaged when he refused to consider the death penalty in a hypothetical question about punishment for someone who raped and murdered his wife. There was one vice-presidential debate.

In 1992 incumbent President George Bush considered not debating. The Clinton campaign pressed for debates, and had a campaign worker dressed as a chicken appear at Bush's campaign events. Bush finally agreed to debate, and there were a series of three debates, using different formats. Independent candidate Ross Perot was invited to participate, and he did the best of the three candidates in the first two debates. Clinton was at his best in the more informal debate format, used in the third debate, where the candidates responded to undecided voters. Bush did not appear to be engaged in that debate. He was caught by the camera looking at his watch. There was one vice-presidential debate in 1992.

In 1996 the Commission on Presidential Debates, after negotiating with representatives of the candidates, determined that there were to be two debates for the presidential candidates, and one for the vice-presidential candidates. The commission decided that Ross Perot should be excluded from these debates. They determined that Perot could not win because his poll numbers were so low. The Perot campaign filed a federal lawsuit, which they lost. The candidates seek the edge in negotiating the debate format. The negotiated format of the 1996 debates included the duration, which was to be 90 minutes, at the urging of the Clinton campaign, who hoped the older Bob Dole would tire. The Clinton campaign also pushed for a town meeting format for the second debate, which had been Clinton's forte in 1992. The Clinton campaign also wanted an early date for the second debate, to allow time for Clinton to recover, if there was any negative fallout from that debate. The Dole campaign was able to have Perot excluded. The 1996 presidential debates were uneventful. The format allowed the candidates to play it very safe. The media have criticized the 1996 debate format as too protective of the candidates. The television ratings for the presidential debates dropped in 1996. *See*: PRESIDENTIAL ELECTION CAMPAIGN.

References: Robert V. Friedenberg, "The 1992 Presidential Debates," in *The 1992 Presidential Campaign: A Communication Perspective*, Robert E. Denton, Jr., ed. (Westport, Conn.: Praeger, 1994); Nelson W. Polsby and Aaron Wildavsky, *Presidential Elections: Strategies and Structures in American Politics*, 9th ed. (Chatham, N.J.: Chatham House, 1996).

PRESIDENTIAL ELECTION CAMPAIGN. Campaigning for president, by the party nominees, started in the twentieth century. Throughout most of the nineteenth century, it was the political parties that campaigned on behalf of their standard bearers. In the presidential election of 1840, William Henry Harrison actually campaigned for himself; he gave speeches in his home state of Ohio. Harrison was criticized for it, and it was many years before a presidential candidate campaigned for himself again. At the end of the nineteenth century, presidential candidates developed the customary practice of receiving visitors at their homes and speaking to them from their front porches.

Presidential campaigning changed significantly with the introduction of electronic media. Warren G. Harding, the last front porch candidate, was the first to speak to the country on the radio, in the campaign of 1920. Franklin D. Roosevelt was the best candidate at delivering his message on the radio. By the 1950s, almost half of American homes had television. That set the stage for the modern electronic, candidate-centered campaign that we know today. In 1952, Republican presidential candidate Dwight D. Eisenhower was the first to use television commercials in his successful campaign against Adlai Stevenson. Eisenhower's running mate, Richard M. Nixon, successfully defended himself from allegations of corruption with his famous televised "Checkers" speech. The first televised presidential debate was in 1960, between John F. Kennedy and Richard M. Nixon. In the 1960s, when electronic media became the central part of the presidential campaign, the political parties were no longer in control of the candidates nor their campaigns.

Television has had a significant impact on modern presidential conventions. The once raucous deliberative national conventions have evolved from being a part of the nominating process to a staged television kick-off of the general election campaign. Images are created for the candidates, and campaign messages are refined for targeted groups of votes. Producers, directors, market researchers, and script writers are now the backroom operators of conventions, rather than the party bosses of the past, and it is the candidate, not the party nor the platform, that is the center of the modern presidential campaign.

The modern presidential campaign is a hierarchically organized, tightly controlled organization, staffed by highly paid professionals, and it is separate from the political party. The function of the party is to serve the campaign. The 1992 Clinton campaign is a textbook case of an effective, modern presidential campaign organization. The daily operation of the campaign was headed by political consultant James Carville. Stan Greenberg was the pollster and strategist. Paul Begala was the principal speech writer and Mandy Greenwald was the top media consultant. David Wilhelm, who would later serve as DNC chair, was in charge of field operations. The campaign operated a ''war room,'' which effectively responded immediately to any negative campaign messages delivered by the Bush campaign. These professionals were hired by and paid by the Clinton campaign. They developed the strategy of the campaign. The Federal Election Campaign Laws reinforced the candidate-centered character of the modern campaign by determining that the public campaign funds, which amounted to $62 million in 1996, would go to the candidate's committee and not the political parties.

There are a number of strategic decisions that a presidential campaign must make. The general election is a contest for Electoral College votes. There are 538 Electoral College votes and a candidate needs 270 to be elected. A presidential campaign must decide what states to compete for, and that determines where the candidates should spend their time, and more importantly, where and how they should spend their money. The party nominees operate from very different Electoral College maps. In the 1980s, political scientists and pundits maintained that the Republicans enjoyed an Electoral College lock. This was based on the fact that the Republicans have an advantage in the West and the South and do well in smaller states, which are overrepresented in the Electoral College. The 1992 and 1996 elections should dispel the notion of a Republican lock on the Electoral College. James Carville said it best—Clinton picked the lock. In the 1990s, the Democrats developed a winning Electoral College coalition based on the East and West coastal states. California was the key to their success. Clinton recognized this and gave special attention to California in his first term. The strategy of a campaign is to shore up the base and then focus on a few targeted, large states. The Dole campaign, trailing badly in the polls, ruminated over whether to target the costly, but Electoral College vote-rich California.

The strategic decision of what states to focus on is only one of the issues a presidential campaign must address. More sophisticated questions surround decisions about the campaign's theme or message. Campaigns deliver both positive and negative messages. Paid electronic advertising is the central medium of delivering the campaign message. Its importance was demonstrated in 1988, when the Bush campaign used the Willy Horton ad, which painted Dukakis as soft on crime. They successfully created Dukakis's image early in the campaign, and Dukakis's campaign failed to respond in a timely and effective manner.

The 1992 presidential campaign is not recognized for skillful use of paid media, but rather Clinton's effective use of free media. Clinton made appearances on *Larry King Live*, *The Arsenio Hall Show*, *Good Morning America*, Phil Donohue, and MTV's *Rock the Vote*. He performed very well in this soft news environment, where he could display his empathy with the concerns of Americans. At first, President Bush avoided this format; when he did venture into using it, he was not able to match Clinton's performance on this new and unusual medium for projecting a presidential candidate's image and message. President Clinton used this media form less often in 1996, preferring the role of incumbent president.

The 1996 campaign also lacked noteworthy campaign commercials, and there were no new and notable uses of the electronic media. The 1996 Clinton campaign was fortunate because Clinton did not have primary opposition and could raise and spend the allowed, maximum amount of campaign funds, to run negative commercials throughout the summer of 1996, tying Dole to the then unpopular Newt Gingrich. The Dole camp had reached the campaign spending limit fighting off challengers in the primary, and could not respond. The Dole campaign, energized by the selection of Jack Kemp as the vice-presidential nominee, was unable to gain momentum with its proposed 15% tax cut. It then moved to the claim that the Clinton administration was soft in the drug war. Next the Dole campaign attempted to make Clinton's character the issue. In 1996 both presidential campaigns seemed to lack focus. Dole continued to reorganize his top staff, hiring and firing his media consultants, reflecting the campaign's continued uncertainty about how to defeat an incumbent president with a high approval rating and a healthy economy. The Clinton campaign lost its brilliant strategist Dick Morris, who had orchestrated Clinton's comeback after the demolishing 1994 Democratic midterm election loss. Morris was forced to resign during the Democratic National Convention, when a tabloid revealed he was having a dalliance with a prostitute, with whom he was sharing campaign tidbits. The Clinton campaign was content to avoid bold moves and ride out its large lead in the polls.

Presidential campaigns use electronic advertising to target certain voter

PRESIDENTIAL ELECTION CAMPAIGN

groups. An example of targeting is the 1996 Clinton campaign spot praising Clinton for promoting the Family Leave Act, which Bob Dole had opposed. This message was directed at working women, a population group with which Clinton did exceeding well. Another example of targeting was the Republican Congress's fall 1996 vote to override the ban on partial birth abortions to force a second Clinton veto. This was a very emotional issue for the Christian Coalition and the Catholic Church. The Republicans hoped to mobilize these voters to its cause.

Neither Clinton nor Dole ran campaigns that were coordinated with the national legislative campaigns. Clinton was content to offer himself as a check on the extremism of the Republican Congress. He did not visibly run a coordinated campaign with House Democrats nor did he campaign extensively for a Democratic Congress. Bob Dole had his troubles with the Republican congressional campaign. A number of Republican House incumbents did not welcome Dole in their districts, and they supported welfare reform, immigration reform, and health care bills in the closing days of the 104th Congress, subjects that the Dole camp did not want settled before the election. Dole wanted to use some of these issues in his campaign. The Republican Congress believed that they needed to have some legislative accomplishments to present to the voters, and they did not heed Dole's request to delay settling some of these issues.

In the modern presidential campaign, the candidates, with the aid of their consultants determine what states to compete for, and this determines where the candidates will spend their time, and where the campaign will invest money in large television buys. The candidates travel around the country, delivering their campaign messages, spending most of their time in targeted states. They try to use free media by appearing on the evening news. Sites are selected and crowds are mobilized, by the advance team, to create good visuals. In 1992 the average quote by a candidate on the nightly news was 8.5 seconds. Seventy percent of the campaign story was told by the reporters. The candidates' press agents have to work closely with the press to attempt to get a favorable story or reduce any damage created by the candidate. The paid media project the same themes that the candidate is focusing on in a particular week.

It is not clear how much effect all of this campaigning has on the outcome of a presidential election. Those who promote the idea of retrospective voting would argue that the 1996 election was a referendum on the past performance of the incumbent administration; with a healthy domestic economy, the voters were satisfied with the Clinton administration and were unwilling to make a change. International events have had little impact on American presidential elections since the collapse of the Soviet Union. *See*: POLITICAL CONSULTANTS; ELECTIONS: 1988, 1992, 1996; PRESIDENTIAL DEBATES; PRESIDENTIAL NOMINATING CAMPAIGNS; RETROSPECTIVE VOTING.

References: Chistopher F. Arterton, "Campaign '92: Strategies and Tactics of the Candidates," in *The Election of 1992*, Gerald Pomper, Chistopher F. Arterton, Ross Baker, and Walter Dean Burnham, eds. (Chatham, N.J.: Chatham House, Inc., 1993); Benjamin Ginsberg and Alan Stone, eds., *Do Elections Matter?*, 3rd ed. (Armonk, N.Y.: M. E. Sharpe, 1996); Thomas E. Patterson, *Out of Order* (New York: Vintage Books, 1994); Nelson W. Polsby and Aaron Wildavsky, *Presidential Elections: Strategies and Structures in American Politics*, 9th ed. (Chatham, N.J.: Chatham House, 1996); Stephen J. Wayne, *The Road to the White House 1996: The Politics of Presidential Elections* (New York: St. Martin's Press, 1996).

PRESIDENTIAL NOMINATING CAMPAIGNS. The campaign for a party nomination for president is an intraparty contest for delegates that are won in primary elections. The actual allocation of the delegates is based on ever-changing party rules. The actual voting for preferred candidates by primary voters and the resulting allocation of state party delegates to the party national conventions occurs in a short period of time. In 1996 it occurred in the winter and early spring of the year of the presidential election.

The presidential nomination campaign begins years before the national party conventions. The campaign for the presidential nomination for 2000 began before the 1996 election was decided. Vice-President Al Gore used the 1996 Democratic National Convention not only to promote President Clinton and their 1996 reelection bid, but also to advance his standing with Democratic voters for the Democratic nomination in 2000. The Republican convention lacked as clear a frontrunner for the future. Jack Kemp, Dan Quayle, and Colin Powell were viewed by many in the audience as possible future candidates if Bob Dole failed in his 1996 bid. Even Republican convention keynoter, Long Island representative Susan Molinari put out "Molinari in 2000" signs to be waved when she spoke. Efforts by prospective 2000 candidates began in earnest as soon as the 1996 election results were tallied.

Arthur Hadley called the early campaign period the "invisible primary." Rhodes Cook called this period the "exhibition season," when many prospective candidates test the water and withdraw before the primaries begin. During the invisible primary, potential candidates travel the country, write and publish books, campaign, and appear at events, all to raise money for their respective parties' organizations and candidates, with the hope of gaining support. During the 1996 invisible primary, Republican candidates such as Bill Bennett, Richard Cheney, Jack Kemp, and Dan Quayle made efforts to start a campaign, and realized that they could neither gain sufficient support nor raise the necessary money to effectively challenge Bob Dole for the nomination. They were casualties of the invisible primary. One candidate who actually announced he was running in 1996, and then withdrew before any ballots were cast, was California governor Pete Wilson.

The most important campaign activity in the years prior to the primaries is raising campaign funds. This is regulated by the Federal Election Campaign

Act laws, and enforced by the Federal Election Commission. The presidential candidates must meet certain requirements in order to qualify for federal matching funds that can be used in the primary. To qualify for the match, a candidate needs to raise at least $5,000 in individual contributions of up to $250 in at least 20 different states. In 1996 the conventional wisdom was that a candidate needs to raise $20 million to be viable. One of the major proponents of that dollar amount was Senator Phil Gramm, who never gained significant momentum in the 1996 race despite his hefty war chest. Raising that amount of money is a herculean task when it has to be done in increments of $1,000 from individuals and $5,000 from groups. Only the first $250 of each donation is matched by the federal fund. Candidates are not required to accept matching funds. If they do not take the matching funds, then they are not subject to the per-state spending caps, and they can donate whatever personal funds they wish. Their personal contribution is limited to $50,000, if they accept the matching money. In 1996 wealthy Steve Forbes did not accept the matching funds and outspent his rivals four to one in the New Hampshire primary, most of it his own money. The only other two candidates who have refused the match since its inception, to avoid the caps, were both Republicans: former Texas governor John Connally in 1980 and televangelist Pat Robertson in 1988. They did not intend to spend their own money, but were able fundraisers, and believed that accepting the matching funds was not worth accepting the spending caps. Money does not guarantee victory, but it is a necessary ingredient of a successful campaign. An effective strategy and good fortune also play an important role.

For the candidates who actually announce and run, the early contests—the Iowa caucuses and the New Hampshire primary—are critical to the candidates' success because of the intensive media scrutiny those events receive. In 1996 these early primary contests gave momentum to Steve Forbes, who in the eyes of the press exceeded expectations, and to Patrick Buchanan, who enjoyed a surprising win in New Hampshire. These two nomination contests also damaged frontrunner Bob Dole, who did worse than expected in Iowa and lost New Hampshire. In 1992, Bill Clinton lost New Hampshire to Paul Tsongas, but Clinton overcame that by creating the impression that he did better than expected, and he named himself the "Comeback Kid." These early primary elections are important in defining the entire primary season. Frontrunners can be damaged by not meeting the expectations, and lesser-known candidates can gain notice and momentum by doing better than expected. The expectations for the candidates are defined by the press.

Presidential candidates pursue different strategies in the nomination contest. Usually, they have to move toward the ideological extreme of their party. In 1996 incumbent President Clinton was fortunate because he did not have a challenge for the Democratic nomination. Consequently, he did not have to move to the political left. This was the first time the Democrats had not had a presidential nomination contest since 1964. Republican presidential hopeful Bob Dole's lead in the early national polls did not scare off all of the challengers. In 1996 almost the entire Republican field took Nixon's sage advice for Republican presidential campaigning; go right in the primary, and back to the center in the general election. Most of the candidates pitched their message to the right of the party. The most influential conservative group in contemporary Republican politics, the Christian Coalition, did not embrace one candidate, and the candidates divided up that vote. Pennsylvania senator Alan Specter attempted to run as a liberal-moderate candidate, but found there was no base vote for that pitch in the Republican Party of the 1990s. The early primaries have a winnowing effect on the field. A number of the GOP candidates including Phil Gramm were knocked out of the nomination contest by their poor showing in these early contests.

The value of the ideological fervent to a presidential nomination campaign is grassroots enthusiasm, a necessary ingredient if the candidate is relying on organization to deliver the vote in low turnout primaries and caucuses. Organization and retail politics, that is, direct personal contact with voters, was the approach of most of the Republican candidates in Iowa and New Hampshire. One candidate who did not build an organization, but relied solely on paid media, was wealthy Steve Forbes, and he had some success in attracting voters. His approach will be taken note of, and perhaps copied, by some of the candidates who seek the nomination in 2000. The longtime frontrunner in 1996, Bob Dole, spent a lot of his money on organization in the early primaries, in which he did poorly. A close win in Iowa, a neighbor of his home state of Kansas, and a loss in New Hampshire almost knocked him out of the race. He recovered by winning in South Carolina, New York, and sweeping ''Super Tuesday'' in the South, many of which were winner-take-all primaries. His opponents either ran out of money or, like Steve Forbes, refused to continue to spend their own money. Dole was able to endure these losses and maintain his frontrunner status, because of the reliable support of most of the 32 Republican governors, especially in South Carolina, and in the large states of Ohio and New York.

The rules, and the calendar of the primary nomination contest, change in some degree for every quadrennial election, and the process affects the outcome. The most radical change occurred with the introduction of the McGovern-Fraser reforms for the 1972 Democratic nomination, which brought about the use of the direct primary as the principal method of delegate selection. The Democratic National Committee mandates the use of proportional representation for the distribution of delegates, and that makes it difficult for the Democrats to bring early closure to a contested nomination. Nonetheless, the proportional distribution of delegates and the timing of the declaration of candidate preference by the superdelegates (PLEOs), which made up 18% of the Democratic delegates in 1996, makes it difficult for a candidate to emerge in the late primaries and overtake the frontrunner. The state Republican parties, who followed the Democrats in using the primary for delegate selection, are permitted by the Republican National Committee to use (and a number of Republican state parties prefer) the winner-take-all primary. This creates the possibility of the Republican frontrunner gaining an insurmountable lead in delegates much earlier than the Democratic party favorite. The winner-take-all Republican primary, however, also gives a challenger the opportunity to overcome the frontrunner in later primaries. In 1976 challenger Ronald Reagan almost overcame President Gerald Ford's delegate lead by winning, late in the primary season, the winner-take-all, delegate-rich states of Texas and California.

In 1996 the presidential primary calendar became front-loaded. State party leaders recognized the influence of early primaries on the nomination process, and in 1996 many states moved their primaries into late winter. For example, large states like Ohio and California moved their primaries from May and June to March. In 1996, since President Clinton was unopposed, only the Republicans had to nominate a candidate in this new untested primary calendar. The Republicans were not pleased with the results. The large states that scheduled their primaries earlier in the year enjoyed neither greater attention by the candidates, nor increased voter participation. Also, party leaders became concerned when it appeared that Dole might be eliminated, and they would be left with a weak field of candidates with no opportunity for other candidates to enter the contest. At their 1996 convention, the Republicans changed their primary rules, and offered bonus delegates to states that move their primaries back later in the year, for the nomination contest of 2000. It is the state legislatures that set the day of the primary, at the urging of the parties.

The final step in the nomination process is the national party convention, held by both parties in the late summer of the election year. The conventions have evolved from being deliberative bodies, where the nominee of the national party was not known until the delegates cast their ballots and someone was eventually nominated, into its current role as a ratifying body, reflecting the preferences of the primary voters. The outcome of the conventions is no longer uncertain, and the convention has changed from being a part of the nominating process to serving as the kick-off for the general election campaign. *See*: DELEGATE; FEDERAL ELECTION CAMPAIGN ACT OF 1971; FEDERAL ELECTION COMMISSION; HUNT COMMISSION; IOWA CAUCUS; MCGOVERN-FRASER COMMISSION; NATIONAL PARTY CONVENTION; NEW HAMPSHIRE PRIMARY; PRESIDENTIAL ELECTION CAMPAIGN; SUPERDELEGATE.

References: Emmett H. Buell, Jr. "The Invisible Primary," in *In Pursuit of the White House: How We Choose Our Presidential Nominees*, William G. Mayer, ed. (Chatham, N.J.: Chatham House, 1996); Michael L. Goldstein, *Guide to the 1996 Presidential Election* (Washington, D.C.: Congressional Quarterly Press, 1996); Arthur T. Hadley, *The Invisible Primary* (Englewood Cliffs, N.J.: Prentice-Hall, 1976); Nelson W. Polsby and Aaron Wildavsky, *Presidential Elections: Strategies and Structures in American Politics*, 9th ed. (Chatham, N.J.: Chatham House, 1996); Stephen J. Wayne, *The Road to the White House 1996: The Politics of Presidential Elections* (New York: St. Martin's Press, 1996).

PRIMARY is an election held before the general election to nominate the political parties' candidates for office. The primary was first introduced in Wisconsin in 1902. The Wisconsin primary law was written by Robert M. La Follete, a leader in the Progressive movement. It was later introduced in the South to create competition in that sectional one-party system. All of the states now use the primary in some form; the last state to adopt the primary was Indiana in 1976.

The presidential primary was introduced in Florida in 1904. It was then adopted in thirteen states. President Woodrow Wilson proposed a national primary to select presidential nominees; his proposal did not catch on at the time. The presidential primary is now the dominant method used by political parties for the selection of national convention delegates.

The primary was promoted in the United States in the early twentieth century by the reformist, Progressive movement, to break the control of political machines over party nominations. The argument for primaries was that they placed the nominations of candidates in the hands of the people, and put an end to boss-controlled party caucuses and conventions. The primary was first adopted in the states where the progressive movement was particularly strong, and where party organizations were not well established.

There is a great deal of diversity in the way the direct primary is defined and operated by the states. Thirteen states continue to permit, or in some cases, require the use of a party convention to have a role in the nomination process. For example, in Connecticut, the winner of the party convention vote automatically becomes the party nominee and can only be challenged in the primary by someone who receives 20% of the convention votes. Four states permit the parties to use either the primary or the convention to nominate a candidate. In 1994, Virginia Republicans opted to use the convention method, resulting in the nomination of Oliver North for the U.S. Senate. They then chose to use the primary in 1996 to nominate Senator John Warner.

There is a great deal of variation among the states in the party affiliation requirement for voting in a primary. A number of states require a public declaration of party affiliation prior to the day of the primary, while some states impose no restrictions. Below is a table that identifies the type of primary used by each of the states. *See*: PRIMARY, BLANKET; PRIMARY, CLOSED; PRIMARY, NON-PARTISAN; PRIMARY, OPEN; PRIMARY, SEMI-CLOSED; PRIMARY, SEMI-OPEN.

Types of Primaries: Region and State

Northeast
Connecticut, closed (unaffiliated voters
    may vote in some Republican primaries)
Delaware, closed
Maine, semi-closed
Maryland, closed
Massachusetts, semi-closed
New Hampshire, semi-closed
New Jersey, semi-closed
New York, closed
Pennsylvania, closed
Rhode Island, semi-closed

Border
Kentucky, closed
Oklahoma, closed
West Virginia, closed
Missouri, semi-open

West
Arizona, closed
California, blanket (blanket primary
    adopted by referendum, 1996)
Colorado, semi-closed
Nevada, closed
New Mexico, closed
Oregon, closed
Wyoming, semi-closed

Midwest
Iowa, semi-closed
Kansas, semi-closed
Nebraska, closed
Ohio, semi-closed
South Dakota, closed
Illinois, semi-open
Indiana, semi-open
Michigan, open
Minnesota, open
North Dakota, open
Wisconsin, open
Vermont, open

South
Florida, closed
North Carolina, closed (unaffiliated voters
    may vote in Republican primary)
Alabama, semi-open
Arkansas, semi-open
Georgia, semi-open
Mississippi, semi-open
South Carolina, open
Tennessee, semi-open
Virginia, semi-open
Louisiana, nonpartisan

References: John F. Bibby and Thomas M. Holbrook, "Parties and Elections," in *Politics in the American States: A Comparative Analysis*, 6th ed., Virginia Gray and Herbert Jacob, eds. (Washington, D.C.: Congressional Quarterly Press, 1996); Council of State Governments, *The Book of the States 1994–1995*, vol. 30 (Lexington, Ky.: Council of State Governments, 1994).

PRIMARY, BEAUTY CONTEST is a state primary or party caucus, where prospective party presidential candidates are listed on a primary ballot, and votes are cast. However, there are no delegates selected as a result of this process. A number of American cities attempted to hold presidential beauty contest primaries in 1995, to attract the attention of presidential candidates to the problems of urban areas. The results had no bearing on the selection of national convention delegates. The candidates were uncooperative and the venture was unsuccessful.

PRIMARY, BLANKET. Alaska, Washington, and California have used the blanket primary. It carries the open primary to the extreme. Voters can vote in every party's primary but they can only vote for one candidate for each office. As an example, a voter can vote for a Republican candidate for U.S. Senator, and a Democratic candidate for county sheriff. The blanket primary, also known as the Jungle primary, received a majority of the vote in a 1996 ballot referendum in the state of California. The issue was opposed by both the Democrat and Republican state party organizations in California, but approved by the voters. The proponents argued that the more moderate candidates would become the party nominees under this system. They argued that the closed primary system, which had been used in California prior to the referendum, favored the more extremist candidates. *See*: PRIMARY.

Reference: Benjamin Sheffner, "California Votes to Join the 'Jungle' with New Primary Election Setup," *Roll Call* (April 1, 1996).

PRIMARY, CLOSED. States that use closed primaries for nominating candidates restrict participation to those who declare allegiance to a particular party in advance of the primary election. The declared voters are permitted to vote in only that one party's primary. New York State has a very restrictive closed primary; voters who wish to change parties must do so a year before the primary. In Pennsylvania, voters must declare their party affiliation at least 30 days before the primary election, in order to be eligible to vote.

Closed primaries strengthen political parties. This system requires the voters to select and openly declare a party affiliation. The Democratic National Committee's post-1972 Mikulski Commission imposed a closed primary for the selection of Democratic National Convention delegates. The party has since eased that restriction. The closed primary allows party organizations greater influence in determining their party's nominees. Both the Democratic and Republican state party organizations opposed the 1996 California initiative, which changed the closed primary in California to a blanket primary. *See*: PRIMARY, BLANKET; PRIMARY, OPEN; MIKULSKI COMMISSION.

Reference: L. Sandy Maisel, *Parties and Elections in America: The Electoral Process*, 2nd ed. (New York: McGraw-Hill, 1993).

PRIMARY, NONPARTISAN. The state of Louisiana is the only state that uses this primary form. It was adopted in 1978. All of the candidates appear on the same primary ballot, and they are not separated by party. Louisiana uses this nonpartisan primary for all state and local elections. It was later extended to congressional elections. Louisiana continues to use a closed primary system for presidential nominating contests. The party identity of the candidate may appear on the ballot. If a candidate receives more than half of the votes cast, that candidate is declared a winner. If no candidate receives more than half of the votes cast, then a runoff election is held between the top two. In 1994 all seven of Louisiana's U.S. House incumbents won reelection in the primary because they received more than 50% of the vote.

In 1996 the Fifth Circuit Court of Appeals ruled that federal statutes require members of Congress to be elected on the same day and that the Louisiana system must conform to that law. In *Foster* v. *Love* (1997), the Supreme Court upheld the lower court and declared that states cannot elect members of Congress before the national election day in November. John C. Kuzenski speculates that it is likely that Louisiana will move its primary to the November election day, and schedule the runoffs later. *See*: ELECTION DAY; PRIMARY, RUN-OFF.

References: James Beck, *Party Politics in America* (New York: Longman, 1997); John C. Kuzenski, "The Four—Yes, Four—Types of State Primaries," *PS Political Science and Politics*, Vol. 30 (June 1997).

PRIMARY, OPEN is a primary in which there is no requirement for declaration of party affiliation. A voter selects, in the privacy of the voting booth, the party primary in which he/she wishes to vote. There is neither a required public declaration nor a public record of the voter's party choice. The voter receives only one party's primary ballot.

There are ten states that use the open primary. Proponents of this type of primary argue that all voters should be allowed to participate in this important process of nominating candidates. Political parties are usually not supporters of this type of primary system, because it is difficult to identify party members, and difficult to influence party nominations. The Democratic National Committee did not allow this type of primary in its presidential nomination reforms, and challenged Wisconsin's right to use an open primary. The DNC was supported on this rule by the U.S. Supreme Court. The DNC, despite its court victory, has given up this requirement. *See: DEMOCRATIC PARTY OF U.S. v. WISCONSIN* (1981); PRIMARY.

PRIMARY, REGIONAL occurs when all or most of the states in a geographic region of the country hold their presidential primaries on the same day. Super Tuesday is, in some respects, a regional primary, since many southern states hold their primaries on the same day. In 1996 many midwestern states held their presidential primaries on the same day, and this was called the Big Ten primary by the press. Also in 1996, a number of the New England states scheduled their primaries a week before Super Tuesday. This primary was called Junior Tuesday. Proponents of reform of the primary system have proposed more formal regional primaries.

The first regional primary bill was introduced by Senator Robert Packwood in 1972. There have been at least 28 additional bills introduced since that one. The proposals are all similar. They propose to divide the country into four or six regions. Some plans require the states to hold primaries on those specific dates; other plans require states to use that date if they intend to have a primary. The proponents of regional presidential primaries argue that better candidates would seek party presidential nominations, since the amount of time required would be shortened. Also, candidates would be required to appeal to a broader audience, and the influence of small unrepresentative states like New Hampshire would be reduced. *See*: JUNIOR TUESDAY; SUPER TUESDAY.

Reference: Barbara Norrander, *Super Tuesday: Regional Politics and Presidential Primaries* (Lexington: University Press of Kentucky, 1992).

PRIMARY, RUNOFF is a nominating system in which there is a requirement that the nominee receive a majority of the vote. If this does not occur, a second primary election (called a runoff) is held between the top two finishers. A number of southern states use the runoff primary, including Alabama, Arkansas, Florida, Georgia, Louisiana, Mississippi, North Carolina (in 1989 North Carolina lowered its threshold to 40%), Oklahoma, South Carolina (if there is a tie, South Carolina has a third runoff provision), Tennessee, and Texas. A number of states outside the South also have established a runoff procedure. These include Maryland, Utah (which has given it up), and South Dakota, where it is on the books but has not been used.

A runoff can be required in a primary, where the percentage of the vote required is less than 50%. The New York State legislature adopted a 40% threshold requirement for the City of New York party primaries, after the 1969 mayoral election, and it is still in effect. Runoffs are often required in non-partisan elections.

The goal of the runoff primary is to insure that the nominated candidate is acceptable to a majority of the party members, and is not a product of a narrow or ideological party faction. This was a concern in the one-party South, where until recent years, the Democratic nomination was tantamount to election to the office.

In the 1980s, Jesse Jackson charged that the runoff primary was designed to reduce the opportunity for African Americans to be elected in the South. Jesse Jackson attempted to make the majority-vote requirement, for a Democratic Party nomination, a campaign issue in the 1984 election.

Charles Bulloch and Loch Johnson found, in their study of runoff elections, that 10% of the southern primary contests actually required a runoff. About a third of the gubernatorial primaries in states that require a majority had runoffs, particularly when there was an open seat or an incumbent Republican in office. They found that when there was an open House seat, runoffs were required almost 40% of the time. *See*: PRIMARY; PRIMARY, NONPARTISAN.

Reference: Charles S. Bullock III and Loch K. Johnson, *Runoff Elections in the United States* (Chapel Hill: University of North Carolina Press, 1992).

PRIMARY, SEMI-CLOSED. Ten states use the semi-closed primary. Like closed primary states, semi-closed states require voters to publicly declare allegiance to a party in order to vote in a party's primary, and the voter is restricted to one party's primary ballot. In a semi-closed primary, the voter is permitted to declare or change his/her party identification on the day of the primary. In a closed primary, the party declaration must be made prior to the election. *See*: PRIMARY, CLOSED; PRIMARY, OPEN.

PRIMARY, SEMI-OPEN. Ten states use semi-open primaries. In this type of primary, voters are required to publicly request their preferred party primary ballot on the day of the election, but there is no record kept of their party preference. The political parties have no record of who voted in their primary in the states where this system is used. This is a type of primary used in many southern states. *See*: PRIMARY.

References: John F. Bibby and Thomas M. Holbrook, "Parties and Elections," in *Politics in the American States: A Comparative Analysis*, 6th ed., Virginia Gray and Herbert Jacob, eds. (Washington, D.C.: Congressional Quarterly Press, 1996).

PRIMARY, WHITE. The white primary was used in the South, after the Civil War, to exclude African Americans from voting. In 1944, the U.S. Supreme Court ruled, in *Smith* v. *Allwright*, that the "white primary" was a violation of the Fifteenth Amendment. The case arose over the denial of a Democratic primary ballot to a black resident in Texas. The Court admitted that it had erred in the case of *Grovey* v. *Townsend* (1935), where it allowed the exclusion of blacks from "private" party primaries. The Court argued that the party was actually performing a state function in holding a primary, and that a primary was part of the electoral process. *See: SMITH* v. *ALLWRIGHT* (1944).

PROGRESSIVE MOVEMENT was a political reform movement that occurred in the United States between the 1880s and the 1920s. The Progressive movement was a response to industrialization and urbanization. Progressivism was often merged with the ideas of Populism, which was a rural protest movement in the agricultural areas of the South and West. The Populists were the first to demand that the national government had a responsibility to attend to the common good.

The Progressives favored regulation of monopolies and government intervention to maintain competition. They also favored the regulation of the production and sale of food and drugs. The Progressives were very much in favor of political reform, and this is where the movement had its greatest impact. For the Progressives, the solution to the problems of a democracy was more democracy. They promoted the direct primary, the initiative, the referendum, and recall. Politics was to be replaced by administrative expertise. Merit should be the standard for government employment, not political connections. The application of science to government would bring about greater efficiency and a better life for its citizens. The Progressives thought that good public administration practices could be discovered, taught, and practiced. They promoted municipal reform and the short ballot.

The ideas of the Progressives and Populists had a significant impact on the West, where a number of states were writing their constitutions, at a time when these movements were very influential. The Progressive movement reached its peak in the election of 1912, when Theodore Roosevelt ran as the candidate of the Progressive Party, which was created as a bolt from the Republican Party of William Howard Taft. The split in the Republicans led to the election of Woodrow Wilson, who was also an advocate of a number of the ideas of the Progressives. *See*: BULL MOOSE PARTY; ELECTIONS: 1912.

References: A. J. Beitzinger, *A History of American Political Thought* (New York: Dodd, Mead, 1972); John G. Francis and Clive S. Thomas, "Influences on Western Political Culture," in *Politics and Public Policy in the Contemporary American West*, Clive S. Thomas, ed. (Albuquerque: University of New Mexico Press, 1991).

PROPORTIONAL REPRESENTATION (PR) is a principle of elections applied to election systems that use a multi-member district; that is, where more than one member/delegate is elected from a geographic unit, and a list of candidates for the available offices is provided by each party. The parties are then awarded available seats based on the percentage of the vote that they receive. There are forms of proportional representation that are not party-based. Mathematically, proportional representation is fairer than single-member district plurality, which is used to elect most government officials in the United States.

There are persuasive advocates of proportional representation. Currently, one of the most notable advocates is Douglas J. Amy at Mount Holyoke College. He advocates the use of proportional representation for all elections in the United States. He argues that plurality elections are unfair and undemocratic. According to Amy, proportional representation would revitalize the American political system. Amy argues that the use of proportional representation would give the voters more choices of parties and candidates, it would break the two-party monopoly, more women and minorities would be elected to office, more voices would be represented, and voting turnout would increase. Critics of proportional representation, especially Maurice Duverger, argue that it contributes to multi-partyism and leads to weak governments and political instability.

The Democratic Party requires the use of proportional representation for the selection of national convention delegates. The party requires states to distribute delegates to the candidates in proportion to the vote they receive in congressional and statewide primaries and caucuses.

The Democratic National Committee rules have a threshold requirement, that is, a candidate must attain a certain percentage of the primary vote to be awarded delegates. There has been a debate within the Democratic Party over the threshold requirement, that is, the minimum percentage of the vote a candidate must receive to be awarded delegates. The national Democratic Party currently sets its threshold at 15%. If a candidate receives less than 15%, he/she is not awarded delegates. *See*: DUVERGER'S LAW; LIST SYSTEM; MCGOVERN-FRASER COMMISSION; MIXED MEMBER PROPORTIONAL; PLURALITY; SINGLE-MEMBER DISTRICT; THRESHOLD REQUIREMENT; TWO-PARTY SYSTEM.

References: Douglas J. Amy, *Real Choices, New Voices: The Case for Proportional Representation Elections in the United States* (New York: Columbia University Press, 1993); Kathleen Barber, *Proportional Representation and Election Reform in Ohio* (Columbus: Ohio State University Press, 1995); Douglas Rae, *The Political Consequences of Electoral Laws* (New Haven, Conn.: Yale University Press, 1967).

PROSPECTIVE VOTING is voting based on the promises and programs that parties and candidates say they will carry out in the future. The 1994 House Republican candidates assumed voters were prospective voters when they offered their Contract with America. The Contract was a specific list of programs the Republicans promised they would vote for, if they gained a majority. Many scholars of voting behavior argue that the theory of retrospective voting is a more powerful explanation of voting behavior. *See*: CONTRACT WITH AMERICA; RETROSPECTIVE VOTING.

PROTEST VOTE is a ballot cast for a candidate who has little or no chance of winning, to show dissatisfaction with the other candidates, or express discontent with social and economic conditions. In the United States, many of the votes cast for minor party candidates are interpreted as protest votes. The voters are casting votes against the candidates and programs offered by the two major parties, and the status quo. In European democracies, a vote for the Communist Party was often interpreted as a protest vote, that is, the voters were not in favor of the Communist Party's platform, but were registering their discontent with political, economic, and social conditions.

PROTESTANTS. White Protestants tend to vote Republican. In the 1996 election, exit polls showed that white Protestants voted: 36% for Clinton, 53% for Dole, and 10% for Perot. Bob Dole won two-thirds of the "religious right" vote. The support for Republicans by Fundamentalist/born-again Christians was especially strong. The National Election Survey, since 1990, has divided Protestants into four groups. The two major groups are mainline Protestants and Evangelicals. The white Evangelicals are more concentrated in the South. White Protestants who have a high religious commitment vote at a higher rate than those expressing lower levels of commitment. White Protestants who express a high level of religious commitment are very strong Republican Party voters. *See*: CATHOLIC VOTE; CHRISTIAN COALITION; JEWISH VOTE.

References: Paul R. Abramson, John H. Aldrich, and David W. Rhode, *Change and Continuity in the 1992 Election*, rev. ed. (Washington, D.C.: Congressional Quarterly Press, 1995); John R. Petrocik and Frederick T. Steeper, "Realignment and 1984: New Coalitions and New Majorities?" *Election Politics*, Vol. 2 (Winter 1984–1985).

PUNDIT is one who comments on both public events and the people involved in those events. Today that commentary is found in newspapers, magazines, radio, and television. Punditry is the interpretation of events, rather than simply the reporting of events. William Safire, a pundit of some note, traced the origin of the word to the Hindi phrase for "learned man." As the word developed, and was adopted in the English language, the word pundit took on an occasional pejorative meaning, and American politicians, like George Bush and Jesse Jackson, have criticized pundits for their influence on American public opinion.

Punditry, as a profession, has grown and prospered in recent decades with the growth of cable television. There are numerous cable television programs that feature pundits, some of them performing as irate opponents to each others' views. According to Dan Nimmo and James E. Combs, "news analysis" has evolved from intellectual musing to personalized, entertaining writing and speech. Pollsters have also become part of the modern pundit set, because they have technical information. Some pundits have attempted to capitalize on their public exposure to become politicians. Longtime conservative pundit Patrick Buchanan gave up his role of pundit to seek the Republican nomination for president in 1992 and 1996; and *U.S. News & World Report* editor David Gergen signed on to help improve the image of the early Clinton administration. Neither Buchanan's nor Gergen's efforts were met with much success.

References: Dan Nimmo and James E. Combs, *The Political Pundits* (Westport, Conn.: Praeger, 1992); William Safire, *Safire's New Political Dictionary* (New York: Random House, 1993).

PUSH POLL is a telephone campaign, disguised as a poll, used by campaigns to disseminate negative information about an opponent. For example, the caller would ask a question such as: If you knew that candidate "X" voted ten times to raise taxes, would that lead you to vote for or against that candidate?

Some of the Republican candidates in the 1996 primary disguised the use of negative phone banks as polling operations. They called Republican primary voters to damage particular opponents. The callers disguised themselves as pollsters, to disseminate negative information about an opponent. Republican presidential candidate Steve Forbes claimed his opponents were doing this to his candidacy, to mobilize pro-life voters against him. Democratic state party officials admitted that they used similar tactics against Republican candidate Jeb Bush, in the 1994 gubernatorial election, and they apologized. This practice has been denounced by the American Association of Political Consultants. *See*: PO-LITICAL CONSULTANTS; POLL.

References: Richard Morin, ''When Push Comes to Shove,'' *Washington Post: National Weekly Edition* (July 1–7, 1996): 35; Michael W. Traugott and Paul J. Lavrakas, *The Voter's Guide to Election Polls* (Chatham, N.J.: Chatham House, 1996).

Q

QUAYLE, J. DAN(FORTH) (1947–   ) served as vice-president of the United States under President George Bush from 1988 to 1991. Dan Quayle was born in Indianapolis, Indiana on February 4, 1947. His father, Jim Quayle, was the publisher of the Huntington *Herald Press*. Corinne Pulliam, his mother, was the daughter of Eugene C. Pulliam, the wealthy owner of the Central Newspapers located in Indiana and Arizona.

Dan Quayle graduated from DePauw University in Greencastle, Indiana in 1969, with an A.B. degree in political science. After graduation, he joined the Indiana National Guard, bypassing normal procedures. Quayle's enlistment in the Indiana National Guard became an issue in the 1988 presidential election. It appeared that family influence was exerted so that Quayle could avoid the draft during the Vietnam War.

In 1974, Dan Quayle graduated from Indiana University Law School. He married one of his classmates, Marilyn Tucker, and they practiced law together. He also joined the family-owned business, the Huntington *Herald Press* in 1974. In 1976, Republican Party leaders asked him to run as the Republican candidate for Congress in the Fourth Congressional District against eight-term incumbent J. Edward Roush. Quayle's candidacy appeared to be a hopeless cause. Quayle won a surprising upset, and in 1978 he was reelected. In 1980 the Republicans once again called on him to run against an incumbent. This time Quayle would challenge Indiana Senator Birch Bayh. Qualye won this election with 54% of the vote. The Reagan landslide in Indiana contributed to Quayle's victory. In 1986, Quayle was reelected to the Senate with 61% of the vote.

As a senator, Quayle was practical and pragmatic. His most noted piece of legislation was the Job Training and Partnership Act of 1982. The bill was cosponsored by Democratic Senator Ted Kennedy. As a senator, Dan Quayle was very supportive of the Reagan administration policies.

In 1988, Dan Quayle was the surprising choice of Republican presidential nominee George Bush. The response to the announcement of Quayle's selection at the National Republican Convention was mixed. Quayle had many attractive attributes: He was young, good-looking, represented a new generation, enthusiastic, and quite conservative in his views. On the other hand, many in the press saw him as having questionable credentials and lacking the necessary intellect and experience for national office. The Bush-Quayle ticket easily defeated the Democratic ticket of Dukakis-Bentson in 1988. Dan Quayle was a very loyal vice-president. In the White House he was a voice for more conservative ideas. Quayle was one of the first public figures to take up the ''family values'' issue. The Bush-Quayle ticket was defeated by Clinton-Gore in 1992. Quayle tested the waters for president in 1996 and withdrew. Quayle took charge of Bob Dole's leadership PAC Campaign America in 1996. He is viewed as a potential GOP presidential candidate in 2000. *See*: BUSH, GEORGE HERBERT WALKER; ELECTIONS: 1988, 1992.

Reference: Richard F. Fenno, *The Making of a Senator: Dan Quayle* (Washington, D.C.: Congressional Quarterly Press, 1989).

R

RAINBOW COALITION is a liberal group within the Democratic Party created and led by Jesse Jackson. The Rainbow Coalition was an effort to straddle the racial divide by presenting itself as a progressive movement of African Americans, Hispanics, women, gays, environmentalists, peace activists, and others, to check the influence of the wealthy and powerful in the Democratic Party. Jesse Jackson created the Rainbow Coalition for his 1984 and 1988 bids for the Democratic nomination for president. In 1991, Jackson threatened to lead the Rainbow Coalition into a third-party movement, which he did not do. The future of the Rainbow Coalition looks dim without Jackson's leadership. In Vermont, in the early 1990s, the Rainbow Coalition merged with the city of Burlington's Progressive Coalition to form a third party. *See*: JACKSON, JESSE L.

Reference: J. David Gillespie, *Politics at the Periphery: Third Parties in Two-Party America* (Columbia: University of South Carolina Press, 1993).

REAGAN, RONALD WILSON (1911–) was the fortieth president of the United States. He was born in Tampico, Illinois. He graduated with an A.B. degree in economics from Eureka College in 1932, and began a career in radio as a sports announcer in Davenport, Iowa. The Great Depression had a significant effect on Reagan, since his father, Jack Reagan, was unemployed. Ronald Reagan admired Franklin Roosevelt's efforts to address the country's poor economic conditions.

As a sports announcer, Reagan used the nickname "Dutch," and he had a smooth radio voice. In 1937, Reagan signed a movie contract with Warner Brothers and in 1940 he played the lead role in *Knute Rockne-All American*. This film established him as a serious actor. During World War II, he served in the U.S. Army, making training films. After the war he returned to Warner

Brothers, and in 1947 was elected president of the Screen Actors Guild. In 1962, after decades of identifying with the Democratic Party, Ronald Reagan became a Republican. He was active in Barry Goldwater's presidential campaign in 1964. His activity on behalf of Goldwater attracted the attention and support of a group of wealthy California Republicans who encouraged him to seek the governor's office. He was elected governor of California in 1966.

In 1974, Reagan decided not to run for reelection for governor; instead, he started his quest for the presidency. In 1976 he challenged Gerald Ford for the Republican presidential nomination, and lost by only 60 convention delegate votes. In 1980 he won the GOP presidential nomination. Reagan was very skillful in the 1980 presidential debates. Efforts by the Carter campaign to paint Reagan as an extremist were defused by Reagan's projection of a warm and stable personality on television. Reagan captured voter sentiment in 1980, when he said to the voters: "Ask yourself, are you better off now than you were four years ago?" Americans responded by electing Reagan by a landslide over incumbent president Jimmy Carter. A majority of Republicans were elected to the U.S. Senate that year.

A few months after his election, Reagan was shot in an assassination attempt. He recovered quickly, and then made a dramatic appeal at a joint session of Congress for reform of the tax laws. He was successful in lowering the tax rates. After a recession in the early 1980s, his economic policies led to strong economic growth. His strong leadership and the economic recovery contributed to a landslide reelection over Democratic nominee Walter Mondale in 1984.

In foreign policy, Reagan took a very strong stand against the Soviet Union, which he described as the "Evil Empire." He advocated building a Star Wars defense system against nuclear attack. He pushed for large U.S. defense spending and forced the Soviet Union to try to keep pace with the United States, which contributed to the eventual collapse of the Soviet Union. His administration was marred by the Iran-Contra scandal, which involved illegal sale of arms to Iran, and then funneled money to the Nicaraguan Contra rebels.

After completing his term in office, Ronald Reagan retired to his ranch in California. He remained a very popular political figure after his retirement. His domestic policies, which resulted in economic growth and large federal deficits, will remain controversial. His accomplishments in foreign policy, particularly his assertive foreign policy, which contributed to the collapse of the Soviet Union, will insure his place as one of the most influential figures in the late twentieth century.*See*: CARTER, JIMMY; ELECTIONS: 1976, 1980, 1984.

References: William E. Pemberton, *Exit with Honor: The Life and Presidency of Ronald Reagan* (Armonk, N.Y.: M. E. Sharpe, 1997); Ronald Reagan, *An American Life* (New York: Simon and Schuster, 1990).

REAGAN DEMOCRATS were urban, blue collar voters who voted for Ronald Reagan in 1980 and 1984. They were attracted to Reagan because of his conservative message. These voters had been a key element of the Democratic

Party's New Deal coalition. Their defection to Reagan was a further sign of the break-up of that coalition. Bill Clinton's moderate "New Democrat" campaigns in 1992 and 1996 attracted these Reagan Democrats back to the Democratic Party. Clinton did very well in the milltowns and industrial centers, home of the Reagan Democrats.

Reference: Rhodes Cook, "Election End Results, County by County," *Congressional Quarterly Weekly Report,* Vol. 54 (December 21, 1996).

REALIGNMENT is a fundamental shift in partisan alignments, to such a degree that the minority party becomes the majority party, and the newly created voter alignment persists beyond a single election. An example of a major realignment occurred in the election of 1860: when Lincoln was elected president the newly formed Republican Party became dominant, and the old Whig Party disappeared. The most recent realignment was the election of Franklin D. Roosevelt, and his New Deal Democratic Party in 1932. Both of these realignments were a result of significant social upheaval in the nation. Prior to the election of 1860, the country was torn by the issue of slavery, and it took a major civil war to resolve the issue. Prior to the election of 1932, the country was devastated by an economic depression, from which it did not fully recover until a decade later.

The New Deal coalition persisted into the 1970s. Many observers had expected a new realignment to occur in the 1980s. Despite the success of the Reagan Republicans at capturing the White House for twelve consecutive years, the GOP only gained control of the U.S. Senate for a few of those years in the 1980s, and the Republicans did not capture the House of Representatives until 1994 after the Democrats had won the presidency. Late-twentieth-century partisanship is more accurately characterized as dealignment. *See:* DE-ALIGNMENT; MAINTAINING ELECTION; NEW DEAL COALITION; PARTISANSHIP.

References: Paul Frymer, "The 1994 Electoral Aftershock: Dealignment or Realignment in the South," in *Midterm: The Elections of 1994 in Context,* Philip A. Klinker, ed. (Boulder, Colo.: Westview Press, 1996); Martin P. Wattenberg, *The Decline of American Political Parties: 1952–1988* (Cambridge, Mass.: Harvard University Press, 1990).

REAPPORTIONMENT is the process of determining the number of national legislative seats each state will be allotted. Each state receives two members of the U.S. Senate. Under the Apportionment Act of 1929, the number of members of the House of Representatives was set at 435. After each ten-year census, the number of House of seats that each state receives is apportioned based on that population count. Each state receives one seat before the seat distribution based on population occurs. This decennial process also affects the number of Electoral College votes for each state. As a result of the 1990 census, California gained seven seats, giving that state 52 seats, almost 12% of the House. Also, Florida gained four seats and Texas three seats. Arizona, Georgia, North Carolina, Virginia, and Washington gained one seat each. The states that lost seats after the 1990 census included: New York, three seats, and Illinois, Michigan, Ohio, and Pennsylvania each lost two seats. Iowa, Kansas, Kentucky, Louisiana, Massachusetts, Montana, New Jersey, and West Virginia also lost one seat each. The population shift to the South and the West has resulted in a significant power shift to those sections of the nation.

The state legislatures determine the boundaries of the congressional districts. The congressional districts must be equal in population size. All single-member districts including those used to elect members of state legislatures and city councils are looked at/modified after the census. The states are limited in their redistricting by federal statutes, such as the Voting Rights Act, and numerous Supreme Court decisions. In the 1990s, many states that had created majority-minority districts had to redraw their congressional boundaries as a result of *Miller* v. *Johnson* (1995), which held that redistricting, based solely on race, violated the Constitution. Increasingly, the courts are intruding on the drawing of legislative district boundaries. *See: BAKER* v. *CARR* (1962); GERRYMANDERING; MAJORITY-MINORITY DISTRICTS; *MILLER* v. *JOHNSON* (1995); REAPPORTIONMENT; REDISTRICTING; VOTING RIGHTS ACT.

Reference: David Butler and Bruce Cain, *Congressional Redistricting: Comparative and Theoretical Perspectives* (New York: Macmillan, 1992).

RECALL is an election called to remove an incumbent from office before the term of the office has expired. Recall is permitted in eighteen states. Most of them are located in the western part of the United States. In some of those states, judicial officials and members of Congress are exempt from recall. The signature requirement for a recall petition ranges from 10% in Montana to 40% in Kansas. Over half the states require over 20% of either the eligible vote or the vote cast in a previous election. The period allowed for the collection of signatures ranges from 60 days to 120 days. Even if recall is not addressed in a state constitution, a number of American cities permit recall of municipal officials in their charters. For example, Ohio does not allow recall of state officials or county officials whose duties are defined by state statute. However, the city of Cleveland permits recall in its city charter. In the 1970s, there was an effort to recall Cleveland mayor Dennis Kucinich. The recall question on Mayor Kucinich was placed on the ballot, but it failed. Recall was first authorized in the 1903 Los Angeles city charter. *See*: INITIATIVE; REFERENDUM.

References: Council of State Governments, *The Book of the States: 1996–1997* (Lexington, Ky.: Council of State Governments, 1996); Joseph F. Zimmerman, ''Civic Strategies for Community Empowerment,'' *National Civic Review* (May/June 1988); Joseph F. Zimmerman, *The Recall: Tribunal of the People* (Westport, Conn.: Praeger, 1997).

REDISTRICTING. State legislatures redraw congressional districts in response to the reapportionment of congressional seats among the states. Redistricting also occurs for state legislative districts, after the decennial census, to meet the U.S. Supreme Court required principle of "one man, one vote," as stated in *Reynolds* v. *Sims* (1964). The drawing of legislative districts has become complex in recent years because of the Voting Rights Act of 1965. Efforts to comply with the Voting Rights Act, by states creating majority-minority districts, has been challenged by the U.S. Supreme Court, which has found redistricting based solely on race unconstitutional. *See*: GERRYMANDERING; REAPPORTIONMENT; *REYNOLDS* v. *SIMS* (1964); *SHAW* v. *RENO* (1993); VOTING RIGHTS ACT.

Reference: David Butler and Bruce Cain, *Congressional Redistricting: Comparative and Theoretical Perspectives* (New York: Macmillan, 1992).

REFERENDUM is the process where a proposed state law or constitutional amendment, passed by the state legislature, is placed before the voters for approval or rejection. There are three sources of referenda: (a) a citizen petition (24 states permit citizen petitions), where the citizens may challenge an act of the legislature requiring a vote, before the challenged law goes into effect; (b) voluntary submission to the voters by the legislature of a proposed law; (c) constitutionally required submission by the legislature of a proposed law (usually a bond or tax issue) or a state constitutional amendment (required in all states except Delaware). Local governments are often required to use the referendum for charter reforms and tax and bond issues.

The use of the referendum to challenge an action of the state legislature was first adopted in South Dakota in 1898. The petition referendum suspends the legislation until a statewide vote of the electorate is held. In 1997, Ohio voters rejected a Worker's Compensation reform enacted by the legislature but challenged by a referendum petition circulated by the AFL-CIO in Ohio. The required number of signatures for a referendum challenge to legislation varies, but it is usually expressed as a percentage of the vote cast in a previous general election.

The elements of direct democracy—initiative, referendum, and recall, which are found in a number of state constitutions—were ideas promoted by the Progressive movement in the United States. *See*: INITIATIVE; PROGRESSIVE MOVEMENT; RECALL.

References: David Butler and Austin Ranney, *Referendums: A Comparative Study of Practice and Theory* (Washington, D.C.: American Enterprise, 1978); Council of State Governments, *The Book of the States: 1996–97* (Lexington, Ky.: Council of State Governments, 1996); David B. Magleby, *Direct Legislation: Voting on Ballot Propositions in the United States* (Baltimore, Md.: Johns Hopkins University Press, 1984); Joseph F. Zimmerman, "Civic Strategies for Community Empowerment," *National Civic Review* (May/June 1988).

REFORM PARTY is the political party created by Ross Perot for his second campaign for the presidency in 1996. In his second bid for the presidency, Perot made a serious effort to create a political party. On September 25, 1995, Perot announced that he was creating a new party, on *Larry King Live*. Perot argued that the polls showed that two out of three Americans wanted a new party, and he was responding to that call. The Perot forces made a major effort to get the Reform Party on every state ballot. It is estimated that Perot spent $6.7 million to get the Reform Party on the ballot in all 50 states. After they attained ballot access, the Reform Party held a two-weekend presidential nominating convention. The first session of the convention was held in Long Beach, California on August 11, 1996, and the second part was held in Valley Forge, Pennsylvania on August 18. The Reform Party used Internet and mail voting by party members to nominate its presidential candidate. In the nomination balloting, Ross Perot collected 27,833 votes to Governor Dick Lamm's 11,965 votes. In 1996, like 1992, Perot was unable to attract a viable vice-presidential nominee. In 1996 the Reform Party's vice-presidential candidate was economist Pat Choate. Unlike 1992, Perot did not use his own fortune to finance his campaign. He was entitled to $29 million from the Federal Election Commission. That amount was based on his vote in 1992. Perot and his Reform Party did not have the appeal that they had in 1992. The Reform Party nominee, Ross Perot, garnered only 8.5% of the vote in 1996.

Bob Dole brought a great deal of attention to the Perot candidacy by asking Perot to withdraw from the race and support Dole, in late October of 1996. In the 1996 campaign, Perot focused a great deal of his attention on campaign finance reform. The future role of the Reform Party is not clear. Third parties do not persist in American politics. *See*: ELECTIONS: 1996; PEROT, ROSS.

References: John C. Green and William C. Binning, "Surviving Perot: The Origins and Future of the Reform Party," in *Multiparty Politics in America*, Paul Herrnson and John Green, eds. (Lanham, Md.: Rowman & Littlefield, 1997); http.//www.reformparty.org.

REGISTRATION, VOTER is the process that a citizen must go through to be able to vote. Registration requirements vary by state. Voter registration is required to avoid election fraud. Every state requires registration except North Dakota. Voters were first required to register in Massachusetts in 1800. Voter registration became more common after the Civil War to avoid fraud. Voters are usually required to register to vote prior to the election; only four states permit election day registration.

In most states there is a residency requirement of some duration to register to vote. The 1970 Voting Rights Act Amendments set a maximum residency requirement of 30 days for federal elections. The Supreme Court, in *Dunn* v. *Blumstein* (1972), restricted the length of the residency requirement that states could impose on all elections to 30 days. Registration requirements are seen as a barrier to greater voter participation. *See*: MOTOR VOTER LAW; VOTER TURNOUT.

References: Steven J. Rosenstone and Raymond E. Wolfinger, "The Effect of Registration Laws on Voter Turnout," *American Political Science Review*, Vol. 72 (March 1978); Council of State Governments, *The Book of the States* (Lexington, Ky.: Council of State Governments, 1996).

RENO v. *BOSSIER PARISH SCHOOL BOARD*, 520 U.S. 471 (1997). In response to population changes recorded in the 1990 census, the Bossier Parish School Board redrew the lines of its voting districts. Because the Board was in an area covered by Section 5 of the Voting Rights Act of 1965, any proposed redistricting plans had to first be precleared by either the attorney general or the Federal District Court for the District of Columbia.

The Board eventually adopted the same redistricting plan that the attorney general had recently precleared for use by the parish's main governing body, the Bossier Parish Police Jury. Like the Police Jury plan, the redistricting scheme for the school board contained no districts in which a majority of the population was black. The attorney general, however, denied preclearance, citing an alternative redistricting plan developed by the NAACP which would have provided for the creation of two districts in which the majority of the population was black. This plan was not available to the attorney general when preclearance had been granted to the Jury plan. The school board argued that in failing to grant clearance to the proposed redistricting scheme, the attorney general had improperly invoked a legal standard under Section 5 of the Voting Rights Act which was only applicable under Section 2 of this Act. In order to understand this controversy, it is necessary to review these two sections of the Voting Rights Act.

Section 5 was placed in the Voting Rights Act to prevent a state or political subdivision from evading the spirit of the Act by repeatedly enacting racially biased voting laws which would remain in force until overturned by a court. Although preclearance is an effective means of accomplishing this purpose, it represents a significant federal intrusion into state lawmaking. Although federal judicial review of state lawmaking is quite common, Section 5 negates the requirement that someone actually challenge the law, and effectively makes the federal government a partner in state lawmaking. Because of its intrusiveness, Section 5 may only be used in certain areas which have exhibited a predisposition toward discriminatory voting practices. Moreover, the standards applied before granting preclearance are often quite lenient. Generally, a state or political subdivision need only prove "non-retrogression." That is, they must show that if the voting law is enacted, minority groups will somehow be placed in a less favorable electoral position. The comparison, therefore, is with the position of minority group voters prior to passage of the law.

Unlike Section 5, Section 2 of the Voting Rights Acts is applicable throughout the United States. A violation of Section 2, however, must be established through litigation. Since the risks to federalism raised by preclearance are not present under Section 2, however, it is easier to prove a violation of Section 2. A state or political subdivision may be found to be in violation of Section 2 of the Voting Rights Act if minority voting strength is "diluted" by a voting law. In order to establish dilution, a comparison is made not to previous voting systems but rather, to an ideal system.

In looking to the hypothetical plan proposed by the NAACP, the attorney general had used a Section 2 standard (comparison to and ideal "non-diluted" voting plan) to refuse preclearance under Section 5. Justice O'Connor, writing for a five-member majority in this case, asserted that the attorney general may not "replace the standards of Section 2 with those of Section 5." Although Justice O'Connor argued that evidence of the dilution of minority voting strength may remain relevant to a Section 5 inquiry, she concludes that "the link between dilutive impact and intent to retrogress is far from direct." *See: BEER* v. *U.S.* (1976); PRECLEARANCE; VOTING RIGHTS ACT.

REPUBLICAN NATIONAL COMMITTEE (RNC) was formed at the first presidential nominating convention of the Republican Party in June 1856. The convention adopted a resolution that a national committee, composed of one member from each state and territory, selected by the respective Republican state committees, would constitute the Republican National Committee for the ensuing four years. That committee met immediately after the convention and selected Edwin D. Morgan, from the state of New York, as the first national chairman.

The newly emergent RNC, like the Democratic National Committee, was responsible for financing and conducting the national campaign. Presidential candidates did not campaign for themselves; they relied on the national chairman and the party organizations to conduct their campaigns. It was not until the chairmanship of Will Hayes (1918–1921) that the RNC established permanent headquarters with paid staff. In 1996 the RNC reported a staff size of 250.

The current membership of the RNC continues to reflect the confederal character of the first committee. There is one national committeeman from each of the 50 states; also represented are: the District of Columbia, Guam, Puerto Rico, American Samoa, and the Virgin Islands, for a total of 55. There is one national committeewoman from each of those political-geographic units (adopted after the Nineteenth Amendment); and the party chair from each of them (adopted in 1968), for a total current membership of 165. There are a number of ex-officio members on the committee including party auxiliary units and representatives of various categories of elected officials.

The chairman and the co-chairman (who must be of the opposite sex) are elected by the RNC by a majority of the members present and voting. They are to be full-time, paid employees of the RNC. The officers are to be elected in January of each odd-numbered year. They can be removed from office by a two-thirds vote of the entire committee. There is an executive committee of the RNC, consisting of eleven members. Three are appointed by the chairman, and each of the four regional caucuses elects one man and one woman. The executive committee is empowered to exercise all of the functions of the RNC except: selecting officers, ratifying the election of members to the RNC, calling the national convention, and filling a vacancy for the party's candidate for president or vice-president. The various committees of the RNC are also confederal in their membership; for example, the Standing Committee on Rules must have one member from each state.

The RNC, like the DNC, has taken on the role of service provider to the candidates, since the candidates have taken control of their campaigns. The RNC has regained influence in national elections because it has been able to sucsfully raise a great deal of money, and develop new campaign technologies. According to John F. Bibby, the RNC's staff size has ranged in size from 200 to 600 since 1972. The RNC has been recognized for its innovations in direct mail fund-raising, and utilizing the latest professional campaign techniques. Two of the RNC's most heralded chairs for their organizational development skills were: Ray Bliss, who took the reigns of the party after Goldwater's defeat in 1964; and Bill Brock, who led the party after Gerald Ford's loss in 1976. Both these national chairmen focused on organizational development and the adoption of new campaign innovations. Of course, like the Democrats, when the Republicans control the White House, the president guides the committee in selecting a national chairman. In 1988, President George Bush encouraged the selection of the skillful Lee Atwater as the GOP chair after the successful 1988 campaign.

The RNC, in contrast to the more directive DNC, reflects its confederal character in dealing with its state party organizations. The RNC is able to coordinate state parties by providing them with financial aid, staff resources, and training. A good example of the RNC's approach in dealing with the Republican state parties is its effort to change the dates of the primaries. The Republicans were the only party to test the 1996 front-loaded primary calendar, and they were not pleased with the results. The party's frontrunner, Senator Bob Dole, was seriously damaged in the early contests, losing both New Hampshire and Arizona. The front-loaded primary does not permit other prospective candidates to enter the race if the frontrunner is fatally wounded. The RNC, under Chairman Haley Barbour, created a committee to study the primary calendar and recommended that many of the states move their primaries back into the Spring, as they had been in 1992. The way the RNC hopes to accomplish this is by offering the state parties the carrot of bonus convention delegates if they move their primaries. The chair of the committee that recommended the changes in the primary calendar was the RNC member from Colorado, Jim Nicholson, who was elected in 1997 to replace Haley Barbour, who stepped down. *See*: ATWATER, LEE; BARBOUR, HALEY; DEMOCRATIC NATIONAL COMMITTEE;

FRONT-LOADED PRIMARY; NATIONAL COMMITTEES; NICHOLSON, JAMES R.

References: John F. Bibby, *Politics, Parties, and Elections in America*, 3rd ed. (Chicago: Nelson-Hall, 1996); Committee on Rules and Order of Business of the 1996 Republican National Convention, *The Rules of the Republican Party* (August 12, 1996); Ralph M. Goldman, *The National Party Chairmen and Committees: Factionalism at the Top* (Armonk, N.Y.: M. E. Sharpe, 1990); Philip A. Klinker, *The Losing Parties: Out-Party National Committees, 1956–1993* (New Haven, Conn.: Yale University Press, 1994); Malcolm Moos, *The Republicans: A History of Their Party* (New York: Random House, 1956); Republican National Committee, 310 1st St., S.E., Washington, D.C. 20003; http://www.rnc.org.

REPUBLICAN PARTY is one of the two major political parties in the United States. It was founded in the 1850s by opponents of the expansion of slavery in response to the Kansas-Nebraska Act. The Republican Party eclipsed the Whig Party as one of the two major parties. In 1856 the Republicans nominated John C. Frémont, who was the party's first presidential nominee. Frémont lost to Democrat James Buchanan.

In 1860 the Republicans nominated Abraham Lincoln. They captured the presidency and both houses of Congress. That brought on the Civil War. For decades after the Civil War, the Republicans enjoyed electoral dominance in the North and the animus of the South.

At the end of the nineteenth century, under the leadership of President William McKinley, the Republican Party became a promoter of protectionism of the emerging industries in the North. The Republicans were the majority party until the Great Depression. In the 1930s, the Democrats became the majority party and their dominance lasted through the greater part of the twentieth century.

After World War II, the Republicans reemerged as a presidential party, capturing the White House in the 1950s with General Dwight D. Eisenhower, in the 1970s with Richard Nixon, and in the 1980s with Ronald Reagan and George Bush.

In the 1960s the party of Lincoln was divided over civil rights. The 1964 Republican nominee Barry Goldwater voted against the civil rights legislation, and the Republicans began to make inroads into the South. This sectoral realignment of the South was not complete until the 1990s.

The Republicans have long been the party of limited government, deregulation of the economy, promoters of capitalism, and a balanced budget. In the postwar years, it has promoted free trade.

The Republicans became the majority party in Congress in the stunning general election of 1994. Fifty-two new Republican members of Congress were elected. This was the first time the Republicans had taken a majority in the

House since 1952. The Republicans held their majorities in the House and Senate in the 1996 election. This was the first election in which a Republican majority had been reelected to the House since the 1920s. The architect of this surprising development was Newt Gingrich, who became the Speaker. The switch to the Republicans in the South has contributed significantly to the Republican majorities in Congress.

The political activism of fundamentalist, evangelical Christians has played a significant role in the recent electoral success of the Republican Party. There has been tension between the religious, social conservatives and the more libertarian, economic conservatives in the contemporary Republican Party. *See*: CHRISTIAN COALITION; CONTRACT WITH AMERICA; GINGRICH, NEWT(ON); GOLDWATER, BARRY M.; GOP; KANSAS-NEBRASKA ACT OF 1854; LINCOLN, ABRAHAM; MCKINLEY, WILLIAM; REALIGNMENT; NATIONAL COMMITTEES; SOUTHERN STRATEGY; WHIG PARTY.

References: William E. Gienapp, *The Origins of the Republican Party, 1852–1856* (New York: Oxford University Press, 1987); George H. Mayer, *The Republican Party, 1854–1964* (New York: Oxford University Press, 1964).

RETAIL POLITICS refers to person-to-person campaigning by the candidate. Retail politics has been practiced by presidential candidates in the early primaries and caucuses in Iowa and New Hampshire. In the years leading up to those early events, the candidates spent time in those two states, cultivating the party activists with personal contact. Bob Dole vacationed in New Hampshire in the summer before the 1996 primary. Dole was able to gain the endorsement of the county sheriffs in New Hampshire by personally contacting them. Lamar Alexander walked across a good part of the state, meeting voters. Steve Forbes ignored retail politics in those states and relied on expensive media buys. Emphasizing expensive media buys is referred to as wholesale politics.

RETROSPECTIVE VOTING is voter judgment based upon an evaluation about the past performance of the incumbent party, and then casting a vote based on that evaluation. If the government has performed well in the eyes of the voter, then the voter will vote for the incumbent party. If not, a voter will vote against the party that has been in office. Voters give particular attention to economic conditions. According to this theory, voters do not vote on future promises; they do not give mandates, but cast their vote on past performance.

The theory of retrospective voting is challenged by those who argue that party identification has become so weak in the United States that retrospective voting is not possible. Also, divided government makes it difficult to hold a particular party, and is responsible for recent economic and political conditions.

References: Morris P. Fiorina, *Retrospective Voting in American National Elections* (New Haven, Conn.: Yale University Press, 1981); V. O. Key, *The Responsible Electorate* (Cambridge, Mass.: Harvard University Press, 1966).

REVENUE ACT OF 1971 was signed by President Nixon in 1971. This law had two major provisions: (1) it instituted a check-off on the federal tax form for the funding of presidential elections and (2) it created the Presidential Election Campaign Fund which would provide subsidies to presidential candidates who met certain criteria commencing with the 1976 election. The actual check-offs began to be collected in 1973. The money from this check-off went directly to the candidate and not to the party. The federal fund would match contributions made to candidates seeking presidential nominations.

The Act devised a formula for distributing monies to major party candidates for their general election campaigns, which amounted to $62 million in 1996 for the general election. The amount of money is determined by multiplying the voting age population times the amount (it was fifteen cents at the time of the law), adjusted for inflation. That sum goes to the nominees of the parties that received more than 25% of the vote in the last presidential election. Parties that receive between 5% and 25% of the popular vote in the previous presidential election are eligible for an amount that is calculated as a percentage of the average vote received by the major party candidates. This formula was used to determine that Ross Perot was eligible to receive $30 million for the 1996 general election. Perot's amount was calculated based on the 19% of the vote he received in the 1992 election, against the average vote of the two major parties. Candidates that accept the federal money must also accept the other limiting regulations. They cannot accept any other donations.

The 1971 law also provided for tax credits and tax deductions for political contributions to encourage small donations. The Revenue Act of 1978 did away with the tax deduction and made the tax credit more generous. These tax provisions were repealed in 1986 and currently there is nothing in the federal tax code to encourage small donations. *See*: FEDERAL ELECTION CAMPAIGN ACT OF 1971 AND AMENDMENTS; MATCHING FUNDS; REVENUE ACT OF 1978.

Reference: Herbert E. Alexander, *Financing Politics: Money, Elections, and Political Reform*, 4th ed. (Washington, D.C.: Congressional Quarterly Press 1992).

REVENUE ACT OF 1978 was signed by President Jimmy Carter in November 1978. This law changed the tax deductions and credits for political contributions as defined in the Revenue Act of 1971. The Revenue Act of 1978 eliminated the deduction for political giving and doubled the maximum tax credit to $50 for an individual and $100 for a joint return. This credit was repealed in the Tax Reform Act of 1986. *See*: REVENUE ACT OF 1971.

References: Anthony Corrado, "Money and Politics: A History of Federal Campaign Finance Law," in *Campaign Finance Reform: A Sourcebook*, Anthony Corrado, Thomas E. Mann, Daniel R. Ortiz, Trevor Potter, and Frank J. Sorauf, eds. (Washington, D.C.: Brookings Institution, 1997).

REYNOLDS **v.** *SIMS*, 377 U.S. 533 (1964). This was the first case in which the U.S. Supreme Court held that the Equal Protection Clause of the Fourteenth Amendment required that states apportion both the lower *and* upper houses of their legislature in proportion to population. In *Baker* v. *Carr* (1962) the Supreme Court had declared that malapportionment was a fit subject for judicial review, and in *Wesberry* v. *Sanders* (1964) the Court held that federal congressional districts had to be substantially equal in population. The significance of this case lies in the extension of the principle of "one person, one vote" to state senate districts. Given that the U.S. Senate represents statehood and not population, prior to the Court's decision in *Reynolds* it was at least arguable that the principle of one person, one vote was only applicable to the lower house of a legislature. *See: BAKER* v. *CARR* (1962); *GRAY* v. *SANDERS* (1963); REAPPORTIONMENT; *WESBERRY* v. *SANDERS* (1964).

RIPON SOCIETY is a moderate Republican organization that lobbies for centrist positions in the Republican Party. The organization was founded in 1962 by graduate students on the East Coast. The organization supported the candidacy of Nelson A. Rockefeller for the Republican presidential nomination in 1962 and 1968. It adopted its name from the city of Ripon, Wisconsin, where it is claimed the Republican Party was founded. The Ripon Society challenged the delegate apportionment formula used for the Republican National Convention in federal court in 1976.

ROCKEFELLER, NELSON A. (1908–1979) served as governor of New York from 1958 to 1973, and as vice-president from 1973 to 1976. Nelson Rockefeller was a member of one of America's wealthiest families. After he graduated from Dartmouth College in 1930, Rockefeller served in the Franklin Roosevelt administration as assistant secretary of state for Latin America. Later he served in the Eisenhower administration as an undersecretary in the Department of Health, Education, and Welfare.

In 1958 he was elected governor of New York, defeating Averell Harriman. As governor, Rockefeller defined himself as a social liberal and a fiscal conservative. He was reelected governor three more times. He lost in three bids for the Republican presidential nomination. In 1973 he was appointed vice-president by Gerald Ford. Opposition by conservative Republicans forced Ford to drop Rockefeller from the 1976 GOP ticket and select Bob Dole. *See*: ELECTIONS: 1964, 1968, 1976.

Reference: James Underwood and William L. Daniels, *Governor Rockefeller in New York: The Apex of Pragmatic Liberalism in the U.S.* (Westport, Conn: Greenwood Press, 1982).

ROLL OFF is the drop in voter participation in election contests for offices that are lower on the ballot. For example, the vote cast for president might represent 95% of all voters who cast ballots in a county, while the vote for county recorder includes only 80% of the votes cast. That 15% loss is the roll off, or the voter fall off. In addition to the salience of the election contest, the roll off could be affected by the type of ballot used. The office block ballot appears to contribute to a higher rate of roll off than the party column ballot. The type of election device used also affects the rate of roll off; a paper ballot has less roll off than the voting machine. Voter fatigue sets in if it is a long ballot. *See*: BALLOT, LONG; BALLOT, OFFICE BLOCK; BALLOT, PARTY COLUMN.

ROMER, ROY (1928–   ) was elected general chairman of the Democratic National Committee on January 21, 1996. He was elected without opposition, because he was the choice of President Bill Clinton. At the time of his election Romer served as governor of Colorado.

Roy Romer was born October 31, 1928. He holds a bachelor's degree in agricultural economics from Colorado State, and a law degree from the University of Colorado. He served in the Colorado legislature from 1958 to 1966 and served as chief of staff of Colorado governor Lamm. He was elected governor of Colorado in 1986, and reelected in 1990 and 1994. He was co-chair of the Democratic Platform Committee in 1992 and worked closely with then Governor Bill Clinton on education issues in the National Governors' Association.

Romer shares the duties of party leadership with Massachusetts businessman and former state party chairman Steve Grossman. Prior to Romer's election the party leadership had been split between Senator Christopher Dodd of Connecticut, who served as general chairman, and Don Fowler who ran the day-to-day operations of the party. Roy Romer is seen as a centrist and conciliator. He is expected to serve the interests of President Bill Clinton and Vice-President Al Gore. Romer had to deal with the questions about illegal fund-raising by the DNC during the 1996 election. *See*: DEMOCRATIC NATIONAL COMMITTEE.

References: Alan Greenblatt and Ronald D. Elving, "Nicholson, Romer Picked to Lead National Committees," *Congressional Quarterly Weekly Report*, Vol. 55 (January 35, 1997); Marie Marmo Mullaney, *Biographical Directory of the Governors of the United States, 1988–1994* (Westport, Conn.: Greenwood Press, 1994).

ROOSEVELT, FRANKLIN D. (1882–1945). Four times elected president of the United States, serving longer in that office than any other man, his leadership tested in two of the twentieth century's greatest crises, depression and war,

Roosevelt has emerged as one of the preeminent historic figures of those 100 years claimed as the American Century. Born on January 30, 1882, of a family of wealth and privilege, part of New York's Hudson River aristocracy, Roosevelt was educated by tutors at the family estate, Hyde Park, later at Groton, and subsequently at Harvard, from which he graduated in 1900. Having attended Columbia Law School, Roosevelt was admitted to the state bar in 1907; he joined one of New York City's most prestigious law firms and was placed in the office's admiralty division. Marrying his fifth cousin, Anna Eleanor Roosevelt on March 7, 1905, not dependent upon the law for his livelihood, the young Roosevelt looked to a future career in politics, perhaps influenced by another relative, "Uncle Ted," who happened to be, at the time, president of the United States. When, five years later, Roosevelt was first to run for office, he chose not the party of Theodore Roosevelt, but the Democratic Party, his own father having been a Grover Cleveland Democrat and "Uncle Ted," by 1910, about to take up a political insurgency which would, briefly, alienate him from the Republican Party. Election year 1910 was one of Democratic Party successes in New York and New Jersey. In the former, Democrats captured control of the state legislature, including a seat from a heretofore "safe Republican" Senate district, which sent 28-year-old Franklin Roosevelt to Albany. In New Jersey, reform Democrat and retiring president of Princeton University, Woodrow Wilson, was elected governor. By common cause, if not by personal relationship, Roosevelt became a Wilsonian, and although reelected to the state senate in 1912, resigned the following year to accept appointment by Woodrow Wilson, now president of the United States, as assistant secretary of the navy, a position once held by "Uncle Ted." Even though the United States had been, since the Spanish-American War of 1898, a rising naval power, Franklin Roosevelt's tenure at the Navy Department would no doubt have been unremarkable but for U.S. entry into World War I on April 6, 1917. The assistant secretary's particular contribution to the war effort was his proposal, later implemented, for a North Sea "mine barrage," a 240-mile cordon of anti-submarine mines aimed at the reduction of allied shipping losses. Attention given to Roosevelt was sufficient that at the 1920 San Francisco convention, Roosevelt, of the famous name, was given the vice-presidential nomination, running with Ohio governor James M. Cox, at the head of the ticket. While Democrats across the nation were buried in the "return to normalcy" election results of that year, Roosevelt emerged as a promising figure for the future of the party. Defending the record of the Wilson administration, arguing for U.S. participation in the League of Nations, Roosevelt conducted a vigorous campaign roundly applauded by party leaders. Within a year, however, Roosevelt's political career was to receive a gut-wrenching blow. While on vacation at the family's summer home on Campobello Island off the Maine coast, Roosevelt was stricken with polio. All but retiring from politics, he was to spend the next several years in physical therapy attempting to recover use of his lower limbs, an attempt that was only partially successful. Roosevelt would live the rest of his days in a wheelchair, relying upon heavy leg braces to stand, and the use of crutches to walk short distances. In an age of more restrained media coverage, public attention was not drawn to Roosevelt's disability. Photographers and newsreel cameramen were particularly sensitive, and accommodating, to Roosevelt's physical condition, so much so that large numbers of Americans, even through his presidential years, were not aware of the extent of his disability. His recovery courageous but slow, led Roosevelt to be reluctant to accept the argument of Governor Al Smith, Democratic Party presidential candidate in 1928, that, to strengthen the ticket in New York State, Roosevelt should run as Smith's successor in the gubernatorial race. Ultimately drawn into the contest, Roosevelt emerged, by a narrow margin, as one of the few Democrats surviving the Hoover landslide; Smith, himself, to his great disappointment, failed to carry New York State. Roosevelt's first two-year term as governor was marked by stalemate with the Republican-controlled legislature. Reelected in 1930 with a 725,000 vote plurality, with reduced Republican majorities in the legislature, and with economic depression deepening both in the state and across the nation, Roosevelt turned to pressing questions of policy development to provide for emergency relief, unemployment compensation, and job creation through public works programs, all of which would come to prove a training ground for meeting the larger challenges that would come in 1933. Almost immediately following the 1930 election-day victory, Roosevelt and certain of his closest political advisors such as Louis Howe and Jim Farley began to turn their attention to the national scene and to the securing of the 1932 Democratic presidential nomination. Governor of the nation's most populous state, with his vote-getting ability proven, Roosevelt would have seemed a shoo-in as his party's choice. In fact, the New York governor had an unusually difficult time in securing the nomination: (1) in part, because of the candidacy of the 1928 presidential nominee, Al Smith, former governor and former friend; (2) in part, because of the rule then in effect at Democratic national conventions requiring a two-thirds vote of the delegates in order for a nomination to be won. Not until striking a deal with the Texas delegation assuring John Nance Garner, Speaker of the House, the vice-presidential candidacy did Roosevelt nail down his own fourth-ballot nomination. Concluding that the tidal wave of anti-Republican, anti-Hoover sentiment, evident throughout the country and fostered by the continuing downward spiral of the economy, was sufficient to insure a landslide Democratic victory, Roosevelt waged a strenuous, but issue-cautious campaign. While in his July acceptance speech at the Chicago convention he promised ''a New Deal for the American people,'' his message of recovery and reform on the fall campaign trail was often surprisingly conventional, as in his Pittsburgh speech of October 19, 1932, when he promised reduced governmental spending and a balanced budget, attacking Hoover for contributing to the nation's failure to lift itself out of the depression by his reckless spending schemes and resulting budget deficits. The election-day result, a foregone conclusion, produced not only a Roosevelt presidential landslide, but overwhelming Democratic majorities in House and Senate, and heretofore unmatched party victories across the country, from state capitol to county courthouse. The presidential vote gave the Democratic national ticket a seven-million-vote plurality, Roosevelt-Garner carrying 42 states with 472 Electoral College ballots to but 6 states and 59 votes in the Electoral College for the Republicans. In the four-month interregnum before the March inauguration the economic crisis, particularly in banking, dramatically worsened. Roosevelt, with the great national emergency before him, on March 4, 1933 promised and subsequently was able to deliver upon a hundred days of unprecedented executive department activism. This was designed not simply to meet the immediate crisis in banking, but, as the corps of New Dealers saw it, to save by measures of regulation and reform the economic system, the collapse of which threatened, as well, the established political and constitutional system. Congress was charged in the inaugural address with responsibility for acting quickly and positively on yet unnamed measures, followed by a stern presidential warning which from the assembled crowd drew long and enthusiastic applause,

But in the event that Congress shall fail . . . and in the event that the national emergency is still critical, I shall not evade the clear course of duty that will then confront me. I shall ask Congress for the one remaining instrument to meet the crisis—broad Executive power to wage a war against the emergency, as great as the power that would be given to me if we were in fact invaded by a foreign foe.

Democrats in Congress chose not to fail, but to follow the president: the Emergency Banking Act, the Economy Act, establishment of the Civilian Conservation Corps, the Federal Emergency Relief Act, the Agricultural Adjustment Act, the Emergency Farm Mortgage Act, the Tennessee Valley Authority Act, the Truth-in-Securities Act, the Home Owners' Loan Act, the National Industrial Recovery Act, the Glass-Steagall Banking Act, the Farm Credit Act, and the Railroad Coordination Act; this astounding package of legislation proposed by the executive branch, passed by the legislative branch, took but 104 days, from March 4 to adjournment of the Seventy-third Congress on June 15, 1933. While other significant New Deal legislation would follow later, such as the Social Security Act of 1935, it was the aforementioned package that was to permanently redefine both the scope and weight of national government power and of presidential dominance within the federal system. Putting aside any evaluation of policy result, it was this unparalleled demonstration of an activist, confident, presidential leadership which the American people applauded, and overwhelmingly accepted. Renominated by acclamation at the Democratic convention of 1936, Roosevelt was to be reelected just shy of acclamation: Roosevelt-Garner ran up an unprecedented plurality of more than 11 million votes, carried 46 of the 48 states with 523 ballots in the Electoral College. Only Maine and Vermont supported the Republican ticket of Governor Alf Landon of Kansas and running mate Frank Knox of Illinois, giving the GOP but 8 Electoral College votes. It was the high tide of the New Deal, and perhaps in the resulting ebullience, misleading to Roosevelt and his key advisors. Disgruntled by Supreme Court decisions which had struck down as unconstitutional key provisions in certain pieces of New Deal legislation, Roosevelt, on February 5, 1937, proposed a "reform" of the Court which would allow an expansion of its membership, thereby permitting the president to nominate adequate numbers of New Dealers, provided they secured Senate confirmation, to overcome the Court's perceived conservative majority. Reaction, surprisingly negative given Roosevelt's mandate of three months earlier, was swift in coming; objection not simply from congressional Republicans who were too few in number to matter, but from moderate and conservative Democrats, who, in the House, and particularly in the Senate, did matter. The great confrontation between president and Court burned brightly through the spring of 1937, but ended as, one of Roosevelt's biographers has paraphrased, "not with a bang but a whimper"; the president realized that from within his own party he did not have the votes needed to prevail. For the first time since Inauguration Day in 1933, Roosevelt, on a major issue, had been thwarted. From this point, far more often than not he would continue to win legislative victories, but never again with the same absolute assurance, and never again without the actual possibility of defeat. The latter possibility was made more real by two results of the mid-term congressional elections of 1938: (1) Roosevelt's failed attempt to selectively purge from the party, in Democratic primary elections, perceived anti–New Deal, conservative Democrats; (2) the resurgence of the Republican congressional party with GOP seats in the House increasing from 88 to 170, in the Senate from 17 to 25. Thus, as of 1937, there was once again on Capitol Hill a functioning political opposition, a phenomenon which the president had not heretofore experienced. Not only was the political world at home changed for Roosevelt; it changed too in the larger world as the Fascist threat in Europe and the Japanese threat in the Pacific grew increasingly ominous. In no small part, as the presidential election of 1940 approached, and the third-term question begged, Roosevelt's concerns, day-by-day, became more ones of national defense and foreign affairs than of further New Deal initiatives in domestic policy. By whatever combination of reasons—a sense of duty in the face of pending international crisis, concern with his place in history, personal ambition and indulgence in the sheer joy of politics—Roosevelt resolved in the affirmative the third, and ultimately the fourth, term question. Neither the 1940 or 1944 elections were, however, to repeat the party sweep and the personal acclamation of the earlier victories. In both instances Roosevelt and the Democrats, facing substantial challenge, were to prevail, but the contests were hard fought and the president was to see his popular vote plurality over the Republican competition decline from 11 million votes in 1936 to 5 million in 1940, to 3.5 million in 1944. The Electoral College count in both election years, however, remained overwhelmingly Democratic: in 1940, Roosevelt and vice-presidential nominee, Secretary of Agriculture Henry A. Wallace of Iowa, carried 38 states and 449 ballots to 10 states and 82 votes for the Republican ticket of Wendell L. Willkie of Indiana and New

York, with his running mate Senator Charles L. McNary of Oregon; in 1944, the president and the third of his running mates, Senator Harry S. Truman of Missouri, carried 36 states and 432 Electoral College votes to 12 states and 99 ballots for the Republicans, governors Thomas E. Dewey of New York and John W. Bricker of Ohio. The third term once won became an exercise in leading both members of Congress and the American people, many of whom held strongly isolationist views, first to preparation for war and, after December 7, 1941, to the waging of war. The staggering demands of war leadership—forging and maintaining the Grand Alliance with Great Britain and the Soviet Union; historic meetings with Churchill and Stalin at Teheran in 1943 and Yalta in 1945; all the while more routinely paving the way for Allied military victory and an immediate postwar period to be marked by establishment of the United Nations—took an enormous personal toll on Roosevelt. The winter and spring of 1944–1945 were particularly strenuous; inauguration on January 20, 1945, the long journey to the Russian Crimea in February, the report to Congress on the Yalta Conference on March 1. A month later a war-weary president, in visibly declining health, left Washington for his vacation retreat at Warm Springs, Georgia; there, the afternoon of April 12th, 1945, Franklin D. Roosevelt, age 63, died of a cerebral hemorrhage. Amidst unprecedented national mourning the funeral train returned Roosevelt's body first to Washington and the White House then to the family estate at Hyde Park in New York for burial. *See*: ELECTIONS: 1920, 1932, 1936, 1940, 1944.

References: James MacGregor Burns, *Roosevelt*, 2 vols. (New York: Harcourt, Brace, Jovanovich, 1956–1970); Kenneth S. Davis, *FDR*, 4 vols. to date (New York: Putnam's; Random House, 1971–1993); Frank Freidel, *Franklin D. Roosevelt, A Rendezvous with Destiny* (Boston: Little, Brown, 1990); Arthur M. Schlesinger, Jr., *The Age of Roosevelt*, 3 vols. (Boston: Houghton Mifflin, 1957–1960).

ROOSEVELT, THEODORE (1858–1919) was born of a wealthy, socially prominent New York family on October 27, 1858. Harvard educated, graduating in 1880, Roosevelt attended Columbia Law School but neither completed his study there nor chose to adopt the law as a career. Elected as a Republican to the New York legislature at age 23, Roosevelt served there until 1884. Suffering the death of both his first wife and of his mother on the same day, February 14, 1884, Roosevelt, seeking restoration in the strenuous life, took on a cowboy's existence at his ranch, Chimney Butte, on the Little Missouri River in the Dakotas. Often spending twelve hours a day in the saddle, Roosevelt was to become a convert to, and then an ardent advocate of, the rigorous outdoor life, a commitment he would hold throughout his life. Returning east in 1886, Roosevelt ran, unsuccessfully, for mayor of New York City, where a decade later he was to serve as chairman of the city's police commission from 1895 to 1897. From the very beginning of Roosevelt's political career he staked out a claim as a reformer opposed to machine politics, particularly the machine's practices of job patronage, contract favoritism, and tolerance of government corruption, including police graft. His opposition to the machine was generic, whether Tammany Hall of the Democrats, or the Republican organizations of Roscoe Conkling, or later, Thomas Platt. In this period, Roosevelt also came to have exposure on the national scene, appointed to the U.S. Civil Service Commission by President Harrison in 1889; he was reappointed by Democrat Grover Cleveland in 1893. While serving as commissioner, Roosevelt promoted the following: extension of civil service employment within the federal bureaucracy, thereby reducing the number of jobs available for "spoils" distribution; development and use of the civil service exam for purposes of hiring and promotion; and enlargement of federal government job opportunities for women. Later, at the national level, Roosevelt was to accept appointment by President McKinley as assistant secretary of the navy (1897). As friction with Spain over conditions in Cuba increased, Roosevelt became a "war hawk," often critical of his own president, privately disparaging, as he perceived it, McKinley's timidity and reluctance to take the nation to war. When war came in April of 1898, Roosevelt resigned from the Navy Department, organized a volunteer cavalry regiment which would become known as "the Rough Riders," and accepted the rank of lieutenant colonel. It was of course Roosevelt's leading of the charge of "the Rough Riders" at San Juan Hill in the battle for the capture of the Cuban port of Santiago, along with Admiral Dewey's naval victory at Manila Bay, that captured through the jingoistic press the nation's attention, making popular heroes of both the admiral and the colonel. At the end of the four-month war, the United States being left with a modest empire stretching from Puerto Rico in the Caribbean to the Philippine Islands in the far Pacific, Roosevelt returned to New York and the practice of politics, being narrowly elected that November to the state's governorship. Hardly settled into office, Roosevelt found himself being promoted by Senator Thomas Platt and the New York Republican machine as a candidate for the vice-presidency. Boss Platt and other of New York's leading Republicans, particularly in the business community, finding the new governor unpredictable and unmanageable, concluded that the perfect burial for Roosevelt would be in the political cemetery that was the vice-presidency, an opening on the national ticket having resulted from the death of Vice-President Garret A. Hobart on November 21, 1899. Despite the strong reservations of Senator Mark A. Hanna of Ohio, Republican National Committee chairman and President McKinley's close friend and ally, the New York governor became the first-ballot vice-presidential choice of delegates at the party's national convention in June of 1900. With McKinley assuming the role of an incumbent president, "above the partisan fray," Roosevelt was given the task of embarking on a national campaign tour in behalf of the ticket, an assignment thoroughly enjoyed by the energetic governor. The November Republican victory, in a time of prosperity and with a victorious war recently won, was decisive: McKinley-Roosevelt, with a popular vote plurality of nearly 900,000 over the Democratic ticket of William Jennings Bryan of Nebraska and former vice-president Adlai

E. Stevenson of Illinois, carried 28 states with 292 Electoral College ballots to 17 states and 155 votes in the Electoral College for the Democrats. Within six months of inauguration day (March 4, 1901), as Mark Hanna had feared, "that damned cowboy" became president, made so by an assassin's bullet fired on September 6, 1901, while President McKinley was visiting the Pan-American Exposition at Buffalo, New York, an assault which led to the president's death one week later on September 14. While pledging a strict continuation of McKinley administration policies, Roosevelt yet managed to put his own stamp on the remainder of the term, and that stamp, to the consternation of the Republican "Old Guard," was clearly reformist and progressive. Attorney General Philander Knox was directed to pursue the government's case against the Northern Securities Company, an elaborate railroad trust controlled by E. H. Harriman and J. P. Morgan; a trust that the government argued acted in restraint of trade in violation of provisions of the Sherman Anti-trust Act of 1890. With the government prevailing before the U.S. Supreme Court in 1904, Roosevelt's reputation as a "trust buster" who would take on, as he was later to put it, "the malefactors of great wealth," was firmly established. On the foreign policy front, the new president's nationalism prevailed as he added the Roosevelt Corollary to the Monroe Doctrine of 1823: that the United States would itself militarily intervene in Latin American countries if it were to prevent, thereby, the kind of foreign intrusion prohibited by the longstanding Doctrine. To give substance to the Corollary, and to meet the new responsibilities of the United States in the Caribbean and the Pacific, Roosevelt urged safeguarding of American military power, particularly that of the navy. This emphasis on a strong military posture became popularly identified as expressing Roosevelt's "speak softly and carry a big stick" dictum. In demonstration of this, Roosevelt, frustrated in the attempt to reach agreement with Columbia for the rights to construct a canal across the Isthmus of Panama, promoted the Panamanian Revolution of 1903 which resulted in the establishment of an independent state on the isthmus and one with which the United States quickly concluded an agreement for the building of a canal connecting the Atlantic and Pacific Oceans, a vital link serving American commercial and military interests. Nominated in 1904 for his own term in the presidency, with Senator Charles W. Fairbanks of Indiana as his running mate, Roosevelt was to achieve an election-day victory of historic proportions; the popular vote plurality for the Republican ticket soaring to more than 2.5 million votes over Democrats Alton B. Parker of New York and Henry G. Davis of West Virginia. In the Electoral College, the Republican total stood at 336 ballots from 32 states to 13 states and 140 votes for the Democrats. With his election mandate behind him, Roosevelt was, over the next four years, to turn progressively left. A wide variety of economic regulatory and social welfare measures were signed into law, among which were the Hepburn Act of 1906, revitalizing the Interstate Commerce Commission and granting it authority to set railroad rates; and the Pure Food and Drug Act, also of 1906, establishing federal government inspection and authorization procedures. Roosevelt, adding to his reputation as a conservationist, was able to see during his presidency a doubling of the number of national parks in the United States and the addition of more than 125 million acres to the national forest reserves. With regard to foreign and military policy (1905–1909), Roosevelt emphasized the new role of the United States as one of the world's major powers, in a demonstration of which, and in the face of congressional reservations, the president sent the navy's great White Fleet on a circumnavigation of the globe, showing the American flag and U.S. naval might to the world. Personal recognition in the field of international politics also came to the president as he mediated a conclusion to the Russo-Japanese War of 1904–1905, achieving for his endeavor the Nobel Peace Prize of 1906. As the presidential election of 1908 approached, Roosevelt, with some reluctance, concluded that the unwritten constitutional precedent of a two-term limitation on presidential service, as established by Washington, applied, if not technically at least practically, to his situation. He was, however, anxious to influence the selection of his successor; not wishing the Republican nomination to go to Vice-President Fairbanks, who was the probable choice of the party "Old Guard," he advanced, successfully, the cause of his friend and political associate, Secretary of War William Howard Taft of Ohio, in whose hands he felt the progressive legacy of his administration would be safe. Leaving the country almost immediately following Taft's presidential inauguration on March 4, 1909, Roosevelt went first on safari to Africa, subsequently traveling the grand circuit of European capitals where he was acclaimed everywhere, meeting with reigning monarchs and political leaders as if his tour were that of an official state visit. Returning to the port of New York in June of 1910, the former president was given a hero's welcome. While out of the country and receiving reports from home, Roosevelt had become increasingly dismayed with the record of the Taft administration and the conservative course he perceived it to be pursuing. The two old friends, Taft and Roosevelt, were soon to become new, and bitter, enemies. Outlining, in a speech given in Osawatomie, Kansas in August of 1910, a broad program of social and political reform which he labeled, "the New Nationalism," Roosevelt began his gradual, frequently denied campaign to challenge President Taft for the 1912 Republican nomination. In a rancorous, highly divisive convention, Taft forces, controlling the party organization, captured a first-ballot renomination for the incumbent president, even as Roosevelt arrived in Chicago the clear winner among Republican voters participating in the thirteen presidential primary elections of that year. Claiming that Taft forces had "stolen" the nomination from "the people," Roosevelt and his supporters bolted the Republican cause, forming, out of the existing progressive movement, the "Bull Moose Party," a party that by acclamation at a hurriedly convened August convention gave its presidential nomination to Roosevelt, naming California Governor Hiram W. Johnson as his vice-presidential running mate. Democrats, sensing the high probability of victory over a factionalized Republican Party, nominated an unusually strong national ticket: the reform governor of New Jersey, Woodrow Wilson, as candidate for president and Governor Thomas R. Marshall of Indiana as candidate for vice-president. For Roosevelt the campaign became a crusade, taking its theme from his acceptance speech, "we stand at Armageddon, and we battle for the Lord." Arguing for "an honest and efficient political and industrial democracy," Roosevelt urged a further democratization of American politics, strict governmental regulation of monopolies, and enactment of a host of social welfare and labor measures. His message, however appealing, lacked the needed support of an established grassroots organization. Election day produced the widely anticipated Democratic Party victory: Wilson, securing 41.8% of the total presidential vote cast, carried 40 states with 435 Electoral College ballots; Roosevelt with 27.4% of the vote carried 6 states and 88 votes in the Electoral College, President Taft, running last in the three-way contest, carried but 2 states with their 8 ballots in the Electoral College, having received 23.2% of the total presidential vote. Additionally, some 900,000 American voters cast ballots for Socialist Party candidate Eugene V. Debs. Roosevelt, returning to the Republican Party by 1916, campaigned vigorously but unsuccessfully against the reelection of Woodrow Wilson. With his pronounced anti-German views, Roosevelt was highly critical of Wilson's neutrality policy which, until April of 1917, kept the United States from involvement in World War I. Even with American entry into the war, and while fully supporting the war effort, Roosevelt maintained an unrelenting drumbeat of criticism directed toward Wilson's war leadership. Preparing for, as he put it, "the one last fight left in me," Roosevelt looked forward to the Republican presidential nomination of 1920. Such, however, was not to be. In failing health, never recovering from his son Quentin's death in a wartime flying mission over France, Roosevelt, age 61, died in his sleep of a coronary embolism on January 6, 1919, at his Oyster Bay, New York estate, Sagamore Hill. *See*: ELECTIONS: 1900, 1904, 1912; McKINLEY, WILLIAM.

References: John Morton Blum, *The Republican Roosevelt*, 2nd ed. (Cambridge: Harvard University Press, 1977); H. W. Brands, *T.R.: The Last Romantic* (New York: Basic Books, 1997); Lewis L. Gould, *The Presidency of Theodore Roosevelt* (Lawrence: University Press of Kansas, 1991); Theodore Roosevelt, *An Autobiography* (New York: Macmillan, 1913).

RUNOFF is an election that requires a majority. If no candidate receives a majority on the first ballot, then a second election is held between the two top candidates. The winner can claim to have the support of the majority. The runoff is frequently required in southern primaries. In 1988, Arizona adopted the runoff provision for the general election of the governor. The threshold requirement that requires a runoff may be less than 50%; the New York City Democratic primary requires a runoff if the leading candidate's vote is less than 40%. Tennessee requires a runoff only in the unlikely case of a tie. *See*: PLURALITY; PRIMARY, RUNOFF.

Reference: Charles S. Bullock III and Loch K. Johnson, *Runoff Elections in the United States* (Chapel Hill: University of North Carolina Press, 1992).

RUTAN **v.** *REPUBLICAN PARTY OF ILLINOIS,* 497 U.S. 62 (1990) is a political patronage case in which the Supreme Court virtually outlawed the use of party affiliation as a basis for state employment decisions. This case is significant because it covered not only hiring practices, but also decisions on whether to promote, transfer, or recall laid-off workers.

Republican governor James Thompson of Illinois had issued an executive order requiring a state hiring freeze to which only he could make exceptions. The result was that the governor's office controlled the hiring, transfer, promotion, and recall of most Illinois state employees. There was evidence that when the governor's office considered job requests under the freeze provision, it investigated the party affiliation of the employee or prospective employee. Several current and prospective employees challenged the actions of the governor's office. The Supreme Court ruled against Governor Thompson and the Republican Party.

Justice Brennan, writing for the majority, concluded that penalizing individuals—even if that penalty only amounted to withholding a promotion or a transfer—because of their failure to support a particular political party violated the freedom of association rights guaranteed by the First Amendment. *See:* ASSESSMENT; PATRONAGE.

S

SAFE SEATS are legislative districts in which the incumbent is almost guaranteed reelection. If the incumbent garners over 55% of the vote, then his/her seat is considered safe. The minority party has virtually no chance of gaining the seat. In 1996 nine Republican and six Democratic incumbents had no major party opposition in the general election. Those are very safe seats. Safe seats are also seats where one party is virtually guaranteed to win. The Center for Voting and Democracy points out that only one in five U.S. House seats are won by less than 10%. The Center calls this "monopoly politics" because there is so little competition in most congressional districts.

In 1998, almost 100 congressional districts were not contested by one of the major political parties. *See*: MARGINAL SEAT; TARGETING.

References: Center for Voting and Democracy, http://www.igc.org/cvd; Juliana Gruenwald and Deborah Kalb, "GOP Likely to Yield Seats But Still Control House," *Congressional Quarterly: Weekly Report*, Vol. 54 (September 28, 1996).

SAMPLE. The sample is the key element to successful public opinion polling. A sample is a part, or a subset of the population, whose opinion the pollster is attempting to reflect by the results. In order to conduct a poll the pollster needs a target population. In preelection polls the target population is registered voters, preferably likely voters. The statistical procedures of probability theory are applied to select the sample (subset) of the target population. The pollster will use a random method of selection, usually with the help of a computer to insure that everyone in the target population has an equal chance of being selected. Random-digit dialing is the predominant method of sampling for election surveys. Those who are selected are called respondents, and are usually contacted by phone and given assurance that no harm will come from their participation in the survey. The results of the survey will have a margin of error, reported as plus or minus some small percentage, usually plus or minus 3 or 4%. Since everyone in the target population was not surveyed, but only a sample on that population, the margin of error reflects the chance of error in the findings of the poll. The larger the sample the lower the margin of error.

When polling started, because of the small sample size of polls, usually less than 2,000 for a national poll, and less than 1,000 for a congressional or countywide poll, politicians were reluctant to accept the results of the polls. In recent years most politicians are believers in polls, and every major campaign has a pollster who has a significant role in crafting a campaign. Officeholders, particularly the president, frequently have polls taken, and the poll results appear to have an impact on public policy decisions. *See*: POLL.

Reference: Michael W. Traugott and Paul J. Lavrakas, *The Voter's Guide to Election Polls* (Chatham, N.J.: Chatham House, 1996).

SCOTT, WINFIELD (1786–1866), serving seven presidents as general-in-chief of the U.S. Army (1841–1861), the last three as lieutenant general, the only officer after Washington and before Grant to be given that rank, Winfield Scott became in 1852 the last presidential nominee of the Whig Party. Born on June 13, 1786, at "Laurel Branch," the family estate near Petersburg, Virginia, the young Scott, after a year at the College of William and Mary, took up the study of law, being admitted to the Virginia bar in 1806. Soon, however, Scott opted for a military career, returning only occasionally to civilian law practice (1807–1812). Posted to upstate New York during the War of 1812, Scott received a hero's attention for his courageous leadership of troops at the battle of Lundy's Lane on June 25, 1814. Brevetted at the rank of major general, Scott became commanding general, Eastern Command in 1817, an assignment which he held until 1841 when, at the death of Major General Alexander Macomb, he was promoted to general-in-chief of the U.S. Army. In the 32 years separating the end of the War of 1812 and the beginning of hostilities with Mexico in 1846, Scott was not, other than for the Second Seminole War, a participant in the Indian wars of the period. He was drawn in, however, to one of the saddest episodes in American history, the forced migration in 1838 of thousands of Cherokees from their homes and lands in southeastern United States, under authority of the Jackson administration's Indian Removal Act of 1830. While Scott ordered humane treatment by the military of the Cherokees as they were moved west of the Mississippi River, the mission was not a successful one; thousands of displaced Cherokees suffered illness and death along what became known as the "Trail of Tears." As war became imminent in Texas, Scott sought assignment there. President Polk, aware of the Whig disposition of both Scott and General Zachary Taylor, and equally aware of their likely recruitment to presidential politics should one or the other, or both, become successful in the southwest, searched for a "Democrat" general of equal stature, or, failing that, using his "Whig" generals, playing one off against the other. As the war unfolded, Polk's worst political fears were realized: both generals became national heroes; Taylor with the battle of Buena Vista, Scott with the capture of Mexico City. And indeed, in time, both officers were recruited by the Whig Party; Taylor, successfully, in the presidential election of 1848; Scott failing of success in 1852. Scott, long ambitious for the executive office, had entertained hope for Whig nominations in each election cycle since 1836. Throughout his career, however, Winfield Scott had nurtured a capacity, by word or pen, for giving offense, often making enemies of brother or superior officers, of secretaries of war, even of presidents. Some of the resulting incidents became serious: the court-martial of 1810; the courts of inquiry in 1836 and 1848; the strained relations with Presidents Jackson and Polk. Hence Scott saw the nominations he coveted go instead to General Harrison in 1840, to Clay in 1844, and to General Taylor in 1848. As the election of 1852 approached, Whig leadership revisited the party's one successful formula in presidential politics, the nomination of a national military hero; the sole surviving possibility in that year was the problematic Winfield Scott. The general's nomination, however, was not easily engineered, taking place on the convention's fifty-third ballot on June 18, 1852. Those who had been instrumental in bringing about the Scott nomination, such as Thurlow Weed and William H. Seward of New York, hoped to hold Scott to a vow of silence. Almost immediately, however, Scott broke loose from his handlers, indicating his unqualified support of the Whig platform, among its planks a statement offering endorsement of the Compromise of 1850. It was in regard to this latter commitment, particularly enforcement of the Fugitive Slave Act, that party leaders, not wishing to offend "Conscience Whigs," had anticipated a quick, quiet burial for the platform. They had not allowed for Winfield Scott's penchant for "putting his foot in it." The Whig ticket of Scott and vice-presidential nominee, Secretary of the Navy William A. Graham of North Carolina, went down to resounding defeat: carrying only 4 states with 42 Electoral College ballots, the Whigs trailed Democratic presidential nominee Franklin Pierce of New Hampshire and running mate Senator William R. King of Alabama by more than 200,000 votes, the Democrats carrying 27 states and 254 votes in the Electoral College. While collecting some 150,000 popular votes, the Free-Soilers, now known as the Free Democrats, with a national ticket of Senator John P. Hale of New Hampshire and George W. Julian of Indiana, had little effect on the election outcome, winning neither a state nor an Electoral College ballot. With the election behind him, Scott, who had declined to resign from his army post during the campaign, continued his military career. He was within the decade to make perhaps his most important contribution to the nation: advising President Lincoln during the secession crisis of 1861; raising and preparing Union forces for the coming war. Foreseeing prolonged hostilities, Scott urged on the Lincoln administration adoption of the Anaconda Plan: Union military control of the Ohio and Mississippi rivers, thus separating the main body of Confederate states from Texas and the West; intercession of supply lines to those southeastern states by an ever-tightening naval blockade. Aged, weary of the burden, subject to the criticism and machinations of junior officers, Scott, at 75, retired from active service in November of 1861. In retirement, he traveled to France, wrote his *Memoirs* (published in 1864), and, in full dress uniform, age 78, paid his final respects to the assassinated Lincoln as the body lay in state in New York City in April of 1865. The Civil War was over, and so was the life of the lieutenant general; Scott died on May 29, 1866, at West Point. *See*: ELECTIONS: 1852.

References: John S. D. Eisenhower, *Agent of Destiny: The Life and Times of General Winfield Scott* (New York: The Free Press, 1997); Charles W. Elliott, *Winfield Scott, the Soldier and the Man* (New York: Macmillan, 1937).

SEVENTEENTH AMENDMENT is a 1913 amendment to the U.S. Constitution that provided for the direct election of U.S. Senators. Prior to this amendment, U.S. Senators had been selected by state legislatures.

SEYMOUR, HORATIO (1810–1886). Farmer and businessman, wartime governor of the state of New York (1862–1864), perhaps the most reluctant candidate for president ever nominated by a major political party, Seymour was born on May 31, 1810 at Pompey Hill, New York. Reading the law in Utica, Seymour was admitted to the bar in 1832. Soon thereafter, however, Seymour found that management responsibilities for the extensive landholdings and investments which he had acquired, both by inheritance and marriage, made the routine practice of law impossible. Perhaps it was these same responsibilities that, while much interested in political affairs, made Seymour the most occasional and reluctant of office seekers. Politically well connected, Seymour's father having been part of Martin Van Buren's "Albany Regency," it is not astonishing that New York's fractious Democratic Party should have viewed the young Seymour as intended for a promising political career. Only occasionally, however, did Seymour answer the party's call, serving as military assistant to Governor William Marcy (1833–1839), and allowing himself to be elected to several one-year terms in the state legislature in 1841–1842 and again in 1844–1845, positions which did not significantly interfere with his private enterprise. Separating his legislative terms, in 1842–1843, Seymour served as mayor of Utica, his unpopular fiscal prudence leading voters to reject his bid for a second term. On six occasions the state Democratic Party gave its gubernatorial nomination to the perpetually reluctant Seymour: defeated in 1850, but elected in 1852, again defeated in 1854; elected in 1862, once more defeated in 1864; and finally, in 1876, refusing, absolutely, the "fait accompli" nomination which the party tried to force upon him. It was, however, Seymour's tenure as wartime governor of New York that brought him to national attention. As the nation moved toward Civil War in the winter of 1861, Seymour relentlessly urged the

North to make every possible effort to reach peaceful accommodation with the seceding Southern states. Personally opposed to slavery, Seymour had been, in the prewar period, highly critical of the abolitionist movement as a needlessly disruptive force, arguing that it must, under the Constitution, be left to the slave states, themselves, to move toward eventual emancipation. Once hostilities began, while meeting his responsibilities as a wartime governor, Seymour maintained a harsh drumbeat of criticism of the Lincoln administration, particularly, as he saw it, of Lincoln's myriad violations of constitutionally protected civil liberties. A "peace Democrat," Seymour continued to urge a negotiated settlement of the war under the ambiguous formula, "the Constitution as it is, the Union as it was." As such, the governor argued that Lincoln's Emancipation Proclamation of January 1863 was unconstitutional, as was federally imposed conscription. The latter issue brought Seymour into almost constant disagreement with the War Department over conscription quotas assigned to New York. Given this well-known public disagreement, it is not astonishing that when the New York City draft riots of July 1863 occurred, Seymour should have been accused, if not of actually offering encouragement to the rioters and their supporters, of not having done anything positive to cool passions and promote the restoration of public order. Widely reported in the press, it was this charge against Seymour that did irreparable damage to his cause, both in the gubernatorial election of 1864 and in the presidential election of 1868. Nomination for the presidency came as Democrats assembled in New York City's Tammany Hall. Twice Seymour declined the nomination, but in each instance party leaders and delegates urged the former governor to reconsider. Certain in his own mind of defeat, but bowing to his duty, Seymour took up the nomination. Known to object to the proposed Fourteenth Amendment to the Constitution (as later he would object to the Fifteenth Amendment), Seymour argued against radical reconstruction of the South, arguing that suffrage for the freed blackman should be left to state determination. Correctly assessing the impossibility of his success, Seymour's election defeat was, however, less severe than had been anticipated. Republican nominee, victorious Union general Ulysses S. Grant, with his running mate, Congressman Schuyler Colfax of Indiana, secured a plurality of 300,000 votes over Seymour and Democrat vice-presidential candidate Francis Preston Blair of Missouri. The Electoral College margin, however, was much more to the advantage of the Republicans, 214 ballots from 26 states for Grant and Colfax, but 80 votes from 8 states for Seymour and Blair. With his defeat, Seymour returned once again to private pursuits and, true to form, continued in his role as the reluctant candidate, adamantly refusing his party's gubernatorial nomination in 1876, having one year earlier declined to allow Democrats in control of the New York legislature to elect him, as they fully intended to do, to the U.S. Senate. A decade later, well pleased in those years to have essentially left politics behind him, Horatio Seymour died in New York City on February 12, 1886. *See*: ELECTIONS: 1868.

Reference: Stewart Mitchell, *Horatio Seymour of New York* (Cambridge, Mass.: Harvard University Press, 1938).

SHAW v. RENO, 509 U.S. 630 (1993) is a significant racial gerrymandering case. At issue were two oddly shaped majority black voting districts drawn by the North Carolina legislature. After the 1990 census, North Carolina obtained an additional representative in Congress. The North Carolina legislature reapportioned congressional voting districts within the state in order to create an additional district. Since the redistricting plan affected counties covered by Section 5 of the Voting Rights Act of 1965, North Carolina had to obtain preclearance from the U.S. attorney general.

The attorney general objected to the initial apportionment plan because it created only one majority black voting district. The attorney general suggested that a second majority-minority district be created in the southern part of the state. The North Carolina legislature responded by instead creating a second black district in the northern part of the state. This second majority-minority district was extraordinarily narrow and essentially ran for 160 miles along interstate 85. It was this second reapportionment plan which was challenged in court. Several North Carolina citizens claimed that the legislature's self-conscious effort to create majority-minority districts with no regard to factors such as compactness amounted to an unconstitutional racial classification.

A federal district court, relying on the Supreme Court's decision in *United Jewish Organizations* v. *Carey* (1977), dismissed the case, arguing that discrimination could not be alleged when it was a minority group that was being favored. The only question before the Supreme Court was whether the district court erred when it dismissed the case. In a 5 to 4 decision, the Court announced for the first time that racial classifications, even if used to enhance the rights of minority groups, were presumptively unconstitutional.

Writing for the Court, Justice O'Connor distinguished the redistricting scheme in North Carolina from the New York plan upheld in *United Jewish Organizations*. In the New York case, the districts were relatively compact. As already explained, however, the North Carolina voting districts ignored geographic considerations in favor of racial consolidation. Because the oddly shaped North Carolina districts could only be explained in terms of race, the Court concluded that the residents of North Carolina who challenged the reapportionment statute had a valid case under the Equal Protection Clause of the Fourteenth Amendment. The Supreme Court then sent the case back to the district court to determine whether North Carolina had in fact violated the Equal Protection Clause by using a racial classification that was not narrowly tailored to achieving a compelling state interest. *See*: COMPACTNESS; GERRYMANDERING; MAJORITY-MINORITY DISTRICT; REAPPORTIONMENT; REDISTRICTING; STRICT SCRUTINY; *UNITED JEWISH ORGANIZATIONS* v. *CAREY* (1977); VOTING RIGHTS ACT.

Reference: Richard K. Scher, Jon L. Mills, and John J. Hotaling, *Voting Rights and Democracy: The Law and Politics of Districting* (Chicago: Nelson-Hall, 1997).

SIERRA CLUB is the country's leading environmental public interest group. It was founded in 1892 to preserve the Sierra Nevada Mountain Range. John Muir was its first president. The Sierra Club lobbies for protection of the environment and conservation of nature. The Sierra Club supported the Clean Air and Water Act. It has opposed the siting of nuclear plants, mass transportation projects, and unlimited growth and development. It has opposed and placed limits on the mining and forestry industry in the United States. It monitors and then rates officeholders on their votes on environmental issues. Lobbying and political action are not its only strategies. It has established the Sierra Club Legal Defense Fund, to pursue environmental issues in the courts. The organization offers its members the benefits of adventure trips, books, and greeting cards.

In 1996, like other interest groups, the Sierra Club spent money as an independent group attempting to defeat targeted members of Congress who had cast anti-environmental votes. It focused on ten Senate races and fifty House races. It spent about one million dollars on media, and passed out 1.3 million voter guides. The Sierra Club's media campaign was quite negative; for example, in one of its radio ads against Republican Senator Robert C. Smith of New Hampshire, it said his environmental voting record ''stinks.'' Smith was reelected in a very close election. *See*: SINGLE-ISSUE GROUPS.

Reference: John H. Cushman, ''Environmentalists Ante Up to Sway a Number of Races: Spending Millions to Promote Their Agendas,'' *New York Times National*, October 23, 1996.

SINGLE-ISSUE GROUP is are a type of interest group organized around a particular cause. This type of group has gained influence in contemporary American politics. Single-issue groups not only lobby, but engage in electoral politics. Prominent examples of such groups include: the National Abortion Rights Action League, the National Right-to-Life-Committee, the National Rifle Association, Handgun Control Inc., and the Sierra Club. President Bill Clinton blamed the National Rifle Association for the Democrats losing Congress in 1994. Republican presidential nominee Bob Dole was unable to overcome the resistance of the pro-life group's influence in writing the Republican Party's platform on abortion in 1996. Dole wanted a tolerance plank in the platform and had to settle for his preferred language in the appendix. The dedicated members of these groups often cast their votes solely on the position of the candidate on the one single issue that concerns them. *See*: INTEREST GROUP; NRA; SIERRA CLUB.

Reference: Philip A. Mundo, *Interest Groups: Cases and Characteristics* (Chicago: Nelson Hall, 1992).

SINGLE-MEMBER DISTRICT is a district from which only one member is elected. All national government officials, most state and many local government officials, are elected in single-member districts. The voter is restricted to casting only one vote. Single-member districts contribute to the maintenance of a two-party system. Single-member districts may distort the legislative majorities of parties. The total vote of a party, nationally or statewide, may be 50% or less, but as a result of the use of single-member districts, the percentage of seats in the legislature the party is awarded is often greater than 50%. For example, in 1996 the national vote for Republican congressional candidates was 48.9%, yet they captured 52% of the seats. Single-member districts are often gerrymandered to benefit or harm the electoral fortunes of a political party or a minority group. *See*: MULTI-MEMBER DISTRICT; PLURALITY; PRIMARY, RUNOFF; PROPORTIONAL REPRESENTATION.

References: Douglas Rae, *The Political Consequences of Electoral Laws* (New Haven, Conn.: Yale University Press, 1967); Joseph F. Zimmerman, "Enhancing Representational Equity in Cities," in *United States Electoral Systems: Their Impact on Women and Minorities*, Wilma Rule and Joseph F. Zimmerman, eds. (Westport, Conn.: Greenwood Press, 1992).

SLATE is a list of candidates running together as a team asking voters to vote for all of them. William Safire says they are presented as a "package." In urban machine politics, the party developed a slate for the primary election. The party strived to develop a slate that represented the various ethnic groups that the party relied on for support, with the expectation that all of the ethnic groups would vote for all of the candidates. Statewide party slates, for many years, represented the various geographic regions of the state. Today, state parties that develop a slate of candidates give attention to minority groups and gender. *See*: MACHINE POLITICS; TICKET.

Reference: William Safire, *Safire's New Political Dictionary* (New York: Random House, 1993).

SLATE CARD is a list of the candidates of a particular party that a voter can hold in his/her hand. Slate cards are distributed on election day outside the polling place, and they are often mailed out to party members prior to the election. The party tries to persuade its members to vote the entire slate. They are also referred to as "palm cards."

SMITH, ALFRED E. (1873–1944). Born in a lower east side tenement in New York City on December 30, 1873, "the Happy Warrior" would come to be elected four times to the governorship of New York, and, in 1928 to be selected by the Democratic Party as its presidential nominee. Leaving school at age fourteen, Smith, street-smart, worked at a number of jobs including long hours at the Fulton Fish Market from which, he was later to quip, he earned his F.F.M. degree. As with many sons of immigrant families (Smith's paternal grandparents came from Ireland), he found social and economic opportunity in the service of the urban political machine. His apprenticeship served, Smith became a Tammany Hall regular. Having supported the Murphy faction, it would be Charles Murphy, Tammany Hall "boss," who would groom Smith for his first gubernatorial bid in 1918. Sent by the machine to the state legislature in 1904, Smith was no run-of-the-mill party hack; hardworking and honest, he used his years in the State Assembly (1904–1915), to acquire a comprehensive understanding of the inner workings of state government. With Democratic majorities after the elections of 1910, and until his retirement from the Assembly in 1915, Smith was to serve as majority leader, subsequently as Speaker. Holding offices in both New York County and City until he was moved into the governor's race in 1918, Smith, despite a nationwide Republican trend, was to narrowly win the gubernatorial election. In office (1919–1921), the new governor began to build his reputation as a machine "pol," dedicated to good government, and possessing a deeply rooted social conscience. Some argue that the latter was a result of family experience with disadvantage and hardship, his devout Catholicism, and of the awakening that came as a result of his participation in the legislative investigation of New York City's Triangle Shirtwaist Company fire of 1911, a disaster which claimed 143 lives. The investigation brought the enactment of a number of employee health and safety measures and developed, for Smith, a lifelong commitment to the cause of working men and women. Having won against the Republican tide in 1918, Smith was not so fortunate in 1920, turned out of office as voters in the state, as across the nation, overwhelmingly cast ballots for the Republicans and "a return to normalcy." Smith was, however, to make a quick return to political success, recapturing the governorship in 1922, and being returned to that office in each biennial election through 1926. It was in these years (1923–1929) that the national reputation of the Smith administration was solidified: state governmental reorganization, with agency consolidation, directed toward administrative efficiency and political accountability; emphasis on the development and legislative adoption of reform labor and social welfare measures; planning and legislative approval of extensive public works programs. In these initiatives Smith's approach was to rely heavily on expert investigation, planning and advice, and then, politically, to marshal the resources and provide the leadership for "results." Women, such as Belle Moskowitz and Frances Perkins, opting for careers in governmental service, were encouraged and became important members of the governor's advisory or administrative staffs; later Perkins, as secretary of labor, became during the Roosevelt administration the first woman to head a federal cabinet-level department (1933–1945). As the presidential election of 1924 approached, Smith became a major contender for the Democratic Party's presidential nomination. His major rival was William G. McAdoo, born in Georgia, later of New York City, then of California. The differences between Smith and McAdoo were deep, as much along lines of political culture as divisions characterized by ideology or issue: Smith, self-educated, "up from the city streets," Catholic and "wet," a machine "pol" to the core; McAdoo, university educated, urbane, Protestant, "dry," son-in-law of Woodrow Wilson and former secretary of the treasury. These two unrelenting competitors were to battle one another through more than 100 convention ballots over 15 days in the summer heat of New York City's Madison Square Garden, both sides finally giving way on the 103rd ballot to the nomination of compromise candidate John W. Davis of West Virginia, preordained by the wounds opened and salted at the convention to dutifully move toward an election-day debacle of historic proportions. In the intervening four years, on the strength of his New York election victories and the progressive record of his administration, Smith became in 1928 the first-ballot presidential nominee of the Democratic Party, delegates "balancing" the ticket with Senator Joseph T. Robinson of Arkansas, Protestant and "dry." Smith waged an aggressive campaign, the high point perhaps being his Oklahoma City speech of September 20, 1928, in which he attacked bigotry, whether of the Ku Klux Klan or others, and vigorously defended himself and his Catholicism from the "whispering campaign" which claimed that his victory would undermine religious freedom in the United States, and give the Vatican, through Smith, control of American government and policy. Probably as a determinant of the election result, more significant than either the religious issue or that of prohibition was the state of the national economy; an opposition party in times of economic well-being gains few election victories. On the surface Smith's defeat appeared overwhelming: the Republican ticket of Herbert Hoover and vice-presidential candidate Senator Charles Curtis of Kansas outpolled the Democrats by some six million votes. With the aid of "Hoovercrats," the GOP, for the first time since reconstruction, carried five states of the Old Confederacy. The Republican total in the Electoral College was impressive; 444 votes from 40 states to 87 votes from 8 states for Smith and Robinson; particularly devastating to Smith was the loss of his home state of New York. There in a final irony of the election, the man who had in his 1924 nominating speech dubbed Smith "the Happy Warrior," and whom Smith had recruited to the 1928 New York governor's race, Franklin D. Roosevelt, was, by a slim majority, to be elected as Smith's successor in Albany and from that position, by 1932, to replace Smith as leader of the national Democratic Party. Had Smith's disappointment not been so great, there were features of the 1928 election results promising to the future of the Democratic Party and for which Smith could claim credit. He had brought into the Democratic fold, in great numbers, urban voters of strong ethnic identification, voters who allowed Smith and the Democrats to carry the major cities of the United States and who henceforth in their steadfast support of the Democratic Party would be a key component of the New Deal coalition that would dominate American politics until the Reagan revolution of the 1980s. Smith, defeated in 1928, looked forward to 1932, particularly as the latter year, given the ever-widening economic collapse ushered in by the stock market crash of October 1929, gave enormous promise of Democratic victories. Smith felt himself entitled to one last chance to gain the presidency, this time in circumstances favorable to his cause. His ambition, however, lay directly across the path of the ambition of another New York Democrat, Smith's one-time protégé, now governor of the state, Franklin D. Roosevelt. At the party's 1932 Chicago convention it was payback time for Smith's enemies within the party. When his old nemesis from 1924, William G. McAdoo, chairman of the California delegation, announced the state's switch to Roosevelt on the fourth ballot, the doors closed on any possibility of a Smith nomination. With Governor Roosevelt's nomination, Al Smith began to take his "walk" away from the Democratic Party. Slighted by Roosevelt's failure, as candidate and as president, to seek out his advice or to provide him with any fitting role, the schism between Roosevelt and Smith widened. Soon Smith found, in the New Deal program to which he was opposed, policies, as he saw it, characterized by collectivist tendencies, needless attacks on the free enterprise system, policies aimed not at mitigating class differences but exacerbating them. Smith's "walk," however, did not take him to the Republican Party, but rather in 1934 to the American Liberty League, an alliance of anti–New Deal conservatives, many of whom were Democrats, but unlike Smith, men of considerable wealth and social position. Smith, however strange the political bedfellows, was enthusiastic in supplying the League his leadership and, even more importantly, his public voice. The League, active in its attempt to defeat Roosevelt and the New Deal in the elections of 1936, and despite vast sums of money expended, was spectacularly unsuccessful. But four years later the Liberty League disbanded. Even without organization or forum Smith was to remain a critic of the New Deal; for "the Happy Warrior," at the level of presidential politics, no return to the party which he had once led was possible. At age 70, in New York, the city that he loved, Al Smith died on October 4, 1944. *See*: ELECTIONS: 1928.

References: Edmund G. Moore, *A Catholic Runs for President, the Campaign of 1928* (New York: Ronald Press, 1956); Richard O'Connor, *The First Hurrah: A Biography of Alfred E. Smith* (New York: Putnam's, 1970); George Wolfskill, *The Revolt of the Conservatives: The American Liberty League, 1934–1940* (Boston: Houghton Mifflin, 1962).

SMITH v. ALLWRIGHT, 321 U.S. 649 (1944) is an early voting rights case involving a challenge to a Democratic "White Primary" in Texas. The main question for the Court was whether primary elections could be considered a state rather than a private activity. Less than ten years earlier, the Supreme Court had ruled that racially exclusive rules passed by the Democratic state convention in Texas were not reviewable since the convention was not governed by the state of Texas. In the present case, the Supreme Court reversed itself, and decided that "primary elections are conducted by the party under state statutory authority." The actions of the state through the party were then found to be in violation of Section 1 of the Fifteenth Amendment to the Constitution. *See*: PRIMARY, WHITE.

SOCIALIST PARTY. This party was created in 1901 in Indianapolis, with the merging of two Socialist associations, one of which was led by Eugene V. Debs.

This party reached its peak in 1912, when its nominee Debs garnered 900,369 votes, almost 6% of the vote cast for president. The Socialists held over 1,000 offices in 1912. After 1912, the party suffered a number of major setbacks. The party took an anti-war position during World War I, and Debs was in the federal penitentiary for giving an anti-war speech when he ran for president in 1920.

In 1924 the party joined with other progressive groups and backed Robert LaFollette for president. In the 1930s, Norman Thomas became the standard bearer of the Socialist Party. Thomas collected over 800,000 votes in the election of 1932, but the party was unable to regain its earlier strength. The Socialist Party was not able to deal with the popularity of Roosevelt's New Deal programs. The party continued to nominate presidential nominees until 1972, and maintained pockets of regional and local strength; for example, the city of Milwaukee elected Socialist mayors until the 1960s. *See*: DEBS, EUGENE V.

References: Harry W. Laidler, *History of Socialism* (New York: Crowell, 1968); Steven J. Rosenstone, Roy L. Behr, and Edward H. Lazarus, *Third Parties in America*, 2nd ed. (Princeton, N.J.: Princeton University Press, 1996).

SOFT MONEY refers to campaign funds raised outside the scope of the Federal Election Campaign law. Soft money emerged in federal elections in the 1980s. In the 1974 Federal Election Campaign Act amendments, party contributions and expenditures for federal candidates were subject to strict limits. Campaign activities by state and local parties that indirectly benefited federal candidates were also restricted. Direct contributions by political parties were limited, and money spent on behalf of federal candidates—referred to as "coordinated expenditures"—was limited.

In the 1976 election, a number of traditional party activities, including grass roots campaign activities and materials, were viewed as in-kind contributions. Local and state parties could not purchase presidential campaign paraphernalia, and the campaign committees preferred to spend their money on media. The parties complained, and Congress responded with the 1979 amendments to the FECA. This law excluded monies spent on grassroots political activities, provided that the expenditures were made with FECA-regulated contributions or "hard dollars." This excluded corporate or labor union funds. Spending was restricted to grassroots campaign materials, such as bumper stickers and yard signs; state and local parties were permitted to distribute slate cards, sample ballots, and slate ads offering three or more candidates seeking office in a particular state. It also allowed state and local party committees to conduct voter registration and GOTV drives. These specified hard dollar expenditures by political parties no longer counted as part of the contribution and expenditure limits.

In 1976 the Federal Election Commission declared that a Kansas party could use state corporate and union contributions, allowed by state law, to finance a share of its vote drive as long as it allocated the federal and non-federal shares. This decision opened the door for the use of non-federal money to influence a federal election. The federal contribution limits would not apply to the state share of the cost. Only the less restrictive state contributions would apply.

This non-federal funding became known as "soft money" and national parties began to take advantage of this opportunity in the 1980 election. At first, the allocation formula between hard and soft money for party campaign expenditures was not specific. Common Cause took the FEC to federal court and requested that the FEC be required to issue a clear allocation formula. These regulations were issued on January 1, 1991. A disclosure requirement for soft money was also issued.

Political parties have been creative in finding new ways to spend soft money. The most significant was "issue advocacy" ads, which must follow the mix of hard and soft money requirements of the allocation formula. In the 1996 election cycle, the two major parties raised and spent over $262 million in soft money.

Reformers maintain that soft money has made the federal campaign finance regulations meaningless. Advocates for political parties argue that parties have enjoyed a resurgence as a result of the soft money funds. *See*: FEDERAL ELECTION CAMPAIGN ACT OF 1971 AND AMENDMENTS; FEDERAL ELECTION COMMISSION; HARD MONEY; ISSUE ADS.

References: Anthony Corrado, "Party Soft Money," in *Campaign Finance Reform: A Sourcebook*, Anthony Corrado, Thomas E. Mann, Daniel R. Ortiz, Trevor Potter, and Frank J. Sorauf, eds. (Washington, D.C.: Brookings Institution, 1997); Brooks Jackson, "Financing the 1996 Campaign: The Law of the Jungle," in *Toward the Millennium: The Election of 1996*, Larry Sabato, ed. (Boston: Allyn and Bacon, 1996).

SOPHOMORE SURGE refers to the usual gain in support experienced by freshmen House members running for reelection. For the past quarter century, the surge has been the norm, and few freshmen have lost their seats. In the 1990s this appears to have changed. In 1994 fifteen Democratic freshmen were defeated, and none of the GOP freshmen seeking reelection were defeated. In 1996 the GOP lost twelve freshman seats, and the Democrats lost only one. Rhodes Cook, of *Congressional Quarterly*, speculates that the sophomore surge is now enjoyed by only one of the parties in any given congressional election. Cook also points out that in 1996, 27 GOP freshman were elected with less than 55% of the vote, generally considered the line between a safe and a marginal seat.

Freshmen House members enjoy a number of advantages that accrue to incumbents, which contribute to the sophomore surge. Those advantages include: constituent service, increased name identification, and a significant fund-raising advantage over their challengers.

Reference: Rhodes Cook, "Freshman Job Security No Comfort for GOP," *Congressional Quarterly Weekly Report*, Vol. 55 (February 22, 1997).

SOUND BITE is a small piece of an audio or video tape of a candidate's campaign statement that is aired on the nightly news. The candidate's remark that is aired is only a few seconds long, less than ten seconds, and the newscaster puts the remark into a context. Candidates prepare their remarks to offer catchy sound bites to the media. For televised campaign sound bites, the setting and the crowd size are also very important. *See*: TELEVISION AND CAMPAIGNS.

***SOUTH CAROLINA* v. *KATZENBACH*,** 383 U.S. 301 (1966) is a case which established the constitutionality of some of the more controversial sections of the Voting Rights Act of 1965.

The case began when the state of South Carolina passed a law which extended voting times by one hour. Since it had previously been determined that South Carolina had used a voting test which resulted in less than half of its voting age residents being registered to vote, the state was a "covered area" under the Voting Rights Act. Therefore, any changes in voting laws in South Carolina had to be precleared by either the attorney general of the United States or the Federal District Court for the District of Columbia. In addition, the provisions of the Voting Rights Act allowed the attorney general to call for the appointment of special federal examiners in covered states such as South Carolina. These federal examiners were empowered to register voters within these states.

The state of South Carolina asked the Supreme Court to declare the coverage formula (whereby the attorney general determines when an area is covered by the remedial provisions of the Voting Rights Act), the preclearance requirement for covered areas, and the appointment of federal examiners to be a violation of the federal Constitution. The Supreme Court rejected all the state's claim. Chief Justice Earl Warren, who drafted the majority opinion in this case, certified the constitutionality of these provisions, declaring that "Congress may use any rational means to effectuate the constitutional (Fifteenth Amendment's) prohibition of racial discrimination in voting." *See*: PRECLEARANCE; VOTING RIGHTS ACT.

SOUTHERN STRATEGY was a conscious effort by the Republican Party to gain a foothold in what had been the solid Democratic South. The first sign of a Republican breakthrough in the South was the 1964 election, when Goldwater carried four deep South states in a year when Lyndon Johnson and the Democrats enjoyed a landslide. In 1968, Nixon was not able to fully exploit the southern strategy because of the sectional candidacy of George Wallace. The southern strategy began to yield large dividends for the GOP in 1972, when Richard Nixon carried all eleven southern states. Since then, the South has been the strongest section of the country for the GOP.

The GOP's southern strategy formally began with the Republican National Committee's program "Operation Dixie." It openly promoted a more conservative states' rights position after Nixon's 1960 defeat. The opportunity was present because of the passage of civil rights legislation by the Democratic Congress and president in 1964. Since 1964, African Americans have become a key part of the Democratic Party in the South, and whites slowly migrated to the Republican Party. In addition to racial politics, the population of the South changed with the immigration of Cuban refugees to Florida, and the migration of northerners to the South. The economy of the South became more industrialized, creating new economic groups. The Republican Party made efforts to draw on all of these changing social forces in the South to their cause.

The South has become more Republican, not only in presidential politics, but also in congressional elections. As the more senior southern Democratic members of Congress retired, the Republicans won many of the open seats, and in 1994, for the first time since the Civil War, a majority of the members of Congress from the Old Confederacy were Republican. The South's recent impact on the Republican Party can be seen with Newt Gingrich of Georgia as Speaker of the House; and Trent Lott of Mississippi, as Senate majority leader. *See*: ELECTIONS: 1964, 1968, 1972, 1980.

References: Joseph A. Aistrup, *The Southern Strategy Revised: Republican Top-Down Advancement in the South* (Lexington: University Press of Kentucky, 1996); Alexander P. Lamis, *The Two Party South* (New York: Oxford University Press, 1988).

SPECIAL ELECTION is an election that is scheduled to be held on a date other than the dates of the regularly scheduled elections. This type of election is also referred to as a by-election. The opportunity to hold a special election is defined by state law. In most states, special elections are held to fill a vacated congressional seat for the remainder of the term. The date is usually scheduled by the governor of the state. Some states limit the dates when special elections can be held. In California, there has been an increase in the number of special elections because of the effects of term limits on members of the state legislature. Members faced with term limits resign early, requiring that special elections be held to fill the vacated offices. Frequently, members of the lower house in California compete for vacated state senate seats, which then requires another special election. *See*: GENERAL ELECTION.

Reference: Stanley M. Caress, ''The Impact of Term Limits on Legislative Behavior: An Examination of a Transitional Legislature,'' *PS Political Science & Politics*, Vol. 29 (December 1996).

SPLIT-TICKET VOTING is voting for candidates of different parties for different offices in the same election. Ticket-splitting has increased in American elections in recent decades. In the 1920 election only 3% of the congressional districts had split election outcomes; that is, a plurality voted for the presidential candidate of one party, and a candidate of a different party won the congressional seat. In 1992, 25% of the congressional districts had split election outcomes. This split-ticket voting is evidence of the decline of partisanship in the American electorate. In 1996 voters in 30 House districts voted to reelect Bill Clinton president, while supporting a Republican for Congress. In nineteen districts, voters voted for Bob Dole for president and for a Democratic member of the House. *See*: COATTAILS; PARTISANSHIP.

References: Rhodes Cook, "Actual District Votes Belie Ideal of Bipartisanship," *Congressional Quarterly Weekly Report*, Vol. 15 (April 12, 1997); Norman J. Ornstein, Thomas E. Mann, and Michael J. Malbin, *Vital Statistics on Congress, 1992–1994* (Washington, D.C.: Congressional Quarterly Press, 1994); Jerrold D. Rusk, "The Effect of the Australian Ballot Reform on Split Ticket Voting: 1896–1908," *American Political Science Review*, Vol. 64 (December 1970).

SPOILER is a candidate who runs for office, not to win, but to diminish the opportunity for a political rival or enemy to win an office. Seldom do third-party candidates run with the motive of spoiling some other candidate's chance to win, even if they cannot win the office; they run to promote their cause. In 1992, Ross Perot denied Bush the opportunity to win a few more states, but Perot did not run to spoil Bush's chance of winning. Some believe that Theodore Roosevelt did run as a third candidate in 1912 to spoil President Taft's chance of being reelected. Certainly, Roosevelt played the role of spoiler for Taft in that election. Some opponents are tagged as spoilers because they challenge the frontrunner in the primary and weaken that candidate in the general election. President Bush tagged Patrick Buchanan as a spoiler in the 1992 Republican primary contest. Buchanan had little chance of winning; but he damaged Bush's chance of winning the general election. *See*: ELECTIONS: 1912.

Reference: William Safire, *Safire's New Political Dictionary* (New York: Random House, 1993).

SPOILS SYSTEM refers to a style of politics practiced where the jobs, appointments, and contracts are used to reward the supporters of candidates and parties that win elective offices. The phrase is most closely identified with the administration of Andrew Jackson, who was criticized for appointing Martin Van Buren as ambassador to Great Britain. Senator William Macy of New York, in defense of the appointment of Van Buren, said that, "to the victor belongs the spoils of the enemy." The term "spoils" is seldom used today. The slightly less pejorative term "patronage" is used in referring to the rewards given to supporters in politics today. *See*: PATRONAGE.

Reference: Anne Friedman, *Patronage: An American Tradition* (Chicago: Nelson-Hall, 1994).

STALKING HORSE is a candidate put forward to conceal another candidate's ambition, or to deadlock a convention. The stalking horse is a decoy for another candidate, used to test voter response to a particular ideology or region. George McGovern was treated by the press as a stalking horse for Ted Kennedy, which, of course, he was not. The term "stalking horse" was descriptive of the type of tactics that could be employed in the presidential nominating system that existed before 1972. In today's nominating system that relies on a candidate-centered primary, there are no stalking horses.

Reference: William Safire, *Safire's New Political Dictionary* (New York: Random House, 1993).

STATE PARTY COMMITTEES direct their respective party activities in their states. In all but five states, the state statutes define state party organizational structures. The two major parties have a state central committee and a state chair in every state. The members of the state committee are selected by county central committees, by party conventions, or party primaries. John Bibby reports that the size of these state committees varies from 20 in Iowa to over 1,000 in California.

The activities of state committees vary, but most of them adopt state policies and platforms. For example, many GOP state party committees adopted a copy of the Contract with America for their states in the 1994 election. These committees engage in fund-raising, and assist in candidate recruitment. The lower the opportunity for victory, the greater the responsibility for the party to find a standard bearer to challenge a formidable incumbent. A few states are legally mandated to hold pre-primary endorsements. A few state parties can offer direct ballot access without petitions, and are able to award favorable ballot positions to their statewide candidates. Other states engage in extra-legal pre-primary endorsements for statewide office, but this is becoming less common. State parties do not have hierarchical control over the county committees in their state. They make an effort to coordinate party programs and state campaigns with the county party committees in the state.

Approximately two-thirds of state party chairs are elected for a two-year term, and the remainder for a four-year term. State party chairs, like national party chairs, are more visible and influential when the party does not control the office of the governor in a particular state. When a party controls the office of governor, then the governor is seen as the leader of that party in the state. Also, the state committees frequently defer to the wishes of the governor in selecting a state party chair. With the rise of candidate-centered campaigns in the states, and the decline of patronage for the parties, the relationship between the state party organization and the governor has become separated.

The political influence of state party committees has eroded with the onset of primaries for the selection of national convention delegates. There are no longer favorite-son candidates, nor uncommitted state delegations at national party conventions. The state party's role in statewide election contests has been diminished with the rise of the candidate-centered campaign at the state level. The growth and enforcement of civil service law, ethics law, and U.S. Supreme Court decisions, such as *Rutan* v. *Republican Party* (1990) restricting patronage, have eroded the control and influence of state parties in the United States.

State political parties, like the national committees, have adapted to the new political environment by developing the role of service-provider to the candidates. State political parties are able to: raise substantial funds, maintain a year-round office, and many of the larger states are able to hire a large full-time staff with technical expertise. They are also able to develop technical capabilities such as opposition research, media production, polling, targeting, and direct mail fund-raising.

State political parties are well integrated with the national committees. The national committees, particularly the Republicans (although the Democrats are catching up with them), provide technical assistance, staff, and money to state party organizations to carry out coordinated campaigns. Large amounts of soft money are transferred from the national committees to the state parties, to conduct Get-Out-the-Vote campaigns in support of federal and state candidates in battleground states. *See*: GOTV; NATIONAL COMMITTEES; PRE-PRIMARY ENDORSEMENT; *RUTAN* v. *REPUBLICAN PARTY OF ILLINOIS* (1990).

References: John F. Bibby and Thomas M. Holbrook, ''Parties and Elections,'' in *Politics in the American States: A Comparative Analysis*, 6th ed., Virginia Gray and Herbert Jacob, eds. (Washington, D.C.: Congressional Quarterly Press, 1996); Malcolm E. Jewell and David M. Olson, *American State Political Parties and Elections*, rev. ed. (Homewood, Ill.: The Dorsey Press, 1982).

STATES' RIGHTS DEMOCRATIC PARTY. This party, also known as the Dixiecrats, was a sectional party that nominated South Carolina governor Strom Thurmond as its candidate for president in 1948. The party was formed by southern Democrats who walked out of the July 1948 Democratic National Convention, when it adopted a liberal civil rights plank. These disaffected Democrats, mostly from Mississippi and Alabama, nominated South Carolina governor Strom Thurmond; he was listed on the ballot in four states as the Democratic nominee. Those states were: Mississippi, Alabama, South Carolina, and Louisiana. These bolting southern Democratic Party leaders were unhappy not only with the National Democratic Party's position on civil rights, but also the attention that was given to cities and labor unions by the National Democratic Party. Truman down-played his civil rights positions in the 1948 campaign, and Thurmond only carried four states, garnering 38 Electoral College votes. Strom Thurmond would later become a Republican U.S. Senator from South Carolina. This break in the ranks of southern Democrats was a precursor of the eventual realignment of the South. *See*: SOUTHERN STRATEGY; THURMOND, STROM.

References: J. David Gillespie, *Politics at the Periphery: Third Parties in Two-Party America* (Columbia: University of South Carolina Press, 1993); Steven J. Rosenstone, Roy L. Behr, and Edward H. Lazarus, *Third Parties in America: Citizen Response to Major Party Failure*, 2nd ed. (Princeton, N.J.: Princeton University Press, 1996).

STEVENSON, ADLAI E. (1900–1965). Grandson of a vice-president of the United States, for whom he was named, father of a U.S. Senator, to whom he gave his name, Adlai E. Stevenson was twice the presidential nominee of the Democratic Party. Born on February 5, 1900, in Los Angeles, California, where his father had accepted an executive position with the Hearst newspaper chain, Stevenson was to return with his parents six years later to the family home in Bloomington, Illinois. Educated at Choate (1916–1918), Stevenson was subsequently to attend Princeton University from which he graduated in 1922. His law degree, after an unpromising two years at Harvard Law School, was to come from Northwestern University in 1926, following upon which he joined what he referred to as "the old Sedley firm," one of Chicago's long established and prestigious law partnerships. Stevenson, himself, was made a full partner in 1935. In this period he became active in a number of civic organizations, including the Chicago Council on Foreign Affairs, of which he was later to become president. With the coming of the New Deal, Stevenson was to interrupt his Chicago law practice for two brief periods of service in Washington, D.C. (1933–1935), first as legal counsel with the Agricultural Adjustment Administration, later with the Federal Alcohol Control Administration. He was not to return to federal government service until 1941 when he joined fellow Chicagoan Frank Knox, secretary of the navy, as legal advisor and key aide. With Knox's death in 1944, Stevenson transferred to the State Department, becoming deeply involved in administration efforts to establish the United Nations. Disappointed at not being appointed one of the American delegates to the first meeting of the United Nations General Assembly in London, Stevenson nonetheless accepted assignment as the delegation's senior adviser. Following his resignation from the State Department in February of 1946, Stevenson returned briefly to the United Nations in the fall of that year, serving as an alternate delegate for the United States at meetings of the General Assembly. Stevenson was now to return to Illinois: to the law, to civic affairs, and to launch a career in elective politics. Stevenson had long harbored interest in his party's nomination for the U.S. Senate. Standing in his way, however, was University of Chicago economics professor Paul Douglas, better known to both the party organization and the public. Leaders of the Democratic machine, sensing the need to put "good citizen" types on the 1948 ballot, and none too confident of Democratic fortunes in what was surmised to be a Republican year in state and nation, persuaded a reluctant Stevenson to accept the gubernatorial nomination, allowing Douglas to seek the Senate seat. Some observers regarded both nominations as sacrificial ones, allowing the party organization to ride out the anticipated Republican tide. Neither Stevenson nor Douglas subscribed to such a strategy, both campaigned as citizen-politicians, committed to "good government." The Republican organization, grown complacent with success, plagued with charges of corruption and mismanagement in state government, was unable to withstand the surge of voters who throughout the midwest returned to the Democratic Party fold in the fall of 1948. Election day gave Harry S. Truman a statewide plurality of 34,000 votes in the presidential contest; Douglas, a more handsome plurality; and Stevenson, leading the ticket, a record-breaking 600,000 vote plurality over the incumbent Republican governor. Once inaugurated, Stevenson's emphasis was on executive administration that was honest, competent, and fiscally prudent. Here his marks were fairly high. His record of success in having the Illinois House and Senate adopt his legislative program was far more modest. Stevenson's supporters, however, would cite progressive accomplishments in the fields of public education, mental health care, and mine safety. As the 1952 elections approached, Stevenson cautiously, others overtly, began to discuss a presidential bid. Although announcing in January of that year that his sole political objective was reelection as governor of Illinois, and even as he refused President Truman's attempts to recruit him to the presidential contest, Stevenson, through efforts of the "Draft Stevenson" movement, became on the convention's third ballot the presidential nominee of the Democratic Party; his running mate was Senator John Sparkman of Alabama. The urbane Stevenson, socially and economically advantaged, well educated and widely traveled, was seen by many as the quintessential Roosevelt New Dealer. More so than the "accidental" Truman, he was viewed as the appropriate heir, and defender, of F.D.R.'s legacy. Prominent among Democrats sharing this view was the late president's wife, the respected and influential Eleanor Roosevelt, who became a devoted supporter of Stevenson, arguing for his presidential candidacy not only in 1952 but again in 1956 and 1960. In the 1952 campaign, Stevenson had the difficult task of promoting the New Deal while yet distancing himself from the Truman administration; an administration that had grown increasingly unpopular with the American public. As the campaign wore on the friction between the White House and the Stevenson camp became greater and more damaging. Stevenson, with his penchant for foreign policy issues, urged the necessity of the United States finding areas of accommodation with the Soviet Union so as to reduce international tensions and, thereby, the risks of nuclear war. The governor also argued for a strengthening of the United Nations, particularly as to its humanitarian efforts. It was also through the United Nations that Stevenson saw the best hope for a negotiated settlement of the Korean War (1950–1953). On the campaign trail, Stevenson repeatedly attacked as divisive and damaging to civil liberties what he considered to be the reckless attempt by Senator Joseph McCarthy, Republican of Wisconsin, to control subversive, allegedly "un-American," activities. For all Stevenson's efforts, burdened by the unpopularity of the Truman administration, faced with the Republican candidacy of the much admired World War II hero, General Dwight D. Eisenhower, the election spelled defeat for the Democratic Party, bringing to an end 20 years of uninterrupted New Deal presidential victories: Eisenhower and Republican vice-presidential candidate Senator Richard M. Nixon of California, running up a popular vote plurality of more than six million votes, carried 39 states, including a number of those in the Democratic "Solid South," emerging with an Electoral College total of 442 ballots; Stevenson-Sparkman carried but 9 states and 89 votes in the Electoral College. Stevenson, now freed of the responsibilities of the Illinois governorship, was to become the most visible and articulate voice of the opposition Democrats. So dominantly did he play that role, and so unfaltering was the allegiance of the liberal, New Deal wing of the party, that Stevenson again became in 1956, this time on the first ballot, the presidential nominee of the Democratic Party. Setting aside the usual practice whereby a presidential candidate simply dictates the name of his vice-presidential running mate, Stevenson declared an "open convention" which resulted in delegates narrowly choosing Senator Estes Kefauver of Tennessee over the challenge of the youthful John F. Kennedy, Senator from Massachusetts. In introducing the tactic of the "open convention," Stevenson intended to draw a sharp contrast with the Republican convention later in August, which, in machine-like fashion, would renominate Vice-President Richard M. Nixon. In particular Stevenson also wanted to draw attention to Nixon, long anathema to liberal Democrats and thought by them to be generally unpopular with the American voter, as someone who might succeed to the presidency if Eisenhower were reelected and should die in office, given the fact of the president's heart attack in September of 1955. In many respects the campaign of 1956 was a reprise of that of four years earlier: Stevenson advocated an expansion of certain New Deal domestic policies; took a cautious stance on civil rights issues, declining to endorse the use of federal force to compel public school racial desegregation; and, once more, focused on foreign policy issues and the need to reduce American-Soviet tensions. Among his proposals on the latter score were ones for banning the further testing of nuclear weapons and for ending the military draft. Just as the themes of the 1956 campaign were similar to those of 1952, so were the election results: the Republican national ticket, improving on its 1952 showing, gained a popular vote plurality of more than nine million votes, carried 41 states with 457 Electoral College ballots to 7 states and 73 votes in the Electoral College for Stevenson-Kefauver. Even as Stevenson announced that he would not again seek the presidency, the most ardent of his supporters began to plan for 1960. The Stevenson campaign in that year was, however, something of a sentimental journey. Not until late in the day, perhaps sensing a possible convention stalemate between forces of John F. Kennedy and of Lyndon B. Johnson, did Stevenson, again at the urging and with the enthusiastic support of Eleanor Roosevelt, enter the fray. For the older generation of Roosevelt New Dealers, it was the last hurrah; the nomination went to Senator John F. Kennedy of Massachusetts, age 43. With Kennedy's subsequent election victory, Stevenson as party elder statesman, and with his well-known and long-standing interest in foreign policy, anticipated an invitation to join the cabinet as secretary of state. The invitation did not come; instead Stevenson was offered the post of U.S. ambassador to the United Nations, serving with cabinet rank. Stevenson accepted. While pleased to return to the world organization whose birth he had witnessed earlier in his career, pleased to be a part of the milieu of international diplomats and administrators, Stevenson came to feel his voice and views on foreign policy questions were not generally valued by the president and the State Department. With some frequency he found himself in the difficult position of defending publicly, as well as within inner circles of the United Nations, administration policies, whether of Kennedy, or later of Johnson, which he privately opposed. Ironically, Stevenson, age 65, who had been on the scene of the United Nations' First General Assembly meeting in London in the spring of 1945, died some 20 years later on July 14, 1965, having returned to London from a meeting of the United Nations Economic and Social Council in Geneva, Switzerland. The body was returned to the United States for burial in Illinois. *See*: ELECTIONS: 1952, 1956.

References: Kenneth S. Davis, *The Politics of Honor: A Biography of Adlai E. Stevenson* (New York: Putnam's, 1967); John B. Martin, *The Life of Adlai E. Stevenson*, 2 vols. (New York: Doubleday, 1976–1977).

STRAIGHT-TICKET VOTING is voting for all of the candidates of one political party. Straight-ticket voting is aided by party column ballots. With the decline of partisanship in the United States, straight-ticket voting is diminishing, with a corresponding increase in the number of ticket-splitters in the United States. The long periods of divided government in the federal government—where one party gains the presidency, and in the same election, a majority of the other party is elected to the House of Representatives—is evidence of the decline of straight-ticket voting. *See*: BALLOT, PARTY COLUMN; SPLIT-TICKET VOTING.

STRAW POLLS (STRAW BALLOT) are votes conducted by a party organization at a meeting it has called, the results of which are reported in the press as an indication of the preference of the participants for that party's presidential nomination. Party organizations often schedule straw polls long before the state caucuses and primaries are held. The Iowa Republicans scheduled a straw poll at their 1994 state convention to poll those in attendance on their 1996 presidential preference. In that straw poll, Bob Dole finished first. Emmett H. Buell Jr. notes that the straw poll would have received greater attention by the press had Dole finished second. Lamar Alexander finished second, and his handlers argued that would boost his campaign.

Many of the straw polls conducted by state and local parties are actually fundraising and media events. Prospective presidential candidates are obliged to see that their supporters purchase enough tickets to have a respectable showing in the straw poll. The candidates are also expected to make an appearance and give a speech. Some presidential campaigns will make a significant effort and spend a lot of their campaign funds for straw polls in the early primary states. They hope to either impress the media with their organizational strength, or protect their putative frontrunner status. In contemporary presidential nomination politics, straw polls are a part of the invisible primary. *See*: PRESIDENTIAL NOMINATING CAMPAIGNS.

Reference: Emmett H. Buell Jr., ''The Invisible Primary,'' in *In Pursuit of the White House: How We Choose Our Presidential Nominees*, William G. Mayer, ed. (Chatham, N.J.: Chatham House, 1996).

STRICT SCRUTINY is a legal test used by courts when they find that the state has either infringed upon a right deemed fundamental, or has classified individuals based on race, religion, or ethnic background. When courts employ this test, they ask whether the government action is narrowly tailored to advance a compelling state interest. There are, therefore, two parts to this test. The state must first prove that it is trying to accomplish some end which it is absolutely required to achieve. Then the state must show that there was no other way that it might accomplish its goal that might be less intrusive. When a court applies the strict scrutiny standard, the government action being tested is usually found to be in violation of the Constitution.

The strict scrutiny test has become so much a part of constitutional law, that the Congress recently wrote the test into a statute. The Religious Freedom Restoration Act of 1993 ordered courts to use strict scrutiny when reviewing religious freedom cases. Ironically, the Supreme Court later declared that Congress had acted beyond its authority when it passed this law.

Reference: J. W. Peltason, *Understanding the Constitution*, 14th ed. (Orlando, Fla.: Harcourt Brace, 1997).

SUFFRAGE is the right to vote. In the early period of the American political system there were property qualifications to vote. When Andrew Jackson was elected president in the late 1920s, there was universal white male suffrage. African Americans were enfranchised with the Fifteenth Amendment to the U.S. Constitution in 1870. In 1920 the Nineteenth Amendment gave women the right to vote. In 1971 the Twenty-Sixth Amendment lowered the voting age to eighteen. In 1964 the Twenty-Fourth Amendment prohibited poll taxes in federal elections. Poll taxes had been used in the South to discourage African-American voting. The Voting Rights Act of 1965 was enacted to protect the right of minorities to vote. *See*: FIFTEENTH AMENDMENT; NINETEENTH AMENDMENT; POLL TAX; TWENTY-FOURTH AMENDMENT; TWENTY-SIXTH AMENDMENT; VOTING RIGHTS ACT.

Reference: Steven R. Lawson, *Black Ballots: Voting Rights in the South, 1944–1969* (New York: Columbia University Press, 1976).

SUPER TUESDAY. Super Tuesday is an early regional presidential primary made up primarily of southern states. Democratic Party leaders in the South believed that the Iowa and New Hampshire primaries were too heavily influenced by liberal special interest groups, and that the results of those early primaries led to the nomination of candidates like George McGovern and Walter

Mondale, who were too far to the left to be elected in the South. In their view, these liberal candidates were damaging the electoral fortunes of southern Democratic Party candidates. The southern Democratic Party leaders and the Democratic Leadership Council encouraged the southern states to hold their primaries on the same day, early in the primary season. The effort to change the primary schedule was organized by the Southern Legislative Conference. Their goal was to nominate a moderate Democratic Party presidential candidate, and increase the influence of the South in the National Democratic Party.

The first Super Tuesday was held on March 8, 1988; fourteen southern and border states held their primaries on that day. In that primary election, Jesse Jackson ran first, followed by Tennessee Senator Albert Gore. The eventual 1988 Democratic Party nominee, Michael Dukakis, was third in the percentage of total votes cast in the South. Also in 1988, the southern Republicans restored George Bush to his frontrunner status, and set back the charge of Senator Bob Dole. In 1992 the southern Democrats gave their support to a native son, Arkansas governor Bill Clinton, who went on to become the party nominee; he would be the first Democratic presidential candidate elected in twelve years. In 1996 the Super Tuesday primary boosted the fortunes of the troubled campaign of Senator Bob Dole, who had been defeated in New Hampshire by firebrand Patrick Buchanan. Dole captured 349 of the 362 delegates in the seven primaries held on Super Tuesday, 1996. Super Tuesday has lost some of its influence because in 1996, many other states moved their primaries into March to gain the attention of the candidates and influence the presidential nominees. In fact, a number of New England states scheduled their primaries a week before Super Tuesday. That event is called Junior Tuesday. *See*: DEMOCRATIC LEADERSHIP COUNCIL; FRONT-LOADED PRIMARY; JUNIOR TUESDAY; PRIMARY, REGIONAL.

Reference: Barbara Norrander, *Super Tuesday: Regional Politics and Presidential Primaries* (Lexington: University Press of Kentucky, 1992).

SUPERDELEGATE is an unpledged delegate to the Democratic National Convention. Superdelegate is the name given to the Party Leader and Elected Official (PLEO) category of delegates, created by the Democratic National Committee's Hunt Commission. In 1982 the Hunt Commission recommended that a number of party and elected officials be added as automatic delegates to the National Democratic Convention. The superdelegates were created to give a greater voice to Democratic Party and government leaders at their national conventions.

The superdelegates made up 18% of the 1996 Democratic National Convention delegates. The promoters of this delegate group expected that these delegates would remain uncommitted and add to the consensus within the party behind the nominee. However, this group of delegates has tended to commit to the frontrunner early, provoking criticism from challengers. In 1984, Jesse Jackson demanded that the Democratic National Committee reduce the number of superdelegates. *See*: FAIRNESS COMMISSION; HUNT COMMISSION; McGOVERN-FRASER COMMISSION.

References: Nelson W. Polsby and Aaron Wildavsky, *Presidential Elections: Strategies and Structures in American Politics*, 9th ed. (Chatham, N.J.: Chatham House, 1996); Stephen J. Wayne, *The Road to the White House 1996: The Politics of Presidential Elections* (New York: St. Martin's Press, 1996).

SWING VOTER is a term used by journalists to characterize voters that are not strongly attached to political parties. These voters cast their votes for candidates of different parties over time, and determine, or swing, the outcome of an election. V. O. Key used the term "switchers," a group of voters who did not vote for the same party's candidate in the subsequent election, and often determined the outcome of elections. Key argued that these voters determined which party to vote for based upon their perception of the way the government treated them between the intervening elections. *See*: RETROSPECTIVE VOTING; SPLIT-TICKET VOTING.

Reference: V. O. Key, *The Responsible Electorate* (Cambridge, Mass.: Harvard University, 1966).

T

TAFT, WILLIAM HOWARD (1857–1930). Elected to the presidency of the United States (1909–1913), appointed chief justice of the United States Supreme Court (1921–1930), Taft is the only individual, to date, to have held these two most powerful positions in American government. Born in Cincinnati, Ohio on September 15, 1857, his father, Alphonso Taft, was one of the city's most prominent lawyers, having served in the Grant cabinet both as secretary of war and as attorney general. Graduated from Yale in 1878, Taft attended Cincinnati Law School before being admitted to the bar in 1880. Establishing his practice in Cincinnati, Taft was to hold a number of local offices before being appointed in 1887, at age 30, judge of the superior court of Ohio; elected to that same judgeship the following year, Taft was to serve on the Superior Court bench until 1890. In the latter year Taft accepted the appointment of President Benjamin Harrison as solicitor-general of the United States, the Justice Department officer who has, among other responsibilities, the lawyer's role of representing the United States in cases before the Supreme Court in which the government is either a party or is appearing *amicus curiae*, as "friend of the court." Two years later, in 1892, Taft again accepted an appointment from President Harrison, this time to one of the federal judgeships within the Sixth Circuit, a circuit whose jurisdiction embraced the four states of Kentucky, Michigan, Ohio, and Tennessee. Judge Taft was to remain on the circuit court bench until 1900, when he was asked by President McKinley to go to the Philippine Islands, recently acquired by the United States as a result of the Spanish-American War of 1898, to assist in establishing a civil government replacing the Spanish colonial administration. A prerequisite to the functioning of civil government was the termination of the guerrilla warfare which had erupted in 1899 against the American occupation forces, warfare waged by Filipinos who no more savored the prospect of U.S. rule than continuation of that of the Spanish. First as president of the Philippine Commission, then as civil governor, Taft was to serve in Manila through the collapse of the insurgency in 1902, and the establishment of an American civilian authority which looked toward internal improvements, social and education reform, judicial reform, and eventual self-rule. Increasingly committed to his "beautiful islands," Taft twice declined the call of President Theodore Roosevelt to return to Washington to accept appointment to the U.S. Supreme Court. Finally in 1903, the president could be put off no longer. Governor Taft boarded the *S.S. Korea* for the United States on December 23, 1903, returning not to the Supreme Court, as his interest and ambition directed him, but to the president's cabinet as secretary of war, where, in addition to the War Department's routine administration, Taft became, in the words of one of his biographers, "Roosevelt's trouble-shooter," taking on a wide variety of assignments for the president, reaching considerably beyond the normal jurisdiction of the War Department. As the presidential election of 1908 approached, and as Roosevelt concluded that he should not break George Washington's precedent and seek what in effect would be a third term, it became obvious to all who could see and would hear that "Will" was the heir-apparent, someone in whose hands, Roosevelt concluded, the progressive legacy of his presidency would be safe. Nominated on the first ballot of the Chicago convention, delegates joined to Taft's name at the head of the Republican ticket that of Congressman James S. Sherman of New York. Taft was to face William Jennings Bryan, for the third time the nominee of the Democratic Party. As with all the presidential campaigns marked by the presence of William Jennings Bryan the issues debated were largely economic; but it was a far more moderate message of economic reform that the Nebraskan offered the American people in 1908 than ever before. Concluding that they saw no reason for change, voters delivered to Bryan his worst defeat. The Taft-Sherman plurality over Bryan and his vice-presidential running mate, John W. Kern of Indiana, reached 1.2 million votes; the Republicans carrying 29 states and 321 ballots in the Electoral College to 17 states and 162 Electoral College votes for Bryan-Hern. Socialist Party presidential candidate Eugene V. Debs, carrying no states, improved only slightly over his impressive showing of 1904 when he had gathered 402,000 votes. Inaugurated on March 4, 1909, Taft called Congress into special session to enact tariff reduction. House and Senate, however, sent to the president the Payne-Aldrich bill, compromise legislation giving Taft much less by way of tariff reduction than he had hoped. Disappointing Republican progressives, and perhaps setting an unfortunate precedent so early in his tenure, Taft signed Payne-Aldrich into law. The Taft administration did, however, continue with Roosevelt's courtroom war against the giant trusts and monopolies; the Taft Department of Justice nearly doubling, over the Roosevelt years, the number of cases prosecuted under the Sherman Anti-Trust Act of 1890. Most significant perhaps were the government's Supreme Court victories over the Standard Oil and American Tobacco companies in 1911. Two constitutional amendments, the first since Reconstruction, were proposed by Congress during the Taft presidency, both endorsed by the president: the Sixteenth Amendment allowing for a federal income tax, ratified by the states shortly before Taft left office in 1913, and the Seventeenth Amendment providing for the direct popular election of U.S. Senators, ratified by the states in May of 1913. The Taft foreign policy became labeled "Dollar Diplomacy," based on the administration's penchant for reliance upon the nation's economic might to reinforce, particularly in Latin America, the influence and power of the United States. The president was not reluctant, however, to employ if necessity seemed to dictate, the Roosevelt "big stick," as with American military interventions in Nicaragua and Honduras (1910–1912). All-in-all the Taft record, other than perhaps in the field of conservation, ought not to have become anathema to former president Theodore Roosevelt. But it did. Returning from an African safari and an extended European tour in 1910, Roosevelt became increasingly critical of Taft, his leadership, and the policies of his administration. As election year 1912 approached, Roosevelt decided to marshall progressive forces within the Republican Party and challenge Taft's renomination. Even as Roosevelt came to the Chicago convention in June of 1912 the winner in the Republican presidential primary elections held that year, it was clear that Taft forces, controlling the majority of state party organizations, would prevail in the delegate count. As Taft was renominated, Roosevelt delegates crying "foul," "a stolen nomination," bolted the convention. Two months later the "Bull Moose" Progressive Party was born, with Roosevelt as its presidential nominee and Governor Hiram W. Johnson of California as "T.R." 's running mate. With the Republican Party divided, the opening for the Democrats was clear. Election-day results gave the Democratic national ticket of New Jersey governor Woodrow Wilson, and Indiana governor Thomas R. Marshall 41.8% of the total presidential vote cast, 40 states, and 435 Electoral College ballots; Roosevelt-Johnson received 27.4% of the vote, 6 states with 88 Electoral College votes; President Taft and the Republican vice-presidential nominee gathered 23.2% of the presidential vote, winning in but 2 states, with 8 Electoral College ballots. The Socialist Party ticket headed once again by Eugene V. Debs captured over 900,000 votes, 6.0% of the total vote cast. Leaving the presidency in March of 1913, Taft, age 56, accepted a professorship at Yale Law School. Writing numerous articles for both the popular press and for professional journals, publishing in 1916 his study of the American presidency, *Our Chief Magistrate and His Powers*, Taft's post-presidential years were extraordinarily productive ones. Giving his support to the World War I effort, Taft accepted, in 1917, President Wilson's appointment as joint chairman of the War Labor Board. And finally in 1921, Taft came to that position which had so long been the object of his ambition, always more so than the presidency, a seat on the U.S. Supreme Court, an appointment by President Harding, made yet more appealing by the fact that the seat was that of the chief justice. A conservative, self-restraint jurist, Taft's considerable contributions to the Court over the next decade, more than in the development of constitutional law doctrine, were to be measured in terms of his leadership skill and administrative ability. In rapidly declining health, the respected chief justice resigned from the Court on February 3, 1930. But a month later on March 8, William Howard Taft, age 73, died at his Washington, D.C. home. *See*: ELECTIONS: 1908, 1912.

References: Paolo E. Coletta, *The Presidency of William Howard Taft* (Lawrence: University Press of Kansas, 1973); Alpheus Thomas Mason, *William Howard Taft: Chief Justice* (New York: Simon and Schuster, 1965); Henry F. Pringle, *The Life and Times of William Howard Taft*, 2 vols. (New York: Farrar, Rinehart, 1939).

TAFT-HARTLEY ACT of 1947 was also known as the Labor Management Relations Act of 1947. This law prohibited the use of labor union treasury funds for candidate contributions. This law was passed by the Republican-controlled Congress, which was elected in 1946, and matched the ban on the use of corporate funds for campaign contributions enacted in 1907. *See*: TILLMAN ACT OF 1907.

TAMMANY HALL was a New York City–based political organization tied to the Democratic Party. It came to epitomize machine politics in urban America. Tammany started as a social club in 1789, it was named after Saint Tammany, a legendary Delaware Indian chief, known for his wisdom. The leader of Tammany was called the Grand Sachem and its headquarters was called the Wigwam. It developed as an ally of the Democratic-Republican Party in New York State politics in the early nineteenth century, under the leadership of influential governor DeWitt Clinton. One grand sachem of Tammany was Martin Van Buren, who was elected president in 1836.

Tammany gained its reputation as a political machine when William March Tweed, who had been elected party chairman of the Democratic Party Central of New York County, became grand sachem of Tammany.

In the late nineteenth century, the Tammany-based Democratic Party Organization cultivated the support of the waves of new immigrants coming to New York City. The Tammany Democrats would offer jobs, money, food baskets, and social events to these new immigrants who became loyal supporters of the Tammany-centered Democratic Party organization. Another legendary figure in Tammany's history was George Washington Plunkett, who prided himself on benefiting from what he called ''honest graft.'' Tammany Hall controlled the mayor's office of New York City throughout most of the late nineteenth and early twentieth centuries. Tammany Hall became a foil for reformers. Tammany's control over the city was finally ended with the election of the popular and reform-minded New York mayor, Fiorello La Guardia, in 1933.

Tammany's ability to earn the loyalty of the lower socioeconomic classes of New York was lost with the rise of the New Deal. The entitlements of the New Deal were delivered by a government bureaucracy, and one no longer had to be a supporter of the local party to receive government benefits. *See*: MACHINE POLITICS.

Reference: William L. Riordan, *Plunkitt of Tammany Hall* (New York: Dutton, 1963).

TARGETING is a practice of legislative campaign committees, political parties, and PACs, which focus scarce financial resources on either candidates that have a good chance of winning, or on incumbents that appear to be vulnerable. For example, in 1996 the AFL-CIO targeted a number of Republican House freshman, and spent $35 million to try to defeat them. Legislative caucuses target open seats. Campaigns target particular voter groups that are critical in determining the outcome of an election. For example, in 1996 the Clinton campaign focused its message on the concerns of women and the elderly.

TASHJIAN v. REPUBLICAN PARTY OF CONNECTICUT, 479 U.S. 208 (1986) is a case in which the Supreme Court decided that the First Amendment forbids states from requiring primary voters to be registered with the party in whose primary they are participating. The case began in 1984 when the Republican Party in Connecticut adopted a rule allowing indepedent voters to participate in that state's Republican primary. Since this party rule was in violation of a Connecticut election statute which forbade non-party members from voting in party primaries, the Republican Party went to court seeking a declaration that the Connecticut statute was unconsitutional. By a 5 to 4 vote, the Supreme Court supported the position of Connecticut's Republican Party.

Justice Thurgood Marshall, writing for the majority, concluded that the state of Connecticut had infringed upon the freedom of association, guaranteed by the First and Fourteenth Amendments to the Constitution. Since the right to associate is considered to be fundamental, Marshall applied the strict scrutiny test. In order to survive strict scrutiny, a state must prove that the law in question is narrowly tailored to advance a compelling state interest. In this case, Connecticut suggested that its law restricting participation in primary elections was intended to acomplish four related goals: (1) reducing the cost of primary elections; (2) preventing one party from ''raiding'' the primary election of another party; (3) minimizing voter confusion; and (4) maintaining the integrity of the two-party system. The Court concluded that, although all of these goals were significant, they did not provide the compelling justification necessary when fundamental rights are jeopardized. *See*: PRIMARY, CLOSED; STRICT SCRUTINY.

TAYLOR, ZACHARY (1784–1850) was born of a prominent Virginia family on November 24, 1784, as his parents, staying with friends, were in the process of emigrating to the western frontier of Kentucky. Home-educated, Taylor at age 23 decided on a career in the U.S. Army. His first assignments were within the Northwest Territory, serving with William Henry Harrison in engagements with the Indian confederation. Following the War of 1812, garrisoned to a number of frontier posts, Taylor was in 1832 to participate in the Black Hawk War. Subsequently reassigned to Florida, Taylor there led troops against the Seminoles. In 1841, Taylor was given command of the army's southern division, headquartered at Baton Rouge. While in Louisiana, Taylor became a planter, eventually acquiring large holdings in land and in slaves. Taylor's military career would draw him into what was to become the Mexican War (1846–1848). Sent to Texas in 1845 by President Polk to protect the recently annexed state from an anticipated Mexican invasion, Taylor, once war was declared the following year, led troops to several initial and attention-gathering victories. Polk, perhaps sensitive to the possibilities of a Whig presidential recruitment of the rising military hero, assigned to General Winfield Scott, not Taylor, responsibility for the invasion of Mexico, leading to the capture of Mexico City. Even though given a far more restricted assignment, Taylor yet managed to secure a number of well-publicized victories, particularly at Buena Vista in 1847. These victories solidified Taylor's reputation as a national military hero and made of him, as presumably Democrat Polk had feared, a target for Whig leadership recruitment to the presidential nomination of 1848. While Taylor found the notion of occupying the presidency enticing, he did not find the demands of party politics equally appealing. Essentially apolitical, Taylor tested the possibility of a nonpartisan bid for the presidency. Becoming convinced, however, that such an approach was not realistic, he allowed himself to be captured by the Whigs, becoming their presidential nominee on a national ticket shared with former congressman Millard Fillmore of New York as the party's vice-presidential candidate. Devoid of some of the hoopla, the 1848 campaign was nonetheless a reprise of that of 1840. Whig leaders offered to the American people an authentic war hero, "Old Rough and Ready," while playing down issue divisions that existed both within the nation and within the Whig Party itself. Taylor and the Whigs were to secure a relatively modest election-day victory: each of the two major parties carried 15 states, the Electoral College advantage was, however, with the Whigs, 163 ballots to 127 for Lewis Cass and the Democrats. The election result was made more problematic because of the campaign waged by a newly organized, anti-slavery third party, the Free-Soilers, who stood unequivocally for adoption into law of the language of the Wilmot Proviso prohibiting the extension of slavery into any of the territories newly acquired from Mexico. The Free-Soil ticket of former president Van Buren and Charles Francis Adams as vice-presidential candidate, gathered nearly 300,000 popular votes to Cass's 1,220,000 and Taylor's 1,360,000. Some political analysts have suggested that the Free-Soil ticket siphoned sufficient numbers of votes from the Democrats, particularly in Massachusetts and New York, to deliver the election to the Whigs. Inaugurated on March 4, 1849, Taylor was to serve but sixteen months in the presidency, dying at the White House on July 9, 1850. During his short tenure, Taylor wrestled with the question of slavery's extension. A cautious, case-by-case determination evolved as the president's approach, allowing each territory or would-be state to make its own decision on slavery. Thus, even though himself a slave holder, Taylor, citing reasons unrelated to the slavery issue, signaled his strong support for California's admission to the Union as a free state. He also expressed, equally strongly, his objection and probable veto of the complex legislation on the slavery issue being crafted by his party in Congress under the leadership of Henry Clay. That package of legislation, the Compromise of 1850, was to be signed into law by his successor, President Fillmore, in September of 1850, but two months after Taylor's death. *See*: ELECTIONS: 1848.

References: K. Jack Bauer, *Zachary Taylor: Soldier, Planter, Statesman of the Old Southwest* (Baton Rouge: Louisiana State University Press, 1985); Frederick J. Blue, *The Free Soilers* (Urbana: University of Illinois Press, 1973); Holman Hamilton, *Zachary Taylor*, vol. I, *Soldier of the Republic*; vol. II, *Soldier in the White House* (Indianapolis: Bobbs-Merrill, 1941, 1951); Elbert B. Smith, *The Presidencies of Zachary Taylor and Millard Fillmore* (Lawrence: University Press of Kansas, 1988).

TELEVISION AND CAMPAIGNS. Television is the dominant media in national elections. Most Americans receive their news from television, and political campaigns spend most of their money on television advertising.

The modern political campaign is designed for television. Campaign advance people look for good visual effects for their candidates. President Clinton had striking visual backdrops as he signed environmental legislation protecting national parks during the 1996 campaign. Campaign speeches by candidates are written and delivered with the nightly news in mind. The candidate delivers lines that the campaign speech writers expect will result in effective sound bites on television. The national party conventions have become media productions for television. Candidates rehearse for their televised debates, and the tone and the themes are tested before focus groups. Bob Dole was restrained in his attacks on Bill Clinton in the 1996 presidential debates because of focus group feedback, which indicated that harsh criticism was viewed negatively, particularly by women.

Television news treatment of the candidates is uneven. A content analysis of evening newscasts on ABC, CBS, and NBC for September 1996 found that 54% of the comments about President Clinton were positive, while only one in three were positive about Bob Dole. Also, in September 1996, there were 194 stories about Clinton compared to 77 about Dole. The positive remarks about Clinton were on his issue positions, the negative remarks concerned issues about his character. The Dole stories focused on his inept campaign, with little attention to his issues. The study was conducted by the Center for Media and Public Affairs. The lack of interest in the 1996 general election led networks to reduce coverage in the month of September by 40% from the coverage given in 1992. The Merkle Foundation calculated that in September 1992 the three national networks ran 304 newscasts on the presidential election, compared to 171 campaign stories in September 1996.

Television advertising is the center of the modern campaign; that is where most of the campaign budget is spent. The campaigns produce and air both positive and negative advertisements that have been market tested. Television advertising was first used in the campaign of Dwight D. Eisenhower in 1952.

In 1996 the AFL-CIO, which had long focused its political activities on phone banks, voter registration, and getting out the vote, spent $35 million on television, airing negative ads targeted at vulnerable freshmen Republican congressmen. As televised campaigns became more sophisticated, they began targeting the message of the advertisement at particular voter groups.

The key decision in a national presidential election in the closing weeks of a campaign, when most of the money is expended, is for the campaign managers to decide what states they will target with their media buys. In 1996 the Dole campaign spent weeks ruminating over whether they should target the Electoral College–rich, but very expensive, state of California. *See*: MASS MEDIA; PRESIDENTIAL ELECTION CAMPAIGN; PRESIDENTIAL DEBATES.

Reference: Stephen Ansolabehere, Roy Behr, and Shanto Iyengar, *The Media Game: American Politics in the Television Age* (New York: Macmillan, 1993).

TERM LIMITS. In 1990 the citizens in states with the initiative began voting overwhelmingly to limit the number of terms for members of their state legislatures. Twenty-two states have now established term limits for their state legislatures. In thirteen states, the limit is eight consecutive years per chamber. In three states, it is twelve. In the rest, it varies by chamber from six to twelve years. Arizona and Florida actually limit individuals to eight consecutive years, whether they serve in one or more chambers. Oklahoma limits individuals to twelve years. Missouri and Ohio allow eight years in each chamber for a total of sixteen years.

The referenda frequently included limits on terms for members of the U.S. House of Representatives, and also placed limits on the number of terms a person may serve in the U.S. Senate. The U.S. Supreme Court, in *U.S. Term Limits* v. *Thorton*, ruled that states could not add requirements for members of Congress beyond the language of the Constitution. The Republicans promised a term limit amendment to the U.S. Constitution in their Contract with America. They could not muster the necessary votes in the 104th Congress to put forward a proposed amendment, offering term limits for the national legislature. *See*: CONTRACT WITH AMERICA; INITIATIVE; *U.S. TERM LIMITS* v. *THORTON* (1995).

References: Gerald Benjamin and Michael J. Malbin, eds., *Limiting Legislative Terms* (Washington, D.C.: Congressional Quarterly Press, 1992); Stanley M. Caress, ''The Impact of Term Limits on Legislative Behavior: An Examination of a Transitional Legislature,'' *PS Political Science & Politics*, Vol. 24 (December 1996).

THIRD PARTIES. In American politics, third parties are often expressions of discontent with the two major parties and their candidates. Historically, minor parties have served a variety of functions in the political system. They have been a source of policy innovation. Women's suffrage, direct election of U.S. Senators, prohibition, abolition of slavery, and the income tax have all been issues promoted by third parties. All of these ideas were eventually adopted by the major parties after they demonstrated voter appeal. The 1992 independent candidacy of Ross Perot made the balanced budget a central issue in national politics. Third parties serve as a safety valve of the electoral process; voters can vent their frustrations and discontents through third parties.

Third parties have been formed as bolt movements from a national party. The 1912 Bull Moose Progressives of Theodore Roosevelt was a bolt movement from the Republicans. They had the greatest success of any third party, garnering 27% of the vote, and 88 Electoral College votes. A more recent party, which formed as a splinter group, was the States' Rights Democrats (Dixiecrats), which was a sectional party resulting from a southern state delegation bolt from the 1948 Democratic National Convention. They nominated Senator Strom Thurmond and he carried four southern states. This 1948 bolt is now viewed as an indication of the beginning of the end of the dominance of the Democratic Party in the South.

Most third parties in the United States are short-lived. Every significant third party has had its best showing in its first national election, with the exception of the Socialist Party led by Eugene Debs, which had its best showing in 1912 with 6% of the national vote, after its first attempt in 1900. Some parties like the Socialist Party had international origins. Most American minor parties are indigenous social movements, bolts from the major parties, or the creation of an individual candidate's ambition. The plurality electoral system makes it very difficult for the third parties to sustain themselves over time. There have been over 1,100 minor parties in the United States since the early nineteenth century. The Libertarian and Natural Law parties, which receive little press attention, have been quite persistent in recent elections. *See*: BALLOT ACCESS; PLURALITY; TWO-PARTY SYSTEM.

References: Paul A. Beck and Frank J. Sorauf, *Party Politics in America*, 7th ed. (New York: HarperCollins, 1992); Steven J. Rosenstone, Roy L. Behr, and Edward H. Lazarus, *Third Parties in America: Citizen Response to Major Party Failure*, 2nd ed. (Princeton, N.J.: Princeton University Press, 1996).

THORNBURG v. GINGLES, 478 U.S. 30 (1986). In *City of Mobile* v. *Bolden* (1980) the U.S. Supreme Court decided that, in order to establish a violation of Section 2 of the Voting Rights Act, plaintiffs had to prove that a state or political subdivision had intended to discriminate against a protected minority group. In response to *Bolden*, Congress amended the Voting Rights Act and specified that, even in the absence of discriminatory intent, a violation of Section 2 of the Voting Rights Act ''is established if, based on the totality of circumstances, it is shown that the political processes leading to nomination or election in the

State or political subdivision'' led to a discriminatory effect. The importance of *Gingles* is that it represents the first attempt by the Court to apply this amended version of Section 2.

The case began when several black voters in North Carolina challenged that state's legislative redistricting plan. The voters claimed that North Carolina's use of multi-member districts diluted minority voting strength in violation of Section 2 of the Voting Rights Act. A federal district court ruled in favor of the black voters, and the Supreme Court for the most part affirmed the lower court's decision invalidating the multi-member districts. Writing for the Court, Justice Brennan established that in order to prove that multi-member districts result in the dilution of minority voters, it must be demonstrated that majority voters vote as a bloc and are ''usually able to defeat candidates supported by a politically cohesive, geographically insular minority group.'' *See: MOBILE, CITY OF*, v. *BOLDEN* (1980); MULTI-MEMBER DISTRICT; VOTING RIGHTS ACT.

THRESHOLD REQUIREMENT has been a point of contention within the Democratic National Committee over the rules for delegate distribution. The threshold is the required percentage of the vote a candidate must reach to be awarded delegates under the proportional representation system used by the Democrats. If a candidate does not reach the threshold, then the candidate is not entitled to any delegates. In the 1984 Democratic primaries, the candidate needed to garner 20% of the vote to be awarded delegates. Jesse Jackson objected to that threshold requirement, arguing it was too high and that it discriminated against certain candidates. After the 1984 defeat, Democratic National Committee chair Paul Kirk appointed the Fairness Commission to revise the rules. The major rule change instituted by this commission was to reduce the threshold from 20% to 15%. *See*: FAIRNESS COMMISSION; PROPORTIONAL REPRESENTATION.

Reference: Philip A. Klinker, *The Losing Parties: Out-Party National Committees, 1956–1993* (New Haven, Conn.: Yale University Press, 1994).

THURMOND, J. STROM (1902–) is the senior U.S. Senator from South Carolina. In March 1996, at the age of 93, he became the oldest person ever to serve in Congress. His career influenced and reflects the changing politics in the South and in the nation.

Thurmond grew up in Edgefield, South Carolina. In 1929 he was elected to the state legislature and was elected Democratic governor in 1947. In 1948 he led a bolt of southern Democrats from the Democratic National Convention as a protest of the Democrats' civil rights plank, and in that year he was the nominee of the States' Rights Party (Dixiecrats), winning 39 Electoral College votes.

In 1954 he was elected U.S. Senator as a write-in candidate. He joined the

Democratic caucus. In 1957 he filibustered Civil Rights legislation for a record 24 hours. Thurmond switched to the Republican Party in 1964. He held the South for Richard Nixon at the 1968 Republican National Convention. After 1965 he softened his position on race issues. In the 105th Congress, Thurmond served as the chairman of the Armed Services Committee.

In 1996 Thurmond faced opposition both in the primary and in the general election. In the general election, Democratic nominee Elliot Close spent almost a million dollars of his own money, and he tried to make an issue out of Thurmond's advanced age. Thurmond won 53% to 44%. *See*: ELECTIONS: 1948; STATES' RIGHTS DEMOCRATIC PARTY.

Reference: Nadine Cohodas, *Strom Thurmond and the Politics of Southern Change* (New York: Simon and Schuster, 1993).

TICKET is a group or slate of candidates running as a team. Political parties offer a ticket for every office. A party organization that engages in pre-primary endorsement will build a balanced ticket. They will then encourage party members to vote for a straight-ticket for all of the endorsed candidates. The party column ballot encouraged straight-ticket voting in general elections. The adoption of the office block ballot predisposes voters to split their tickets. *See*: BALLOT, OFFICE BLOCK; BALLOT, PARTY COLUMN; PRE-PRIMARY ENDORSEMENT; SLATE; SPLIT-TICKET VOTING.

TILDEN, SAMUEL J. (1814–1886). Corporation lawyer, governor of New York (1875–1877), by his claim "president-elect" of the United States in 1876, Tilden was born on February 9, 1814, in New Lebanon, New York. His father, Elam Tilden, counted among his political associates and friends Martin Van Buren and Silas Wright, house guests who often invited the young and precocious Tilden to join in their after-dinner conversations, cultivating in him an early affection for politics and a virtually uninterrupted identification with the Jacksonian Democratic Party. Attending Yale, but never feeling himself to be in robust health, Tilden returned from New Haven after but one year (1834). Later enrolled in New York University (1838–1841), Tilden took up the study of law and was admitted to the bar in the latter year. Throughout the remainder of his life Tilden's great passion was to be his law practice, and the wealth it brought. Politics would be an interesting, occasionally fascinating avocation, not a substitute career. Given his long-standing political connections, and as he struggled to establish his practice, the young Tilden, age 27, accepted election by the New York Common Council to the position of legal counsel for New York City in 1843. In 1846 Tilden was to be elected to the New York legislature and, from June to October of that same year, to serve as a member of the constitutional convention drafting a new basic law for the state. Since his youth, a supporter of his father's friend Martin Van Buren, Tilden followed the "Little Giant" and the anti-slavery "Barnburners" out of the Democratic and into the

Free-Soil Party of 1848. Always opposed to slavery, Tilden would nevertheless attribute his more radical abolitionist statements of this period to youthful exuberance, and while other of the "Barnburners" would eventually gravitate toward the new, anti-slavery Republican Party of the 1850s, a more moderate Tilden returned to the Democrats. For the next decade and through the years of Civil War (1861–1865), Tilden devoted himself to his increasingly lucrative law practice, coming to represent a number of major businesses, particularly in the fields of railroading and mining. In 1866 Tilden again became politically active assuming, as state chairman, leadership of the New York Democratic Party. Initially working in cooperation with New York City's Tammany Hall, as evidence of the corruption practiced by Boss Tweed and his "ring" mounted, Tilden called for reform, supporting Tweed's prosecution in 1872–1873. With Tweed's influence on the wane, Tilden returned to Tammany Hall membership, becoming in 1875 one of the machine's "sachems." Receiving both state and national recognition as a reformer, Tilden accepted the Democratic nomination for governor in 1874. Elected, and with his ambition set on the presidency, Tilden proved himself to be an unusually able administrator: state expenditures were reduced, government agencies efficiently operated, and taxes cut. Corruption, such as that associated with the "canal ring," was exposed and the officials involved prosecuted. Tilden's record, in Albany, of honesty, reform, and administrative competence, became particularly appealing to national Democrats who in 1876 were seeking a nominee who could take advantage of the exposed corruption and scandals of the Grant administration. Nominated on the second ballot at the party's St. Louis convention in June of 1876, Tilden was joined on the Democratic national ticket with Thomas A. Hendricks of Indiana. The campaign was a raucous one with Democrats pointing to the evidence of extortion, bribery, and theft which, they claimed, characterized the Grant presidency. For their part, the Republicans, in support of the party's ticket (Governor Rutherford B. Hayes of Ohio and Congressman William A. Wheeler of New York), again waved "the bloody shirt," pointing to the passive role played by Tilden in support of the war effort, sitting in his New York City office, as they saw it, becoming a man of wealth while General Hayes and countless others were fighting the Union cause on the battlefields of the Civil War. The election itself was to produce, to date, the one disputed result in American presidential election history. Election evening in November 1876 suggested a decisive Tilden victory with Democrats carrying New York State, its large block of Electoral College votes, and seemingly, thereby, the election itself. Within days, however, Republican leaders challenged the returns from Florida, Louisiana, and South Carolina, claiming in each of those three southern states widespread fraud in the counting and reporting of the vote, and, as well, the systematic intimidation of black males, many of whom were prevented from participating in the elections and casting their presumed Republican ballots. Tilden, the clear popular vote winner, sought to have the presidential election thrown into the U.S. House of Representatives where, with Democrats in the majority, his candidacy would prevail. Contrarily, Republican leaders argued that Tilden electors from Florida, Louisiana, and South Carolina should be disqualified and replaced by certified Hayes electors; that accomplished, the Republican ticket, having an Electoral College majority, could be declared officially elected, and Hayes could then proceed, constitutionally and legitimately, to inauguration. After weeks of negotiation in Washington, and as inauguration day (March 4, 1877) approached, a compromise solution was adopted: Congress established a special Electoral Commission, seven members to be appointed by the Democratic House, seven members to be appointed by the Republican Senate, and with a final, presumably non-partisan, member to be selected from the U.S. Supreme Court. Justice Joseph P. Bradley of New York, an appointee of President Grant in 1870, was chosen as the Commission's fifteenth, and decisive, member. On each crucial decision taken by the Commission, Bradley voted with the Republicans, to the effect that from all three southern states Hayes electors replaced those of Tilden, giving to the Republican ticket, when Electoral College ballots were ultimately counted, a majority of one: Hayes-Wheeler carrying 21 states with 185 Electoral College votes to 17 states and 184 ballots for Tilden-Hendricks. Tilden was, however, to have the satisfaction of remaining the popular vote winner, the Democratic plurality standing at more than 250,000 votes. The long-standing question has been asked as to why congressional Democrats would have agreed to the Electoral Commission proposal. History has suggested that a compromise was struck: congressional Democrats were willing to concede the presidency to the Republicans if Hayes, once inaugurated, would end military reconstruction in the South, thereby allowing the reestablishment of all-white Democratic Party regimes in the states of the defeated Confederacy. It should be noted that in support of this theory, President Hayes, in April of 1877, issued an executive order withdrawing federal troops from the South, thus bringing to an end the period of military reconstruction. Tilden, claiming to be the rightful winner of the 1876 election, the true "president-elect," looked forward to the election of 1880 for both political revenge and justice's reward. Neither came to him. Expecting to be the Democratic Party nominee by acclamation and, subsequently, to be "reelected" to the presidency, Tilden found his stock greatly diminished by the summer of 1880. Two events in particular seem to have contributed to Tilden's demise: charged with income tax evasion during the Civil War period, prosecuted by federal authorities, Tilden was not to reach a settlement in the pending case until 1882; furthering the damage was the discovery and disclosure of the so-called "cipher telegrams" which suggested that Democrats had plotted in December of 1876 to "buy influence" with certain of those individuals who might come to be certified as eligible to cast Florida's Electoral College votes. Tilden, realizing that the 1880 Democratic nomination would not come to him on his preferred terms, released a letter asking to be "honorably discharged" from the party's consideration. Perhaps more quickly and decisively than Tilden had expected, the party, taking him at his word, honored his request. Talked of again in 1884, Tilden again declined to be considered for the presidential nomination. Increasingly devoting his time, energy, and wealth to the building and improvement of his vast mansion, Greystone, in Yonkers, New York, and to the enlargement of his book collection and private library, Tilden, long in declining health, died at his estate, on August 4, 1886. He left his $5 million fortune, enormous by the measurement of his time, in trust for the purpose of establishing a great New York City library, but his will was, just as the election of 1876, disputed. The final resolution in 1890 provided but one-third of the estate, some $2.5 million, to the creation of what would become, in 1901, the New York Public Library. *See*: ELECTIONS: 1876.

References: Alexander C. Flick, *Samuel Jones Tilden: A Study in Political Sagacity* (New York: Dodd, Mead, 1939); Paul J. Haworth, *The Hayes-Tilden Disputed Presidential Election of 1876* (Cleveland, Ohio: Burrows, 1906).

TILLMAN ACT OF 1907 was the first significant campaign finance reform act passed by Congress. This federal law prohibits corporations and national banks from making political contributions to federal campaigns; it remains in effect today. The ban on the use of labor union treasury funds for federal campaign contributions was permanently adopted in 1947 with the Taft-Hartley Act. In recent years these prohibitions have been undermined by "soft money" contributions to political parties. The Tillman Act was part of the reaction to the political excesses of the Gilded Age, and reflects the influence of the Progressive Era in early twentieth-century American politics. *See*: FEDERAL CORRUPT PRACTICES ACT OF 1910 AND 1911; FEDERAL ELECTION CAMPAIGN ACT OF 1971 AND AMENDMENTS; SOFT MONEY; TAFT-HARTLEY ACT.

References: Herbert E. Alexander, *Financing Politics: Money, Elections, and Political Reform*, 4th ed. (Washington, D.C.: Congressional Quarterly, 1992); Anthony Corrado, Thomas E. Mann, Daniel R. Ortiz, Trevor Potter, Frank J. Sorauf, eds., *Campaign Finance Reform: A Sourcebook* (Washington, D.C.: Brookings Institution, 1997).

TIMMONS **v.** *RAMSEY,* No. 95–1608 (1997) is a case which tested the constitutionality of Minnesota's ban on what are known as "fusion" candidacies. A fusion candidate is an individual who runs for office as a candidate of more than one political party.

The case was brought by the New Party, which alleged that the ban violated party members' First and Fourteenth Amendment associational rights. Although the Supreme Court agreed that associational rights had been burdened, the Court claimed that the burden was not very significant. Justice Rehnquist, writing for a five-member majority, argued that anti-fusion laws merely "reduce the universe of potential candidates" available to a party, thereby imposing burdens which "though not trivial—are not severe."

Because associational rights were not found to be heavily burdened, the Court declined to use the stringent legal standard known as "strict scrutiny." Under strict scrutiny, Minnesota would have been required to show that its ban on fusion candidates was narrowly tailored to serve a compelling state interest. Since the Court found that no severe burden had been placed on the right to associate, the Court required only that Minnesota's interests be "sufficiently weighty," rather than compelling. The Court concluded that Minnesota's asserted interests in "avoiding voter confusion and overcrowded ballots, preventing party splintering and disruptions of the two party system, and being able to clearly identify the election winner" satisfied this reduced standard. Consequently, the Minnesota law was found constitutional. In reaching this conclusion, however, the Court was careful to point out that its ruling did preclude states from adopting fusion systems, should they be so inclined. Based on this case, states are free to either allow or disallow fusion candidacies. *See*: FUSION TICKET; STRICT SCRUTINY.

TRACKING POLLS are preelection surveys conducted by campaigns to measure the effectiveness of television advertisements, issues, and the public's attitude toward the candidates. There are only a few questions in a tracking poll. They are brief and administered on a regular basis. A series of separate polls gives the campaign a sense of the changes that are occurring in the campaign. Some tracking polls use a small sample each night, and add the results to the previous nights results, which creates a running average. The campaigns adjust to the information from the poll results. Tracking polls are known to be imprecise in predicting the outcome of the election. In 1992, George Bush's tracking polls had him ahead of Bill Clinton in the closing weeks of the campaign. *See*: BENCHMARK POLL; POLL; SAMPLE.

References: Nelson W. Polsby and Aaron Wildavsky, *Presidential Elections: Strategies and Structures in American Politics*, 9th ed. (Chatham N.J.: Chatham House, 1996); Michael W. Traugott and Paul J. Lavrakas, *The Voter's Guide to Election Polls* (Chatham, N.J.: Chatham House, 1996).

TRADE ASSOCIATION is an alliance of businesses in the same industry or sector that unite to pursue a common political agenda. As a group, they have particular concerns about tax law, trade law, and regulatory law that affect their industries. They share mutual political interests, and lobby government to achieve their goals. Trade associations have the largest number of offices in Washington of all of the interest groups. There are over 2,000 trade associations in Washington, D.C. Many trade associations organize PACs and are a major source of funds for congressional campaigns. *See*: LOBBYIST; POLITICAL ACTION COMMITTEE.

References: Philip A. Mundo, *Interest Groups: Cases and Characteristics* (Chicago: Nelson-Hall, 1992); Paul S. Herrnson, Ronald G. Shaiko, and Clyde Wilcox, eds., *The Interest Group Connection: Electioneering, Lobbying, and Policymaking in Washington* (Chatham, N.J.: Chatham House, 1998).

TRUMAN, HARRY S. (1884–1972). His father a farmer and mule trader, Harry was born on May 8, 1884, in Lamar, Missouri; the family later moved to a farm near Independence, the small town which Truman would regard as "home" throughout his long life. Not able to afford a college education, the young Truman, age 22, took on management of his grandmother's 600-acre farm near Grandview, Missouri, in 1906. With the U.S. entry into World War I, Truman, a Missouri National Guard volunteer, was to experience combat duty in France, after his unit was brought into the U.S. Army as the 129th Field Artillery Regiment. Promoted to the rank of captain in June of 1918, later recommended for the rank of major, Truman was mustered-out on May 6, 1919. Returning to Missouri, Truman and an army buddy opened a men's clothing store in Kansas City; the postwar recession, however, led to its failure by September of 1922. That same year, long interested in Democratic Party politics, the emerging Pendergast machine looking to put at least a few "honest," "good citizen" types on the ballot, Truman was recruited to the race for judge of the Jackson County Court (the three-member county court being not a judicial body but a general governing body akin to boards of county commissioners in other states). Elected that year, he was defeated in 1924 but returned victorious two years later, elected as presiding judge in 1926. Personally honest, honest in office, but maintaining close ties with the machine, Truman became in 1934 Tom Pendergast's candidate for the U.S. Senate. Successful in both the primary and general elections, Truman entered the Senate as a committed New Dealer and a loyal supporter of the president. Franklin Roosevelt and other key administration figures, however, held Truman at some considerable distance, uneasy because of his association with the Kansas City machine, particularly by the spring of 1939 when Pendergast came under a multi-count federal indictment, the most serious charge being that he had failed to report large sums of bribe money as income. From Washington, Senator Truman lamented the indictment: "He has been a friend to me when I needed it. I am not one to desert a ship when it starts to go down." And go down it did; on May 29 Pendergast, having entered a guilty plea, entered Leavenworth federal penitentiary. Truman, caught in the undertow, also came very close, politically, to going under. Facing reelection to the Senate in 1940 labeled as the Pendergast candidate, but now without the machine's former clout to assist him, Truman remarkably survived both primary and general elections, in the latter no doubt benefiting from the coattails of the candidate at the top of the ballot that year, Franklin D. Roosevelt. Returning to the Senate in 1941, now largely free of the Pendergast albatross, the Senator was to gain a national reputation as chairman of the "Truman Committee," a special committee set up by the Senate as the prewar military build-up gained momentum to investigate the national defense program. The particular focus of the committee was on fairness in the awarding of defense contracts and, subsequently, on the performance integrity of those coming to hold the contracts. Over the life span of the committee, Truman, committee members, and staff would come to argue that "we saved the taxpayers about fifteen billion dollars." In 1944, in the midst of his war leadership, Roosevelt sought renomination and reelection. He and his most trusted political advisors decided on the necessity of dropping Vice-President Henry A. Wallace from the Democratic national ticket, Wallace having come to be regarded by many within the party, particularly those in its conservative wing, as too liberal, too pro-Soviet, too idiosyncratic. Balancing the ticket with a midwesterner (the chairman of the Senate's Truman Committee), delegates at the Chicago convention gave Roosevelt the third of his vice-presidential running mates, Harry S. Truman of Missouri. Roosevelt, reelected in November, inaugurated for his fourth term on January 20, 1945, war-weary and in rapidly declining health, died while on vacation in Warm Springs, Georgia on April 12, 1945, some 80 days into his new term. World War II moving to its conclusion, all of the enormous problems of the postwar world confronting him, never taken into Roosevelt's inner circle of policy making, Truman was to remark, as he was informed of the president's death, that he "felt like the moon, the stars, and all the planets had fallen on him." Truman's inner strength, a hard core of feisty self-confidence, was, however, to prevail. The first Truman administration, 1945–1949, remained essentially a war administration, bringing to a close European hostilities on May 8, 1945. This was followed by the Potsdam Conference at Berlin in July which determined, not only for occupied Germany but for Europe itself, the respective allied spheres of influence that, within a year (as Winston Churchill had warned in 1946) would come to be defined by a Soviet-imposed "iron curtain" descended across the heart of Europe. In the Pacific theater, to bring an end to hostilities there, Truman made what he later came to regard as the most difficult decision of his presidential tenure: authorization to the American military to use newly developed atomic bombs over the Japanese cities of Hiroshima and Nagasaki in August of 1945; a decision vindicated, in Truman's perspective as commander-in-chief, as one necessary to quickly terminate the war with Japan, thereby saving countless thousands of American lives which would be lost if a full-scale invasion of the main Japanese islands were required. That decision was questioned by some then, many later, on its moral grounds in terms of the death and destruction brought to the largely civilian populations in those cities. Truman's decision had its anticipated effect: Japanese surrender on September 2, 1945. Almost immediately the president's attention was returned to Europe where the Soviet Union, bringing much of eastern and central Europe under communist control, now extended the threat to Greece and Turkey in the Mediterranean. Out of this Soviet ambition emerged the U.S. policy of containment, beginning with promulgation of the Truman Doctrine early in 1947, which offered economic and military aid not only to Greece but to other countries faced with Soviet-supported communist insurgencies; adoption of the European Economic Plan ("the Marshall Plan"), to assist in the rebuilding of western European economies thereby safeguarding political stability; and later, in 1949, creation of the North Atlantic Treaty Organization (NATO), a defense alliance of western European states, eventually to include a re-armed and sovereign Federal Republic of Germany. These undertakings in the field of international politics were not wholly to dominate over domestic political and policy considerations: 1948 was a presidential election year; the Republicans, having regained control of House and Senate in the congressional elections of 1946, were poised to recapture the presidency, nominating their 1944 standard bearer, Governor Thomas E. Dewey of New York and, as his running mate, Governor Earl Warren of California. Truman, not only confronted with the problems associated with the economic and social adjustments which come with a nation shifting from war to peace, faced a disintegrating Democratic Party. Angered by the president's executive order ending racial segregation in the armed forces and by his further pledges in support of civil rights legislation aimed at racial equality before the law, conservative southern Democrats bolted the Philadelphia convention to form the Democratic States' Rights Party, the "Dixiecrats," nominating Governor J. Strom Thurmond of South Carolina and Mississippi governor Fielding L. Wright as their ticket, both governors strongly committed to the defense of racial segregation. On the Left, some liberal Democrats, joining with leftists of a wide variety, came to support the Progressive Party candidacy of former vice-president Henry A. Wallace and his running mate, U.S. senator Glen Taylor of Idaho. Thus buffeted by the foreign policy problems of an increasingly polarized world, the domestic problems of a war economy in transition to one of peacetime, with his party factionalized along ideological lines, Truman, nominated at the Philadelphia convention in July of 1948, with Senator Alben W. Barkley of Kentucky as his vice-presidential running mate, was thought by virtually everyone, except Harry S. Truman, to be a sure November loser. Beginning with his acceptance speech in Philadelphia, Truman pledged himself, if reelected, to an extensive "Fair Deal" agenda of legislative initiatives leading to expanded social security coverage, a program for national health insurance, public housing, advancements in civil rights, full employment and an increased minimum wage, economic controls to fight inflation, and, for organized labor, repeal of the Taft-Hartley Act of 1947. Further, in that same acceptance speech, Truman called the Republican-controlled 80th Congress back into special session so that the Republicans, who at their own convention had pledged themselves to a moderately progressive platform, could immediately deliver, turning promise into law. The special session was, as Truman anticipated, largely unproductive. The president then took to the campaign trail, whistlestopping across the country, an estimated 31,000 miles, castigating the Republican "Do Nothing" Congress and, urged on by increasingly large and enthusiastic crowds, "giving 'em hell." In late September and through October, against all predictions and survey findings, the Democrats began to surge, particularly in the states of the midwest where falling farm prices began to trigger memories of the "Republican" Great Depression of the 1930s. Truman's spectacular upset victory, Election Day 1948, was probably as much the result of the latter phenomenon as of Truman's advocacy of the "Fair Deal," or of his feisty, "man of the people" campaigning. The Truman-Barkley ticket ran up an amazing two-million-vote plurality over Dewey-Warren, the predicted winners. The Democratic national ticket carried 28 states with 303 Electoral College ballots to 16 states and 189 votes in the Electoral College for the Republicans. The two third parties which were expected to be fatally damaging to Truman failed to live up to advanced billing: the Dixiecrats and the Progressives drew about equal numbers of popular votes, each with some 1,150,000 ballots; the Thurmond-Wright ticket managing to carry four deep South states with 39 votes in the Electoral College. For Truman it was a vindicating personal victory won against great odds, and made all the more satisfying by restored Democratic majorities in House and Senate. Inaugurated on January 20, 1949, Truman's second administration, during which he had hoped to see accomplished much of his proposed "Fair Deal" program, turned almost immediately, as with his first four years, into a war administration, dominated at first by an ever more threatening "cold war" with the Soviet Union, and subsequently, after June 1950, by the hot war in Korea. Only the Housing Act of 1949 was to stand as testimony to the "Fair Deal"; the other initiatives were either blocked in Congress by the Republican-southern Democrat coalition, or shelved by the administration on the basis of "butter or guns" decision making. Truman, himself, was to suffer greatly in terms of lost popular standing. Two events in particular seemed to turn the tide of public opinion against the president: (1) in 1951 Truman felt compelled, in order to preserve constitutionally mandated civilian control of the military, to remove World War II hero General Douglas MacArthur from his command in Korea on the basis of the general's refusal to follow administration policy and, more directly, specific presidential orders; (2) in 1952 the U.S. Supreme Court held, in *Youngstown Sheet and Tube Co.* v. *Sawyer*, that President Truman had exceeded his constitutional authority in ordering federal government seizure and operation of the nation's steel industry about to be shut down by a threatened strike. Truman's argument, that to prevent such a strike which would affect war production and be felt on the battlefields of Korea was within the president's constitutionally unspecified "emergency powers," was rejected both by a divided Court and, within the public arena, by a divided nation. Announcing on March 29, 1952 his decision not to seek renomination and reelection, Truman had earlier that January attempted to recruit Illinois governor Adlai E. Stevenson to the presidential race. Stevenson, while ultimately becoming the Democratic nominee, equivocated, presumably not wishing to be seen as Truman's hand-picked successor. Further distancing himself from the Truman administration during the 1952 campaign, Stevenson's tactic was unrewarding in that the November elections returned Republicans to the White House for the first time since Herbert Hoover's departure on March 4, 1933. With the inauguration of his successor, General Dwight D. Eisenhower, Truman returned to Independence, Missouri, and an active retirement. Continuing a lively interest in policy and politics, Truman also devoted time to the writing of his presidential memoirs, published in 1955–1956. Living to age 88, Truman died on December 26, 1972, in hospital in Kansas City, Missouri. *See*: ELECTIONS: 1944, 1948; ROOSEVELT, FRANKLIN D.

References: Robert J. Donovan, *The Presidency of Harry S. Truman*, 2 vols. (New York: Norton, 1977–1982); Alonzo L. Hamby, *Man of the People, A Life of Harry S. Truman* (New York: Oxford University Press, 1995); Donald R. McCoy, *The Presidency of Harry S. Truman* (Lawrence: University Press of Kansas, 1984); Harry S. Truman, *Memoirs*, 2 vols. (Garden City, N.Y. Doubleday, 1955–1956).

TWELFTH AMENDMENT is the 1804 amendment to the U.S. Constitution that required the members of the Electoral College to vote separately for president and vice-president. Prior to that, the vice-presidency was given to the runner-up in the presidential election. The amendment also reduced the range of choices for the House to the top three vote-getters, if one candidate did not attain a majority of the Electoral College votes. This amendment was a result of the confusion created by the election of 1800, in which Thomas Jefferson was tied with his own party's vice-presidential candidate, Aaron Burr. The election went to the House, which eventually selected Jefferson as president and Burr as vice-president. This amendment was adopted to accommodate the emerging party system that had not been foreseen by the founding fathers. *See:* ELECTORAL COLLEGE; ELECTION: 1800.

TWENTY-FOURTH AMENDMENT is a 1964 amendment to the U.S. Constitution that forbids the levying of a poll tax in primary and general elections for national offices. *See*: POLL TAX.

TWENTY-SECOND AMENDMENT is the 1951 amendment to the U.S. Constitution that provides that no one person can be elected president more than two times. This was enacted to prevent a repetition of what Franklin D. Roosevelt was able to accomplish. He was elected president four times (in 1932, 1934, 1936, and 1940). There had been a tradition of a two-term presidency since George Washington. Every president had respected that tradition except Roosevelt. It was the Republican Congress of 1946, the first GOP Congress since the New Deal, that promoted this amendment. It is ironic that it was the Republicans who promoted this amendment, because the next president who might have been elected to a third term was the popular Republican, Ronald Reagan.

TWENTY-SIXTH AMENDMENT is a 1971 amendment to the U.S. Constitution that lowered the voting age to eighteen. The voting age had already been lowered to eighteen by the Voting Rights Act of 1970, but the U.S. Supreme Court, in *Oregon* v. *Mitchell* (1970), ruled that Congress had the authority to lower the voting age for national elections but not for state and local elections. This created the need for a constitutional amendment. The Democratic Party was very supportive of this amendment, anticipating that it would benefit from this newly enfranchised vote. This age cohort of voters has a very low turnout rate. In fact, enfranchising this age group has contributed to the lower turnout rate in the United States. *See*: VOTER TURNOUT.

TWENTY-THIRD AMENDMENT is a 1961 amendment to the U.S. Constitution that allots three electoral votes to the District of Columbia. The residents of the nation's capital city had no voice in national elections because the Constitution (Article II, Section 1) states that only "states" can appoint college electors. This amendment addressed that for the District of Columbia. The residents of the District of Columbia frequently lobby for full representation in the U.S. House and Senate. In 1978, Congress approved a constitutional amendment to repeal the Twenty-Third Amendment and authorize full representation to the District of Columbia, but the amendment was not ratified by the states.

TWO-PARTY SYSTEM is a party system in which only one of two parties has the opportunity to gain control of the major offices of the national government. The United States has had a two-party system throughout its history. The Democratic Party has its origins in the founding period of the Republic with Thomas Jefferson. The emergent Republican Party outpolled the Whig Party in the presidential election of 1856, and the Whigs faded. The two parties have been very competitive at the national level. From 1888 to 1992, the Democrats won the presidency in twelve elections, and the Republicans captured the office of the president fifteen times in that period. At the state and congressional levels, the competitiveness between the two parties is not as balanced. Since the Civil War, the South had been solidly Democratic. However, in recent decades the Republicans have become more competitive in the South. In many congressional districts around the country, one party is so dominant that the minority party has almost no chance of winning.

There are a variety of explanations for the two-party character of the American party system. One common explanation is the plurality election system. In almost every election in the United States, including Electoral College votes for president, U.S. Senator, U.S. Representative, governors, most state legislators, county officials, mayors, and city council, members are elected in a plurality system. A plurality system is one in which the top vote-getter wins. A majority is not required. That, combined with the use of single-member districts for the election of most offices, where only one member is elected from each district, contributes to the maintenance of a two-party system. It is very difficult to create and sustain a third party in the United States under the current electoral system. Third-party voters begin to believe their votes are wasted.

State and federal law also supports the two parties in the United States. The Federal Election Campaign Act awards to the two parties, defined as those parties that receive 25% of the vote in the previous election, both federal grants to hold national conventions and the maximum level of funding to their candidates for the general election. The Commission on Presidential Debates, which sponsors the debates, was organized by the national committees of the two major parties. This Commission refused to allow Ross Perot to participate in the 1996 presidential debates, restricting the debates to the two major party candidates. *See*: DEMOCRATIC PARTY; FEDERAL ELECTION CAMPAIGN ACT OF

1971; PLURALITY; PROPORTIONAL REPRESENTATION; REPUBLICAN PARTY; RUNOFF; WHIG PARTY.

References: John F. Bibby, *Politics, Parties, and Elections in America*, 3rd ed. (Chicago: Nelson-Hall, 1966); Leon Epstein, *Political Parties in the American Mold* (Madison: University of Wisconsin Press, 1986).

TWO-THIRDS RULE. A super-majority of two-thirds of the delegates required for presidential nominations was adopted by the Jacksonian Democratic-Republican Party for its first convention in 1832. The rule led to a convention deadlock in 1844. Martin Van Buren attained a majority of the delegates, but was unable to attain two-thirds. Consequently, the first dark horse nominee, James K. Polk, was nominated on the ninth ballot. The rule had been used by the southern Democrats to protect their interests at Democratic National Conventions. The two-thirds rule was finally abrogated at the 1936 Democratic National Convention. At the 1948 Democratic convention, the southern Democrats offered a minority report to the rules committee with a proposal to reinstate the two-thirds rule. It was not accepted.

Reference: Ralph M. Goodman, *The National Party Chairmen and Committees: Factionalism at the Top* (Armonk, N.Y.: M. E. Sharpe, 1990).

TYLER, JOHN (1790–1862), the first vice-president to succeed to the executive office at the death of an incumbent president, was born in Greenway, Virginia on March 29, 1790. Educated at the College of William and Mary from which he graduated in 1807, he read the law under the tutelage of his father, then serving as governor of Virginia. Admitted to the bar in 1809, Tyler almost immediately began what was to be a lifelong career in Virginia politics. Elected, at age 21, to the Virginia House of Delegates, the youthful Jeffersonian Republican served there until 1816, when voters sent him to the U.S. House of Representatives. In 1823, Tyler resumed his career in state politics, first returning to the House of Delegates, subsequently to the governorship (1825–1827). In the latter year the state legislature elected him to the U.S. Senate where he was to serve until his resignation in 1836; a resignation prompted by his refusal to follow instructions from the Democrat-controlled Virginia legislature directing him to vote in support of President Andrew Jackson, to whom Tyler had become increasingly opposed. This break with the state Democratic Party led Tyler to identification with the Whigs. As he switched parties Tyler did not, however, abandon the Jeffersonian republican principles which he had long espoused. He continued a strong advocacy of states' rights, stopping short, however, of an endorsement of the doctrine of nullification. A spokesman for southern interests and slavery, he remained skeptical of national government, and particularly of presidential, exercise of power. John Tyler's conversion to the Whig Party was thus born more out of antipathy to Andrew Jackson than of any wholesale subscription to Whig policy. Nonetheless, Whig leadership came in 1840 to view

Tyler as someone who would, by both his views and his political experience "balance," as a vice-presidential nominee, a ticket headed by the military hero, "Ole Tippecanoe," William Henry Harrison. The raucous campaign of that year resulted in comfortable popular and Electoral College vote margins for the Whig ticket. The party's expectations for a Harrison administration cooperatively joined with, if not actually guided by, the Whig congressional leadership were shattered by the president's death just one month following his inauguration on March 4, 1841. By claiming all of the perquisites and powers of the executive office, Tyler set an important constitutional precedent, negating the argument of those who maintained that at the death of an incumbent the vice-president merely became the "acting" president, with restricted authority. By assuming the former role, and with his opposition to Whig proposals to reestablish a Bank of the United States, Tyler brought himself into open warfare with his party in Congress. It was the second veto of the bank measure in September of 1841, that led (except for Secretary of State Daniel Webster) to the dramatic resignation of the entire cabinet. At that point Tyler became a man, more significantly a president, without a party. Failing to establish a new states' rights party, Tyler's hopes for a second term vanished. Leaving office in March of 1845, Tyler returned to Virginia, there to remain a strong voice in support of states' rights. While holding to the constitutional prerogative of a state to secede, Tyler yet sought ways to preserve the Union. On the eve of civil war, Tyler presided over a "last resort" effort to ward off hostilities, prevent additional states from seceding, perhaps even to restore the Union through the Washington Peace Convention of February 1861. With the convention's failure, John Tyler followed Virginia into the Confederacy. That November, Tyler, a member of the provisional body, was elected to the first regularly constituted Confederate Congress. In Richmond, waiting to be seated, John Tyler died on January 18, 1862. *See*: ELECTIONS: 1840.

References: Oliver P. Chitwood, *John Tyler: Champion of the Old South* (New York: Appleton-Century, 1939); Norma L. Peterson, *The Presidencies of William Henry Harrison and John Tyler* (Lawrence: University Press of Kansas, 1989).

U

UNDECIDED refers to a group of respondents to a poll who say they have not made up their minds about which candidate will receive their vote. The number of undecided respondents decreases as election day draws closer. Some public opinion experts predict that the undecided will break against the incumbent. In the last two presidential elections, a large proportion of the undecided went for Perot. Some public opinion experts argue that the late undecided vote will vote against the incumbent. This unexpected voting behavior by undecided voters has led to a number of inaccurate predictions by public pollsters.

National polling firms often ask the undecided a series of questions to determine which way the respondents are leaning. The frequently cited Gallup/CNN/ *USA Today* poll has not been exact in predicting the results of recent presidential elections because of the way it has distributed the undecided. In 1996 the Reuters/Zogby poll was the most accurate, actually predicting the percentages the candidates received. *See*: POLL.

References: Rhodes Cook, ''Clinton's Easy Second-Term Win Riddles GOP Electoral Map,'' *Congressional Quarterly*, Vol. 54 (November 9, 1996); Michael W. Traugott and Paul J. Lavrakas, *The Voter's Guide to Election Polls* (Chatham, N.J.: Chatham House, 1996).

UNION PARTY. The Union Party was the name adopted by the Republican Party for the election of 1864. President Lincoln was seeking Democratic support in this election during the Civil War.

There was also a Union Party in the 1936 election. It was a minor party promoted by the controversial radio priest, Father Charles E. Caughlin. The Union Party's presidential candidate in 1939 was North Dakota congressman

Charles Lemke, who received 1.96% of the vote in 1936. This minor party promoted radical ideas from both the left and the right, making its ideology difficult to classify.

References: J. David Gillespie, *Politics at the Periphery: Third Parties in Two-Party America* (Columbia: University of South Carolina Press, 1993); Malcolm Moos, *The Republicans: A History of Their Party* (New York: Random House, 1956).

UNIT RULE is a rule, adopted by state delegations at national party conventions, that binds all delegates to vote with the majority of the state delegation. If adopted, the entire delegation of a particular state is be required to vote with the majority of the delegates from that state on nominations and issues brought before a convention. Several state delegations imposed the unit rule at the 1968 Democratic National Convention. After their 1968 loss, the Democratic National Committee created a Commission on Party Structure and Delegate Selection, which prohibited the use of the unit rule in state delegations. The Republicans have never sanctioned nor condoned the use of the unit rule. At the 1976 Republican National Convention, the Mississippi delegation adopted a unit rule, which helped President Ford fend off the challenge of Ronald Reagan for the Republican nomination.

References: Philip A. Klinker, *The Losing Parties: Out-Party National Committees, 1956–1993* (New Haven, Conn.: Yale University Press, 1994); Stephen J. Wayne, *The Road to the White House 1996: The Politics of Presidential Elections* (New York: St. Martin's Press, 1996).

UNITED JEWISH ORGANIZATIONS* v. *CAREY, 430 U.S. 144 (1977) is a case in which the U.S. Supreme Court upheld a state legislative redistricting scheme which was designed to enhance the representation of minorities.

Several counties in New York were required under Section 5 of the Voting Rights Act of 1965 to submit their redistricting plans to the attorney general for preapproval prior to their implementation. Following the rejection of the 1972 reapportionment statute, the New York State legislature passed a law (in 1974) creating three majority-minority state senate districts, and seven majority-minority assembly districts. This is the same number of majority-minority districts as were created under the 1972 statute. The only difference between the 1972 and the 1974 statutes was that under the latter, all of the majority-minority districts were at least 65% non-white. Under the 1972 plan, the non-white population in some of these districts was as low as 53%. The 1974 plan, however, called for a district line that essentially divided in half the Hasidic community in the Williamsburg section of New York.

The United Jewish Organizations of Williamsburg, representing the Hasidic Jews, challenged the redistricting plan, asserting that the value of their vote was being diluted because of their race, in violation of the Fourteenth and Fifteenth Amendments. The Supreme Court ruled in favor of the state of New York, affirming the lower court's holding that the Hasidic community did not have a constitutional right to have their votes consolidated within one district. Furthermore, the Court acknowledged that race must be considered when states are attempting to comply with the Voting Rights Act of 1965, and therefore concluded that race-conscious redistricting plans were not necessarily discriminatory.

Although the Supreme Court has not formally overturned *United Jewish Organizations, Shaw* v. *Reno* (1993) severely limited the effects of this case. *See*: GERRYMANDERING; PRECLEARANCE; REDISTRICTING; *SHAW* v. *RENO* (1993); VOTING RIGHTS ACT.

UNITED WE STAND AMERICA was a front group for Ross Perot's independent candidacy for president in 1992. There remained a few state and local chapters of United We Stand after the 1992 election. There was, however, considerable internal bickering over money, leadership, and Ross Perot's role in the organization. Ross Perot created the Reform Party for his 1996 bid for president. *See*: PEROT, ROSS; REFORM PARTY.

U.S. TERM LIMITS **v. THORTON**, 514 U.S. 799 (1995) is a significant case which provided the U.S. Supreme Court with its first opportunity to evaluate the constitutionality of term limits legislation. As part of growing national movement, the state of Arkansas had amended its constitution to include restrictions on the number of times that an individual might be elected to the Senate and House of Representatives. Under the amendment, members of the House of Representatives who had served three terms, and senators who had served two terms, were prohibited from appearing on the ballot. A number of registered voters in Arkansas brought suit, claiming that the law ran afoul of the U.S. Constitution.

The Supreme Court, by a vote of five to four, agreed with Arkansas voters. According to the Court, the term limit amendment amounted to an addition to the "qualifications clauses" in Article I, Sections 2 and 3 of the U.S. Constitution. These clauses set out rather minimal age, citizenship, and residency requirements for members of Congress. According to the Court, the Founding Fathers intended these standards to be exclusive; that is, they represent all that may be required of those who would seek election to Congress. In this way, the Framers guaranteed a large pool of potential legislators. Any measure which would make one who met these criteria ineligible would contradict the intent of the Framers, and the plain words of the U.S. Constitution. The majority felt that this is precisely what the people of Arkansas did when they attempted to place term limits on their representatives in Congress. In effect, the Arkansas amendment would, for example, disqualify an otherwise qualified candidate for the House of Representatives based on the fact that the individual had already served three terms.

Although this case involved a state term limits law, the reasoning would clearly extend to any federal law having the same effect. The Court decision means, therefore, that absent the formal amending of the U.S. Constitution, no limits may be placed on the number of terms that one may serve in the Senate and the House of Representatives. *See*: TERM LIMITS.

V

VAN BUREN, MARTIN (1782–1862) was born in the Dutch settlement of Kinderhook, Columbia County, New York on December 5, 1782. Becoming, in the 1820s, one of the principal organizers of the Jacksonian Democratic Party, it is alleged that the young Van Buren acquired an early interest in politics listening to the debate about candidates and issues among the farm and village patrons of his father's tavern. Largely self-educated, Van Buren, age fourteen, began the study of law with a local attorney, later continuing that study in New York City. Admitted to the bar in 1803, Van Buren practiced in Columbia County, appointed surrogate there in 1808. Four years later he was elected to the New York Senate where he served, with rapidly rising influence, until 1821. In this period Van Buren became increasingly active in the factional politics that constituted Jeffersonian Republicanism in New York State. Never forgiving Dewitt Clinton for his brief flirtation with the Federalists, accepting that party's presidential nomination in 1812, Van Buren battled the Clintonians to the very day of Governor Clinton's death in February of 1828. Despite some largely personal victories scored by Clinton in the 1820s, it was Van Buren who by that time controlled New York politics, having organized a statewide political machine under his personal leadership and that of a council of selected partisans known as the "Albany Regency"; the machine relying heavily on the use of a strict patronage distributed on the basis of party (i.e., factional) loyalty, a tightly controlled state legislative caucus, and a dedicated and talented governing elite. It was these superb organizational and manipulative skills, combined with his modest height, that were to earn Van Buren the nickname the "Little Magician." It was, however, this same ability and emphasis that led to a lifelong perception of Van Buren as a man more interested in politics as a pragmatic means to power than as a principled means to policy. Secure in the assessment that the

"Regency" would function effectively in his day-to-day absence, Van Buren, in 1821, allowed himself to be elected by the New York legislature to a seat in the U.S. Senate. There his Jeffersonian Republicanism, even as that coalition was disintegrating, prevailed: a cautious advocacy of states rights; opposition to elaborate schemes for nationally funded internal improvements; skepticism of the wisdom of high protective tariffs and of the Bank of the United States. Overarching these views was a more generalized commitment to a democratic politics, shaped and directed by *party*. Even though supporting Secretary of the Treasury William H. Crawford of Georgia in the presidential election of 1824, it is not astonishing that Van Buren soon found his political hero, as the nation had found its popular hero, in Andrew Jackson of Tennessee. A prime mover in organizing Jacksonian forces as the Democratic Party (1825–1828), Van Buren resigned his Senate seat in the latter year to return to New York to manage the Jackson campaign there and, so as to strengthen the ticket, to become the Democratic Party's gubernatorial nominee. Both he and Jackson were to be successful. His term as governor, however, was a brief three months; Van Buren resigned in March of 1829 to join the Jackson cabinet as secretary of state. As the divisions over states' rights issues made enemies of Jackson and Vice-President John C. Calhoun of South Carolina, the alliance between the president and his secretary of state grew stronger. With the approach of the presidential election of 1832, Jackson made clear his determination that delegates to the Democratic National Convention were to ratify his choice of running mate, namely, Martin Van Buren. This they did. The election results of that year produced a landslide Democratic victory, encouraging Jackson, now supported by his new vice-president, to move energetically and successfully against administration opponents, whether South Carolina nullificationists or last-ditch defenders of the Bank of the United States. Just as Jackson had dictated Van Buren's vice-presidential nomination so, as the 1836 election approached, he designated the New Yorker as his presidential heir. Going one step further, he also made certain that delegates to the party's convention in Baltimore, in May of 1835, added to the national ticket as vice-presidential nominee the name of Congressman Richard M. Johnson of Kentucky, a candidate whose personal life caused distress, if not outright objection, among many delegates and party leaders. By design the Whig Party in 1836 declined to nominate a national ticket, adopting instead the tactic of encouraging a number of regional candidacies to be advanced so as to deny to any one nominee, primarily Van Buren, an Electoral College majority, thereby throwing the presidential election into the U.S. House of Representatives where Whig leaders concluded a candidate of their choice might prevail. The tactic failed; Van Buren easily outpolled the Whig frontrunner, General William Henry Harrison, by more than 200,000 popular votes, carrying 15 states with 170 Electoral College ballots, a clear majority. An interesting footnote to the election result, however, was that the combined Whig popular vote, shared by Harrison, Senator Daniel Webster of Massachusetts, and Hugh White of Tennessee, was all but equal to that given to Democrat

Van Buren. Perhaps because of Democratic divisions over vice-presidential nominee Richard M. Johnson, the Whig tactic did result in no one candidate for that office securing an Electoral College majority, the election being transferred, as provided by the Constitution, to the U.S. Senate. There Johnson prevailed, securing the vote of 33 senators to 16 who supported the Whig, Francis Granger of New York. Inaugurated on March 4, 1837, President Van Buren was soon entangled in the problems of the prolonged economic depression initiated by the Panic of 1837, a panic which Whig adversaries argued was the result of the widespread state and local bank speculation which followed closure of the Bank of the United States. As is historically the case, politics follows economics, and Van Buren suffered all the discomforts of presidents, past and future, unfortunate enough to be in office at a time of economic collapse. He was, nonetheless, unanimously renominated at the Democratic National Convention of 1840. The Whigs selected their most popular vote-getter of 1836, "Ole Tippecanoe," William Henry Harrison, joining with him as vice-presidential candidate a recent convert to Whigism, John Tyler of Virginia. Van Buren found himself ill-suited for the campaign ahead, one of the most raucous in American political history. Slogans and songs, gimmicks, torch light parades, and mass meetings prevailed over substantive discussion of national issues. Voters decided for "Tippecanoe and Tyler too" over "Van, Van, a used-up man," giving the Whig ticket a plurality over the Democrats of nearly 150,000 votes, Harrison carrying 19 states with 234 Electoral College ballots to Van Buren's 7 states and 60 votes in the Electoral College. Returning to New York, the "Little Magician" was soon again deeply involved in the factional politics of that state, eventually becoming leader of the "barnburners," an anti-slavery faction that was (in 1848) to bolt the state and national Democratic Party. Rejected by the Democratic National Convention in 1844 as he sought its presidential nomination, Van Buren, as a "barnburner," now became in 1848 the nominee of the Free-Soilers, an anti-slavery party committed to the provisions of the Wilmot Proviso of 1846 (proposed legislation which, if adopted, would prohibit the extension of slavery into territories acquired as a result of the war with Mexico, 1846–1848). As the nominee of the Free-Soil Party, with Charles Francis Adams as vice-presidential candidate, the ticket polled nearly 300,000 popular votes, but carried no states nor gained any Electoral College ballots. Many argue, however, that by siphoning votes away from the Democratic ticket of Cass and Butler, particularly in Massachusetts and New York, the Free-Soilers delivered the election to the Whig presidential nominee, General Zachary Taylor of Louisiana and his running mate Millard Fillmore of New York. By 1850, factional differences largely repaired, Van Buren and most of the barnburners returned to the Democratic Party. There the "Little Magician" remained, in the party he had been so instrumental in forming a quarter of a century earlier. Van Buren, supportive of President Lincoln and the unionist cause, died in the second year of the Civil War, on July 24, 1862. *See*: ELECTIONS: 1836, 1840, 1848.

References: Frederick J. Blue, *The Free Soilers, Third Party Politics, 1848–54* (Urbana: University of Illinois Press, 1973); John Niven, *Martin Van Buren: The Romantic Age of American Politics* (New York: Oxford University Press, 1983); Martin Van Buren, *Autobiography*, John C. Fitzpatrick, ed. (Washington, D.C.: U.S. Government Printing Office, 1920); Major L. Wilson, *The Presidency of Martin Van Buren* (Lawrence: University Press of Kansas, 1984).

VICE-PRESIDENTIAL SELECTION. Presidential nominees select vice-presidential nominees to help them win the general election. Frequently, the running mate is selected to achieve geographic or ideological balance. John F. Kennedy selected Lyndon B. Johnson to help secure Texas and votes in the South. Also in 1960, Californian Richard Nixon selected Henry Cabot Lodge of Massachusetts to help garner votes in the East. In 1980, Ronald Reagan, a strong conservative, selected the more moderate George Bush to balance the ticket and heal the wounds from the primary battle. Balancing the ticket can go beyond geographic regions and ideology: Jimmy Carter selected Senator Walter Mondale, and Michael Dukakis selected Texas Senator Lloyd Bentson. In order to deal with the concern that the presidential nominees were Washington "outsiders," they selected Washington "insiders" as their running mates.

Some interesting recent vice-presidential selections include: Walter Mondale's choice of Geraldine Ferraro as the first female vice-presidential nominee in 1984. The Democrats were trying to exploit the emerging gender gap and give momentum to their campaign by this bold move. In 1988, George Bush selected the young, inexperienced, conservative junior senator from Indiana, Dan Quayle, with the expectation that he would attract younger voters and female voters. Both the Ferraro and Qualye selections led to some degree of controversy during the campaigns.

The most recent vice-presidential selections, including Democrat Bill Clinton's selection of Al Gore, and Bob Dole's 1996 pick of Jack Kemp, gave their respective party tickets a boost when the vice-presidential nominees were announced. Clinton's selection of Al Gore in 1992 emphasized the youth and moderation of this winning baby boomer ticket. Bob Dole's selection of critic and philosophical foe Jack Kemp showed Dole's willingness to overlook past differences with Kemp to invigorate his fledgling campaign.

For many, the vice-presidency has been a road to the presidency. Almost one-third of American presidents were once vice-presidents. Five were elected president, and nine succeeded to the office because of death or resignation of the president.

References: Nelson W. Polsby and Aaron Wildavsky, *Presidential Elections: Strategies and Structures in American Politics*, 9th ed. (Chatham, N.J.: Chatham House, 1996); Stephen J. Wayne, *The Road to the White House 1996: The Politics of Presidential Elections* (New York: St. Martin's Press, 1996).

VNS (VOTER NEWS SERVICE). Voter News Service was formed in 1993. It is sponsored by a consortium of networks, including ABC, CBS, CNN, and

NBC. The purpose of VNS is to gather election data, in particular, exit polling data. The data is given to the networks, who use them to do their own analyses and election night predictions. This consortium saves the networks a great deal of money. *See*: EXIT POLLS.

Reference: Michael W. Traugott and Paul J. Lavrakas, *The Voter's Guide to Election Polls*. (Chatham, N.J.: Chatham House, 1996).

VOTE-BY-MAIL is an election innovation approved for testing by the state of Oregon in 1981. In 1987, Oregon made vote-by-mail an option for local and special elections. A majority of Oregon counties now use it because it reduces the cost of election administration. In 1983 vote-by-mail was used for a statewide ballot.

In 1995, as a result of Senator Robert Packwood's resignation from the U.S. Senate, Oregon used the vote-by-mail for both the primary and the general election. The primary ballots were mailed in mid-November, the voters had until December 5 to return their ballots by mail or drop them off at a specified site. Identical procedures were used for the general election in January. The rate of turnout of eligible voters was 58% in the primary, and 66% of eligible voters in the general election.

A study by two professors in the Department of Political Science at the University of Oregon of the mail-in voters found that vote-by-mail format does raise voter turnout. They found that the demographics of the additional voters generated by the vote-by-mail procedures are more similar to the traditional voters than they are to the non-voters.

In 1996 the state of North Dakota held the first vote-by-mail presidential primary. The state also offered traditional on-site voting with one location in each county. Like Oregon, North Dakota also experienced greater voter participation with vote-by-mail.

The use of vote-by-mail impacts on the timing of political campaigns, since the candidates and the parties do not know when the voters will mail in their ballots. The campaigns need to intensify their efforts over a longer period of time.

The major barrier to increased vote-by-mail, which has a number of advantages including increased turnout and lower cost, is the fear of ballot tampering. *See*: ABSENTEE BALLOT; VOTER TURNOUT.

References: Priscella L. Southwell and Justin Burchet, ''The Effect of Vote-By-Mail on Turnout: The Special Senate Election in the State of Oregon,'' Prepared for delivery at the American Political Science Association Annual Meeting, August 29–September 1, 1996, San Francisco, CA; Oregon Secretary of State, http://www.sos.state.or.us/executive/other.info.

VOTER TURNOUT is usually measured as the percentage of the voting age population that votes in a particular election. On occasion, the press reports it as a percentage of the registered vote that cast ballots. European democracies have much higher rates of participation, when compared to the United States. The turnout rate in the United States for the 1992 presidential election was 55.2% of the voting age population (VAP). The turnout rate in 1992 was a gain over the 50.1% turnout in 1988. This uptick in the turnout in 1992 was a result of Ross Perot's candidacy. In 1996 the turnout in the presidential election reached a postwar record low of 48.8%. This was calculated to be the lowest turnout since 1924, when women, who had been given the right to vote in 1920, did not vote in significant numbers.

The turnout for midterm elections is lower than in the presidential year. In the midterm election of 1994, the turnout was 38%. In the nineteenth century in the United States, the turnout rate was much higher; it was closer to the European countries that have a turnout rate of over 80%.

One explanation for the lower rate of turnout in the United States is the voter registration requirement. In European democracies, it is the responsibility of the government to register the eligible voters. In the United States it is the citizens' responsibility to register to vote. Registration in most states must occur 30 days before the election, a period when there is not a great deal of interest in politics. There is also a state residency requirement to be eligible to vote. In 1972 the U.S. Supreme Court limited the residency requirement to 30 days. The mobility of Americans limits voter participation by some estimates of up to 9%. States that have election-day registration, such as Minnesota, often have a turnout rate of over 70%.

Certain groups are not permitted to vote, such as aliens and felons. Some states, like Delaware, never allow convicted felons to vote, while others, like Massachusetts, allow felons to vote while they are serving their sentence.

There is tremendous variation in voter turnout by state. In 1996, Minnesota had the best rate of turnout at 67%, followed by Maine and Montana with over 60%. New York State had a poor showing of only 42%. Georgia and South Carolina had a turnout rate of 41% in 1996.

Certain demographic groups are better voters than others. Socioeconomic characteristics associated with high turnout rates include: higher income, higher levels of education, middle age, Catholic, Jewish, and white. The low rate of voting by 18-to 21-year-olds, granted the franchise by the Twenty-Sixth Amendment, contributes to the lower rate of turnout in the United States. Level of education is the best predictor of voting. Eighty-four percent of citizens with four years of college or more reported they voted. One-half of the citizens with a high school diploma reported they voted. In recent presidential elections females have voted at a rate slightly better than males.

Primary elections have a very low rate of participation. A study of statewide contested primaries over a 26-year period showed only a 30% participation rate. The average turnout in presidential primaries is 25%. Primary voters have a strong sense of partisan identity, and are more ideological. *See*: MOTOR VOTER LAW; REGISTRATION, VOTER.

References: Walter Dean Burnham, "The Turnout Problem," in *Elections American Style*, James A. Reichley, ed. (Washington, D.C.: Brookings Institution, 1987); Malcolm Jewell and David Olson, *Political Parties and Elections in American States* (Chicago: Dorsey, 1988); Harold W. Stanley and Richard G. Niemi, *Vital Statistics on American Politics*, 5th ed. (Washington, D.C.: Congressional Quarterly Press, 1995).

VOTING RIGHTS ACT was passed by Congress in 1965. It was extended and expanded in 1970, 1975, and 1982. The 1965 Voting Rights Act was designed to expand suffrage to African Americans in the South. At the end of reconstruction, southern states wrote state constitutional provisions intended to restrict black voting, without violating the Fifteenth Amendment. The literacy test was one of these provisions. In Mississippi, for example, prospective voters had to read sections of the state constitution or interpret the meaning of sections that were read to them. This was done by state-appointed officials, with wide discretion. The 1965 Voting Rights Act banned the literacy test for voter registration. In addition, in states and counties where less than 50% of the population was registered, federal registers and voting examiners were sent in to register voters and supervise the conduct of the elections. Section 5 of the 1965 law required that the affected state and counties submit to the Justice Department, or a federal district court judge, changes in "any voting qualifications or prerequisites to voting" different from that which had been in effect. This preclearance requirement became important in the reapportionment after the 1970 census. Multi-member districts were not permitted where there were sizable black populations. The Voting Rights Act was viewed by many as quite successful on expanding the right of African Americans in the South to register and vote. By the end of 1967 over half a million new African American voters were enrolled in the seven covered states.

The 1970 extension of the Voting Rights Act lowered the voting age to eighteen, and banned residency requirements for voting longer than 30 days. The eighteen-year-old franchise was tested in the U.S. Supreme Court, and in *Oregon v. Mitchell* (1970) the Court ruled that Congress did not have the authority to lower the voting age to eighteen to vote in state elections. The Court did uphold the national government's right to ban literacy tests.

The 1975 extension of the Voting Rights Act addressed the concerns of foreign-language-speaking minorities. It required bilingual ballots in jurisdictions where 5% of the population did not speak English as their native language. This had its greatest impact where there were large Hispanic populations. In 1975 the preclearance requirement of Section 5 was expanded to Hispanics and other groups. The Voting Rights Act was extended in 1982 for 25 years.

The Voting Rights Act also addressed issues beyond voting. The revised language of Section 2 states that members of racial and language minorities "have less opportunity than other members of the electorate to participate in the political process and to elect representatives of their choice." This led states to draw majority-minority districts after the 1990 census. The U.S. Supreme

Court has come to view districts drawn on the basis of race alone as unconstitutional. This issue continues to be litigated, and districts continue to be redrawn to meet the Court's changing view on the issue. *See*: MAJORITY-MINORITY DISTRICT; *MILLER* v. *JOHNSON* (1995); *MOBILE, CITY OF*, v. *BOLDEN* (1980); *OREGON* v. *MITCHELL* (1970); *SHAW* v. *RENO* (1993); *THORNBURG* v. *GINGLES* (1986).

References: Bernard Grofman, Lisa Handley, and Richard G. Niemi, *Minority Representation and the Quest for Voting Equality* (New York: Cambridge University Press, 1992); Richard K. Scher, Jon L. Mills, and John J. Hotaling, *Voting Rights and Democracy: The Law and Politics of Districting* (Chicago: Nelson-Hall, 1997).

W

WALLACE, GEORGE CORLEY (1919–1998) was a four-term Democratic governor of Alabama, and three-time presidential candidate. George Wallace gave voice to those fearful of the changes that occurred in the 1960s and 1970s in the United States.

George Wallace was born on an Alabama farm. He earned a law degree from the University of Alabama. In 1948, as a delegate to the Democratic National Convention, Wallace did not join the southern bolt from the convention in protest of the civil rights plank. In 1958 he lost the Democratic nomination for governor of Alabama, and many interpreted this loss as a result of his soft position on race issues. Wallace did win the Alabama governorship in 1962, and in his inaugural address he pledged to defend segregation.

As governor, Wallace stood at the door of the University of Alabama to block the registration of two African-American students. President John Kennedy called out the National Guard to integrate the university.

In 1964, Wallace ran for the Democratic nomination for president and won 25% of the vote in the Wisconsin primary. In 1968 he ran as the candidate of the American Independent Party, and carried five states and 46 Electoral College votes. He ran again in 1972, but left the race after an assassin's bullet left him paralyzed; he had won the Florida and Indiana primaries before he withdrew. He campaigned briefly for president in 1976, but withdrew when it was obvious his candidacy was not going to catch fire. *See*: AMERICAN INDEPENDENT PARTY; ELECTIONS: 1968.

Reference: Dan T. Carter, *The Politics of Rage: George Wallace, The Origins of New Conservatism, and the Transformation of American Politics* (New York: Simon and Schuster, 1995).

WARD. Many cities are divided into wards for the election of their city council members. The local political party organizations recognize ward boundaries, and organize themselves according to wards. There are ward leaders in local party organizations. There is also the pejorative term "ward healer," which implies a party operative who fixes legal problems and doles out jobs and favors to constituents in return for support for the party ticket. Wards were important when political machines were influential in urban politics. The reformers of the early twentieth century viewed the ward system as aiding the bosses in controlling city government. The reformers promoted the at-large system for the election of members of city councils. *See*: BOSS; MACHINE POLITICS.

Reference: Steven P. Erie, *Rainbow's End: Irish-Americans and the Dilemmas of Urban Machine Politics, 1840–1985* (Berkeley: University of California Press, 1988).

WASHINGTON, GEORGE (1732–1799). Given command by the Continental Congress (June 15, 1775) of "all forces raised or to be raised for the defense of American liberty," the hero of the Revolutionary War became, more than a decade later, the new nation's first president under the Constitution of 1787. Born on February 22, 1732, at Wakefield, a modest plantation on Pope's Creek in northern Virginia, Washington was of a land-owning, slave-holding family. In no small part Washington was self-educated and sufficiently so that while yet in his teens he was to work as a surveyor on the western frontiers of Virginia. These experiences led him in 1752 to service with the Virginia Militia. Youthful and militarily inexperienced, but with the influence of family, Washington soon was promoted to lieutenant colonel. His military career at this time, the beginning of the French and Indian War, was, as to success, anything but remarkable. Following the "Jumonville affair" and the subsequent surrender of troops under his command at Fort Necessity, Washington returned to Virginia and in 1754 resigned his commission. A year later, however, he returned to military service on the frontier as aide-de-camp to Maj. General Edward Braddock, and achieved the rank of colonel from which he resigned in 1758 to accept election to the Virginia House of Burgesses, his first direct exposure to political life. In the House of Burgesses, Washington developed that political persona which was to be nurtured through the rest of his life: cautious observation of the political terrain, development of cordial relationships among his colleagues, emphasis on conciliation; all of which allowed him to ride well above damaging issue controversies and personal animosities. Washington was drawn slowly, and initially not altogether irrevocably, to the patriot cause. Years later Thomas Jefferson would write of the thought processes of Washington that they were "slow in operation, little aided by invention or imagination, but sure in conclusion." As he calculated Virginia interests, and to a lesser degree formed and calculated American interests, Washington decided for the patriot cause. Committed at first to accommodation with Great Britain, he was prepared, as his deliberate logic would dictate, to go the step beyond: *independence*. Elected to the First Continental Congress in 1774, Washington reprised his role as House of Burgesses delegate: quiet, cautious, cordial and non-controversial; gaining the esteem of most and the animosity of none. A year later, Congress, with need to balance New England interests against those of the middle states and of the South, turned to the Virginian, offering him the commission of commanding general of the Continental Army. Given Washington's quite modest estimate of his military experience, his reluctance to leave Mount Vernon, it is remarkable that he should have accepted the assignment, one which he, himself, characterized as "too boundless for my abilities and far, very far beyond my experience." While driving ambition is to be dismissed as an explanation, a finely developed sense of duty is not. The following eight years of military leadership were to both confirm and deny Washington's initial assessment of his own abilities. From the early triumph at Boston to the successes at Trenton and Princeton in 1776–1777; from the debacle of Long Island and the loss of New York City in 1776 to the suffering of the winter encampment at Valley Forge in 1777–1778, to the decisive victory of the allied French and American forces at Yorktown on September 19, 1781, Washington was to demonstrate himself as an able strategist. More importantly, he was a near genius in the ability to hold together by administrative skill, personal example, and exhortation an army often struggling under the most extreme of recruitment, training, supply, and morale problems. Rejecting (in 1782–1783) attempts by army officers to stage a military coup ousting congressional authorities and yet other attempts to place him on an American throne, and with the signing of the Treaty of Paris (September 3, 1783), formally ending hostilities with Great Britain and giving full recognition to American independence, Washington retired to Mount Vernon. During this period he slowly was brought to recognition of the need to make adjustments to the political system established by the Articles of Confederation; adjustments which would control the most problematic features of state separatism through a significant strengthening of national authority. With his usual caution Washington agreed to be one of the representatives from Virginia to the convention called for the spring of 1787 in Philadelphia. The result of the convention was not suggested amendments to the Articles of Confederation but rather proposal of an entirely new national Constitution. Washington's contribution to the making and ratification of this proposed Constitution was true to form. His national reputation led to his election as president of the convention over which he presided with even-handedness, assisting in the cooling of tempers when they flared, encouraging agreement for the needed compromises as occasion and political realities demanded. While essentially taking no part in the debate, he was known to favor the strengthening of national authority vis-à-vis the state governments, particularly as to congressional powers to provide for and regulate a national economy and to secure the national defense. He was also known to support the argument for an executive branch presidency assigned with real powers and to function institutionally within a tripartite separation-of-powers system. During the hard-fought ratification battles in the several states (1787–1788), Washington lent his quiet support to the nationalist cause. With those battles won he became by an overwhelming national consensus the man whom the Electoral College was expected to recruit to the newly created presidential office. The electors unanimously did that which was so widely anticipated of them: Washington became the nation's first president, inaugurated in New York City, with John Adams as vice-president, on April 30, 1789. His first term was marked by Congress's acceptance of the comprehensive economic program developed by Secretary of the Treasury Alexander Hamilton: assumption by the national government of state debts incurred as the Revolutionary War had been fought; funding of the national debt with creation of a Bank of the United States; implementation of the taxing power of the national government; stimulation of commercial and manufacturing interests relative to agrarian ones. In the field of foreign affairs Washington attempted to steer the nation on a course of strict neutrality among competing and increasingly belligerent European powers. While he wrestled with the aforementioned policy questions he yet safeguarded his personal reputation and prestige so as to lend weight to both the presidency and to national authority. Washington's success in this endeavor was made easier because he was in his first term a president free of party. As with so many of his successors in the presidential office, Washington's second term, to which he was again unanimously elected in 1792, proved increasingly more difficult in policy terms and immensely less satisfying in personal ones. The policy controversies between agrarians and supporters of Hamilton's economic program grew more sharply defined. Foreign policy divisions nurtured by Hamilton's advocacy of the British cause and Secretary of State Thomas Jefferson's ardent argument for support of Revolutionary France divided the administration, the Congress, and the nation; these latter divisions were brought to a head by Jefferson's formal resignation as secretary of state on December 31, 1793, and the subsequent ratification in 1795 of the Jay Treaty with Great Britain. Washington, now subject to increasing criticism, found himself politicized, a metamorphosis against which his whole personality desperately fought. Facing a rapidly emerging party system of Federalists and Jeffersonian Republicans, harassed by the party press of the latter, tired of office and controversy, Washington vigorously rejected all arguments that he stand for a third term. He was, however, to leave the presidency with a number of constitutional precedents firmly set, among them the development of the cabinet as the structural mechanism for executive branch policy development and implementation; the interpretation that the "advice and consent" clause of Article II ôf the Constitution required the president to secure the approval of the Senate to negotiated treaties but not to solicit its ongoing participatory *advice*; the interpretation (which at a later date was to be rejected) that the executive veto was restricted in its use to legislative proposals of questionable constitutionality; and the principle that occupancy of the presidency was to be limited to two terms, a part of the unwritten constitution that, when violated in the mid-twentieth century, resulted in adoption of the Twenty-second Amendment. Further, Washington was to entrench in American political culture two themes both alive and well more than two hundred years after his Farewell Address first appeared in a Philadelphia newspaper on September 19, 1796. The indictment of party and partisanship as impediments to the enacting of policy truly in the national interest was forcefully argued. The abiding suspicion which Americans have toward parties and partisan solutions grows in no small part from Washington's definition of ''the baneful effects of the Spirit of Party.'' Further, the warning given by the first president that foreign and defense policy ought ''to steer clear of permanent Alliances'' trusting to ''temporary alliances'' to meet ''extraordinary emergencies,'' has fostered the enduring skepticism many Americans feel when confronted with the acceptance of treaty commitments or of appeals for military interventions abroad. Ironically, Washington's final years of retirement at Mount Vernon were interrupted by frequent calls for support of the Federalist Party cause, and even for a dramatic return to public service when, in 1799, facing the possibility of war with France, President John Adams urged Washington to again take command of the American army. The likelihood of war, however, diminished as the year drew to a close; unexpectedly, so with the life of Washington. Contracting a severe throat infection in early December, the seriousness of which rapidly developed, Washington, the patriarch, died at Mount Vernon on December 14, 1799. *See*: ELECTIONS: 1788, 1792.

References: Douglas Southall Freeman, with John A. Carroll and Mary W. Ashworth, *George Washington: A Biography*, 7 vols. (New York: Scribner's, 1948–1957); Forrest McDonald, *The Presidency of George Washington* (Lawrence: University Press of Kansas, 1974); Willard S. Randall, *George Washington: A Life* (New York: Holt, 1997).

WEDGE ISSUE is a divisive issue selected by a candidate or a party to divide voters in a way that benefits the candidate or party promoting that issue. The social issues of the Christian Coalition—abortion, prayer in school, and school choice—are wedge issues that divide voters. In 1996, Republican presidential nominee Bob Dole endorsed Proposition 209, a California initiative which would repeal affirmative action. Dole's support for Proposition 209 is an example of a candidate taking a stand on an issue that divides voters. Wedge issues are not always effective for the candidate. Proposition 209 passed in California, but Dole lost California. The Republican attention to immigration issues in 1996 could also be considered a wedge issue.

Reference: John Harwood, ''Dole Presses Hot-button Issues to Try to Rouse GOP Activists Missing From the Campaign So Far,'' *Wall Street Journal*, October 22, 1996.

WESBERRY v. SANDERS, 376 U.S. 1 (1964) is the first case in which the U.S. Supreme Court formally reviewed and rejected a state's apportionment of federal congressional voting districts. This is significant, since the Court's required redrawing of voting district lines would likely result in electoral difficulties for members of a co-equal branch of government: the U.S. House of Representatives.

At issue was Georgia's Fifth Congressional District which had a population three times as large that of the state's smallest district. Relying on *Colegrove* v. *Green* (1946), a three-judge federal district court had dismissed the original challenge. In agreeing to hear the case, the Supreme Court made it clear that *Colegrove* was no longer a reliable precedent. Justice Black, who had dissented in *Colegrove*, wrote for the majority in this case. Relying on an extensive review of the intent of those who drafted and designed the Constitution, Black argued that Georgia had diluted the votes of some of its citizens, in violation of Article I, Section 2 of the Constitution. Black also reaffirmed the holding of *Gray* v. *Sanders* (1963) that the applicable standard in apportionment cases was "one person, one vote." *See: BAKER* v. *CARR* (1962); *COLEGROVE* v. *GREEN* (1946); *GRAY* v. *SANDERS* (1963).

WHIG PARTY. This party was founded in 1834 by groups who were opposed to President Andrew Jackson's policies. It was the major party in opposition to the Democratic Party of Andrew Jackson. From 1834 until the 1850s, there was a period of party competition between the Whigs and the Democrats. The Whigs favored military heroes as presidential candidates; they won their first presidential election with the nomination of William Henry Harrison in 1840, and won the presidency again in 1848 with Zachary Taylor.

Many former Anti-Mason Party leaders joined the Whigs, including Thurlow Reed of New York State. Another prominent Whig was Horace Greeley. The influential Henry Clay was the leader of the Whigs in Congress. The Whigs were not a sectional party. They enjoyed the support of commercial interests in the North, and slave holders in the South.

The Whigs collapsed when they tried to settle the festering issue of slavery with the Compromise of 1850. The party was badly beaten in the election of 1852, and disintegrated after that. Many prominent Northern Whigs including Thurlow Reed and Horace Greeley joined the newly created Republican Party. The collapse of the Whigs marked the end of what is termed the second-party period. The Republican Party replaced the Whigs as one of the two major parties in the two-party system.

Reference: A. James Reichley, *The Life of the Parties: A History of American Political Parties* (New York: The Free Press, 1992).

WILLKIE, WENDELL L. (1892–1944). Sometime Democrat, successful corporation lawyer and utility executive, emerging critic in the 1930s of the domestic policies of the New Deal, Willkie became, in 1940, the presidential nominee of the Republican Party. Born in Elwood, Indiana on February 18,

1892, of parents both of whom were practicing lawyers, Willkie, as did they, found in Woodrow Wilson an advocate of those progressive policies to which the family was intensely committed. In 1920 the 28-year-old Willkie, having received his law degree but four years earlier from Indiana University, and following military service in France (1918–1919), gave serious consideration to seeking the Democratic Party nomination in the Indiana Eighth Congressional District, a campaign which if undertaken would allow him to defend Wilson policies and promote U.S. membership in the League of Nations. Ultimately bowing to political realities which in 1920 held little promise of Democratic victories in traditionally Republican Indiana, Willkie chose to abort this flirtation with elective politics and instead to give full attention to the building of a career in law. This decision led him to move from Indiana to Akron, Ohio; first, joining the legal staff of Firestone Tire and Rubber Company, subsequently, becoming a partner in the firm of Mather, Nesbitt and Willkie. It was in this latter context that Willkie came to the attention of utility magnate Bernard C. Cobb. Impressed with Willkie, and upon forming in 1929 the utility holding company, Commonwealth and Southern, Cobb recruited the 37-year-old lawyer to New York City to become, in the firm Weadock and Willkie, legal counsel for Commonwealth and Southern. When ill health forced Cobb's retirement in 1933, Willkie, his protégé, became his successor as president of the vast holding company. It was in this position that Willkie was to build a national reputation as perhaps the foremost spokesman for the cause of private enterprise in its confrontation with what was seen by many, particularly in business circles, as the attempt of the New Deal to bring about, by gradual encroachment, state ownership of much of American industry. In the struggle between Commonwealth and Southern and the Tennessee Valley Authority (TVA), the New Deal's initiative in public power development, the battle was joined. While the Roosevelt administration was to prevail, it was at the cost of a $78 million settlement with Commonwealth and Southern in 1939. Willkie supporters were to claim that it was largely on the basis of his efforts that the New Deal was prevented from undertaking further excursions into other areas of traditional private enterprise. Thus as the presidential election year of 1940 approached, portrayed by the national press as the most credible of the critics of the New Deal, with the conventional ranks of Republican leadership thinned by eight years of New Deal election-day victories, Wendell Willkie, yet nominally a Democrat, became touted as the one man best suited to take on the "champ," as Willkie himself labeled President Franklin D. Roosevelt. To some significant degree the 1940 Republican presidential nomination was ripe for the picking: Herbert Hoover and Alf Landon were discredited by their respective landslide losses in 1932 and 1936; emerging party leadership could only offer the recently elected U.S. senator from Ohio, Robert A. Taft, son of the former president and chief justice, and the crime-busting prosecutor Thomas A. Dewey of New York, someone who had, to date, been successfully elected to no office higher than that of district attorney. Into this political vacuum a small, dedicated group of enthusiasts, supported by friends in the press, introduced Wendell Willkie. From the quickly organized associated Willkie Clubs across the nation came a deluge of letters and telegrams reaching Republican delegates as they assembled in Philadelphia for their party's national convention in June of 1940. Willkie, himself, joined by hundreds of his volunteer supporters, converged on the city to cajole delegates in hotel lobbies and restaurants, in taxis and busses, wherever they could be found. From the galleries at the convention hall, from the city's streets, came the seemingly perpetual chant, "We Want Willkie," "We Want Willkie." By the sixth ballot, delegates succumbed, giving to those enthusiasts in the galleries, in the city, and across the nation what they so desperately wanted: Wendell Willkie, but a short time ago a Democrat, was made the presidential nominee of the Republican Party. As vice-presidential candidate, the delegates chose U.S. senator Charles L. McNary of Oregon. Willkie hoped not simply to wage a campaign but rather to lead a great crusade against the ever increasing concentration, and, as he saw it, misuse of political power in Washington; power in the hands of New Deal planners and the president, with FDR so ambitious to maintain that power that he would violate the long-standing "no third term" precedent set by Washington. Within the parameters of such a broad theme, Willkie expected to endorse any number of New Deal domestic policy initiatives, among them social security coverage and unemployment compensation for workers; minimum wage and maximum hour standards; government regulation of utilities, banks, and security markets; and protection for labor's right to organize; the Willkie argument being that his administration would provide more prudent and efficient implementation of these policies and programs. In no small part, however, Willkie was to be captured by events far beyond his control. Fascist aggression had, in the late summer of 1939, taken the shape of war across virtually the whole of Europe: France had fallen in June as Willkie was being nominated; the Battle of Britain was to rage as he conducted his fall crusade. To urge a rapid build-up of America's military forces, to argue the moral imperative to aid Great Britain, short of actual entry into war, was for Willkie no easy task in the face of entrenched isolationist, anti-war forces within his own newly adopted party. Through the weeks of October, and as Roosevelt, himself, took to the hustings, the strong inclination of American voters to stay with proven leadership in a crisis situation, particularly where war threatened, clearly came into evidence. Willkie's defeat on election day 1940 was decisive: Roosevelt-Wallace carried 38 states and 449 votes in the Electoral College to 10 states and but 82 Electoral College ballots for the Republican ticket. In losing, however, Willkie had brought to the Republican Party a new energy and appeal, dramatically improving its popular support: Willkie's presidential vote of more than 22 million ballots was a million votes greater than in Hoover's decisive victory of 1928 and was a Republican presidential vote total not to be bettered until Eisenhower's landslide of 1952. Perhaps for this reason, among others, Willkie did not take his November 5 defeat as a signal to withdraw from politics and national leadership, particularly once the United States entered World War II. As a result of his 50-day tour of global trouble spots in 1942, Willkie, by magazine articles, lectures, and his book, *One World* (published in 1943), attempted to prepare party and nation for postwar internationalism. So as to control the Republican Party's presidential wing, Willkie committed himself to a campaign for the 1944 presidential nomination. Believing that he had to demonstrate, early on, his ability to prevail over isolationist forces in the party, Willkie entered the presidential primary election in Wisconsin, a state claimed by some as ''the most isolationist in the Union.'' Should he win there, so Willkie and his advisors felt, it would prove that he could win among Republican voters anywhere in the nation; he would be, they calculated, unstoppable. But stopped he was. Wisconsin Republicans, on April 4, 1944, most frequently elected national convention delegates pledged to the candidacy of New York governor, Thomas E. Dewey; neither in at-large or district contests did they give one delegate to Willkie. From Omaha, Nebraska, the evening following the Wisconsin debacle, Wendell Willkie withdrew from the 1944 presidential contest. Speculation was fueled that he would now abandon the Republican Party to form a new, internationalist third party, or that he would rejoin the Democrats, waiting until 1948 to seek their nomination. Speculation was to end, however, but six months after the Wisconsin defeat. Willkie, exhausted, suffering for some time from the symptoms of heart disease, entered Lenox Hill Hospital in New York City where, on October 8, 1944, he died of coronary thrombosis. *See*: ELECTIONS: 1940.

References: Ellsworth Barnard, *Wendell Willkie, Fighter for Freedom* (Marquette: Northern Michigan University Press, 1966); Donald B. Johnson, *The Republican Party and Wendell Willkie* (Urbana: University of Illinois Press, 1960).

WILSON, WOODROW (1856–1924). Noted educator, president of Princeton University (1902–1910), reform governor of New Jersey (1911–1913), president of the United States in peace and in war (1913–1921), Wilson was born, son of a Presbyterian clergyman, in Staunton, Virginia on December 28, 1856. First attending Davidson College in North Carolina, he transferred to Princeton in 1875 and graduated from that institution in 1879. Studying law at the University of Virginia the following year, Wilson was admitted to the bar in 1882. After a brief period in law practice in Atlanta, Georgia, Wilson chose to do graduate study in the fields of history and government at Johns Hopkins University, being awarded his doctoral degree in 1886. Serving as his dissertation for the latter degree was Wilson's first book, *Congressional Government*, published in 1885 and immediately receiving scholarly recognition and critical acclaim. Read yet today for its valuable insights, *Congressional Government* explored the growth in the power of Congress, and its committees, relative to the diminished power of the presidency in the post–Civil War period. Leaving Baltimore, Wilson was to hold faculty positions at Bryn Mawr College and at Wesleyan University before joining the Princeton faculty in 1890. Moving from the classroom, where he was known as a brilliant teacher, to the office of president of Princeton in

1902, Wilson instituted major curriculum reforms, introduced the preceptorial system, and strove to reorganize the Graduate School, the latter attempt leading to an intra-university conflict which resulted in Wilson's resignation in 1910. Wilson was not, however, to leave New Jersey. Democrats looking for a reform candidate for governor settled on the soon to be retired president of Princeton. Elected to the governorship in November of 1910, Wilson accomplished election reform with introduction of the primary system, public school organizational reform, public utility regulation, and legislative enactment of New Jersey's first workmen's compensation law. This progressive record made Governor Wilson an appealing figure to many Democratic Party leaders as the national convention of 1912 approached. When frontrunner Champ Clark of Missouri, Speaker of the U.S. House, stalled in convention balloting, and with the switch of influential party leader William Jennings Bryan from Clark to Wilson, the governor emerged, on the forty-sixth ballot, as the presidential nominee of the Democratic Party. Exhausted delegates then chose Governor Thomas Riley Marshall of Indiana as Wilson's running mate. Because of a Republican Party split between its conservative and progressive wings, 1912 presented Democrats with an unusual opportunity for presidential election victory. Wilson, campaigning by train across the country, promoting his ideas of reform as the "New Freedom," took every advantage of being in a three-party race: to his right, the incumbent president William Howard Taft, the Republican candidate; to his left, having bolted the Republican Party, former president Theodore Roosevelt, leading the crusade of the "Bull Moose" Progressive Party. Holding the core Democratic Party vote, Wilson coasted to an easy election-day victory: the Wilson-Marshall ticket received 41.8% of the total presidential vote cast, carrying 40 states with 435 Electoral College ballots; Progressives Theodore Roosevelt and vice-presidential candidate Governor Hiram W. Johnson of California took 27.4% of the popular vote with 6 states and 88 votes in the Electoral College; trailing the three-party field was the Taft-Sherman Republican ticket with 23.2% of the presidential vote, carrying but 2 states and 8 Electoral College ballots. Socialist Party presidential candidate Eugene V. Debs, more than doubling his vote totals of 1904 and 1908, gathered nearly one million ballots, 6.0% of the total vote cast. Inaugurated on March 4, 1913, with his party in the majority in both House and Senate, often meeting with the Democratic caucuses on Capitol Hill, Wilson moved quickly to see enacted into law the "New Freedom" agenda: in 1913, the "reform and reduction" Underwood Tariff Act, provisions of which included the fixing of a graduated tax on personal incomes (the Sixteenth Amendment to the Constitution having been ratified in February of 1913); the Federal Reserve Act, which reorganized the government's central banking system, with creation of the quasi-independent Federal Reserve Board; in 1914, the Clayton Anti-Trust Act, strengthening provisions in the Sherman Anti-Trust Act of 1890; establishment of the Federal Trade Commission; and in 1916, the Adamson Act which, in fixing the eight-hour workday for railroad employees, signaled federal government endorsement of the eight-hour standard for American industry. With the outbreak of World War I across Europe in August of 1914, Wilson's attention turned dramatically from domestic to foreign policy. Developing a position of "strict neutrality," Wilson was to run for reelection in 1916 with his party using the slogan, "He kept us out of war." He faced in that year a reunited Republican Party with a formidable national ticket: Charles Evans Hughes of New York, leaving the U.S. Supreme Court, became the party's presidential nominee and, as vice-presidential candidate, convention delegates chose Charles W. Fairbanks of Indiana, vice-president of the United States from 1905 to 1909. The Electoral College vote proved to be surprisingly close: Wilson-Marshall took 49.2% of the total presidential vote cast and carried 30 states with 277 Electoral College ballots; Hughes-Fairbanks received 46.1% of the vote with 18 states and 254 votes in the Electoral College. The second Wilson administration, with U.S. entry into the war in April of 1917, was transformed into a war presidency. Congress, responding to Wilson's war leadership, authorized the exercise of broad executive powers so that the president might effectively mobilize the economy and the military to the war effort, as with passage in 1917 of the Lever Food-Control Act and the Selective Draft Law. Also enacted that same year were controversial measures restricting peacetime civil liberties, the Espionage Act, and the Trading-with-the-Enemy Act of October 6, 1917. Looking forward to the postwar world, Wilson released on January 8, 1918, his, now famous "Fourteen Points," a plan by which he intended to shape the peace settlement, redraw the political map of Europe in terms of nationality considerations, and establish a new international order committed to the preservation of peace through a League of Nations. Following the armistice of November 1918, Wilson, a month later, setting a presidential precedent, left the United States for Paris, to personally participate with other allied leaders in drafting that set of treaties which, if adopted, would not only bring to a formal conclusion belligerency with Germany and Austro-Hungary, but which would also effectuate much of the president's "Fourteen Points" agenda. Returning to the United States in July 1919, Wilson was to encounter a greatly altered political world; in both the House and Senate Republican majorities, as a result of the midterm elections of 1918, now held sway. Crucial to the Senate's ratification of the negotiated treaties was the Senate Foreign Relations Committee, chaired by Senator Henry Cabot Lodge of Massachusetts. As Lodge and other Republican senators were soon to indicate, they had "reservations." Unwilling to accept the treaty alterations which Senate Republicans seemed intent on making, Wilson decided on recourse to public opinion and the American people. Embarking on an extensive cross-country tour on September 2, 1919, Wilson intended to raise popular support for both his leadership and for ratification of the treaties. With clear signs of the president's deteriorating health, the last segment of the tour was canceled and the presidential train hurriedly returned to Washington, arriving there September 28. Early in October, at the White House, Wilson suffered a massive stroke which was to leave him significantly impaired for the remaining eighteen months of his term. It is suggested that in the first months of his partial recovery, the president's wife, Edith Bolling Wilson, in effect functioned as acting president. Politically, Wilson's final months in the presidency brought few victories and little satisfaction. In November 1919 the Senate was to reject the Treaty of Versailles; in November 1920 the American voter was to reject Wilson's party, sending Republicans back to the White House in the "return to normalcy" election of that year. With the inauguration of U.S. Senator Warren G. Harding of Ohio on March 4, 1921, Wilson retired to his Washington home on S Street. Never fully recovering his health, he died there on February 3, 1924. *See*: ELECTIONS: 1912; 1916.

References: Kendrick A. Clements, *The Presidency of Woodrow Wilson* (Lawrence: University Press of Kansas, 1992); August Heckscher, *Woodrow Wilson* (New York: Scribner's, 1991); Arthur S. Link, *Wilson*, 5 vols. (Princeton: Princeton University Press, 1947–1965); Woodrow Wilson, *Congressional Government*, orig. pub. 1885 (Baltimore: Johns Hopkins University Press, 1981).

WINNER-TAKE-ALL SYSTEMS. *See*: PLURALITY.

WINOGRAD COMMISSION of the National Democratic Committee, was created by chair Robert Strauss before the Democratic Convention of 1976, to study the problem of the proliferation of primaries for delegate selection. The Commission was chaired by Morley Winograd of Michigan. The role of the Commission was expanded by the Democratic National Convention. However, the Commission put off its work until after the presidential election. In November 1976 the Democratic presidential nominee Jimmy Carter was elected. Representatives of the White House were added to this party Commission. The charge of this Commission was then redefined to enhance the opportunity for President Jimmy Carter to be renominated in 1980. The Winograd Commission instituted a three-month "window" in which primaries and caucuses could be held. This would benefit the incumbent president. The threshold for proportional representation was raised from 15% to 25%.

Other provisions of the Winograd Commission included the bound delegate rule, that is, delegates were bound to support the candidates they were pledged to on the first convention ballot. They also created the 10% add-on of at-large delegates appointed by the state parties. This was designed to get party regulars and elected officials back into the nomination process. This would later be enhanced with the superdelegates idea of the Hunt Commission.

The Winograd Commission never fully addressed the issue it was originally charged to resolve—the proliferation of primaries. *See*: FAIRNESS COMMISSION; HUNT COMMISSION; McGOVERN-FRASER COMMISSION; MIKULSKI COMMISSION.

Reference: David E. Price, *Bringing Back the Parties* (Washington, D.C.: Congressional Quarterly Press, 1984).

WOMEN'S SUFFRAGE. The Continental Congress debated the right of women to vote, and decided to leave that issue to the individual states to decide.

Women were denied the right to vote throughout the nineteenth century in the United States. The campaign for women's suffrage began in July of 1848, when the first women's rights convention was held in Seneca Falls, New York. The delegates in attendance decided that attainment of the franchise should be their primary goal. They adopted a Declaration of Sentiments, and saw their list of demands as similar to the Declaration of Independence. In the Seneca Falls Declaration, they listed what they saw as the ''injuries and usurpations on the part of men towards women.'' Many notable Americans of the day supported their cause, including Horace Greeley, but they met a great deal of resistance to their demand and were unsuccessful.

It was not until 1890, when the National American Woman Suffrage Association was formed, that women begin to make some progress on this issue. Early in the twentieth century a number of states permitted women to vote. Colorado granted women the right to vote in 1893, California in 1911, and New York in 1917. In 1919, Congress approved the Nineteenth Amendment which stated that: ''The right of Citizens of the United States to vote shall not be denied or abridged by the United States or by any State on account of sex.'' It was ratified by 36 states and became effective in August of 1920.

The rate of women voting was lower than men until 1980. Voter turnout by women has been greater than male turnout in every presidential election since 1984. *See:* GENDER GAP; NINETEENTH AMENDMENT.

Reference: M. Margaret Conway, Gertrude A. Steuernagel and David W. Ahern, *Women and Political Participation: Cultural Change in the Political Arena* (Washington, D.C.: Congressional Quarterly Press, 1997).

WRITE-IN CANDIDATE is a candidate whose name does not appear on the printed ballot. The write-in candidate's supporters must write the name of the candidate on the designated ballot line. States may require a filing of a declaration by the candidate in order to have the write-in votes counted. One of the more notable write-in campaigns was the successful 1964 write-in campaign on behalf of Henry Cabot Lodge of Massachusetts over the declared Republican presidential candidacies of Barry Goldwater and Nelson Rockefeller. Usually, write-in campaigns are unsuccessful.

Y

YOUNG DEMOCRATS OF AMERICA. The Young Democratic Clubs were founded by James Farley, who was the DNC chairman during the Roosevelt administration, to attract young people to the Democratic Party. In 1975 the organization changed its name to the Young Democrats of America. In the 1960s the clubs were very supportive of Eugene McCarthy, Robert Kennedy, and the anti–Vietnam War movement. They also advocated gay rights, the legalization of marijuana, and legal abortion in that period. Many of those positions were not favored by the senior Democratic Party activists.

The Young Democrats of America are entitled to two seats on the Democratic National Committee. The organization receives support from the DNC but is not controlled by the DNC. Many members of Congress and members of the Democratic National Committee had been active in the Young Democrats of America. The organization restricts membership to those 35 years old and younger. The organization maintains that the organization: ''Seeks to encourage young men and women to take an active part in politics and become members of the Democratic party.'' *See*: DEMOCRATIC NATIONAL COMMITTEE.

Reference: Paul Allen Beck, *Party Politics in America*, 8th ed. (New York: Longman, 1997).

YOUNG REPUBLICAN NATIONAL FEDERATION. This auxiliary organization of the Republican National Committee was founded in 1931 by Robert H. Lucas, who was the Executive Director of the RNC. There are local chapters throughout the country, and there is often a state federation of Young Republicans. The organization serves as a starting point for young Republican activists.

Like the Young Democrats of America of the 1960s, which was more liberal than the national party, the Young Republicans have been more conservative than the senior Republican Party. The Young Republican National Federation was very supportive, and was a major organizing grid of the very conservative Barry Goldwater campaign of 1964. Later, the Young Republicans were very supportive of conservative Ronald Reagan. The Republican National Committee provides the Young Republican National Federation ex-officio membership on the executive committee of the RNC.

Membership is restricted to those between the ages of eighteen and forty. The organization claims that it: ''Seeks to further the aims of the Republican party among young people.'' *See*: REPUBLICAN NATIONAL COMMITTEE; YOUNG DEMOCRATS OF AMERICA.

Reference: John F. Bibby, *Politics, Parties, and Elections in America*, 3rd ed. (Chicago: Nelson-Hall, 1996).

Appendix:
Presidents, Vice-Presidents, and Party Control of Congress, 1789–Present

Term	President and Vice-President	Party of President	MAJORITY PARTY House	Senate	Congress
1789–1797	**George Washington**	None	(N/A)	(N/A)	1st
	John Adams		(N/A)	(N/A)	2nd
			(N/A)	(N/A)	3rd
			(N/A)	(N/A)	4th
1797–1801	**John Adams**	Federalist	(N/A)	(N/A)	5th
	Thomas Jefferson		Federalist	Federalist	6th
1801–1809	**Thomas Jefferson**	Republican	Republican	Republican	7th
	Aaron Burr (1801–1805)		Republican	Republican	8th
	George Clinton (1805–1809)		Republican	Republican	9th
			Republican	Republican	10th
1809–1817	**James Madison**	Republican	Republican	Republican	11th
	George Clinton (1809–1812)		Republican	Republican	12th
	Elbridge Gerry (1813–1814)		Republican	Republican	13th
			Republican	Republican	14th
1817–1825	**James Monroe**	Republican	Republican	Republican	15th
	Daniel D. Tompkins		Republican	Republican	16th
			Republican	Republican	17th
			Republican	Republican	18th
1825–1829	**John Quincy Adams**	National-Republican	Admin.	Admin.	19th
	John C. Calhoun		Jacksonian	Jacksonian	20th
1829–1837	**Andrew Jackson**	Democrat	Democrat	Democrat	21st
	John C. Calhoun (1829–1832)		Democrat	Democrat	22nd
	Martin Van Buren (1833–1837)		Democrat	Democrat	23rd
			Democrat	Democrat	24th
1837–1841	**Martin Van Buren**	Democrat	Democrat	Democrat	25th
	Richard M. Johnson		Democrat	Democrat	26th
1841	**William H. Harrison**	Whig			
	John Tyler (1841)				
1841–1845	John Tyler	Whig	Whig	Whig	27th
	(VP vacant)		Democrat	Whig	28th
1845–1849	**James K. Polk**	Democrat	Democrat	Democrat	29th
	George M. Dallas		Whig	Democrat	30th
1849–1850	**Zachary Taylor**	Whig	Democrat	Democrat	31st
	Millard Fillmore				
1850–1853	**Millard Fillmore**	Whig	Democrat	Democrat	32nd
	(VP vacant)				
1853–1857	**Franklin Pierce**	Democrat	Democrat	Democrat	33rd
	William R. D. King (1853)		Republican	Democrat	34th
1857–1861	**James Buchanan**	Democrat	Democrat	Democrat	35th
	John C. Breckinridge		Republican	Democrat	36th
1861–1865	**Abraham Lincoln**	Republican	Republican	Republican	37th
	Hannibal Hamlin (1861–1865)		Republican	Republican	38th
	Andrew Johnson (1865)				
1865–1869	**Andrew Johnson**	Republican	Union	Union	39th
	(VP vacant)		Republican	Republican	40th

Term	President and Vice-President	Party of President	MAJORITY PARTY House	Senate	Congress
1869–1877	**Ulysses S. Grant**	Republican	Republican	Republican	41st
	Schuyler Colfax (1869–1873)		Republican	Republican	42nd
	Henry Wilson (1873–1875)		Republican	Republican	43rd
			Democrat	Republican	44th
1877–1881	**Rutherford B. Hayes**	Republican	Democrat	Republican	45th
	William A. Wheeler		Democrat	Democrat	46th
1881	**James A. Garfield**	Republican	Republican	Republican	47th
	Chester A. Arthur				
1881–1885	**Chester A. Arthur**	Republican	Democrat	Republican	48th
	(VP vacant)				
1885–1889	**Grover Cleveland**	Democrat	Democrat	Republican	49th
	Thomas A. Hendricks (1885)		Democrat	Republican	50th
1889–1893	**Benjamin Harrison**	Republican	Republican	Republican	51st
	Levi P. Morton		Democrat	Republican	52nd
1893–1897	**Grover Cleveland**	Democrat	Democrat	Democrat	53rd
	Adlai E. Stevenson		Republican	Republican	54th
1897–1901	**William McKinley**	Republican	Republican	Republican	55th
	Garret A. Hobart (1897–1899)		Republican	Republican	56th
	Theodore Roosevelt (1901)				
1901–1909	**Theodore Roosevelt**	Republican	Republican	Republican	57th
	(VP vacant, 1901–1905)		Republican	Republican	58th
	Charles W. Fairbanks		Republican	Republican	59th
	(1905–1909)		Republican	Republican	60th
1909–1913	**William Howard Taft**	Republican	Republican	Republican	61st
	James S. Sherman (1909–1912)		Democrat	Republican	62nd
1913–1921	**Woodrow Wilson**	Democrat	Democrat	Democrat	63rd
	Thomas R. Marshall		Democrat	Democrat	64th
			Democrat	Democrat	65th
			Republican	Republican	66th
1921–1923	**Warren G. Harding**	Republican	Republican	Republican	67th
	Calvin Coolidge				
1923–1929	**Calvin Coolidge**	Republican	Republican	Republican	68th
	(VP vacant, 1923–1925)		Republican	Republican	69th
	Charles G. Dawes (1925–1929)		Republican	Republican	70th
1929–1933	**Herbert Hoover**	Republican	Republican	Republican	71st
	Charles Curtis		Democrat	Republican	72nd
1933–1945	**Franklin D. Roosevelt**	Democrat	Democrat	Democrat	73rd
	John N. Garner (1933–1941)		Democrat	Democrat	74th
	Henry A. Wallace (1941–1945)		Democrat	Democrat	75th
	Harry S. Truman (1945)		Democrat	Democrat	76th
			Democrat	Democrat	77th
			Democrat	Democrat	78th
1945–1953	**Harry S. Truman**	Democrat	Democrat	Democrat	79th
	(VP vacant, 1945–1949)		Republican	Republican	80th
	Alben W. Barkley (1949–1953)		Democrat	Democrat	81st
			Democrat	Democrat	82nd

Term	President and Vice-President	Party of President	MAJORITY PARTY House	Senate	Congress
1953–1961	**Dwight D. Eisenhower** Richard M. Nixon	Republican	Republican Democrat Democrat Democrat	Republican Democrat Democrat Democrat	83rd 84th 85th 86th
1961–1963	**John F. Kennedy** Lyndon B. Johnson (1961–1963)	Democrat	Democrat	Democrat	87th
1963–1969	**Lyndon B. Johnson** (VP vacant, 1963–1965) Hubert H. Humphrey (1965–1969)	Democrat	Democrat Democrat Democrat	Democrat Democrat Democrat	88th 89th 90th
1969–1974	**Richard M. Nixon** Spiro T. Agnew (1969–1973) Gerald R. Ford (1973–1974)	Republican	Democrat Democrat	Democrat Democrat	91st 92nd
1974–1977	**Gerald R. Ford** Nelson A. Rockefeller	Republican	Democrat Democrat	Democrat Democrat	93rd 94th
1977–1981	**Jimmy Carter** Walter Mondale	Democrat	Democrat Democrat	Democrat Democrat	95th 96th
1981–1989	**Ronald Reagan** George Bush	Republican	Democrat Democrat Democrat Democrat	Republican Republican Republican Democrat	97th 98th 99th 100th
1989–1993	**George Bush** J. Danforth Quayle	Republican	Democrat Democrat	Democrat Democrat	101st 102nd
1993–	**William J. Clinton** Albert Gore, Jr.	Democrat	Democrat Republican Republican	Democrat Republican Republican	103rd 104th 105th

Selected Bibliography

Abramson, Paul R., John H. Aldrich, and David W. Rhode. *Change and Continuity in the 1992 Elections*. Rev. ed. Washington, D.C.: Congressional Quarterly Press, 1995.

Aldrich, John H. *Why Parties? The Origin and Transformation of Political Parties in America*. Chicago: University of Chicago Press, 1995.

Alexander, Herbert E. *Financing Politics: Money, Elections, and Political Reform*. 4th ed. Washington, D.C.: Congressional Quarterly Press, 1992.

Amy, Douglas. *Proportional Representation: The Case for a Better Election System*. Northampton, Mass.: Crescent Street Press, 1997.

———. *Real Choices, New Voices: The Case for Proportional Representation Elections in the United States*. New York: Columbia University Press, 1993.

Ansolabehere, Stephen, and Shanto Iyengar. *Going Negative: How Political Advertisements Shrink & Polarize the Electorate*. New York: The Free Press, 1995.

Asher, Herbert B. *Presidential Elections and American Politics: Voters, Candidates, and Campaigns Since 1952*. 5th ed. Pacific Grove, Calif.: Brooks/Cole, 1992.

Barone, Michael. *Our Country: The Shaping of America from Roosevelt to Reagan*. New York: The Free Press, 1990.

Barone, Michael, and Grant Ujifusa. *The Almanac of American Politics 1998*. Washington, D.C.: National Journal, 1997.

Batchelor, John C. *"Ain't You Glad You Joined the Republicans?" A Short History of the GOP*. New York: Henry Holt, 1996.

Beck, Paul Allen. *Party Politics in America*. 8th ed. New York: Longman, 1997.

Bibby, John F. *Politics, Parties, and Elections in America*. 3rd ed. Chicago: Nelson-Hall, 1996.

Binkley, Wilfred E. *American Political Parties: Their Natural History*, 4th ed. New York: Knopf, 1963.

Boller, Paul F., Jr. *Presidential Campaigns*. Rev. ed. New York: Oxford University Press, 1996.

Bullock, Charles S. III, and Loch K. Johnson. *Runoff Elections in the United States.* Chapel Hill: University of North Carolina Press, 1992.

Ceaser, James W., and Andrew E. Busch. *Losing to Win: The 1996 Elections and American Politics.* Boulder, Colo.: Rowman & Littlefield, 1997.

Chase, James S. *Emergence of the Presidential Nominating Convention, 1789–1832.* Urbana: University of Illinois Press, 1973.

Clubb, Jerome M., William H. Flanagan, and Nancy H. Zingale. *Partisan Realignment: Voters, Parties, and Government in American History.* Beverly Hills, Calif.: Sage Publications, 1980.

Congressional Quarterly. *Presidential Elections, 1789–1992.* Washington, D.C.: Congressional Quarterly Press, 1995.

———. *Selecting the President from 1789 to 1996.* Washington, D.C.: Congressional Quarterly Press, 1997.

Conway, M. Margaret, Gertrude A. Steuernagel, and David W. Ahern. *Women and Political Participation: Cultural Change in the Political Arena* Washington, D.C.: Congressional Quarterly Press, 1997.

Corrado, Anthony, Thomas E. Mann, Daniel R. Ortiz, Trevor Potter, and Frank J. Sorauf, eds. *Campaign Finance Reform: A Sourcebook.* Washington, D.C.: Brookings Institution, 1997.

Edsall, Thomas B., and Mary D. Edsall. *Chain Reaction.* New York: W. W. Norton, 1992.

Erie, Steven P. *Rainbow's End: Irish-Americans and the Dilemmas of Urban Machine Politics, 1840–1985.* Berkeley: University of California Press, 1988.

Flanigan, William H., and Nancy H. Zingale. *Political Behavior of the American Electorate.* 8th ed. Washington, D.C.: Congressional Quarterly Press, 1994.

Freedman, Anne. *Patronage: An American Tradition.* Chicago: Nelson-Hall, 1994.

Gienapp, William E. *The Origins of the Republican Party, 1852–1856.* New York: Oxford University Press, 1987.

Gillespie, J. David. *Politics at the Periphery: Third Parties in Two-Party America.* Columbia: University of South Carolina Press, 1993.

Gimpel, James. *National Elections and the Autonomy of American State Party Systems.* Pittsburgh: University of Pittsburgh Press, 1996.

Goldman, Ralph M. *The National Party Chairmen and Committees: Factionalism at the Top.* Armonk, N.Y.: M. E. Sharpe, 1990.

Graham, Gene. *One Man, One Vote: Baker* v. *Carr and the American Levellers.* Boston: Little, Brown, 1972.

Green, John C., and Daniel M. Shea, eds. *The State of the Parties.* 2nd ed. Boulder, Colo.: Rowman & Littlefield, 1996.

Grofman, Bernard, and Arend Lijphart, eds. *Electoral Laws and Their Political Consequences.* New York: Agathon Press, 1986.

Havel, James T. *U.S. Presidential Candidates and Elections: A Biographical and Historical Guide.* New York: Macmillan, 1996.

Herrnson, Paul S. *Congressional Elections: Campaigning at Home and in Washington.* 2nd ed. Washington, D.C.: Congressional Quarterly Press, 1998.

Herrnson, Paul S., and John Green, eds. *Multiparty Politics in America.* Boulder, Colo.: Rowman & Littlefield, 1997.

Herrnson, Paul S., Ronald G. Shaiko, and Clyde Wilcox, eds. *The Interest Group Con-*

nection: Electioneering, Lobbying, and Policymaking in Washington. Chatham, N.J.: Chatham House, 1998.

Hill, Kathleen Thompson, and Gerald N. Hill. *Real Life Dictionary of American Politics.* Los Angeles: General Publishing Group, 1994.

Key, V. O., Jr. *American State Politics: An Introduction.* New York: Knopf, 1956.

Klinker, Philip A. *The Losing Parties: Out-Party National Committees, 1956–1993.* New Haven, Conn.: Yale University Press, 1994.

Lichtman, Allan J. *The Keys to the White House, 1996.* Lanham, Md.: Madison Books, 1996.

Maisel, L. Sandy. *Parties and Elections in America: The Electoral Process.* 2nd ed. New York: McGraw-Hill, 1993.

Mayer, George H. *The Republican Party, 1854–1964.* New York: Oxford University Press, 1964.

Mayer, William G. *The Divided Democrats: Ideological Unity, Party Reform, and Presidential Democrats.* Boulder, Colo.: Westview Press, 1996.

Mayer, William G., ed. *In Pursuit of the White House: How We Choose Our Presidential Nominees.* Chatham, N.J.: Chatham House, 1996.

Milkis, Sidney M. *The President and the Parties.* New York: Oxford University Press, 1995.

Miller, Warren E., and J. Merrill Shanks. *The New American Voter.* Cambridge, Mass.: Harvard University Press, 1996.

Moos, Malcolm. *The Republicans: A History of Their Party.* New York: Random House, 1956.

Murphy, Walter F., James E. Fleming, and Sotirios A. Barber. *American Constitutional Interpretation.* 2nd ed. Westbury, N.Y.: Foundation Press, 1995.

Mutch, Robert E. *Campaigns, Congress, and the Courts.* New York: Praeger, 1988.

Nelson, Michael, ed. *The Elections of 1996.* Washington, D.C.: Congressional Quarterly Press, 1997.

Norrander, Barbara. *Super Tuesday: Regional Politics and Presidential Primaries.* Lexington.: University of Kentucky Press, 1992.

Plano, Jack, and Milton Greenberg. *The American Political Dictionary.* 10th ed. Fort Worth, Tex.: Harcourt Brace College Publishers, 1997.

Polsby, Daniel D. "*Buckley* v. *Valeo*: The Special Nature of Political Speech." *Supreme Court Review* (1976).

Polsby, Nelson W. *Consequences for Party Reform.* New York: Oxford University Press, 1983.

Polsby, Nelson W., and Aaron Wildavsky. *Presidential Elections: Strategies and Structures in American Politics.* 9th ed. Chatham, N.J.: Chatham House, 1996.

Rae, Nicol. *Southern Democrats.* New York: Oxford University Press, 1994.

Reichley, A. James. *The Life of the Parties: A History of American Political Parties.* New York: The Free Press, 1992.

Reichley, A. James, ed. *Elections American Style.* Washington, D.C.: Brookings Institution, 1987.

Renstrom, Peter G., and Chester B. Rogers. *The Electoral Politics Dictionary.* Santa Barbara, Calif.: ABC-CLIO, 1989.

Roseboom, Eugene H. *A History of Presidential Elections.* New York: Macmillan, 1957.

Rosenkranz, E. Joshua. *Voter Choice '96: A 50-State Report Card on the Presidential*

Elections. New York: Brennen Center for Justice of the New York School of Law, 1996.

Rosenstone, Steven J., Roy L. Behr, and Edward H. Lazarus. *Third Parties in America: Citizen Response to Major Party Failure.* 2nd ed. Princeton, N.J.: Princeton University Press, 1996, p. 658.

Rule, Wilma, and Joseph F. Zimmerman, eds. *United States Electoral Systems: Their Impact on Women and Minorities.* Westport, Conn.: Greenwood Press, 1992.

Safire, William. *Safire's New Political Dictionary.* New York: Random House, 1993.

Salmore, Barbara G., and Stephen A. Salmore. *Candidates, Parties, and Campaigns: Electoral Politics in America.* 2nd ed. Washington, D.C.: Congressional Quarterly Press, 1989.

Scher, Richard K., Jon L. Mills, and John J. Hotaling. *Voting Rights and Democracy: The Law and Politics of Districting.* Chicago: Nelson-Hall, 1997.

Schlesinger, Arthur M., Jr., ed. *History of U.S. Political Parties.* 4 vols. New York: Chelsea House, 1973.

Shafritz, Jay. *The HarperCollins Dictionary of American Government and Politics.* Concise ed. New York: HarperCollins, 1993.

Shea, Daniel M. *Campaign Craft: The Strategies, Tactics, and Art of Political Campaign Management.* Westport, Conn.: Praeger, 1996.

Simpson, Dick. *Winning Elections: A Handbook of Modern Participatory Politics.* New York: HarperCollins, 1996.

Southwick, Leslie H. *Presidential Also Rans and Running Mates, 1788–1980.* Jefferson, N.C.: McFarland, 1984.

Stanley, Harold W., and Richard G. Niemi. *Vital Statistics on American Politics.* 5th ed. Washington, D.C.: Congressional Quarterly Press, 1995.

Stanwood, Edward. *A History of the Presidency from 1788 to 1897.* Boston: Houghton Mifflin, 1898.

Traugott, Michael W., and Paul J. Lavrakas. *The Voter's Guide to Election Polls.* Chatham, N.J.: Chatham House, 1996.

Ware, Alan. *The Breakdown of the Democratic Party Organization, 1940–1980.* New York: Oxford University Press, 1985.

Wayne, Stephen J. *The Road to the White House 1996: The Politics of Presidential Elections.* New York: St. Martin's Press, 1996.

Wilson, James Q. *Political Organizations.* Princeton, N.J.: Princeton University Press, 1995.

Zimmerman, Joseph F. *Participatory Democracy: Populism Revived.* New York: Praeger, 1986.

———. *The Recall: Tribunal of the People.* Westport, Conn: Praeger, 1997.

Index

Note: Page numbers set in **bold** indicate the location of a main entry.

About the Authors

WILLIAM C. BINNING serves as Chair of the Political Science Department at Youngstown State University. He earned a Ph.D. from Notre Dame University. Binning has published a number of essays on state and local parties in the United States. In addition to his scholarly interest in parties, Binning has been actively involved in political parties. He served as the Chair of the local county Republican Party for a decade, and was a delegate to three Republican National Conventions. He is listed in *Who's Who in American Politics*.

LARRY E. ESTERLY is professor emeritus at Youngstown State University after teaching American Politics for over twenty-five years. He did his graduate work at Johns Hopkins University. While at Youngstown State, he was named a University Distinguished Professor. In 1996, he was appointed by Ohio Governor George Voinovich to serve as a Trustee of the University for a nine-year term.

PAUL A. SRACIC has taught Constitutional Law and Political Theory at Youngstown State University since 1992. He has a Ph.D. from Rutgers University. In 1998, he was named Outstanding Professor of the Year. He regularly contributes book reviews and articles on the Supreme Court to the *Philadelphia Inquirer* and *Commonweal*. He has written articles on the Supreme Court and on American Politics for the *Washington Post*, the *Philadelphia Inquirer*, and *Commonweal*.

ISBN 0-313-30312-6

HARDCOVER BAR CODE